MADNESS, RELIGION AND THE STATE IN EARLY MODERN EUROPE

From the ideological crucible of the Reformation emerged an embittered contest for the human soul. In the care of souls, the clergy zealously dispensed spiritual physic – for countless early modern Europeans, the first echelon of mental health care. During its heyday, spiritual physic touched the lives of thousands, from penitents and pilgrims to demoniacs and mad persons. Ironically, the phenomenon remains largely unexplored. Why?

Through case histories from among the records of more than a thousand troubled and desperate individuals, this regional study of Bavaria investigates spiritual physic as a popular ritual during a tumultuous era of religious strife, material crises, moral repression and witch-hunting. By the mid-seventeenth century, secular forces ushered in a psychological revolution across Europe. However, spiritual physic ensconced itself by proxy upon emergent bourgeois psychiatry. Today, its remnants raise haunting questions about science and the pursuit of objective knowledge in the ephemeral realm of human consciousness.

DAVID LEDERER is Lecturer at the National University of Ireland. His research focuses on early modern Central Europe, the history of psychiatry and suicide studies.

NEW STUDIES IN EUROPEAN HISTORY

Edited by

PETER BALDWIN, University of California, Los Angeles
CHRISTOPHER CLARK, University of Cambridge
JAMES B. COLLINS, Georgetown University
MIA RODRÍGUEZ-SALGADO, London School of Economics
and Political Science
LYNDAL ROPER, University of Oxford

The aim of this series in early modern and modern European history is to publish outstanding works of research, addressed to important themes across a wide geographical range, from southern and central Europe, to Scandinavia and Russia, and from the time of the Renaissance to the Second World War. As it develops the series will comprise focused works of wide contextual range and intellectual ambition.

For a full list of titles published in the series, please see the end of the book.

MADNESS, RELIGION AND THE STATE IN EARLY MODERN EUROPE

A Bavarian Beacon

DAVID LEDERER

CAMBRIDGE
UNIVERSITY PRESS

CAMBRIDGE UNIVERSITY PRESS

Cambridge, New York, Melbourne, Madrid, Cape Town, Singapore, São Paulo

Cambridge University Press
The Edinburgh Building, Cambridge CB2 2RU, UK

Published in the United States of America by Cambridge University Press, New York

www.cambridge.org
Information on this title: www.cambridge.org/9780521853477

© David Lederer 2006

First published 2006

Printed in the United Kingdom at the University Press, Cambridge

A catalogue record for this publication is available from the British Library

ISBN-13 978-0-521-85347-7 hardback
ISBN-10 0-521-85347-8 hardback

For Max

Fearlessly the idiot faced the crowd,
Smi-i-i-i-iling.
Merciless the magistrate turns round,
Fro-o-o-o-owning.
And who's the fool who wears the crown?

David Gilmour and Roger Waters, *Fearless*

Contents

Plates

Figures

Maps

.

Tables

Preface

This book explores the obscure origins of modern psychology and psychiatry in early modern Europe. Specifically, it investigates regional practices and beliefs employing interdisciplinary tools from the history of medicine, cultural anthropology and religious sociology in addition to traditional historical methods. Given that readers may come from other areas of interest, a basic introduction is offered here simply to clarify certain underlying assumptions. Obviously, its brevity requires indulging in some crude generalizations. Persons already familiar with the early modern period or the history of psychology/psychiatry may therefore find this preamble largely superfluous and can skip it entirely without the slightest danger of miscomprehension.

As the expression suggests, the early modern period in Europe (broadly defined as the years from 1450 to 1789) witnessed the birth of philosophies, inventions and institutional practices regularly associated with standard definitions of modernity and progress. For historians of ideas, these include the Renaissance and the Enlightenment. As regards technological advances, science recognizes innovations like the printing press, the magnetic compass and the telescope, to mention but a few. Scholars of religion point to the consequences of the Reformation and the Catholic reform movements for social and political development in the West. Sociologists invoke the appearance of systematized bureaucracies, mass culture and rationalization as symbols of modernity. In the grander scheme of things presumably progressive, all these developments moved history forward at various levels. Ultimately, the presumption of a modern civilization remains one of something qualitatively unique and different from preceding eras.

Until the First World War, this understanding of modernity pinned the hopes of humankind on the ideals of material, social and intellectual progress. Accordingly, Western civilization confidently accepted certain goal orientations – the consolidation of the nation state with a secure monopoly of violence based in law rather than superstition, the eradication of disease and the achievement of material prosperity. The history of the twentieth century, the cruelest on record for its inhumanity, sorely tested positivist aspirations. On the one hand, the Great Wars and the Holocaust, not to mention continuing threats of nuclear annihilation, recurrent genocide, unforeseeable global pandemics, terrorism and economic instability, have sorely vexed blind faith in human progress as teleological or unidirectional. On the other hand, unconditional surrender to the vagaries of absolute relativism is, at best, oxymoronic and dilettantish, at worst – as more recent events clearly demonstrate – patently dangerous. No one seriously disputes how novel technologies extend life expectancy (at least in some societies) and make living more comfortable. Things are less clear, however, when operating in subjective arenas such as quality of life or normalcy, for example, requiring subtle value judgments that defy simple quantification. Healthy skepticism and sober debate over the precise nature of progress as intrinsically good and unidirectional ("damn the torpedoes, full speed ahead," as Farragut said) is clearly in the public interest. In order to conduct effective public debate, we require evidence. Technical studies like this one contribute empirical and circumstantial evidence, anecdotal examples and cognitive models for evaluation and the formation of informed, rather than intuitive, value judgments. Though not necessarily an exhortation to conservatism, this approach certainly favors erring on the side of caution in our critical reflection of where we are now and how we came to be here. Therein rests the merit of the humanities in general and history in particular.

For example, psychology, psychiatry and psychoanalysis are remarkably complex and controversial disciplines worthy of historical investigation. Their story is too often presented in extremes: either as one of unfettered and heroic progress from the nineteenth century onwards or, alternatively, as verification of omnipresent repression and abuses of power in a nightmarish post-modern society embodied in Edvard Munch's *The Scream*. I subscribe exclusively to neither view. However, if one defines psychology, psychiatry and psychoanalysis as modern disciplines, then (not unlike modern banking practices) it seems prudent to seek their genesis in the *early* modern period. In fact, the terms "psychology" and "psychiatry" first emerged in the sixteenth century, the OED notwithstanding.

Logic recommends an examination of early modern developments as potentially relevant to our ability to understand current institutions and practices. Early modern history also allows us to contextualize with a measure of detachment. Although disconcerting issues are raised in this study – the role of political exigency, religious ethics, social norms and public perceptions in the genealogy of scientific knowledge – no major drug contracts, sweeping institutional reforms, redundancies or recommendations for the confinement of abnormal behavioral types ride explicitly on its outcome. Hence, I submit the following argument for your critical consideration. Although focused on the regional analysis of one highly specialized form of early modern mental health care, it presents a trenchant and compelling story with broader historical significance.

Initially, this book began as a village reconstitution of a local cult shrine dedicated to the treatment of madness in southeastern Germany. Gradually, its course changed and I pursued ceaseless meanderings with inquisitive wonder. A book is a journey no author completes alone. At its end, custom obliges reflection on and thanks to colleagues, institutions, friends and loved ones for help along the way. Needless to say, so many munificent individuals contributed so many kindnesses that it would take more than a lifetime to repay them all in full. Hopefully, these acknowledgments offer some recompense, however slight.

Books are not written, they are produced, and several academic and philanthropic organizations indulged in financial and material support for this endeavor. The Fulbright Commission provided for an initial research stay of seventeen months in Munich, while the Volkswagen Foundation afforded an additional year for comparative study in Augsburg, hosted by the Institute for European Cultural History. The University of Massachusetts at Amherst and New York University awarded grants-in-aid and scholarships. The German Academic Exchange Service facilitated a return visit to Munich, hosted by the Max-Planck-Institute for Psychiatry. The staffs of the Institute for Bavarian History, the Bavarian Central State Archives and the Bavarian State Library gave repeatedly of their time and facilities, the latter providing a study carrel for six months. At Cambridge University Press, I thank Michael Watson for his forbearance and collegiality over the past months, as well as Jackie Warren, Carol Fellingham Webb and the other members of the production staff for their industry and care. The administration of the National University of Ireland of Maynooth granted a leave of absence, patiently awaiting the end product.

To my academic mentors, Ronnie Po-Chia Hsia, Hans-Christoph Rublack, Winfried Schulze and Walter Ziegler, I express deep respect for their sensible guidance over many years. Lyndal Roper and Wolfgang Behringer encouraged my efforts at every turn and suffered repeatedly through less felicitous versions of the present text. Other scholars tendered insightful critiques on portions thereof, including Tom Tentler, H. C. Erik

Midelfort and T. A. Brady. Sarah Ferber shared her ideas on demonic possessions. Among psychiatrists and their historians, Sono Shamdasani brought the medieval interests of Jung to my attention, as well as the true wonders of London: jazz, Fortnum & Mason's and the collection at the Wellcome Trust Centre for the History of Medicine. Zvi Lothane and Paul Vitz both proffered sound advice on Freud's affinity for the occult. In Munich, I thank Ferdinand Kramer and Joachim Wild for their collegial advice, as well as Walter Jaroschka for putting me through the ropes, paleographically speaking. Mathias Weber and Wolfgang Burgmair opened the doors of the former Kräpelin Institute for Psychiatry (now the Max-Planck-Institute) for my investigations into the Heinrich-Laehr Collection and the tastefully decorated cerebral museum. In Augsburg, Johannes Burckhardt and Wolfgang Weber deserve especially amiable mention for their contributions to a whole community of scholars. Energy and gentle prodding came from students, especially Georgina Laragy and Paul Clear at Maynooth and the participants at a Catholic University of America seminar on the history of medicine held in conjunction with the National Library of Medicine, National Institutes of Health. In spirit and memory remain three influential scholars: Heiko Obermann, Roy Porter and Bob Scribner. We are all poorer for the loss.

A number of dear friends deserve special mention. To my friend, Otto Feldbauer, who helped both personally and professionally, fond regards as always. Together with Eric Mader, Elisabeth Schepers and Stephan Breit, we engaged in heated historiographic debates at the Atzinger in Schellingstrasse many years before construction began on the *Historicum* across the street. Martin Ott continues to facilitate civilization, diplomacy and the long-distance transfer of materials selflessly and without hesitation. In Stuttgart and Tübingen, Sabina Holtz will recall the glory days of the *Oberseminar*. She and Stephan Zauner continue to tend the fire there. Claudia Stein has moved on to Warwick, Craig Koslofsky to Champaign-Urbana. In Augsburg, I joined for a time with a number of ex-pats and locals (not least among them Sibylle Backmann, Duane Corpis, Hans-Jörg Künast, Benedikt Maurer, Kathy Stuart and Ann Tlusty) in a fruitful and exciting renaissance of cultural history. To all my colleagues at the Department of History Maynooth, many thanks for welcoming a traveler into their midst without reservation, introducing me gently to the Celtic tiger. Ulinka Rublack, dear friend, provided important last-minute advice on the history of the emotions. To Paul Hebert, also a product of the MPP program for gifted children during another lifetime in North Tonawanda: Thanks for reading the draft – who'd have guessed how things would turn out? Maktub.

Finally, to my parents and family, thanks for love and hope. Throughout, for better or worse, from beginning to end, Irene has accompanied me.

This journey is over, finished and done; another begins. Any errors are purely my own . . .

Cill Droichead

Abbreviations

ABA	*Archiv des Bistums Augsburg*
ADB	*Allgemeine Deutsche Biographie*
AEM	*Archiv des Erzbistums München*
AMB	Anastasia Miracle Book
BayStaBi	*Bayerische Staatsbibliothek*
BB	*Benediktbeuern*
BlK	*Blechkasten*
Cgm	*Codex germanicus monacensis*
Clm	*Codex latinus monacensis*
DSM	*Diagnostic and Statistical Manual of Mental Disorders (DSM IV)*
EG	*Erscheinungen von Geistern*
Fasz.	*Faszikel*
Geist. Rat	*Geistlicher Rat*
GR	*General Register*
GW	Freud, Sigmund, *Gesammelte Werke*, ed. Anna Freud, 19 vols. (London, 1952–1987).
HGS	*Heiliggeistspital*
HK	*Hofkammer*
HR	*Kurbayern Hofrat*
HStAM	*Bayerisches Hauptstaatsarchiv*
ICD	*The International Classification of Diseases*
Jes.	*Jesuitica*
KL	*Klosterliteralien*
KU	*Kloster Urkunde*
LaT	*Landesarchiv Tirol*
Thk	*Lexikon für Theologie und Kirche*
MGH	*Monumenta Germaniae Historica*
PMB	Pürtner Miracle Book
RL	*Rentmeister Literalien*

RM	*Rentamt München*
SE	Freud, Sigmund, *The Standard Edition of the Complete Psychological Works of Sigmund Freud*, ed. James Strachey, 24 vols. (London, 1953–1974).
SStBA	*Staat- und Stadtsbibliothek Augsburg*
StAA	*Stadtsarchiv Augsburg*
StAM	*Staatsarchiv München*
UAM	*Universitätsarchiv München*
ZBLG	*Zeitschrift für bayerische Landesgeschichte*
Zedler	Zedler, Johann Heinrich, *Grosses vollständiges Universal-Lexikon* (Halle & Leipzig, 1732–1754; reprint: Graz, 1964), 68 vols.

Plate 1. "Bavarian Beacon – St. Anastasia, Life and Martyrdom, Translation, Wonders and Good Deeds." St. Anastasia atop a lighthouse, her reliquary bust held by a monk to the upper right, below several sufferers including the mad, who pray for her help; a ship in peril, one of the signs of her martyrdom; the head of the devilish sea monster appears in their lower left; upper left, the monastery of Benediktbeuern.

From the title page of Aemilian Biechler, *Bayerischer Pharos: S. Anastasia von Gott in Obern-Bayern vor 600 Jahren in dem Closter Benedictbaiern angeszundet . . .* (Augsburg, 1663), copper etching by Bartholome Kilian. (Permission of the Bavarian State Library, Munich.)

CHAPTER I

On the soul

And, if it be said, that the cure of men's minds belongs to sacred divinity, it is most true; but yet moral philosophy may be preferred unto her as a wise servant and humble handmaid.

Francis Bacon, *The Advancement of Learning*

SPIRITUAL PHYSIC

In early modern Europe, one specific form of mental health care fell within the purview of the clergy. Known as spiritual physic, Christian sects recognized and practiced it throughout Europe. Above all, spiritual physic aimed at restoring equilibrium in the souls of troubled individuals. Its practitioners treated afflictions ranging from simple tribulations (the most common form) to suicidal despair and demonic possession. Since the 1965 translation of *folie* from the title of a French monograph as "madness," historians have tended to lump this broad band of afflictions together under one comprehensive banner.[1] In fact, a relatively small proportion of contemporary sufferers complained of madness, preferring instead a subtle and differentiated vocabulary derived largely from biblical and classical sources. For most, spiritual physic represented the first echelon of mental health care in early modern Europe. The clergy, in turn, enthusiastically dispensed a pastoral service that witnessed a heyday during the sixteenth and seventeenth centuries, touching the lives of thousands of psychically troubled Europeans. Ironically, scholars have yet to treat the subject directly. Standard histories of psychology (the discipline of charting the psyche) and psychiatry (the practice of treating it) pass over the period as an unimportant hiatus between the superstition of the Middle Ages and the advent of enlightened

---

[1] Michel Foucault, *Madness and Civilization. A History of Insanity in the Age of Reason* (New York, 1965), the abridged translation of his *Histoire de la folie à l'âge classique* (Paris, 1961). On the advantages of the heuristic imprecision offered by applying the term "madness," see H. C. Erik Midelfort, *The Mad Princes of Renaissance Germany* (Charlottesville, 1994), 3–7.

empiricism.[2] In the few specialized accounts, spiritual physic receives little explanation, if any at all.[3] Why?

Perhaps one exception explains the deficit. In the late nineteenth century, spurred on by public curiosity, the theosophical movement and esotericism, liberal intellectuals conducted important historical studies of witchcraft, demon possession and exorcism. One scholar, Andrew D. White, an American diplomat and first president of Cornell, campaigned vehemently to limit sectarian influence at the fledgling university. He employed a historical argument to rail against religious interference in the sciences. White published his complaints in a blistering attack on the stifling influence of Christianity, disparaging spiritual physic as fetishism and a theological retardant to the evolution of medicine and psychiatry.[4] White and other liberal cultural historians took it for granted that modern psychiatry emerged *ex nihilo* from the scientific revolution, but only after Europeans abandoned medieval superstition to embrace reason.[5] For these scientific positivists, our ability rationally to comprehend the human psyche rested entirely upon one major historic prerequisite – the utter detachment of secular thought from religion by the Enlightenment.

[2] Spiritual physic is regularly ignored by textbook histories of psychiatry and psychology. Henri F. Ellenberger, *The Discovery of the Unconscious. The History and Evolution of Dynamic Psychiatry* (New York, 1970) glosses over the pre-nineteenth-century history of psychoanalysis superficially. The otherwise detailed work of Werner Leibbrand and Annemarie Wettley, *Der Wahnsinnn. Geschichte der abendländischen Psychopathologie* (Freiburg, 1961) lacks any reference to spiritual physic.

[3] The concluding section of Michael MacDonald's portrait of mental disorders in early modern England, *Mystical Bedlam: Madness, Anxiety, and Healing in Seventeenth-Century England* (Cambridge, 1981), 217–231, is entitled "Spiritual Physic." Here, MacDonald vaguely suggests analogies between the practice of the astrological physician Richard Napier and the ideas of Puritan Evangelists, without protracted analysis. Philip Soergel treats the subject purely metaphorically: see his "Spiritual Medicine for Heretical Poison: The Propagandistic Uses of Legends in Counter-Reformation Bavaria," *Historical Reflections* 17 (1991), 125–149; extended in Soergel, *Wondrous in his Saints. Counter-Reformation Propaganda in Bavaria* (Berkeley, 1993), 159–216. In an essay, "The Patient in England, c.1660–c.1800," in: Andrew Wear (ed.), *Medicine in Society: Historical Essays* (Cambridge, 1992), 96–97, Roy Porter briefly alludes to spiritual physic as "self-dosing" (i.e. self-treatment) or "medicine without doctors."

[4] Andrew D. White, *A History of the Warfare of Science with Theology in Christendom* (New York, 1896; reprint: Buffalo, 1993), Book 2, 1–167, a lengthy history of medicine, miracles, psychiatry and demonic possession.

[5] The so-called "Soldan paradigm" of late nineteenth-century witchcraft studies, shared by scholars such as White, George Lincoln Burr and Henry Charles Lea. The pejorative adjective "medieval," commonly employed by liberal nationalist historians of the nineteenth century, derided popular folk beliefs and Catholicism as baseless superstition. A critique of the Soldan paradigm is found in William Monter, "The Historiography of European Witchcraft: Progress and Prospects," *Journal of Interdisciplinary History* 2 (1971/1972), 435–453; Wolfgang Behringer, "Witchcraft Studies in Austria, Germany and Switzerland," in: Jonathan Barry, Marianne Hester and Gareth Roberts, *Witchcraft in Early Modern Europe: Studies in Culture and Belief* (Cambridge, 1996), 65–67; see also Behringer, *Witches and Witch-Hunts: A Global History* (Cambridge, 2004), 5.

Today, most historians of science accept the ideological struggles with theology and magic as the necessary preconditions to modern secularism in the West. Clearly, without these struggles, what we now know as the natural sciences would be unrecognizable. However, the dynamic of historic change may have been less dialectical than is generally supposed. Several modern sciences developed directly out of brushes with the supernatural, products of an evolutionary quantum leap or paradigm shift in the seventeenth century:[6] from astrology came astronomy, from alchemy, chemistry, from natural philosophy, psychology and, in our case, out of spiritual physic emerged psychiatry. In the course of these metamorphoses, arcana from religious and magical systems of thought seeped into the secular realm surreptitiously and ensconced themselves in Western scientific orthodoxy. White himself cautiously acknowledged a "vast system of 'pastoral medicine', so powerful not only throughout the Middle Ages, but even in modern times, both among Catholics and Protestants."[7] Today, prudent observers seek productive and open, if consciously critical dialogue between religion and science. There is an increased willingness to take culturally relative factors into account and recent research has yielded exciting insights into the notoriously ephemeral realm of human consciousness.[8]

With that in mind, the present study proposes to redress a considerable deficit in our understanding of the historical development of mental health care. It proposes to do so through a cultural history of spiritual physic in the Duchy of Bavaria. One could justify such a study for reasons of historical accuracy alone. However, the significance of spiritual physic extends far beyond any antiquarian fetish for pre-empirical quackery, esoteric religiosity or politically correct folk belief. The history of spiritual physic is significant for two important reasons. First, it reminds us that attitudes toward mental health care are conditioned by particular political, religious and social constellations. The culture of insanity manifests itself in a community relating through shared values on normal behavior. Second, early modern spiritual physic also exerted a formative influence on the ideological

---

[6] Ibid., 9.   [7] White, *A History of the Warfare*, Book 2, 27–30.

[8] A prominent example of such collaboration is the work of the Mind and Life Institute in Dharamsala; see Daniel Goleman, *Destructive Emotions: How Can We Overcome Them? A Scientific Dialogue with the Dalai Lama* (New York, 2003). In 2004, research conducted by Richard Davidson, a psychologist, and Matthieu Ricard, a Buddhist monk and molecular biologist, at the University of Wisconsin, Madison suggested the positive effects of meditation on the brain. However, not all neuroscientists are equally enthusiastic. Some opposed the specter of religious influence in the sciences through a boycott of the 2005 annual meeting of the Society of Neuroscience in Washington, D.C., where the Dalai Lama was scheduled to lecture. They denied any ulterior motives. According to the *Guardian* (July 27, 2005), 7: ". . . many of the scientists who initiated the protest are of Chinese origin, but say their concern [*sic*] are not related to politics."

crucible of the seventeenth century, out of which modern psychiatry arose in the West.

In the course of this study, I argue that spiritual physic broaches the nexus not only of religion and science (still recognized as interconnected systems of knowledge and practice at that time), but also of madness, early modern politics and mentalities. Politically, the history of spiritual physic in Bavaria elucidates the broader historical processes of state building, confessionalization and social disciplining, where the state instrumentalized it to promote a homogeneous religious identity. It helped to reify the "self" according to the dictates of a normative social code, defining some individuals as normal and others as troubled, mad, tempted or possessed in a manner consistent with perceived patterns of behavioral abnormalities. The decline of spiritual physic in the seventeenth century demonstrates how perceptions of mental health depended upon social relations and material circumstances. For example, the normative model of spiritual physic promoted by the ruling elite did not always correspond with popular understanding and ritual practice, because consumption involves expropriation and does not necessarily imply consensus on meanings.[9] Culture is produced, but it is also lived and undergoes changes. Like psychiatry today, contemporaries viewed spiritual physic as an emotionally charged issue. Were that not the case, we could reduce its history – and that of mental health in general – to White's vitriolic narrative of objective progress and intellectual achievement.

Alternatively, Michel Foucault located the history of madness within the confines of an illusive and threatening discourse on power. This is not the place to enter partisan debate over "the master of the history of madness."[10] Probing minds of greater agility have elsewhere adequately dealt with the implications of his work.[11] Suffice to say, madness delimited power in both discursive and tangible ways. This study makes abundantly clear that, as with most other public policies, the ruling elite integrated spiritual physic into their strategic policy considerations for a variety of motives, not all intentionally harmful or bent on repression. More often than not, the historical records reveal a true sense of frustration and helplessness

---

[9] Some prominent examples include Michel de Certeau, *The Practice of Everyday Life* (Berkeley, 1984); Roger Chartier, *Cultural History: Between Practices and Representations*, trans. Lydia G. Cochrane, (Ithaca, 1988); Stephen Greenblatt, *Marvelous Possessions: The Wonder of the New World* (Chicago, 1991).

[10] Georges Minois, *History of Suicide: Voluntary Death in Western Culture* (Baltimore, 1999), 77.

[11] For critical opinions of Foucault's work on madness, see Gary Gutting, "Foucault and the History of Madness," in: Gutting, *The Cambridge Companion to Foucault* (Cambridge, 1994), 47–70; H. C. Erik Midelfort, "Madness and the Problems of Psychological History in the Sixteenth Century," *Sixteenth Century Journal* 12 (1981), 5–12; Winifred Barbara Maher and Brendan Maher, "The Ship of Fools: *Stultifera Navis* or *Ignis Fatuus*?," *American Psychologist* 37 (July 1982), 756–761.

among sufferers, kin, neighbors and rulers alike. Together they turned to spiritual physic, which offered a semblance of hope. The authorities expressed paternalistic concern for their "poor senseless" subjects and alarm about dangers to public safety, not to mention maltreatment at the hands of callous relatives and communities. In the ensuing translation of their strategic policies into action, however, methods of communications and patterns of consumption often dictated practical outcomes far removed from the original intent.

Communications and consumption are two oft-ignored variables in strategic planning. The early modern media of social and cultural communications complicated policy implementation in peculiar ways. If the authorities could access novel print technology, the bulk of the populace still relied heavily on an oral culture. Occasionally, the history of spiritual physic allows us to track the otherwise murky lines of oral communications. We can actually chart tactical methods of consumption at the popular level, fostered by specific material circumstances, wants, needs and aspirations. Even when subjects read, they read selectively and differently from courtiers. In the practice of everyday life, people consumed spiritual physic to their own advantage, often with little concern for the strategically innovative policies of the ruling elite.

I also contend that the history of early modern spiritual physic explains the emergence of bourgeois psychiatry in the late eighteenth century and the continuing influence of religion on psychology, psychiatry and psychotherapy from the nineteenth century to the present. Therefore, just as Andrew White suggested over a century ago (and as today's providers of pastoral care throughout the world will readily acknowledge), facets of spiritual physic remain with us. For these reasons, spiritual physic is hardly a historical eccentricity. It is both relevant and immediate, not only to the cultural, political, religious and social history of early modern Europe, but for psychologists, psychiatrists, psychoanalysts, philosophers of mind and current providers of pastoral care. And yet, despite a multitude of arguments in favor of its recollection, the history of spiritual physic remains obscure. Why?

The vocation of its practitioners is of prime importance, since they offend our secular boundaries between science and religion, between knowledge and belief, and between the profane and the sacred. For example, in a discussion of lawyers, religiosity might not appear particularly germane until we recall that vigorous practices still operate in the vast arena of canon law. For historical purposes, we might also recall the classic bifurcation of law in early modern Europe, when lawyers held doctorates in either canon or

Roman law – or proudly bore both titles. Even less is understood about the classically observed bifurcation of medicine into its corporal and spiritual branches. Though not officially conferred in university degrees per se, spiritual physic none the less recognized those disciplinary boundaries. Professional competencies sometimes overlapped, but the clergy's authority over the psyche proved tenacious, because the care of souls traditionally fell under their sway. In sheer numbers, spiritual physicians outnumbered university-trained mad-doctors, reflected in the absolute volume of patients.

Not surprisingly, early modern theologians most vocally advocated spiritual physic as an independent branch of medicine concerned with the mind–body relationship. In Italy, the Minorite friar and exorcist Girolamo Menghi[12] sharply contrasted corporal physicians (*medici corporali*) with spiritual physicians (*medici spirituali*), charging the latter with the care of the soul and the former with bodily ailments – incidentally, a matter considered secondary in importance.[13] In England, John Downame's *Spiritual Physicke* (1600) depicted the tripartite division of humankind into body, affections and soul as the very essence of humanity. In chapters four and twenty of his highly successful *Devotions on Emergent Occassions* (1624), John Donne acknowledged "the necessity of two physicians . . . the bodily and the spiritual physician" for their disparate contributions to the health of the whole person; like Menghi, Donne too preferred spiritual physic. In the Low Countries, the Spanish jurist and demonologist Martin Del Rio, SJ coined the unique expression "*Christus Psychiatrus*" (the first-known mention of a psychiatrist) in conjunction with spiritual physic:

But by means of this spiritual physic [medico animarum], the cure of all pestilence and wounds is facilitated by him, whose will alone, has created the soul and alone can heal it very easily. Just because there is no balm in Galaad, can one say he fails to provide the Church, his bride, with a suitable drug [de pharmacis idoneis] for healing its sons? Anyone who acknowledges this in their mind or words is ignorant of our sacraments and religion. Therefore we fail ourselves when we neglect what Mother Church proposes and the remedies which CHRIST, the healer of souls [CHRISTUS Psychiatrus], prescribes for our treatment. We sad and miserable creatures: there is surely no one who does not feel or admit that they are in need of

---

[12] On Menghi, see Mary R. O'Neil, "Sacerdote ovvero strione: Ecclesiastical and Superstitious Remedies in 16th Century Italy," in: Steven L. Kaplan (ed.), *Understanding Popular Culture* (New York, 1984), 53–55; David Gentilcore, *From Bishop to Witch: The System of the Sacred in Early Modern Terra d'Otranto* (Manchester, 1992), 94–127; Christian Gottlieb Jöcher, *Allgemeines Gelehrten-Lexicon*, vol. III (Leipzig, 1751), 433–434.

[13] See his introductory *Il Stampatore alli Lettori* in the *Compendio dell'Arte Essorcistica et possibilità a delle mirabili & stupende operationi delli demoni & de Malefici* (Bologna, 1576).

purification. Who can deny this? Every day, we struggle with the filth of our own flesh; the foul dirt of earthly ambition constantly stains us; we continuously daub ourselves with the infernal pitch of dishonesty, mixed by the demons themselves.[14]

Related by marriage to Michel de Montaigne, Del Rio held a doctorate of law from the University of Salamanca and professorships at universities in Douai, Liege, Louvain and Graz.[15] He and other moralists and demonologists encouraged Europeans periodically to cleanse their souls from the misery of "everyday struggles": the blackness of deceit and the soil of earthliness (two characteristic signs of melancholy), corruptions of the body, and the interventions of evil spirits. Martin Luther, too, described "daily" dangers to the soul, hinting at the genetic inheritability of madness:

For, first, free-will led us into original sin, and brought death upon us: afterwards, upon sin followed not only death, but all manner of mischiefs, as we daily find in the world, murder, lying, deceiving, stealing, and other evils, so that no man is safe in the twinkling of an eye, in body or goods, but always stands in danger. And, besides these evils, man is afflicted with yet one greater, as is noted in the gospel – namely, that he is possessed of the devil, who makes him mad and raging. We know not rightly what we became after the fall of our first parents; what from our mothers we have brought with us. For we have altogether, a confounded, corrupt, and poisoned nature, both in body and soul; throughout the whole of man is nothing that is good.[16]

Corporal physicians throughout Europe agreed with moralists. The eminent English medicus Thomas Browne emphatically reminded readers of his *Religio medici* (1642) that the concerns of the soul far outweighed those of the body; a hugely successful book, it went into multiple editions and found numerous imitators.[17] Throughout his home medical encyclopedia, *The Terrible Desolation of the Human Race* (1610), the Austrian Hippolyt Guarinonius, personal physician to Emperor Ferdinand II, consistently associated both bodily and spiritual health with personal salvation. The German physician Theodorus Corbeius subordinated nosology (the systematic categorization of diseases) to etiology (the enumeration of the

---

[14] Martin Del Rio, *Florida mariana* (Antwerp, 1598), 160–161.
[15] André Rayez, "Del Rio," in: *Dictionnaire de spiritualité ascetique et mystique*, vol. III (Paris, 1957), 131–132.
[16] A slightly modified version of the translation of William Hazlitt (ed. and trans.), *The Table Talks of Martin Luther* (London, 1895), 119. Demonologists also believed that the devil caused disease and spiritual afflictions, such as melancholy, epilepsy, paralysis, blindness, deafness, imaginations causing love and hate, and other mental disturbances: David Gentilcore, *Healers and Healing in Early Modern Italy* (Manchester, 1998), 161.
[17] The concept is the subject of a recent volume by Ole Peter Grell and Andrew Cunningham (eds.), *Religio Medici: Medicine and Religion in Seventeenth Century England* (Aldershot, 1996).

causes of disease). By way of clarification, he explained how the causes of all diseases clearly fell under one of two headings – either medical or theological, the latter clearly requiring the intervention of the clergy.[18] Some physicians deferred to their ecclesiastical counterparts out of sincere Hippocratic concerns for the welfare of the human spirit. However, an ominous ideological tension existed, one which has poisoned the relationship between empirical science and religious belief ever since. Perhaps the most infamous example from the natural sciences is the trial of Galileo for heresy and his recantation. Similar threats confronted those who delved into the mechanisms of the human soul. The prevailing system of Galenic medicine still subordinated the body to the soul and medical authors usually passed decorously over the problematic mind–body relationship. If one insisted that God did not impose life upon the human body for religious purposes or that it represented an inherent characteristic of the organism itself, one risked charges of heresy.[19]

The influence of religious orthodoxy on medicine during the early modern period raises uncomfortable questions about natural science as an objective pursuit. To be sure, historians have long distanced themselves from the Rankean ideal of absolute empirical objectivity. Nor can post-Enlightenment medicine, psychology or psychiatry – or any other branch of science, for that matter – claim to be entirely value-free. As disciplines, they are trapped within specific economic, political, social and contextual dimensions. In other words, they have a history. The question of objectivity in psychology is especially perplexing because of its reflexive nature, since the object of study, i.e. the human psyche, is also the subject of analysis.[20] To a certain extent, the logic of psychology is precariously circular. Despite this challenge, the history of spiritual physic also offers a strong argument of tradition in favor of psychology and psychiatry as legitimate branches of human knowledge.

Universalistic claims to a metahistorical understanding of the human psyche remain the chief obstacle to any contextual history of mental health care. Etiological characterizations of mental illness as genetically coded, biologically static and universally comprehensible hamper historical investigations. Presumably, some illnesses disappear without a trace in the course of

---

[18] Theodorus Corbeius, *Pathologia* (Noribergum, 1647), 19. See also Gentilcore, *Healers*, 204–207.
[19] Ole Peter Grell and Andrew Cunningham, "Medicine and Religion in Seventeenth-Century England," in: Grell and Cunningham, *Religio Medici*, 5.
[20] For an insightful discussion of the reflexive problem in psychology, see Sonu Shamdasani, *Jung and the Making of Modern Psychology: The Dream of a Science* (Cambridge, 2003).

natural selection, preventing biological reconstitution, but leaving us with the nagging difficulty of explaining the phenomena.[21] Culturally, medical anthropologists recognize that perceptions of illness are conditioned by belief systems. These attitudes have already made deep inroads into medical practice. For example, clinical psychiatrists in training are now instructed to determine whether a suspected mental illness "is a true delusion or is widely held by members of a religious group and therefore not a delusion."[22] Nevertheless, as Sarah Ferber warns us, we need to remain vigilant about the legal and ethical ramifications of accepting occult dinosaurs uncritically into our midst, out of place and out of time, in the name of recondite populism or absolute relativism, an oxymoronic concept.[23] There are some aspects of the Enlightenment, like universal human rights, well worth preserving. Hence, this study seeks to contribute to our historical understanding of spiritual physic as one form of mental health care with lasting ramifications rather than to justify it.

One example of the potential for atavisms in our current understanding is the etymology of a common German expression for mental illness – *Geisteskrankheit*, literally a malady of the spirit or soul, whether of organic or inorganic origin. One ethnographic encyclopedia specifically defines "spiritual afflictions," as the "unsolicited and malevolent attention of the spirit world . . . thought to be the result of human agency, in some cases, divine in others" and distinct "from natural illness."[24] The late medieval Alsatian preacher Geiler von Kaysersberg described many spiritual afflictions in his German sermons.[25] At that time, all illnesses were vaguely associated with the Christian notion of sin, even if contemporaries recognized a plurality of causes and a punitive relationship (illness as a God-sent punishment for

---

[21] St. Vitus dance, for example; see H. C. Erik Midelfort, *A History of Madness in Sixteenth-Century Germany* (Stanford, 1999), 32–49.

[22] Michael Gelder, Dennis Gath and Richard Mayou, *Concise Oxford Textbook of Psychiatry* (Oxford, 1994), 13.

[23] In her *Demonic Possession and Exorcism in Early Modern France* (London, 2004), 1, Ferber begins with a disturbing account invoking Australian solicitors who entered evidence from a seventeenth-century account of demonic activity in a 1993 murder trial. It is unclear whether this "evidence" was actually accepted by the court. Perhaps more disturbing – and more complex – are rising incidents of persecutions for witchcraft throughout Africa, as well as the inclusion of anti-witch statutes on the law books of some African nations.

[24] Vieda Skultans, "Affliction: An Overview," in: Mircea Eliade, *The Encyclopedia of Religion*, vol. 1 (New York, 1987), 51–55. See also Bruce Kapferer, *A Celebration of Denons: Exorcism and the Aesthetics of Healing in Sri Lanka* (Bloomington, 1983); I. M. Lewis, *Ecstatic Religion: An Anthropological Study of Spirit Possession and Shamanism* (Harmondsworth, 1971).

[25] Johann Geiler von Kaysersberg, *Das irrig Schaf. Sagt von kleinmütikeit und verzweiflung* (n.l. [Strasburg], c.1510).

sinful behavior) was never definitive.[26] Erasmus of Rotterdam considered the causes (etiology) of insanity as twofold; it arose either from the visitations of demons from hell, which stirred the passions of the soul to evil deeds, or from folly, which freed the soul from anxious cares through the visitations of happy mental aberrations.[27] Nevertheless, ill humors were regularly described as peccant (i.e. corrupt), from the Latin "peccare," to sin. Conversely, healthiness, holiness and well being (*salus*) too were semantically related.[28]

Although mental illnesses could just as easily have purely organic causes, they might also be interpreted as a providential test of faith or a halo of sanctity. In England, Calvinist interpretations of providence justified spiritual physic in an allusion to insanity as a manifestation of God's will, a curse to the wicked and a blessing to the godly.[29] Among corporal physicians, religion seriously influenced perceptions of mental disorders until the mid-seventeenth century. That influence persisted much longer in the minds of many ordinary people. As late as the eighteenth century, Simon Browne (a Dissenting minister from Portsmouth, England) still described his own insanity, which left him "a brute animal without consciousness," as the murder of his soul.[30]

The scope of spiritual physic extended well beyond demonic possession to include mundane conditions.[31] However, despite any association

---

[26] Weakness (*Schwäche, Schwachheit*) appears as the primary definition of illness (*Krankheit*) in the standard encyclopedic dictionary of the German language, Grimm's *Deutsches Wörterbuch*, vol. v (Leipzig, 1879; – reprint Munich, 1984), 2038. It offers an etymology of illness from sin as a sign of weakness of character: "*mhd. kranchheit (s. krank 1): wenn sie einen psalmen oder gebett gesprochen haben on gegenwirtige warnemung, sunder mit ausschweifung des gemüts, die mönschliche kranckheit ausz ir selbs nit vermeiden mag. Keiserberg irrig schaf; gott, der da weiszt und bekent unser aller gröszeste krankheit und neigung zu dem bösen. dreieck. spieg . . .*" However, an absolute association of sin with illness is highly tentative; see Raymond Klibansky, Erwin Panofsky and Fritz Saxl, *Saturn and Melancholy: Studies in the History of Natural Philosophy, Religion and Art* (New York, 1964), 67; Dirk Matejovski, *Das Motiv des Wahnsinns in der mittelalterlichen Dichtung* (Frankfurt a.M., 1996), 84–85. On the early modern period, see Gentilcore, *Healers*, esp. 6, 11–12, 192.

[27] Desiderius Erasmus, *Praise of Folly* (London, 1993), 58–59.

[28] Gentilcore, *Healers*, 6.

[29] David Harley, "Spiritual Physic, Providence and English Medicine, 1560–1640," in: Ole Peter Grell and Andrew Cunningham (eds.), *Medicine and the Reformation* (London, 1993), 101–117.

[30] David Berman, "Simon Browne: the Soul-Murdered Theologian," *History of Psychiatry* 7 (1996), 257–263. Berman suggests a coincidence between the "soul murder" of Browne and that of Daniel Schreber in the nineteenth century. Schreber described his own treatment at the hands of the psychiatric community as "soul murder"; see Zvi Lothane, *In Defense of Schreber: Soul Murder and Psychiatry* (Hillsdale, 1992).

[31] Michael Kutzer, *Anatomie des Wahnsinns. Geisteskrankheit im medizinischen Denken der frühen Neuzeit und die Anfänge der pathologischen Anatomie* (Hürtgenwald, 1998), 13–18. However, Kutzer's critique of ecclesiastic treatments (esp. pp. 21–30) contradicts some of his views on Weyer. The clergy also treated organic matters and many corporal physicians harbored strong theological convictions and popular beliefs.

of mental health with providence, most ordinary sufferers expressly consulted spiritual physicians for this-worldly solace. The methods employed by practitioners were a mix of official Christian sacraments and semi-official sacramentals, offering sufferers hopes of effective alleviation in the here-and-now. By examining case histories, we unearth clues to the physical and social conditions associated with mental suffering in a pre-industrial society. Contemporary etiology, psychopathology (the science of the origin, nature and course of mental illness studied from a psychological perspective) and nosology applied a cornucopia of seemingly contradictory terms and therapies. At times, they mystify modern observers, leaving some pining romantically for the rational shelter of twenty-first-century classification – ostensibly offered by the *ICD* or the *DSM*.[32] If the "inchoate state" of early modern psychiatry[33] confuses us with its easy and apparently irreconcilable mixture of magical, religious and scientific concepts, then spiritual physic was more transparent to contemporaries, for whom its cosmological and eschatological implications were all too immediate.[34] Thus, this seemingly inconsistent and arbitrary system actually possessed an internal logic all its own, or at least just as much of one as we have come to expect from present-day psychiatry and its competing schools. For that reason, perceptions of spiritual physic also tell historians a great deal about the translation of religious cosmology and medical ideology into the mentalities of ordinary people.

In the sixteenth century, advocates of spiritual physic took great pains to systematize procedures for treating afflictions of the soul. Menghi, for example, compiled an exhaustive list of ecclesiastical remedies (*medicine ecclesiatiche*), a repertoire consisting of auricular confession, communion and pilgrimage, the laying on of hands and relics, and exorcisms, the most powerful of all. For Catholics, the parish priest as father confessor typically stood in the vanguard of care. In Spain, the status of the father confessor as a "doctor of souls," who administered "suitable spiritual medicine," was greatly enhanced in post-Tridentine Catholicism.[35] According to the collegial and provincial reports of Austrian Jesuits, auricular confession in conjunction with the reception of the Eucharist proved the most effective

---

[32] The *International Classification of Diseases* and the *Diagnostic and Statistical Manual of Mental Disorders*; for example the *DSM IV* (Washington, 1994).

[33] MacDonald, *Mystical Bedlam*, 7.

[34] Most recently: Stuart Clark, *Thinking with Demons: The Idea of Witchcraft in Early Modern Europe* (Oxford, 1997), 401–434; Denis Crouzet, "A Woman and the Devil: Possession and Exorcism in Sixteenth-Century France," in: Michael Wolfe (ed.), *Changing Identities in Early Modern France* (Durham, N. C., 1997), 191–215.

[35] Stephen Haliczer, *Sexuality in the Confessional. A Sacrament Profaned* (Oxford, 1996), 22, 35.

form of spiritual physic in their arsenal of "soul remedies" (*Seelenarznei*).[36] The two rituals had been integrated since 1215, when Innocent III ordered all Christians to cleanse themselves yearly by shriving prior to the reception of grace through consumption of the body of Christ at Easter time.[37] The cathartic confession as a therapy of the word[38] and the Eucharistic therapy of communal reintegration[39] followed a compelling logic, with ritual purification from corruption celebrated by reintroduction into the community of believers during a shared feast. Successful treatments helped to validate the power of ritual sacraments like penance and transubstantiation, a matter of considerable propagandistic import during the Reformation.

In book six of his legendary *Disquisitiones magicarum*, Del Rio specified the duties of the confessor as the dual roles of a judge and a physician. In the latter, he noted, "A doctor must know the causes, types, and cures of diseases. The diseases of the mind are sins . . ." whose types and causes he elaborated in the preceding five books.[40] In his discussion of remedies, Del Rio detailed superstitious or illicit remedies and a systematic list of twelve licit or supernatural remedies emanating from God and the church and virtually identical to Menghi's.[41] He proposed an orthodox and pious life as the first step to spiritual well being. The sacraments (especially baptism and penance) provided more serious ecclesiastical remedies, as did the intercession of saints, pilgrimage and miracles, with exorcisms comprising

[36] Gernot Heiss, "Konfessionelle Propaganda und kirchliche Magie. Berichte der Jesuiten über den Teufel aus der Zeit der Gegenreformation in den mitteleuropäischen Ländern der Habsburger," *Römische Historische Mitteilungen* 32 and 33 (1990/1991), 122–125. Books on consolation (*Trostbücher*) and spiritual physic (*Geistliche Arznei*) had an enormous appeal in the sixteenth century; for example, Urbanus Rhegius, *Seelenarznei* (Augsburg, 1529).

[37] W. David Myers, *"Poor Sinning Folk": Confession and Conscience in Counter-Reformation Germany* (Ithaca, 1996), 29–38, 58, 146–153.

[38] One should distinguish between the orality of Catholic auricular confession and the Protestant "therapy of the word," e.g. readings from the Bible.

[39] Generally: Ronnie Po-Chia Hsia, *The World of the Catholic Renewal 1540–1770* (Cambridge, 1998), 198–201. On the refusal to take communion as a reflection of communal discord in an evangelical village in Württemberg, see David Warren Sabean, *Power in the Blood: Popular Culture and Village Discourse in Early Modern Germany* (Cambridge, 1984), 37–60. In Catholic Bavaria, non-participation in communion could be considered a criminal offense; see Rainer Beck, "Der Pfarrer und das Dorf. Konformismus und Eigensinn im katholischen Bayern des 17./18. Jahrhunderts," in: Richard van Dülmen (ed.), *Armut, Liebe, Ehre. Studien zur historischen Kulturforschung* (Frankfurt am Main, 1988), 107–143.

[40] Martin Del Rio, *Disquisitiones magicarum Libri Sex* (Antwerp, 1599–1600). Later editions from Antwerp (1608) and Mainz (1617) were also consulted for this study. For example, this section comes from Del Rio, *Disquisitiones* (1608), 504–527 – Bk. 6 "*De officio confessarii.*" (Notably, the first authority cited by Del Rio in this section was the famous Italian physician Battista Codronchi.) Wherever possible, however, I have made use of the most recent abridged edition and translation of P. G. Maxwell-Stuart, *Martín Del Rio: Investigations into Magic* (Manchester, 2000), here 243.

[41] Ibid., 262–270, on the twelve forms of licit remedies.

an extreme ecclesiastical tonic. Others included merciful works and sacramentals, such as the invocation of Christ or the Virgin, genuflection, relics and holy water, benedictions of bread, salt or grain, blessings, pious charms and amulets and the tolling of sacred bells. Menghi, Del Rio and the German Jesuit Peter Thyraeus distinguished ecclesiastical physicians not only from their lay counterparts, but from the practitioners of vile popular superstition as well. However, their definition of superstition differed fundamentally from our own. They characterized superstition as efficacious and evil magic, tasking the clergy to combat unauthorized practices with religiously orthodox ones. Thyraeus produced what has been called the first "scientific"[42] (i.e. systematic) research on modern exorcism, based in part on the experiences of Peter Canisius, a close colleague of his brother Herman Thyraeus, SJ, at the universities of Ingolstadt and Dillingen. Peter Thyraeus revealed his contempt for unauthorized healers in the ancient past and unfavorably compared their motivations with those of corporal physicians:

For they were not Christians – who would render this kind of service free and without any contract for payment – but infidels, mountebanks, and peddlers, who went around the towns and made use of superstitions, and, like medical healers tending the body, made a money-spinning racket of it . . . But God wished to be called on by possessed persons to heal through his power. For although He is, above all, the healer of souls, and seeks, before all, their salvation, He by no means neglects the welfare of the body, and removes things that are hurtful to it – as are troubles caused by spirits – for the sake of His kindness and benevolence towards the human race; and this aid was all the more to be expected from Him, in that He alone was able to help.[43]

Several points are worth noting here. Not surprisingly, Thyraeus prioritized salvation over bodily health like his fellow demonologists Menghi and Del Rio, and, as we have seen, many contemporary physicians. By putting spiritual welfare ahead of physical health, he clearly implied the superiority of spiritual physic, over not only superstitious peddlers, but racketeering medical professionals as well. In etiological terms, he too presumed a significant causal role of supernatural agency in spiritual afflictions. Perhaps surprisingly, Thyreaus also emphasized the ability of spiritual physicians to cure bodily illnesses, as well as the power of evil spirits to cause physical

---

[42] "Le dernier thème abordé par Thyraeus concerne la POSSESSION et l'EXORCISME. A ce sujet, il ne faut pas oublier que, à côté d'une recherche scientifique, l'auteur voulait aider ceux qui étaient affligés de ces maux": Constantin Becker, "Thyraeus," in: *Dictionnaire de Spiritualité* vol. xv (Paris, 1991), 913–916.

[43] Petrus Thyraeus, *Daemoniaci, hoc est: de obsessis a spiritibus daemoniorum hominibus* (Colonia Agrippina, 1598), 107, 113.

harm. One seventeenth-century pamphleteer specifically prescribed spiritual physic as a remedy for the plague.[44] As devout Catholics, Menghi, Del Rio and Thyraeus all insinuated that priests were institutionally empowered by God as healers in accordance with the Petrine doctrine on the keys of loosing and binding and the apostolic succession, the cornerstones of sacramental penance and papal legitimacy.[45] In doing so, they claimed the ability to treat physical maladies in addition to purely spiritual afflictions. Nor was the practice limited to Catholicism. In England throughout the seventeenth and eighteenth centuries, some divines openly practiced corporal medicine in remote areas suffering a scarcity of corporal physicians, while others authored treatises on self-medication to guide the laity, such as Hugh Smythson's *Compleat Family Physick* and the *Primitive Physick* of John Wesley (founder of the Methodists), a self-help manual for the poor.[46]

Furthermore, the competition between unofficial and official healers represented another source of tension. Therefore, the history of spiritual physic is the flip side of the unauthorized treatment of spiritual afflictions by laypersons. The cultural dominance of the clergy in spiritual physic was part of a larger religious and political campaign against popular culture and superstitious practices, integral to the wider Reformation and Catholic Reform movements. Spread in part through catechism, in part through criminal prosecution, the fight against unauthorized practices was most visible in the area of demonic possession and exorcism.[47] Popular competitors, such as the exorcist of Santena, Giovanni Baptista Chiesa,[48] fell foul of systematic repression. They were charged with the illicit performance of sacred rituals (such as exorcising without an episcopal license) or, fatefully, practicing superstitious magic with the aid of Satan. It was irrelevant that members of the clergy were "repeatedly found guilty of complicity in the very errors they were charged to eradicate,"[49] since they cured by virtue of their office with institutional authority. Nevertheless, the public's thirst for healers, both official and unofficial, proved insatiable. The public craving for access to physic of all sorts grew steadily, reflected in the popular

---

[44] Anonymous, *Geistliche Artzney in Zeit der Pest, ansteckenden Kranckheiten, und betrübten Zeiten* (n.l., n.d.) is a Marian eulogy, perhaps from the time of the Thirty Years War.

[45] On the role of the keys in penance, see Myers, *"Poor Sinning Folk," passim*; Thomas N. Tentler, *Sin and Confession on the Eve of the Reformation* (Princeton, 1977), *passim*.

[46] Porter, "The Patient in England," 98.

[47] Clark, *Thinking with Demons*, 395.

[48] For Chiesa's story, see Giovanni Levi, *Inheriting Power: The Story of an Exorcist*, trans. Lydia G. Cochrane (Chicago, 1988). Levi, *Inheriting Power*, 177, fn. 4, intimates that Chiesa may have read a book on spiritual physic by P. A. Giustoboni, *Il medico spirituale al punto, aggiuntovi in questa impressione dallo stesso autore L'esorcista istrutto* (Milan, 1694).

[49] O'Neil, "Sacerdote ovvero strione," 56.

canonizations of healer-saints, which eclipsed the image of the heroic missionary martyr by the eighteenth century.[50] In this sense, spiritual physic is one example of what David Gentilcore has aptly termed "medical pluralism."[51] As the records of the *protomedicato* of Naples and applications for canonization (the records of *Miracolati*) to the Neapolitan Congregation of Rites in the eighteenth century demonstrate, early modern Europeans wholeheartedly supported medical pluralism to keep all their options open. Resilient popular attitudes toward spiritual physic throve side-by-side with a growing desire for care provided by healing professionals, while official policies gradually (though never completely) diminished the taste for the remedies of unauthorized healers.[52]

The Catholic clergy were certainly not the only official practitioners of spiritual physic in Europe. At first glance, the rejection of sacramental penance by some Protestants might appear to have posed a serious obstacle, but this is hardly the case. Martin Luther himself admitted the efficacy of auricular confession in evangelical pastoral care.[53] One staunch evangelical moralist, Andreas Celichius, made an ardent plea for the spiritual treatment of demoniacs in 1594/1595, claiming to have personally witnessed at least thirty cases of actual possession in the previous twelve years.[54] In England from 1580 onward, people displayed greater concern with spiritual afflictions than ever before and the reading public developed a remarkable taste for classical medical psychology, a shift sometimes attributed to demographic growth and economic change.[55] The rediscovery of classical teachings on mental health by civic and Christian humanists in a pan-European movement dubbed the "*De anima* Renaissance" sparked further interest.[56] In England, Puritans led the way as physicians of the

---

[50] Hsia, *Catholic Renewal*, 134–137. For a detailed treatment of this process, see Albrecht Burkardt, *Les clients des saints; maladie et quête du miracle à travers les procès de canonisation de la première moitié du XVIIe siècle en France* (Rome, 2004).

[51] Gentilcore, *Healers*, passim.

[52] Some of the Neapolitan records are examined in David Gentilcore, "Contesting Illness in Early Modern Naples: Miracolati and the Congregation of Rites," *Past and Present* 148 (1994), 117–148. On the office of the *protomedicato*, see Gentilcore, *Healers*, 29–55; see also Giovanni Romeo, *Inquisitori, esorcisti e streghe nell'Italia della Controriforma* (Florence, 1990), 219–220.

[53] Luther's doctrine of penance is outlined in Susan Karant-Nunn, *The Reformation of Ritual: An Interpretation of Early Modern Germany* (London, 1997), 91–107. For a provocative social history of Lutheran confession in Franconia, see Hans-Christoph Rublack, "Lutherische Beichte und Sozialdisziplinierung," *Archive for Reformation History* 84 (1993), 127–155.

[54] H. C. Erik Midelfort, "The Devil and the German People: Reflections on the Popularity of Demon Possession in Sixteenth Century Germany," in: Steven Ozment, *Religion and Culture in the Renaissance and Reformation* (Kirksville, 1989), 106; Midelfort, *A History of Madness*, 59; Clark, *Thinking with Demons*, 405.

[55] MacDonald, *Mystical Bedlam*, 2–3.   [56] Midelfort, *A History of Madness*, 140–181.

soul.[57] Their leaders and writers reminded the rank-and-file clergy to attend to infirm souls and admonished the community of true believers to accept the religious significance of mental illnesses.[58] Religious authors like Downame incorporated contemporary Galenic and Aristotelian theories of the human soul into their religious works.[59] He stressed the underlying structural unity of mind and body, refusing to accord the soul any sort of dualist autonomy from the affections. Of course, Puritan divines like Downame preferred non-institutionalized rituals of healing, such as fasting, prayer and peer support, and they outwardly opposed most Catholic rituals.

The creation of a class of seminary-trained clergy and the massive catechizing of the people (a process alternatively known as Christianization or confessionalization) promoted demand for and access to spiritual physic from the later sixteenth century until the mid-seventeenth century. Both the dissemination of a penitential ideology of internalized self-discipline and the availability of larger numbers of qualified clergy fueled the growth of spiritual physic. Confessional competition and exaggerated claims by Catholics and Protestants encouraged demand by raising public expectations. As competitors, practitioners engaged in a propaganda war and, subsequently, found themselves at ideological loggerheads during the period of violent religious wars which rocked Europe at that time.

In Catholic propaganda, spiritual physic served as a weapon of social psychology in the post-Tridentine campaign against superstition and the contagion of heresy. In 1600, for example, Daniel Baradinus characterized orthodox pastoral care as an efficacious remedy for heretical poison, defending the healing power of ritual pilgrimage against Protestant attacks on the power of the saints.[60] While English Puritans eschewed most Catholic rituals, some invoked astrological treatments for spiritual afflictions. The English divine Richard Napier and his imitators treated thousands of patients in the first half of the seventeenth century. Throughout Europe, practices swelled, as did the ranks of identifiable sufferers and demoniacs. As part of a larger political and religious conflict, the competition between spiritual, corporal and folk healers became an intense and, at times, dangerous struggle, both for practitioners and sufferers alike.

---

[57] MacDonald, *Mystical Bedlam*, 217–231.
[58] Michael MacDonald, "Religion, Social Change, and Psychological Healing in England, 1600–1800," in: W. J. Sheils (ed.), *The Church and Healing* (Oxford, 1982), 103–104.
[59] However, the suggestion that early modern "spiritual physicke" is synonymous with psychotherapy is clearly anachronistic: see Richard Hunter and Ida Macalpine, *Three Hundred Years of Psychiatry 1535–1860* (London, 1963), 55.
[60] See Daniel Baradinus, *Geistliche Artzne für Ketzergifft* (Munich, 1600); considered in Soergel, "Spiritual Medicine."

Mental anguish, whether socially constructed or historically contingent, is also an individual and human condition. There can be little doubt that persons who sought spiritual physic actually suffered distress, but they framed the nature of their suffering within the limits of their understanding. Therefore, their case histories go far beyond the simple retelling of an age-old saga. Perceptions of suffering and the vocabulary used to express it tell us a great deal about the specific pressures of everyday life in a specific historical context. Sufferers came from every social category, from the nobility to common servants, and their stories reflect gender and familial status, as well as perceptions of contemporary morality. Religious morality played a major role in explanations for madness and, in spiritual physic, the moral casuistry of mental distress. Casuistry gradually developed into a science from the thirteenth century and achieved a high level of sophistication in the sixteenth century. It can be defined as

The application of general principles of morality to definite and concrete cases of human activity, for the purpose, primarily, of determining what one ought to do, or ought not to do, or what one may do or leave undone as one pleases; and for the purpose, secondarily, of deciding whether and to what extent guilt or immunity from guilt follows on an action already posited.[61]

A legalistic sense of guilt formed an essential part of the early modern pathology of mental anguish. An epistemological nexus between the casuistry of moral theology and humoral pathology had existed since the Middle Ages, transmitted from Arab science via Constantinus Africanus and systematized by Avicenna in the eleventh century.[62] Wilhelm of Conches, probably the most influential scholastic to treat the subject, associated humoral imbalance with sin as early as the twelfth century.[63] Further, casuists like Hughes de Fouilloi had already expounded upon the physical effects of immorality upon the four humors:

For the doctors say that the sanguine are sweet, cholerics bitter, melancholics sad, and phlegmatics equable. Thus in contemplation lies sweetness, from remembrance of sin comes bitterness, from its commission grief, from its atonement equanimity. And one must keep watch lest spiritual sweetness be tainted by worldly bitterness or the bitterness arising from sin corrupted by fleshly sweetness, lest wholesome grief be troubled by idleness or weariness or the equable spirit brought into confusion by unlawfulness.[64]

---

[61] The authorized Catholic definiton: http://www.newadvent.org/cathen/03415d.htm (10 December 2004).
[62] Klibansky et al., *Saturn and Melancholy*, 75–102.   [63] Ibid., 67–74, 102–112.   [64] Ibid., 107.

According to casuists, both individual morality and group behavior influenced social order. In an age when catastrophes – war, plague, famine or mental disorder – were commonly perceived as an expression of celestial displeasure, casuists constantly reprimanded the laity and admonished them to research their consciences for residual moral turpitude. They, in turn, felt obliged to express their anxieties in moral terms. Presumably, not only did individual moral failings cause spiritual afflictions, but sin corrupted the bodily humors physically. During the Black Death, for example, sin was equated with humoral corruption:

Whenever anyone is struck down by the plague they should immediately provide themselves with a medicine like this. First let him gather as much as he can of bitter loathing towards the sins committed by him, and the same quantity of true contrition of the heart, and mix the two into an ointment with the water of tears. Then let him make a vomit of frank and honest confession, by which he shall be purged of the pestilential poison of sin, and the boil of his vice shall be totally liquefied and melt away.[65]

However, most sufferers expressed fewer fears for their individual salvation or the state of the common weal than for their own peace of mind. Spiritual physic offered hope of an alleviation from distress arising from physical illnesses, affairs of the heart, familial problems, financial setbacks, evil spirits or more complex circumstances. For the average person, spiritual physic represented an important and accessible means to bring the soul back into harmony.

Casuistry developed broad social and political aspirations. Widespread individual imbalance, if left unchecked, represented a threat to public order. For example, the neo-stoicist Justus Lipsius compared the struggle between mind and body for control over the soul with two commanders in a military campaign, one of sound reason, the other acting upon unsound opinion.[66] Lipsius, one of the greatest political theorists of his age, was influential in many other ways as well.[67] For example, after he had left the Catholic fold and subsequently converted to Lutheranism and Calvinism, his life-long

---

[65] Mary Lindemann, *Medicine and Society in Early Modern Europe* (Cambridge, 1999), 43–44.
[66] Justus Lipsius, *De constantia*, trans. Florian Neumann (Excerpta Classica edition, Mainz, 1998), 32. In the original text, the pair is *Ratio* and *Opinio*. Florian Neumann translates *Opinio* as *Wahn*, unreason or madness. The translation makes sense if taken in the context of neo-stoicist thought; Lipsius considered madness the alternative to self-discipline and social control. On this passage, see also Gerhard Oestreich, *Neostoicism and the Early Modern State*, ed. Brigitta Oestreich and Helmut Georg Koenigsberger, trans. David McLintoule (Cambridge, 1982), 18–19, which translates *Opinio* as "vain imaginings," associating reason with the divine and opinion with earthliness and the body.
[67] In art, for example; see Mark Morford, *Stoics and Neostoics. Rubens and the Circle of Lipsius* (Princeton, 1991).

friend Martin Del Rio reconverted him to Catholicism in Louvain. Del Rio acted as his father confessor during the reconversion and the two met frequently to discuss subjects as varied as literature, dreams, the apparition of spirits, witches and, of course, politics.[68] Lipsius, perennially suspicious of the mob, considered public disorder and popular uprisings as manifestations of collective mania. Theories of statecraft reflected notions of sympathy between individual behavior and international politics, between the microcosm and macrocosm. In Bavaria, the ducal father confessor, Adam Contzen, SJ, borrowed directly from his role model Lipsius, employing a neo-stoicist metaphor.[69] Both Lipsius and Contzen explicitly compared resistance, revolt and civil war in the body politic to mania, epilepsy, convulsions and madness in the individual body.

Among his various descriptions of melancholiacs and persons suffering from fantasies, the Bavarian court secretary and librarian, Aegidius Albertinus related the amusing anecdote of Urbin, the mad stable boy who believed he was emperor. Each day, Urbin hung a painted sheet on the stable wall depicting the pope, cardinals, kings, princes, lords and knights of the Empire in council. He then donned a paper crown, legislated against the Turks, struggled with devils and wooed scores of courtesans, dancing and springing about the stable. These "councils" continued until his master spied the peculiar proceedings and cried out in the midst of one session, "I am most pleased of your fortune, which has made a lord and emperor out of a stable hand." Urbin responded by ripping the sheet from the wall and taking leave of his master for good.[70] By implication, Albertinus accused subjects of the Empire who sought to rise above their status of causing discord. Obviously, they were mad and no longer a part of the social order. Grimmelshausen's *Simplicissimus* (1664) leveled similar charges against social climbers he held responsible for the madness of the Thirty Years War.[71]

For, despite the early support of the authorities and just as the practice peaked in popularity, there were definite signs that, by the mid-seventeenth century, the heyday of spiritual physic had passed. It had always been contentious even before falling under negative scrutiny by elite skeptics. The authorities found spiritual physic and supernatural afflictions too difficult

---

[68] Del Rio, *Disquisitiones* (1617), 597 – Bk. 4, ch. 3, ques. 6.
[69] Adam Contzen, *Politicorum libri decem* (Mainz, 1620), 1–3; my thanks to Eric Mader for this reference.
[70] Aegidius Albertinus, *Lucifers Königreich und Seelengejaidt* (Augsburg, 1617). Here, I have cited a later edition by Rochus von Liliencron (Berlin, 1883), 345.
[71] It is hardly far-fetched to claim that this is the crux of the book, which begins by describing the folly of the parvenu.

to regulate and too politically charged. Its elite supporters, usually uncompromising and radical hardliners, clamored for public exorcisms, the violent eradication of heresy, the persecution of witches, holy war and continued legal sanctions for suicides. In the end, they threatened the peace and social stability painfully achieved after brutal wars of religion. Sufferers, whose unruly pilgrimages and demonic possessions disturbed public order, challenged the authorities' will by claiming direct access to metaphysical avenues of empowerment. General support for moral policing also decayed as criminal prosecution focused on crimes against the state and property.[72]

The ruling elite became receptive to policies and philosophies that vanquished the capricious interdictions of the supernatural from this world. In England, spiritual physic became too closely associated with popular dissent and religious Puritanism to avoid political suspicion.[73] Ruling elites exhibited greater faith in the empirical methods of corporal physicians and a policy of confinement for the mad, both of which lacked the political volatility of religious cures. In philosophy, Cartesian Dualism encouraged intellectuals to separate metaphysical causes from medical etiology and to think in purely physical terms. The reputation of auricular confession also suffered greatly after Blaise Pascal's scathing attack on laxism and Jesuit casuistry. After 1650, the insanity defense gained momentum throughout Europe. It could rely on a physical etiology of mental illness rather than subjective and contentious interpretations of moral turpitude or demonic agency. A pronounced ideological paradigm shift had set in.

From that time onward the tendency toward the internment of the insane was incessant and culminated in the institutional victory of the asylum – but only at the end of the *ancien régime*. By the mid-eighteenth century, many at court preferred the fledgling psychiatric profession over spiritual physic. Of course, there were exceptions, chief among them the treatment of mad King George III by the English divine Rev. Dr. Francis Willis. For the sufferers themselves, official rejection first of popular healers and then of spiritual physic considerably narrowed therapeutic options. In the

[72] Wolfgang Behringer, "Mörder, Diebe, Ehebrecher. Verbrechen und Strafen in Kurbayern vom 16. bis 18. Jahrhundert," in: Richard van Dülmen (ed.), *Verbrechen, Strafen und soziale Kontrolle. Studien zur historischen Kulturforschung III* (Frankfurt/a.M., 1990), 85–132, 287–293.

[73] In England, "It was, however, the shock of revolution that transformed the ardent rationalism of the scientists and philosophers into the outlook of a whole class. Horrified by the proliferation of radical sects with politically subversive doctrines, the governing elite developed a powerful and lasting aversion to religious groups that claimed special powers of holiness and revelation. They fashioned a polite culture, founded on rational religion, natural philosophy, and neoclassicism that repudiated the intellectual bases of spiritual healing": MacDonald, "Religion, Social Change," 119.

seventeenth century, the ideological triumph of academic physicians and formalized Galenic medicine "blunted the use of case histories, of detailed clinical reporting, and of categories of disease drawn from philosophy and theology – notably disorders brought on by guilt and demon possession."[74] However, the reappearance of moral treatment, notably at the York retreat founded by the Quaker Tuke family in 1792, demonstrated the enduring appeal of spiritual physic even among the learned upper classes.[75]

It proved impossible to eradicate religious perceptions of mental health root and branch at the popular level. In 1842, huge crowds still gathered to witness the public exorcisms of Gottlieb Dittus by Johan Christoph Blumhardt, an evangelical pastor in Wurttemberg. When he reported the incident to his superiors in the Upper Consistory, they forbade him from extending his pastoral duties into the realm of medicine in the future.[76] As late as 1999, a Swiss psychiatrist, Samuel Pfeiffer, examined 343 psychiatric outpatients who considered themselves "religious," noting a marked propensity to suspect demonic agency behind their mental illness in over 25 percent of those interviewed (56 percent among schizophrenics).[77] He concludes that:

beliefs in possession or demonic influence are not confined to delusional disorders and should not be qualified as a mere delusion. Rather they have to be interpreted against the cultural and religious background which is shaping causal models of mental distress in the individual.[78]

EARLY MODERN PSYCHOLOGY

To better highlight the contours of spiritual physic against a specific cultural, religious and historical backdrop, let us consider early modern psychology. Psychology is certainly no more anachronistic a historical tool than, say, sociology. In fact, psychology was an innovation of the sixteenth century. First mentioned in a lost manuscript of 1520 attributed to the Dalmatian humanist Marcus Marulus, it figured prominently in the title of

[74] H. C. Erik Midelfort, "Sin, Melancholy, Obsession: Insanity and Culture in 16th Century Germany," in: Steven L. Kaplan (ed.), *Understanding Popular Culture* (New York, 1984), 124.
[75] Andrew Scull, *The Most Solitary of Afflictions: Madness and Society in Britain 1700–1900* (New Haven, 1993), 96–174.
[76] The pastor's report to the consistory is available as Johann Christoph Blumhardt, *Die Krankheitsgeschichte der Gottliebin Dittus*, ed. Gerhard Schäfer (Göttingen, 1978).
[77] Samuel Pfeiffer, "Demonic Attributions in Nondelusional Disorders," *Psychopathology* 32 (1999), 252–259.
[78] Ibid., 252.

his *Psichologia: de ratione animae humanae.*[79] In 1590, psychology was the subject of a detailed treatise, *Psychologia: that is on the Perfecting of Man, on the Soul and its location* by Rudolf Göckel the elder.[80] His *Psychologia* began with an orthodox discussion of Aristotelian faculty psychology and Galenic humoral pathology. He praised the superiority of the intellective faculty of the soul, which spiritually elevated humans above simple plants and animals, despite the potential for material corruption by the four bodily humors contaminated by sin.[81]

Bavaria, a Catholic region of the Holy Roman Empire where spiritual physic was practiced methodically, offers an outstanding and plastic example of early modern psychology. There, in the banquet hall of Benediktbeuern (an abbey at the foot of the Alps, from which the *Carmina Burana* draws its name), a fresco allegorically illustrates the machinations of the human psyche. Graphically centered within a larger cycle of ceiling frescoes, the allegory of the human soul is literally situated at the heart of the cosmos. Painted between 1672 and 1675, the concept behind this cosmological map derives from a published dissertation. Co-authored by Francis and Phillip Taxis, brothers and Augustinian canons studying at the nearby University of Dillingen, it bore the descriptive title *A Disputation on Sacro-Profane Philosophy as the Intercourse of Logic, Physics and Metaphysics* (1664).[82] Both the cycle of frescoes and the Taxis dissertation mix common motifs from classical mythology and philosophy with Christian thought. These cultural artifacts provide us with unique keys to the charting of the early modern psyche. For example, by positioning the human soul at the heart of the cosmos, the authors engendered the mind–body continuum with transcendental meaning, physically and metaphysically linking the human microcosm to a logically consistant universe.[83]

---

[79] Morton Hunt, *The Story of Psychology* (New York, 1994), 59; David J. Murray, *A History of Western Psychology* (Englewood Cliffs, 1988), 77.

[80] Here, a later edition was consulted: Rudolf Goclenius, ΨΥΧΟΛΟΓΙΑ: *hoc est de Hominis Perfectione, Animo, ortu Huius* (Marburg, 1594).

[81] Ibid., esp. 6–21. Göckel, a dyed-in-the-wool Protestant Aristotelian and humanist, was professor of physics at Marburg and taught mathematics, logic and ethics in Bremen, Herborn, Lemgo and Wittenberg. His son, Rudolf Göckel the younger, wrote on the related concepts of sympathy and magnetism.

[82] Hereafter referred to as the Taxis dissertation: Sebastianus Franciscus and Philippus Constantinus Guilielmus Taxis, *Philosophia sacro-profana logicam, physicam et metaphysicam disputationem complexa* (Dillingen, 1664), with copper etchings by Matthäus Küsel. The Taxis dissertation was composed under the supervision of Ferdinand Visler, SJ, a prominent professor of philosophy at Dillingen. The entire cycle of ceiling paintings is presented in art historical terms by Leo Weber, *Der frühbarocke Festsaal und seine Deckenbilder im Kloster Benediktbeuern* (Munich, 1996).

[83] An evocative and precise analytical concept borrowed from Esther Cohen, "The Animated Pain of the Body," *American Historical Review* 105 (2000), 41–47.

Along the outermost perimeter of the cycle, the physical foundations of the universe rest squarely upon four cornerstones of fire, water, earth and air – the four irreducible elements of contemporary physics. Between the cornerstones, figures from classical mythology are subordinated to Jesus in four christological poses. He is: 1) crowned master of the heavens by Helios, 2) assisted by Neptune as he fishes for souls, 3) portrayed on the cross bleeding profusely onto the earth from whence springs its bounty of flora, and 4) depicted with a musket, hunting for souls as the celestial tamer of its fauna. The next concentric ring alternates between medallions and rectangles representing eight virtues/vices and the twelve months of the agrarian calendar respectively. Each successive ring approaches the central feature – *The Triumphal Chariot of the Rational Soul*,[84] the crowning achievement in God's creation (Plate 2). As the only aspect of the cycle with a teleological rationale, the depiction of the psyche embued the entire composition with its fundamental historical and psychological relevance.

The allegoric *Triumphal Chariot* had Platonic roots. In the *Phaedrus*, Plato likened the soul to a chariot driven by two steeds, the obedient spirit and unruly desire, harnessed by reason.[85] In the Benediktbeuern fresco, the rational soul (*anima rationalis*) sits perched atop the chariot and bears the star of revelation on his head. In the accompanying text of the Taxis dissertation, the problem of the rational soul is resolved as the combined structure of mind and body. It emphasizes the wholeness of the rational soul as a logical proposition greater than the sum of its parts.[86] The text offers a specific rhetorical example to illustrate the unity of the soul: "Peter is learned" (*Petrus est doctus*).[87] Here, body and mind figure as two equally substantial points in the equation. In grammatical terms, they are subject and predicate of a sentence literally explained as "glued together" (*conglutinatur*) by the verb of being. In other words, the rational soul represents an existential proposition, consisting of the physical body (in this case, *Petrus*) and a mental quality (*doctus*) joined together through action. Specifically, the verb reflects the Aristotelian quality of "becoming," also known as entelechy or actualization. In this variation, the mind–body problem of early modern psychology is solved structurally, rather than ontologically.

[84] *Triumphwagen der anima rationalis*, details in Georg Paula and Angelika Wegener-Hüssen (eds.), *Denkmäler in Bayern, Band I.5: Landkreis Bad-Tölz-Wolfratshausen* (Munich, 1994), 102–104.
[85] Plato's tripartite division of the soul is often compared to Freud's concepts of ego, id and superego.
[86] Taxis, *Philosophia*, 136. On the *anima rationalis* and Galenic influences on the early modern dispute over the nature of body and spirit, see Kutzer, *Anatomie*, 55–60.
[87] Taxis, *Philosophia*, 3–4, *In Primam Mentis Operationem Logicae Aristotlicae*.

Aristotelian specialists and theologians explained the structural relationship of mind and body through hylomorphism. The doctrine of hylomorphism treated form and matter as equally substantial elements of existence,
connoting the interconnectedness of mind and body. In theology, hylomorphism also explained other mysteries of faith, such as transubstantiation,
the hypostatic union and the nature of the trinity. Hylomorphism invoked a
holistic approach toward treatments for the soul, justifying equal attention
to both spirit and body.

Aristotelian actualization (entelechy) combined with Christian soteriology to justify human existence through goal orientation. Justification
engendered the Christian way of life with a goal or *telos*. Therefore, entelechy provided the logical glue, soteriology the moral, to justify life and
grant it transcendental meaning. Again, the verb of being (the *actualization* in the mind–body relationship) rhetorically assumed this function.
Salvation actualized justified human existence on both the material and the
spiritual levels. Salvation required correct moral comportment and a proper
balance of the two. Immoral behavior affected the soul at both levels and
threw it out of balance, with serious implications for spiritual well being
and sanity, not to mention salvation. Most Christian moralists agreed on
this point, whether they followed Luther's doctrine of justification through
faith alone or the Catholic doctrine of good works.

Like Jean-Paul Sartre, contemporary moralists too reified human "being"
by juxtaposing it ontologically with "nothingness," though, again, adopting
a stance more in tune with Christian soteriology and Aristotelian physics
than modern existentialism. In his *Christ's Kingdom and Hunt for Souls*,
which predates the same motif from the cycle of ceiling frescoes in Benediktbeuern, the moralist Aegidius Albertinus posed immorality as an existential
dilemma in a section entitled, "On the Horror of *Nihili* or the Nothingness
that is Sin":

What is this Nothingness, through the recognition of which we become so wise
and clever? It is nothing other than an infirmity, a vice, a shock and a deprivation:
in other words, this deprivation (says Aristotle) is nothingness. Augustine says,
peccatum nihil est, sin is nothingness. Blessed are those who recognize this, but
unhappy are those who neither know nor recognize this. *Initium salvatis est
cognitio peccati* [the start of salvation/well being is the recognition of sin], says
Seneca.[88]

[88] Aegidius Albertinus, *Christi Königreich und Seelengejaidt* (Munich, 1618), 60. Cohen, "The Animated
Pain," 42–52, synopsizes the nexus between Aristotle, Augustine and Stoicism in scholastic theology.

For the moralists then, sin represented a deficiency in Christian actualization. Albertinus further described sin as the "death of the soul" and persons who fail to recognize their sins as "ignorant."[89] By way of another rhetorical explanation, he grammatically declined sin into the six cases of Latin nouns.[90] Perhaps Luther was right, when he once complained that the Catholic concept of the soul was heavily, if not overly dependent on rhetorically disciplined logic.[91] Whether or not Albertinus subscribed to an extreme neo-scholastic stance need not detain us for the moment. His explanation on the nature of the soul is simply offered here as independent corroboration, another unambiguous example of the structural nexus between contemporary morality and psychology. Theologians study that nexus as moral casuistry and they treat deficiencies in moral comportment through spiritual physic.

The *Triumphal Chariot* skillfully incorporates moral casuistry into the Christian teleology of psychological actualization.[92] The rational soul (the chariot itself) drives onward through the theater of the world (*theatrum mundi*) toward the gates of eternity. The wheels of the chariot embody the four cardinal elements of classical physics that also comprise the material substance of the human body – in canonical order: air, fire, earth and water. These elements, in turn, correspond to the so-called *naturals*, i.e. the four Galenic humors – again, in canonical order: blood, choler (i.e. yellow bile), black bile and phlegm. Spiritual physicians seamlessly interwove Galenic naturalistic physiology (i.e. the classic theory of the humors) and humoral pathology into Christian doctrine by stressing the immanent morality of actions played out through the human body.[93] Through their sympathetic attraction (or antipathy) to other people, objects or celestial bodies, the four corruptible elements of the body caused motions or emotions in the soul. Thus, a physical as well as metaphysical linkage existed between the human microcosm and the universal macrocosm.

In the Benediktbeuern fresco, the linkage between microcosm and macrocosm allegorically depicts how external influences (the so-called non-naturals) upset the balance of the soul. The charioteer (described in the Taxis dissertation as blind) connotes the predominance of free will as the controlling force behind the rational soul in Catholic theology. The free will reins in the affects, alternatively known to contemporaries as appetites,

---

[89] Albertinus, *Christi Konigreich* 57, 61.　　[90] Ibid., 64–66.

[91] Midelfort, *A History of Madness*, 84–85. Not surprisingly, Luther also emphasized the centrality of the word (*sola scriptura*) in spiritual physic.

[92] A uniform standard encountered in Luther and Paracelsus as well: Ibid., 81–82.

[93] And, therefore, closely related to Elizabethan psychology; MacDonald, *Mystical Bedlam*, 178.

Plate 2. *Triumphal Chariot of the Rational Soul*, Central Ceiling Fresco, Festsaal, Benediktbeuern, *c*.1675. (Courtesy of the Salisians of Benediktbeuern; photograph by Foto Thoma, Benediktbeuern.)

affections, emotions, motions or passions: love (Eros), anger (Ares), hope (Athena) and sorrow (Hephaestus).[94] Thus harnessed, the passions pull the chariot onward, coaxed by the five external senses – allegorized as five women with four animals (from left to right: touch; hearing/the deer; taste/the monkey; smell/the hound; and sight/the eagle). While the free will struggles to control the affects, sensual attractions tug at them and drive them.[95] Divine reason flies overhead with a torch to provide an inner light for the blind charioteer and assist him in controlling the passions without losing sight of his ultimate goal, which can only be achieved through the inner eye of blind faith. Death (*Thanatos*) and Judgment await the rational soul at the end of the procession. In this psychological model, all physical and metaphysical components of the soul are understood as essentially neutral, interdependent and, if held in balance, benevolent parts of the mind–body continuum. Given free rein, the passions could topple the chariot. On the other hand, reining the passions too tightly hindered progress on the road toward salvation. A breakdown in the material under-carriage threatened to bring the entire procession to an abrupt halt. Any of these imbalances, brought on by temptations of the senses or internal cor-ruptions of the humors, justified the intervention of the spiritual physician.

Inspired by the *Triumph of the Church* (now in the Prado in Madrid) of Peter Paul Rubens (an intimate of Justus Lipsius), the psychological impli-cations of the allegoric procession of the human soul would have been self-evident to most contemporaries, in our case the Benedictine monks

---

[94] Hephaestus was the father of Eros, the unsuccessful suitor of Athena and the rival of Ares for the affections of his wife, Aphrodite. I purposefully refrain from engaging the problem of concupiscible and irascible emotions. Sorrow is related to fear, sadness, grief and despair in Thomistic philosophy. Aquinas offers eleven different passions, but argues that hope, fear, pleasure and pain are the four principal passions and that all passions derive ultimately from love: Frater Antonius Senensus Lusitanius, sacra Theol. Bach., Ordinis Fratrum Praedicatorum, *Quaestiones disputatae S. Thomae Aquinatis Doctoris Angelici: de potentia die, de malo, de spiritualibus creaturis, de anima, de daemonibus, de angelis, de Veritate, et pluribus alijs quaestionibus, ut in tabula contietur* (Antwerp, 1569), 134–135, *De Passionibus animae*, Art. V. See also Margaret Hamilton Wagenhals, "Report on Saint Thomas Aquinas' Concept of the Emotions as Contained in the Summa Theologica, I–II, Quaestiones XXII–XCVIII," (MA Thesis, Smith College, 1907). Baruch Spinoza's related monist interpretation of the emotions found in his *Ethics* need not detain us here, but a systematic treatment is available in: David B. Low, "Religious Affects in Spinoza: A Topology of Emotions Understood as a System of Spirituality" (Ph.D. dissertation, Temple University, 1998). A good critical history of the early modern emotions is a major research desideratum. For a treatment at the level of high theory, see Susan James, *Passion and Action. The Emotions in Seventeenth-Century Philosophy* (Oxford, 1997). Many thanks to Ulinka Rublack for this reference. For a consideration of the more practical implications of the emotions, see Ulinka Rublack, "Fluxes: The Early Modern Body and the Emotions," *History Worship Journal* 53 (2002), 1–16.

[95] As Justus Lipsius also warned his readers: *De Constantia*, 18.

and their esteemed dinner guests.[96] The sixteenth century had already witnessed a broad psychological movement, sometimes dubbed the "*De anima*" Renaissance. No fewer than forty-six commentaries appeared on Aristotle's *De anima* and his psychological theories spread from the university and pulpit to reach large segments of European society.[97] Theologians like Juan Luis Vives and Philip Melanchthon wrote their own *De animae*.[98] The *De anima* Renaissance reinforced the hold of Aristotle on early modern interpretations of the mind–body relationship in schools from Oxford to Rome and Istanbul.[99]

The *De anima* Renaissance lasted well into the eighteenth century, informing basic curricula on moral and natural philosophy, ethics and metaphysics – required courses in arts faculties at schools and universities across Europe, notably in France after the revocation of the Edict of Nantes.[100] The *De anima* Renaissance was actually part of a broader behavioralist literature, popularized in vernacular penitentials and moralist tracts. In the case of Sebastian Brant's illustrated *Ship of Fools* (1494) and, to a lesser extent, in Erasmus' *Praise of Folly* (1509), immorality and foolishness are synonymous. Ignatius Loyola's *Spiritual Exercises* (1548) provided readers with specific instructions and meditations to assure sound decision-making and behavior. Aegidius Albertinus' Bavarian *Brain Grinder*, originally published in 1618, (see Plate 3) offered solace and moral advice for self-improvement in

[96] Weber, "Der *frühbarocke Festsaal*," 26. On the personal relationship between Rubens and Lipsius, see Morford, *Stoics, passim*.

[97] Hermann Schüling, *Bibliographisches Handbuch zur Geschichte der Psychologie des 16. Jahrhunderts* (Hildesheim, 1967).

[98] Vives' pioneering work in empiricist psychology was the most thoroughly systematized account of the human emotions until Suarez. It later influenced Descartes' *Les passions de l'âme* (1649). A summary of Vives' contribution to modern psychology is found in Murray, *Western Psychology*, 61–62. On Vives' concept of the emotions, see Juan Luis Vives, *The Passions of the Soul: The Third Book of the De anima et vita*, ed. and trans. Carlos G. Noreña (Lewiston, 1990). On Melanchthon's *Liber de Anima*, see Jürgen Helm, "Die Galenrezeption in Philipp Melanchthons De anima (1540/1552)," *Medizinhistorisches Journal* 31 (1996), 891–902; Marion Lischka, "Der Mensch zwischen Humanismus und Reformation. Die Anthropologie Philipp Melanchthons und ihre Bedeutung im Zeitalter der Konfessionalisierung (MA thesis, Bochum University, 1993). Melanchthon's stoic approach to Aristotle is sometimes referred to as "Lutheran scholasticism." Oxford remained a center of Aristotelian learning until the mid-seventeenth century, whereas Cambridge supported a more Ramist/Platonic outlook. Thomas Hobbes wrote a digest of the *Rhetoric* and steeped his psychological profile of the state of nature in Aristotelian notions of the passions.

[99] The *De anima* remained a standard university text and Aristotle dominated the curriculum at many European universities, as at the Collège de France from 1703 to 1720: see Liam Chambers, "Defying Descartes: Michael Moore (1639–1726) and Aristotelian Philosophy in France and Ireland," in: Stephen Harrison (ed.), *The Medieval World and the Modern Mind* (Dublin, 2001), 11–26. (Not surprisingly, Moore also owned copies of works by Martin Del Rio and Justus Lipsius; many thanks to Liam Chambers for this information.)

[100] Gary Hatfield, "Descartes' Physiology and its Relation to his Psychology," in: John Cottingham (ed.), *The Cambridge Companion to Descartes* (Cambridge, 1992), 339.

Plate 3.   Copper etching, title page from *The Brain Grinder* of Aegidius Albertinus (*Der Hirnschleifer*, 1645 edition). Note the variety of hats: the celestial gristmill of mental pressure weighed down heavily upon all members of society. This copy had been acquired by the Jesuit College of St. Michaels in Munich in 1661. (Courtesy of the Bavarian State Library, Munich.)

an age of crisis.[101] Steeped in the Christian humanist tradition, all harkened back to the fifteenth-century *Imitatio Christi* of Thomas á Kempis. Human reason and an idealistic belief in the ability of humankind to better itself were two central psychological tenets of humanism. Ultimately, by cultivating reason one became more human, akin to angels and God, distancing oneself from base plants and animals.[102]

The main aspects of the rational soul are detailed in the original Dillingen Taxis dissertation as a microcosmic reflection of the universal order in reference to Aristotle's *Physics* and his *Metaphysics*, a view clearly shared with natural philosophers and physicians in Bavaria, indeed throughout Europe.[103] The naturalistic view of humankind employed a crude anthropomorphism[104] and conceived of "sympathies and concordances between the mind and body,"[105] another traditional aspect of the Aristotelian/Galenic doctrine of the four cardinal elements and the four

---

[101] Aegidius Albertinus, *Der Hirnschleifer* (Munich, 1618). See also Albertinus, *Lucifers Königreich*, v–xix; Guillaume van Gemert, *Die Werke des Aegidius Albertinus (1560–1620). Ein Beitrag zur Erforschung des deutschsprachigen Schriftums der katholischen Reformbewegung in Bayern um 1600 und seiner Quellen* (Amsterdam, 1979), 573–575, 589–590.

[102] Hans Baron, *In Search of Florentine Civic Humanism. Essays on the Transition from Medieval to Modern Thought* (Princeton, 1988), 29–42; Peter Burke, *The Italian Renaissance: Culture and Society in Italy* (Oxford, 1986), 178–203.

[103] For example, the Regensburg physician Joannes Freytag, *Kurzer Bericht von der Melancholia Hypochondriaca* (Frankfurt am Main, 1643), 313–393 ("*Anologia Macro- & Microcosmi*"): "man is a little world." Or the physician Oswald Croll's *Tractat von den innerlichen Signaturen oder Zeichen aller Dinge* (Frankfurt, 1623). The concept occurs in the works of Paracelsus as well; see for example his *Vom Licht der Natur und des Geistes. Eine Auswahl aus dem Gesamtwerk* (Stuttgart, 1993), 163–164. MacDonald, *Mystical Bedlam*, 26, notes that "The purpose of this astral cartography was to situate the patient in the cosmos, placing him at the vortex of the natural forces that impelled the universe, discovering the correspondences that linked microcosm and macrocosm." The term "vortex," though colorful, implies an unintended analogy with Cartesian physics, where the vortex represented a gravitation-like force arising from the revolution of heavenly bodies and resulting in physical attraction between them as opposed to the doctrine of natural sympathy. On 179, MacDonald, *Mystical Bedlam*, also cites Burton, who invokes a political allusion: man is "Microcosmus, a little world, a model of the world, sovereign lord of the earth, viceroy of the world, sole commander and governor of all the creatures in it." MacDonald bases part of his discussion of Renaissance physiology and psychology on two classic studies of English literature: a systematic survey of ideas and images from the age of Shakespearean and Jacobean drama by Lawrence Babb, *The English Malady. A Study of Melancholia in English Literature from 1580 to 1642* (East Lansing, 1951), esp. 1–20, and a series of published lectures on medieval and Renaissance cosmology by C. S. Lewis, *The Discarded Image* (Cambridge, 1964), esp. 139–174. In an eighteenth-century woodcut published by the famous Flemish printer Jan Moretus, a tripartite division of the cosmos into the natural world, the faculties of the soul and the universal qualities of astronomy was employed to stress the influence of the stars on the human microcosm. This woodcut still decorates the Moretus print museum in Antwerp: Phillip Guerry, SJ, *Philosophia universi* (Antwerp, 1738).

[104] Herschel Baker, *The Image of Man: A Study of the Idea of Human Dignity in Classical Antiquity, the Middle Ages, and the Renaissance* (New York, 1961), 275–276.

[105] Francis Bacon, *The Advancement of Learning* (London, 1605) Book, II.ix.§1.

universal causes.[106] Natural sympathy or concord (antonym = antipathy/discord) between human microcosms and the universal macrocosm underscored a universal interdependence, rendering individual morality relevant to the state of the commonwealth, just as the position of the stars influenced events in the world and personal behavior. Just how, exactly, sympathy between sublunary and heavenly substances or between mind and body actually functioned remained secondary to the structure of the causal relationship between form and substance (hylomorphism). Contemporaries found it far more interesting to note the natural sympathy between the faculties of the soul and the parts of the body than attempt to locate the nodal connection between sensory perception and conscious thought. Furthermore, the sympathetic relationship could be paralleled poetically and facilely with analogous relationships on other planes of existence. The emphasis on sympathy and correspondence between various planes in the overarching cosmological structure played like a symphony to popular conceptions of medical psychology. Furthermore, links between the soul and a broader cosmology supported political and social interpretations of links between disturbances in the individual mind and disturbances in the natural order of things.[107] As Francis Bacon – the famous empiricist and self-declared opponent of Aristotelian pragmatism – admitted, "For the consideration is double: either how far the humors and affects of the body do alter or work upon the mind; or again, how and how far the passions or apprehensions of the mind do alter or work upon the body. . . ."[108] His interpretation reflected widespread attitudes toward individual mental health and social order.

The doctrine of natural sympathy prompted the authors of the Taxis dissertation to other structural analogies: "Man is a microcosm, whose soul is heaven, in which the sun is reason, the moon is the free will . . ."[109]

---

[106] Baker, *The Image of Man*, 277–279, describes this as "a kind of physiological monism." Despite the tendency to view the cosmos and the mind–body problem holistically, early modern Aristotelianism was partly dualist, if more ambivalently so than Platonism, because it differentiated between substance and form, while insisting on their overarching structural unity. Hence, the term "ultradualist" is sometimes employed to describe radical Platonic and Cartesian philosophy.

[107] MacDonald, *Mystical Bedlam*, 183. A haunting account of sympathy and its sway over seventeenth-century cosmology is Umberto Eco, *The Island of the Day Before* (New York, 1995). Historical accounts of natural sympathy have been less sympathetic: Keith Thomas, *Religion and the Decline of Magic* (London, 1970), treats its properties as incoherent. However, they did have an inherently logical structure, even if lacking an empirical basis.

[108] Bacon, *Advancement of Learning*, Book II. ix. §3 and xii. §1. In these two subparagraphs, Bacon outlines circumstances under which the authority and ability of "religion or superstition . . . do exceed" the power of medicine to "clarify the wits."

[109] Taxis, *Philosophia*, 139, "De Vivente Rationali, seu Homini." For an example of an Aristotelian explanation for male dependability (reason) and female capriciousness, see Heidi Wunder, *He is the Sun, She is the Moon: Women in Early Modern Germany* (Cambridge, Mass., 1998).

Table 1.1 *Galenic humoral pathology (in cardinal order)*

Temperament (humor)	Substance: nature	Color	Taste	Emotional state	Vegetal function
Sanguine (blood)	Air: warm and moist	Red	Sweet	Sensual	Nourishes muscles, distributed through the veins and arteries, and warms the body.
Choleric (yellow bile)	Fire: hot and dry	Yellow	Bitter	Angry	Stimulates intestinal tract and dilutes phlegm to aid in digestion and excretion.
Melancholic (black bile)	Earth: cold and dry	Black	Sharp and acid	Sad	Stimulates appetite, nourishes spleen and bones.
Phlegmatic (phlegm)	Water: cold and moist	White	Sweet or tasteless	Childish, senile	Nourishes brain, tempers blood, and greases limbs and joints to ease movement.

They compared sublunary substances to bodily fluids, organs and tissues: skin to earth, blood to water, vital breath to air, bile to fire, the heart to gold, the brain to silver, senses to gems, passions to meteors, tears to rivers, and so on. They associated the four humors (blood, choler, black bile, phlegm) each in canonical order with a cosmic element (air, fire, earth, water) and a particular consistency (warm and moist, warm and dry, cold and dry, cold and moist) (see Table 1.1).[110] Contemporary medical theory associated each humor with a particular organ of the body (heart, liver, spleen and brain). Humors were paired off with a corresponding passion, implying an even stronger affective connection between conscious perception and the senses as physical receptors.[111] General interpretations regularly and sympathetically associated each humor with a season (spring, summer, fall, winter), a time of the day (morning, afternoon, evening, night) or an ascendant planet (Jupiter, Mars, Saturn, Neptune or the Moon), implying a connection between circumstance and mood. It was also not uncommon to associate humors (again, in canonical order) with an age of humankind (childhood, youth, middle age, old age) and temperament.

---

[110] Taxis, *Philosophia*, see table on the page preceding 71.
[111] MacDonald, *Mystical Bedlam*, 186. In the case of the fresco, the associations are choler to ire, black bile to sadness, blood to Eros and phlegm to hope.

As the Tyrolean physician Hippolyt Guarinonius explained, despite the presence of an immortal soul, human beings were, like animals, unable to live in corporal form forever because of the presence of:

the four corruptible elements composing the human body, which not only change their quality, form, gestalt and energy during the course of life, but must also change as often as shifts of concerns and the complete array of desires and moods. Humans carry the nature of moist warm air [sanguine] with them at birth and keep it during their childhood and the onset of youth, at which time the moisture is dried by the element of fire [choleric], whose reign brings a strength to the body that is increased and completed by about the thirty-fourth year of life, at which time the heat gradually depletes and humans, like the earth, become dry and cold [melancholic] until once again gradually . . . they become dull and weak from a loss of energy and from a certain age are completely moist [phlegmatic] . . .[112]

Every person possessed a fundamental physical and psychological complexion or temperament – either one of the simple universal temperaments (sanguine, choleric, melancholic, phlegmatic) or a compound one, made up of any two dominant humors, for a total of eight possible. A ninth complexion – the "golden temperament" – was a perfect mix, but practicably unattainable for all but the saints.[113] Experts recognized no "normal" temperament, only transitory tendencies or deviations from an idealized norm. The exact humoral balance at any given time decided a person's momentary temperament.[114]

For example: a person with a dominant sanguine humor, considered the noblest and most perfect of the four, was thought to be agreeable, jovial (in reference to the ascendant planet Jupiter, i.e. (Jove)), amiable, kind, amorous, intelligent and courageous, and fleshy with fair hair and a ruddy facial complexion owing to a healthy profusion of blood throughout the

[112] Hippolyt Guarinonius, *Die Grewel der Verwüstung Menschlichen Geschlechts* . . . (Ingolstadt, 1610), 31.
[113] Babb, *The English Malady*, 9. Freud too conjectured that all human beings are imperfect, that all persons exhibit some form of perversion. Richard Webster's revisionist synthesis, *Why Freud was Wrong: Sin, Science and Psychoanalysis* (New York, 1995), 318, compares Freud to Jonathan Swift. He describes Freud's accusation of universal perversion among humans as a reinterpretation of original sin. The passage is chock-full of Aristotelian inference: "The animal impulses and appetites which he located in the self were characterized in predominantly negative terms. The most obscene levels of the sexual imagination were not, according to Freud, to be affirmed or incorporated into the whole identity and liberated as part of the riches of the self. Rather they were to be intellectually acknowledged and then controlled and sublimated through the power of reason." Webster goes on to compare Freud's typology of perverts to the grotesque monsters painted by Brueghel for the *Temptation of St. Anthony*.
[114] In Matejovski, *Das Motiv des Wahnsinns*, 37 and especially Klibansky et al., *Saturn and Melancholy*, 55–66, complexion and temperament are allocated slightly different meanings, whereas elsewhere, as in MacDonald, *Mystical Bedlam*, 186–187, Lewis, *Discarded Image*, 170–174, as well as the OED, they are defined synonymously.

body. Michel de Montaigne regarded his own complexion as a sanguine–melancholy compound, an otherwise harmonious mix (*eukrasia*) unless an excess of black bile upset the humoral balance (*dyskrasia*), rendering him liable to fits of genius or lunacy.[115] Normally, the body evacuated excess humoral fluids naturally through an associated excretory orifice or duct (nose – blood; ears – yellow wax, i.e. choleric bile; eyes – melancholic tears; and mouth – phlegm) to help prevent unhealthy residues, build-ups or pressures. An unhealthy humoral imbalance called for phlebotomy (venesection, cupping, application of leeches, etc.), performed by a barber-surgeon, or for purgatories (cathartics, clysters, vomitories, etc.), prescribed by a physician and purchased from an apothecary to cleanse the body and restore harmony. Alternatively, an imbalance resulting from moral turpitude could be checked by spiritual physic.

Aristotle further subdivided the human soul into three constituent levels: the vegetative, sensitive and rational souls.[116] This widely accepted principle of Aristotelian faculty psychology has gone largely ignored by historians, who prefer to dwell on Galenic humoral pathology, but is of inestimable importance to any understanding of contemporary psychology. The faculties invoked a decided hierarchy of abilities among living creatures. Plants had only vegetal faculties, animals a soul with vegetal and sensitive faculties, while humans and divine beings shared a rational soul.[117] The vegetative faculty of the soul, which had its locus in the liver, allowed for simple nutritive functions like digestion, growth and reproduction. Shared by all forms of life, it was the source of natural heat in the body and necessary for the production of the humors. The animal, sensitive or sensual faculties allowed for sensation, movement and motivation (i.e. the power of locomotion and the emotions).[118] The rational or intellective faculty, the highest of

---

[115] M. A. Screech, *Montaigne and Melancholy: The Wisdom of the Essays* (Selinsgrove, 1983), 22–41.

[116] Taxis, *Philosophia*, 140; Aristotle, *De anima* (New York, 1986), 158–210; Lewis, *Discarded Image*, 152–156; MacDonald, *Mystical Bedlam*, 178–179. The Jesuits were particularly keen on the structured model of three human faculties. For Ignatius Loyola, they were so self-evident that he mentioned them only *en passant* in the *Spiritual Exercises*; see *The Spiritual Exorcises of Ignatius Loyola*, ed. and trans. George E. Ganss, SJ (St. Louis, 1992), esp. 98, "On the Three Powers [as the translator notes in the index, the precise term is "faculties"] of the Soul" and "On the Five Senses of the Body." In fn. 133, Ganss identifies the faculties with the internal senses of memory, intellect and will instead of the Aristotelian breakdown into vegetative, animal and rational. See also Franciscus Suarez, *Opera Omnia*, vol. III (Paris, 1856), the *Liber de anima*.

[117] This explains the historical genealogy of the vegetative nervous system in present-day clinical psychiatry, or why we still refer to a coma as a vegetative state, or to persons driven by sensual pleasures as animals, or why plants and animals cannot enter the kingdom of heaven according to Christian theology.

[118] Contrary to the James–Lange theory of emotions (i.e. an emotion is simply a perception of a state of being), here the emotion is physically affected by the senses and in turn physically affects changes in the body.

the three, connoted the possession of human reason and, in Catholicism, free will. This faculty expressed itself in advanced spiritual functions of free will and intellect, such as language and philosophy. These areas were most closely associated with morality.[119]

After 1586, all Jesuit colleges were supplied with an outline of standard curriculum stipulating, "In logic, natural philosophy, ethics and meta-physics, Aristotle's doctrine is to be followed."[120] Francis Borgia, General of the order, issued this stern warning about curricula at the order's schools just after the conclusion of the Council of Trent, which reiterated the fun-damental structural unity of faculties:

Let no one defend or teach anything opposed, detracting, or unfavorable to the faith, either in philosophy or in theology. Let no one defend anything against the axioms received by the philosophers, such as: there are only four kinds of causes [material, efficient, formal and final]; there are only four elements; there are only three principles of nature . . . The intellective soul is truly the substantial form of the body . . . [it is] not numerically one in all men, but there is a distinct and proper soul in each man . . . [it] is immortal . . . There aren't several souls in man, intellective, sensitive, and vegetative souls, and neither are there two kinds of souls in animals, sensitive and vegetative souls, according to Aristotle and the true philosophy. The soul, whether in man or in animals, is not in fuzz or in hair. Sensitive and vegetative powers in man and animals do not have their subject in prime matters. Humors are, in some manner, part of man and animals. The whole being of composite substance is not solely in form, but in form and matter.[121]

The possession of a rational soul composed of all three faculties (vegetal, animal, intellectual) furthered the sympathetic association between humans and all other living creatures, i.e. plants and animals.[122] However, the divine spark of the rational soul distinguished human beings and they shared it with angels alone. As beings without elemental substance, angels were uncorrupted by the vegetative and sensual faculties, placing humanity in a liminal position between animals and angels.[123] The loss of human reason reduced one to the status of an animal, the loss of sense and motion to that of a vegetable. As noted above, the five external senses figure allegorically in the ceiling frescoes at Benediktbeuern. Together with the external senses, five internal senses made up the cognitive properties of the human soul. The internal senses (or wits) included fantasy, imagination, memory, thought and common sense.[124]

---

[119] Lewis, *Discarded Image*, 156–158.
[120] Roger Ariew, "Descartes and Scholasticism: The Intellectual Background to Descartes' Thought," in: John Cottingham (ed.), *The Cambridge Campanion to Descartes* (Cambridge, 1992), 64–65.
[121] Ibid.   [122] Lewis, *Discarded Image*, 153.   [123] Guarinonius, *Die Grewel*, 161–163.
[124] Baker, *The Image of Man*, 281, and Babb, *The English Malady*, 3, list only three internal senses, while Lewis, *Discarded Image*, 161–165, admits two others, fantasy and estimation (common sense,

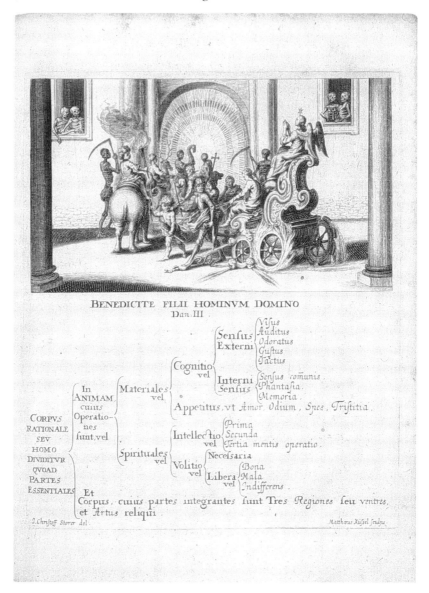

Plate 4. *Triumphal Chariot of the Human Soul*, copper etching from the original Taxis dissertation (1664). This chart details the functional psychology of the human soul according to standard categories derived from the *De Anima* of Aristotle. (Permission of the Bavarian State Library, Munich.)

In the infamous *Malleus maleficarum*, the author described demonic delusions and their potential impact upon the internal senses:

although it has been treated of before, where Alexander of Hales says that a Prestige, properly understood, is an illusion of the devil, which is not caused by any material change, but exists only in the perceptions of him who is deluded, either in his interior or exterior senses. With reference to these words it is to be noted that, in the case we are considering, two of the exterior senses, namely those of sight and touch, are deluded, and not the interior senses, namely, common-sense, fancy, imagination, thought and memory. (But St. Thomas says they are only four, as has been told before, reckoning fancy and imagination as one; and with some reason, for there is little difference between imagining and fancying. See St. Thomas, I, 79.) And these senses, and not only the exterior senses, are affected when it is not a case of hiding something, but the causing of something to appear to a man whether he is aware or asleep.[125]

If this psychological complex seems hermetic to us, it remained self-evident to most contemporaries, already present in iconographic representations in medieval art.[126] Classical notions of the mind–body relationship embedded in humoral pathology and the psychic hierarchy of the faculties influenced Europeans since the Renaissance, when "there was available for the common man as for the savant a convenient body of knowledge and a convenient terminology to explain man's functioning."[127] They became common currency with the arrival of print technology, when "a vast number of cheap manuscripts, broadsheets, almanacs, and popular pamphlets" made information on types of temperament and the correspondence between morality, the humors, the seasons and the ages of man available, "to the humblest cottage"; based on popular proverbs, one historian concludes, "Galenism found its way into all strata of society."[128] By the sixteenth century, even the Friulian Miller Domenico Scandella demonstrated proficiency in this

imagination or fantasy and memory) and goes on to characterize common sense: "According to Albertus Magnus, it [common sense] has two functions: (a) 'It judges of the operation of a sense so that when we see, we know we are seeing'; (b) it puts together the data given by the five senses, or Outward Wits, so that we can say an orange is sweet or one orange is sweeter than another. Burton, centuries later, says 'this common sense is the judge or moderator of the rest, by whom we discern all differences of objects; for by mine eye I do not know that I see, or by mine ear that I hear, but by my common sense'. Common sense is that which turns mere sensation into coherent consciousness of myself as subject in a world of objects."

[125] *Malleus maleficarum*, Pt. II, ques. I, chap. VII, "How, as it were, they Deprive a Man of his Virile Member."

[126] Rolf Sprandel, "Die Seele der Analphabeten im Mittelalter," in Gerd Jütteman, Michael Sonntag and Christoph Wulf (eds.), *Die Seele. Ihre Geschichte im Abendland* (Weinheim, 1991), 97–103.

[127] MacDonald, *Mystical Bedlam*, 3. Citation from Baker, *The Image of Man*, 275.

[128] Klibansky et al., *Saturn and Melancholy*, 112–123, esp. 116. The authors claim these concepts were already part of the "general fund of knowledge of north-west Europe" in the seventh century: 102.

area.[129] Popular broadsheets demonstrate how Galenic humoral pathology influenced perceptions of something as seemingly banal as alcoholic intoxication. It was common to typologize four different types of drunkards, each affected by alcohol according to their complexion. Drunken cholerics were prone to discord, phlegmatics to lose control of their bodily functions (vomiting, flatulence, loss of consciousness, etc.), melancholics to act irrationally and the sanguine to become jovial and affectionate. Hans Sachs, the shoemaker-poet of sixteenth-century Nuremberg, addressed just that theme in his *Four Wondrous Qualities and Effects of Wine*.[130] Therefore, drunkenness offered small defense for immoral behavior, as it merely reflected a caricature of one's true self. Similar depictions appeared in popular drinking songs, Shrovetide plays and woodcut illustrations.

Similarly, the doctrine of sympathy was also largely self-evident to early modern Europeans. For example, writers incorporated sympathy into theories about the childlike state of the inhabitants of the New World, whom they considered prone to a phlegmatic complexion (the most demeaning temperament). They blamed this condition on the ascendancy of certain planets and stars looming over the Western Hemisphere, which sympathetically drew its inhabitants toward a feminine and docile temperament, offering a psychological rationalization for European paternalism.[131] According to contemporary interpretations, women were also disproportionately prone to a phlegmatic humor. In a section of the *Praise of Folly* devoted to sex and psychology, Erasmus pondered a classical argument, which questioned whether women possessed reason and, indeed, whether they were human at all.[132] Folly, the narrator of the tract, explicitly refers to herself as female throughout.

A physical body comprising four elemental humors, a mind divided into three hierarchically defined faculties, all structurally justified in hylomorphic balance, progressing onward toward the goal of Christian actualization: did this picture of sanity really make sense to contemporaries? David Gentilcore implies that it did, suggesting how well the sick of early

[129] Carlo Ginzburg, *The Cheese and the Worms: The Cosmos of a Sixteenth-Century Miller* (New York, 1980), 71–76.

[130] Ann Tlusty, *Bacchus and Civil Order. The Culture of Drink in Early Modern Germany* (Charlottesville, 2001), 59–61.

[131] Jorge Cañizares Esguerra, "New World, New Stars: Patriotic Astrology and the Invention of Indian and Creole Bodies in Colonial Spanish America, 1600–1650," *American Historical Review* 104 (1999), 33–68.

[132] Erasmus, *Praise of Folly*, 30. One debate on the humanity of women raged for almost 175 years: see Manfred P. Fleischer, "'Are Women Human?' – The Debate of 1595 between Valens Acidalius and Simon Gediccus," *The Sixteenth Century Journal* 12 (1981), 107–120.

modern Europe understood their therapeutic options, encouraging the humblest to take an active role in the diagnosis and treatment of their own illnesses, both mental and physical.[133] We might debate the actual proficiency of the average European in the highly disciplined rhetoric of Aristotelian faculty psychology or Galenic humoral pathology, or the extent to which peasants and townsfolk were actually cognizant, or were made cognizant of their daily participation in a macrocosmic order. Nevertheless, as the present study indicates, when it came to their own mental health or that of their kin, early modern Bavarians were acutely aware of the dangers of immoral behavior, the pulls of the affections and the assaults of demonic temptation both for themselves and for society around them. When they suffered afflictions and imbalances of the soul, they turned to spiritual physic for comfort, consolation and cures.

A BAVARIAN BEACON

In his classic study of the English astro-physician Richard Napier, Michael MacDonald once compared the early modern history of mental health to an "intellectual Africa"; an unfortunate Victorian cliché, perhaps, but one that connotes the slight extent of our knowledge.[134] MacDonald persuasively voiced the neuroses of an entire society through the office notes of one practitioner. In a synthetic bricolage of cases from sixteenth-century Germany, Midelfort evidenced characteristic attitudes toward madness in a series of vignettes illustrating cultural, legal, religious, medical and social aspects. This study profits greatly from the work of both scholars, but is located at an intermediate level. On the one hand, this approach is intended as a broader validation of MacDonald's individual case study of Napier. On the other, it fleshes out some of Midelfort's ideas through detailed contextualization.

In order to achieve an intermediate position, compact regional analysis is preferred here as the method of observation favored by medical anthropologists or historians who study a related phenomenon – witchcraft persecutions.[135] It is hardly surprising that Midelfort began his career with a regional study of the witch-hunt.[136] The present study can also benefit from another excellent regional history of witchcraft persecutions, the

---

[133] Gentilcore, *Healers*, 204–205.
[134] MacDonald, *Mystical Bedlam*, 1.
[135] E.g. Kapferer, *A Celebration of Demons*; Alan Macfarlane, *Witchcraft in Tudor and Stuart England* (London, 1970).
[136] See his pathbreaking study, *Witch-Hunting in Southwest Germany, 1562–1684: The Social and Intellectual Foundations* (Stanford, 1972).

spadework of Wolfgang Behringer, who conducted an exhaustive analysis of the phenomenon in Bavaria.[137]

Behringer too believed that an analysis limited to a medium-sized geographic region offers the historian a number of advantages. It obviates charges of peculiarity sometimes leveled at individual micro-histories and allows for well-founded comparisons with MacDonald's results. At the same time, the evidence is drawn from a limited geographic entity, presenting a unified and comprehensive whole. Thus, we can safely draw on Midelfort's supra-regional inspiration without the threat of diffusion. Certainly, without his "post-holes," significant portions of my intellectual scaffolding would lack strong foundations.[138] Most importantly, we want to identify spiritual physic as a coherent set of practices, highlighting the lives of the afflicted, their neighbors and kin, the ideologies of healers and the learned elite, as well as the political problems facing local and central authorities. To achieve that end, this study also adapts a method from psychoanalysis, the use of individual case histories. However, rather than trying to employ the analytic principles of psycho-history, the use of case histories is limited here to the attempt to locate individuals within a web of contributory social and material circumstances, as well as within the contemporary terms of spiritual physic. In conjunction with ethnography, regional economic history and demographic data, the contours of the political, religious and social landscape of madness in Bavaria are then brought into greater relief. Taken together, these methods yield a chromatic image of the region for synchronic comparison with other parts of Europe. Diachronically, the methods facilitate an analysis of change over time, suitable for the exposition of a chronological model.

Bavaria, the geographic and demographic object of this regional analysis, was one of the largest and most politically compact territories of the Holy Roman Empire (see Map 1). Dynastically partitioned since the Middle Ages, the autonomous duchies of Upper and Lower Bavaria had been reunified in 1505 following the brief, but bloody War of the Bavarian Succession. Except for a few isolated enclaves (i.e. the bishoprics of Freising and Regensburg, the tiny counties of Haag, Hohenwaldeck and Ortenburg, and Free Imperial Regensburg), Bavaria was unbroken by intervening jurisdictions, facilitating a high degree of centralization. Munich became the sole ducal residence and the administrative center of the region after 1545. Northward lay the Margravate of Ansbach-Kulmbach and mighty Free

---

[137] Wolfgang Behringer, *Witchcraft Persecutions in Bavaria: Popular Magic, Religious Zealotry, and Reason of State in Early Modern Europe*, trans. J. C. Grayson and David Lederer (Cambridge, 1997).
[138] Midelfort, *A History of Madness*, 17.

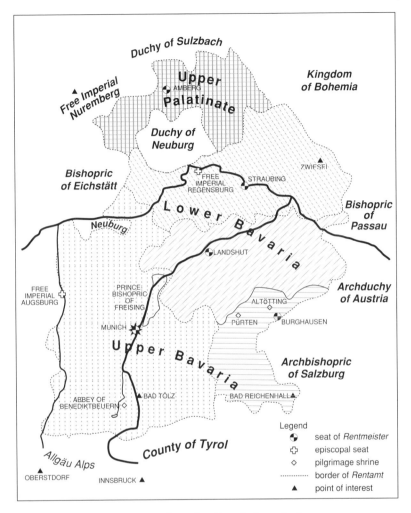

Map 1. Early modern Bavaria (by author)

Imperial Nuremberg. To the south was the Habsburg County of Tyrol, part of Bavaria until 1363; not surprisingly, cultural ties between the two regions remained close. In the east, Bavaria bordered the Prince-Bishopric of Salzburg, the Provostship of Berchtesgaden, the Archduchy of Austria and the Kingdom of Bohemia. The wealthy city of the Fuggers, Augsburg, and the Prince-Bishopric of Augsburg lay just across the Lech River to the west.

In Upper and Lower Bavaria, real administrative authority devolved onto four governments (*Regierungen*) subordinate to Munich, the fiscal provinces (*Rentämter*): Burghausen and Munich in Upper Bavaria and Landshut and Straubing in Lower Bavaria. A provincial administrator, the *Rentmeister* or *Vize Dominus*, governed each *Rentamt*. In 1623, the Holy Roman Emperor elevated Duke Maximilian I (r. 1597–1651) to the status of Prince-Elector as a reward for faithful service in the Thirty Years War, at which time Bavaria also annexed a fifth *Rentamt*, Amberg, the administrative seat of the Upper Palatinate. These five provinces in turn contained some 120 local administrative units, the district or county courts. In 1600, most of the approximately 900,000 inhabitants of Bavaria lived in rural areas pursuing pasturage and subsistence agriculture. Munich, the most heavily populated urban area in the Duchy, counted some 20,000 dwellers and was dwarfed by the neighboring (and suspect) bi-confessional, Free Imperial City of Augsburg, with over 60,000 residents. By the time of the Swedish occupation (1632–1634), plague and warfare had reduced the regional population by about one-third.

Confessionally, all the inhabitants of Bavaria were nominally Catholic, according to the provisions of the Imperial Peace of Augsburg (1555). This meant that, officially, the practice of spiritual physic was doctrinally unified and ostensibly consistent. Ecclesiastically, Bavarian territory fell within the jurisdiction of the sees of Augsburg, Bamberg, Chiemsee, Eichstätt, Freising, Regensburg and Salzburg. However, primary responsibility for the confessionalization of the Duchy rested with the secular rulers of the Wittelsbach dynasty, who proved more zealous reformers than the regional episcopate. Duke Wilhelm IV (r. 1508–1550) insured that Bavaria remained Catholic during the early years of the Reformation by granting Johann Eck, rector of the territorial University of Ingolstadt, full support in his theological struggle with Martin Luther. Wilhelm IV also initiated the merciless persecution of Anabaptism and enlisted the aid of the fledgling Society of Jesus to reform the Duchy. With Peter Canisius (known as the catechizer and second apostle of the Germans after St. Boniface) at their head, they made Ingolstadt the new headquarters of a Jesuit province. Duke Albert V (r. 1550–1579) expelled the Jews, adopted a strict policy of censorship to suppress heterodox ideas and, after the defeat of the confessionalist movement (the so-called "Bavarian Fronde"), he restricted the rights of the evangelical estates. In 1583, Duke Wilhelm V (the Pious, r. 1579–1597) concluded a concordat with the papacy, extending the power of the Wittelsbach dynasty over the territorial church and laying the groundwork for the introduction of Tridentine reforms. In 1605, Duke Maximilian I assumed the leadership of the Catholic League and transformed Bavaria into the bulwark of Catholicism in the Holy Roman Empire.

Chronologically, this study treats the early modern period. Some of the earliest records of spiritual physic date from reports of miracles at the dynastic cult shrine at Altötting from 1495. Earlier sources from the late Middle Ages were consulted as well and the work concludes with speculation on eighteenth-century developments, including the origins of the Royal Bavarian Insane Asylum in Giesing (Munich), founded contemporaneously with Montgelas' program of secularization in 1803. However, there is a clear chronological focus on the century from 1579 until 1679, which corresponds precisely to the reigns of three generations of Wittelsbach rulers, Duke Wilhelm V, Elector Maximilian I and Elector Ferdinand Maria, and to an unbroken chain of Jesuit father confessors as their advisors.

One problem much bemoaned by historians of early modern mental health is a deficit of documentary evidence. Sometimes this problem arises from the unjustified assumption that the serious history of mental health care is limited to the story of university-trained medical professionals. This is a modern prejudice. Given the contemporary regime of phlebotomies, vomitives and clysters employed by corporal physicians, one has to question whether such methods truly deserve to be privileged over the analytic case histories of spiritual physic. Also, returning to the issue of sources, we sometimes underestimate the efficiency of early modern bureaucracies. The Bavarian bureaucratic reforms of the late sixteenth and early seventeenth century produced a unique run of documentation on madness and spiritual physic, greatly facilitating the present study. In the end, it proved possible to access a wide range of sources and, in fact, not all of the voluminous examples could be included here. The decision to privilege some case histories over others is based upon the depth of the information and their relevance to the larger picture. Further, the selection seeks to illuminate the changing complexion of mental health care from as many angles as possible, from the perspective of the ruling elites, local, central and civic administrators, the higher and lower clergy, university professors, natural philosophers, physicians, theologians, practitioners and healers, as well as the afflicted men, women and children, their kin and their village communities.

The bureaucrats of the *Rentamt* of Munich produced an abundance of rich and fortunately well-preserved archival materials. Although less extensive, records from other administrative provinces, as well as those of the surrounding imperial territories (the Habsburg Archduchy of Tyrol, the Prince-Bishoprics of Augsburg, Freising, Passau and Regensburg, as well as the Free Imperial Cities of Augsburg and Regensburg), were examined.

In fact, the amount of material often proved daunting – more than two thousand case histories of spiritual afflictions were examined, including demoniacs, pilgrims, madpersons, suicides and asylum patients, not to mention printed and codified sources with a normative character. In the end though, not even a thorough examination of a limited geographic region can claim to be completely exhaustive, nor would it have been prudent to incorporate into the present work all of the materials consulted. There are certainly other cases of madness to be found in the recesses of the Bavarian State Archives, while I have reserved a considerable body of research on suicide for a wider study of that phenomenon in the Holy Roman Empire.[139]

Serial documents proved valuable sources of information. These include the records of pilgrimages to two cult centers dedicated solely to the ambulatory treatment of spiritual afflictions: St. Anastasia in Benediktbeuern and the Beata Alta in Pürten (see Map 1). In a hagiographic miracle book, the *Bavarian Beacon*, the cult custodian of Benediktbeuern, Aemilian Biechler, recommended his shrine as a "help and consolation to the suffering, the troubled in spirit, yes even the possessed . . ."[140] Access to rare, unpublished manuscript miracle books proved significant, providing a basic pool of almost fifteen hundred case histories which detail the spiritual afflictions of each pilgrim in entries ranging from a brief sentence to several pages. This basic pool of case histories was corroborated and enlarged through the systematic examination of other serial sources, such as parish registers, criminal files and administrative protocols. For example, the protocols of the Bavarian Aulic Council provided another essential trove of consistently reported serial documentation. In his study of witchcraft trials, Behringer also effectively exploited these protocols, an almost unbroken record of internal affairs for the whole of the seventeenth century. The councilors in Munich placed a high priority on the reporting of suicides and the care

---

[139] Initial findings have appeared as David Lederer, " Verzweiflung im Alten Reich. Selbstmord während der kleinen Eiszeit," in: Wolfgang Behringer, Hartmut Lehman and Christian Pfister, *Kulturelle Konsequenzen der kleinen Eiszeit* (Göttingen, 2005), 255–280; Lederer, " '. . . welches die Oberkeit bey Gott zuverantworten hat.' Selbstmord im Kerker während der frühen Neuzeit," *Comparativ* 5/6 (2003), 177–188; Lederer, "De cultuurgeschiedenis van de zelfdoding in Vlaanderen: een uitdaging," *Archieflink* 2 (2002), 4–5;. Lederer, "Selbstmord im frühneuzeitlichen Deutschland: Klischee und Geschichte," *Psychotherapie* 4 (1999), 196–202; Lederer, "The Dishonorable Dead: Elite and Popular Perceptions of Suicide in Early Modern Germany," in: Sibylle Backmann, Hans-Jörg Künast, B. Ann Tlusty and Sabine Ullmann (eds.), *Das Konzept der Ehre in der Frühen Neuzeit* (Augsburg, 1998), 347–363; Lederer, "Aufruhr auf dem Friedhof. Pfarrer, Gemeinde und Selbstmord im frühneuzeitlichen Bayern," in: Gabriela Signori (ed.), *Trauer, Verzweiflung und Anfechtung. Selbstmord und Selbstmordversuche in mittelalterlichen und frühneuzeitlichen Gesellschaften* (Tübingen, 1994), 189–209.

[140] Aemilian Biechler, *Bayerischer Pharos: S. Anastasia . . .* (Augsburg, 1663).

of "senseless" persons; some 450 additional cases were identified through the systematic exploitation of the Aulic Council's quarterly volumes. The protocols of the Ecclesiastical Council of the Prince-Bishopric of Freising identified exorcists and demoniacs who came to the attention of the authorities as well. Rich criminal and financial records from the Free Imperial City of Augsburg contain valuable supplementary materials.

Ultimately, the reconstitution of elusive case histories cannot depend on protocol entries alone. This leaves the historian at the mercy of their investigative instincts, obliging the eclectic consultation of unexpected sources among the miscellanea stacked arbitrarily in archival cubbyholes. Spy reports, academic theses, university matriculation records, legal briefs written as expert testimony for use in criminal and civil court cases, the records of religious orders and special administrative deputations on ghosts, apparitions, plagues and asylum care, executioners' receipts for dishonorable burials, as well as the correspondence of exorcists, the afflicted and skeptics, have all been drawn upon for the present study. Such chance references range from passing mention in a letter to files on individual demoniacs several hundred pages in length.

Among printed sources, sermons, catechisms and penitentials expose the message of morality, guilt and consolation, which theologians attempted to inscribe upon the popular conscience. Published hagiographies and printed miracle books offer normative characterizations of spiritual afflictions and have, in the past, proved invaluable for the compilation of statistics on pilgrimage in early modern Bavaria. However, the pilgrims are seldom named in full and this anonymity prohibits the type of independent confirmation possible in cases of persons named in full in the manuscript miracle books. Printed miracle books were also polemical and propagandistic in character, whereas the manuscripts list failures as well as triumphs. Contemporary law codes, decrees, encyclopedias (Besold's *Thesaurus* or Zedler's *Universal Lexikon*) and chronicles rank highly as tools for the categorization of normative stereotypes and the identification of spectacular cases. A number of iconographic representations (oil paintings, votive art, copper etchings, etc.) add a visual dimension to the written perceptions of officials, theologians and commoners.

Chapter 2 addresses the reinvigorated post-Tridentine ritual of auricular confession, a penitential ritual of atonement and self-flagellation, during a time of general crisis. It examines normative perceptions of mental health and deviance, while introducing the dynastic history of Bavaria and the influential role of the Society of Jesus as the early masters of spiritual physic. Confession had three important functions in early modern Bavaria:

consolation, political consultation and social control. Canisius and other theologians spread casuistry through the media of sermons and print technology, depicting penance and sin in humoral terms. Father confessors at court embodied a century-long political alliance between the Jesuits and the Bavarian Wittelsbachs, while criminal enforcement of a penitential regime was intended to combat the "poisonous" spread of heterodoxy. Chapter 3 assesses the relationship of geographic mobility to mental health care. Through the reinvigoration of ritual pilgrimage and the veneration of the special dead, the confessional state intended the construction of a regional identity through sacred geography, the *Bavaria Sancta*. The Wittelsbachs patronized a Marian program of state in pursuit of both foreign and domestic policy agendas, such as internal political centralization and the rehabilitation of claims to the imperial title. On the other hand, the popular tradition of local veneration also benefited from the revival of the cult of the saints. Local traditions emphasized specialist saints and common Bavarians continued to access them, largely for personal reasons rather than dynastic ideology. This chapter also introduces the two regional shrines dedicated exclusively to the treatment of spiritual afflictions, the cults of St. Anastasia at Benediktbeuern and the Beata Alta at Pürten. An analysis of their manuscript miracle books illustrates the contractual nature of early modern devotion, spontaneous methods of oral transmission, the hopes and aspirations of pilgrims in their day-to-day struggles with mental disorders, as well as the local, regional and supra-regional significance of a popular geography of the sacred.

Chapter 4 characterizes the different types of spiritual afflictions, detailing specific complaints of the mental ailments and the phenomenology of their treatment. Contemporaries contested the power to name mental disorders, but nosology had concrete legal and social implications beyond the pale of psychiatry. Additionally, this section systematically analyzes the case histories of individual sufferers, including two particularly rich case histories in their relationship to social and gender status. Chapter 5 traces the decline of supernatural explanations for mental disorder and the rise of a secular insanity defense in the hotly contested arena of ritual exorcisms, perhaps the most dramatic form of spiritual physic. It develops a chronology of exorcism from the early days, when Peter Canisius defied his Jesuit superiors and promoted a spate of exorcisms in Augsburg and Altötting. The chronology then follows the spread of demonic possessions in the region and the histories of popular healers until the practical implementation of a secular insanity defense in cases of madness and demonic possession by another Jesuit and father confessor at the Bavarian court, Bernhard Frey. Reason-of-state policies, a decline in support for diabolical explanations of madness and a rising mistrust of a metaphysically based spiritual physic as ideology of care initiated a psychological revolution at court. The limits of the absolutist state are explored in the last substantive chapter. By focusing on changing patterns in the spatial segregation of the corpses of suicides and the bodies of the dangerously insane, chapter 6 exposes the open opposition faced by the state in its attempts to implement rationalized and secularized policies on mental well being. Resistance came chiefly from local communities, town councils and the representatives of the church, who fought to retain their traditional privileges over corporate spaces. Clearly, changing patterns in decisions concerning the location of burials in cases of suicide preferred the insanity defense over diabolical explanations, and the history of confinement for madness moved from a parish-based system of poor relief to early attempts at centralized institutionalization at the Holy Spirit Hospice. Both decisions were heavily influenced by the consideration of state sovereignty (*Herrschaft*) over the bodies of its subjects.[141] However, popular beliefs continued to dog absolutist policies about the final resting place of suicides, manifest in open resistance to suicide decisions. Further, although relatives and communities supported the principle of removing the mad to a central repository at the Holy Spirit Hospice in Munich, they balked at requests for financial support. The town council of Munich also obstructed the policy on the grounds of corporate privilege. Ultimately, structural limitations on the absolutist state insured that the ideological origins of the Great Confinement remained ideological, an intention completely lacking in sound institutional and economic foundations until the end of the *ancien régime.*

Chapter 7 concludes with a re-evaluation of the evidence, to include afterthoughts on the historical significance of madness, religion and the early modern state. A tentative résumé of developments in eighteenth-century Bavaria looks beyond the psychological revolution to consider the potential influence of enlightened discourse, ending in the foundation of the first public insane asylum in Bavaria. Finally, a speculative excursus on Freud's analysis of the seventeenth-century Bavarian demoniac Johann Christoph Haizmann considers the legacy of spiritual physic in the nineteenth and twentieth centuries. Freud employed a method known as retrospective medicine, the use of historical case studies to prove the timeless and universal nature of psychic dysfunction. By turning retrospective medicine on its head, elements of spiritual physic are identified in the genesis of modern psychiatry.

---

[141] For an excellent discussion of the multiple meanings of *Herrschaft*, see Sabean, *Power in the Blood*, 20–27; although he avoids the term "sovereignty," I find it a useful tool, especially given its contemporary connotations in political theories on the nature of the absolutist state.

Long before Emil Kraepelin systematized twentieth-century psychiatric thought and opened a research clinic in Munich with American financial backing, long before Ernst Rüdin contracted an unholy alliance with the National Socialists as the promoter of sterilization for "life not worth living,"[142] Bavaria figured prominently in the history of the psyche. However, the story of spiritual physic warrants more than a simple reduction to yet another tedious aspect of an inevitable German *Sonderweg*.[143] The history of spiritual physic demonstrates that early modern Bavaria had much in common with its European neighbors, both Catholic and Protestant. Furthermore, the activities of Jesuits like Bernhard Frey and Adam Tanner contributed positively to the European debate ending large-scale witchcraft persecutions through the systematic application of a secular insanity defense. As a major center of spiritual physic, it became home to one of the earliest state-operated asylums in Germany. Bavaria continued to play a leading role in the history of German psychiatry in the nineteenth century, another legacy of a longstanding regional interest in mental health care. The story of spiritual physic in Bavaria offers valuable insights into contemporary cosmology, mentalities, the evolution of modern psychiatry and, not least of all, German social and political history. Far from arcane or hermetic, spiritual physic contributed to a psychological paradigm shift in the seventeenth century, permitting the emergence of bourgeois psychiatry in the eighteenth century while insuring a pastoral tradition that survives to the present.

---

[142] Dirk Blasius, *"Einfache Seelenstörung." Geschichte der deutschen Psychiatrie 1800–1845* (Frankfurt am Main, 1994), 145–197. Rüdin also supported the T-4 euthanasia program morally, although he was reluctant to back it officially, since euthanasia rendered professional psychiatry redundant; see Mathias M. Weber, *Ernst Rüdin. Eine kritische Biographie* (Berlin, 1993), esp. 270–280.

[143] Although Blasius, *"Einfache Seelenstörung,"* offers a good synthesis of the history of modern German psychiatry, its central argument is far too simplistic in its anti-positive teleology of a German psychiatric *Sonderweg*.

CHAPTER 2

Sackcloth and ashes

> Exomologesis is the discipline of prostrating and humbling men in
> habit, in living, to lie in sack and ashes.
>
> Heinrich Bullinger, *Decades*

CRISIS AND ATONEMENT

Norms and perceptions are perhaps the most significant indicators of mental health in any society. During the late sixteenth and early seventeenth centuries, Europeans perceived themselves in the midst not only of a crisis of values, but of a general crisis with decidedly material manifestations. Historians still debate the nature and extent of the general crisis. Hugh Trevor-Roper first associated the extended period of religious wars (both civil and international) with atavistic larges and poor governing policies among the ruling elite.[1] Alternatively, others emphasize either the long-term effects of the sixteenth-century price revolution, or Malthusian positive checks on demographic growth, or the mounting social pressures of absolutist state building on the brittle society of orders, or a climatic disaster during the worst decades of the Little Ice Age.[2] Whatever reasons we ascribe, one thing is certain; contemporaries too acknowledged a crisis, but their

---

[1] Hugh Trevor-Roper, *Religion, the Reformation and Social Change* (London, 1967).
[2] The literature of the late sixteenth- to early seventeenth-century crisis is extensive. After Trevor-Roper, the debate was taken up in Geoffrey Parker and Lesley M. Smith (eds.), *The General Crisis of the Seventeenth Century* (London, 1978). The structural inadaquacies of absolutism are highlighted in Perry Anderson, *Lineages of the Absolutist State* (London, 1974). More generally: Henry Kamen, *The Iron Century* (London, 1971), reprinted as *European Society 1500–1700* (London, 1992); Winfried Schulze, "Untertanenrevolten, Hexenverfolgung und 'kleine Eiszeit': Eine Krisenzeit um 1600," in: Bernd Roeck, Klaus Bergdolt and Andrew John Martin (eds.), *Venedig und Oberdeutschland in der Renaissance. Beziehungen zwischen Kunst und Wirtschaft* (Sigmaringen, 1993), 289–309. Evidence for the adverse effects of an environmental catastrophe is mounting. See Hartmut Lehmann, "Frömmigkeitsgeschichtliche Auswirkungen der 'Kleinen Eiszeit'," in: Wolfgang Schieder (ed.), *Volksreligiosität in der modernen Sozialgeschichte* (Göttingen, 1986), 31–50; Wolfgang Behringer, Hartmut Lehman and Christian Pfister, *Kulturelle Konsequenzen, des "Kleinen Eiszeit"* (Gottinger, 2005).

perceptions of normalcy distilled different meanings from it. Haunted by the rapacious four-horsemen of famine, disease, warfare and death, moralists reproached society at large and urged repentance in preparation for the impending apocalypse. They admonished Europeans to assume collective blame and personal guilt. Convinced that the confessional divide and subsequent disasters harbingered the coming of the Antichrist, moralists preached a doctrine of mass atonement to a receptive audience. The sullen humor of normative and proscriptive literature has led those historians with an appreciation for social psychology to dub the era an age of melancholy or even despair.[3] Georges Minois, a historian of suicide, characterizes the years from 1580 to 1620 as the "first crisis of conscience" in Western European society.[4] Evidence of a normative state of emergency is nowhere more prevalent than in the wash of flailing incitements to guilt and penance, particularly in, but not limited to, Catholic regions. Concrete measures taken by the authorities to intensify the experience of auricular confession as a cathartic method of spiritual physic manifest their determination to employ every possible means to unite society and overcome present adversities.

In the late sixteenth century, Bavaria witnessed widespread measures designed to proselytize auricular confession and criminalize noncompliance with the established yearly requirement. What were the psychological, political and social ramifications of this policy? Historians began theorizing on the function of auricular confession in late medieval and early modern Europe more than a century ago. Henry Charles Lea[5] and other liberal Protestants condemned enforced auricular confession as an aberration of papal spiritual autocracy,[6] greatly resented by the laity as a hateful burden, a source of anxiety and a psychological intrusion.[7] Contrarily, Catholic apologists have concentrated on the need to resolve

[3] Midelfort, *A History of Madness*; MacDonald, *Mystical Bedlam*; Lederer "Verzweiflung im Alten Reich."
[4] Minois, *History of Suicide*, 86–115.
[5] Henry Charles Lea, *History of Auricular Confession and Indulgences in the Latin Church*, 3 vols. (Philadelphia, 1896).
[6] Ibid., v. And yet Lea's anti-papal stance is complex. His father was a Quaker, but his mother was Catholic. During the anti-Catholic riot of 1844, the Philadelphia publisher and historian took arms to defend a local Catholic church; Dumas Malone (ed.), *Dictionary of American Biography* (New York, 1933), vol. XI, 67–69.
[7] As late as 1975, Steven Ozment echoed Lea's condemnation, depicting pre-Reformation confession as an instrument of ecclesiastical repression resented by the laity: *The Reformation in the Cities* (New Haven, 1975), e.g. 15–28. Two years later, Tentler, *Sin and Confession* reconstructed late medieval penance through an analysis of confessors' manuals; see also Karant-Nunn, *The Reformation of Ritual*, 101, 105. Also of interest is Alexander Murray, "Confession as a Historical Source in the Thirteenth Century," in: R. H. C. Davis and J. M. Wallace-Hadrill (eds.), *The Writing of History in the Middle Ages. Essays Presented to Richard William Southern* (Oxford, 1981), 275–322.

the inchoate state of late medieval practice and on the positive psychic and social aspects of confession. Together with communion, they argue, it defused local conflict and relieved individual fears and guilt through pastoral consolation.[8] Social and cultural historians locate auricular confession within the framework of Elias' "civilizing process," depicting it as a novel method of identity formation designed to efficiently inculcate individual self-discipline and a social conscience.[9] Most histories of auricular confession and penance rely heavily on normative sources, such as confessors' manuals, limiting their ability to elucidate actual practices. Recent innovative studies employ less orthodox methods, examining previously untapped sources (e.g. criminal interrogations, lay penitentials and saints' hagiographies) to gain new perspectives on the mentality of confession and penance.[10] At the end of the day, conjectures about the extent of coverage, levels of appropriation of the penitential message or the actual penetration of the "inner self" during the Confessional Age, though tantalizing, remain conjectures.

While all of these commonsense speculations probably contain a kernel of philosophical truth, we can empirically ascertain at least three functions of auricular confession in early modern Bavaria. First and foremost, theologians touted penance as a source of consolation and spiritual physic. Second, Jesuit father confessors played an influential role at court as political advisors to the Wittelsbach dynasty. Third, the rulers of Bavaria strategically instrumentalized the sacrament to monitor their subjects and fight heterodoxy. Penance and auricular confession truly represented a *confessio* in the patristic sense: a witnessing and public profession of orthodoxy.

[8] For example, John Bossy, "The Social History of Confession in the Age of the Reformation," *Transactions of the Royal Historical Society* 25 (1975), 21–38; Lawrence G. Duggan, "Fear and Confession on the Eve of the Reformation," *Archive for Reformation History* 75 (1984), 153–175. Bossy (and subsequently Myers) depicted the yearly requirement as a ritual of communal purification not unlike biblical scapegoating, while Duggan emphasizes the easy access to absolution as a weapon against contemporary angst.
[9] Norbert Elias' variant of the Weberian modernity thesis also builds upon Ferdinand Tönnies, *Gemeinschaft und Gesellschaft. Abhandlung des Communismus und des Sozialismus als empirischer Kulturformen* (Leipzig, 1887), translated as *Community and Civil Society* (Cambridge, 2001). Other references are found in Michel Foucault, *The History of Sexuality, vol. I: An Introduction* (New York, 1980).
[10] An excellent, but oft-overlooked study is Günther Pallaver, *Das Ende der Schamlosen Zeit. Die Verdrängung der Sexualität in der frühen Neuzeit am Beispiel Tirols* (Vienna, 1987). Other innovative accounts include Jodi Bilinkoff, "Confessors, Penitents, and the Construction of Identities in Early Modern Avila," in: Barbara Diefendorf and Carla Hesse, *Culture and Identity in Early Modern Europe (1500–1800). Essays in Honor of Natalie Zemon Davis* (Ann Arbor, 1993), 83–100; Oscar di Simplicio, *Peccato, Penitenza, Perdono: Siena 1575–1800. La formazione della coscienza nell'Italia moderna* (Milan, 1994), synopsized in his, "Confessionalizzazione e identità collettiva – Il caso italiano: Siena 1575–1800," *Archive for Reformation History* 88 (1997), 380–411. In her overview of Lutheran confession, Karant-Nunn, *The Reformation of Ritual*, 100–106, recognizes consolation, but emphasizes the disciplining aspects of penance and auricular confession.

For the Wittelsbach dukes, it acted as a guarantor of religious homogeneity according to the precepts of the Peace of Augsburg. They viewed confession as a moral control intended to protect against civil disorder and mobilize the population for external conflicts. And yet, despite any repressive motives on the part of the secular authorities, auricular confession achieved huge popularity from the late sixteenth century onwards. That popularity can be explained only through the consoling function of confession. Battered by the material misfortunes of the general crisis, ordinary subjects accessed auricular confession in ever-increasing numbers as a valuable method of spiritual physic.

A proclamation of March 13, 1598 exemplifies the perception of crisis and the spirit of atonement. Three months after the melancholic Emperor Rudolf II,[11] formally invested him with the title to Bavaria, Duke Maximilian I issued his first public legislation – a sweeping religious mandate on public morality. Heralded by couriers and then officially posted in each market, town and district court throughout the Duchy, his Inaugural General Mandate of 1598 commenced with a bleak assessment of current affairs:[12]

First, it is unfortunately apparent that the present anger and afflictions of God, manifest in looming and recurrent outbreaks of war, pestilence and all manner of dangerous epidemics and illnesses, are not on the decline, but instead grow steadily longer, more virulent and more terribly numerous, not only in many other places, but partially in our own princedom as well. This situation is primarily attributable to the sinful vices which daily gain the upper hand in the present-day, godless, vile world. However, if anything is certain, we have no other means at our disposal to escape the anger and wrath of God than righteous, true, serious penance. We therefore desire herewith and it is our serious opinion that those who care for souls and parish priests everywhere should constantly and with all industry admonish the people in their sermons to abandon their sinful ways, repent and mourn them. And without any further hesitation (indeed most especially now at this Easter time) hurry to prepare themselves for a healing confession and receive the most reverend sacrament of the altar in order that they might once again enter into the grace of God. And they should also present proper attestation in the

---

[11] The nature of Rudolf's melancholic obsession with the occult and necromancy is discussed in Robert John Weston Evans, *Rudolf II and his World. A Study in Intellectual History, 1576–1612* (Oxford, 1973), 90f, 196–242. In 1591, the court portraitist, Giuseppe Arcimbaldo, composed a floral study of the emperor as Vertumnus, the Roman spirit of change and transition. However, despite Arcimbaldo's earlier anthropomorphic sequences of the four seasons and the four elements, there is no definitive evidence to indicate that Arcimboldo's portraits of either *Autumn* or *Earth* (both allusions to melancholy) were supposed to represent Rudolf.

[12] Walter Ziegler (ed.), *Dokumente zur Geschichte von Staat und Gesellschaft in Bayern. Abteilung I: Altbayern vom Frühmittelalter bis 1800*, vol. II: *Altbayern von 1550–1651* (Munich, 1992), 612.

form of a certificate of confession [*Beichtzettel*] to their respective local authorities. Furthermore, wherever disobedient persons [i.e. those not making a confession] are found, the local authorities should make a list available to our representatives as soon as possible.

In his Inaugural Mandate, Maximilian implicitly sought to address concrete concerns readily manifest to contemporaries. A bloody civil war between Catholics and Huguenots in France had just ended that same year with the Edict of Nantes. The United Provinces had only recently gained independence from Spain after decades of atrocities during another internal religious struggle. Certainly, the Empire enjoyed over forty years of superficial calm after the Peace of Augsburg established territorial sovereignty in matters of religion after 1555. However, religious tensions churned just beneath the surface and sporadically escalated into open conflicts, threatening the status quo. In 1583, during the War of the Cologne Succession, the Wittelsbachs gained the Rhineland prince-bishopric and its electoral title as a virtual secundogeniture. In 1584, Protestant opposition and mob violence against Gregorian calendar reforms developed into street violence in the neighboring city-state of Augsburg. In 1607, Duke Maximilian formally annexed Free Imperial Donauwörth on the pretense that Protestants obstructed local Catholic processions. In the prelude to thirty years of internecine war in Central Europe, mounting religious tensions split the Empire into a Protestant Union (1608) and a Catholic League (1609), the latter headed by Maximilian himself. Shortly thereafter, he took an active role in the Jülich-Cleve succession crisis (1609–1614), negotiating the scandalous conversion of the Protestant heir-apparent to Catholicism through a marriage alliance; a European conflagration was narrowly averted.

The prolific moralist Aegidius Albertinus harped on religious troubles closer to home. In his translation of Florimund de Raemund's *History from the Origins to the Decline of Heresy and what sort of Awesome Changes, Widespread Suffering, Emergencies and Extreme Dangers it has caused all over the World since 1500*, Albertinus recounted the initially enthusiastic popular reception of Protestantism in Bavaria.[13] However, peasant revolt in nearby Salzburg and religious wars in France had already convinced Maximilian's grandfather, Duke Albrecht V, to put an end to religious toleration.[14] In the 1560s, Albrecht officially expelled the Jewry, withdrew

[13] Aegidus Albertius, *Historia vom Ursprung/ auff abnemmen der Ketzereyen/ und was sie seyter Anno 1500 schief aller orten in der Welt . . . für wunderbarliche veränderungen/ weitläuffigkeiten/ jammer/ noth und höchste gefarlichekeiten verursacht* (Munich, 1614).
[14] Albrecht's original comments on the French Wars of Religion, the peasant revolt in the Pinzgau and the confessionalist movement are reproduced in Ziegler, *Dokumente*, 337–339.

support for clerical marriage and smashed a regional Utraquist movement in a pre-emptive strike against noble "confessionalists" (i.e. supporters of the 1530 Confession of Augsburg) during the Bavarian Fronde.[15] Culturally, a new austerity at court accompanied religious intolerance.[16] The days of Renaissance mirth, when guests danced to the madrigals of Orlando di Lasso at Albrecht's sumptuous wedding feast, had passed; thereafter, di Lasso's primary commissions required him to compose dour penitential hymns. In a visible mood swing in fashion at the court in Munich, the Duke and his courtiers adopted formalized Spanish ceremony, ascetic manners and the sombre dress usually associated with Puritanism. Here too, the melancholic temperament became the courtier's coat-of-arms.[17]

In direct reference to the Bavarian Fronde and the French Wars of Religion, Duke Albrecht candidly confided in his son, the future Duke Wilhelm V, "when it comes to religious negotiations . . . act enthusiastically and seriously, never turning a blind eye. For experience has shown that, up to now, turning a blind eye in matters of faith has resulted in much apostasy."[18] Wilhelm V (as well as his melancholic spouse, Renata of Lorraine[19]) experienced an intense religious awakening, earning him the accolade "the Pious." With the help of zealous émigrés and converts, he conducted a concerted campaign against internal heterodoxy, popular religious practices, clerical ignorance and concubinage. When Wilhelm abdicated to pursue the cloistered existence of a hermit, his son, Maximilian I, assumed control over a confessionally homogenized nascent absolutist state.[20]

Of course, perceptions of crisis were not limited to court. Natural catastrophes and wars reinforced brooding apocalyptic paranoia about celestial

---

[15] Dietmar Heil, *Die Reichspolitik Bayerns unter der Regierung Herzog Albrechts V. (1550–1579)* (Munich, 1999), esp. 249–292. Alois Knöpfler, *Die Kelchbewegung in Bayern unter Herzog Albrecht V* (Munich, 1891), is also still useful.

[16] On the changing mood at the Wittelsbach court, Behringer, *Witchcraft Persecutions*, 410; Behringer, "Weather, Hunger and Fear: Origins of the European Witchhunts in Climate, Society and Mentality," *German History* 13 (1995), 1–27.

[17] MacDonald, *Mystical Bedlam*, 150–160.

[18] Max Spindler (ed.), *Handbuch der bayerischen Geschichte*, vol. II (Munich, 1988), 387.

[19] On Renata's melancholy, see Heinz Dotterweich, *Der Junge Maximilian. Jugend und Erziehung des bayerischen Herzogs und späteren Kurfürsten Maximillian I. von 1573 bis 1593* (Munich, 1962, reprint: 1980), 39.

[20] Generally: Felix Stieve, *Die kirchliche Polizeiregiment in Baiern unter Maximilian I. 1595–1651* (Munich, 1876), 10–30. On the suppression of the evangelical movement in the diocese of Freising, see Hans Rößler, *Geschichte und Strukturen der evangelischen Bewegung im Bistum Freising 1520–1571* (Nuremberg, 1966); Claus-Jürgen Roepke, "Die evangelische Bewegung in Bayern im 16. Jahrhundert," in: Hubet Glaser (ed.), *Wittelsbach und Bayern II/1: Um Glauben und Reich. Kurfürst Maximilian I. Beiträge zur bayerischen Geschichte und Kunst 1573–1657* (Munich, 1980), 101–114. The persecution of suspected Anabaptists in Munich was the most severe since the pogroms against the Jews in 1285 and 1349: Claus-Peter Clasen, "The Anabaptists in Bavaria," *Mennonite Quarterly Review* 39 (1965), 243–261; Hans Rößler, "Wiedertäufer in und aus München 1527–28," *Oberbayerisches Archiv* 85 (1962), 42–53.

displeasure over human behavior in society as a whole. Contemporary moralists had good cause to characterize their times as troubled and Maximilian's millenarian warning of 1598 reflected a sincere spirit of atonement. Again, Aegidius Albertinus' prolific writings are indicative of that spirit. A Catholic refugee from Deventer in the former Spanish Netherlands, he fled the bloodshed of the Dutch revolt to a warm reception in Munich. Albertinus translated innumerable Catholic tracts from French and Spanish into vernacular German.[21] His chiliasm sprang from personal experience. Apart from sectarian struggles in the Netherlands and France, Albertinus augured portentous signs in inauspicious weather and outbreaks of contagion, a sensibility heightened exponentially by the prevailing millenarian climate.

Therefore, the penitential legislation contained in Duke Maximilian's Inaugural General Mandate of 1598 was no idle harangue issued simply to mark his accession. His grave perceptions of a crisis threatening the social order should not be underestimated.[22] The previous decade bore desperate witness to an identifiable conjuncture of crop failures, spiraling inflation of grain prices, and a spate of suicides and trials for magic in neighboring Augsburg.[23] In his foretelling of the coming debacle in Central Europe of the Thirty Years War, Maximilian demonstrated astounding prescience at a time when famines and disease passed from epidemic to endemic proportions. He subsequently released a barrage of plague decrees in 1599, 1606, 1613, 1625, 1634 and 1649, all coinciding with severe regional outbreaks.[24] After 1618, the war wrought chronic havoc. A vicious cycle of crop failures resulted in severe grain-price fluctuation; currency devaluation during the Kipper and Wipper years (1621–1622) brought hyperinflation; famines (Grimmelshausen's accounts of cannibalism are not far off the mark) contributed to dietary insufficiencies, further exposing the population to catastrophic effects of infectious disease. Almost as soon as it

---

[21] E.g. Aegidues Albertinus, *Von den Sonderbaren Geheimnusse deß Anti Christi* (Munich, 1604) – see also Clark, *Thinking with Demons*, 354–357; *Flagellum Diaboli, oder des Teufels Gaissl* (Munich, 1602); *Historia vom Ursprung/ auff abnemmen der Ketzereyen/ und was sie seyter Anno 1500 schief aller orten in der Welt . . . für wunderbarliche veränderungen/ weitläuffigkeiten/ jammer/ noth und höchste gefarlichekeiten verursacht* (Munich, 1614). Albertinus was one of the most popular and prolific secular writers and translators in Bavaria at that time: see ADB, vol. I, S. 217–219; van Gemert, *Die Werke*. He probably translated the anonymous and apocalyptic tale of possession, *Erschröckliche doch warhaffte Geschichte/ Die sich in der Spanischen Statt/ Madrileschos genannt/ mit einer verheuraten Weibsperson zugetragen/ welche von einer gantzen Legion Teuffel siben Jar lang besessen gewest* (Munich, 1608). For his translation of Mateo's *Gusman de Alfaryr* in 1615, he is recognized as the originator of the German picaresque novel, upon which Grimmelshausen based his later works.

[22] See Theodore K. Rabb, *The Struggle for Stability in Early Modern Europe* (Oxford, 1975).

[23] Lederer, "Verzweiflung im Alten Reich," 262–264.

[24] HStAM *Kurbayern Mandatensammlung* 1599 x 4; 1606 IX 9; 1613 IX 5; 1613 IX 24; 1634 VIII 19; 1649 XI 1. The Decree of 1634 is reprinted in Ziegler, *Dokumente*, 1073–1078.

subsided, the devastation wrought by the horrific plague of 1623 was surpassed by the next in 1627/1628, convincing Maximilian of the need to
establish an ad hoc commission (the Deputation on Infection) to monitor
its progress.[25] After the plague of 1649, Maximilian organized a standing medical commission (the Council on Contagion) to fight pandemics.
Swedish occupation brought yet another terrible plague in 1634/1635, when
villages and towns reported losses of up to one-third of their remaining
populations. In absolute numbers of victims, that plague would surely have
been far worse had not the Duchy already suffered from near demographic
exhaustion.

Epidemiological disasters weighed heavily upon the guilt and fears of a
society already programmed for the excesses of self-flagellation.[26] An education with the Society of Jesus conditioned the responses of a whole generation of Catholic rulers and intellectuals like Maximilian and Albertinus.
Jesuit pedagogy mixed austere Christian morality with anti-Machiavellian
humanism and neo-stoicist political theory, exhorting princes to exercise
reason and to control individual passions to insure stability in the commonwealth.[27] Post-Tridentine Jesuit teaching in Bavaria called for a strict
schooling of the will and the internal sense of fantasy to avoid sin.[28] Maximilian's pedantic mentors demanded many spiritual exercises of him as a
young boy.[29] He joined the Brotherhood of the Servants of the Most Holy
Virgin in his youth, assumed the office of Prefect in 1584 and later headed the
congregation for the entire Empire.[30] In instructions to his primary school
tutors, Duke Wilhelm insisted they teach the young Maximilian to diminish the desires and affections as part of a virtuous humanist education. They
built upon one specific principle: unity derived from coherent upbringing,

---

[25] The voluminous protocols of the *Infektionsdeputation* are found in HStAM HR 215–217.
[26] Jean Delumeau, *Sin and Fear: The Emergence of a Western Guilt Culture 13th–18th Centuries* (New York, 1990).
[27] Despite more recent work on the subject, Dotterweich, *Der Junge Maximilian* is still a fascinating explication of Maximilian's Jesuit humanist upbringing. On neo-stoicist values, see Baker, *The Image of Man*, chap. 18, "Sixteenth-Century Ethics and the Development of Neostoicism. 'Right Reason as an Instrument of Christian Virtue.'" Justus Lipsius was very influential at the court in Munich. In 1592, Wilhelm V attempted to attract Lipsius to the University of Ingolstadt: Oestreich, *Neostoicism*, 100. For discussions of the common weal, see Hans-Christoph Rublack, "Political and Social Norms in Urban Communities in the Holy Roman Empire," in: Kaspar von Greyerz (ed.), *Religion, Politics and Social Protest: Three Studies on Early Modern Germany* (London, 1984), 24–60 and Winfried Schulze, *Vom Gemeinnutz zum Eigennutz: über den Normenwandel in der ständischen Gesellschaft der frühen Neuzeit* (Munich, 1987).
[28] Dotterweich, *Der Junge Maximilian*, 66.
[29] One banal example: misbehaving at age eleven, Maximilian had to write this verse a hundred times: "Take it for better, take it for worse, to honor the virtues, that is my wish, may God grant me this"; Stieve, *Die kirchliche Polizeiregiment*, 10.
[30] Maria Angela König, *Weihegaben an U. L. Frau von Altötting vom Beginn der Wallfahrt bis zum Abschluss der Säkularisation* (Munich, 1939), 245.

discipline and control, not the sum of disparate parts.[31] Consequently, and despite their traditional division into "the ecclesiastical authorities, who watch over souls [and] the secular authorities, who care for and administer the political,"[32] religion and government interwove in the same coarse sackcloth. An anecdote from Maximilian's biography, written by his father confessor, Vervaux, illustrates the Duke's internalization of religious values. In his biography, published under a pseudonym, Vervaux described a hair shirt and whip found locked in a small chest inside Maximilian's personal chambers. In life, Maximilian carried the key to the chest on a chain about his neck at all times and it was only opened after his death.[33] According to Vervaux, the instruments of flagellation displayed signs of repeated use.

A policy of overlapping institutional competency between the religious and secular spheres filled gaps in a bureaucratic infrastructure overextended by dwindling human resources, diminished by war, social disruption, famine and disease. Maximilian's regime continued to encourage the recruitment of foreigners as well. In their search for order, these hardset bureaucrats exhibited limited moral tolerance. One particular method employed to economize morality efficiently, penance, emerged as a defining trait. From the late sixteenth century, in a "confessionally oriented society with a heightened awareness of sin, increased frequency of confession . . ." was an approved method of social control and crisis management in Catholic Europe.[34] In Bavaria during the reign of Maximilian I, that translated into hard legislation. For the good of the commonwealth, the individual expurgation of sin through auricular confession came to punctuate the yearly routine of ordinary people no less tenaciously than the unremitting cyclical crises of the age.[35]

The Fourth Lateran Council institutionalized the religious requirement for penance prior to the reception of Easter communion in 1215.[36] In light of the Peace of Augsburg, however, the procedure for monitoring compliance

---

[31] Ibid., 54–55, 76.   [32] Albertinus, *Lucifers Königreich*, 1.

[33] Sigmund Riezler, *Geschichte Bayerns, 1597–1651*, vol. v (Gotha, 1903), 6–8. Vervaux had to compose the biography under a pseudonym because of his sympathetic stance toward Emperor Louis the Bavarian, presumably at the suggestion of Maximilian. The elimination of the stain of Louis' excommunication on the honor of the Wittelsbach dynasty is a recurrent preoccupation in court-sanctioned literature of the period.

[34] Haliczer, *Sexuality in the Confessional*, 22.

[35] On this point, my evidence is in total agreement with Myers, *"Poor Sinning Folk,"* 87, 145–146, 158–181, esp. 192–193. Archival evidence points conclusively to rigorous confessional practices instituted during the reign of Duke Maximilian I.

[36] For a thought-provoking sociological history of confession as part of Elias' "Civilizing process" see Alois Hahn, "Zur Soziologie der Beichte und anderer Formen instititionalisierter Bekenntnisse: Selbstthematisierung und Zivilizationsprozess," *Kölner Zeitschrift für Soziologie und Sozialpsychologie* 34 (1982), 407–434. The text of the Lateran provisions for Easter confession issued in 1215 (*Utriusque Sexus*) can be found in Oscar D. Watkins, *A History of Penance*, vol. ii (London, 1920), 748f.

invoked by the Inaugural General Mandate comprised significant legislation. Martin Luther spotlighted the centrality of the Catholic sacrament
of penance in his ninety-five theses.[37] In their simplicity, the ninety-five
theses threatened the very foundation of papal authority, which responded
literally by engraving the "Tu est Petrus" clause in the stone of St. Peter's
cathedral in Rome. Luther's challenge forced a painstaking re-evaluation of
penance and its eventual renewal at the fourteenth session of the Council of
Trent on November 25, 1551. The Council ultimately buttressed the institutional authority of penance through an attritionist compromise. Attrition-
ists emphasized the outward performance of ritual. They underscored the
mechanical value of sacramental penance "through the operation itself" (*ex
opere operato*) over sincere contrition, the performance of satisfaction, or the
immediate moral state of the priest granting absolution.[38] A retrenchment
of papal authority, attritionism rested on the power of the keys of loosing and binding based on Matthew 16.[39] In 1583, Nuncio Felix Ninguarda
(1524–1595) anxiously negotiated a political concordat to facilitate the implementation of these and other Tridentine reforms in Bavaria.[40] Ninguarda
himself published a set of penitential instructions for the lower clergy in
Bavaria, his *Manual for Parish Priests and Others Charged with the Care of*

[37] Luther's position on penance developed over a number of years and is outlined in Karant-Nunn, *The Reformation of Ritual*, 91–107; Rublack, "Lutherische Beichte," 127–155. The theological implications of Luther's later works for Catholic penance are briefly considered in Haliczer, *Sexuality in the Confessional*, 12–13 and Karant-Nunn, *The Reformation of Ritual*, 95. J. C. Wolfart details a local evangelical struggle over penance in "Why was Private Confession so Contentious in Early Seventeenth-Century Lindau," in: Robert Scribner and Trevor Johnson (eds.), *Popular Religion in Germany and Central Europe, 1400–1800* (London, 1996), 140–165. See also Mary Jane Haemig, "Communication, Conso-lation and Discipline: Two Early Lutheran Preachers on Confession," in: Katherine Jackson Lualdi and Anne T. Thayer (eds.), *Penitence in the Age of Reformations* (Aldershot, 2000), 30–48.

[38] J. Waterworth (ed.), *The Council of Trent: Canons and Decrees* (Chicago, 1848), 14th Session, chapter 3: "The holy synod doth furthermore teach, that the form of the sacrament of penance, wherein its force *principally* [emphasis – added] consists, is placed in those words of the minister, I absolve thee, &c: to which words indeed certain prayers are, according to the custom of holy Church, laudably joined, which nevertheless by no means regard the essence of that form, neither are they necessary for the administration of the sacrament itself." See also Hubert Jedin, *Geschichte des Konzils von Trient*, vol. III (Freiburg, 1970), 315–337. A clear summary of the late medieval debate on satisfaction, contrition, attrition and absolution is found in Myers, *"Poor Sinning Folk,"* 15–33. On the essence of the Tridentine resolutions, ibid., 107–113.

[39] Tentler, *Sin and Confession*, esp. 281–301.

[40] This was the year of the near loss of electoral Cologne to the Protestant cause and Bavaria's victory in the War of the Cologne Succession, resulting in a virtual Wittelsbach secundogeniture over both the archbishopric and its electoral title until the eighteenth century. The Calendar Struggle of 1584 in bi-confessional Augsburg only exacerbated tensions; see Bernd Roeck, *Eine Stadt in Krieg und Frieden. Studien zur Geschichte der Reichsstadt Augsburg zwischen Kalenderstreit und Parität*, vol. 1 (Göttingen, 1989), esp. 133–189. Hence, Ninguarda was anxious to see Tridentine reforms implemented quickly in Bavaria, the papacy's principal ally in the Empire: Spindler (ed.), *Handbuch*, esp. 391, 396, 705–707; Walter Brandmüller (ed.), *Handbuch der bayerischen Kirchengeschichte*, vol. II (St. Ottilien, 1993), 55–59.

.

Souls.[41] The Bavarian Concordat of 1583 enhanced Wittelsbach dynastic control over ecclesiastical discipline and the moral policing of the laity.[42] It paved the way for the type of secular regulation of the penitential regime mandated by Maximilian in 1598.

THE SOUL DOCTORS

Consolation, roughly speaking, the cure of anxieties, best characterizes the psychological function of penance from the late Middle Ages.[43] The late medieval penitential ideal was essentially circular.[44] In this hermetic system, ultimate institutional authority for both defining and absolving sin rested with the church and its representatives. Although the institutionalized ideal of auricular confession as spiritual consolation dates from the Fourth Lateran Council of 1215, the reality of late medieval penance was ad hoc

---

[41] Felicianus Ninguarda, *Manuale Parochorum et aliorum curam animarum habentium* (Ingolstadt, 1582); this process is described in detail by Myers, *"Poor Sinning Folk,"* 123–131. It was presumably intended for instruction at the seminary; the value of a Latin handbook for the pre-Tridentine parish clergy in Bavaria would have been slight indeed.

[42] The text of the Concordat is found in Ziegler, *Dokumente*, 490–495.

[43] Tentler, *Sin and Confession*, xvi, 12–16, 347–349, identifies consolation along with discipline or social control as the fundamental organizational principles of his study. Twentieth-century theologians are quick to point out the benefits that Catholic confessors can derive from a better understanding of psychotherapy. Some, such as Balthasar Gareis, *Psychotherapie und Beichte* (St. Ottilien, 1988) and Andreas Snoeck, *Beichte und Psychoanalyse* (Munich, 1960), suggest a more open dialogue with their psychiatric counterparts, while others, like Eugen Drewermann, undertake professional psychiatric training and achieve official status as psychoanalysts. Drewermann promotes an eclectic blend of psychotherapy and less-formalized confessional ritual as a better-suited pastoral treatment for repressed fears and guilt engendered by traditional morality of Western Christianity. See his *Psychoanalyse und Moral Theologie 1: Angst und Schuld* (Mainz, 1982). In 1975, the sociologist Erik Berggren published an important study, *The Psychology of Confession* (Leiden, 1975), which analyzes similarities between the Catholic sacrament of auricular confession and the clinical procedure of psychotherapy. He applies the methodological rigor of Weberian ideal types in order to demonstrate how the ritual encounter between priest and penitent resembles not just the form, but also the curative phenomenology of exchange between therapist and patient. Berggren argued that guilt feelings associated with sin engender "psychic pressure" among Catholics, repressible to a certain extent, but eventually making "the need to find release through confession a powerful force." Confession, a talking cure that recognizes the power of the spoken word, ostensibly releases psychic pressure and alleviates symptoms of trauma and hysteria. The sacrament hinges on an intimate bonding experience that maintains social distinctions of hierarchical authority. This relationship liberates the penitent/patient from the isolating and inhibiting effects of repressed sin/guilt and offers new perspectives, critique and, especially in the case of the sacrament, a final absolution representing the transference of guilt onto the confessor. Interesting for our present consideration is Berggren's identification of the sources of clerical charisma which strengthen the bond of trust between the penitent/analysand and confessor/therapist. These include formal attire (more pronounced in the case of the priest), the creation of a special, private space away from the mundane activities of everyday life and the attainment of professional training enhancing an aura of virtuosity. The widespread conformity to these procedures on the part of the clergy only occurred as a result of the Council of Trent.

[44] For example, see Euan Cameron, *The European Reformation* (Oxford, 1991), 79–82.

at best, at worst confused and, all too often, contradictory.[45] It took centuries to establish a uniform doctrine and the Protestant challenge to Catholic sacraments provided the major developmental impetus for the Tridentine renewal of auricular confession.[46]

With the introduction of movable type, a consoling image of shriving as spiritual physic confronted the laity en masse for the first time. Books of consolation in the vernacular (*Trostbücher*), especially those dedicated to consolation of the sick and dying (*ars moriendi*), were a very popular genre of sixteenth-century literature. In Bavaria, the young Maximilian's tutor at Ingolstadt, Johann Christoph Fickler, composed a lengthy manuscript with the apocalyptic title *Consolation and Physic for the Soul, not merely for the Infirm and the Dying, but also for healthy Christians in these Recent and Dangerous Times.*[47] Fickler chastized those who ran to their corporal physician to recover their physical health at any price, but balked at the care of their souls in a state of sin.[48] Books of consolation, like Albertinus' translations of the *Compass for the Soul* and *The Art of Dying for Princes and Potentates*,[49] offered readers rational explanations for untimely misfortunes as either a test of one's faith or a punishment for sin to help the faithful overcome spiritual apprehensions.[50] They regularly prescribed auricular confession as an effective physic for tribulations, pusillanimity, temptations or despair arising from pangs of conscience.[51]

---

[45] Myers, *"Poor Sinning Folk,"* 57. Duggan, "Fear and Confession," 167, refers to attempts to limit the choice of confessor and retain reserved cases as "a mess."

[46] On the thesis of "Christianization" in Europe and the practical implementation of Tridentine doctrine during the late sixteenth and seventeenth centuries, see Jean Delumeau, *Le Catholicisme entre Luther et Voltaire* (Paris, 1970).

[47] On Fickler's influence on the future Duke/Elector with special reference to his views on spiritual physic, the devil and witchcraft, see Dotterweich, *Der Junge Maximilian*, 115–125; Clark, *Thinking with Demons*, 486. Fickler also authored works on witchcraft: Behringer, *Witchcraft Persecutions*, 219–220, 237.

[48] BayStaBi: Cgm *c.*1309, 207–245.

[49] Aegidius Albertinus, *Der Seelen-Compaß. Das ist: von den Vier letsten dingen deß Menschen: Vom Todt/ Jüngsten Gericht/ der Höllen und Ewigen Leben* (Munich, 1617); Albertinus, *Der Fürsten und Potentaten Sterbekunst* (Munich, 1599).

[50] Johann Henrick Zedler, *Grosses vollständiges Universal-Lexikon* vol. XLV (Halle and Leipzig, 1745), 1182–1201.

[51] E.g. Adam Walasser, *Trostbüchlein für die Krancken und Sterbenden* (Dillingen, 1597); Anonymous, SJ, *Geistliches Trost-Büchlein/ . . . doch wegen unterschidlicher Zufäll und Scruplen geängstigte Seel trösten und auffmunteren soll/ zu sonderbarem Trost und Hülff viler betrübten Gemüther* (Munich, 1699). Books of consolation were also popular among evangelicals for, to paraphrase Luther, those who have received the gospel have a joyful consolation and are full of hope to combat melancholy, timid, pusillanimous and troubled spirits: Grimm, *Deutsches Wörterbuch*, vol. XXII, 905–906, entry for *Trost*. The colloquial German expression, "Are you unconsoled?" (*Bist Du nicht beim Trost?*) is literally a question of one's sanity, i.e. "Are you mad?"

Medieval theology, such as the manuscript *On the Physic of the Soul* (*De medicina animae*) by Hugues de Fouilloi, had already recommended confession as a remedy for tribulations and melancholy as early as the twelfth century.[52] However, printing enabled early modern moralists such as Albertinus to reach a wide audience in the vernacular. Albertinus chided sufferers of despair for not availing themselves of the physic of auricular confession, which could restore them to full spiritual health.[53] Confession offered Catholics access to institutionalized consolation based on formalized hierarchical authority and steeped in the casuistry of moral theology. We can juxtapose their methods with Protestant forms of spiritual healing contingent upon faith alone, grace or a healer's individual charisma.[54] In sixteenth-century Bavaria, three prominent theologians dealt specifically with the moral casuistry of sin and guilt, and the remedial value of sacramental penance. Like Albertinus, all three originated from outside the Duchy – Dr. Johann Eck (1486–1543) from the hinterland of Memmingen, Peter Canisius (1521–1597) from the Netherlands, and the Swabian Dr. Martin Eisengrein (1535–1578). Motivated in part by confessional polemics, in part by missionary fervor, these three authors produced the most influential sixteenth-century vernacular works on penance for the Bavarian laity – sermons, catechisms and lay penitentials – in addition to their work as prominent preachers, pedagogues and administrators at the territorial University of Ingolstadt.[55]

Sermons represented the first uniform lessons on penance to reach the Bavarian populace. As early as 1530, Duke Wilhelm IV tasked Eck to compose a four-volume standard edition of orthodox sermons in German. The Duke ordered an emissary to distribute Eck's sermons to every parish in the Duchy at a cost of $1\frac{1}{2}$ fl. per volume. Priests claiming indigence were ordered to procure funds from their ecclesiastical superiors.[56] Eck, renowned arch-rival of Luther at the Disputation of Leipzig (1519), had

---

[52] Klibansky et al., *Saturn and Melancholy*, 107–109. [53] Albertinus, *Lucifers Königreich*, 420.
[54] Ellenberger, *Discovery of the Unconscious*, 43–46.
[55] The penitential works of the Jesuits Gregor de Valencia, Jacob Gretser and Adam Tanner were in Latin and therefore limited in terms of their intended audience. Valencia's *De Poenitentiae Sacramento* (Ingolstadt, 1585), Gretser's *De Sacramento Poenitentiae* (Ingolstadt, 1591) and Tanner's *De Poenitentiae Virtute et Sacramento* (Ingolstadt, 1611) justified penance and good works against the attacks of Luther, Melanchthon and Calvin. Valencia, 17–18, does suggest that Protestants might be more prone to despair without access to confession. Otherwise, these works were meant as polemics and not as practical guides.
[56] Karl-Ludwig Ay (ed.), *Dokumente zur Geschichte von Staat und Gesellschaft in Bayern. Abteilung I: Altbayern vom Frühmittelalter bis 1800*, vol. II (Munich, 1977), *Altbayern von 1180–1550*, 284–285. The emissary's name was Erasmus Schwaiger. The protest of the bishops of Freising, Passau and Regensburg against this and other measures is subsequently recorded on 285–289.

studied theology in Heidelberg, Tübingen, Cologne and Freiburg before he assumed a professorship at the University of Ingolstadt in 1510. He eventually rose to the posts of rector and vice-chancellor at the institution. A leading Catholic theologian throughout the Reformation era, Eck played a pivotal role at all critical imperial diets on religious matters, including Augsburg (1530) and Regensburg (1541). In 1534, he released the fourth volume of his collected sermons, dedicating no fewer than fourteen sermons to the themes of confession and penance.[57] His defense of the Catholic sacraments against Luther echoed his earlier polemical tracts.[58] Eck employed pure scholastic exegesis from gospels, psalms and works of the early church fathers (especially St. Augustine) to refute Luther. His sermons thirty-eight through fifty-one addressed the sacramental nature of confession, absolution and penance. The first sermon on auricular confession began with the admonition:

You devout and chosen in Christ, just as we have lost godly favor and grace through mortal sin, so too has the merciful Lord provided us with a remedy to heal this injury, the sacrament of penance.[59]

Eck went on to outline three types of confessions: first, the inner examination of one's conscience on each Sunday and on holy days; second, the ritual transference of sin and guilt onto a scapegoat by the children of Israel; and third, the oral tradition of narrating sins either privately to a priest or publicly before the assembled congregation. For Eck, confession offered a vomitive to expel moral impurities from the body:

Now see what scripture teaches us. No one should conceal sin inwardly, for perhaps, like those who have indigestible food within or some kind of slime or moisture, which causes the stomach discomfort, so too can you be eased and made fit and therefore healthy. If you hide and repress the sin within you, so will you suffer internal pressure and even come near to choking on the slime of sin, whereas if one becomes the accuser and accuses oneself of sin and confesses, then sin, the cause of indigestion, can be released.[60]

The origin of his catharsis of the spoken word was largely patristic. Eck, the consummate scholastic, cited Origen, Jerome, Cyril and biblical

[57] Johann Eck, *Der viert tail Christlicher Predigen von den siben H. Sacramenten nach außwesung Christlicher Kirchen und grund Byblischer gschrifft/ den alten frummen Christen zu gut* (Ingolstadt, 1534).

[58] Johannes Eck, *Enchiridion* (Ingolstadt, 1529), 62v–65v; Eck, *De poenitentia et confessione secreta semper in Ecclesia Dei observata, contra Lutherum* (Ingolstadt, 1533). On the debate between Eck and Luther over the sacrament of auricular confession, see Heinrich Schnauerte, *Die Bußlehre des Johannes Eck* (Münster, 1919).

[59] Eck, *Der viert tail Christlicher Predigen*, 73r.   [60] Ibid., 74v.

passages.[61] He accepted the church's authority to forgive sin according to the doctrine of the keys, emphasizing that those bitten by the snake of the devil must not be ashamed to expose their wound to their spiritual physician in confession. Only then could the doctor recognize the internalized poison of sin, "for he cannot cure what he cannot see."[62] These metaphors, neither novel nor original, were organized into a coherent agenda of anti-evangelical propaganda in support of the Catholic sacrament of penance. Volume four of the orthodox sermons was undoubtedly the first depiction of auricular confession as spiritual physic transmitted to a wide audience in Bavaria through the effective combination of two mass media, vernacular print and standardized preaching.

Later tracts on penance concentrated less on a defense of the sacrament, instead inviting the individual to explore their conscience fully for moral failings. This is the case with Peter Canisius, who actively employed the motif of the father confessor as a spiritual physician in his subsequent catechisms. Canisius occupied the vice-chancellorship of the University of Ingolstadt from 1549 to 1552.[63] In 1566, he became the first provincial of Upper Germany, headquartered at the university. In his *Confession and Communion Booklet* of 1569, Canisius went beyond Eck's patristic interpretations, insisting that the healing power of the priest in confession was greater than that of his medical counterpart.[64] Canisius prescribed confession as the most effective remedy for afflictions of the soul.[65] Previously, he outlined the healing function of the priest in his enormously successful

---

[61] Eck, *Enchiridion*, 64r–65r, concurs with Tertullian that exomologesis can restore physical as well as mental health. Eck also cites the *De oratione* of Origen on "incurable" sins. Later he suggests confession as a remedy (*medicina*), citing a biblical source (James) and explicitly calls the priest-confessor a "physician." Similar references are found in the works of Ambrose, who discusses confession in reference to laying hands on the sick, Victor Tununensis ("confession is thy medicine . . .") and Caesarius of Arles, among others; see Watkins, *History of Penance*, vol. i, 116–117, 132–142, 430–435, and vol. ii, 565–566.

[62] Eck, *Der viert tail Christlicher Predigen*, 75r, 77r. Trent took up this theme as well, e.g. Waterworth, *The Council of Trent*, 14th Session, Chap. 5 b, "for if the sick be ashamed to show his wound to the physician, his medical art cures not that which it knows not of."

[63] The post had been vacant since Eck's death in 1543. On Canisius' early life and his associations with Nicholas of Esch and the Beguine Maria of Osterwijk, both followers of the *devotio moderna*, and Justus Landsberg, a mystic Carthusian, see Engelbert Maximilian Buxbaum, *Petrus Canisius und die kirchliche Erneuerung des Herzogtums Bayern, 1549–1556* (Rome, 1973), 69–80. Also see Julius Oswald, SJ and Peter Rummel (eds.), *Petrus Canisius – Reformer der Kirche. Festschrift zum 400. Todestag des zweiten Apostels Deutschlands* (Augsburg, 1996).

[64] These citations are taken from a later edition, Petrus Canisius, *Beicht und Communion Büchlein* (Dillingen, 1579), 10r–11v. In the sixteenth century, the medicinal metaphor became popular among the Jesuits whose penitential practices are characterized by Bossy, "Social History of Confession," 28, as the "psychological school."

[65] Myers, *"Poor Sinning Folk,"* 147–148, 154, 156.

Great and *Little Catechisms*, reprinted in dozens of vernacular editions as the standard catechistic work of the Duchy.[66]

> It is foremost appropriate that the sinner humble himself before God and God's Church and make use of the sacrament of penance as Christ established it, namely as a truly necessary remedy and ecclesiastical medicine for consolation, strength, and redemption . . .[67]

Here, the father confessor acted primarily in a diagnostic role as the penitent's spiritual physician, but he also held the secondary legal authority of a judge.[68] Like marriage, Canisius noted, the sacrament of penance had a legalistic character, but only after the authorized priest pronounced the judicial phrase of absolution, "ego te absolvo."[69] Canisius insured that widespread catechizing reinforced the status of the confessor as a spiritual physician already present in Eck's standard sermons. By the end of the sixteenth century, catechism classes for children were mandatory in Bavaria; during the reign of Maximilian I, children were enticed with trinkets to attend.[70] According to Canisius, the penitent should approach the confessional

> . . . with a completely innocent, humble, sad, and honorable heart: that he approaches like an invalid or one seriously wounded, who stands before his physician: or like an indebted prisoner desirous of mercy, who appears before his judge.[71]

A *Confession Book* by the polemicist Dr. Martin Eisengrein, a close friend and collaborator of Canisius, appeared one year after his death in 1579. Eisengrein consistently referred back to the Tridentine decrees to develop the concept of spiritual physic according to the new conciliar guidelines.[72] Born to an evangelical family in Stuttgart, Eisengrein studied in Tübingen, Ingolstadt and Vienna. He converted to Catholicism in 1558 under the influence of the Jesuits, most likely Canisius himself. Eisengrein served as

---

[66] Buxbaum, *Petrus Canisius*, 192–196; Clark, *Thinking with Demons*, 500–501, is also pertinent.

[67] Canisius, *Beicht*, 3r; Canisius, *Der kleine Catechismus* (Ingolstadt, 1584), 246.

[68] As Duggan, "Fear and Confession," 164, points out, this title was secondary to the confessor's role as a physician. See also Anne T. Thayer, "Judge and Doctor: Images of the Confessor in Printed Model Sermon Collections, 1450–1520," in: Katharine Jackson Lualdi and Annet Thayer (eds.), *Penitence in the Age of Reformations* (Aldershot, 2000), 10–29.

[69] Josef Andreas Jungmann, SJ, *Die lateinischen Bußriten in ihrer geschichtlichen Entwicklung* (Innsbruck, 1932), 1; LThK, 129–130. The judicial comparison is patristic as well.

[70] Stieve, *Die kirchliche Polizeiregiment*, 34.

[71] Canisius, *Beicht*, 12r. A faint echo of Tridentine pronouncements, e.g. Waterworth, *The Council of Trent*, 14th Session, Canon IX: "If any one saith, that the sacramental absolution of the priest is not a judicial act . . . let him be anathema."

[72] Martin Eisengrein, *Beichtbuch* (Ingolstadt, 1579), an abridged version of his 1577 Latin penitential.

court preacher in Vienna to Emperor Maximilian II until called in 1562 to Ingolstadt, where he acted as rector, dean and superintendent, founding the university library. He is most remembered for his immensely popular account of exorcisms at Altötting, where Canisius personally conducted the ritual.[73]

Eisengrein's *Confessional Book* justified penance and good works as unavoidable remedies for both spiritual and physical illnesses, implying that Christ himself compared the physicians of the soul to the physicians of the body.[74] In an explication of the moral casuistry of sin, he noted that:

through the confession of sins and the expulsion of burdens, the heart is cleansed of the bitter bile from inward bitterness of sin resulting from human desires of the flesh – just as from an injurious food, as if something impure and bitter had gathered in the heart. When a person expels such bitterness from himself, he saves himself from even greater dangers and afflictions of the body.[75]

In his penitential, Eisengrein warned that those who conceal or repress their sins suffer from anxiety and are choked with malevolent humors and the retention of bodily waste. If bitterness arose from pangs of guilt, contemporaries knew that yellow bile, or choler, had a bitter flavor and that the recollection of sin stimulated "the expelling operation of the intestines and dilutes the phlegm inside them, for excremental as well as alimentary purposes."[76] Therefore, Eisengrein's injunction to the penitent to seek proper treatment for their sin-stained soul in the care of a qualified spiritual physician was more than a passing reference. It epitomized the revival of Galenic humoral pathology after the Council of Trent as part of the second scholastic and neo-stoicist movements.[77] Eisengrein went beyond the attritionist stance and ritual confession, which represented only one aspect of sacramental penance. The penitent should also be contrite, refrain from sin in the future and perform proper satisfaction as adjudicated by the priest. Otherwise, poor wretched sinners could never fully recover from their spiritual afflictions.[78]

Eisengrein, a fiery preacher, also employed sermons to promote the image of sacramental penance and auricular confession as consolation and a remedy for uncontrollable urges, external temptations and the demonic infections of sin causing humoral imbalance. Sermons offered him the twin

---

[73] Martin Eisengrein's *Unser Lieben Fraw zu Alten oetting* (Ingolstadt, 1571) went into at least six editions by 1625. On Canisius' participation, see Brandmüller, *Handbuch*, 888.

[74] Eisengrein, *Beichtbuch*, 15.   [75] Ibid., 69.

[76] Delumeau, *Sin and Fear*, 218–219. See also Klibansky et al., *Saturn and Melancholy*, 107–109.

[77] Ariew, "Descartes," 60.   [78] Eisengrein, *Beichtbuch*, 20.

advantages of reaching a wide audience through printing and engaging listeners personally through the charismatic medium of the spoken word. In
his *Faithful Admonition*, a sermon given in Ingolstadt, Eisengrein emphasized the paired relationship between purity and shame and the struggle
between a good conscience and the devil. By repressing the basic need to
confess sins verbally, he added, one adversely affected one's God-given sense
of reason. To withhold sins from the father confessor altogether might result
in the retention of bodily wastes and exert actual humoral pressures within
the body.[79] Such pressures required release through the physic of the word
to restore a proper spiritual and physical balance. Potentially, denial and
repression ended in *insania*, literally equated with a loss of reason induced
by a build-up of humoral pressure:

> The saintly teacher Bernhard once said (and it is surely true), "Insania est quod
> pudet ablui & non pudet coinquinari" – that is, it is unreason to be ashamed to
> wash, but not be ashamed to make oneself unclean. The sinner stains himself and
> makes himself unclean, but those who confess cleanse themselves. If you weren't
> ashamed to sin, well then in God's name don't be ashamed to wash yourself, drive
> out the devil of dumbness and confess your sins so that you are free of them and
> your conscience will be calmed.[80]

In Bavaria, lay penitentials continued to characterize penance as spiritual
physic until the eighteenth century.[81] One *New Confessional Form* published
anonymously in Munich in 1635 reminded its readers that the priest alone,
through heavenly grace and the authority of his office, could easily heal
infirmity and cure sickness in the soul.[82] The author maintained that it
was, in fact, a sin against the first Commandment to depend more on a
secular physician than on the confessor, who, as the mediator of heavenly
grace, was preferable as the healing instance of first recourse.[83] Penitentials
and guides to penance in catechisms, previously little more than endless
indices of sins based on the Ten Commandments, now included detailed
instructions to guide the penitent through the difficulties of researching
their conscience. Confession was touted as an effective means not only to
purge sins, but also to achieve peace of mind and maintain physical health.

Aegidius Albertinus once dubbed penance a true theriac (that mythical
panacea) and righteous antidote for the poison of sin.[84] The Neapolitan

---

[79] Martin Eisengrein, *Trewherzige Vermanung an alle Catholische Christen/ das sie sich/ durch den Teuffel
und seine Diener/von der Beicht nit lassen abwendig machen* (Ingolstadt, 1566), 7v.
[80] Ibid., 12v–13r.   [81] LThK, vol. II, 126, 131.
[82] Anonymous, *Newer Beichtform* (Munich, 1635), B2r–v. See also Canisius, *Kleine Catechismus*, 241.
[83] Anon., *Newer Beichtform*, D3v.   [84] Albertinus, *Christi Königreich*, 82.

protophysician Giovanni Filippo Ingrassia cited it and other forms of spiritual physic as the sole effective remedies against magical spells, while demonological works (e.g. Menghi, Del Rio, Thyraeus, or the 1608 *Compendium maleficarum* of Francesco Maria Guazzo, which cited Galen and Avicenna) extolled the advantages of confession and spiritual physic in patently humoral language.[85] A papal *motu proprio* of Pius V in 1566 and a decree issued by Archbishop Carlo Borromeo formally legitimized penance as spiritual physic; both prohibited physicians from treating seriously ill persons prior to confession.[86] In Naples, one physician-surgeon was denounced to the Inquisition in 1640 for regularly having done so.[87] In his 1596 text on medical ethics, the Italian physician Battista Codronchi also encouraged his professional colleagues to have patients confess prior to treatment. The hylomorphic bond between body and soul insured that shriving cured the soul and cleansed the body as a "physical medicament."[88]

The attitudes of the renowned Tyrolean physician and Catholic moralist Hippolyt Guarinonius (1571–1654) are also relevant to our present consideration, since he was an acknowledged expert on health care in neighboring Bavaria. Son of the personal physician to Emperor Rudolf II, Guarinonius was born in Trent and later served as a page to the Tridentine patron of penance, Borromeo, in Milan.[89] After completing medical studies in Prague and Padua, he served as personal physician to a Moravian cardinal and, from 1607, to the Habsburg archduchesses Maria Christiana and Leonora of Styria at the imperial convent of Hall in Tyrol. There, he also filled a vacant post as civic medicus until his death. Today, Guarinonius is also remembered as a footnote to the legend of Andreas of Rinn (near Innsbruck). Largely through his documentary efforts, "Anderl" became one of only two alleged child-victims of Jewish ritual murder ever to be

---

[85] Gentilcore, *Healers*, 23, 161–163, 208. Del Rio cited Codronchi as well; see *Investigations into Magic*, ed. and trans. P. G. Maxwell-Stuart (Manchester, 2000), 240–248. For a lengthy discussion of scientific explanations for witchcraft and demonic activity, to include medicine and humoral theory, see Clark, *Thinking with Demons*, esp. 151–311.

[86] Andriano Prosperi, "Beichtväter und Inquisition im 16. Jahrhundert," in: Wolfgang Reinhard and Heinz Schilling, *Die katholische Konfessionalisierung* (Güterslohe, 1995), 129. Also see Thomas Deutscher, "The Role of the Episcopal Tribunal of Novara in the Suppression of Heresy and Witchcraft, 1563–1615," *The Catholic Historical Review* 77 (1991), 403–421. Actually, this was part of canon law as early as the fourteenth century; many thanks to Tom Tentler for this observation.

[87] Gentilcore, *Healers*, 11–12.

[88] Ibid.; Lynn Thorndike, *A History of Experimental Magic and Science, vol. VI: The Sixteenth Century* (New York, 1941), 544–547.

[89] Jürgen Bücking, "Hippolytus Guarinonius (1571–1654), Pfalzgraf zu Hoffberg und Volderthurn," *Österreich in Geschichte und Literatur* 12 (1968), 65–80.

officially recognized by the papacy.[90] Efforts to publicize other legendary child-victims played a role in devotion and spiritual physic in Bavaria.

For contemporaries, Guarinonius became famous for his talents as a Counter Reformation physician after the publication of his voluminous moral treatise *The Abomination of the Desolation of the Human Race*, intended as a home medical encyclopedia. If the subtitle, "completely useful, very necessary and also quite enjoyable for all, ecclesiastical and lay, learned and unlearned, and persons of high and low estate," denoted his desired target audience, the hefty leather-bound tome (1,330 pages), organized into two distinct books, was expensive and acquired largely by religious and educational institutions. The apocalyptic title, drawn from Matthew 24:15, refers to Daniel's interpretation of Nebuchadnezzar's dreams concerning the four ages of man and the prophecy of the end of the world. Dedicated to Rudolf II, the treatise commenced with this advice on general health: "diseases and illnesses afflicting the putrefying human body mean less than nothing when compared to the adulteration and loss of the most precious soul."[91] His introduction commenced with a dismal assessment of the political health of the Empire, noting that despite its material riches, the German nation suffered from its worst period of rising prices and dearth in living memory, while young persons of both sexes appeared pitiably weak and deathly pale.[92]

Guarinonius devoted book one to God as the fountain of good health, to consolation as a vital means of attaining it, and to the superiority of the soul over an "impure, greedy, unchaste, sotted, drunken, stinking body."[93] In the second book, on temperament, he reinforced the theme of consolation and penance as the two best means to combat troubles, fear and tribulations affecting the body with physical afflictions.[94] Published in Ingolstadt in 1610, the *Abomination* sported an approbation from the university theology faculty and a poem dedicated to Philip Menzel, MD (d.1613), poet laureate and professor emeritus at the faculty of medicine. The university and the Jesuit College of St. Michael's in Munich, indisputably the two most important academic institutions in Bavaria, both owned copies (see Plate 6). Guarinonius enjoyed especial esteem in Bavaria, influencing the work of Albertinus and Jeremias Drexel.[95] His other publications included

---

[90] Ronnie Po-Chia Hsia, *The Myth of Ritual Murder: Jews and Magic in Reformation Germany* (1988), 218–222.

[91] Guarinonius, *Die Grewel, Dedicatio.*   [92] Ibid., 2.   [93] Ibid., 10, 110.

[94] Ibid., e.g. 292–303.

[95] Dieter Breuer, "Hippolytus Guarinonius als Erzähler," in: Herbert Zeman (ed.), *Die österreichische Literatur. Eine Dokumentation ihrer literarhistorischen Entwicklung* (Graz, 1986), 1117–1133, esp. 1120.

Plate 5. Hippolyt Guarinonius, 1607, at age 37. (Taken from the *Admiration of the Desolation*, Courtesy of Sturzflug Press.)

Plate 6. Copper etching, title page, *The Abomination of the Desolation of the Human Race* by Hippolyt Guarinonius (Ingolstadt, 1610); originally acquired by the Jesuit College of St. Michael's in Munich. (Permission of the Bavarian State Library, Munich.)

a practical guide on plague, a moral tract on Christian marriage and a translation of a hagiography of Borromeo. Guarinonius' brand of "moral medicine," a dogmatic blend of physic and casuistry, was vehemently anti-Machiavellian and pro-Lipsian. The author openly referred to himself as a "worldly Jesuit."[96]

More than any other group, the Jesuits reinforced the idea of sacramental penance as spiritual physic through consolation. They prescribed it for physical as well as spiritual afflictions and spread that image through printed ecclesiastical and medical texts, in sermons, through catechistic activities and as part of university curricula. Although impossible to gauge accurately the extent of reception, it would have been difficult for any ordinary child, man or woman in the Duchy of Bavaria to escape the message by the end of the sixteenth century. With the aid of the printing press, the polemic activities of counter-reformers like Eck, Canisius and Eisengrein and the pedagogical efforts of the Jesuits at their regional colleges and the University of Ingolstadt reached a mass audience in Bavaria in a systematized fashion.[97] However, consolation was only one aspect of their penitential message. In political terms, father confessors also played a central role as personal confidants and spiritual advisors. Here, too, the Jesuits had their part to play. For an unbroken period of a hundred years, from 1579 to 1679, the Jesuits tenaciously held the coveted post of father confessor to the Wittelsbach Dukes, earning themselves both political power and the envy and enmity of their rivals at court in Munich.

JESUIT FATHER CONFESSORS: SPIRITUAL PHYSIC FOR THE HEAD OF THE BODY POLITIC

Another Tyrolean, Nicholas of Cusa, once described the political common-wealth as a living organism with a soul, contending that every king needed a "physician of state."[98] In line with that philosophy, father confessors

---

[96] Jürgen Bücking, *Kultur und Gesellschaft in Tirol um 1600. Des Hippolytus Guarinonius' "Grewel der Verwüstung Menschlichen Geschlechts" (1610) als kulturgeschichtliche Quelle des frühen 17. Jahrhunderts* (Lübeck, 1968), 9; Guillaume van Gemert, "Tridentinische Geistigkeit und Moraldidaxis in Guarinonius' 'Grewel'. Der Arzt als geistlicher Autor," in: Elmar Loche (ed.), *Hippolytus Guarinonius im interkulturellen Kontext seiner Zeit* (Bozen, 1995), 45–64.
[97] For Euan Cameron, this is a defining aspect of the European Reformation as a coherent ecumenical event: "The Reformation gave large groups of people across Europe their first lessons in political commitment to a universal ideology. In the sixteenth century, religion became mass politics. Other ideologies, ultimately more secular in tone, would take its place. The Reformation was the first" (*The European Reformation*, 422). By Reformation, I take him here to include the Catholic renewal.
[98] The medieval mystic philosopher and Archbishop of Brixen, Nicholas of Cusa; see Klibansky et al., *Saturn and Melancholy*, 194–195.

assumed a crucial role in Bavaria as political counselors, especially after the arrival of the Jesuits. Duke Wilhelm IV, father of Albrecht V, struck an initial bargain with Ignatius Loyola in 1548 to fill three vacant professorships at Ingolstadt, a turning point in the political and intellectual life of the Duchy.[99] Canisius was one of those three theologians arriving in 1549. As a result of the Reformation, the university had already lost one-third of its students, most from the faculty of the *"artes,"* the traditional training ground for the parish clergy.[100] The innovative teachings of Protestantism, which included not least provisions for marriage, lured applicants away. Qualified parish priests and monastic novitiates became scarce. In return for dispatching the three fresh theologians, Ignatius Loyola received direct assurances providing for a Jesuit college in Ingolstadt. When Albrecht V succeeded his father and assumed an initially tolerant religious posture, he reneged on the pledge. Immediately, Ignatius withdrew his theologians,[101] forcing Albrecht's hand. Thus in 1555, the first Jesuit college in Upper Germany came to cohabit with and dominate academic life at the territorial university. The headquarters of the newly created Jesuit Province of Upper Germany made its home in Ingolstadt and was headed by Canisius for its first thirteen years. Albrecht established another college at the vacant Augustinian monastery in Munich in 1559. These Jesuit colleges laid the foundation for a regional school system, which retained its form long after the order's dissolution in 1773. Canisius, who hand-carried the decrees of the Council of Trent from Rome to the south German bishops, personally undertook the religious indoctrination of the educated elite at Ingolstadt.[102]

Albrecht V also assigned his son, Wilhelm V, a Jesuit as his father confessor. Jesuits continued to occupy the office of father confessor to the rulers of Bavaria without interruption until 1679. At first, Jesuit superiors in Upper Germany were reluctant to assign one of their order to a post at court on a permanent basis. Some of the order's superiors suspected the temptations of court life, which might conflict with the strict hierarchical structure and vows of obedience demanded from its members by the militant society, or that contact with women at court might lead to compromise and scandal.[103]

---

[99] For an estimation of the influence of the Jesuits on intellectual life in Bavaria, see Richard van Dülmen, "Die Gesellschaft Jesu und der bayerische Späthumanismus," ZBLG 37 (1974), 358–415.
[100] Arno Seifert, "Die 'Seminarpolitik' der bayerischen Herzöge im 16. Jahrhundert und die Begründung des jesuitischen Schulwesens," in: Glaser, *Wittelsbach und Bayern*, 125–132.
[101] Stieve, *Die kirchliche Polizeiregiment*, 5–6.
[102] Karl Bosl, *Bayerische Geschichte* (Munich, 1976), 121.
[103] Bernhard Duhr, SJ, *Geschichte der Jesuiten in den Ländern deutscher Zunge*, vol. II, pt. 2 (Freiburg, 1918), 687–697.

Prudent authorities simply feared that bad advice from a Jesuit confessor to his prince could damage the reputation of the fledgling order. However, as early as 1553, Ignatius Loyola rebuked the Administrator of the Portuguese Province for refusing a post as father confessor to King John III. Loyola insisted that the pastoral obligation of the society extended to the mighty as well as the lowly. He employed the metaphor of a sane body politic to illustrate that the performance of high office was of greater importance "since all the parts of the body profit from the well-being of its head, just as all subjects profit from the well-being of their Prince."[104] Later, in his instructions to Jesuit confessors of princes in 1602 (*De confessionariis principum*), General Acquaviva reminded his subordinates to avoid political entanglements and limit themselves to matters of conscience.[105] Hesitantly, the Society of Jesus had embarked on a strategy to achieve political dominance through close association with members of the social elite.

The case of Pater Dominic Mengin illustrates the razor's edge walked by the Jesuits in a dual attempt to retain both their autonomy and influence at court. Pater Mengin was Duke Wilhelm V's first father confessor. Whereas Wilhelm IV and Albrecht V had tacitly supported the new order, Wilhelm V now favored them outright, a sentiment directly attributable to Mengin's personal influence.[106] A French Jesuit from the diocese of Toul, he was initially appointed as confessor to Duchess Renata (also from Lorraine), who suffered bouts of melancholy during the long absences of her husband.[107]

Canisius initially described Mengin as a good and simple priest, but ignorant of theology.[108] Mengin assumed a post as rector at the Jesuit college in Munich in 1565. In 1568, Paul Hoffaeus, Canisius' successor as provincial, accused Mengin of cultivating an overly intimate relationship with the Duchess of Lorraine when he accepted a secondary post as her chaplain. There were visible indications that courtly life adversely affected his personal conduct: he drank intemperately and over-indulged in creature comforts. Hoffaeus described his behavior in coarse terms: "If he [Mengin] goes on in this fashion, it will give the appearance that he leads the life of a pig rather than a member of the order."[109] In 1578, he had Mengin relieved

---

[104] Ibid., 685.

[105] Dieter Albrecht, *Maximilian I von Bayern 1573–1651* (Munich, 1998), 325–326.

[106] On Wilhelm V: "He was blindly devoted to the Jesuits and filled with such fanatic bigotry, that he was eventually moved through their influence to abdicate and fulfill a desire to secure his access to heaven by retiring to a life of monastic penitence" – here, one should take Stieve, *Die kirchliche Polizeiregiment*, 9, with a grain of salt, as a liberal representative of the *Kulturkampf.*

[107] On Renata's melancholy, see Dotterweich, *Der Junge Maximilian*, 39–40.

[108] Duhr, *Geschichte der Jesuiten*, vol. II, pt. 2, 689–690; James Broderick, SJ, *Petrus Canisius, 1521–1597* (Vienna, 1950), 493–495.

[109] Ibid., 492.

as rector of the college. Hoffaeus then allied himself with Canisius in a bid to remove Mengin as father confessor to Wilhelm, still in his minority, but poised to inherit the Duchy.[110] The two felt uncomfortable with Mengin's close relationship to the heir-apparent, which compelled them to pay lip-service to Mengin in clear breach of Jesuit hierarchical discipline. Hoffaeus complained that the couple "venerate him like a deity and do not wish to see him troubled."[111]

Canisius traveled to Munich to negotiate Mengin's immediate recall to Rome. Dismayed, Wilhelm reacted sharply, dispatching a letter directly to the society's General in Rome. Pater Mengin, he indicated, performed his office dutifully for many years and his life and manners were nothing less than a living lesson on piety and scrupulousness.[112] He acted as father confessor not only to the Duke and his wife, but also to numerous courtiers and to his own father, Albrecht V, who loved P. Dominic (Mengin) so much, he would hardly accept a replacement. If the society placed any value at all on the good will of the Duke, they should see to it that P. Dominic continued in his office as long as deemed fit. Simple thankfulness for the charitable actions of the Duke on behalf of the college demanded that common courtesy. The closing remark was a veiled threat concerning a grandiose construction project on behalf of the order, which Wilhelm made public several months later.

The threats alarmed Provincial Hoffaeus, who suddenly shifted blame onto Canisius for having misjudged Mengin. Hoffaeus traveled to Munich himself in 1580 to patch up what he now referred to as Canisius' botched diplomacy.[113] Mengin triumphed with the support of the Duke and Duchess, as well as Wilhelm's mother, herself a daughter of Emperor Maximilian II. Mengin retained his post at court as father confessor. Hoffaeus had Canisius ignominiously transferred to Switzerland after the latter fell into disfavor, first with Duke Wilhelm over the Mengin affair and then with his own superiors for performing unauthorized exorcisms.

Hoffaeus continued to complain about Wilhelm's attempts to draw the society into active participation in political affairs until the Duke named him president of his newly formed Ecclesiastical Council.[114] In spite of accusations of moral turpitude, Mengin's influence at court paid off. In 1581, Wilhelm announced his intention to construct a proper structure to house the Jesuit college in Munich; construction began two years later. The society convinced Wilhelm to construct an impressive monument

---

[110] Duhr, *Geschichte der Jesuiten*, vol. II, pt. 2, 688–690.
[111] Broderick, *Petrus Canisius*, 493–504.   [112] Duhr, *Geschichte der Jesuiten*, vol. II, pt. 2, 691.
[113] Broderick, *Petrus Canisius*, 497–498, 500.   [114] Duhr, *Geschichte der Jesuiten*, vol. II, pt. 2, 693.

symbolizing Catholic unity.[115] St. Michael's was consecrated by Wilhelm on July 6, 1597, but Mengin did not survive to witness the dedication. His successor, P. Casper Torrentius, SJ, held the post of father confessor to Wilhelm for the next three decades.[116] Spurred on by political successes, the society shifted to a policy of active involvement at court.

The Tyrolean historian Matheus Rader, SJ (1561–1634) and the Swabian dramatist Jacob Gretser, SJ (1562–1625) officially dedicated St. Michael's to Duke Wilhelm in their *festschrift, The Bavarian Trophy, Saint Michael the Archangel.*[117] Michael, the warrior saint who cast Lucifer and his rebellious angels from heaven, was strongly associated with the militant image of the Society of Jesus locked in mortal combat against the forces of the devil. St. Michael's combined balanced proportion with an interplay of light to create a homogeneous and uninterrupted space that exuded unity, harmony and moderation, making it the first truly baroque house of worship in Germany.[118] It remains the penultimate architectural embodiment of Jesuit pedagogy north of the Alps.[119] Steeped in the Ignatian program of humanist education, its architectural plan reflected the sequence of Loyola's *Spiritual Exercises*, inviting worshipers on a spiritual pilgrimage through three stages: purgation, illumination and union. The Ignatian exercises combined deep sensualism with psychological self-awareness training. They appealed explicitly to the senses, above all sight and imagination (the mind's eye).[120] Upon entering the nave of St. Michael's, two chapels confronted the worshiper with paintings intended to encourage self-examination and memory: the *Penitent Mary Magdalen* and the *Martyrdom of St. Ursula*. The latter saint, martyred in Cologne, was intended as a reminder of Bavaria's victory in the recent war of 1583. Several feet away, confessionals adorned the piers between the nave chapels. The Jesuits were among the first to introduce the confessional to Bavaria; design plans for confessionals date from as early as 1591.[121]

---

[115] Heinz Jürgen Sauermost, "Zur Rolle St. Michaels im Rahmen der Wilhelmisch-maximilianischen Kunst," in: Glaser, *Wittelsbach und Bayern*, 167–174.

[116] Duhr, *Geschichte der Jesuiten*, vol. ii, pt. 2, 700–702, 784.

[117] Matheus Rader and Jacob Gretser, *Trophaea Bavarica Sancto Michaeli Archangel. In templo et gymnasio societatis Jesu dicata* (Munich, 1597).

[118] Erich Hubula, "Vom europäischen Rang der Münchner Architektur um 1600," in: Glaser, *Wittelsbach und Bayern*, 141–151.

[119] Jeffrey Chipps Smith, *Sensuous Worship: Jesuits and the Art of the Early Catholic Reformation in Germany* (Princeton, 2002), 80–81.

[120] Ignatius distinguished between the affective (external) and cognitive (internal) senses: ibid., 35–40.

[121] Ibid., 80–85; Smith, characterized confession here as "one tool that the Jesuits actively wielded in their desire to build a Catholic state in Germany."

In 1597, Wilhelm V abdicated to his son, Maximilian I, an event that also ushered in a strategic shift toward reason-of-state policies.[122] Unlike his father, Maximilian I was a disciplined administrator and spent his energies perfecting the bureaucracy created by his grandfather, Albrecht V. A tireless worker, Maximilian micro-managed policy decisions and involved himself in the day-to-day operations of the central government.[123] He differed significantly from Wilhelm in his skeptical attitude toward religion. In a letter to his aging father, the new Duke stated bluntly, "My life long, I will not trust Romanists." Blind support of Rome, Maximilian continued, had cost the Duchy much in monies and damage, adding almost cynically, "I believe that in spiritual as well as worldly affairs, only the reason of state is observed, and only those who have much land or much money are respected."[124] Nevertheless, it would be wrong to label Maximilian a secular ruler in the modern sense. As Friedrich Meinecke once noted, religious and political ideologies were stressfully interwoven during the confessional age. Political decisions remained questions of conscience and honor, and rulers often felt torn between the dictates of practical Machiavellian politics and the anti-Machiavellian teachings of the pulpit and the confessional.[125] Furthermore, Maximilian relied heavily on ecclesiastical institutions to govern effectively. A paragon of Catholic virtue in the Empire, he founded the League and led the Catholic cause throughout much of the Thirty Years War. While on campaign, he continued to hear mass daily and confessed at least once a week. Maximilian was attended by three consecutive father confessors over his fifty-year reign as Duke and (after 1623) Prince-Elector, all of whom performed simultaneous public duties as political advisors, foreign emissaries and policy makers.[126]

Johannes Buslidius, SJ from Luxembourg was assigned to Maximilian and his first wife, Elisabeth of Lorraine, by his father in 1594.[127] Maximilian

---

[122] Spindler, _Handbuch_, 405–406. Speculation over his abdication centers on Wilhelm's generous support of the Jesuits, which contributed to a state of bankruptcy: Benno Hubensteiner, "Maximilian I," in: Glaser, _Wittelsbach und Bayern_, 186.

[123] Robert Bireley, SJ, _Maximilian von Bayern, Adam Contzen, SJ und die Gegenreformation in Deutschland 1624–1635_ (Göttingen, 1975), 47–48.

[124] A veiled reference to Wilhelm V's support of the Jesuits and their costly building projects, which nearly bankrupted the state: Ziegler, _Dokumente_, 634.

[125] Albrecht, _Maximilian I_, 324; Friedrick Meinecke, _Die Idee der Staatsräson in der neueren Geschichte_ (Munich, 1976), 140.

[126] On the activities of father confessors as political advisors, see Robert Bireley, _The Counter-Reformation Prince. Anti-Machiavellism or Catholic Statecraft in Early Modern Europe_ (Chapel Hill, 1990); Bireley, "Hofbeichtväter und Politik im 17. Jahrhunderts," in: M. Sievernich and G. Switek, _Ignatianisch. Eigenart und Methode der Gesellschaft Jesu_ (Freiburg, 1990), 386–403; Winfried Müller, "Hofbeichtväter und geistliche Ratgeber zur Zeit der Gegenreformation," in: Müller (ed.), _Universität und Bildung_ (Munich, 1991), 141–155.

[127] Albrecht, _Maximilian I_, 324–325.

called on him for advice in countless matters of religious doctrine and political affairs. Buslidius was a vocal advocate of witchcraft persecutions, having once met the demonologist Martin Del Rio in Graz to discuss the unrestrained use of torture on suspected witches. A charter member of the radical Jesuit party at court, he intransigently preached for a holy war against Protestantism and took an active part in Maximilian's invasion of Bohemia in 1620 during the White Mountain campaign.[128] Buslidius also acted in a diplomatic capacity, accompanying the heir-apparent of the County Palatine of Neuburg and Duchy of Jülich-Cleves, Wolfgang Wilhelm, to Rome after Maximilian negotiated his conversion from Lutheranism to Catholicism and sealed it with an arranged marriage to his sister, Magdalena.[129] This was a major blow to the Protestant cause and Buslidius was a crucial figure in the conversion, acting as Wolfgang Wilhelm's father confessor, teacher of conscience and catechizer.[130]

Maximilian's second father confessor was the renowned author on anti-Machiavellian statecraft, Adam Contzen from Mainz. In 1620, Contzen published his *Politicorum libri decem*, a pro-absolutist, anti-Machiavellian poem on statecraft designed to assist Catholic rulers in practical matters of government based upon the four cardinal virtues of prudence, justice, temperance and fortitude central to neo-stoicist philosophy.[131] In the work, Contzen laid out a pragmatic program for the effective operation of an early absolutist mercantile state, offering advice on such diverse topics as rationalized agriculture, moderate taxation, the conduct of warfare, and internal production for the market economy, including state monopolies. Contzen was a vehement opponent of reformed Calvinism and his *Politicorum libri decem* earned him a dubious international reputation as a papist conspirator in places as far away as England, where an anti-Contzen tract appeared in 1641.[132]

Contzen accompanied Maximilian constantly during his tenure as father confessor, whether at imperial diets or on campaign during the Swedish invasion and occupation of Bavaria from 1632. Contzen returned in triumph

---

[128] Behringer, *Witchcraft Persecutions*, 238, 261–265.
[129] Hans Schmidt, "Pfalz-Neuburgs Sprung zum Niederrhein. Wolfgang Wilhelm von Pfalz-Neuburg und der Jülich-Klevische Erbfolgestreit," in: Glaser, *Wittelsbach und Bayern*, 77–89.
[130] Buslidius' report to Pope Paul V on the stages of the conversion and the spiritual guidance he provided appears in Ziegler, *Dokumente*, 774–780.
[131] An in-depth analysis of the political writings of Contzen and their relevance to contemporaries is provided in Ernst Albrecht Seils, *Die Staatslehre des Jesuiten Adam Contzen, Beichvater Kurfürst Maximilian I. von Bayern* (Lübeck, 1968).
[132] Anonymous, *Looke about you: The Plot of Contzen, the Moguntine Jesuite, to cheate a Church of the Religion Established therin and to serve in Popery by Art, without noise or tumult; As it is by him drawne out in his 18. and 19. Chapters of his second Booke of Politickes, Translated by a Catholicke Spy* (London, 1641).

with the Prince-Elector to Munich in 1635, dying shortly thereafter.[133] Max-imilian confessed to him on a weekly basis, addressing political subjects in close connection with moral and religious ones. Contzen acted as a political advisor and regularly reviewed matters of state, including the affairs of the Privy Council, thereby influencing virtually every sector of government. He advised Maximilian on taxation and was appointed to a territorial com-mission on hunting rights in 1627.[134] His capacity as personal advisor often detrimentally associated the Jesuit order with unpopular policies, provok-ing the resentment and envy of political rivals at court, not to mention the other religious orders.

At court, Contzen allied himself with other powerful Jesuits like Gretser, Rader, Drexel and Gregor of Valencia. The society advised Maximilian into many a hopeless situation during the Thirty Years War because of their extreme hawkish stance on holy war.[135] Opponents refered to them to as "zealots" or "the theologians" and juxtaposed them with their factional rivals in the Aulic Council, whom they in turn derided as Machiavellian politicians (*politici*) and publicly blamed for setbacks in the war.[136] For the members of the Jesuit party, these setbacks did not originate from their own implacable policies, but instead manifested celestial displeasure, because the *politici* lacked determination for the fight against the poisons of heresy and failed to back their campaign against witchcraft.[137] Motivated by the apoc-alyptic spirit of atonement, this so-called Catholic phalanx promoted stern sacramental disciplining and several witchcraft persecutions. Contzen con-sciously patterned his own political work after Lipsius' *Politicorum libri* of 1589 when he compared a state in which subjects resisted the central author-ities to a monstrous body whose appendages fought against the head. In his own *Politicorum libri decem*, he depicted this suffering body as a maniac and epileptic, contorted against its will by seizures, violent convulsions and madness, resulting in dangerous deformities analogous to discord, civil war and corruption in the body politic.[138]

When Contzen died in 1635, Bavaria itself was in a monstrous state, plundered by both Swedish and imperial troops. Plague, the ever deadly companion of military campaigns, annihilated over one-third of the population, while occupations left behind a legacy of desolation and

---

[133] Bireley, *Maximilian*, 48.   [134] Ibid., 48–55.
[135] Albrecht, *Maximilian I*, 182–184; Behringer, *Witchcraft Persecutions*, 237–239.
[136] Bireley, *Maximilian*, 52, 152–154; Duhr, *Geschichte der Jesuiten*, vol. II, pt. 2, 141–143.
[137] Behringer, *Witchcraft Persecutions*, 238, fn. 97.
[138] See above, chapter 1 on the connection to Lipsius. As Tom Tentler also informs me, the reference stems from Plutarch and is repeated in Shakespeare's *Coriolanus* as well.

terror.[139] Contzen's successor, the moderate Pater Johannes Vervaux from Lorraine, shared Maximilian's shock over the results of the war. During his prior tenure as father confessor to Maximilian's wife, the Electress Elisabeth, Vervaux proved himself inured to political intrigue and factionalism.[140] He willingly compromised in pursuit of peace even at a cost to the hard-line stance of the Jesuit phalanx. Vervaux represented a new breed of moderate Jesuits. Maximilian eagerly employed him as a foreign envoy and, having previously studied in Paris, Vervaux was the logical choice to conduct secret negotiations there in 1645 aimed at obtaining French protection for Bavaria and the Wittelsbach secundogeniture in Cologne.[141] The talks broke down when the Swedes invaded Bavaria again, this time with French backing, but Vervaux eventually negotiated the cease-fire of Ulm in 1647. When war hawks later convinced Maximilian to break the cease-fire, it was Vervaux alone who stood firm against a breach of peace.[142]

Vervaux also acted as father confessor to the heir-apparent, Ferdinand Maria, supervising his education. At Maximilian's request, Vervaux composed the *Monita paterna* in 1639, a "prince's mirror" (*Fürstenspiegel*) for his son.[143] Like Contzen's *Libri decem*, it was decidedly anti-Machiavellian and neo-stoicist in tone.[144] The *Monita* outlined a three-part program on proper comportment in matters of religion, private life and state administration, with particular attention paid to jurisprudence, counsel, bureaucracy, finance and the military.[145] However, the *Monita* went one step further, incorporating classical authors, the Bible, Lipsius and Contzen into a practical guide to reason of state. It admonished the young prince to fear God, who reigned alone above all other princes, to diligently receive the sacraments of confession and communion, to avoid corrupt libidinous desires, and to promote justice, common welfare and Christian discipline among his subjects,[146] but also to strive for peace and order. In closing, Maximilian, through the pen of Vervaux, reminded his son to study industriously.

Vervaux expressed concern about Ferdinand Maria's academic progress at an early age and it was rumored he too suffered from a melancholic

---

[139] On the demographic losses in Germany and Bavaria during the Thirty Years War, see Rudolf Schlögl, *Bauern, Krieg und Staat. Oberbayerische Bauernwirtschaft und frühmoderner Staat im 17. Jahrhundert* (Göttingen, 1988), 71–81; Schlögl, "Zwischen Krieg und Krise," *Zeitschrift für Agrargeschichte und Agrarsoziologie* 40 (1992), 133–167

[140] Albrecht, *Maximilian I*, 329–331.

[141] Vervaux's activities in Paris are summarized in Andreas Kraus, *Maximilian I. Bayerns Großer Kurfürst* (Regensburg, 1990), 269–273. The electoral see of Cologne (like Freising and other bishoprics) had been occupied by members of the Wittelsbach dynasty since the Cologne War of Succession in 1583.

[142] Ibid., 291–294.   [143] Albrecht, *Maximilian I*, 346–351.   [144] Kraus, *Maximilian I*, 42–45.

[145] The text of the *Monita* is reproduced in Ziegler, *Dokumente*, 1116–1126.

[146] Myers, *"Poor Sinning Folk,"* 117–118, emphasizes the latter.

disposition.[147] His mother, Maximilian's second wife, Maria Anna of Austria, ruled during his minority. Ferdinand Maria's wife, Henriette Adelaide of Savoy, exercised great influence over him as well. Initially, Maria Anna attempted to extend the minority and assigned Henriette Adelaide a Jesuit father confessor, Pater Luigi Montonaro, who tyrannically monitored her personal affairs. Through the intrigues of Henriette Adelaide, leading figures at court persuaded Maria Anna to step down in 1654. Ferdinand Maria's majority marks another subtle, yet fundamental shift in court policy, away from religious radicalism toward secular reason of state. The shift is largely attributable to his wife. Henriette Adelaide promoted the arts and raised the level of court culture by ordering a variety of ambitious secular construction projects.[148] She replaced the austere Spanish ceremonial of Maximilian's court with Italian manners, importing French absolutist iconology with its pseudo-religious mystification of the prince and an arsenal of symbols, emblems and literary motifs, intended to promote reason of state over religious dogmatism, all indications of significant changes in political and intellectual culture immediately after the Thirty Years War.[149]

Vervaux stayed on as Ferdinand Maria's father confessor until his death in 1661. He was briefly replaced by Leopold Mancini and, subsequently, in 1673, by Pater Bernhard Frey. Frey represented the last of the continuous line of Jesuit father confessors to the rulers of Bavaria. He proved a skeptical judge in cases of witchcraft and demonic possession. Again, it was the ambitious Henriette Adelaide who ended Jesuit primacy in elite circles. From the very first, she incited a political campaign to have Cajetan of Thiene and Francis of Sales canonized.[150] After her husband gained his

---

[147] Ludwig Hüttl, *Max Emanuel. Der Blaue Kurfürst 1679–1726* (Munich, 1976), 13. Roswitha von Bary cites the allegorical depiction of Ferdinand Maria as a lonely Greek deity: *Henriette Adelaide von Savoyen. Kurfürsten von Bayern* (Munich, 1980), plate 21, with a description on 248. Perhaps the deity is Saturn, the personification of melancholy. Surely the moon in the background, another symbol of melancholy, supports her interpretation, though the official guide to the Munich residence identifies the representation in the painting as Jupiter, patron of the arts and sciences, and as such would indicate a jovial = sanguine humoral complexion: Gerhard Hojer and Elmar Schmid, *Nymphenburg* (Munich, 1991), 24, 68, plate 5. For a related analysis of the melancholy discourse in the early modern period, see Wolfgang Weber, "Im Kampf mit Saturn. Zur Bedeutung der Melancholie im anthropologischen Modernisierungsprozeß des 16. und 17. Jahrhunderts," *Zeitschrift für Historische Forschungen* 19 (1992), 154–192.

[148] Spindler, *Handbuch*, 641, 1074–1077. Most of the cultural projects were commissioned at the insistence of Henriette Adelaide and reflect an intimate understanding of coterminous developments at the French court. She hired the Italian architects Barelli and Zucalli to oversee construction of the summer palace at Nymphenburg, the Theatine church, and the expansion of the hermitage at Schleißheim, a perfect example of mirrored husband/wife courts described by Norbert Elias in his *Court Society* (New York, 1983), 41–65.

[149] Bosl, *Bayerische Geschichte*, 130. On state building in France, see James B. Collins, *The State in Early Modern France* (Cambridge, 1995).

[150] Bary, *Henriette Adelaide*, 139–142.

Table 2.1 *A century of Jesuit father confessors to the rulers of Bavaria.*

Wittelsbach ruler (reign)	Father confessor	Tenure
William V	Dominic Mengin, SJ	(1564–1594)
(1579–1597)	Casper Torrentius, SJ	(1594–1624)
Maximilian I,	Johannes Buslidius, SJ	(1595–1623)
Duke (1597–1621)	Adam Contzen, SJ	(1624–1635)
Elector (1621–1651)	Johannes Vervaux, SJ	(1635–1651)
Ferdinand Maria	Johannes Vervaux, SJ	(1651–1661)
Elector (1651–1679)	Bernhard Frey, SJ	(1661–1679)
Maximilian Emmanuel	Don Antonio Spinelli, OTheat	(from 1673)
Elector (1679–1726)		

majority, she convinced him to support the campaign for canonization and, after 1655, both dispatched numerous entreaties to Rome to that end. Through her close association with the Theatine and Salesian orders in Savoy, both were invited to Munich.[151] Her personal struggle with her subsequent Jesuit confessor, Pater Montonaro, intensified when she flatly refused to obey his demands to stop gambling and dancing ballet.[152] In 1659, he relinquished his post in frustration, opening the way for the Italian Theatines at court.

That same year, the childless electoral couple took a vow to Cajetan, promising to erect an imposing edifice to his memory in return for an heir. In 1660, Henriette Adelaide gave birth to the first of her four children, Maria Anna, named after her mother-in-law. In 1661, the couple negotiated with Pope Alexander VII to transfer the postulator and biographer of Cajetan (incidentally Henriette's former father confessor in Savoy), Don Stefano Pepe of the Theatines, to Munich to establish a house for the order there. He arrived in 1662 and reassumed his duties as her confessor until his death in 1665, when she replaced him with Don Antonio Spinelli, also a Theatine.[153] The couple had already ordered the construction of the monumental Theatine church and monastery dedicated to Cajetan directly across from their Munich residence, laying the cornerstone together in 1663; a group of noblewomen founded the Congregation of the Servants of Maria at St. Cajetan in that same year.[154] In its size, elegance and physical proximity to political power, St. Cajetan's easily eclipsed St. Michael's. During an

[151] Spindler, *Handbuch*, 1074.
[152] Bary, *Henriette Adelaide*, 143; Duhr, *Geschichte der Jesuiten*, vol. II, pt. 2, 846–849.
[153] Bary, *Henriette Adelaide*, 192–198.
[154] Hugo Schnell, *Der baierische Barock. Die volklichen, die geschichtlichen und die religiösen Grundlagen sein Siegeszug durch das Reich* (Munich, 1936) 58.

audience with the architect Barelli on October 7, 1662, Henriette Adelaide
was rumored to have remarked:

Pay special attention that it will be a most beautiful and valuable Church, like no
other in the city. The church must be worthy of the [Theatine] order, which is the
foremost in the world. One must also consider who is building it and for what
reasons.[155]

The rumor touched off a testy pamphlet war between the Jesuits and the
Theatines.[156] Ferdinand Maria displayed open mistrust toward the Jesuits,
accusing them of brokering too much power and of abusing his confidentiality.[157] After 1666, Henriette persuaded him to assign Don Spinelli as their
children's catechizer, much to the ire of the Jesuits. The Jesuit monopoly
on access to power had been symbolically broken by the transfer of the
office of father confessor to the heir-apparent to the Theatines. Maximilian Emanuel, nicknamed the Blue Elector, took control of Bavaria after his
father's death in 1679 and retained his Theatine father confessor. After that,
the office of father confessor remained an object of competition between
religious orders, but lost much of its former significance, as Maximilian
Emanuel vacillated between pro-Habsburg and pro-French appointments
to suit his mood and political exigencies.[158] The Jesuits managed to regain
the office again in the eighteenth century, but the position of father confessor had suffered a considerable loss of political influence and was, by that
time, largely ceremonial.

DISCIPLINING THE PEOPLE: A PENITENTIAL REGIME?

Sacramental penance and confession also functioned as methods of social
control.[159] The initial wave of confessional discipline under Albrecht V
and Wilhelm V targeted the educational and behavioral standards among
the elite and the elimination of heterodoxy. Maximilian I effectively established a number of efficient bureaucratic mechanisms to police religious
orthodoxy among the populace. During his reign, strategic policies of social

---

[155] Bary, *Henriette Adelaide*, 119.
[156] Romuald Bauerreiss, OSB, *Kirchengeschichte Bayerns*, vol. VII (St. Ottilien, 1977), 24–25.
[157] Bary, *Henriette Adelaide*, 198.   [158] Hüttl, *Max Emanuel*, 315.
[159] Tentler, *Sin and Confession*, xvi. For an analysis of the disciplining aspects of auricular confession in
Milan, hometown of Borromeo, see Wietse de Boer, *The Conquest of the Soul. Confession, Discipline,
and Public Order in Counter-Reformation Milan* (Leiden, 2001); summarized in de Boer, "The Politics
of the Soul: Confession in Counter-Reformation Milan," in: Katherine Jackson Lualdi and Anne
T. Thayer (eds.), *Penitence in the Age of Reformations* (Aldershot, 2000), 116–133.

disciplining achieved new heights. In this regard, the enforcement of ritual confession set out in the Inaugural General Mandate of 1598 served several purposes. It equipped the authorities with a tool to rigorously monitor compliance with the yearly requirement for the first time since its enactment in 1215. It also provided parish priests with a regular source of income, the confessional penny, as well as an annual opportunity to settle other financial accounts, since the clergy were in the habit of lending money to parishioners for interest. Finally, and most importantly for the central authorities in Munich, auricular confession was instrumentalized to identify religious dissidents and potential heretics. The new policy vectored subjects within multiple networks of social control – those of the local judges, the parish priests and territorial officials.

According to the stipulations of the Inaugural General Mandate of 1598, parishioners were required to purge themselves of sin in confession at least once a year prior to the reception of communion on Easter Sunday.[160] Pastors kept track of attendance at the confession, distributing certificates of compliance (*Beichtzettel*: see Plates 7a and b) during Lent in return for a penny or, quite literally, an Easter egg, a regular portion of the parish priest's yearly income.[161] Penitents retained their certificates both as evidence of confession and as payment receipts, returning them prior to the reception of the Eucharist on Easter Sunday. Communally, confession was a pacifying ritual not unlike the yearly custom of scapegoating among the ancient Hebrews, designed to purge discord, reunite the community during the subsequent ritual feast and console troubled souls.[162] Participation symbolized spiritual harmony in the parish and averted communal discord or the dangers of celestial displeasure, manifest in natural or man-made disasters, individual spiritual afflictions and demonic assaults.

The ecclesiastical hierarchy had long targeted those not fulfilling their duty of "Christian obedience" for sanctions, prohibiting them from legitimate marriage, burial in hallowed ground and admittance to hospices.[163] Pope Pius V elevated the identification of heretics for prosecution by the

---

[160] Myers, *"Poor Sinning Folk,"* 101–102, 145–158, demonstrates that more frequent confession was desirable and probably practiced, but apart from travel abroad and marriage, the *confessio bina* does not appear to have been enforced by the state.

[161] The custom of the confessional penny was common in Lutheran areas of Franconia and Saxony as well: see Rublack, "Lutherische Beichte," 141–142, 151–153; or Karant-Nunn, *The Reformation of Ritual*, 106. Karant-Nunn assumes that, in places where the practice lapsed, other forms of monetary substitution made up for the lost income. The custom persisted in Bavaria well into the twentieth century; LThK, vol. II, 131.

[162] The refusal to participate in Sunday communion was indicative of local conflict: Sabean, *Power in the Blood*, 37–60; also Karant-Nunn, *The Reformation of Ritual*, 106–107.

[163] As did some Evangelicals; see Rublack, "Lutherische Beichte," 135–136.

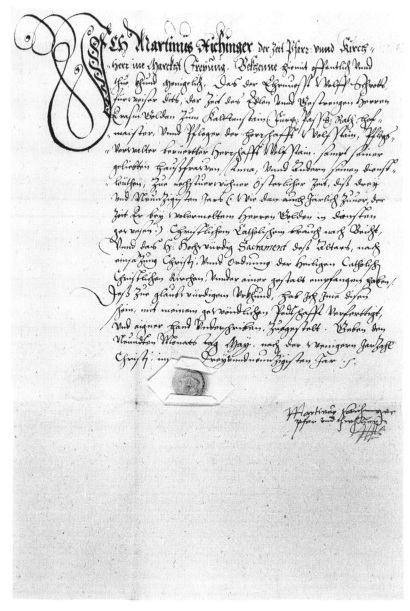

Plate 7a.   Confessional certificate for citizenship, Passau. (HStAM, BlK 34; permission of Bavarian Central State Archives, Munich.)

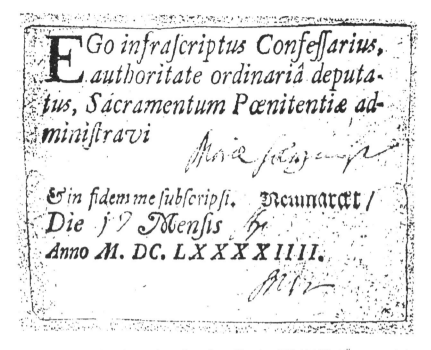

Plate 7b. Nuptial confessional certificate from Altötting (HStAM KL AÖ 52; permission of Bavarian Central State Archieves, Munich.)

Holy Inquisition to a main priority of auricular confession in the mid-sixteenth century.[164] In the Empire after the Peace of Augsburg, participation in yearly confession quickly came to symbolize politico-religious reliability in a Catholic principality.[165] In Bavaria, Maximilian I gave his penitential admonition disciplinary teeth in secular law. Whether or not all sins were a crime (as many sins surely were[166]), not to confess one's sins at Easter was a serious offense punishable by the intermediary administrators, the *Rentmeisters*. It also had to be brought to the attention of the Aulic Council in Munich. The Inaugural Mandate of 1598 ordered parish priests to compile lists of the disobedient (i.e. those who failed to confess) and

[164] Prosperi, "Beichtväter," 126–128.   [165] Pallaver, *Das Ende*, 70–72.

[166] An interesting aspect of criminal history initially taken up by Geoffrey R. Elton, "Crime and the Historian" in: J. S. Cockburn (ed.), *Crime in England, 1550–1800* (Princeton, 1977), 1–14, and subsequently revisited in an article on early modern Germany by Heinz Schilling, "'History of Crime' or 'History of Sin?' – Some Reflections on the Social History of Early Modern Church Discipline," in: E. J. Kouri and T. Scott (eds.), *Politics and Society in Reformation Europe. Essays for Sir Geoffrey Elton on his 65th Birthday* (London 1987), 289–310.

hand them over to the local district judges, who, in turn, sent them up to their respective *Rentmeister*. In practice, as a method of surveillance, the yearly requirement engaged both the secular and ecclesiastical authorities in a mutually hierarchical relationship that favored the former. Prosecutions by the church authorities were rare, usually occurring at the impulse of the state. Theoretically, penitential discipline touched every man and woman in Bavaria, as well as children from the age of their first communion, anywhere from seven to twelve years.

Certificates of confession (or confessional receipts) fulfilled several purposes. For the ruling elite in Bavaria, they established eligibility for seats on civic councils and in the ducal government.[167] Analogous procedures in neighboring Catholic territories are well documented, as in the Tyrolean diocese of Brixen.[168] Some 1,100 certificates of confession survive from the Prince-Bishopric of Passau alone,[169] largely from persons applying for citizenship between 1570 and 1630.[170] The authorities sought to identify potential heretics; secondarily, the certificates of confession served to insure the payment of civic entry-fees.[171] In Passau, parish clergy also returned certificates to the secular arm of the prince-bishop responsible for meting out judicial punishment in matters of religious discipline. Fiscal records from 1649 to 1655 confirm that the survivors of persons in abeyance of fines for non-conformity had to pay for their deceased kin. The certificates and subsequent lists composed by parish priests in rural areas around Passau indicate further that father confessors noted whether penitents were utraquists, i.e. if they had requested communion *sub una* (*sic*) or *unius speciei* (*sic*), confirming lingering fears of the chalice movement and Anabaptism.[172]

An examination of the Munich Aulic Council protocols regarding certificates of confession reveals the extent of surveillance in Bavaria and the rigorous treatment of moral delinquents during Maximilian's reign. In 1616, for example, four residents in the local judicial district of Kösching were reported for dereliction of their duty of obedience to the Christian Catholic Church, i.e. for not confessing at Easter time.[173] The Council ordered two of them to appear at the next session of the *Rentmeister*'s itinerate court, to

---

[167] Hsia, *Catholic Renewal*, 76.   [168] Pallaver, *Das Ende*, 72–74.   [169] HStAM BlK 35.
[170] Gertraud K. Eichhorn, *Beichtzettel und Bürgerrecht in Passau 1570–1630. Die administrativen Praktiken der Passauer Gegenreformation und den Fürstbischöfen Urban von Trenbach und Leopold I., Erzherzog von Österreich* (Passau, 1997).
[171] Ibid., 16–17.
[172] Ibid., 19. Lists from the surrounding countryside are found in HStAM BlK 34. NB, these lists are from the Prince-Bishopric of Passau and not from Bavaria, as Myers, *"Poor Sinning Folk,"* 120, seems to indicate.
[173] HStAM HR 131, 170r–171r.

pay a fine and to confess to their parish priest within the next three days without hesitation or face expulsion from the Duchy. The Aulic Council remanded the other two to custody for five days on bread and water, ordering them to confess to a priest immediately under analogous threats of exile. The council also instructed the district judge of Kösching to keep an eye out for any subjects attending mass in nearby Lutheran areas or individuals possessing or reading heretical books. In 1618, Bartholomew Dollinger took Easter communion without prior confession.[174] He was arrested, but later released on condition that he follow proper procedure in the future and present a certificate of confession to the authorities upon request or face banishment. When Martin Rieger's dead body was discovered in the district of Schongau in 1621, the authorities ordered an investigation into the apparent murder and made conditional provisions for his burial in the parish cemetery, if it could be proved that he had complied with the Easter requirements of confession and communion.[175] In 1624, the Aulic Council received a report from the district judge of Schwaben concerning Christina Kharzmayer's excuse for not confessing at Eastertime.[176] They dropped the case, since she subsequently resolved the matter with her parish priest and procured a certificate of confession, but reminded her that those who failed to confess because of illness were still required to make up the yearly sacrament after regaining their health.

Other delinquents were remanded to the custody of the Society of Jesus, sent on pilgrimages, fined, put on public display or shamed in the pillory before the parish church on Sunday, exiled, or threatened with public flogging and torture, depending on their reasons for non-compliance.[177] Fines and honorific punishments were usually reserved for those guilty of simple negligence. If a person was suspected of heterodoxy or heresy, the authorities initially sought their rehabilitation. A Protestant chronicler, Jörg Siedler of Augsburg, has left us with a graphic, if somewhat partisan account of this aspect of the penitential regime. He narrates the case of Conrad Seybold, who left his native Landsberg, Bavaria to cross the Lech River and work in nearby Augsburg as a weaver.[178] In 1615, Seybold refused to comply with the yearly requirement to confess, having since embraced evangelical Protestantism. He was reported to the authorities in Landsberg and subsequently

[174] HStAM HR 141, 72v.   [175] HStAM HR 170, 297v.   [176] HStAM HR 193, 417v.
[177] For example HStAM HR 221, 125v–126r, 154r–v; 231, 367v; 252, 151r; 254, 304r; 264, 169r; 272, 136r–v.
[178] StAA RC 20, 312r–320v, the chronicle of Jerg Siedler; many thanks to Benedikt Mauer for bringing this case to my attention. See his extensive research on Augsburg chroniclers: *"Gemain Geschrey" und, "teglich Reden." Georg Koelderer – ein Augsburger Chronist des konfessionellen Zeitalters* (Augsburg, 2001).

the Aulic Council in Munich, which requested and obtained his extradition from Augsburg. The Privy Council secretary, Dr. Christoph Gewold, questioned him for five hours, intending to release Seybold, but instead had him clapped in irons for his impertinence and sent to the city prison, the Falkenturm, for further interrogations. Gewold, a Catholic convert from Hesse, close friend of Aegidius Albertinus and an associate member of the Catholic phalanx at court, was so extreme in his views on heresy and witchcraft that the Augsburg chronicler Siedler mistakenly identified him as a Jesuit.[179] Gewold had Seybold's belt and suspenders confiscated, presumably to prevent a suicide, whereupon a smuggled translation of the New Testament and an evangelical catechism were discovered secretly sown into his garments. During his incarceration, Seybold sang Protestant songs, consoling his fellow inmates, some of whom faced execution. He was forced to dispute with a high judge and several Jesuits, who coaxed him with special concessions to persuade him to convert, offering an immediate and unconditional pardon. They discussed his attitude toward the Catholic Church, asking whether or not Lutherans considered the Pope to be an Antichrist, whereupon Seybold answered: "I let the Pope be who he is, I am now and here my own person and don't need to defend the Pope." The Lutheran weaver also demonstrated an excellent knowledge of scripture. When questioned about the doctrine of good works, he begged in the name of Jesus to be set free, because he too had once done a good deed. Seybold then capably disputed the veneration of the Virgin and the saints, suggesting a venerable tradition did not automatically put Catholics in the right, insisting that scripture alone was authoritative. The prison warden and his wife once invited Seybold to dinner. After he explained Lutheranism to them, they expressed bewilderment at how differently everything had been put to them in the past. After three weeks of incarceration, Seybold was paroled in Munich, but remained at the beck and call of Gewold and the other judges. They required him to attend a Jesuit sermon, after which he retorted, "my coat has been sprayed full of snot and drool." Shortly thereafter, the unrepentant Lutheran was transferred back to Landsberg (presumably to forfeit any claims to his inheritance, dowry or birth certificates) and sent packing out of Bavaria to his new home in Augsburg in keeping with the spirit of the Peace of 1555.

In light of this incident, it should hardly surprise us that Maximilian I was especially sensitive to the immanent dangers of heretical poison penetrating his lands from neighboring Protestant territories and infecting his subjects. Mandates and correspondence with judges in border districts harped on the need for redoubled vigilance to prevent the entry of heretical literature and restrict transit by suspected heretics, most of all the Anabaptists, whether leaving Bavaria to attend evangelical services or simply engaging in a trade.[180] However, despite decrees and repeated persecutions, it proved impossible to seal off the Duchy hermetically. It was the Wittelsbach dynasty, and not the people of Bavaria, who were primarily responsible for keeping the Duchy within the Catholic fold.[181] Bavaria's rural character – often erroneously posited as the sociological cornerstone of Catholic conservatism among the peasantry – paradoxically insured the importation of heterodox ideas along with manufactured goods from nearby free imperial cities such as Nuremberg, Augsburg and Regensburg, all officially bi-confessional, but overwhelmingly Protestant. Furthermore, apart from agricultural products, Bavaria's chief export was labor. Peasants and craftsmen flocked to border cities like Augsburg in search of training and employment. The authorities worried that poor struggling artisans might literally sell their souls in return for jobs and advantageous marriage arrangements.[182] That is another reason why nuptial certificates of confession were required from betrothed couples before they might marry. The apprehensions of the authorities were not entirely unfounded. The case of Conrad Seybold highlights the role of wandering apprentices as part of the transmission network for heterodox ideas in Bavaria.[183] Repeated embargoes could exert political pressure on neighboring cities, but the exigencies of trade always forced the borders to reopen, calling for different strategies to fight the ideological contagion of heresy.[184]

Maximilian's Inaugural Mandate of 1598 clearly recognized the need for young people to travel abroad in pursuit of a career.[185] Before doing so, however, they were to be catechized on the dangers of deviation from the

---

[180] On general work prohibitions and heresy, see Ziegler, *Dokumente*, 616–618; several specific examples are HStAM HR 131, 170r–171r; 219, 260r–v; 265, 380r–381v.
[181] Initially, Protestant ideas met with a receptive audience in Bavaria. Many members of the nobility and urban burgers supported the confessionalist movement during the reign of Albrecht V and there was wide support among the laity for the innovation of clerical marriage, especially in the countryside.
[182] Stieve, *Die kirchliche Polizeiregiment*, 22.
[183] Rößler, *Geschichte und Strukturen*; summarized in Rößler, "Kontakte und Strukturen als Voraussetzung für die evangelische Bewegung des 16. Jahrhunderts im Herzogtum Bayern," ZBLG 32 (1969), 355–366.
[184] Wolfgang Wüst, "Kurbayern und seine westlichen Nachbarn. Reichsstadt und Hochstift Augsburg im Spiegel der diplomatischen Korrespondenz," ZBLG 55 (1992), 255–278.
[185] Ziegler, *Dokumente*, 617–618.

authorized practices of the Catholic Church before obtaining the official birth certificate required from local authorities. The procedure for obtaining a birth certificate was detailed in a 1606 mandate and, if an individual's religious practices were suspect, officials had the right not only to refuse to issue one, but also to notify the *Rentmeister* at the provincial level.[186] Countless applications for birth certificates recorded in the protocols of the Aulic Council in Munich verify this procedure. After registering with district officials at home, the applicant was required to register upon arrival with one of the religious agents (*Religionsagenten*) posted since 1606 in suspect cities such as Kaufbeuren, Memmingen, Regensburg and Augsburg. In Augsburg, a bustling center of trade, for example, the agency operated out of the Piagetti house on Jesuit Allee #7–9 until the dissolution of the order in 1773. A similar agency was operated in Augsburg by the Habsburg authorities between 1607 and 1665.[187] Most Bavarian "children abroad" (*Kinder ausser Lands*, expatriates without regard to age) in Augsburg engaged in crafts, especially the lucrative silversmith, goldsmith and printing trades as skilled apprentices.[188]

The religious agents, Jesuits more often than not, had several duties. They insured that the religious freedom of Catholics was respected and attempted to set laborers up with jobs in reliable Catholic workshops. Failing in that, they investigated the moral integrity or proselytizing intent of Protestant employers.[189] Should a compromising situation arise, the agent had official authorization to intervene with the respective town council or the local bishop. In case of complications, district judges from border towns might be called upon to intervene, as occurred in Memmingen in 1638 and Augsburg in 1639, when it emerged that Protestant masters were encouraging their apprentices to attend evangelical services.[190] The agents collected certificates of confession from the children abroad, reported to Munich once a year on Whitsuntide regarding their religious reliability and pursued the extradition of delinquents for punishment. Surveillance operated within a triple security system. The agents reported religious deviance directly to the Aulic Council in Munich, while sending the certificates of

---

[186] In general, see Stieve, *Die kirchliche Polizeiregiment*, 26; Ziegler, *Dokumente*, 617. In practice, see HStAM HR 121, 327r–v; 260, 295v–297r.

[187] Riezler, *Geschichte Bayerns*, 23; Wüst, "Kurbayern," 262; Pallaver, *Das Ende*, 75–76. The agents in Kaufbeuren, Regensburg and Augsburg are mentioned, for example, in HStAM HR 262, 162v–164v, and 459r–v. Stieve, *Die kirchliche Polizeiregiment*, 25, also cites an agent in Memmingen from a ducal mandate dated September 1606 calling for the hiring of Jesuit religious agents in the free imperial cities of Augsburg and Regensburg.

[188] Wüst, "Kurbayern," 259–260.

[189] Stieve, *Die kirchliche Polizeiregiment*, 27; Pallaver, *Das Ende*, 77–78.

[190] HStAM HR 259, 32r–v; 264, 467r–468r, 510r–v.

confession on to local district judges. The judges, in turn, compiled their own lists of offenders and also sent the names on to the Aulic Council. The Ecclesiastical Council in Munich too appears to have composed an index of its own. Unfortunate delinquents fell under the direct scrutiny of Maximilian's father confessor and were subsequently reported to the *Rentmeister* or the Aulic Council for direct disciplinary action.[191] The Habsburg religious agent in Augsburg required his "children" to report to him twice a year, at Easter and Michaelmas (September 29).[192] Back at home, local officials employed religious spies; they too sent their quarterly reports on conformity directly to the *Rentmeister*.[193]

As with all aspects of the penitential regime, the surveillance system of religious agents suffered from frequent deficiencies. However, the central authorities kept close tabs on the system and made concerted efforts to redress its shortcomings. In 1624, the parish priest of Haidhausen, a suburb of Munich, was earnestly reprimanded and ordered to issue proper certificates of confession, contacting the secular authorities to assist in the proper identification of delinquents.[194] The Aulic Council constantly reiterated to district judges their responsibility to obtain the certificates of confession of children abroad directly, either from a religious agent or the penitents themselves. The Council intervened when the district judge of Starnberg failed to request certificates from his subjects living abroad in religiously suspect parts of Austria in 1612.[195] Even the relatively autonomous town council of Munich was severely taken to task when it failed to register applicants' certificates before the distribution of birth certificates and travel papers. The Aulic Council deemed their reports of four, five, or a maximum of eleven children abroad (for the years in which they bothered to report at all) grossly underestimated.[196] The district judge of Aibling found himself in an embarrassing situation when he neglected to report on the obedience of an individual who had subsequently taken leave of his senses in 1636, since a father confessor might have been able to shed light on the nature of the affliction.[197] The district judge of Friedberg, a border town narrowly separated from the contado of Augsburg by the Lech River, seems to have had an insurmountable task and ran afoul of the central authorities

---

[191] Stieve, *Die kirchliche Polizeiregiment*, 54–56; Wüst, "Kurbayern," 260. The institutional practice can be gleaned from entries in the Aulic Council protocols, e.g. HStAM HR 103, 104r–v; 253, 113r; 258, 52v–53v; 259, 35v; 262, 162v–164v. See also the instruction for the Ecclesiastical Council of 1629 in Ziegler, *Dokumente*, 397–400.
[192] Pallaver, *Das Ende*, 75.   [193] Stieve, *Die kirchliche Polizeiregiment*, 58–61.
[194] HStAM HR 191, 110v.   [195] HStAM HR 103, 104r–v.   [196] HStAM HR 212, 327r–v.
[197] HStAM HR 253, 113r.

on all-too-numerous occasions.[198] The system was maintained through episcopal assistance, the zealousness of the Jesuits and the casual diligence of district judges, supposedly acting in concert. The parish clergy were incessantly reminded to sermonize to their obstinate charges using Eck's standard sermons.[199] In the end, the massive level of bureaucratic coordination necessary to manage the penitential regime established by Maximilian I proved unsustainable. By the mid-seventeenth century, receipts from confession were only required on special occasions, e.g. marriage. Nevertheless, despite its bureaucratic deficiencies, the penitential regime functioned on a perfunctory bureaucratic level for a time and after a fashion. Nearly every Bavarian was exposed to the penitential regime during the reign of Maximilian I. Whether they slept through catechism classes, attended to the Easter requirement in an inebriated state, or obtained a confessional certificate simply to comply with nuptial requirements and legitimize their sexuality cannot be sufficiently answered here.[200]

How sincerely did Bavarians accept the exomologetic message of penance in the face of impending crisis and under the pressure of systematic coercion? Might excessive probing into the catalogue of sins by father confessors actually teach lascivious behavior, as some feared, or were gregarious penitents liable to dwell in the confessional on the sins of their neighbors rather than their own?[201] In his annual visitation reports on the state of religious practices in individual parishes, the *Rentmeister* of Burghausen certainly noted frequent deviations from official policies on sacramental discipline. These included low attendance at catechisms and mass, consumption of brandy during the mass, excessive wedding celebrations and the keeping of concubines by parish priests, all blatant violations of repeated ducal decrees. Where he discovered deviance, strong action was taken to restore church discipline.[202] However, negative inducements could hardly be expected to win more than mechanical and formal compliance. Certainly, the constant repetition of religious mandates after 1598 implies both

[198] HStAM HR 258, 52v–53v; 259, 35v; 262, 459v; 264, 467r–468r, 510r–v; 265, 380r–381v; 272, 136r–v, 453v.
[199] Elfriede Moser-Rath, *Dem Kirchenvolk die Leviten Gelesen. Alltag im Spiegel süddeutscher Barockpredigten* (Stuttgart, 1991), 177–179.
[200] The *Rentmeister* of Burghausen complained repeatedly about the consumption of brandy during mass in his annual itinerate reports (*Umritte*) of 1600 and 1601; HStAM RL 80, 359, 361. Although the number of complaints declined by the time of his annual rounds in 1631, the *Rentmeister* still fined a pregnant woman 2 lb. of pennies for drinking brandy before a wedding and vomiting during the mass; HStAM RL 80, 363, 63r–v.
[201] Bossy, "Social History of Confession," 24.
[202] *Relationen der Rentmaister Umbreitens Rentamt Burghausen in Geistlichen Sachen* 1600, 1601, 1631 (HStAM RL 80, 359, 361, 363).

the tenacity of the authorities and complacency of the population at large.[203] As outsiders in the community, parish priests had a tentative hold over their flock and often remained dependent upon communal good will for some portion of their livelihood.[204] For that very reason, priests and communities often presented a unified front, resisting inquisitive intrusions by the central authorities into local affairs. At other times, individuals and whole communities did not get along with their parish priests at all. Visitations noted how some individuals feared to confess in their own parish, presumably because of the priest's pivotal role in factional intrigues.[205] Some communities openly mistrusted their parish priest, as did the congregation of Altenhohenau in 1631, which registered with the visitor a formal complaint against him for his overt worldliness.[206] The office of father confessor, with its aura of secrecy and intimacy, also had the potential for abuses of power, damaging to the reputation of sacramental penance. As in Spain, solicitation and sexual abuse occurred in Bavarian confessionals.[207] Even the vaunted confidentiality of the confessional had its limits: the Aulic Council in Munich found occasion to request written testimony from confessors as professional witnesses to a parishioner's state of mind prior to committing the crime of self-murder.[208] Given the chiliastic mood of the times and the novel rigor of the authorities, the post-Tridentine penitential regime ought to have been a much greater source of spiritual anxiety than its late medieval ancestor.

This makes the immense popularity of auricular confession and penance all the more baffling.[209] If Jesuit statistics on the distribution of the Eucharist in Munich during the seventeenth and eighteenth centuries are any measure of prior confession, then many people confessed more than once annually.[210] In 1615, five hosts were distributed for every inhabitant of the city. By 1690, the figure reached a ratio of seven to one. A similar rise in the reception of the Eucharist was recorded for Ingolstadt, where, in a city of

---

[203] Myers, *"Poor Sinning Folk,"* 197–198; Stieve, *Die kirchliche Polizeiregiment*, 63–64.
[204] Beck, "Der Pfarrer," *passim.*   [205] Bossy, "Social History of Confession," 24.
[206] HStAM RL 80, 363, 41v.
[207] In 1610 the Ecclesiastical Council of Freising charged a father confessor with fornication and impregnation: AEM GR 31, 156, 179. On solicitation in Spain, see Haliczer, *Sexuality in the Confessional.*
[208] HStAM HR 221, 251r–v; 261, 109v–110v; 339, 137v, 351v–352r; 373, 69r. Lutheran pastors may have abused confidentiality in the confessional as well; see Karant-Nunn, *The Reformation of Ritual*, 102. Many thanks to Tom Tentler for sharing his as yet unpublished paper, "Sacramental Privacy: The Myth, Law, and History of the Seal of Confession, 1215 to 1965." On the seal in Lutheranism, see Ronald K. Rittgers, "Private Confession and Religious Authority in Reformation Nürnberg," in: Katherine Jackson Lualdi and Anne T. Thayer (eds.), *Penitence in the Age of Reformations* (Aldershot, 2000), 49–70.
[209] Myers, *"Poor Sinning Folk,"* 189.   [210] Ibid.

some 7,000 inhabitants, 15,000 hosts were distributed in 1615, 59,000 in 1673, 35,500 in 1700 and 72,900 in 1715.[211] Obviously, one must exercise caution when extrapolating numbers of confessions from the distribution of hosts: however, the general implication of the Jesuit statistics is clear – participation, voluntary or otherwise, was on the rise. Given the coercive measures laid out in the Inaugural General Mandate of 1598 and countless other grounds for misapprehensions on the part of penitents, how can we explain the rising popularity of auricular confession and penance?

The Tridentine reform of the parish clergy and the improved reputation of the sacrament partially explain the increased popularity of confession. The introduction of a novel penitential technology, the confessional, also effectively privatized the ritual.[212] A Tridentine invention of Cardinal Charles Borromeo of Milan,[213] the confessional booth was introduced gradually by the Jeusits, but only became widespread in Bavaria during the eighteenth century. Borromeo recommended placing a meshed screen in the booth with holes no larger than a pea to prevent physical (and sexual) contact between priest and penitent, as well as hanging graphic depictions of the crucifixion above the screen facing the penitent to heighten feelings of contrition and guilt. Stained glass portraits and copper etchings hung up in Bavarian churches brought home the problems of conscience; one portrayed a penitent in a confessional flanked by an angel on one side, imploring a pious confession, and the devil on the other, trying to hinder it.[214] The legend of Johannes Nepomuk of Prague (thrown off the Charles Bridge for refusing to reveal the secrets of his confidants and later canonized as the patron of auricular confession) became a popular theme of confessional devotion in the late seventeenth and early eighteenth centuries, embodied in a gruesome church dedicated to the saint in Munich. Hideously bejeweled with skulls, skeletons, instruments of death and putti, it was designed by the famous rococo architects Egid and Quirin Asam, who chose to erect the monument to Nepomuk between their own private dwellings in the city center.[215] Confidentiality and privacy: these were two novel hallmarks of post-Tridentine penitential practice.

We have seen how, supported by the Wittelsbach dynasty and theological moralists, the post-Tridentine Catholic renewal reached the common

[211] Ibid., 190.   [212] Ibid., 133–143.
[213] See Wilhelm Schlombs, *Die Entwicklung des Beichtstuhls in der katholischen Kirche: Grundlagen und Besonderheiten im alten Bistum Köln* (Düsseldorf, 1965), 134–138, for a synopsis of the provisions.
[214] Ibid., 79.
[215] Now simply referred to as the Asamkirche. On the veneration of St. Nepomuk in Bavaria, see Schnell, *Der baierische Barock*, 61, 160.

people through preaching, catechism and the printed word. The echoes of the doctrinal message continued to reverberate in the population long after the complex system of surveillance and enforcement established by Maximilian I had been abandoned. The traditional message was also one of personal consolation and internalized discipline, or at the very least external compliance with the ideal. As Steven Ozment suggests in reference to the psychological aspects of Jesuit theology, it "prepared individuals for new states of mind and morality by playing directly on their basic emotions of fear and love."[216] The psychological pangs of guilt and the need for consolation were mutually reinforcing emotional aspects of the penitential regime. However, the appeal to internalized emotional control proved too onerous or repressive for some and helps to explain rising reports of spiritual afflictions and demonic possessions since the late sixteenth century. In extreme cases, instead of providing consolation, the call to penance gnawed at the conscience of the sufferers, spiraling into a vicious devil's circle of mental anguish and requiring more powerful spiritual physic than auricular confession.

Such is the case with Katharina Rieder, a demoniac treated at St. Joseph's Hospice in Munich from 1667 to 1669. The intimate details of her story will interest us below, but one point is worth mentioning here. Initially complaining of tribulations and pusillanimity, she was committed to the care of a Jesuit confessor for observation. In her own autobiographical letters, she insisted that his shriving failed to alleviate her symptoms, instead complicating them because he failed to believe her. On the brink of despair, convinced she had been baptized improperly, Katharina recalled how the devil entered her body one night when, at age nine, she awoke screaming to find a man in black standing by her bed.[217] She prayed constantly to the Virgin, the blood of Jesus Christ, St. Francis Xavier and Simon of Trent (a purported child-victim of Jewish ritual murder) for relief. She penned a vow to conduct a pilgrimage. When her father confessor expressed reservations, Katharina confessed demonic copulations to him and left two copies of a pact with the devil – barely visible on slips of paper – in the confessional for him to find. The first read, "Because of my false confession, I now surrender myself to the devil totally and completely with body and soul, with possessions and blood, irretrievably" (Plate 8a) On the second, she penned, "I surrender myself wholly and completely to the devil, with body and soul, with possessions and blood, irreversibly" (Plate 8b)

---

[216] Steven Ozment, *The Age of the Reformation, 1250–1550* (New Haven, 1980), 412; here, Ozment is referring specifically to the message of Loyola's *Spiritual Exercises*.

[217] I decline to entertain the possibility of incest without further evidence.

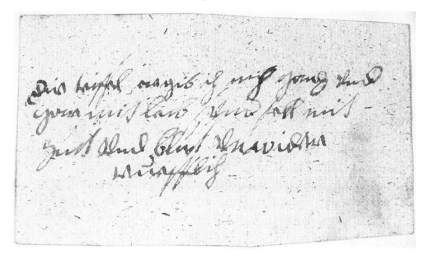

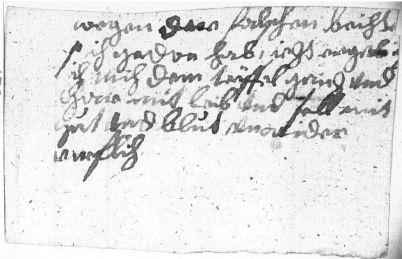

Plate 8.   Katharina Rieder's pacts with the devil (HStAM *Jesuitica* 527; permission of the
Bavarian Central State Archives).

Katharina was certain of two things. First, Satan, sacrilege, her own
sinful behavior and a false confession were causing her terrible emotional
sufferings. Second, only the spiritual physic of a sympathetic confessor, an
exorcist, or the intercession of the Virgin Mary and the saints at a cult shrine
could relieve her from her tribulations, faintheartedness, terror and suicidal

despair. In the face of her desperation and her father confessor's skepticism, how could she possibly trust in his ability as a spiritual physician?

CONCLUSIONS

The sixteenth century systematized the etiology of sin and guilt, disseminating knowledge through sermons, catechism and penitentials. According to the casuists of moral theology, immoral behavior unbalanced the humors thereby affecting the intellective faculty and leading to spiritual afflictions. Auricular confession offered the suffering a means of self-help, albeit with the assistance of a properly designated spiritual physician. In their role as father confessors, they offered a consoling purge for a bad conscience through shriving, forgiveness through absolution and healing through penance. Father confessors both defined and treated psychic abnormality. Of course, the individual had to want to change, to turn from the path of immoral behavior. The onus of responsibility lay with the sufferer, turning the inability to achieve positive results through confession and penance into evidence of insincerity, closet moral turpitude or irrepressibly dark and deeply rooted passions.

Katharina Rieder's case is emblematic of both the successes and failures of the penitential regime to inculcate a self-disciplined perception of normal behavior. Auricular confession simultaneously performed a number of apparently contradictory functions in early modern Bavaria. Intended by theologians as a ritual of consolation, confession provided an acceptable outlet for psychological sufferings. However, the examination of conscience promulgated in sermons, catechism and lay penitentials also encouraged a level of self-awareness and self-criticism that evoked deep pangs of guilt, based as it was upon a strict moral code. Further, the state employed surveillance of attendance at auricular confession to track down non-conformists and backsliders as potential heretics.

Still, despite the disciplinary components of the penitential regime, its rising popularity indicates that consumers bought into the message of auricular confession as spiritual physic. Whether this talking cure delivered on its promises overall, successfully consoling some or offering a moral cathartic for others, must remain a matter of conjecture. We can, at best, review the results of individual case histories. As the message of consolation reached people at an early age through catechism, the elements of sin, guilt and absolution mutually reinforced one another. The psychological circle of angst and an attendant need for its relief was inherent in the ritual. Nevertheless, the logic of the system appears to have been acceptable to many.

At first, sacramental penance appealed to the ruling classes. Many realized the advantages of an internalized rationale of self-discipline to facilitate social and political advancement, either by the mechanical performance of formalized ritual or through the actual inculcation of a critical self-awareness dictated by religious conventions. In any event, the penitential regime contributed to a legalistic culture on a mass basis, a truly modern collective consciousness. And, as David Myers has pointed out, similar attitudes spread gradually among Bavarian burgers during the seventeenth and eighteenth centuries. The extent of its penetration at the popular level is open to debate.

Consolation remained the defining popular justification of auricular confession as a method of spiritual physic. Simultaneously, confession worked in tandem with another form of spiritual physic, ritual pilgrimage and devotion to the cult of the saints. Interest in spiritual physic at cult shrines, also pronounced from the end of the sixteenth century, reflected a marked increase in canonizations for healer-saints to meet a swell of expectations.[218] Those shrines dedicated to spiritual physic as a treatment for madness and other spiritual afflictions derived special benefit from the impetus to confess and conduct pilgrimages at the shrine. If confession to a parish priest provided basic consolation, shriving at pilgrimage shrines offered the additional benefit of access to a saint's direct intercession.

Travel to a shrine was time consuming and more expensive than confession in one's own parish. However, at shrines where certificates of confession were issued, pilgrimage also fulfilled the yearly requirement while insuring greater privacy in unfamiliar surroundings. Travel to shrines for auricular confession raises the issue of traditional competition between the regular and secular clergy, but there were also definite signs of cooperation. Faced with difficult cases, parish priests regularly encouraged sufferers to seek help from qualified practitioners at dedicated cult shrines. With the help of the saints, soul doctors tapped directly into the treasury of merit and invoked powerful spiritual physic. The healing shrines where spiritual physic was dispensed, especially Benediktbeuern and Pürten, exemplified a blossoming sacred economy and geography in the region.

---

[218] Hsia, *Catholic Renewal*, 134–137. Confession was also popular as spiritual physic in England; see Kenneth Parker, "Richard Greenham's 'Spiritual Physicke': The comfort of Afflicted Consciences in Elizabethan Pastoral Care," in: Katherine Jackson Lualdi and Anne T. Thayer (eds.), *Penitence in the Age of Reformations* (Aldershot, 2000), 71–83.

CHAPTER 3

Bavaria Sancta

If they can get but a relic of some Saint, or the Virgin Mary's picture,
or the like, that city is forever made, it needs no other maintenance.
Robert Burton, *The Anatomy of Melancholy*

PILGRIMS ON THE MOVE

Travel can be liberating, but geographic dislocation can give rise to anxieties. During the general crisis, ordinary Europeans took to the roads in record numbers. Demographic pressures fueled internal and external migration. By the sixteenth century, the European population had fully recovered from the Black Death and surpassed its pre-plague density. Demographic growth, an influx of Spanish gold from the New World and declining agrarian productivity combined to cause a price revolution.[1] Competition intensified pressures on labor markets. Skilled craftsmen worked for less as jobs became scarce, consigning journeymen to a permanent proletarian state. Runaway inflation, lower real wages and the labor surplus impacted adversely on productive and reproductive relationships. Journeymen's organizations jealously guarded the shop floor, excluding women from even the most menial tasks; guilds forced masters' widows to remarry younger men, themselves struggling for economic independence.[2] Limited employment

---

[1] Historical processes outlined by Peter Kriedte, *Peasants, Landlords, and Merchant Capitalists: Europe and the World Economy, 1500–1800* (Cambridge, 1983). The Swiss historian of climate Christian Pfister and his team of researchers have compiled impressive empirical evidence to argue for the climatic shift in late medieval and early modern Europe regularly known as the Little Ice Age. He characterizes these specific years as the second and, because of its temperature anomalies, the worst phase: "Die . . . weitaus umfangreichste [kalte Anomalie] umfasst die Jahre 1566–1635 und zeigt um 1570 einen markanten Kippeffekt: Am meisten war der Hochsommer betroffen": Christian Pfister, *Raumzeitliche Rekonstruktion von Witterungsanomalien und Naturkatastrophen, 1496–1995* (Zürich 1998), 38–43.
[2] For general overviews of worsening social conditions and their impact on the labor market during the course of the sixteenth century, see Robert Jütte, *Poverty and Deviance in Early Modern Europe*

99

prospects swelled the ranks of the itinerant poor, severing communal ties and leaving them and their families socially and geographically adrift.

Religious intolerance exacerbated an already acute situation. After 1555, the Peace of Augsburg required confessional dissenters in the Empire physically to relocate. Wars and civil unrest in France and the Low Countries added waves of refugees to the chaos. In the late sixteenth and early seventeenth centuries, Central Europe experienced a migratory torrent.[3] Moralists such as Peter Canisius, Aegidius Albertinus and Martin Eisengrein, as well a number of artists, fled to Bavaria to escape religious unrest and start a new career. During the Thirty Years War, huge armies clogged the roads of the Empire with hundreds of thousands of foreign troops. On campaign throughout the region, armies on both sides extorted supplies from local populations in systematic levies or "contributions" to support the war effort. They pillaged, looted, and left a wake of devastation in their path. They disrupted productive activities and left countless peasants and burgers homeless.

Perhaps C. V. Wedgewood exaggerated the level of suffering in her classic analysis of the Thirty Years War. Certainly, recent accounts such as those of Rudolf Schlögl and Govind Sreenivasan underscore the remarkable adaptability of peasant societies when confronted by the devastations of war, plague and famine in the sixteenth and seventeenth centuries.[4] In Malthusian or Darwinian terms, one might even view the long-term demographic consequences as a positive check. By causing the deaths of millions, war undoubtedly eased population pressures. Indeed, after 1648, real wages actually recovered, prices fell and agricultural production witnessed an "economic miracle."

However, to me at least, Malthusian rationales for human suffering ring a bit hollow.[5] Certainly, those who weathered the storm failed to derive

(Cambridge, 1994); Merry Wiesner, *Working Women in Renaissance Germany* (New Brunswick, 1986); Johannes C. Wolfart, *Religion, Government and Political Culture in Early Modern Germany: Lindau, 1520–1628* (London, 2001).

[3] Witnessed by a never-ending flood of mandates, decrees and trials against begging, gypsies, wandering Jews, disbanded mercenaries and other "riff-raff." This phenomenon was not limited to Bavaria, and Peter Blickle characterizes a situation in which hundreds of thousands of Central Europeans took to the roads during the seventeenth century; see his *Deutsche Untertanen. Ein Widerspruch?* (Munich, 1981), 109–110 (translated as Peter Blickle, *Obedient Germans? – A Rebuttal: New View of German History*, trans. Thomas A. Brady (Charlottesville, 1998)). On the impact of criminal justice on migration, see also Robert Scribner, "Mobility: Voluntary or Enforced? Vagrants in Württemberg in the Sixteenth Century," in: Gerhard Jaritz and Albert Müller (eds.), *Migration in der Feudalgesellschaft* (Frankfurt am Main, 1988), 64–88.

[4] C. V. Wedgewood, *The Thirty Years War* (London, 1938); Schlögl, *Bauern, Krieg und Staat*; Govind P. Sreenivasan, *The Peasants of Ottobeuren, 1487–1726: A Rural Society in Early Modern Europe* (Cambridge, 2004).

[5] Reminiscent of the nigological argument of Professor Pangloss to explain the catastrophic Lisbon earthquake of 1755 in Voltaire's *Candide*.

comfort from their lot and the perception of a crisis lingered long after in the collective consciousness. Complacency severely retarded structural, economic and social change in Central Europe for generations.[6] In psychological terms, the general crisis engendered an enduring climate of terror and despair, leaving society a nervous wreck. Even after death and interminable suffering on a massive scale had subsided, ordinary Bavarians continued to vote with their feet and undertook pilgrimages in unprecedented numbers. Although dynastic support in Bavaria proved crucial initially, Marc Forster notes a significant level of spontaneous popular enthusiasm for popular devotion in the German southwest as well, lasting into the eighteenth century.[7] Even after their time of need had passed, Bavarians turned to the saints in large numbers. As the early modern period drew to a close, travel to cult shrines still offered tens of thousands of Europeans hope and psychic consolation through spiritual physic.

Duke Maximilian's first legislative act – the Inaugural General Mandate of 1598 – affirmed the authorities' commitment to penitential discipline. His first ceremonial act – an arduous pilgrimage from Munich to the Chapel of Our Lady of Grace at Altötting (*c*.80 km) – sought to channel and control the outpouring of popular devotion. Imbued with an astute appreciation for sacred histrionics,[8] Maximilian orchestrated a magnificent procession to mark the event. His inaugural procession, participatory theater on a grand scale, reified social hierarchy and distanced the ruling elite from the common people. Accompanied by representatives from the territorial estates, Maximilian assumed the leading role in an awesome spectacle of the three orders for an audience of common subjects en route. When he arrived at Altötting, he placed a mysterious cylindrical vessel of silver on the altar as an offering to the Virgin Mary. Fifty years later, Maximilian's heart was also laid to rest in Altötting, in accordance with his last wishes.[9] Thereupon, in 1652, Dean Gabriel Küpfferle sealed the cardiotaph (a special tomb for the extracted heart) and opened the silver vessel at the behest of Maximilian's widow, the Electress Maria Anna. Inside, Küpfferle found a scroll declaring, "Into your servitude I dedicate and consecrate myself

[6] Ronald G. Asch, *The Thirty Years War. The Holy Roman Empire and Europe, 1618–1648* (London, 1997), 186–188.
[7] Marc R. Forster, *Catholic Revival in the Age of the Baroque: Religious Identity in Southwest Germany, 1550–1750* (Cambridge, 2001), 83–105.
[8] Theater was another specialty of the Jesuits. Maximilian's university tutor at Ingolstadt, Gregor de Valencia, SJ, was a master of devotional theater and the dramatist, Jacob Gretser, SJ, was an intimate confidant. The role of theater in Jesuit pedagogy is examined by Ronnie Po-Chia Hsia, *Society and Religion in Münster 1535–1618* (New Haven, 1982).
[9] As was the heart of Field Marshal Tilly. The chapel at Altötting is still affectionately referred to as "the heart of Bavaria."

In mancipiu tuum
me tibi dedico consacroque
Virgo MARIA
hoc teste cruore atq; chyro=
grapho ,
Maximilianus peccatorum
coryphæus

[A.o 1634.]

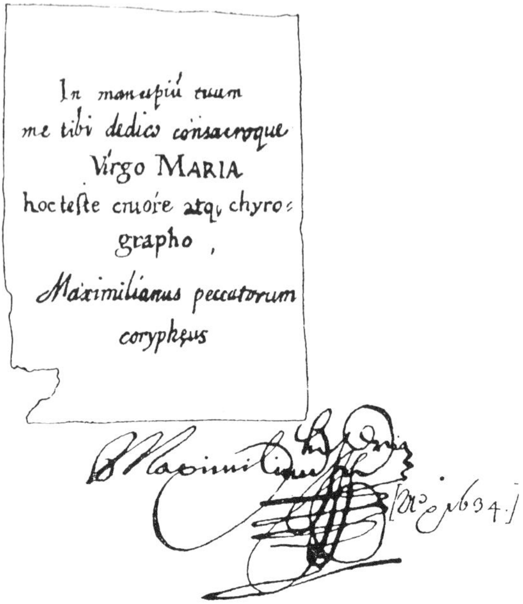

Plate 9a. Blood pact of Maximilian I with the Virgin Mary; below right, a comparative handwriting sample. (Latin, 1634; from König, *Weihegaben*, Table 32, Courtesy of Lentner'sche Bookshop, Munich.)

In Mancipium tuum me tibi
consacro Virgo Maria
hoc teste cruore atq chirographo

Ferdinandus Maria
peccatorum maximus

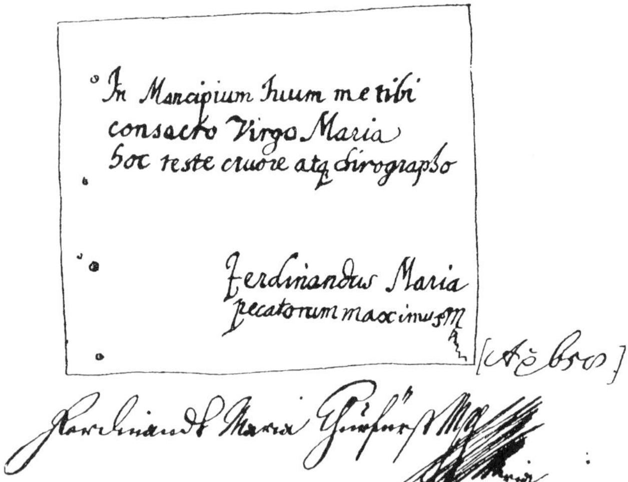

Plate 9b. Blood pact of Ferdinand Maria with the Virgin Mary; below right, a comparative handwriting sample. (Latin, 1658; from König, *Weihegaber*, Table 32, Courtesy of Lentner'sche Bookshop, Munich.)

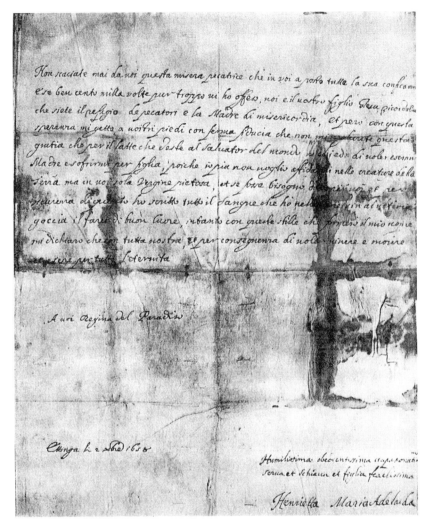

Plate 9c. Blood pact of Henriette Adelaide with the Virgin Mary. (Italian, 1658; from König, *Weihegaben*, Table 33, Courtesy of Lentner'sche Bookshop, Munich.)

to you, Virgin Mary, this testified in my own blood, [signed] Maximilian, a sinful leader" (Plate 9).[10] Küpfferle examined the covenant, authenticated it, and resealed the cylinder. In 1898, it was reopened. The intact vessel still

---

10 "In mancipium tuum me tibi dedico consacroque, Virgo Maria, hoc teste cruore meo, Maximilianus peccatorum coryphaeus": Anton Wilhelm Schreiber, *Maximilian I. der Katholische, Kurfürst von Bayern und der dreißigjährige Krieg* (Munich, 1868), 24; Otto von Schaching, *Maximilian I, der Große, Kurfürst von Bayern* (Freiburg, 1876), 23–24.

contained Maximilian's blood pact, although the second seal of 1652 had been broken to add two similar pacts from his son, Ferdinand Maria, and his son's wife, Henriette Adelaide, in 1658. Investigators prepared copies and resealed the cylinder for a third time. It is still stored at the Chapel of Our Lady in Altötting to the present day.

Were it not so, we might dismiss a ceremonial blood pact with the Virgin Mary as demented monkish fantasy, just as we might be tempted to do with Katharina Rieder's pacts with the devil. The documents do exist, even if positivist, nationalist or bourgeois decorum might prefer to relegate these grotesque curios to the ossuary of baroque history. The pacts' intrinsic cultural strangeness actually provides us with a key to a cryptic gateway into the seventeenth-century mind. As covenants, we can juxtapose the devotional pacts of Maximilian I, Ferdinand Maria and Henriette Adelaide to the Virgin with Katharina Rieder's devil's pact; symbolically antipathetic and yet similar in form.[11] Rieder's pacts manifested a desperate blasphemy, while contemporaries justified Maximilian's macabre blood pact as an extreme, but contrite act of hope, a perfectly legitimate response to extraordinary circumstances. However, both types of pacts assumed the substance of a contract. Although a physical contract was an unusual votive offering, pilgrims regularly took vows to saints. As a standard feature of religious devotion by the sixteenth century, the vow reflected the resurgence of Roman contractual law in the popular consciousness. Delivered at the end of his pilgrimage to Altötting, Maximilian's blood pact concretely reaffirmed his devotion to the moral order in a contractual vow to the Virgin to save the Duchy from impending peril.

Ascetically, physical pacts embodied a pervasive spirit of melancholy. A notorious temperament, melancholy populated the sufferer's dreams and imaginings with denizens of the subterranean order – snakes, demons in caves, ghosts and corpses in graveyards.[12] Associated with the element "earth," it preoccupied the mind of the sufferer with thoughts of the dead. In a melancholy age, the popularity of the saints is not so surprising. The cult of the special dead witnessed a long series of ups and downs since its beginnings in late antiquity, but it achieved its peak during and after the general crisis.[13] The popularity of Christian saints stagnated in the late Middle Ages, declining considerably after reformers from Erasmus to Karlstadt

[11] König, *Weihegaben*, 310–316, suggests that Maximilian's blood pact with the Virgin was intended to evoke this very imagery in the minds of his subjects.
[12] Del Rio, *Disquisitiones* (1617), 593; Kutzer, *Anatomie*, 74. Katharina Rieder's devil's pact, on the other hand, expressed moral resignation and despair.
[13] The most convincing synthesis remains Peter Brown, *The Cult of the Saints. Its Rise and Function in Latin Christianity* (Chicago, 1981).

exposed unscrupulous practices, badly tarnishing the public image of pilgrimage.[14] Aegidius Albertinus recognized the challenge to Catholic saints, reminding Bavarians that no good had come of it.[15] By his day, however, the cult of the saints had recovered and even begun to exceed its former levels of popularity.

With the revival of cultic devotion, one genre of literature witnessed a renaissance. Miracle books – ledgers kept at shrines to record wonders – had indicated collapsing numbers of miracles and a consequential decline in pilgrimages during the first half of the sixteenth century.[16] Counter Reformation miracle books sought to combat decline, combining prurient hagiography with highly successful anti-Protestant propaganda into histories of wonder and a novel code of conduct for pilgrims.[17] Propagandistic miracle books and dynastic patronage encouraged a renewal of post-Tridentine devotion, as the cult of the saints gradually regained and ultimately surpassed its medieval incarnation. The miracle book kept at St. Rasso in Wörth (later called Grafrath), for example, faithfully charts changes in patterns of devotion in late medieval and early modern Bavaria. Between 1444 and 1499, an average of ninety miracles were recorded there annually,[18] but then wonders dropped off significantly, falling to only five per year between 1500 and 1560. After 1560, however, reported miracles became progressively more frequent, on average twenty-eight per year from 1561 to 1594. Following a forty-five year lacuna in the ledger, wonders averaged thirty-nine miracles per annum from 1639 to 1691. Finally, from 1692 to 1728, miracles (on average 102 per annum) surpassed late medieval levels during the age of reason.

Dynastic patronage played a crucial role in the revitalization of cultic devotion in early modern Bavaria. The revitalization of ritual pilgrimage began under Duke Albrecht V, who linked it to the politics of confessionalization, state building and foreign policy. He invested heavily in pilgrimage during his struggle against the chalice movement and the Bavarian Fronde. Albrecht appointed the convert Martin Eisengrein as provost to the Wittelsbach Chapel at Altötting in 1567. Eisengrein worked feverishly to restore devotional activity. In 1571, just as the Duke outlawed utraquism,

[14] Eliade Mircea (ed.), *The Encyclopedia of Religion*, Vieda Skultans, "Afflictions: An Overview," vol. VIII (New York, 1987), 338–340.
[15] Albertinus, *Flagellum diaboli* (1602), 43–44.   [16] Soergel, *Wondrous in his Saints*, 44–74.
[17] Rebekka Habermas, "Wunder, Wunderliches, Wunderbares: Zur Profanisierung eines Deutungsmusters in der frühen Neuzeit," in: Richard van Dülmen (ed.), *Armut, Liebe und Ehre: Studien zur historischen Kulturgeschichte* (Frankfurt am Main, 1988), 38–66.
[18] K.-S. Kramer, "Die Mirakelbücher der Wallfahrt Grafrath," *Bayerisches Jahrbuch für Volkskunde* (1951), 80–81.

Eisengrein published his famous miracle book, *Our Lady of Altötting*, an embittered defense of spiritual physic, the Catholic sacraments, pilgrimage and exorcism against Protestant propaganda.[19] *Our Lady of Altötting* promoted a thinly veiled propagandistic message. Eisengrein praised nearby towns and villages, exaggerating their unshakeable loyalty against the confessionalist movement.[20] His miracle book combined history with a mythical ethnography of ancient Bavaria, endowing the region with an aura of pristine Catholic space associated with the saints. His historical account of the body politic located the Chapel of Our Lady of Altötting at the geographic heart of a devotional covenant, safeguarding faithful Bavarians from invading pagans and natural catastrophes for over a thousand years.[21] Maximilian's later inaugural pilgrimage, his blood pact with the Virgin and his bequest to have his heart interred at Altötting literally embodied the renewal of that contract.

While Eisengrein promoted the cult of Altötting, Albrecht V sought to further the active association of the Wittelsbach dynasty with the cult of the saints. In a controversial move, he arranged for the translation of the relics of St. Benno from Saxony in 1576. Martin Luther personally condemned Benno's canonization in 1524, but the Bishop of Meissen moved the relics to safekeeping, saving them from radical iconoclasts.[22] One half-century later, Albrecht smuggled Benno's remains to Munich and interred them next to the tomb of the medieval Emperor, Louis the Bavarian, in the civic church of Our Lady. Propagandistically, the reburial served to rehabilitate Louis, who died excommunicate. Concerned with the reputation of his lineage and the ancestral claim to the imperial title, Albrecht made the Benno

---

[19] Eisengrein, *Unser Lieben Fraw*.
[20] According to Soergel, "Spiritual Medicine," 132, this was a direct reference to urban support for Duke Albrecht during the crisis of the chalice movement. His conclusion is based on Eisengrein's (1571), *Vorrede* – last two pages (unnumbered): "wie nun mehr in die 1000 Jar/ in Bayrn/ kein anderen glaub unnd Gottß dienst/ als eben der so noch heüttigs tags/ nach ordnung der Catholischen Röm. Kirchen im gang ist/ gehalten und getriben worden . . . ," a state of affairs Eisengrein attributes generally to the inhabitants of the region. In fact, many Bavarian towns supported a more moderate version of demands for toleration based on the articles of the ducal declaration of 1556: see Ziegler, *Dokumente*, 218–219 (Declaration of 1556), 336–337 (composition of factions); Anton Landersdorfer, *Das Bistum Freising in der bayerischen Landesvisitation des Jahres 1560* (St. Ottilien, 1986), 165.
[21] Soergel, "Spiritual Medicine," 132–134 The chapel at Altötting was spared destruction from the Hungarians in 907. On the Black Madonna of Altötting, see Monique Scheer, "From Majesty to Mystery: Change in the Meanings of Black Madonnas from the Sixteenth to Nineteenth Centuries," in *American Historical Review* 107 (2002), 1412–1440.
[22] Martin Luther, *Wider den neuen Abgott und alten Teufel der zu Meisen soll erhoben werden* (Wittenberg, 1524). The iconoclasts acted on the orders of Andreas von Bodenstein, alias Karlstadt. Outbreaks of iconoclasm were a motivating factor behind Luther's return from the Wartburg and Karlstadt's expulsion from Wittenberg.

shrine a central object of dynastic devotion.[23] Eventually, during the reign of Maximilian I, the first printed St. Benno miracle book appeared in 1601, followed by annual installments until 1643; a compendium of miracles appeared in 1697.[24] Like Eisengrein's *Our Lady of Altötting*, the literary attention showered on the Benno cult evidences dynastic patronage. With Wittelsbach support, miracle books kept at dynastic shrines reported an analogous rise in popular response to the peregrinational summons. At the new shrine of the Marian Star at Taxa, for example, the number of devotees rose nearly every year from 1642 to 1659, from 2,564 to 8,610.[25] By the eighteenth century, pilgrims visiting shrines during annual processions measured in the tens of thousands, calculated according to the distribution of the Eucharist.[26]

The cult of the saints continued to reverberate the late medieval denial of worldliness (*contemptus mundi*) and, enhanced by the millenarian tone of the age, the morose fascination with baroque necrolatry grew.[27] The Wittelsbach dynasty amassed such a ghoulish array of bones and skulls for display in ornate monstrances at their Munich residence that a separate chamber had to be built to house them.[28] Wilhelm V was one of the most avid collectors of relics in the Empire. He hired agents to comb the charnel houses of Central Europe in search of trophies. Wilhelm was particularly crestfallen when his spies reported their failure to steal relics from a church in Nuremberg, because all the civic locksmiths (who were devout Evangelicals)

---

[23] Karin Berg, "Der ehemalige 'Bennobogen' der Münchner Frauenkirche," in: Glaser, *Wittelsbach und Bayern*, 312–317; Robert Böck, *Volksfrömmigkeit und Brauch. Studien zum Volksleben in Altbayern* (Munich, 1990), 19–59.

[24] Hermann Bach, "Mirakelbücher bayerischer Wallfahrtsorte (Untersuchung ihrer literarischen Form und ihrer Stellung innerhalb der Literatur der Zeit)" (unpublished Ph.D. dissertation, Munich, 1963), 210: reports covering each preceding period were published in 1602 (three), 1603, 1604 (two), 1608, 1609, 1615, 1617, 1622 and 1643; see also Böck, *Volksfrömmigkeit*, 26.

[25] Böck, *Volksfrömmigkeit*, 147.

[26] For example, Böck, *Volksfrömmigkeit*, 148, 50,000 pilgrims at Maria Stern in 1798; Schnell, *Der baierische Barock*, 52, 71–76: e.g. 345 at the centennial celebration of 1734 at Mariahilfberg near Amberg, 13,000 yearly at Tuntenhausen, 48,000 at Maria-Dorfen, 20,000 at Marienberg near Burghausen.

[27] The spirit of baroque necrolatry is vividly evoked in a film by Peter Greenaway, *The Baby of Macon* (Darwin, 1993).

[28] Still housed in a large, purpose-built security vault near the house chapel. For a list of the relics, including the bones of children, see Herbert Brunner, Gerhard Hojer and Lorenz Seelig, *Nymphenburg: Residenz München* (Münchweiler, 1986), 113–119. At this time, numerous Bavarian monasteries inventoried and catalogued their relics for publication, an aspect of the early modern passion for collection. Not surprisingly, Evangelicals expressed interest in death through the written word rather than devotion to relics, leading to a proliferation of books on how to die with dignity and printed funerary eulogies; see Craig Koslofsky, *The Reformation of the Dead. Death and Ritual in Early Modern Europe, 1450–1700* (London, 2000).

refused his bribes.[29] His son, Maximilian I, elevated baroque necrolatry to
new and ironic heights; legend has it that money he spent stubbornly saving
relics from Protestants later went to purchase the cannon turned against
his own troops during the Thirty Years War.

Moralists worked hand-in-hand with the composers of miracle books
and the Wittelsbach dynasty to reinvigorate pilgrimage. They blamed
the breakdown of Christian unity for the Turkish conquest of Eastern
Europe, runaway inflation, hunger, earthquakes, comets, monstrous births
and witchcraft. In a sermon of 1563, Peter Canisius complained:

> Everywhere witches are punished, but still increase remarkably. Their outrages are
> horrifying . . . formerly one never saw people in Germany yield themselves up to
> the Devil and sign pacts with him so often . . . They bring many to their deaths
> through their devilish arts, raise storms and bring frightful harm to the country
> folk and other Christians. Nothing seems secure against their terrible arts and
> powers . . .[30]

Catholic moralists made desperate appeals for the vigilant observation of
sacraments and ritual pilgrimages as the only hopes of salvation.[31] Eisengrein
too responded to Protestant attacks on the veneration of the saints by inte-
grating pilgrimage into an articulate anti-Protestant propaganda campaign.
He insisted upon the efficacy of miracles as proof of the sacred power focused
in holy places and on holy objects.[32] Aegidius Albertinus explicitly recommended pilgrimage as a social remedy for sin, illness and the assaults of
Satan.[33] Daniel Baradinus prescribed pilgrimage as ecclesiastical medicine
to cure the poison of heresy. He attacked "Lutheran lies," proclaiming
the efficacy of miracles and the apparition of saints as proof of Catholic
doctrine.[34] Countless broadsheets, published miracle books, sermons and
historical tracts propagated confessional polemics, manipulated chiliastic
fears with vague promises of cures through pilgrimage and devotion to the
saints.

Catholic physicians too promoted the invocation of saints and the healing powers of their relics. Hippolyt Guarinonius (ever popular in Bavaria)

---

[29] Uwe Miller, "Der Versuch Herzog Wilhelm V. von Bayern, das Reichsheiltum in seinen Besitz zu
bringen," *Mitteilungen des Vereins für Geschichte der Stadt Nürnberg* 72 (1985), 117–135.
[30] Behringer, *Witchcraft Persecutions*, 109.
[31] E.g. Jacob Feucht, *Fünff kurtze Predige/ zur Zeit der grossen Theurung/ Hungersnot/ und Ungewitter . . .*
(Cologne, 1573).
[32] On the propaganda of pilgrimage and miracles in Counter Reformation literature, see Soergel,
"Spiritual Medicine," 125–145 and *Wondrous in his Saints*. The published accounts of exorcism and
miraculous faith healing also tended to be of a propagandistic nature; see D. P. Walker, *Unclean
Spirits. Possession and Exorcism in France and England in the Late Sixteenth and Early Seventeenth
Centuries* (Philadelphia, 1981).
[33] Albertinus, *Flagellum Diaboli*, 41–44.   [34] Baradinus, *Geistliche Artzne*.

published a version of the play *Theophilus*, depicting the fall of a priest who signed a pact with the devil in his own blood, only to be saved through the miraculous intervention of the Virgin Mary.[35] According to a 1655 broadsheet, Guarinonius employed the sleeve of Peter Canisius' shirt in Hall to treat pregnant women in danger of miscarriage. The broadsheet detailed other relics used by Guarinonius. In 1634, the Tyrolean physician hung a letter from Canisius around his own neck, enabling him to treat plague victims without contracting the contagion himself. In 1646, at the age of seventy-six, Guarinonius prayed to Canisius, who interceded to cure his own severe ailments; Guarinonius had a silver plaque engraved to commemorate the incident.[36] All of this was part of a broader movement to have Canisius canonized as a healer-saint for his abilities as a casuist and exorcist.

THE *PATRONA BOIARIAE*

There were an estimated 288 pre-Reformation shrines dedicated to a plethora of saints and their relics in Bavaria, with numerous post-Tridentine additions.[37] However, Wittelsbach interest was highly selective. The dynasty patronized cults through pious donations and interments of family members (or their body parts) at shrines, reinforcing popularity through dynastic association.[38] Among them, shrines to the Virgin were by far the most important. Five dynastic shrines were associated directly with the cult of the Virgin: the Holy Mountain at Andechs, St. Rasso at Grafrath, Our Lady of Altötting, St. Benno in the Church of Our Lady in Munich and the Marian Star of Taxa.[39] Marian veneration limited the need

---

[35] Originally composed by Mattheus Rader: Bücking, *Kultur and Gesellschaft*, 126.

[36] HStAM, Jesuitica 513/III contains a copy of *Kurtzer Inhalt Der Sonderbaren Gnaden und Gutthaten/ welche Gott der Herr R. P. Petro Canisio Societattis Iesu Theologio durch sein Fürbitt anderen Persohnen/ so wol vor als nach seinem Todt eryeigt hat . . . getruckt zu Freyburg in Ochtland bey David Irrbisch Anno 1655.* Located among materials used to support canonization efforts on Canisius' behalf, the broadsheet from Freiburg underscores Guarinonius' authority among Catholics throughout the Empire.

[37] Lionel Rothkrug suggests this figure in his "Religious Practices and Collective Perceptions: Hidden Homologies in the Renaissance and Reformation," *Historical Reflections* 7 (1980), 206–213. See also Steven Sargent's review which considers the basis of verification: "A Critique of Lionel Rothkrug's List of Bavarian Pilgrimage Shrines," *Archive for Reformation History* 80 (1989), 351–358.

[38] Maximilian and Count Tilly both left cardiotaphs at the chapel of Altötting: König, *Weihegaben*, 255–264.

[39] These shrines are the subjects of the following: Altötting – Soergel, *Wondrous in his Saints*; Grafath – Kramer, "Die Mirakelbücher der Wallfahrt Grafath," 80–103; St. Benno and Maria Star – Böck, *Volksfrömmigkeit*, 19–59, 106–178. On the dynastic relationship of the Wittelsbach family and the Counts of Andechs-Merian see Karl Bosl (ed.), *Andechs: der heilige Berg; von der Frühzeit bis zum Gegenwart* (Munich, 1993).

for functional diversity, because Mary did not specialize like other saints; she was a panacea, a wondrous thyriac.

Dynastic attention revolved around Marian pilgrimage shrines located at strategic points throughout the Duchy. The Wittelsbachs sought an alliance with the Virgin to domesticate the special dead hierarchically under her central banner. Analogous policies aided centralization in a number of Catholic states during the sixteenth and seventeenth centuries.[40] By promoting dynastic association with the cult of the Virgin, the policy simultaneously sought to diminish the prestige of local saints.

Maximilian invested heavily in the artistic and literary association of the Virgin with Bavaria's sacred landscape. Generally loath to add to a calendar saturated by holy days disrupting the work regimen of his subjects, Maximilian unwaveringly sanctioned the Feast of the Immaculate Conception (1629) and the Marian Assumption (1638) at the urgings of Jesuit advisors.[41] His son Ferdinand bore the popular matronymic "Maria." For all intents and purposes, the Virgin Mary emblemized Bavaria's flag under the reign of Maximilian. Mary, according to Aegidius Albertinus, became the Duchy's "compass of the soul" (*Seelencompass*).[42] Her virginity, a potent symbol, manifested the purity of the Wittelsbach state.[43] Virginity not only was linked to state formation, but is a recurrent motif in the regional history of madness; both the hagiography of St. Anastasia and a number of madwomen who visited her shrine for spiritual physic specifically recalled threats to their virginity. Immaculatism spread an image of Mary (indeed of women in general) as a spiritual rather than physical being.[44]

Politically, the Marian program of state pursued both internal and expansionist goals. Internally, dynastic Marianism yoked the triumphal mannerism of baroque art to project the majesty and purity of the central state. As with moral propagandists, non-Bavarians (specifically the Flemish artists Peter Candid, Peter-Paul Rubens and Hubert Gerhard) undertook much of the work. Maximilian's artistic program achieved fruition under the direction of Hans Krumper (1570–1634), a native-born pupil

[40] Political centralization achieved through a cultural policy of disenfranchising local saints and advancing Marian devotion was not limited to Bavaria, but was also practiced by the Austrian Habsburgs. On similar policies under Phillip II of Spain in the mid-sixteenth century, see William Christian, *Local Religion in Sixteenth-Century Spain* (Princeton, 1981), esp. 153–157.
[41] Stieve, *Die kirchliche Polizeiregiment*, 35. The public proclamation ordering observance of the Immaculate Conception is reproduced in Ziegler, *Dokumente*, 1034–1035.
[42] Albertinus, *Der Seelen-Compass*.
[43] On female sexual purity and state building in early modern Bavaria, see Ulrike Strasser, *State of Virginity. Gender, Religion and Politics in an Early Modern Catholic State* (Ann Arbor, 2004).
[44] On immaculatism and the early modern spiritulization of the Virgin, see Donna Spivey Ellington, *From Sacred Body to Angelic Soul: Understanding Mary in Late Medieval and Early Modern Europe* (Washington, DC, 2002).

of Gerhard. Krumper's plastic representations evoked a sense of hierarchical unity well suited to Maximilian's purpose.[45] Appointed court architect in 1609, Krumper oversaw extensive renovations and expansions of the Munich residence, and Candid's magnificent ceiling in the vaulted *Antiquarium*. Candid's frescoes portrayed the 102 cities, markets, castles and palaces of Bavaria as one community united under the cope of heaven. In 1616, Krumper allegorized the four cardinal virtues (Fortitude, Justice, Prudence and Temperance) as reclining women above the main portals of the western façade of the residence, facing the main street for all passers-by to see. They embodied the cardinal points on the Lipsian compass of neostoicist/anti-Machiavellian statecraft. Between them, Krumper later added his now-famous Madonna with child enthroned above the inscription: "*Patrona Boiariae*. We flee to your protection under which we live securely and happily." Maximilian officially elevated Mary to patron saint of Bavaria that same year.[46] In a blatant violation of civic privilege, he commissioned Krumper to erect a gilded Marian column in the market square before the city hall of Munich in 1638. The *Mariensäule* (the first of its kind in Central Europe) commemorated the city's deliverance from plague and Swedish occupation during the Thirty Years War.[47] At its dedication, Maximilian appealed: "Virgin Mary, preserve the substance, the ruler, the regime, the region and the religion of your Bavaria."[48]

Externally, the spiritual direction of the Marian program was expansionist and imperial. It echoed from the White Mountain in 1621, where Maximilian, founder and leader of the imperial Catholic League, opened the first major conflict of the Thirty Years War with the battle cry "Maria."[49] The etymology of the antiquated usage "*Boiariae*" (Krumper's inscription for the façade of the residence), rather than the contemporary "*Bavariae*," recalled the historic borders of the Duchy when it included Tyrol, Upper and Lower Austria, and the prince-bishoprics of Salzburg, Freising, Regensburg and

[45] On Krumper and his work, see Spindler, *Handbuch*, 1069–1071; Dorothea Diemer, "Hans Krumper," in: Glaser, *Wittelsbach und Bayern*, 279–311; Schnell, *Der baierische Barock*, 40, 58, 71, 80, 93, 120, 206.

[46] Brunner et al., *Nymphenburg*, 4, 8, 15; Ziegler, *Dokumente*, 827: "Patrona Boiariae. Sub tuum praesidium confugimus, sub quo secure laetique dedimus."

[47] Peter Bernhard Steiner, "Der gottselige Fürst und die Konfessionalisierung Altbayerns," in: Glaser, *Wittelsbach und Bayern*, 259. Marian columns, or plague columns (*Pestsäulen*) as they are sometimes known, appeared throughout Central Europe thereafter, e.g. in Eichstätt, Freising, Innsbruck, Prague and Vienna.

[48] "Rem, Regem, Regimen, Regionem, Religionem, Conserva Bavaris Virgo Maria tuis": Ziegler, *Dokumente*, 1101. Distances from Munich have been measured from the column in the market square before the city hall (now simply known as the *Marienplatz*) ever since; Schnell, *Der baierische Barock*, 41.

[49] Steiner, "Der gottselige Fürst," 254–155. He builds on inferences by Schnell, *Der baierische Barock*, 41–47. On the role of the Bavarian army at the Battle of the White Mountain, see Riezler, *Geschichte Bayerns*, vol. IV, 170–177.

Passau during the Middle Ages. Here, Maximilian consciously employed the Marian program of state to revive ancient claims to independent Catholic prince-bishoprics and neighboring Habsburg possessions in the seventeenth century.[50] Dynastic rivalry between the Habsburgs and Wittelsbachs had a long tradition, involving not only claims for former lands, but the imperial title as well. Maximilian harbored imperial aspirations; he strove tirelessly to rehabilitate the last Wittelsbach Emperor, Louis the Bavarian. Through the annexation of the Upper Palatinate and the County Palatine of the Rhine in 1623, Maximilian captured a coveted electoral title, moving the dynasty one step closer to the purple.[51]

In addition to productions in the plastic arts, court historiography resiliently promoted the Marian program of state. Maximilian invited prominent Catholic literary figures from all over Europe to Munich to embellish his program in writing. They reconstituted regional history, masterfully weaving territorial and dynastic aspirations with religious orthodoxy into an aesthetic whole.[52] Under Wittelsbach patronage, a multi-volume regional history was commissioned in 1595, but slow progress prompted Maximilian to reassign the project to Matheus Rader, SJ in 1602.[53] He composed the most famous Bavarian geography of all time.

---

[50] Steiner, "Der gottselige Fürst," 255.
[51] After the Middle Ages, the Wittelsbachs were the only dynasty briefly to break the Habsburg hold on the imperial title when Elector Karl Albrecht reigned as Emperor Karl VII from 1742 to 1745.
[52] Spindler, *Handbuch*, 911.
[53] Initially, the Augsburg humanist Marcus Welser received the commission. On Maximilian's political program of historiography, see Alois Schmid, "Geschichtsschreibung am Hofe Kürfurst Maximilians I. von Bayern," in: Glaser, *Wittelsbach und Bayern*, 330–340; Martin Ott, *Die Entdeckung des Altertums. Der Umgang mit der römischen Vergangenheit Süddeutschlands im 16. Jahrhundert* (Kallmünz, 2002). Rader counted Justus Lipsius and Martin Del Rio among his intimate correspondents and friends. He joined the Society of Jesus in Innsbruck at age twenty in 1581. An internationally recognized philologist, he taught rhetoric to a generation of significant baroque preachers like Jeremias Drexel and Jacob Bidermann at the Jesuit College in Munich: Steiner, "Der gottselige Fürst," 252–255. Rader also completed three volumes of a dynastic history extending into the seventeenth century, but his apologetic treatment of Louis the Bavarian led his Jesuit superiors to suppress the publication. A subsequent history by Rader's own student, fellow Tyrolean and Jesuit Andreas Brunner, met a similar fate in 1637. Maximilian fought hard to cleanse the name of his emperor-ancestor, finally succeeding after direct negotiations with the Curia in Rome. See, for example, Maximilian's appeal to Pope Gregory XV in 1622 in response to the degradation of Louis by the Polish Dominican Abraham Bzowski in the *Annales Ecclesiastici*: Ziegler, *Dokumente*, 931–932. Nevertheless, not until Vervaux published the *Annales Boicae Gentis* in 1662/1663 under the pseudonym Chancellor Johann Adlzreitter did a laudatory grand history appear. In their attempts to rehabilitate Louis and Duke Arnulf "the wicked," and to develop a direct lineage from Charlemagne to the Wittelsbach dynasty, Bavarian historians resorted to meticulous archival research. Vervaux's *Annales* were highly praised by Leibniz and eighteenth-century scholars: Spindler, *Handbuch*, 912; Schmid, "Geschichtsschreibung," 337.

Rader's *Bavaria Sancta et Pia* appeared in four separate volumes, a first in the Duchy's history. Together they conjured a mythical image of Bavaria as a holy land replete with its own autonomous cult of martyrs and relics.[54] A copper etching on the title page sported a map of Bavaria presented by St. Michael (warrior patron of the militant Jesuits) to the Virgin Mary, enthroned as the *Patrona Boiariae* (*sic*). The map clearly delineated the boundaries of the Duchy according to the four Rentamts of Burghausen, Landshut, Munich and Straubing, but its hagiographies deliberately included saints associated with former Wittelsbach possessions now in Habsburg hands.[55] The dedication to Maximilian in volume one topographically explained the sacred quality of Bavaria as internally (and to the above extent, externally) ubiquitous:

For if you examine all parts of the Bavarian landscape, you will hardly find a place unmarked by shrines and religion; cities, castles, markets, districts, villages, fields, forests, mountains and valleys all breathe and proclaim the traditional Catholic religion in Bavaria . . . So great a portion of the landscape is subsumed by holy places, it would be tedious to list them all, because the whole region is nothing other than religion and manifests a complete communal folk-church.[56]

Needless to say, the sheer geographic intention, politically to subsume every regional shrine into the *Bavaria Sancta*, was a daunting project. Rader also displayed consummate discrimination by only choosing saints, monasteries and shrines favorably associated with the Wittelsbach dynasty. Each handsome folio volume was adorned with oversized copper etchings, beginning with St. Lucius' mission during the Roman occupation. The last volume, the *Bavaria Sancta*, the *Pia*, ended with gruesome illustrations of St. Michael from the County Palatinate of the Rhine (annexed by Bavaria in 1623) and six children from Regensburg, all mythical victims of Jewish ritual murder; another victim of ritual murder, Simon of Trent, figured

---

[54] Matheus Rader, SJ, *Bavaria Sancta et Pia* (Munich, 1615, 1624, 1627 and 1628). The first three volumes were published prior to the annexation of the Upper Palatinate and Maximilian's accession to the electoral title.

[55] Steiner, "Der gottselige Fürst," 255. The title of this section, *De Finibus Bavariae*, indicates Rader was aware of the contemporary usage, but consciously and purposefully chose the archaic form for use in the caption – "Parua sed alma Dei praesignat dextera BOIAM, Propinat totum VIRGO parensque DEUM. Tutatur MICHAEL coelesti inisite campos; INDIGETES seruant oppida, BOIA times?" (emphasis added): Rader, *Bavaria Sancta*, vol. 1 (1615), 9r–10r.

[56] Ibid., vol. 1 (1615), 4v–5r: "Nam ut omnes Boicae terrae partes circumspicias, nullum ferè locum inuenies, vbinon illustria sanctitatis religionisque vestigia deprehendas; urbes, oppida, fora, pagi, vici, agri, silvae, montes, valles, Catholicam & priscam religione Bavaria spirant & ostendunt . . . Magnam denique in Boica, terrae partem sacra obtinent, ut labor sit singulorum numeruminire, cum toto regio, nil nisi religio, & unum quoddam commune gentis templum videatur."

prominently in several regional cases of demonic possession.[57] Rader's goal, rationally to organize the sacred under the cope of the *Patrona Boiariae*, imitated the militant hierarchy of the Jesuits: his sacred geography literally and pictorially mobilized the corps of the special dead into a regional command structure under the Virgin Mary. The *Bavaria Sancta* achieved huge success as a source of regional pride and, like Krumper's statues of the *Patrona Bavariae*, the literary *Bavaria Sancta* still conceptually motivates regional pilgrimage today, an enduring monument to the Marian cultural program.[58]

Devotion to the saints was serious business. Pilgrimages and processions not only secured confessional unity in the Duchy, but also played an important role in foreign policy. Again, the incident at Donauwörth is instructive. Maximilian encouraged divisive displays of Catholic devotion in the bi-confessional town on Bavaria's northern border. When Catholic representatives on the town council accused Protestants of disrupting their public processions, Maximilian used the quarrel as a pretext to annex the free-imperial city in 1607. In doing so, he nearly fomented a war and provoked the Protestant estates to form an imperial defensive alliance of their own, the Union, only adding to religious and political tensions in the Empire on the eve of the Thirty Years War.

PILGRIMS AND RIFF-RAFF

The secular authorities and the authors of miracle books, hagiographies and sacred geographies envisioned processions and pilgrimages as orderly and disciplined affairs.[59] Their scope ranged from the St. Leonhard processions held in rural communes to bless animals to the urban Corpus Christi

---

[57] Ibid., vol. III (1627), 174–182; vol. IV (1628), 189; on the use of blood for maleficent magic, 3, 174. Concerning accusations of ritual murder against the Jews in the Holy Roman Empire, see Hsia, *The Myth*. A most famous victim of alleged ritual murder, Simon of Trent is the subject of Hsia, *Trent 1475: Stories of a Ritual Murder Trial* (New Haven, 1992). A theoretical connection between Marian devotion and anti-Semitism is posited by Lionel Rothkrug, "Holy Shrines, Religious Dissonance and Satan in the Origins of the German Reformation," *Historical Reflections* 14 (1987) 143–286.

[58] After a second edition of Rader's original, there followed a German translation by the Bavarian Jesuit Maximilian Rassler in 1714, a romantic reinterpretation by Joseph von Obernberg in 1818, an edition embracing saints from annexed territories in Franconia and Swabia by Magnus Jocham in 1861/1862, that of the patriotic folklorist Ludwig Rosenberg in 1948 and, most recently, a grand three-volume edition by Georg Schwaiger, Director of the Institute for Church History at the University of Munich. For references to the aforementioned publications see Georg Schwaiger (ed.), *Bavaria Sancta. Zeugen des christlichen Glaubens in Bayern*, 3 vols (Regensburg, 1970–1973), 17.

[59] Soergel, "Spiritual Medicine," 126–128, vol. I.

parades of Munich, complex and hierarchical events.[60] Impressed by the pageantry of the Corpus Christi procession in Munich, one Italian musician (a member of Orlando di Lasso's court orchestra) reported in detail on the opulent variety of competing biblical floats entered in the parade by local guilds, state officials and musicians.[61] At times, however, they may have been sad affairs. Wilhelm V and Maximilian I vehemently rebuked courtiers and town councilors for inadequate demonstrations of devotion, fining them for failure to provide a proper contingent to carry the canopy of heaven, for example.[62] The authorities also expressed concerns about the preservation of public order. Wild carnival processions lampooned social hierarchy through temporary inversion.[63] The authorities opposed incessant outbreaks of jubilance, prohibiting unseemly parodies with penalties for masquerading, dancing and fiddle-playing.[64]

Legally, pilgrimage served a disciplinary or, if one prefers, rehabilitating function. For example, Melchior Funckh, a fifty-six-year-old cotter charged with failure to perform his Easter confession, traveled to St. Benno, confessed and obtained a certificate of confession as proof of penance to his local authorities.[65] Anna Liglin was charged with superstitious practices after she profaned a consecrated maypole by urinating on it. She had to pay a fine and conduct a pilgrimage to the Holy Mountain at Andechs, confessing and taking communion there; certification was required.[66] In at least one case, however, the rehabilitative effect of pilgrimage failed to make a lasting impression on the delinquent, highlighting the questionable value of

---

[60] The former were annual blessings of livestock by parish priests not unlike a local fair, symbolizing communal solidarity against outside influence and internal rivalry, while the latter served publicly to replicate the society of orders. Public processions served a similar purpose throughout Catholic Europe, as in Italy and Lyon: Richard Trexler, *Public Life in Renaissance Florence* (New York, 1980), and Philip Hofman, *Church and Community in the Diocese of Lyon 1500–1789* (New Haven, 1984). On the St. Leonhard procession, see Steven Sargent, "Religion and Society in Late Medieval Bavaria: The Cult of St. Leonard," (unpublished Ph.D. Dissertation, University of Michigan, 1988); Leo Weber, *St. Benedikt zu Benediktbeuern als Wallfahrtsort* (Benediktbeuern, 1981), 12–14.

[61] Cerbonio Besozzi: see Ziegler, *Dokumente*, 332–333: "et al tempo dil sacratissimo corpo di Christo si fa una solennissima et delle belle processioni, che dalla religione Romana si possi fare, nella città di Monaco tutta quanta con gli misteri del vechio et nuovo testamento in figura . . ."; he also comments on the consumption of meat on holidays and the presence of Lutheran princes at a recent baptism, fully conscious of the confessionally contentious implications.

[62] The visitation of 1584 noted that not all households in the town of Aibling observed processions: HStAM RL 40, 8v. The visitation of 1601 criticized processions on Whitsuntide in the market town Kraiburg, and Maximilian personally took the inner town council of Munich to task for failing to carry the "heaven" in the procession of 1636: HStAM RL 80 #361, 5v; HStAM HR 254, 299v–300r.

[63] Although raucous carnivalesque inversions probably did more to validate the existing social hierarchy, as suggested by Natalie Zemon-Davis, "The Reasons of Misrule," in: Zeman-Davis, *Society and Culture in Early Modern France* (Stanford, 1965), 97–123.

[64] On the repression of carnival activities in Landshut: HStAM HR 157, 51v, 172r.

[65] HStAM RL F. 26 #108, 31r.   [66] Ibid., 28r–v.

engaging pilgrimage as a tool of discipline. In 1631, the ordinary of Passau sentenced vicar Adam Sachreuter of Uttendorf and an accomplice to three days' confinement on bread and water and a pilgrimage to Salzburg with confession and communion; again, certificate required. Witnesses accused Sachreuter of concubinage, fathering several children, and fornication with married women.[67] Sachreuter developed a routine: he would gamble with a husband, encourage him to drink to the point of stupor, and then escort his wife in a carriage to the vicarage, admitting her through a concealed entrance. His sentence made little impression, nonetheless. After their pilgrimage to Salzburg, Sachreuter and his colleague stopped at a local tavern long enough to initiate a drunken brawl with a local forester.[68]

The authorities sought to regulate pilgrimage and processions by creating confraternities to organize and lead them. Confraternities subordinated to religious orders like the Jesuits adopted similar initiation rites and hierarchical command structures.[69] In practice, however, pilgrimage proved an ambivalent ally in the campaign to discipline and mobilize the population, since geographic mobility sorely tested networks of social control.[70] Pilgrimage denoted perambulation – even for heads of state like Maximilian. Apart from his inaugural pilgrimage to Altötting, he hiked annually in penitential garb to Ramersdorf and Thalkirchen near Munich, and to distant shrines at Tuntenhausen and Andechs, several days on foot from his residence.[71] The authorities were already overwhelmed to track the innumerable "children abroad," especially apprentices traveling to religiously suspect imperial cities like Augsburg and Regensburg. Itinerant peddlers hawking heretical literature, Jews (expelled by Albrecht but nevertheless entering the Duchy illegally), gypsies,[72] plague-carrying beggars, bandits, ex-soldiers and, most insidious of all, Anabaptists, complicated the

---

[67] In particular, the wife of a weaver from Münchstein, of a miller from Wasen and of a farmer near Mauerkirchen.

[68] HStAM RL 80, 101r–103v.

[69] Louis Chatellier, *The Europe of the Devout* (Cambridge, 1989).

[70] Specifically regarding immigration/emigration, see Stieve, *Die kirchliche Polizeiregiment*, 17; Ziegler, *Dokumente*, 785.

[71] Riezler, *Geschichte Bayerns*, 7. Even during a three-year regime in exile in Braunau during the Swedish occupation of Munich, Maximilian was an all-weather participant in weekly processions: Stieve, *Die kirchliche Polizeiregiment*, 37.

[72] Gypsies were targeted by the authorities probably more often than any other ethnic group during the reign of Maximilian I. For a few examples from the protocols of the Aulic Council, see HStAM HR 141, 71r; 159, 144r; 166, 246r; 177, 214v–215r; 191, 139r; 195, 222v–223r; 200, 51v–r. Apart from gypsies and Jews, other ethnic categories included French and Turkish soldiers, as well as Bohemian and Italian itinerants.

impossible task of controls and internal surveillance. Bavaria needed outsiders, as the careers of Canisius, Eisengrein, Rubens and Candid suggest.

Early modern authorities throughout Europe waged an endless battle
to restrict travel. In their exuberance to promote the cult of the special
dead, however, Bavarian authorities now faced the paradox of controlling
veritable armies of pilgrims. The atmosphere at shrines and church fairs
was festive, to say the least, accompanied by excessive drinking, gambling
and dancing – conduct against which local, provincial and central officials
struggled time and again, usually to no avail.[73] Outraged by immoralities
occurring during the massive yearly procession to the Holy Mountain at
Andechs, the authorities fought to curb them year after year with little
success. Sometimes, they blamed each other for a lack of vigilance. The
Abbot of Andechs refused Maximilian's request to construct small huts
on the slopes of the Holy Mountain to house "common" pilgrims on the
grounds that "those same wicked people" would get into trouble, especially at night.[74] Later, Maximilian levied a fine of eight talers against the
same abbot after he failed to prevent public dancing at a local inn.[75] From
1640 until 1682, Maximilian, Ferdinand Maria and Maximilian Emanuel
repeated an annual warning to the high judge of the Munich town council, describing the processional pilgrimage to Andechs on the Feast of the
Ascension in these words:

Recalling the order prepared for him one year ago . . . he should now travel
on the Feast of the Ascension to the Holy Mountain; herewith it is therefore
mercifully ordered, that he proceed there with all possible industry at this the feast
time and command his subordinate overseers and officials to pay close attention,
that attendant peddlers, inn-keepers, beer-sellers, bakers, cooks and others do not
take advantage of the pilgrims, that they respect the official weights and measures
and currency, and that violators are properly prosecuted. Furthermore, particular
attention should be given to the presence of riff-raff, who undertake all manner
of evil and, should any of the same be disorderly or suspected of a common
crime or something more serious, they should be arrested by the county judge of

---

[73] A cursory quantification of the local court protocols (*Briefprotokolle*) for the Hofmark of Benediktbeuern alone, taken at ten-year intervals between 1643 and 1703, indicates about one dozen offenses
each year, especially at the yearly parish fair (*Kirchtag*), though the prosecution of moral offenses
witnessed a general decline; see StAM *Briefprotokolle, Gericht Tölz, Hofmark Benediktbeuern*. Brawls
broke out at church fairs and drunks attending mass vomited in churches: HStAM RL F. 26 #108,
29v, 197v. For some examples of serious moral crimes and their penalization at the central level
during the reign of Maximilian, see HStAM HR 155, 240r–v, forbidding dancing during carnival;
175, 266v–267v, gambling at the parish fair; 200, 38v–39r, excessive dancing, drinking, pipe smoking
and eating at the parish fair.
[74] HStAM KL Andechs, F.41, ff. 3–9.   [75] HStAM HR 212, 262v, 334v–335r, 385r–386r, 411r–v.

Weilheim, who will be on hand, taken to the jail in Weilheim and there subjected to interrogation, with reports sent to the Aulic Council in Munich . . .[76]

Viewed as a means of ideologically mobilizing popular piety against the dangers of heretical infections in the body politic, pilgrimage ironically provided enterprising individuals with an opportunity to circumvent social controls. During large annual processions and pilgrimages, the otherwise taut net of vigilance slackened to a sieve. Thievery, pickpockets and violence were not uncommon. As the above instruction suggests, the inadequacy of official control mechanisms in the face of mass gatherings encouraged not only disorderly conduct and criminal activity, but free trade as well, with local economies benefiting from an effective deregulation of commerce. Inns and hospices, both legal and illegal, prospered along the routes and at the shrines themselves. Itinerant vendors set up shop, purveying foodstuffs and alcoholic beverages or hawking rosaries, medallions and other religious souvenirs at inflated prices.[77] Prices for accommodations varied according to categories of luxury and seasonal demand. At Andechs, "honorable visitors" lodged directly at the guest facilities of the monastery and thus avoided an onerous and repetitive ascent of the Holy Mountain each new day, as well as the discomfort of staying at one of the many overcrowded local inns and taverns in the village below among the "common rabble" and "vulgar pilgrims."[78] For many small communities, the success of a shrine brought seasonal prosperity in its wake as local sodalities arranged bed and breakfast for jubilant pilgrims. Printed miracle books competitively advertised the miraculous powers of their respective shrines in a bid to attract travelers. Pilgrimage and processions to shrines were good for local business. In turn, the journey held capital of another kind for pilgrims to take home. In an age under constant threat of disease, warfare, famine and death, the morbid fascination of relics acted as a bizarre form of social capital. Like pilgrimage itself, direct contact with a saint's remains conferred local status through association with the sacred. The value of this status sometimes appears repugnant and even puerile to us. For example, the Corpus Christi Brotherhood of St. Peter's in Munich sent a supplication to the Abbot of Andechs on the eve of the annual procession to the Holy Mountain in 1652. The confraternity complained that the Brotherhood of Our Lady at

---

[76] HStAM HR 271, 196r–197r. The order for the preceding year defines "riff-raff" as "those beggars and persons who are unworthy of alms and should be driven from our lands": HStAM HR 267, 544r–545r. A copy of both orders was sent to the Abbot of Andechs to insure his cooperation. For successive decrees issued on a yearly basis throughout the reign of Ferdinand Maria, see HStAM KL Andechs F. 41 ff. 15r–29r.

[77] HStAM HR 212, 262v, 334v–335r, 385v–386r, 411r–v.   [78] HStAM KL Andechs F. 41 ff. 3–9.

Altötting had already carried the holy sweat-cloth in the procession last year and insisted that now it was their turn.[79]

THE BEATA ALTA AND ST. ANASTASIA: "HELP AND CONSOLATION TO THE SUFFERING, THE TROUBLED IN SPIRIT, YES EVEN THE POSSESSED . . ."

In spite of the twin centripetal and expansionist designs attendant to the Marian program of state, local non-dynastic shrines also profited from the renewal of pilgrimage. Locals patronized them because of their communal significance and outsiders journeyed to them as a result of their reputation for dealing with specific ailments. Two particular shrines won regional and even supra-regional acclaim for their specialization in spiritual physic for the care of mental sufferers: the cults of the Beata Alta at Pürten and St. Anastasia at Benediktbeuern. Both rose to prominence as the most important ambulatory centers for the treatment of mental afflictions in Bavaria during the general crisis and peaked in the mid-seventeenth century, mirroring a proliferation of spiritual afflictions, reports of demonic activity and witchcraft persecutions.

The origins of the cult of the Beata Alta are obscure. Secular clergy attended her shrine at a minor church, but they never composed a hagiography or published a miracle book. The shrine's success is attributable to its location near Waldkraiburg on the main pilgrimage route from Munich to Altötting. According to legend, Alta (a pious virgin) belonged to an early medieval French royal dynasty. In the tenth century, she suffered an indeterminate terminal illness, but the Virgin Mary appeared to her in a dream to encourage her to travel to Bavaria.[80] She died en route, but instructed her escorts to continue the journey and bury her at the exact spot where two asses pulling her carriage stopped. The animals halted at Pürten, where she was interred. Her most prized possession, a beautifully illuminated evangelistary, or book of the gospels, was donated to the humble church.[81] By the sixteenth century, rumors spread about its powers to cure epilepsy, demonic

---

[79] HStAM KL Andechs F. 41, ff. 32r–35v.

[80] The date of the journey is not mentioned in the account of Anton Mayer and Georg Westermayer, *Statistische Beschreibung des Erzbisthums München-Freising*, vol. II (Regensburg, 1880), 161–167. However, the daughter of the tenth-century Archbishop of Salzburg, Adalbrecht, was named Alta and her evangelistary is generally dated to the tenth century as well.

[81] The gospel book, presently the object of art historical veneration, is kept in the manuscript collection of the Bavarian State Library in Munich: BayStaBi Clm 5250. See also Katharina Bierbrauer, *Die vorkarolingischen und karolingischen Handschriften der bayerischen Staatsbibliothek* (Wiesbaden, 1990), 131–132.

possession and other mental ailments, and the book subsequently became the fetish of cult veneration.

The second shrine, devoted to St. Anastasia, was located at Benedikt-beuern, a Benedictine monastery some fifty kilometers south of Munich. The legend of St. Anastasia originated in classical antiquity and was first treated in the hagiography *A Bavarian Beacon*.[82] Born into the noble Prae-textatus family in ancient Rome, she was baptized a Christian at birth. However, her parents promised her in marriage to Publius, a pagan friend of the Emperor Diocletian. The well-intentioned marriage arrangements went awry after Anastasia demanded her new husband convert before con-summating the union – an act that might have cost him a good deal more than his position during Diocletian's persecutions. Anastasia visited fel-low Christians imprisoned by Diocletian until her anxious spouse had her locked away for months at a time with only the barest of necessities. She obstinately withstood his continued advances and finally gained her free-dom after Publius died on campaign in Persia. While evangelizing with a confidant, Chrysogonus, both became victims of persecutions. After all manner of tortures and unspeakably erotic temptations at the hands of a pagan sorcerer and his female apprentices, Anastasia still refused to sacrifice to the Emperor.[83] In prison, the spirit of St. Theodota fed and consoled her until she was condemned to die with pagan criminals aboard a sinking penal ship. Then Theodota appeared and guided the ship to safety, where-upon all of the criminals converted. On December 25, AD 304, Diocletian had her staked to the ground and roasted alive during a mass execution of 270 martyrs.

In 1053, Abbot Gotthelm of Benediktbeuern dispatched Presbyter Gottschalk to carry a petition to the Bishop in Verona. Gottschalk lodged at the nearby abbey of St. Maria Organa, where the abbot woefully con-fided that the cloister's dismal finances prevented the worthy care of relics, including the remains of St. Anastasia.[84] During the abbot's sermon, Gottschalk stole away to the crypt, vowing then and there to commit a

---

[82] Biechler, *Bayerischer Pharos* (1663), 4–41; see also Karl Meichelbeck, *Leben/ Leyden/ Todt/ Erhebung/ . . . der grossen Heiligen Martyrin Anastasiae . . .* (Munich, 1710), 8–72.
[83] On the allusions to her female temptresses, again see Biechler, *Bayerischer Pharos* (1663), 4–41.
[84] *Monumenta Germaniae Historica, Scriptores* 9, 224–229: "Tunc quoque tempore supradictus abbas Gotthelmus misit quendam presbyterum suum nomine Gotschalcum in civitatem Veronam ad eundem pontificem cum aliis suis nunciis, petens solatium victualium, quia fames tunc temporis cepit esse in terra Bauwariorum per decem annos, et maxima multitudo cruciabatur fame illis temporibus. Isdem namque frater Gotschalcus veniens in civitatem Veronam et non inveniens ibi episcopum, ad monasterium sancte Marie Organa dictum divertit, ad abbatem lici illius nomine Engelberonem, qui et ipse erat ex familia sancti Benedicti." Benediktbeuern, founded in the eighth century and one of the oldest Benedictine monasteries in Bavaria, lay at that time in the ecclesiastical province of Verona.

holy theft (*furta sacra*).[85] Caught *in flagrante delicto* by the custodian of relics, who threatened to inform the abbot, Gottschalk bribed him with twenty soldes.[86] On his return journey over the Brenner Pass, seven signs attested to the miraculous powers of the saint. In one incident, Gottschalk met a demoniac named Gisilbirga, who touched the relics and howled, "Anastasia burns me, Anastasia's intercession is too hot for me!" – a reference to her martyrdom at the stake.[87] This is the earliest reference to the role of the cult in the treatment of a demoniac. Five centuries passed before another case documented the Anastasia cult. It appeared in a 1537 entry from the miracle book at Tuntenhausen, noting that a woman robbed of her senses had previously journeyed to Benediktbeuern, but had obtained no relief there.[88]

The patient records from both shrines are found in their own manuscript miracle books, which register biographic information on the sufferers, their symptoms, attempted cures, results and votive offerings. Entries range from a brief sentence to more detailed accounts over several handwritten pages. They are systematic in so far as they generally cite the date of a visit, the person's name, place of origin and affliction. The miracle book of Pürten is less well organized, but chronologically longer, spanning the years from 1621 to 1866. However, the bulk of regular entries fall in the period from 1653 to 1710 (226 entries for individual pilgrims),[89] including annotations at the end of the main register (Table 3.1). Twenty scattered accounts from 1621 to 1635 are followed by an eighteen-year gap, while several hundred entries for the period after 1710 offer little more than perfunctory lists of pious donations with no details of sufferers and their maladies.

The miracle book from the St. Anastasia cult at Benediktbeuern covers a shorter time-span, but is more dense, systematic and thorough in its accounting. The records date from the period 1657 to 1668 (1,099 visits), as well as three chance entries from 1683 and one from 1692 appended at the very end of the book (see Table 3.2). Information provided in published hagiographies indicates that other ledgers may have existed, but have since

---

[85] The holy theft of relics was a popular literary motif used to explain the translation of relics under dubious circumstances; see Patrick Geary, *Furta Sacra. Thefts of Relics in the Central Middle Ages* (Princeton, 1990), 14–15 on the Anastasia story.

[86] MGH SS 9, 227: "Accipe, domine pater, istos denarios cum reliquiis his, et noli detegere reatum meum abbati tuo, et neque fratribus tuis dicas pecatum meum."

[87] Ibid., 228; Biechler, *Bayerischer Pharos* (1663), 52; K.-S. Kramer, "Ein Mirakelbuch der heiligen Anastasia in Benediktbeuern," *Bayerisches Jahrbuch für Volkskunde* (1991), 111–112.

[88] Ibid., 113; Irmgard Gierl, *Bauernleben und Bauernwallfahrt in Altbayern. Eine kulturkundliche Studie auf Grund der Tuntenhausen Mirakel-Bücher* (Munich, 1960), 108–109.

[89] Therefore, single entries and visits appear to be synonymous in the case of the Pürten miracle book, while the Anastasia miracle book includes five pilgrims who visited on at least two separate occasions.

Table 3.1 *Recorded visits to the Beata Alta shrine at Pürten*

Year	Visits	Year	Visits	Year	Visits	Year	Visits
1653	13	1667	7	1679	22	1693–1694	0
1654	3	1668	4	1680	11	1695	1
1655	1	1669	0	1681	26	1696–1697	0
1656–1658	0	1670	8	1682	4	1698	21
1659	4	1671	4	1683	14	1699	8
1660	2	1672	14	1684	17	1700	12
1661	0	1673	15	1685	2	1701	13
1662	10	1674	5	1686	1	1702–1705	0
1663	17	1675	0	1687	3	1706	2
1664	7	1676	0	1688	2	1707–1708	0
1665	8	1677	2	1689–1691	0	1709	1
1666	8	1678	17	1692	1	1710	5

Table 3.2 *Recorded visits to the Anastasia shrine at Benediktbeuern.*[a]

Year	Visits	Year	Visits	Year	Visits
1657	84	1662	105	1667	76
1658	109	1663	73	1668 (to June)	72
1659	119	1664	84		
1660	104	1665	116	*1683*[b]	*3*
1661	76	1666	79	*1692*[b]	*1*

[a]Note that these total figures differ slightly from Kramer, "Ein Mirakelbuch," 118. There are several reasons for this, the most obvious being that Kramer counted entries, not visits, and therefore usually counted two pilgrims mentioned in the same entry as one. Shortly before his death, Prof. Kramer kindly permitted access to his notes, enabling careful checking of both our accounts. Regrettably, Prof. Kramer, who had retired, passed away two days before we were finally to meet, an occasion we had both looked forward to very much.
[b]Data from two years added after the main body of the miracle book.

been lost, perhaps as a consequence of the secularization of the monastery in 1803, when it was transformed into a military barracks. Most records were removed to the state archives in Munich at that time, though some were misappropriated or destroyed outright. The Anastasia miracle book survived in the parish archives until Theresa Leichtweis, the parish priest's sister, inherited it in 1877. She subsequently presented it to a government official as a gift in 1878.[90]

[90] BayHStM, Klosterliteralien Benediktbeuern 121$\frac{1}{2}$. Hereafter referred to as the Anastasia Miracle Book = AMB; in this case, the reference is to the title page.

Although both manuscript ledgers commence in the seventeenth century (as do the earliest references to miracles in published Anastasia hagiographies), the reputation of both shrines was already on the rise by the late sixteenth century, when they attracted the fleeting attention of the Wittelsbach dynasty. In August 1592, Wilhelm V requested and received a perfunctory report on the origins and powers of Alta's evangelistary from the Abbot of Au.[91] An official communiqué dated September 11, 1624 from the district judge of Waldkraiburg to Maximilian detailed cures performed on the spiritually afflicted at Pürten. In 1629, Maximilian's brother (Albrecht) wrote the Archbishop of Salzburg about the shrine at Pürten as well. Initial signs of dynastic interest in the Anastasia cult occurred simultaneously. In 1602, Maximilian ordered the abbey to compile a complete list of all available relics. In 1608 and again in 1613, he forbade the abbot from relinquishing any portion of Anastasia's relics (as a regional treasure) and subsequently ordered him to deliver them up to the provisional capital in Burghausen during the Swedish occupation to prevent them from falling into enemy hands.[92] Maximilian's brother (Ernst) requested the relics to assist in the treatment of a "distinguished person" in Munich in 1630.[93] In 1701, the Bavarian court cartographer, Michael Wening, described Benediktbeuern in his official topographical catalogue as the place where

the sacred body of St. Anastasia rests . . . and many good deeds are done to this day through the intercession of that saintly virgin on behalf of those who desire help, as is especially experienced by the possessed, out of whom the demons of hell are often driven after the sacred head is placed upon them.[94]

During the reign of Maximilian, popular interest in both shrines grew significantly, reflecting the heightened popular interest in accessing shrines specifically devoted to spiritual physic for troubled minds. At Pürten, spiritually afflicted pilgrims began donating a fine collection of ex-votos after 1620 (coinciding with the first entries in the manuscript miracle book).[95] By the end of the sixteenth century, popular enthusiasm for the Anastasia cult in Benediktbeuern had overshadowed the principal cult of St. Benedict,

[91] Mayer and Westermayer, *Statistische Beschreibung*, 166–168.
[92] Josef Hemmerle, *Die Benediktinerabtei Benediktbeuern* (Berlin, 1991), 254–255.
[93] Weber, "St. Benedikt," 8.
[94] Michael Wening, *Historico-Topographica Descriptio*, vol. 1 (Munich, 1701; reprint Munich, 1974), Rentamt München, 120, Benedictbeyrn: "allwo der H. Leib der H. Anastasiae ruhet . . . und werden durch Fürbitt dieser H. Jungfrauen biß auff heutigen Tag den jenigen /so hülff begehren / vil Gutthaten erwisen / wie dann solche sonderbar die Besessene erfahren /auß welchen öffters die Höllische Geister in Auffsezung deß H. Haupts vertrieben worden / wie dann ein eygnes Buech darvon außgangen."
[95] Mayer and Westermayer, *Statistische Beschreibung*, 166.

the original patron saint of the abbey. At the beginning of the seventeenth century, the abbot felt obliged to request the construction of a new, separate chapel to receive the ever mounting influx of mad pilgrims (see Plate 10).[96] The Lateran Chapter of St. Anastasia in Rome authorized the new Anastasia Chapel in 1603. Construction was completed three years later and the Bishop of Augsburg consecrated the chapel in 1609.[97] Both shrines continued to attract popular attention as late as the early twentieth century. In 1872, the apothecary of Pürten suggested that most of the humble parish's income still derived from the care and accommodation of the mentally ill, who came in droves from many distant lands.[98] Until renovations were conducted on the sacristan's dwellings in 1919, one could still view the iron rings and chains used to restrain sufferers during treatment.[99] Reference was made to Benediktbeuern as a popular locus for the treatment of chronic headaches as late as 1910.[100]

Although the social network disseminating knowledge of these cults defies systematic reconstitution, the means of dissemination are clearly discernible in the case of the Anastasia cult.[101] Its specificity of purpose acted as a magnet, attracting pilgrims from an expansive geographic reservoir. At the height of its popularity, the custodians of St. Anastasia's relics kept a book on over a thousand pilgrims seeking spiritual physic within a decade (1657–1668), as compared with Andechs, where only 221 reports of madness, demonic possession and other spiritual afflictions appear for the entire period from 1454 to 1657, or Tuntenhausen and Altötting, where absolute numbers were far less.[102] Therefore, although the annual volume of total recorded miracles (ninety) was moderate in comparison with the shrines

---

[96] Weber, "St. Benedikt,", 11; Hemmerle, *Die Benediktinerabtei*, 263.

[97] Privileges were renewed and extended in several papal and episcopal decrees: HStAM, Kloster Urkunde (KU) Benediktbeuern (BB) 1272, 1275, 1286, 1317. See also Hemmerle, *Die Benediktinerabtei*, 43–44. The St. Anastasia Church in Rome became a regular appointment for Bavarian ecclesiastics, carrying with it the title of cardinal, e.g. Cardinal G. Häffelin and Cardinal Karl August, Count of Reisach, former Archbishop of Munich-Freising.

[98] Mayer and Westermayer, *Statistische Beschreibung*, 165–167.

[99] *Waldkraiburger Nachrichten*, 3.iii.1993, 24.

[100] Marie Andree-Eysn, *Volkskundliches aus dem bayerisch-österreichischen Alpengebiet* (Braunschweig, 1910), 120.

[101] On the geographic spread of devotional knowledge in two French examples, see Michel de Certeau, *The Possession at Loudun* (Chicago, 1996), 109–121; Jean-Claude Schmitt, *The Holy Greyhound: Guinefort, Healer of Children since the Thirteenth Century* (Cambridge, 1983).

[102] The manuscript HStAM KL Andechs 40, 4r, 31v–32r mentions seventeen spiritual afflictions from 1624 to 1644; the anonymously published miracle book, *Denkwürdige Miracula . . . unser Lieben Frawen Gottshauß und Pfarrkirchen zu Tundenhausen* (Munich, 1646), records some two dozen spiritual afflictions for the period 1584–1643. They appear sporadically in manuscript and printed miracle books from Altötting as well.

Plate 10. *The Veneration of St. Anastasia*, Benediktbeuern, oil on canvas, 1685 by Hans Georg Assam, father of Quirin and Aegid Assam. A typical scene of piligrimage from the seventeenth century. From left to right: Devotees gather to venerate the Anastasia bust around the altar of her chapel; mad pilgrims and demoniacs flail about in the foreground, awaiting the application of relics; a madman is carried to the shrine; a pious pilgrim shops for mementos, while a young boy steals a bottle of wine from his basket; a procession approaches with the Alps in the background. (Courtesy of the Salisians of Benediktbeuern; photograph by Foto Thoma, Benediktbeuern.)

of Altötting, Andechs or Taxa, the caseload was virtually limited to spiritual afflictions. The famous Marian shrines certainly attracted more pilgrims each year, whereas organized processions to Benediktbeuern were largely local affairs limited to feast days in September, December and January. Most pilgrims trickled in on their own or in the company of friends and family.[103] Competition was fierce. For example, the custodian of the miracle book of Tuntenhausen took obvious pleasure recounting the story of a senseless woman who suffered such terrible tribulations "that she had also been taken to Benediktbeuern and other places, but God had without doubt reserved [her] relief [from the affliction] for the worthy house of God at Tuntenhausen" in 1643.[104] Nevertheless, and despite the lack of dynastic patronage and competition from a number of other major Marian shrines, the market for spiritual physic at Benediktbeuern was extraordinarily expansive and growing in the seventeenth century.

Michel de Montaigne, normally an astute observer, took no notice of Benediktbeuern as he passed on his way to Italy in 1580.[105] Eighty years later, however, the Anastasia cult did not fail to impress another nobleman returning from a study tour (*peregrinatio academica*) to Italy, where he had lost his senses.[106] Its location on a major transalpine thoroughfare insured the cult extensive dissemination. In fact, based upon each pilgrim's place of origin, the geographic renown of the St. Anastasia shrine in the mid-seventeenth century extended far beyond the core regions of other Bavarian shrines; lacking a significant center of attraction, pilgrims were just as likely to gravitate from its immediate environs (thirty-three), as from the Munich area (fifty-five), or from neighboring Habsburg Tyrol (116), from whence a wave of emigration to Bavaria filled the demographic vacuum brought about by plague and the Thirty Years War.[107] Pilgrims came from Württemberg, Ulm and Augsburg (more than thirty), Switzerland, the Alsace and as far afield as England, Italy, the Netherlands, Prague and Vienna.[108] In comparison,

[103] Hemmerle, *Die Benediktinerabtei*, 263; Weber, "St. Benedikt," 10.
[104] *Denkwürdige Miracula . . .* , 17–18.
[105] Michel de Montaigne, *Journal du Voyage de Michel de Montaigne en Italie, Par la Suisse et l'Allemagne en 1580 et 1581* (1775), 111. His reference to a steep mountain pass and the lake beyond en route to Mittenwald undoubtedly refers to the Kesselberg and the Walchensee, indicating that he undoubtedly passed by Benediktbeuern.
[106] His case is dealt with in detail below: AMB 600301: dates from the ledger are hereafter abbreviated for the seventeenth century as year-month-day, e.g. 600301 = entry for March 1, 1660.
[107] Hermann Hörger, *Kirche, Dorfreligion und bäuerliche Gesellschaft: Strukturanalysen zur gesellschaftsgebundenen Religiosität ländlicher Unterschichten des 17–19. Jahrhunderts, aufgezeigt an bayerischen Beispielen*, vol. 1 (Munich, 1978/1983), 42–46.
[108] The noblewoman from the Netherlands, mentioned by Biechler, *Bayerischer Pharos* (1663), 84–86, was likely the embellished account of an arrival reported by the president of the Aulic Council in Munich in 1604: HStAM Gen. Reg. F. 1190, #63.

pilgrimage to the Wittelsbach shrine of St. Rasso at Grafrath grew in numbers, but continuously declined in the extent of its geographic attraction
since the late Middle Ages to little more than the area around Munich.[109]
From the beginning of the seventeenth century, the fame of the Anastasia cult as an ambulatory treatment center for spiritual afflictions spread
orally and spontaneously. The sheer volume of pilgrimage from the jurisdiction of other Benedictine monasteries is indicative of the order's active
role in the dissemination of knowledge.[110] Informational networking was
a common facet of monasticism since the early Middle Ages and itinerant
monks (like the sacred thief Gottschalk) regularly lodged with members
of their own order while travelling.[111] Benedictine monks from outside the
area recommended the Anastasia cult to their constituents either in person
or in sermons.[112] In 1660, a pilgrim accompanied by her mother and father
was directed to Benediktbeuern to seek treatment for her melancholic condition by the Benedictine monks at Andechs.[113] In 1666, a demonically
possessed woman visited the Benedictine abbeys of Benediktbeuern, Ettal
and St. Emmeram in Regensburg in search of alleviation.[114] The oral propagation of Anastasia's miraculous healing power by the brethren was part
of a pattern of competition between monastic orders. Other orders also
networked to promote their shrines. For example, Abraham à Santa Clara
reported from Vienna that the Augustinian order had communicated news
of the Marian Star of Taxa to their colleagues as far afield as Altomünster
and Prague.[115]
Pilgrims too transmitted the news of shrines after returning to their communities.[116] One pilgrim claimed to have heard of Anastasia's miraculous
powers from other pilgrims who had been there.[117] The fact that parents,
spouses or friends accompanied sufferers magnified the spread of information. They recounted their experiences to acquaintances and relatives,
enhanced the reputation of the shrine and encouraged others to seek help

---

[109] Kramer, "Ein Mirakelbuch," 118–122.
[110] Other Benedictine monasteries referral from which is specifically mentioned in the ledger include
Andechs, Ettal, Metten, Rott am Inn, Scheyern, Seeon, Tegernsee, and Wessobrunn. Most larger
cities mentioned in the Anastasia miracle book (i.e. Salzburg, Augsburg, Regensburg) had Benedictine cloisters as well.
[111] Inter-regional monastic networking during the early Middle Ages is detailed by Friedrich Prinz,
*Frühes Mönchtum im Frankenreich. Kultur und Gesellschaft in Gallien, den Rheinland und Bayern am
Beispiel der monastischen Entwicklung (4. bis 8. Jahrhundert)* (Munich, 1988).
[112] In general, see Böck, *Volksfrömmigkeit*, 28–30. The role of sermons in promoting pilgrimages is
discussed by Moser-Rath, *Dem Kirchenvolk*, 180–184.
[113] AMB 600301.   [114] AMB 660825; BayStBi Cgm 2620, 120–126.
[115] Böck, *Volksfrömmigkeit*, 152.
[116] On the similar oral transmission of the Benno cult, see ibid., 27–31.   [117] AMB 630308.

there. Successive pilgrims from one locality often followed others within a month.[118] In some communities, devotion to the cult exhibited signs not only of continuity, but also of outright emulation. In Wolfratshausen, for example, pilgrims traveled to Benediktbeuern in at least five of the twelve years during which the manuscript ledger was maintained.[119] The brewery in Wolfratshausen was particularly plagued with evil spirits. The brewer tied his daughter to a wagon and transported her to the shrine in December 1663 after she became tempestuous (*ungestümm*) at the approach of her wedding.[120] Her recovery there caused her father to weep with joy. One month later, a servant from the same brewery arrived at Benediktbeuern in a state of fear displaying symptoms of demonic possession.[121]

Oral transmission conquered distance through family networking as well. One month after Christina Gremminger traveled to the St. Anastasia shrine, Susanna Gremminger followed her lead.[122] Bavarians living and working abroad also acted as ambassadors for the cult. In 1665, a Bavarian woman working as a servant in Linz recommended the shrine to a local, who later traveled there.[123] Heavy immigration after the Thirty Years War may account for the over-representation of Tyroleans at the shrine. One woman (originally born near Andechs) recalled the shrine and traveled there from Württemberg, where she had resided for the past fourteen years.[124]

Popular notoriety achieved through oral transmission encouraged interest in the shrine and resulted in referrals. In 1604, a distraught Flemish noblewoman visiting the court of the Archduchess in Innsbruck learned of "a relic in a monastery where many people had been helped," whereupon she journeyed to Benediktbeuern.[125] In 1626, the Ecclesiastical Council of Munich ordered the chaplain of Oberalting to refer anyone requesting his services as an exorcist in the future directly to Benediktbeuern.[126] In 1623 and again in 1631, the criminal court of Munich recalled that two persons (one possessed, the other suicidal) had been referred to the Anastasia chapel for treatment.[127] Two further cases of possession recorded in the published miracle books of St. Benno for the years 1617 and 1696 revealed individuals who had been treated in Benediktbeuern.[128] In 1670, the Ecclesiastical Council of Freising allowed the father confessor of the monastery

---

[118] For example: AMB 590930, 591025 (Schonhausen in the county of Dachau); 610628, 610701 (Oberpeissenberg); 620718, 620809 (Weil in the county of Landsberg).
[119] AMB 570719, 610218, 610728, 631212, 640116, 650616, 650507.
[120] AMB 631212.   [121] AMB 640116.   [122] AMB 590809, 590913.   [123] AMB 650612.
[124] AMB 650616.   [125] HStAM Gen Reg F. 1190.   [126] AEM GR 62, 44.
[127] Böck, *Volksfrömmigkeit*, 45–46.   [128] Ibid.

of Altomünster to hear the confession of a demoniac, but then directed him to accompany her to Benediktbeuern for exorcism rather than performing the ritual himself – this despute the fact the shrine was located outside the Prince-Bishopric of Freising, not to mention in a separate diocese (Augsburg) and archdiocese (Mainz).[129]

THE DEVOTIONAL CONTRACT

The renewal of pilgrimage in post-Tridentine Bavaria according to the Marian state program also revitalized local and popular adoration of the saints and their relics. The rise in popularity of the St. Anastasia cult at the end of the sixteenth century was an ancillary result. As the nascent absolutist state invested its cultural resources into devotion, it enhanced the status value of shrines throughout the Duchy. What the ruling elite viewed as a centralizing measure also provided local communities associated with shrines (there were many) with a transcendental escape clause, because direct access to sacred power enabled them to shore up communal authority.[130] Communities gained influence and wealth through their association with the cult of the special dead. Furthermore, a central policy of renewing devotion created individual avenues of social empowerment.[131] For individual pilgrims, the experience of travel temporarily confounded the regimen of surveillance and released them from their immediate social constraints – witness the mirthful atmosphere during pilgrimages, processions and at the shrines themselves. Therefore, expressions of baroque piety were, at best, an ambivalent ally of Wittelsbach centralization.

Moreover, if their rulers were successful in justifying the cult of the saints, Bavarians sometimes viewed the saints as more powerful allies than their own rulers, able to intercede on their behalf, protect them from impending catastrophes and heal. Early modern communities were heavily dependent on agricultural production. They regularly invoked saints rather than their rulers to protect them against threats to agrarian fertility and harvest failures resulting from dry spells, hail storms or excessive precipitation and the ever-present danger of warfare and pestilence to people and

---

[129] AEM GR 87, 211.
[130] On the economy of the sacred and the usurpation of salvific power through "sacred performances" (*actiones sacrae*), see Robert Scribner, "Cosmic Order and Daily Life: Sacred and Secular in Pre-Industrial German Society," in: Kaspar von Greyerz (ed.), *Religion and Society in Early Modern Europe 1500–1800* (London, 1984), 17–32.
[131] Ibid., 17–25. On mysticism as a response to political apathy, see Michel de Certeau, *Heterologies. Discourse on the Other* (Minneapolis, 1986), 84.

livestock.[132] Therefore, devotional trends were not simply dictated by the whims of the elite, but were also closely related to conjunctural crises. The most famous regional example of devotion arising from the general crisis of the seventeenth century is the passion play of Oberammergau, an alpine community of Upper Bavaria. The devastation of the Swedish invasion of 1632–1634 reached into the upland communities and, in 1633, communal leaders vowed penance in the form of a passion play, performed in perpetuity each decade in return for deliverance from plague. Legend has it that no further inhabitants died of plague after the vow, still performed today by the community.[133] Similarly, the village community of Bichl near Benediktbeuern commemorated its deliverance from plague in 1634 with an impressive votive painting dedicated to the patrons of plague sufferers, St. Sebastian and St. Rochus.[134] Of course, like Maximilian's pact with the Virgin Mary, vows were contracts and only valid if reciprocal. This was one of the main arguments used against the viability of pacts with the devil. Since the monies or other considerations offered by Satan in the exchange were illusory, Johann Weyer (an opponent of witch trials) held that any pact with the devil was void according to the principles of Roman law as a leonine contract, from which only one party benefited.[135] Similarly, devotees expected saints to help in return for their pledges and held them accountable if wished-for relief was not forthcoming. For example, the Bavarian Mandate against Superstition and Witchcraft of 1612 condemned the popular habit of throwing saints' statues into rivers if the weather was poor on their name day.[136]

---

[132] Or they resorted to illegal magic: Wolfgang Behringer, *Mit dem Feuer vom Leben zum Tod. Hexengesetzgebung in Bayern* (Munich, 1988), 164–191.

[133] Otto Huber, Helmut Klinner and Dorothea Lang, "Die Passionsaufführungen in Oberammergau in 101 Anmerkungen," in: Michael Henker, Eberhard Dünninger and Evamaria Brockhoff (eds.), *Hört, sehet, weint und liebt. Passionsspiele im alpenländischen Raum* (Munich, 1990), 163–180; Gottfried O. Lang, "Die Wechselwirkung wirtschaftlicher und nicht wirtschaftlicher Faktoren im Fortbestand der Oberammergauer Passionsspiele," in: Henker et al., *Hört, sehet, weint und liebt* 203–210; Schalom Ben-Chorin, "Die Polster, das Schwarzbrot und der Antisemitismus. Randbemerkungen zum Oberammergauer Passionsspiel," in: Henker et al., *Hört, sehet, weint und liebt*, 215–220. Saul S. Friedman offers a polemic assault on the internationally renowned passion play and its role in the German anti-Semitic tradition in his *The Oberammergau Passion Play: A Lance against Civilization* (Carbondale, 1984). His charges are moderated somewhat by James Shapiro, *The Troubling Story of the World's Most Famous Passion Play* (New York, 2000). The play still contributes significantly to the local economy despite these criticisms.

[134] According to the parish register of Benediktbeuern, the number of communicants fell from 1,270 in 1634 to 967 in 1635: *Pfarrarchiv Benediktbeuern, Pfarrmatrikel*.

[135] Midelfort, *A History of Madness*, 206–211.

[136] Behringer, *Mit dem Feuer*, 181.

Pilgrimages corresponded closely to the agrarian calendar, often motivated by cyclic as well as conjuncture crises. A tabular comparison of annual rates of pilgrimages with population statistics taken from the local parish registers of Benediktbeuern reveals the contours of a demographic regime analogous to the one discovered in Giessen and its environs for the same period by the Imhof research team.[137] Marriage practices in agrarian communities in the early modern period were conditioned by the schedule of work and by religious prohibitions. Weddings peaked in February (just before Lent), followed by November (after the harvest), June/July (between planting and harvest), and January. December (Advent), March (Lent), April and May (planting), and August to October (preparations for harvest) were the least preferred months for wedlock. Accordingly, conception peaked from early spring to early summer and ebbed as harvest approached, with the consequence that most births occurred during the difficult winter months. Infant mortality was especially high at these times and highest among all age groups from February to April, when hygienic conditions were poor, the weather was cold and winter stores ran low.

Patterns of mortality in the parish registers reflected patterns in pilgrimages reported in the Anastasia miracle book, albeit with allowances for a lag between illness, death, trauma and the fulfilment of a vow; occasionally, pilgrims postponed their journey for several years. Nevertheless, we can speculate on some trends (illustrated below, Table 3.3). The warm summer months May through July ranked highest as times of pilgrimage to Benediktbeuern because this was the best time for travel, particularly for pilgrims crossing the Alpine pass from the Tyrol via Innsbruck and Mittenwald. The peak season in pilgrimage is also attributable to a lull in the agrarian work cycle following spring planting. Emotionally, it manifested a reaction to the suffering, grief and tribulations of the long hard months when illness and mortality took their greatest toll. If autumn harvests were a time for jubilation and winter a time of suffering, summertime provided the occasion for psychological consolation and closure. Visits by women suffering postpartum afflictions (the so-called *Kind-* or *Wochenbett*, as well as traumas resulting from still birth or early infant death[138])

---

[137] *Pfarrarchiv Benediktbeuern, Pfarrmatrikel*; Arthur Imhof (ed.), *Historische Demographie als Sozialgeschichte: Giessen und Umgebung vom 17. zum 19. Jahrhundert* (Darmstadt, 1975), esp. 245–253.

[138] See also MacDonald, "Religion, Social Change," 38, 108–109; Gabriela Signori, "Aggression und Selbstzerstörung. 'Geistesstörungen' und Selbstmordversuche im Spannungsfeld spätmittelalterlicher Geschlechterstereotypen (15. und beginnendes 16. Jahrhundert)," in: Signori

Table 3.3 *Annual cycle of all pilgrimages to Benediktbeuern (rounded to nearest percentage point).*

Winter	Visits (%)	Spring	Visits (%)	Summer	Visits (%)	Fall	Visits (%)
December	3	March	8	May	15	August	8
January	5	April	8	June	15	September	7
February	5			July	13	October	7
						November[a]	7

[a]Demographic data justify the inclusion of November in the autumn harvest season, reflecting the time of relative plenty after the slaughter-feast of St. Martin before the arrival of harsh winter weather near the end of the month.

illustrate the lag between the occurrence of trauma and the attempt to seek help. Winter brought a cruel coincidence of birth and infant mortality rates, which climaxed from January to March, but the twenty-five women who journeyed to Benediktbeuern suffering postpartum afflictions only arrived months later – five in May, four each in June and July and seven in August. Only two came in February and one each in January, October and December respectively over a period of ten years.

Since saints could not perform miracles themselves, devotees needed to negotiate with them to petition with Christ for divine intervention on their behalf. Obviously, as his mother, the Virgin Mary had a particular advantage. The saints procured divine intervention in return for their own accumulated good works, making a withdrawal from their metaphysical savings account at the treasury of merit.[139] The invocation of a saint was binding with a vow to perform a pilgrimage or some other obligation, such as the donation of a votive offering, representing the legal consideration. This and other forms of supernatural contractual negotiations were quite familiar to early modern Europeans, villagers, townsfolk and members of the ruling elite alike – again, witness Maximilian's compact with the Virgin Mary.[140] Thus, the devotional contract mixed early modern metaphors of

(ed.), *Trauer, Verzweiflung und Anfechtung. Selbstmord und Selbstmordversuche in mittelalterlichen und frühneuzeitlichen Gesellschaften* (Tübingen, 1994), 113–148, 141–148; Eva Labouvie, *Andere Umstände. Eine Kulturgeschichte der Geburt* (Vienna, 1998), 176–186.
[139] Jacques Le Goff, *The Birth of Purgatory* (Aldershot, 1984).
[140] Or pacts with the devil. On devotional contracts in early modern Spain, see Christian, *Local Religion*, 23–69. Wolfgang Behringer demonstrates that contractual law played an important role in other cases of supernatural beliefs as well; see his *Shaman of Oberstdorf: Chonrad Stoeckhlin and the Phantoms of the Night*, trans. H. C. Erik Midelfort (Charlottesville, 1998), 12–16. District court records suggest that most Bavarian villagers attended the spectacle of legal justice at some point in their lifetime, either as defendants, aggrieved parties, witnesses or, at the very least, part of the audience at their local

material and legal negotiations. Individuals entered into the same form of contractual relationships with saints as did communities, but for highly personal reasons. The precise title of the handwritten Anastasia miracle book reflected the personal nature of pilgrimage to that shrine: "Index of those Persons, who made a vow to the worthy sanctuary of St. Anastasia or who were themselves there."[141]

Generally, the devotional contract recorded in manuscript miracle books consisted of four essential parts: an invocation, a vow, performance and witnessing. Devotional contracts were initiated when affliction or misfortune motivated devotees to invoke a saint, which could occur virtually anywhere from their own place of residence to the shrine itself. The choice of saint or relic was limited by both special needs and the local availability of knowledge. An invocation proceeded directly into a vow, whereby the devotee negotiated the conditions of intercession – usually a pilgrimage or a votive offering. Martin Kreuz and Anastasia Reiser both recovered immediately after vowing a pilgrimage to Benediktbeuern, which was not uncommon.[142] Vows were taken vicariously on behalf of an incapacitated loved one by spouses, parents or in-laws.[143] Some devotees vowed to sponsor a mass at the St. Anastasia shrine.[144] Appolonia Kreinerin, who suffered swelling over her whole body, pledged to sponsor a mass at Benediktbeuern and recovered.[145] A husband obtained relief for his wife, who had lost her wits, after promising both a pilgrimage and a mass.[146]

Apart from pilgrimages and donations to sponsor masses, devotees commissioned votive offerings, such as the silver cylinder offered at Altötting by Maximilian I. One published hagiography of St. Anastasia refers to woodcarvings, while the manuscript ledger records numerous donations, like the wax chains offered by Wolfgang Raid on his pilgrimage to Benediktbeuern in 1663.[147] Chains symbolized madness, just as the instruments of martyrdom were associated with portrayals of the saints. Pilgrims commonly donated wax chains as votive offerings at both Benediktbeuern and Pürten.

---

courts. They were important local affairs and local courts were overwhelmed with yearly criminal proceedings, property transactions, and proceedings for indebtedness or inheritance disputes. These copious legal records are amazingly rich, thick enough to support a cultural-anthropological study of village life on the scale of David Warren Sabean, *Property, Production, and Family in Neckarhausen, 1700–1870* (Cambridge, 1990). For example, a massive study of economic and social structure is available for one village in Bavaria: Rainer Beck, *Unterfinning. Ländliche Gesellschaft vor Anbruch der Moderne* (Munich, 1993).

[141] AMB, title page: "Verzaichnuß deren Person, die sich zu dem würdigen Hailtumb Anastasiae verlobt oder selbst da sein gewesen."

[142] AMB 570521, 600501. [143] E.g. AMB 600614, 630500, 630809, 631026, 650101, 650923.

[144] In all 103, according to Kramer, "Ein Mirakelbuch," 134. [145] AMB 610306.

[146] AMB 600614. [147] Biechler, *Bayerischer Pharos* (1663), 77; AMB 630514.

Occasional lame pilgrims offered wax feet.[148] Ex-votos, paintings depicting the circumstances of suffering or the intercession of the saint, were popular, but costly. Many still adorn the walls at Bavarian pilgrimage chapels like Altötting or have made their way into the extensive collections of the Bavarian National Museum.[149] Existing votive paintings depicting sufferers of spiritual afflictions (madness, possession, tribulations, etc.) are far fewer than those for other types of physical ailments or material disasters, but they are hardly unknown. The miracle books of Benediktbeuern and Pürten indicate many were donated, but only about a dozen survive in the present community center of Waldkraiburg from the Beata Alta shrine at Pürten (see Plate 11), with a handful from Altötting and even fewer from Benediktbeuern. Votive iconography was generally commissioned and produced locally by craftsmen and furniture painters and then transported to the shrine, as the miracle books suggest.[150] It is unlikely that they were done on site by itinerants, since they required no small investment in labor, time and materials, generally necessitating a commission ahead of time.

Performance of the vow was crucial to the devotional contract. Those pilgrims seeking help at a shrine combined invocation, the vow and performance all in one tidy package. Some sufferers, unable to travel themselves, sent others to fulfill their promises. A woman too ill to make the relatively short journey from Andechs to Benediktbeuern sent a servant in her stead.[151] In 1663, a father went on behalf of his daughter, just as a husband did for his wife in 1665.[152] Since recovery often proceeded "on credit," it was not unusual to postpone performance of pilgrimages or other vows. Ursula Lartin, for example, delayed her pilgrimage because of pregnancy, fulfilling it directly thereafter.[153] Occasionally, pilgrims delayed performance for longer periods, perhaps too long, with unexpected consequences.

After a four-year delay, Paul Mayer fulfilled his vow to undertake a pilgrimage to Benediktbeuern, where he received a stern reprimand for his sloth.[154] The honorable weaponsmith Simon Hasenweg vowed a

---

[148] AMB 660602; PMB 640603. For other examples of wax figures shaped after the afflicted portion of the body, see Böck, *Volksfrömmigkeit*, 49, 94, 174.

[149] Printed catalogs of votive folk art include: Edgar Harvolk, *Votivtafeln* (Munich, 1979); Lenz Kriss-Rettenbeck, *Das Votivbild* (Munich, 1958); Kriss-Retterbeck, *Bilder und Zeichen religiösen Volksglauben* (Munich, 1971); Kriss-Retterbeck, *Ex Voto. Zeichen, Bild, und Abbild im christlichen Votivbrauchtum* (Munich, 1972); William Theopold, *Votivmalerei und Medizin* (Munich, 1981); Theopold, *Mirakel. Heilung zwischen Wissenschaft und Glauben* (Munich, 1983).

[150] Siegfried Seidl, "Der volkstümliche Maler Johann Bapt. Reisbacher sen. in Kollnburg bei Viechtach (Bayer. Wald)," *Bayerisches Jahrbuch für Volkskunde* (1980/1981), 29–30.

[151] AMB 610830.   [152] AMB 631113, 650727.   [153] AMB 600614.

pilgrimage, a pound of wax, a holy mass, as well as attendance at auricular confession and communion all on behalf of his wife, Margaretha, who suffered from tribulations during her pregnancy in 1662.[155] He and two other townsmen finally made the journey in 1665, "with great joy . . . that she might once again get better," since she had fallen into renewed tribulations in the interim. In 1665, a dyer conducted a pilgrimage three years after he invoked Anastasia, but only after he was visited by a dream that his illness would surely return if he failed to keep his promise. A published account in an Anastasia hagiography reported a similar dream-state reprimand delivered to a woman in 1640: "From which we learn only too well that the vows taken should not be put off if we do not wish to infuriate the saints."[156] The author emphasized his warning with another tale of a man who delayed for five years, after which St. Anastasia employed pressure tactics, revisiting him with back pains.[157]

Witnessing concluded the devotional contract. Frequently, parish priests were called upon to testify on behalf of devotees. The parish priest of Wessobrunn accompanied one of his charges to Benediktbeuern to witness an exorcism.[158] The dean of the collegiate church in far-away Speyer sent a written testimonial with a pilgrim to the shrine confirming his miraculous recovery, not an uncommon practice.[159] Other pilgrims arrived with written testimonials recording the performance of exorcisms at other shrines.[160] In one case, a man recovered completely from his spiritual affliction after making a vow to travel to St. Anastasia, a claim witnessed in writing by his entire community.[161] Margaretha Hasenweg's entire town officially witnessed her recovery in writing. Yet other pilgrims arrived with written attestations from their local secular authorities.[162] Witnessing, a common rhetorical device in literature, established credibility.[163]

The truth of the devotional contract lay in the power of the saint to intervene on behalf of any and all that petitioned her. The ultimate authority was the same, whether invoked by Maximilian to legitimize an idealized corporate society or by a humble pilgrim to remedy spiritual afflictions, even if the saints sometimes varied. Saints demanded deference, but remained intimate and influential friends, addressed by all devotees with the familiar "*Du*"-form of the second-person singular.[164] This was the irony behind

---

[154] AMB 610212.   [155] AMB 650527.   [156] Biechler, *Bayerischer Pharos* (1663), 89.
[157] Ibid., 94.   [158] AMB 670307.   [159] AMB 640317; see also 630821, 660929.
[160] AMB 660825, 660825.   [161] AMB 630500.   [162] AMB 650612; PMB 670401.
[163] Compare Greenblatt, *Marvelous Possessions*, 122.
[164] See "Ein Gebett zu der heiligen Martyrin Anastasia" in Biechler, *Bayerischer Pharos* (1663), 107–108.

Plate 11a. Ex-voto, Pürten: district judge, Wolfgang Khaiser, suffered tribulations and was cured by the application of the evangelistary of the Beata Alta, 1660. (Courtesy of the Parish Archive of Pürten; photograph by author.)

Plate 11b. Ex-voto, Pürten: a "certain person" long suffered tribulations, pusillanimity and was confused in the head (*in Köpf verwürth*), but immediately regained her reason and health after using the evangelistary of Beata Alta. The Beata, left, reads from her book. (Courtesy of the Parish Archive of Pürten; photograph by author.)

Plate 11c. Ex-voto, Pürten: Adam Laethner of Lanzing devoted this ex-voto on behalf of his wife, who regained her reason "from day to day" when she slept on the evangelistary. (Courtesy of the Parish Archive of Pürten; photograph by author.)

Plate 11d. Ex-voto, Pürten: Thomas Hüeber, town councilor, burger and rope-maker of Erding, prays for his daughter, who completely lost her reason for fifteen weeks and had tried many other worldly and spiritual remedies, 1728. Note the use of the book as a headrest. (Courtesy of the Parish of Pürten; photo by author.)

post-Tridentine worship; its popularity lent it a subtly subversive quality.[165] Common people discovered they too could contract with the Virgin Mary and the saints. If that proved unsuccessful, early modern Bavarians also knew of other contractual options, such as the devil's pact of Katharina Rieder.

The case history of another demoniac, Anna Puchmayer, deserves special mention here as an apt illustration of the difficulties encountered by early modern authorities in their attempts to control geographic mobility while caring for the mad. Through a careful analysis of disparate official, criminal and ecclesiastical papers, we can reconstruct her movements in detail. Her case demonstrates the lasting psychological effects of the general crisis of the seventeenth century, long after relative stability returned to the region. Anna Puchmayer, a carpenter's daughter, was born near Baierbach during the Thirty Years War and raised in Neufraunhofen, a nearby village south of Landshut in Lower Bavaria (Map 2). Anna returned to Baierbach to marry a local smith, but then the couple moved on to Rottenburg a.d. Laaber, thirty-five kilometers to the north, where their son, Adam, was born. She had long suffered from melancholy and tribulations, but after her husband died in 1657, a spirit had entered her body, a fact she later confided in her daughter, Christina.[166]

In 1664, Anna and her daughter moved to a hostel Munich. Shortly thereafter, Christina resigned her position as a servant to provide full-time care for her mother, who suddenly began to rave uncontrollably. In 1666, Anna and Christina made a pilgrimage to St. Emmeram, a Benedictine monastery in Regensburg, where she underwent initial exorcisms and very nearly committed suicide. From Regensburg, the duo – urged on by the Benedictines of St. Emmeram – traveled to Benediktbeuern, arriving on August 25, 1666.[167] After further exorcisms there, they journeyed to the Benedictine monastery of Ettal for yet more exorcisms.[168] From Ettal, they proceeded to the abbey at Schlehdorf, staying for fourteen days of exorcisms. Anna Puchmayer wintered in Munich, traveling to Freising the following spring. There, her disruptive behavior came to the attention of the Prince Bishop, who took a personal interest in her case. As she was a subject of Bavaria, he ordered an examination of witnesses and the demoniac herself in Munich on June 1, 1667. At one point, Anna suffered a fit, screaming

---

[165] Masterfully demonstrated by Werner Freitag, *Volks- und Elitenfrömmigkeit in der Frühen Neuzeit. Marienwallfahrten im Fürstbistum Münster* (Paderborn, 1991), who uses the example of the sponta-neous renewal of pilgrimage in Westphalia.
[166] BayStaBi Cgm 2620, ff. 120–126, testimony of witnesses, June 1, 1667.
[167] AMB 660825.   [168] BayStBi Cgm 2620, ff. 120–126.

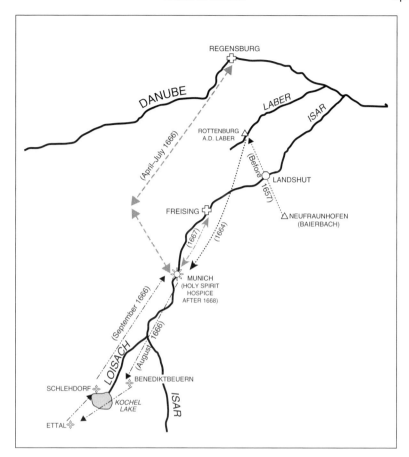

Map 2. The peregrinations of the demoniac Anna Puchmayer, 1657–1667 (by author)

"Phooey, phooey to the soldiers, we have to travel" (perhaps a reference to an experience during the Thirty Years War?) and fell into exhaustion. On June 13, the ecclesiastical authorities remanded her to the care of corporal physicians. After months of written protests, she finally succeeded in having herself committed to a court hospice in Munich, St. Joseph's, on February 11, 1668. On April 19, the Aulic Council had her transferred to the civic hospice of the Holy Spirit; thereafter, she disappears from the records and her ultimate fate is unknown.[169]

---

[169] AEM GR 84, 218, 236, 307, 319–320, 337, 355; HStAM HR 375, 231v; 377, 162r; 378, 76v, 154v–155r; 379, 426r; 380, 236r.

CONCLUSIONS

Travel to cult shrines offered ordinary individuals access to a powerful form of spiritual physic, but the authorities viewed it with increasing mistrust. Both the case of Katharina Rieder devil's pact and that of Anna Puchmayer's saga of pilgrimage suggest the extent to which ordinary Bavarians still viewed mental health in religious terms even after the crises of the early seventeenth century and the devastations of the Thirty Years War passed. Although economic and demographic pressures gradually subsided, psychological horrors remained firmly implanted in the individual and collective consciousness. The populace insured the resilience of the cult of the saints long after the general crisis, thoroughly convinced by the hope of intervention by the special dead.

Simple piety and devotion were surely manifest, but beyond salvific concerns, material adversity dominated in the motivation to travel and seek spiritual physic at cult shrines. With the passing of the general crisis, the afflicted conducted pilgrimages not to unite in a fight against the apocalypse, but rather for mundane personal concerns, the dangers associated with liminal stages of life, cot deaths and infant mortality or other shocks and setbacks. One might suggest that the social pressures on mental health remained largely the same, both during and after the crisis. For most Bavarians, the peregrinational summons resounded a message of hope, which they interpreted to their own advantage. Part of that advantage lies in physical dislocation, an officially sanctioned loophole discovered by ordinary people in the taut net of social discipline. Despite the proliferation of published miracle books, popular transmission poached its own meanings from pilgrimage and religious devotion, which retained a significant oral and informal component focusing on the individual or the communal, rather than the confessional state. Spiritual physic at shrines provided them with psychic comfort and consolation from the moral pressures of everyday society. For communities involved in the provision of care, it also held manifold economic benefits. Specialist shrines provided a major source of local income in a competitive environment. The reputation of shrines, often dispensed by word of mouth, was paramount.

Both cases also demonstrate the increasing antagonism of the authorities toward challenges to public disorder, whether in popular pilgrimage or in public displays of religious madness. For a brief time, pilgrimage had proved politically expedient for the Wittelsbach dynasty. In the years after the Peace of Augsburg (1555), the Dukes patronized shrines to discourage internal heretical infection, threatening the body politic with the potential madness of a religious civil war. They domesticated sacred geography in a policy of centralization. In the case of civic processions, they even succeeded in disciplining some forms of public devotion. In the end, however, their overall successes were measured. The policy of encouraging pilgrimage ended just as ambivalently as attempts to discipline penance and auricular confession. As individual affairs, pilgrimages proved difficult to control, especially in the countryside. Specialist saints remained hugely popular. The geographic mobility inherent in pilgrimage proved an unreliable ally, bringing with it a host of new problems. With the restoration of internal order after the crisis, sufferers might still wander freely to pilgrimage shrines in search of a cure. That is, of course, until they drew the attention of the authorities for causing public disorder, especially in urban centers close to the government, like Freising and Munich. Whereas the popular consciousness continued to embrace religious madness, spiritual physic in its extreme forms became an irritant at court. They embarrassed the authorities and challenged the ability of the absolutist state to enforce order. As in the case of Anna Puchmayer, the ecclesiastes, who increasingly found themselves on the defensive over issues like spiritual physic, joined with the secular authorities to restore order. Nevertheless, mad pilgrims and demoniacs continued successfully to hinder the struggle for public order. Most mad pilgrims fell through the cracks unless their abnormal behavior provoked a public spectacle and they were detected.

Popular notions of spiritual afflictions and religious madness also digressed from authoritative definitions, the latter largely legalistic in their designs. Sufferers, their kin and their neighbors expressed their afflictions in a religious vocabulary expressive of a complex battery of spiritual afflictions. Initially, it had the approbation of the representatives of the state. Sufferers or the loved ones who accompanied them to shrines demonstrated cognizance of symptoms and potential cures in their conscious pursuit of appropriate ecclesiastical remedies. Instead of describing themselves as mad (usually employed as a blanket legal term), they made subtle distinctions between categories of tribulations, melancholy, pusillanimity, despair and demonic possession. Success at pilgrimage shrines for spiritual physic contributed to the proliferation of a common understanding of these distinctions. Many Bavarians identified the origins of their mental maladies in moral and religious terms, just as they had been taught to do and for which they could hardly be held to task by the authorities. Again, initially, the state encouraged spiritual physic as an alternative to the overburdened judiciary. For the populace, the heavenly court held a sympathetic (and fiscal) appeal beyond the scope of the secular judicial machinery. The nosology of spiritual afflictions offered ordinary people manifold alternatives to define themselves and their suffering in the public arena, leaving them yet another ideological space for expression and maneuver.

CHAPTER 4

Spiritual afflictions

I leave aside simple folk, for whom fear sometimes conjures up visions
of their great grandsires rising out of their graves still wrapped in their
shrouds, or else of chimeras, werewolves or goblins . . .

Michel de Montaigne, Essays

A REPRESENTATIVE SAMPLE

The power to name reveals much about a culture, its values and its beliefs.
For example, medical nosology, the systematic naming of illnesses, has
a markedly political dimension.[1] Early modern Europeans expressed the
moral and religious nuances of mental disorders in a rich vocabulary,
describing disequilibria of the soul causing behavioral abnormalities. For
historians and psychiatrists, the temptation to translate these past disorders into familiar terms is intense. Nonetheless, the nosology of spiritual
physic resists simplistic, albeit well-intentioned efforts to unmask demonic
possessions as schizophrenia, melancholy as depression, or all psychiatric
categories as the ultimate tools of repression.[2] If suicidal urges are ubiquitous, only the subjective notion of despair remains fairly common to
most societies. The translation of mood disorders or organic mental disturbances as cognates for past complaints often disintegrates under closer
scrutiny. Nevertheless, the persistence of historians and psychiatrists in their

[1] The relationship between medical nosology and politics, or "noso-politics," in the early modern period,
is considered in Michel Foucault, "The Politics of Health in the Eighteenth Century," in: Foucault,
Power/Knowledge: Selected Interviews and Other Writings, 1972–1977 (New York, 1980), 166–182.
[2] Probably the most famous example of early modern psycho-history is Erik Erikson's *Young Man
Luther* (New York, 1958). The works of Richard Hunter and Ida MacAlpine embody both the benefits
of an interdisciplinary engagement with the history of psychiatry, as well as its potential pitfalls; see
Hunter and MacAlpine (eds.), *Schizophrenia 1677. A Psychiatric Study of an Illustrated Autobiographical
Record of Demoniacal Possession* (London, 1956). The pioneering pair have also edited several impor-
tant collections of source documents: Hunter and MacAlpine (eds.), *Memoirs of my Nervous Illness*
(Cambridge, Mass., 1988); Hunter and MacAlpine (eds.), *Three Hundred Years of Psychiatry 1535–1860*
(London, 1963).

search for useful comparisons is defensible on several grounds, not least of which is heuristic. Certainly, we jump over our own shadow at the peril of anachronism. This was the central failing of nineteenth-century retrospective medicine, a positivist tenet operating under the naturalistic guise of universal knowledge. Nonetheless, alternatively, without some attempt to translate past disorders into a comprehensible form, we equally run the grave risk of antiquarianism. The problem is one of tension: we want to understand past states of psychic disturbance and yet find ourselves limited by our own horizons. However, this need not deter our analysis of early modern psychiatric nosology, since this tension is inherent to all historical endeavors. In fact, rather than posing a discouragement, the tension between past and present provides an intellectual dynamic, a dialectic force constantly driving historical analysis toward novel perspectives. Fortunately we have an ally in historical context. Make no mistake, the analysis of names is no mere taxonomical game. It clarifies social relationships to material and immaterial factors among the people doing the naming.

Admittedly, any attempt to classify early modern mental disorders poses a number of methodological challenges. Europeans recognized a wide variety of mental disorders with meanings contingent upon moral attitudes in an agrarian society. Comparisons with secular morality in an urban and industrialized setting are tenuous. Today, the wonders of psychopharmacology favor biological explanations. However, genetic comparisons between past and present diseases with psychic symptoms are fraught with hermeneutic pitfalls, given the former predominance of an introspective medical paradigm (Galenicism), changes in attitudes toward afflictions such as hypochondria, the gradual elimination of disorders like hysteria from psychiatric vocabulary, and the potential for genetic mutations in diseases, not to mention the veritable extinction of certain maladies, such as St. Vitus' dance.[3] Above all, however, the deepest chasm separating modern and past explanations remains epistemological. In an era "*before* our familiar vision of the division between mind and body – our Cartesian heritage – was articulated,"[4] Europeans explained the relationship of mind and body to society and the universe in structurally different ways. In reference to the sympathetic and antipathetic relationships within and without the soul,

---

[3] Midelfort, *A History of Madness*, 32–49; Julia Schreiner, *Jenseits vom Glück. Suizid, Melancholie und Hypochondrie in deutschsprachigen Texten des späten 18. Jahrhunderts* (Munich, 2003).
[4] Lyndal Roper, *Oedipus and the Devil. Witchcraft, Sexuality and Religion in Early Modern Europe* (London, 1994), 21.

they took a holistic, a hylomorphic view. Our modern preoccupation with the mind/body "problem" was, for contemporaries, less problematic and based on a complex structural relationship between God, humans and the physical universe. Simply put, early modern Europeans deployed a nosology that, over time, has became largely alien.

Methodologically quick-fix solutions are unsatisfactory, born alternately of positivism, biological determinism or apathy. While some historians and psychiatrists psychoanalyze the past in modern terms, others distance themselves from it entirely. Both extremes cheat us of important clues about cultural and social forces at play in the determination of psychic abnormalities. They obscure normative codes, condescend toward popular beliefs and erode our own historical sensibilities. What early modern person could not immediately have recognized a pallid countenance, a solitary demeanor or morbid paraphernalia portrayed in art or literature as definite signs of a melancholic temperament? How often do researchers gloss over literary depictions of tribulations and despair as metaphorical or self-explanatory? In order to understand spiritual afflictions as a component of contemporary mentality, we have to take common complaints as seriously as grave ones.

First and foremost, by extending our vista beyond the narrow confines of madness, melancholy, disease and genetics to embrace the full range of spiritual afflictions, we learn about daily experiences of a wider variety of emotional states and mental disturbances, from the mundane to the radical. Undoubtedly, the language of early modern mental disorders was a legacy of the Judeo-Christian and classical heritage revitalized by the humanist movement. Regional studies of common practices and beliefs also provide building blocks for comparative analyses, pieces of a larger puzzle insoluble through a survey of intellectual discourse alone. As an appropriation of learned opinion, popular perceptions modified them. Popular perceptions also witness a shared vocabulary of spiritual afflictions throughout Europe.[5] Beyond anachronism and antiquarianism, the tension between theory and practice – the very foundation of moral casuistry – reiterates the important function of popular belief, which identified the theoretical relationship of moral norms and the individual soul, but judged that relationship in concrete everyday situations. Once again, context is our ally,

---

[5] In a comparison of spiritual physic between Puritan divines and Napier's ordinary patients, MacDonald, *Mystical Bedlam*, 217, notes, "The Puritan evangelists used language and ideas very similar to those voiced by Napier's troubled clients."

Table 4.1 *Commonly reported afflictions in early modern Bavaria*

Affliction	Pürten[a] (1651–1710)	Benediktbeuern (1657–1668) (female/male)	TOTAL
Tribulations	84	191 (128/63)	275
Mad (loss of reason/sense)	51	94 (46/48)	145
Maleficium	–	111 (67/44)	111
Terror	2	82 (56/26)	84
Evil thoughts	–	68 (43/25)	68
Demonic possession	2	58 (48/10)	60
Corrupt humor	2	54 (20/34)	56
Suicidal temptations[b]	7	48 (26/22)	55
Mad (raving, furious, manic)	4	39 (21/18)	43
Fearful	–	41 (25/16)	41
Melancholy	8	32 (16/16)	40
Confused/deranged	11	25 (7/18)	36
Despair	–	27 (14/13)	27
Agitated	–	14 (6/8)	14
Fever/frenetic	–	13 (8/5)	13
Demonic obsession	–	10 (6/4)	10
Pusillanimous	1	8 (6/2)	9
Headache	–	8 (6/2)	8
Epilepsy/*Frais*	–	7 (2/5)	7
Ghost/specter	–	7 (6/1)	7
Sad	1	4 (2/2)	5
Dejected	–	5 (3/2)	5
Hypochondriac	–	3 (2/1)	3
Total	173	949 (564/385)	1,122

[a] *Gender distinctions are too sporadic to support a breakdown for Pürten*
[b] *Suicidal inclinations*

accessible through the study of individual case histories. Through a comparative analysis of categories employed by other European studies and a contextual examination of specific afflictions in individual case histories, we can overcome many serious obstacles to our understanding of past mental disorders.

Before embarking upon categorization, let us consider the sources at our disposal. Miracle books are one important source of information on spiritual afflictions. For example, Table 4.1, based upon the manuscript miracle books from the Beata Alta shrine at Pürten for the period 1651 to 1710 (173 complaints) and the St. Anastasia shrine at Benediktbeuern for the period 1657 to 1668 (949 complaints), graphically illustrates the types and frequency of afflictions.[6] These 1,122 complaints represent the largest pool of information on mental disorders for early modern Bavaria. The two specialized shrines predominated as the most important regional centers for the ambulatory treatment of spiritual afflictions in a very competitive regional environment; neither Benediktbeuern nor Pürten had Marian or dynastic ties. Although composed independently by several different spiritual physicians over extended periods, the two manuscripts display commonalities. The information recorded in each entry describes the afflictions, date of visit, gender and place of origin of pilgrims on a case-by-case basis. Age, profession and other details are sometimes proffered as well. In the main, pilgrims were commoners. The gender ratio of female to male is immediately striking. At 564/385, women suffered spiritual afflictions more often than men (NB, henceforth all ratios are given as female/male). Most complaints were not directly attributed to demonic agency.

It is difficult to resist the temptation to analyze a uniquely representative sample of evidence statistically and offer generalizations. Statistics never speak for themselves; they are always a matter for interpretation. The historical statistician often attributes meanings with only vague reference to the circumstances of a source's production or its intent. This is especially true when the sources are generated in an age before statistical analysis was common. Once again, we confront a hermeneutic problem and caution is advised. These statistics are not intended in an absolute sense, they merely represent trends, but trends corroborated by other historians and qualitative evidence. As manuscript sources, the data in the miracle books of Benediktbeuern and Pürten are raw, unedited, and were never intended for public consumption in that form. Fortunately, miracle books placed great store in numbers. Custodians at these and other cult shrines collected stories avidly, albeit with partisan intent. For the Anastasia cult, scraps of heavily edited raw data eventually found their way into two hagiographies after a process of deliberate selection and conflation, whereby stories underwent cosmetic improvements. Certainly, printed miracle books utilized sheer numbers to overwhelm skeptics and convince the pious of the competitive value of their shrine. In their original form, however, the manuscript miracle books are remarkably uniform and, unlike the anonymous stories of pilgrims from the subsequent printed versions, the cases in the manuscripts are verifiable through independent corroboration. In conjunction with a variety of other

---

[6] The absolute number of entries differs from the total number of complaints. This is because some pilgrims suffered multiple complaints, while others visited the shrine on more than one occasion, and a fractional minority reported only physical complaints, and as such are not considered here.

primary sources, the manuscripts also facilitate the full reconstitution of several individual case histories.

Statistical analysis frequently raises almost as many questions as it answers. Comparative analysis equips us with an additional interpretive tool of inestimable value, enabling several definitive conclusions. For example, an analysis of published miracle books from shrines not directly devoted to the cure of mental disorders through spiritual physic confirms the gender ratios and ordinal frequency of the spiritual afflictions set out in Table 4.1. The earliest printed miracle books kept at any shrine in Bavaria are those of Our Lady of Altötting from 1495 to 1497. Additional accounts from 1540 and 1623, as well as an inventory of ex-votos donated at Altötting confirm that at least forty-three pilgrims were treated there for spiritual afflictions, both major and minor.[7] To these, we can add the descriptive accounts from the quarterly manuscript protocols of the Bavarian Aulic Council from 1610 to 1679 (more than 350 cases of madness and suicide) and from diverse chronicles, criminal documents and the records of hospices. The qualitative outcome: sufferers, university-trained monks at Benediktbeuern, Andechs and Tun enhausen, the humble rural sextons at Pürten and the secular authorities in Munich all interpreted spiritual afflictions in an analogous and coherent fashion. As for the sufferers themselves, one might debate whether or not their testimonials represent their own complaints or the opinion of the recorders. Here, however, criminal interrogatories and autobiographical accounts corroborate a diagnostic familiarity with the common symptoms of spiritual afflictions, indicating that concepts from Galenic humoral pathology, Aristotelian faculty psychology, moral casuistry and magical explanations for spiritual afflictions played a formative role in contemporary perceptions. Ultimately, the claims made here are based upon a pool of evidence conservatively estimated at 1,500 cases.

Comparisons are available in the secondary literature, which is mounting. H. C. Erik Midelfort has quantified a number of printed miracle books, and these bear closer scrutiny. His analysis of a 1644 printed miracle book

---

[7] For Altötting, several edited miracle books and articles by Robert Bauer, a curator of the shrine, provide specific primary information: Bauer, "Das älteste gedruckte Mirakelbüchlein von Altötting," *Ostbairische Grenzmarken. Passauer Jahrbuch für Geschichte, Kunst und Volkskunde* 5 (1961), 144–151; Bauer, "Das Büchlein der Zuflucht zu Maria. Altöttinger Mirakelberichte von Jacobus Issickemer," *Ostbairische Grenzmarken. Passauer Jahrbuch für Geschichte, Kunst und Volkskunde* 7 (1964/1965), 206–236; Bauer, "Die Altöttinger Votivtaferl," *Ostbairische Grenzmarken. Passauer Jahrbuch für Geschichte, Kunst und Volkskunde* 13 (1971), 176–183; Bauer, "P. Johannes Saller SJ– Das ausgegraben Oeting. Die Mirakelberichte 1623," *Ostbairische Grenzmarken. Passauer Jahrbuch für Geschichte, Kunst und Volkskunde* 35 (1993), 54–108.

from Altötting limited to dramatic afflictions (in particular, madness, suicidal tendencies and demonic possessions) identifies fifty-six complaints.[8] A Tuntenhausen miracle book published in 1646 (condensing the years from 1588 to 1645) adds another fifty-three cases of madness, temptations to suicide and demonic possession.[9] However, based on a more comprehensive survey of annual miracle books from Tuntenhausen tracking the previous years 1527–1589, Midelfort emphasizes that only fifty-six cases of madness and demonic possession are found among a total of 800 miracles (i.e. 7 percent of the total case-load).[10] All told, his analysis of the non-specialist Marian shrines Tuntenhausen and Altötting suggest that only 8 percent of the total cases concerned madness; shrines such as St. Salvator of Bettbrunn and St. Leonard of Inchenhofen[11] drew some 10 percent of their pilgrims from among the mad. Therefore, at non-specialist shrines, the relative volume of mad pilgrims remained low. In comparison, the case-load at the two specialized shrines of Pürten and Benediktbeuern was limited, with a few rare exceptions, to spiritual afflictions. Occasionally, the records show that pilgrims visited both specialist and non-specialist shrines. However, in absolute terms, most Bavarians continued to turn to specialist saints for treatment of spiritual afflictions.

Among cases of spiritual afflictions, indications of direct involvement of the devil were even slighter. A little over 15 percent of the Tuntenhausen and Altötting cases of madness involved the devil, with only a handful of outright demonic possessions. For the later period (1588–1645), the miracle books of Tuntenhausen identify only seven cases of possession out of fifty-three mad persons (less than 8 percent).[12] At 31 percent of the total case-load, incidences of demonic involvement were much higher at Benediktbeuern – 111 cases of maleficium, 68 of evil thoughts, 48 temptations to suicide, 10 obsessions and 58 cases of demonic possession. Nevertheless, the records of Benediktbeuern and Pürten only mollify Midelfort's claim that "the vast majority of madnesses reported in the sixteenth century . . . did not involve any supposed demonic attack."[13] At Benediktbeuern, which dealt exclusively with spiritual afflictions, almost 70 percent of spiritual afflictions had nothing directly to do with the devil; at Pürten, 95 percent of spiritual afflictions were non-demonic. The evidence is conclusive. The vast majority of spiritual afflictions in early modern Central Europe were not directly

---

[8] Midelfort, *A History of Madness*, 319; based on Jacob Irsing, SJ, *Historia von der weitberühmten lieben Frawen Capell zu Alten-Oeting in Nidern Bayern* (Munich, 1644).

[9] *Denkwürdige Miracula*, 14–19. For a quantification, see Midelfort, *A History of Madness*, 315.

[10] Ibid., 309, examined nineteen different printed miracle books from Tuntenhausen for the years 1527–1589.

[11] Ibid., 316–317.   [12] Ibid., 315.   [13] Ibid.

connected with the devil. Further, dramatic afflictions like madness and melancholy were far less pervasive than one might expect. Mundane afflictions were far more pervasive, but considered serious enough to motivate a pilgrimage.

Gabriela Signori's list of spiritual afflictions based on nine Central European miracle books from the late fifteenth to the early sixteenth century is also instructive.[14] From approximately 3,000 entries, only 173 cases of spiritual afflictions were reported (less than 6 percent), verifying Midelfort's percentages of mad pilgrims visiting shrines with non-specific attributes. Again, women and girls predominated over men and boys (95/74, four indefinite "children"). Signori's statistics distinguish two sub-categories for 78 of the 173 afflictions: demonic possession (30/14) and ten varieties of affective/mood disorders (27/7). Again, however, demonic possessions (44) make up only about one-quarter of all spiritual afflictions (173); if one includes a further 12 persons suffering suicidal tendencies, a condition usually associated with the devil, then only about 29 percent of all afflictions she reports were linked directly to demonic agency. This figure, closer to the 31 percent of demonic afflictions from Benediktbeuern, is still far from a majority. Once again, women predominate, demonic agency is hardly dominant and the volume of spiritual afflictions at non-specialist shrines (173 out of 3,000) pales in comparison with the absolute numbers at Benediktbeurn and Pürten, a further testimony to their popularity.

Michael MacDonald's analysis of Sir Richard Napier's 767 English patients from manuscript practice notes (1598–1634) remains, by far, the most compatible pool of evidence for comparison. Napier's practice too was specialized on spiritual afflictions. Thus, it affords grounds for not only thematic, but also European comparison. MacDonald details afflictions by symptoms and stress factors, as well as frequency and gender.[15] As noted below, the present representative sample of 1,500 cases from Bavaria compares favorably, both qualitatively and quantitatively, with his. For categorical definitions, we can also refer to the eighteenth-century *Universal Lexicon* edited by the Protestant encyclopedist of Saxony, Johann Heinrich Zedler. Despite the confessional divide, there are striking similarities. The popular medical treatise of Hippolyt Guarinonius is also instructive as a reference manual. For Italy, parallels can be drawn from the work of Giovanni Levi, who analyzed the notes of the Piedmontese exorcist Giovanni Battisti

---

[14] Signori, "Aggression," 126, 140.
[15] Compare the categories given below with the symptoms described in the study of Napier's casebooks in MacDonald, *Mystical Bedlam*, 112–148, as well as his statistical breakdown, 238–251.

Chiesa.[16] In France and the Netherlands, rare, but similar complaints have been traced to dozens of late medieval pilgrimage sites by Henri Beek.[17] All of the aforementioned works display pronounced qualitative similarities to Bavarian sources in their application of psychopathological nosology, indicating a basic uniformity in perceptions of spiritual afflictions throughout Western Europe.

Historians categorize early modern illnesses in different ways. David Gentilcore recognizes three categories of illnesses delineated by the purview of the healer: popular, medical and ecclesiastical, the latter being the focus of our present concern.[18] Levi, on the other hand, employs an etiological dichotomy that differentiates between personalistic and naturalistic causes of sickness:

> If by a personalistic system we mean a culture in which people believe that sickness may be the effect of the intervention of a conscious agent (divine, supernatural, or human), acting with varying degrees of energy and purpose, the sick person will be seen as the object of aggression (occasionally of self-aggression) and punishment aimed at him as an individual. Thus these systems are concerned not only with the how of his illness but also with who is sick and why. In naturalistic systems, on the other hand, illness is explained in impersonal terms, as if the physical elements that make up the body come to be found in a situation of disorder or disturbed equilibrium, and the cause of this disturbance could be fully explained in natural terms.[19]

For Levi, the category of mental disorder is secondary to material circumstances and social relations. Bavarians too expressed spiritual afflictions in personalistic as well as naturalistic terms. All manner of suffering, even outbreaks of plague, were attributed to immoral behavior, as the Inaugural General Mandate of Maximilian I suggests. In practice, spiritual physicians dealt with both physical complaints and imbalances of the soul. Pilgrimage shrines treated all manner of ailments, from broken bones to epilepsy. However, our present attention is limited to purely mental disorders, broken down here into six basic categories.[20] These six categories include:

---

[16] Levi, *Inheriting Power*, 1–28.
[17] Henri Hubert Beek, *De Geestesgestoorde in de Middeleeuwen. Beeld en Bemoeienis* (Haarlem, 1969), 184–186.
[18] Gentilcore, *Healers*, 3.   [19] Levi, *Inheriting Power*, 20–22.
[20] In his statistical appendices, MacDonald, *Mystical Bedlam*, 242–245, conflates symptoms with disorders, complicating their definitive assignment to the specific categories employed here. I have conservatively assigned the disorders to these categories only when they correspond closely to the descriptions provided in Bavarian sources, choosing to err on the side of caution and therefore excluding some symptoms from his list. Our categories correspond as follows; madness = mad, lunatic, mania, frenzy, raging, furious, senseless (399 complaints); fear, terror and shocks during and

1 Madness
2 Somatic disorders (humoral disorders, fevers and plagues)
3 Fear, terror and shocks and pregnancy
4 Affective disorders
5 Evil thoughts, demonic temptations and despair
6 Obsession and possession.

AFFECTS AND AFFECTIONS

1   Madness

Historians grant madness pride of place if for no other reason than its usefulness as a collective headline for all pre-modern mental disorders. The
collective term has, however, overshadowed other pervasive complaints,
causing misunderstandings and distortions. This is especially true of vari-
ations between legal, medical, theological and popular explanations. Madness is a contentious term and did not hold the same "useful, untechnical
vagueness" for early modern Europeans as it does for us.[21] Contemporaries applied it judiciously under specific and recognizable parameters.
In Bavaria, for example, the authorities applied the terms senseless (*sinnlos*), nonsensical (*unsinnig*) or robbed of their senses (*ihre Sinnen beraubt*)
or slipped from reason (*vom Verstand verrückt*)[22] in a largely legalistic
fashion to describe what we in English might refer to as raving madness or what contemporaries also referred to as mania. Sufferers came to
the attention of the authorities because they posed an immanent danger
to society through potentially destructive behavior, or because sufferers
endangered themselves or were victimized by others. First and foremost,
madness implied a potential for violence. The general association of madness with mania (*Raserei*) was a standard legal category, used by jurists
to describe persons "out of their senses." Persons described as mad faced
special social controls. Traditional historiography is often based on legal
documentation. For that reason, perhaps more than any other, the juridical

after pregnancy = took fright, terrifying dream (225 complaints); affective disorders = melancholy,
mopish, troubled in mind (1,526 complaints); evil thoughts, demonic temptations and despair =
tempted to kill self, just "tempted," tempted to despair, evil thought, despair (440 complaints). Elsewhere (199), MacDonald, *Mystical Bedlam*, indicates that 264 patients suspected harmful witchcraft
as the cause of mental disturbance, while another 148 persons "who suffered psychological symptoms
were believed to be haunted or possessed." It should be noted that the numbers he offers for each
symptom refer to complaints; most of Napier's 767 clients entertained more than one complaint.
[21] Midelfort, *Mad Princes*, 3.   [22] The original meaning of today's usage for "*verrückt*."

usage explains the wholesale adoption of "madness" as a category by some historians.[23]

The legal identification of individuals as mad connoted immanent danger. Of all spiritual afflictions, it was primarily a concern for legal authorities. Therefore, it should come as no surprise that the vast majority of non-suicidal mental disorders dealt with by the Aulic Council, the central high court of Bavaria, fell under the rubric of madness (*Sinnlos* or *Unsinnig*). Arguably, the inclusion of these cases from the Aulic Council can skew statistics in three significant ways. First, the jurists of the Aulic Council grossly underrepresented other disorders in their deliberations. Second, even when the Aulic Council identified other afflictions, they were often subsumed under madness to lend them a recognized legal stature. By placing sufferers under a standard legal heading, the authorities addressed a potential threat to life, limb and property. Ironically, a sincere, if paternalistic concern to protect otherwise harmless subjects from degradation and abuse at the hands of relatives and neighbors often resulted in legal action to rob sufferes of their majority. Third, men clearly predominated (29/64) in the Aulic Council protocols on madness, probably as a function of their legal status. However, even when legal action did not involve conflicts over property, the disposition of the sufferer and the adjudication of responsibility for care were a tantamount concern. Madwomen proved just as dangerous as madmen, but they appeared far more often in the records of non-legal sources since the *pater familias* assumed immediate legal responsibility for their care. For example, 145 senseless persons were treated for madness at the shrines in Pürten and Benediktbeuern, with an additional 43 descriptions of mania, ranking madness as the second most common category of affliction. Nonetheless, the ratio of women to men was nearly equal (67/66) at the shrines, while, among Napier's English patients, women predominated at his private practice by a significant margin (235/164). Therefore, the type of historical document used to analyze a specific ailment heavily influences quantitative analysis, making it essential to understand the circumstances of a source's production.

Madness implied a lack of reason. As late as the eighteenth century, Zedler still defined madness (*Unsinnigkeit*) as "nothing other than the

---

[23] This is certainly the case with R. A. Houston's *Madness and Society in Eighteenth-Century Scotland* (Oxford, 2000). As Houston points out, his principal sources for a social history of madness in Scotland are legal and first become available in the late seventeenth century. Despite this limitation, Houston employs legal sources in a number of innovative ways and is able to identify many popular "colloquialisms" (331–355) used to identify degrees of madness.

highest degree of mania, but never that connected to a fever."[24] According
to his *Universal Encyclopedia*, the senselessly mad uttered foolishness, were
constantly restless, averse to hunger and cold, displayed the terrible strength
of many, shredded clothes and bedding, and wandered about naked (a sure
sign of their uncivilized animal nature), entertaining wicked, scandalous
and murderous intentions. While some mad persons developed melancholy
as a consequence of mania, melancholics were not automatically mad. Possession of reason and common sense, indications of the presence of the
intellective faculty of the soul, were an essential human trait. Possession of
reason intimated the acquired accoutrements of civilized society necessary
to participate in material and social exchanges and to achieve full majority.
In contrast, the lack, loss or theft of one's reason or sense reduced people to a
wild-natured state akin to the beasts, as stated in indirect references to Aristotelian faculty psychology.[25] Dehumanizing traits attributed to pilgrims
robbed of their senses illustrate these perceptions. Georg Heusel's fourteen-
year-old daughter lost her senses, threw off her clothes and went into the
woods to live with the animals before a pilgrimage to Altötting in 1497.
Other pilgrims had literally taken to the forests, foraging for subsistence
and living like wild animals.[26] They shed their clothing and walked about
naked.[27] Catharina Penz arrived at Benediktbeuern bound and chained
with her hair flying in the wind and barefoot, reminiscent of an image on a
votive painting contributed by a madwoman at Altötting.[28] Anna Wider-
mann, who slept on a pile of manure, was "in very awful shape."[29] The
mad emitted terrible onomatopoeic screams compared to the bellowing of
calves or oxen and wrestled about like livestock.[30] The cowherd Michael
Habt, brought to the Anastasia shrine in the hope of a cure, "died like an
animal in the stables."[31] The Aristotelian imagery of a mad person reduced
to the animal faculty was especially accessible to a society in daily contact with farm animals and dependent upon husbandry for subsistence. By
equating the lack of reason or sense with creatures regarded as less than
human, communities reacted within logical boundaries of experience to

[24] Zedler, *Universal-Lexikon* (hereafter Zedler) vol. XLIX, 2046–2047; see also "*Raserey*," in ibid., vol.
XXX, 899–903.
[25] Houston, *Madness*, 202–208; on the metaphor of the "wildman" as madman in the Middle Ages, see
Beek, *De Geestesgestoorde*, 19–23.
[26] Bauer, "P. Johannes Saller," 90; AMB 620303, 620415, 660814.
[27] ABM 620415, 640506, 650819.
[28] ". . . sovil gebundten, eben die hendt mit strikhen gebundten, daß haar ganz fliegendt im Lufft,
paarfiessig auch noch dazrue schon lange Zeit an einer köten gelegen": AMB 651121. The ex-voto
from Altötting also adorns the dust cover of Midelfort, *A History of Madness*.
[29] ". . . gar Übl bestelt . . .": AMB 650620.   [30] ABM 620811, 640501, 650611, 650815.
[31] ". . . wie ein Vieh im Stall gestorben . . .": AMB 620418.

those unpredictable persons unable to contribute to village life and who endangered their precarious existence. Bestialization was part and parcel of popular attitudes toward mental health. Europeans also denigrated the corpses of suicides to the level of beasts, ritually denying them every aspect of human dignity.[32] In a traditional society, going over the edge of reason literally robbed a person of human status and placed them beyond the bounds of common sense.

Admittedly, some mad persons undoubtedly exhibited dangerous behavior. The potential for suicide or self-mutilation represented a direct threat to the sufferers themselves, confronting communities with heavy emotional, material and metaphysical burdens. Maria Blauenschmidt became so rebellious after she gave birth that she chopped off a finger and presented it to her husband amidst her ravings.[33] Then there was the danger to other persons, especially children, as well as to private property and the community at large. When Jörg Lästrider's wife went mad, she threatened to kill her two infants.[34] Seventeen-year-old Barbara Lauß physically assaulted children in her village.[35] A woman known only as "mad Maria" was imprisoned for her dangerous behavior. In a sad twist of events, she lost custody of her own child (whom she kept with her in her cell) after she was accused of fornicating with her jailers.[36] Mad Matheus Diechtel injured seventy-year-old Wolf Reitter so badly on his way home from Vohburg that he died shortly thereafter.[37] The danger of fire was a paramount concern.[38] Anna Buecher ran from house to house in her senselessness with the expressed intent of burning her village to the ground. Wolf Veith's mad wife threatened her entire community with conflagration.[39] The Aulic Council specifically ordered Georg Lehner to take his brother into custody in order to protect the community from fire or other vague dangers.[40] Some mad persons were utterly harmless, like the senseless smith deluded by "great fantasies of buying and selling."[41] However, raving persons were reputed to possess

---

[32] Lieven Vandekerckhove, *On Punishment. The Confrontation of Suicide in Old Europe* (Leuven, 2000), 43–47.
[33] AMB 600815.
[34] The votive painting celebrating her recovery still hangs at the Chapel of Our Lady at Altötting and is reprinted in Philipp Halm, "Die Mirakelbilder zu Altöting," *Bayerischer Heimatschutz* (1925), 1–27. See also fn. 28 above.
[35] AMB 650523.   [36] HStAM HR 352, 111v, 179v.   [37] HStAM HR 159, 197r–v.
[38] On the fear of arson, see Robert Scribner, "The Mordbrenner Fear in Sixteenth-Century Germany: Political Paranoia or the Revenge of the Outcast?," in: Richard J. Evans (eds.), *The German Underworld: Essays in the Social History of Crime in German from the Sixteenth Century to the Present* (London, 1988), 29–56
[39] AMB 650605; HStAM HR 333, 270r–v.   [40] HStAM HR 283, 279v–280r.
[41] PMB 790604: symptoms of *Wahnwitz*, see Zedler, 467–468.

incredible strength and endurance, capable of withstanding temperature extremes with impunity.[42] The escape of the mad peasant Jacob Deiniger, restrained with iron bands in his jail cell in Starnberg, rightly astonished the Aulic Council in Munich, which called for an immediate manhunt and a full investigation.[43] In 1604, the town council's spies in Munich confirmed that a traveling noblewoman suffered terrible fits, during which "twenty, even thirty men were burdened to restrain her."[44] She had refused a marriage proposal and fallen victim to a love potion; for years, she had wandered in search of a cure. Raving individuals, both men and women, often taxed the strength of two or more large men attempting to restrain them at the Anastasia shrine.[45] For example, in 1665, Anna Leiner arrived at Benediktbeuern from the territorial university town, Ingolstadt: "locked up at home for half a year, [she] raged terribly here . . . showing herself so strong, that [she] dragged two rude and strong men around like a beast of burden, giving the appearance, as if she were possessed. It was said that a student had enchanted her."[46]

Madness, a potent social symbol, implied the loss of humanity as well as legal majority. However, by conflating all other afflictions into one, by confining our attention to cases of outright mania, we ignore the vast majority of spiritual afflictions and trivialize them. In purely functionalist terms, even minor spiritual afflictions disrupted orderly communal relations and were a cause for local, if not legal concern.

2 Somatic afflictions

If madness, as a legal category, has come to the attention of historians who study legal sources, historians of medicine and psychiatry are quicker to acknowledge physical illnesses affecting the mind. Again, this is partially a product of their traditional choice of sources. Diseases particularly interest protagonists of the theory of mental disorders as essentially biological.[47] Physical afflictions also provide a home playing field for champions of retrospective medicine, since their apparent objective status is suited to positivist interpretations of academic psychiatry as the victory of empirical medicine

---

[42] Ibid., vol. xxx, 899–903; vol. xlix, 2046–2048.   [43] HStAM HR 334, 468r–v.
[44] HStAM GR F. 1190.   [45] AMB 620418, 660825, 670331.
[46] ". . . zu haus ein halbes Jahr eingespert gewesen, alhie grausam gewietet . . . also starckh sich erzaiget, daß zwei grobe und starckhe Menner hin und her geschlaipft wie ein vich, Es hatt daß Ansechen gehabt, als wan sie besessen were. Sie ist von einen Studenten, wie man gesagt hat, verzaubert worden": AMB 650518.
[47] This is the working premise of Edward Shorter's *A History of Psychiatry. From the Era of the Asylum to the Age of Prozac* (New York, 1997).

over superstition. In Bavaria, somatic afflictions involved complaints of humoral corruptions and diseases.[48] Four specific types are mentioned in legal, medical and religious sources: non-specific humoral corruptions; the falling sicknesses of *Frais* and epilepsy; the Hungarian fever and other plague-related fevers; and chronic headaches. In total, somatic afflictions represented a far smaller proportion of the sample than madness. At eighty-four, illnesses actually ranked last among all complaints registered at the two cult shrines, probably because somatic illness fell clearly within the purview of corporal medicine. Obviously, practitioners of spiritual physic held that they too could cure physical complaints, but ordinary people might view it as a treatment of last resort, when all else failed or the sufferer lacked the means to consult a university-trained physician. Significantly, somatic afflictions are the only category of complaint at the Anastasia shrine suffered less often by women than men (36/46). Like madness, which had a legal basis, physical illness supplied a medical rather than moral explanation for male mental deviance.

Humoral corruptions were the most common form of somatic complaint. A gender ratio of 20/34 at the Anastasia shrine confirms contemporaries ascribed humoral corruption to women less often than men. Since moral and demonic explanations predominated at pilgrimage shrines, the custodians infrequently attributed spiritual afflictions to humoral imbalance. Humoral sufferers probably opted for corporal medicine in this case. Nevertheless, the implication that women displayed a higher incidence of moral corruption is borne out there as well. Galenism underscored the influence of temperament upon a person's emotional state. Apart from the legal criteria for madness, the Munich Aulic Council also emphasized humoral pathology in its examinations, connoting the influence of university medicine at court. And, once again, men predominated in judicial accounts of humoral afflictions.

Falling sicknesses included epilepsy[49] and the *Frais*, a regional term for a convulsive childhood illness.[50] The contemporary definition of epilepsy closely matches our own understanding, or, perhaps better, has shaped it. A physical affliction rarely mentioned at the cult shrines, epilepsy also affected fewer females than males (2/5). Fits might strike repeatedly during the course of the day and persist for years, though contemporaries did not necessarily view the condition as chronic.[51] A peddler from Traunstein arrived at Benediktbeuern complaining of the *Frais*, which he blamed

[48] Matejovski, *Das Motiv des Wahnsinns*, 60. [49] Ibid., 55–60. Zedler, vol. VIII, 1341–1405.
[50] Johann Andreas Schmeller, *Bayerisches Wörterbuch*, vol. 1 (Munich, 1872–1877; facsimile reprint, 1985), 826.

on witchcraft, but reportedly recovered from his convulsive fits after the visit.[52]

Of the fevers, two types, the Hungarian or camp fever[53] and plague-related fevers (*Phrenitis* or *Hirnwütten in hitzigen Fiebern*),[54] greatly concerned the Aulic Council because of the danger of contagion. Surprisingly, given the military origins of this somatic affliction, women predominated slightly as sufferers of fever-related afflictions (8/5), especially the Hungarian fever (6/2). The Augsburg practitioner Raymund Minderer, personal physician to Maximilian I, traced the *Hungarica Febris* (*Febris castrensis, Teutsch feldfieber, Soldatenfieber*) to an initial outbreak in Hungary among imperial troops fighting the Ottomans. Later, soldiers transmitted the disease to the civilian population upon their return to Germany.[55] Minderer identified certain circumstances conducive to the spread of the disease: wet summers (a characteristic of the Little Ice Age), a disorderly life-style (e.g. a military encampment), foul water, or air contaminated by *Totendampf*, the miasma emitted in close proximity to graveyards or through contact with garments stolen from the dead on battlefields. In its terminal stages, chronic symptoms included delirium and madness, as the infected tossed about violently uttering gibberish and suffering fantasies until they became suicidal and had to be restrained to prevent them from "throwing themselves out a window or jumping into a body of water or injuring themselves with some weapon."[56] In other words, a phrenetic raving person posed a greater threat to the self than to others, distinguishing fevers from madness. Corporal physicians recommended a sweating cure, while spiritual physic at pilgrimage shrines helped others, but most were beyond hope.[57] The Hungarian fever caused sleeplessness, severe nosebleeds and had dangerous side-effects like the *Frais*. Agatha Kheull suffered a serious bout of Hungarian fever and subsequently evil and suicidal thoughts vexed her. However, suicidal behavior attributed directly to fevers was considered unintentional (*non compos mentis*), as in the case of Maria Schuester, who suffered so severely that she "unknowingly sprang into a deep well."[58] Chronic headaches or

[51] AMB 650112, 680408.   [52] AMB 650101.   [53] Zedler, vol. XIII, 1223–1224.
[54] Ibid., 195–196.
[55] The Hungarian fever is detailed in Raymund Minderer, *Consilium oder Räthliches Gutachten. Die jetzt schwebende/ und under den Soldaten mehrertheils grassirende Sucht betreffendt* (n.l., 1620); see also Zedler, vol. XIII, 1223–1227. Hans Zinsser identifies the Hungarian disease as typhus: *Rats, Lice and History. A Study in Biography* (New York, 1934), 268–269.
[56] Minderer, *Consilium*, 8–9; for an example, see the *Miracula und Wunderzaichen . . . zu Tundenhausen*, 14–15.
[57] AMB 580426, 580630, 680531.   [58] AMB 660911.

madness completely robbed sufferers of their reason or senses, driving them to fits of mania.[59] Relatively few persons complained of hypochondria. A psychic infirmity with physical origins, it resulted from prolonged physical inactivity, such as sitting at work. The compression of the stomach caused the spleen to secrete acids, which formed a waxy material after coming into contact with phlegm. The material congealed and blocked circulation. Untreated, hypochondria could lead to serious complications, such as *melancholia hypochondriaca*, though in practice, sources do not report a single case.[60] Hypochondriacs fantasized or complained of physical ailments with no apparent foundation, an element of hypochondria retained by modern medicine. The hypochondriac Hans Obehauser complained he no longer had a stomach, lung or liver, but recovered all three after several days at the Anastasia shrine.[61] Margaretha Grözl suffered recurring bouts of hypochondria.[62] The affliction was serious enough for the Ecclesiastical Council in the neighboring Bishopric of Freising to excuse the administrative lethargy of the parish priest of Ried before the district judge of Wasserburg on account of "*effectu hypocondriaco*" in 1670.[63]

3 Fear, terror and shocks and pregnancy

One hundred and twenty-five persons complained of fears and terrors. At the Anastasia shrine, women predominated by a ratio of nearly two to one (81/42); Napier's English patients displayed an even higher gender ratio of three to one (120/43); Signori's figures are exclusively female (8/0). Hippolyt Guarinonius dedicated a whole chapter of his household medical encyclopedia to fear and terror. As he explained, both ultimately arose from an instinctive desire for self-preservation and an innate repugnance to death (including the fear of ghosts at night). Further, the Tyrolean physician extended his discussion to include fear of material loss or terror at natural phenomena, e.g. thunder or lightning.[64] Custodians at the shrines described individuals afflicted with fears as timorous (*furchtsam, timorata/us*), timid (*ängstlich, timida/us*) or terrified (*erschreckt, territa/us*).

---

[59] Anon., *Denkwürdige Miracula*, 14.   [60] Kutzer, *Anatomie*, 105–111   [61] AMB 650413.
[62] AMB 570518.
[63] AEM GR 87, 178r. Stefan Breit, a historian at the Bavarian State Archives, recounted to me the case of a court scribe in Munich who excused an absence from work in writing, claiming a bout of hypochondria. Cases like these contributed to the growing disrepute of this somatic affliction. On the eighteenth-century discourse of hypochondria, see Schreiner, *Jenseits vom Glück, passim*.
[64] Guarinonius, *Die Grewel*, 304–311. See also David Gentilcore, "The Fear of Disease and the Disease of Fear," in: William Naphy and Penny Roberts (eds.), *Fear in Early Modern Society* (Manchester, 1997), 184–208.

Fear (a chronic condition of anxiety) originated when the free will fixed upon a particular object.[65] Sufferers like Agatha Neumayer complained of restlessness and insomnia. She journeyed to Benediktbeuern out of great fear, which gave her no respite in the home.[66] Late medieval and early modern Europeans were quite literally afraid of the dark.[67] Fear overcame at least fourteen persons at night. Mathias Wolf from Kochel fell into a great nocturnal fear followed by the apparition of St. Anastasia.[68] He visited the shrine immediately thereafter and recovered from all his fears. Fear prevented Maria Bernhardt from sleeping peacefully unless a candle burned by her side the whole night through.[69] A wheelwright accompanied his young son to Benediktbeuern after he fell into a state of unrelenting fear following a shameful fit of screaming in the night.[70] Christoph Holzhauser, who thought he saw something in the night, was afraid to get out of bed.[71] A miller from the district of Mindelheim refused to say a prayer before retiring one evening. Relations found him half an hour later hiding under his bed and completely crazed with fear.[72] For the custodian at the Anastasia shrine, it seemed unusual and highly noteworthy that fear struck Eva Hohenleitner in broad daylight.[73]

Fear connoted apprehensions about a particular threat. Some feared persecution by witches. One local claimed witches plagued him. The thought froze him with fear and made him unfit to travel to the shrine from a neighboring village. He had a mass read to St. Anastasia on his behalf in absentia.[74] Hans Grudl, a farmhand, arrived at Benediktbeuern in a state of restlessness accompanied by his father, fearing that evil people sought to

---

[65] In Zedler vol. IX, 2324–2326, there arises debate over fear as an affective disorder: "Daß es ein Adfect sey, ist daher zu beweisen, weil allezeit bey der Furcht eine Bewegung in den Willen vorgehet, die auf ein künfftig anzuschertdes Objectum zielet."

[66] AMB 610824: "wegen grosser Forcht . . . allweil sie khain bleibende Statt in Haus gehabt . . ."

[67] As Jean Delumeau points out in *Fear in the West* (New York, 1989); see also Gentilcore, "The Fear of Disease." On a fifteenth-century sufferer from Nuremberg, see Bauer "Das Büchlein," 125. The Jesuit exorcist Petrus Thyraeus, *Daemoniaci*, considered the dangers of nocturnal terror at length in an appendix, "Libellus De Terrificationibus Nocturnis," 326–352.

[68] AMB 641222: "in der Nacht ein grose Forcht ankhomen, so ist ihme erschinen S. Anastasia . . ."

[69] AMB 620809: "lange Zeit kheinen Schlaf khinen haben, und von wegen grosser Forcht die ganze nacht ein liecht hat brenen miessen . . ."

[70] AMB 641004: "das er gar schändlich habe aufgeschrieen in der Nacht, und hat ihn vast geforchtet . . ."

[71] AMB 680606: "vermeint hat, er sehe etwas, und ist ihm ein soliche Forcht ankhommen, das er ihm nit aus dem Bött heraus gethrauet . . ."

[72] AMB 670117.

[73] AMB 640116: "ist ihr etwas umb S. Andreas Tag ankhomen mit einer Forcht bei lichten Tag, das sie hernach khein ruche noch frid khinen haben . . ."

[74] AMB 650112: "er furcht gar sehr die Hexen und sezen ihm gar starck zu das er nit fahren khont, last ein H. Meß lesen."

do him harm by poisoning his food or drink.[75] Many victims of witchcraft displayed symptoms of possession, others spat forth the tools of *malefi-cium* (e.g. bloody hairballs, pins or needles, straw, etc.) during exorcisms, another claimed to have evacuated frogs along with blood during her men-struation, while several others found magical charms planted around their homes or in their beds.[76] Still others feared conditions threatening their health or spiritual well being. Although Martin Stobel recovered from a bout of corruption, the fear it might return oppressed him.[77]

Sufferers attributed terror, an intensified manifestation of fear, to a one-time incident of a threatening nature, a horrifying emotional experience or some surprising optical encounter.[78] Brief in duration, terror might evolve into a chronic condition of fear. Something terrified Gertrude Schwaiger while she worked in the barn and, as her husband reported, she had suf-fered from relentless fear ever since.[79] Justina Neiner, a young servant woman, sought alleviation from terror suffered after witnessing an accident in a church.[80] Bartholomeus Wallner, terrorized, had witnessed a suicide.[81] Unexpected sightings of threatening animals not infrequently terrorized the populace. One woman was terrified after running across a black dog, another by a black cat taken for the devil.[82] A headless wolf standing upright shocked one shepherd when it attacked his flock; he had to be bound and carried to Benediktbeuern after sighting the werewolf.[83] Animistic beliefs and anthropomorphic costumes played a regular role in early modern pop-ular culture, not just at carnival, but also throughout the year, especially in areas where locals employed rough justice and the charivari.[84] A visit to the modern Tyrolean Museum of Folk Art (*Tiroler Volkskunstmuseum*) in nearby Innsbruck still impresses with its terrific display of demonic carni-val masks and traditional costumes (see Plate 12). Masqueraders during the Benediktbeuern carnival of 1665 terrified participants on two separate occa-sions.[85] That same year, another masked farmhand terrified young Ursula Ludtlin in a meadow.[86] Dreams terrified individuals as well. A man dreamed that an entire horde of warriors ran over him in the night and was struck

[75] AMB 600608: "ist mit seinem Vatter etwas unruehig alhier gewesen, vermeinte bese Leith die spotet und sezten ihm nach (welches ihm bei einem bauer) dem er diente, wider behaftet sein solte durch ainen Trunkh oder Essen ware auch zu forchten von den Leithen."
[76] AMB 631124, 640113, 660417, 660818, 680517, 680609.
[77] AMB 620504: "vor 8 Jahrn sei hie gewesen corrupt, nach welcher er ganz gsundt worden, iezt aber widerumb in ein forcht gefahlen . . ."
[78] Zedler, vol. VIII, 1300.   [79] AMB 630611.   [80] AMB 630612.   [81] AMB 650407.
[82] AMB 570526, 600517.   [83] AMB 640120.
[84] Broadly, see David Lederer, "Popular Culture," in: Jonathan Dewald (ed.), *Europe 1450–1789: Ency-clopedia of the Early Modern World* (New York, 2004), 1–9.
[85] AMB 650224, 650331.   [86] AMB 650923.

Plate 12a. Tyrolean vineyard guard in costume. The purpose? To scare off thieves.
(Courtesy of Tyrolean Museum of Folk Art, Innsbruck.)

Plate 12b. Tyrolean carnival costume, "Luzifer." (Courtesy of Tyrolean Museum of Folk Art, Innsbruck.)

by terror.[87] A woman had a dream that terrified her just after childbirth.[88] The dream of a friend transformed into a cat terrified young Magdalena Denner.[89]

Aristotle held that sights and sounds left indelible marks upon the soul like the imprints of a stylus upon a soft wax tablet. The Aristotelian tradition, transmitted by Protestant (e.g. Luther, Melanchthon[90]) and Catholic theologians alike, translated into popular beliefs. When expectant mothers experienced terror, many feared a trauma might sympathetically affect the unborn child. They feared to pass by the grave of women who had died in childbirth, because the souls of the deceased might try to claim the fetus in compensation for their own. For that reason, their graves were deliberately isolated in a remote corner of the cemetery or outside consecrated ground altogether.[91]

Women regularly referred to unspecified postpartum shocks (*im Kindbett erschrocken*) that led to chronic fear, melancholy, lapses from reason, demonic possession and suicidal tendencies.[92] One terrorized expectant mother claimed she was the victim of an enchantment, while another woman feared witches stole her breast milk.[93] Mothers expressed a deep attachment to newborn infants. High rates of miscarriages, stillbirths, cot deaths and other forms of infant mortality made expectancy and childbirth a period of anxiety. Infertile women made up another group of sufferers at pilgrimage shrines in Bavaria.[94] In one tragic case, a desperate woman pledged herself to a pilgrimage for her sick child and named the newborn Anastasia, but she failed to fulfill the vow after the baby recovered. Two years later, the child became ill again, began to emit a foul stench from her mouth and subsequently died.[95] Her mother, consumed with grief, came to the Anastasia shrine in search of consolation.

---

[87] AMB 640229. Perhaps a vision of the nocturnal horde or "wild hunt"; see Carlo Ginzburg, *Night Battles* (Baltimore, 1983) and a contrary position by Wolfgang Behringer, *Chonrad Stoecklin und die Nachtschar* (Munich, 1994).

[88] AMB 650225.   [89] AMB 600517. Others were terrified in dreams as well: AMB 650525.

[90] Midelfort, *A History of Madness*, 123.

[91] Karant-Nun, *The Reformation of Ritual*, 78, see fn. 39. Robert Scribner refers to fears of the dangers posed by mothers' souls in "The Impact of the Reformation on Daily Life," in: Scribner, *Popular Culture and Popular Movements in Reformation Germany* (London, 1987), 337. Reprinted in Robert Scribner and Lyndal Roper (eds.), *Religion and Culture in Germany, 1400–1800* (Leiden, 2004), 275–301.

[92] AMB 600809, 610723, 600602, 600614, 600722, 650225, 650702, 660620, 660814. Generally, see Signori, "Aggression," 141–148, for a description of postpartum depression and *Kindbett*.

[93] AMB 650702.   [94] For example, AMB 600424, 600602, 600807, 600825, 660809, 671209.

[95] AMB 640520.

4   *Affective disorders*

Long-term affective or mood disorders (*Gemütskrankheiten*) caused disequilibria of the soul. They unbalanced perceptions in a chronic rather than acute fashion, disrupting the rhythms of everyday life on a routine basis. Affective disorders assumed three related forms in a descending spiral of severity: tribulation (*Betrübtheit, tribulata/us*), faint-hearted pusillanimity (*Kleinmütigkeit, pusillanimis*) and melancholy (*Schwermütigkeit, melancholia*). Guarinonius purposefully grouped all three together.[96] In reference to the second faculty of Aristotelian psychology, Guarinonius suggested that, unlike common anger or afflictions born of animal affections (e.g. fear), mood disorders affected the higher faculties as well as the external senses. Strictly limited to humans, one did not encounter them among baser creatures. Since they lacked higher faculties, animals presumably did not suffer mood swings.

In early modern Europe, tribulations represented the most common mood disorder and, indeed, the most common spiritual affliction of all. No fewer than 275 complaints of tribulations appear in the Pürten and Benediktbeuern miracle books. Pilgrims complained of tribulations in the earliest miracle books from Altötting and, with 717 complaints, "troubled in mind" topped the list in Napier's English casebooks as well.[97] Like Napier's patients (458/257), women at Benediktbeuern complained of tribulations by an overwhelming ratio of two to one (128/63), while the ratio offered by Signori is slightly less (4/3).[98] One encounters tribulations in the Bible (Psalms 46.4 and 77.3, Zachariah 9.15), which described a condition of lingering unease, as the disquiet of drunkenness.[99]

Tribulations, a simple affliction, could sorely beset sinners who failed to make use of appropriate spiritual physic, which conquered them through the consoling promise of eternal salvation.[100] Widespread tribulations presented practitioners of spiritual physic with a serious problem in the sixteenth century. A whole new genre of moral literature, books of consolation (*Trostbücher*), made its appearance and specifically targeted tribulations and despair during "these troubled times." The custodians at the cult shrines described many serious cases of tribulations, some of extended duration.[101] Salomon Quirechtmayer suffered tribulations for six years.[102] One troubled

---

[96] Guarinonius, *Die Grewel*, 292–303.
[97] Bauer, "Das Büchlein," 122–139; MacDonald, *Mystical Bedlam*, 117, 148–150.
[98] MacDonald, *Mystical Bedlam*, 243.   [99] Zedler, vol. III, 1558.
[100] Guarinonius, *Die Grewel*, 293–294.   [101] AMB 640414, 640416;   [102] PMB 680612.

individual refused to speak.[103] Nuptial problems sometimes led to tribulations. Caspar Lainger, a Catholic, married a Lutheran woman, but after a
year tribulations sorely tested him and he could no longer perform his trade
as a carpenter.[104] Tribulations visited Leonhardt Mayer after a lost court
case.[105] A father already beset with tribulations went raving mad after his
son hanged himself.[106] Unconsoled, victims of tribulations lost their minds
or fell into despair, becoming suicidal.[107]

Melancholy, a term that has long fascinated historians of art and literature and focused the attention of learned debate among contemporaries,
has also come to subsume a variety of other categories of a afflictions. Recognized by corporal physicians, divines and jurists alike, its explication is
complex and often frustrating. Napier's patients in England, many from
the social elite, accounted for 465 complaints of melancholy, but the disorder was far less frequent in Bavaria. As MacDonald suggests, the social
elite developed a penchant for cultivating melancholy at the end of the
sixteenth century. For common pilgrims at the Bavarian shrines, it simply
ranked as a more serious mood disorder, more commonly mentioned in
conjunction with cases of suicide heard by the Aulic Council in Munich.
Thus, one encounters complaints of melancholy and an associated affective
disorder, pusillanimity (faintheartedness), far less often than tribulations.
The symptoms of melancholy differed only slightly from the other affective
disorders, though contemporaries regarded it as a far more serious condition and maintained a rigid distinction to the point that simultaneous
conditions of melancholy, pusillanimity and tribulations might be diagnosed in the same person.[108] Melancholy, a condition with acknowledged
medical and legal connotations, afflicted both men and women at Benediktbeuern equally, whereas pusillanimity predominated among women (6/2).
A fainthearted brewer's son became melancholic and, when phlebotomy
(i.e. bleeding) failed to improve his condition, his father brought him to
Benediktbeuern, where he still refused to speak or eat.[109] The local school-
master brought Maria Helana, the thirty-year-old daughter of a noble district judge, in a melancholic condition to Pürten, where she refused to speak
either good or evil with anyone.[110] One woman suffered pusillanimity as a
result of wedding and another suffered melancholy after her wedding plans
fell through.[111] After his wedding, Albert Kraidmayer became melancholic

---

[103] AMB 570312.   [104] AMB 620607.   [105] AMB 600608.   [106] PMB 790613.
[107] E.g. AMB 570615, 571021, 571104, 580619, 620716, 640701; PMB 641031, 641127, 660208, 680523,
700819, 701218.
[108] PMB 780831, 840623. Zedler, vol. xv, 906, indicates a graduated progression, with pusillanimity the
least serious, tending toward tribulations, then melancholy and even despair. Geiler van Kaysersberg,
Das irrig Schaf, also treats pusillinamity as an early stage of despair.
[109] AMB 680606.   [110] PMB 660707.   [111] AMB 680505, 600408.

and "didn't want to have his wife" anymore because of her strange desires.[112] Melancholy, like fear, struck women during and after pregnancy.[113] In practice, debts and over-industriousness caused bouts of melancholy as well.[114] These bouts, even when cured, still recurred unexpectedly.[115] Guarinonius devoted considerable detail to melancholy and faintheartedness, whereby he concluded that mature women were especially susceptible to sexual advances and immoral temptations when they became pusillanimous.[116] Zedler defined pusillanimity as general discouragement and meekness arising from a fundamental sense of mistrust.[117] As mood disorders, pusillanimity and melancholy drove some to despair and suicidal thoughts, just as tribulation did.[118]

Victims of mood afflictions complained of a shooting sensation in the head and throat, a heavy heart with the weight of a stone, or the sensation of a living creature in the heart that climbed into the throat.[119] These were early warning signs of demonic possession originating from tribulations, melancholy or pusillanimity. Several women complaining of mood disorders gave the impression of being possessed, a condition that revisited them after years of good health, while other sufferers openly complained that the devil beset them.[120] Official reports associated pusillanimity with suicides. The Aulic Council made a clear distinction between affective disorders and despair in cases of suicide, since the latter was punished by sanctions. It was completely unclear whether Thomas Gambsen drowned himself "out of pusillanimity, despair or from mood confusion"; the council requested further information.[121] The case of Georg Pliembl left no doubt that the servant hanged himself more "out of pusillanimity or confusion than despair."[122] Old widow Horb, who enjoyed an upstanding reputation in Abersdorf, was also found to have taken her own life because of pusillanimity and not desperation.[123]

5 Evil thoughts, demonic temptations and despair

Evil and heavy thoughts vexed many after a terrifying experience. Evil thoughts (*mit bösen Gedanken angefochten, malis cogitationibus vexata/us*) connoted a proclivity to harm oneself, rather than any innate personal

---

[112] " . . . ist melancholisch, will sein weib nit haben": AMB 680604.
[113] AMB 610723.   [114] AMB 600424, 600505, 660326.
[115] AMB 650418. Zedler, vol. xxxvi, 471–472, notes that moral and congenital melancholy recurred chronically. The same held true for tribulations: one woman suffered a recurrence after eight years: ABM 620513.
[116] Guarinonius, *Die Grewel*, 312–320.   [117] Zedler, vol. xv, 906.   [118] AMB 580507, 620528.
[119] ABM 620528, 610723, 570524.   [120] ABM 570220, 660826, 640811, 641029.
[121] HStAM HR 344, 394v.   [122] HStAM HR 346, 351v–352r.   [123] HStAM HR 379, 313r–v.

wickedness or desire directed toward others. As sufferers of evil thoughts, women outnumbered men at the Anastasia shrine by almost two to one (43/25), whereas among persons complaining of or exhibiting outright suicidal tendencies, ranging from parasuicidal temptations (*Anfechtungen*: 26/22) and despair (*Verzweiflung*: 14/13), the gender ratios were nearly even. In England, women also predominated by two to one in evil thoughts (55/24). In terms of actual suicides committed in Bavaria between 1611 and 1670, however, men clearly predominated, making up two-thirds of the victims, in keeping with an established Western custom.[124] Unchecked, repressed evil thoughts led to melancholy, bodily swelling, eating and sleep disorders, or an inability to pray or confess. Numerous pilgrims simply complained that they were sorely beset with evil or heavy thoughts.[125] After a scare, Hans Mayer complained of evil thoughts and suffered a shooting sensation throughout his body.[126] Peter Herger complained of a similar affliction, as if something moved about within his body, accompanied by evil thoughts; restlessness and insomnia resulted.[127] Anna Mayer and Elisabeth Recher both believed that evil thoughts would ultimately rob them of their senses.[128] Apart from the shooting sensation, "as if something traveled about inside the body" ("*fahret etwaß hin und her in dem leib*"), evil thoughts were attended by head and chest pains, such as headaches, earaches or deafness, sore throats and heart palpitations.[129] Barbara Thalmayer actually attempted suicide while still suffering from evil thoughts.[130]

Demonic temptations (*Anfechtungen*) and suicidal despair (*Verzweiflung, desperata/us*) were a level beyond evil thoughts, when one explicitly verbalized thoughts of suicide.[131] Johannes, a twenty-six-year-old from Öttingen, complained he was "badly beset with all sorts of homicidal, desperate and blasphemous thoughts," while Barbara Niedermayer was simply "vexed with heavy tribulations and temptations."[132] Despair represented a distinct form of spiritual affliction, the only type thought to provoke intentionally motivated (*compos mentis*) suicide, and as such it was a condition with

---

[124] This is well in keeping with data from the sixteenth to the twenty-first centuries: men traditionally succeed at killing themselves far more often than women in Western culture, while the parasuicide rate among women is traditionally higher. The suicide rate of women to men was 33 percent/67 percent in early modern Bavaria, a figure based on 300 cases from the Aulic Council protocols, 1611–1670. Behringer's figure of 45 percent female suicides is based on a single bill for services submitted to the authorities by the executioner of Munich, Hans Georg Fahner, for the disposal of one dozen suicides; Behringer, "Mörder," III, 131–132.

[125] PMB 840907, AMB 600412, 620223, 620924, 621022, 660703, 680221.   [126] AMB 610513.

[127] AMB 620329 (NB, follows entry for 670520); 600525, a two-year case of insomnia; 680517.

[128] AMB 600520, 600726.   [129] AMB 580527, 600412, 600501, 600518, 610422, 610721, 650620.

[130] AMB 621109.   [131] Midelfort, *A History of Madness*, 104–108.

[132] ". . . mit allerlej Mörderischen, Verzweifflischen und Gotteslästerischen Gedanckhen starckh angefochten . . .": PMB 670211. "mit schweren betrüebnus und anfechtung behafft": PBM 720515.

grave metaphysical and social implications. Historians sometimes conflate suicidal despair with melancholy. Some contemporaries certainly linked despair with mood disorders.[133] Long bouts of tribulations and melancholy sometimes culminated in despair.[134] Nevertheless, just as often, some other type of spiritual affliction preceded despair and/or suicidal tendencies. Emphasizing the fact that mood disorders preceded despair as a proclivity to a particular type of suicidal tendency suggests a symptomatic linkage, but the two remained very distinct afflictions. The English divine Robert Burton agreed. He dedicated a special chapter at the conclusion of his *Anatomy of Melancholy* to the causes, symptoms, prognoses and cure of suicidal despair.[135]

In its inquiries, the Aulic Council always distinguished practically between suicides resulting from despair and those resulting from mood disorders like pusillanimity. In 1641, the council requested elaboration from the district judge of Dachau; his report on the suicide of Bartholomew Gennstaller's wife did not provide sufficient detail to determine whether she hanged herself "from real, actual desperation" or, as additional testimony of neighbors might show, "from a poor disposition and melancholy or some other similar condition."[136] Depositions in the case of Joseph Saltner (found dead in the district of Marquartstein in 1651) proved he had not killed himself out of desperation, "but rather that which occurred, occurred more so from melancholy and a condition of childishness resulting from his old age . . ."[137] The central authorities in Munich noted that the local report of a woman who sprang to her death in a well in the district of Wolfratshausen in 1649 failed to address the potential influence of a fever epidemic causing widespread phrenesis and melancholy.[138]

Therefore, the close association of mood disorders with suicide is not entirely out of place. Nearly every type of spiritual affliction was implicated

---

[133] Zedler, vol. xlviii, sometimes defined despair (*Verzweiflung*) as a mood disorder (*Gemüths-Unruhe*): 234.

[134] AMB 570615, 571021, 571104, 580507, 580619, 600830, 610701.

[135] Burton, *The Anatomy of Melancholy*, 770–783.

[136] HStAM HR 271, 114r–v: "ob diser laidige fahl, auß rechter aigentlicher verzweiflung, oder einem anderwertigen zuestandt . . . in gebürende obacht zuenemmen, in allweeg aber, bei deß gennstallers benachbarthen, wie sich sein weib vor Irer strangulierung erzaigt habe, ob Sie etwan auß gmueth und melancholia oder anderen dergleichen zuestandt in dises laidige unhail gerathen sein möchte . . ."

[137] " . . . sondern waß beschechen, teil mehr auß einer melancolei, und der in seinem hochem alter zuegestandner Kindtheit vorbeigangen . . .": HStAM HR 311, 168r–v.

[138] "Dem Pflegsverwalter zu Wolferzhausen wider zuschreiben, weillen auß seinem erstatten bericht nit zuzunemmen, ob solche WeibsPersohn, weillen sie verstandtnermassen einem kranckhen außgewarttet, vermuetlich nit etwan auß einem zuegestandenem dobel, und dermahlen Regierenden hiziger Khrankheit, unnd erlangter Melancolia sich in den Prunnen getrückhte und erttrenckt . . . widrigen fahls aber wann sie sich auß verzweiflung in den Prunnen gestirzt haben wurde [dann] . . .": HStAM HR 303, 234v–235r.

in suicidal behavior at some point and several cases from the ledgers of miracle books confirm the subordinate role of fears, evil thoughts and fevers. Nevertheless, the Aulic Council distinguished legally between these causes and despair. Imbecility, physical pain, illness, madness, epidemic fevers, senility and the Hungarian fever were all juxtaposed with despair as possible causes of suicide or suicide attempts. Why did early modern perceptions of despair elevate it to such an egregious form of suicidal behavior? The answer lies in the grave theological consequences attached to suicide from despair, so clearly and universally understood that neither the secular authorities nor the keepers of the shrines felt obligated to elaborate upon them. Suicide motivated by despair implied a state of apostasy through the loss of hope in the prospect of resurrection and everlasting life. Sufferers who killed themselves in desperation ostensibly turned their back on the hopeful message of salvation and thereby reckoned among the eternally damned. Self-killing out of desperation represented nothing less than a complete rejection of the central salvific tenets of Christianity, threatening to melt the metaphysical glue that held society together and legitimized Christian states in the Confessional Age. As long as the early modern state relied on religious legitimization, successful suicide resulting from despair had to be publicly condemned as treasonous. Along with demonic possession and raving madness, despair was one of the most serious spiritual afflictions.

Evil thoughts and desperate temptations occupied a thin moral space between affective and demonic afflictions. As we have seen, afflictions sometimes manifested themselves somatically, as fevers or humoral corruptions. Preternatural afflictions, however, were caused by witchcraft or the devil and, as such, they were another matter entirely. Probably none were more blatant than cases of demonic obsession and possession. The proselytization of moral theology through preaching, catechism and medical tracts like that of Guarinonius had touched a nerve in the popular consciousness. They appealed to a pathological conceptualization of the body as a porous contaminable object, vulnerable to penetration by bewitchment or the devil. Given his propagandistic value in the war of words between Protestants and Catholics, it is hardly surprising that the devil made his presence known by visiting individual sufferers and turning their bodies into a moral battleground.

6   Obsession and possession

D. P. Walker's comparative study of famous demonic possessions in early modern France and England skeptically treated printed accounts of possessions as propaganda used to validate post-Tridentine Catholicism in the forum of inter-confessional polemics.[139] In practice, he viewed exorcisms as conscious acts of collusion between the possessed and the exorcist to hoodwink the public. In terms of propaganda, few cases described in the handwritten ledgers of the St. Anastasia and Beata Alta miracle books ever found their way into published hagiographies. Indeed, the custodians were loath to describe treatments that failed. Cases with polemical value, like the English convert who had her enchantment "driven out from the mouth along with much blood," were exceptional and seldom exploited.[140] Another woman (a "crypto-Calvinist") underwent an unusually lengthy exorcism during which eight demons were driven out.[141] These possession stories remained locked in unpublished sources and oral transmission, with the struggle between good and evil occurring only at a personal and local level. The short-term relationship between exorcist and possessed at Benediktbeuern and Pürten lends little credence to theories of collusion or swindle. No doubt, these personal relationships entailed potential mutual benefits – exorcists kept their jobs and the possessed were liable to gain a degree of local notoriety – but genuine psychological factors, which neither party totally controlled, were an essential concern.

Stuart Clark also points to reductionism in Walker's argument, since "Whatever insights are gained . . . are achieved, therefore, at the expense of the beliefs and actions of those who, operating with sincerely held notions of reality very removed from our own, regarded possession by demons as a real phenomenon."[142] Clark posits a strategic theory of a binary opposition between good and evil in the contemporary eschatology of demonology, which viewed possession as a sign of the impending apocalypse in an age of crisis.[143] For Sluhovsky, possession remains a complex phenomenon, one highly indicative of contemporary spirituality and devotion.[144] Certainly, the fact that demoniacs frequently conducted pilgrimages underscores his point on the role of devotion in possession. Devotion was a system of exchange as well as pious belief. Individual goals varied and some demoniacs surely sought to tap metaphysical sources of empowerment for this-worldly advantage. However, many ordinary pilgrims and those who accompanied them probably hoped for little more than an end to suffering, primarily

[139] Walker, *Unclear Spirits.*
[140] ". . . ganz bluettig durch den mundt herauß vertriben worden . . .": AMB 660818.
[141] The last demon was hesitant to leave her, "*biß auf 8. Niclaii tag, da sie wurde sunst widerumb Calvinisch . . .*": AMB 650714.
[142] Clark, *Thinking with Demons*, 392–393.   [143] Ibid., 335–345.
[144] Moshe Sluhovsky, "The Devil in the Convent," *American Historical Review* 107 (2002), 1379–1411.

for themselves, but also for their families and their communities. In a sense, it too was a type of empowerment, though no more so than is present in sufferers of disease. Ultimately, as Sarah Ferber correctly observes, demoniacs experienced possession in many different ways and exorcists drove out demons for many different reasons.[145] One might only reiterate here that, more often than not, possession manifested a real and personal problem and the exorcism represented a positive means to resolve it.

Contemporaries presumed that the body was porous, physically open to all manner of moral temptations and corruptions. Despite prevailing medical explanations of disease as a product of endogenous humoral imbalances, common people intuitively interpreted certain conditions as a product of foreign contamination. Contamination might enter the body orally, as in the case of Virgil Paur, who attributed his symptoms to a drink he consumed four years prior, an allusion to an enchantment.[146] Magic provided ready access to the human body and soul. Paul Berzl also blamed his suffering on maleficent magic.[147] Sir Johann Hietman, a student in Augsburg, had suffered greatly as a novitiate in a monastery three years earlier.[148] Tortured by mice, which nibbled on his body during the night, he was advised by his master to hang a crucifix or penny on the door to his cell. Now residing with his parents, his mother complained of his obsessive behavior: he searched every nook and corner of the house both day and night. Again, numerous pilgrims recalled the peculiar sensation of a foreign object moving around inside their body.[149] Besides obvious bodily orifices, afflictions accessed the body through the armpits.[150] Others complained that evil spirits and thoughts externally besieged them, as the devil lurked about trying to gain access to their body during a moment of physical or spiritual weakness.[151] A ghost terrified Catharina Mayer by knocking at her door; now the devil himself severely beset her with evil thoughts.[152] Michael Ecker saw the devil before him at all times.[153] The devils that plagued Margaretha Bauer, Ursula Bernhardt and Christina Keller drove them to tribulations.[154] Christoph Hörmann dreamed that two men fought over his soul, one in white who tried to prevent the other from entering his body.[155]

Demonic obsession was quite distinct from possession. Sufferers complained that the devil threatened them, but from without, never entering

[145] Ferber, *Demonic Possession*, 4–13.   [146] AMB 620920.   [147] AMB 640814.
[148] AMB 660917.
[149] AMB 610201, 610224, 610513, 620505, 640116, 650324, 650518, 650522, 660508, 660620, 660713, 670329, 680309, 680519, 680524.
[150] AMB 620303, 650713.   [151] PMB 731231, 810704, AMB 620306, 620515, 620716, 651128.
[152] AMB 661014.   [153] AMB 610308.   [154] PMB 740326, AMB 640811, 641029.
[155] AMB 651012.

their bodies or controlling their behavior from within. Of the ten persons who complained of obsessions at Benediktbeuern, six were women. However, if the devil succeeded in entering a victim, demonic possession manifested itself in a variety of symptoms. The symptoms of possession usually conformed to an orthodox catalogue laid out in the post-Tridentine *Rituale Romanorum* of 1614, the Roman church's guide to ritual exorcism.[156] The *Rituale* enumerates four basic symptoms, all well known to contemporaries: repulsiveness exhibited toward the application of holy objects, the ability to speak in previously unknown languages, superhuman strength and knowledge of facts hidden or secret. The demoniacs who came to Benediktbeuern for exorcisms were women by a superlative ratio of almost five to one (48/10). Margaretha Koch's possession took a typical course. She arrived with her father, Bartholomeus, and stayed for ten days, undergoing "the usual exorcisms" each day, including the application of the reliquary bust of St. Anastasia.[157] Insufferable Satan cried and wept each time, confessing he would soon be driven out. On the last day, Margaretha finally vomited a devil named "Peibest" from her mouth with a repugnant stench in the presence of many onlookers in the chapel, including the local judge. Later, the custodian received an official attestation from her local authorities confirming that she was fresh and healthy.

Sometimes, non-specialists recognized symptoms of demonic possession even before demoniacs sought the help of an exorcist. Barbara Aingl had already visited other sacred shrines and an evil spirit made its presence known well before she made a pilgrimage to Benediktbeuern.[158] The parents of Sebastian Weselmayer brought him to the shrine of Beata Alta possessed by an "evil guest" and he twice emitted an "inhuman and insufferable stench."[159] Two demons possessed twelve-year-old Margaretha Mayer for twenty weeks after "evil people" (i.e. witches) enchanted her.[160] The "Stürer" devil possessing her raged at Benediktbeuern, calling St. Anastasia

---

[156] See any version of the *Rituale Romanum*, Tit. XI, Kap. 1–3. The earlier *Rituale Augustanum* (Dillingen, 1580) was also on hand in the library at Benediktbeuern: BayStaBi Cgm C.405, vol. I, 28v. Official Catholic practice according to the *Rituale* is outlined in Cecile Ernst, *Teufelsaustreibungen. Die Praxis der katholischen Kirche im 16. und 17. Jahrhundert* (Berne, 1972).

[157] ". . . mit dem laidigen Teufel besessen . . . hie Zehen tag gebliben, sein alle tag die gewohnliche Exorcismen neben aufsezung deß H. Haubts an ihr angewandt worden, hat der laidige Sathan vill heulen und weinen verbracht, und oftermalen bekhent, daß ihn die H. Anastasia wirdt bald herauß treiben, wie dan wir hofentlich sein gewesen, daß sie von solchen sei erlediget worden, da ein grosser brackhen mit einen grosser gestankch aus ihren mundt herauß gangen, in bei sein viller menschen bei den H. Gerichtschriber in der Khurchen, die leut auch gesprochen, ich mein dem Peibest den teufel herauß vermaint sie sein erlediget worden. ist per Atestationem als durch einen schreiben von der Obrigkeit bestetigt, daß sie frisch und gsundt sei": AMB 620817.

[158] AMB 600725.   [159] PMB 660709.   [160] AMB 670114.

"witch-head." He identified his comrade as "Pottsau." The devil possessing
Maria Impler, a soldier's wife, cursed St. Anastasia each time the relics were
laid upon her.[161] In her fits of rage, several persons had difficulty restraining
her. Maria Schapfnacker's husband, also a soldier, brought the possessed
woman to Benediktbeuern. Repulsed by the relics, she raged violently.[162]
The custodian questioned her in Latin and the devil responded through
her in German. Unable to spend the night in a hostel, she slept on the
streets and in a nearby wood in the rain and wind. The demon possessing
Anna Mark actually did speak in Latin and Satan spoke German, Latin,
Greek and Hebrew through the body of Eva Hohenleitner.[163]

At other times, the custodians at a shrine were the first to identify persons as victims of possession. Jörg Raifer emitted shameful noises, twitched
about and, when the spiritual physicians applied the reliquary bust of St.
Anastasia, the devil ultimately made his presence known, raging awfully.[164]
Two unidentified men accompanied Hans Hän to the shrine, where he
shrieked, "quaub, quaub, quaub" day and night.[165] Once again, following the application of relics, the devil began to speak in a rough voice,
complaining that he now must leave the body and return to hell. At first,
Ursula Aigner began to shiver from the proximity of relics, and the exorcist
reported, "every time I ordered it in honor of St. Anastasia, the devil had to
remain still, something that he otherwise never did in the church."[166] The
first time the relics were applied to Maria Schmidt, the devil began to shiver
and, on the next day, he identified himself as "Haasenschreyer," suffering
terribly under the influence of the saint.[167] Only then did he reveal he had
entered her body six months before on the feast of St. Jacob. Catharina
Wörzen came to Benediktbeuern for the second time in several months,
but this time the devil finally revealed himself in the saint's presence, weep-
ing and crying that he must leave the body because St. Anastasia had now
discovered him and plagued him awfully.[168]

Everyone in Hall mistook the possession of the honorable Gertrude
Hofer, wife of a Tyrolean salt merchant, for a fever.[169] She suffered terribly
for twelve weeks and displayed a variety of paroxysms and contortions;
standing, her feet would spread apart so far that one could easily slip between
them and, when she sat, the devil forced her legs together and drew them up
to her mouth. Arriving at Benediktbeuern, she hallucinated in the cemetery,
perceiving that all the doors to the Anastasia chapel were shut tight and her
entry was barred. When Gertrude finally entered the chapel, she began to

---

[161] AMB 620318.   [162] AMB 620530.   [163] AMB 660805.   [164] AMB 650611.
[165] AMB 650614.   [166] AMB 651118.   [167] AMB 640111.   [168] AMB 651012.
[169] AMB 650714.

tremble. The "devil in her" turned up his nose and gazed treacherously at the custodian, who responded:

I addressed him: St. Anastasia will surely find you. Thereupon, the devil spoke to the messenger from Mittenwald: You have saved her, because you know every angle, otherwise I would re-enter her, as [I did] in Tyrol. I asked him, when had he entered this person, and he answered, on Easter Monday, because she had hurried to the Jesuits for the first Mass and forgot to genuflect, at which point I gained the power to enter her: for he had stalked her for some time.[170]

Gertrude remained at the shrine for eight days, during which time the devil repeatedly admitted he must leave her because of the saint's intercession. During the last four days, she exhibited no further symptoms, prompting all involved to believe that the devil had been driven out. However, the exorcist warned her that if any symptoms reappeared she should return immediately. He further promised to read a mass to force the devil to identify himself, if still present. While passing Kochel Lake, the devil indeed made his presence known again and the wagon headed about for Benediktbeuern. The devil screamed under the application of relics, admitting that the mass had forced his hand. Otherwise, Gertrude could have stayed at Benediktbeuern for a whole year and still he would have concealed himself in the hope of diminishing the saint's reputation among the residents (and the Jesuits) of Hall. The devil was finally driven out and she returned home. Later, a fellow monk from Hall sent a letter to Benediktbeuern, substantiating her total recovery. Gertrude was now able to sleep, pray, eat, drink and work, activities previously prevented by her affliction.

SPIRITUAL AFFLICTIONS AND SOCIAL ROLES:
TWO CASE HISTORIES

From the representative sample of sufferers treated by spiritual physicians in early modern Bavaria, two are scrutinized here in order to flesh out the circumstances of specific spiritual afflictions. These biographic reconstitutions are useful and representative for a number of reasons. Pragmatically, they were chosen because both are well documented. In the case of pilgrims originating from a wide geographic catchment area, complete reconstitutions

---

[170] Ibid.: "Ich hab ihme zugesprachen: S. Anastasia wirdet dich schon aufmerckig machen: Gleich darauf sprache der Teufl zu dem Potten von Mittenwald, du hast sie Heraus gekehrt, dan du waist alle winkhl, sonsten were ich widerumb hineingefahren, daß ist in daß thirol. Ich fragt ihn, wan er in dise Persohn sei hineingefahren, antwortet er an Ostermontag, dan sie hat geeilet zu der ersten Mess zu den Hernn Jesuiten, und sich zuvor nit gesegnet, auf daß ich den gewalt bekhommen, hineinzufahern: dan er zuvor ihr lang nach gestellet."

of individual case histories are tedious; they require reference to multiple layers of primary sources scattered in far-flung archives. However, the effort can, occasionally, yield substantial dividends. For instance, one can follow up depictions from the manuscript miracle books through parish registers, secular protocols, criminal records and other forms of documentation. The resultant independent corroboration substantiates the information in the ledger entries to a remarkable degree. The two sufferers in question here, one a wealthy nobleman and the other a servant woman, lived on opposite ends of the social spectrum. Nevertheless, although they illustrate social extremes in terms of status and gender, their specific experiences of spiritual afflictions and spiritual physic were typical. Indeed, both case histories are arguably quite ordinary, since neither achieved prominence beyond the communal or familial level, nor were they the subject of any literary discourse or polemic.

While we might expect a good run of documentation for a nobleman, Sir (*Freiherr*) Leopold Francis Isidor of Taufkirchen was a relatively minor figure and ultimately ended his days in obscurity. The amount of information available for a common serving woman, Anna Maria Streimayer-Arnold is, considering her social and legal status, surprisingly equivalent. Both case histories highlight a precarious liminal stage in the life-cycle, the rite of passage to adulthood, the quandaries of entering the world of work and, in the latter case, courtship. These particular rites of passage, fraught with uncertainties and dangers, exemplify a substantial number of cases from the miracle books.

The account of Leopold Francis Isidor of Taufkirchen portrays the ideal-typical life of a nobleman and his misfortunes in the seventeenth century. A venerable lineage, the Taufkirchen family traced its origins to the ancient nobility of Verona.[171] Despite support for the chalice movement against the Wittelsbach dynasty in 1563, the family later regained the Dukes' good graces, achieving high offices by the early seventeenth century.[172] In 1635, Wolfgang Christoph married Johanna Catharina of Leubelsing; they parented a daughter, Maria Francisca, and a son, Leopold Francis Isidor, both in 1636. Four years later, a second son, Johann Wolfgang, was born. The family's rising star held future honors in store: in 1684, Johann Wolfgang

---

[171] Zedler, vol. XLII, 369–374; Johann Hübner, *Geneologische Tabellen*, vol. III (Leipzig, 1728), table 930; Gabriel Bucelin, *Germaniae Topo-Chrono-Stemmatographicae Sacrae et Profanae*, vol. IV (Ulm, 1699), 278.

[172] Wolf Christoph of Taufkirchen was one of the confessionalists who petitioned for religious parity according to the provisions of the Confession of Augsburg at the territorial Diet of Ingolstadt in 1563: Ziegler, *Dokumente*, 337. Later, both Hochprand of Taufkirchen and his younger stepbrother, another Wolfgang Christoph, were posted as chamberlains to the exchequer (*Hofkammerer*).

(who married into the prestigious Katzenberg family) and his cousin, Wolfgang Joseph (husband of Maria Magdalena Fugger, of the Augsburg banking dynasty), received a joint patent from Elector Maximilian Emanuel, which elevated their domain to an autonomous judicial district.[173] Other family members regularly occupied prominent administrative posts in the Bavarian government well into the eighteenth century – among others, chamberlain, chamber counselor, *Rentmeister* of Burghausen, and *Stadholder* of Ingolstadt.

However, in the seventeenth century, nobility no longer guaranteed a ticket to high office in the territorial administration. An expanding state bureaucracy introduced a uniform legal system and required representatives to familiarize themselves with both new procedures and customary anomalies.[174] Increased pressure to learn novel bureaucratic techniques combined with rising competition from bourgeois jurists, who made up the learned bench of the Aulic Council in Munich and began to intrude on the noble bench by purchasing patents.[175] After 1678, Ferdinand Maria mandated attendance at Ingolstadt as a prerequisite for state service, stressing the importance of regional university education, especially in law.[176] The matriculation records of the territorial university at Ingolstadt demonstrate how the regional nobility took every opportunity to expose their progeny to the benefits of university education: one in six students enrolled at Ingolstadt between 1472 and 1648 came from their highest ranks.[177] The Taufkirchen family was no exception, sending eleven offspring to the University of Ingolstadt from its foundation in 1472 until the signing of the Peace of Westphalia.[178]

Leopold Francis Isidor paid 3fl. to matriculate at Ingolstadt during the winter semester of 1653 as "*Liber Baro de Dafkirch . . . Illustris Dominus*"; he studied logic and later, law.[179] The regimen at the Jesuit-dominated university was strict; in 1655, Ferdinand Maria recommended that the law faculty trim its curriculum and concentrate on legal fundamentals, because

---

[173] Enrst Heinrich Kneschke, *Neues allgemeines deutsches Adels-Lexicon*, vol. IX (Leipzig, 1870: reprint: Neustadt an der Aische, 1995–1996), 148–50.
[174] Rainer A. Müller, *Universität und Adel. Eine soziostrukturelle Studie zur Geschichte der bayerischen Landesuniversität Ingolstadt 1472–1648* (Berlin, 1974), 150.
[175] Ibid., 80; Richard Heydenreuter, *Der Landesherrliche Hofrat unter Herzog und Kurfürst Maximilian I. von Bayern (1598–1651)* (Munich, 1981), 56–59.
[176] Ibid., 82–84.
[177] Müller, *Universität*, 78. If one considers the relatively small proportion of the population they actually constituted, then this figure is all the more impressive.
[178] Ibid., 179.
[179] Götz Freiherr von Pölnitz, *Die Matrikel der Ludwig-Maximilians Universität Ingolstadt-Landshut-München*, vol. II (Munich, 1939), 777–785.

many administrators still lacked essential training.[180] He accused professors of lecturing in monotone and complained that students, required to attend lectures at lunch hour, were falling asleep.[181] Foreign language courses were already established in 1625 as a country club for the nobility – a symbol of their elite status – and Leopold Francis Isidor undoubtedly attended them in addition to his law studies.[182]

In 1656, he participated in a public disputation on philosophy and proposed a thesis, which won him honors.[183] Shortly thereafter, Leopold Francis Isidor successfully completed a *Proberelation*, a legal brief arguing an appellate case before the Aulic Council. The *Proberelation* was a standard requirement to graduate from the law faculty.[184] His handwritten thesis argued a probate dowry case in appeal before the Aulic Council from 1657 to 1658 and demonstrated his acumen in both Roman law and regional customary procedure. Were one to conduct a comparative handwriting analysis of his thesis and that of his cousin, Wolfgang Joseph, submitted in 1649, one might note that Leopold's *Probrelation* suffered from almost manic illegibility. His handwriting is extremely large and disorderly in comparison, and the thesis suffers from organizational problems not present in his cousin's work; Leopold utilized only half-pages and his subsections and paragraphs are ad hoc, indicating frenetic excitability. Leopold Francis Isidor attached a petition to his *Proberelation* addressed directly to Prince-Elector Ferdinand Maria. It acknowledged his successful public defense after five years of university study and requested permission for an academic tour (*peregrinatio academica*) to better his foreign language skills, in anticipation of whatever post might be deemed fitting for his "meager talents."[185] On September 20, 1660, the Aulic Council in Munich authorized his petition to travel abroad,

---

[180] UAM, LI 8, October 23, 1654. A general intensification of pressure on the nobility to serve at court as a source of mental stress is also suggested by Midelfort, *Mad Princes*, 152.

[181] UAM, LI 8, October 23, 1654: "Sonsten ist bishero die Lectio Institutionorum von Zwölff bis ain Uhr gehalten worden . . ."; See also Carl Prantl, *Geschichte der Ludwig-Maximilians Universität in Ingolstadt-Landshut, München* (Munich, 1872), vol. II, Quellen, 446.

[182] Müller, *Universität*, 157.

[183] "Nobilissimae Taufkirchiorum familiae honoribus addere hic iuuat disputationem Philosophicam, quam hoc anno Leopold. Franc. Isidorus L. B. de Taufkirchen publice instituit Praeside Ioanne Stozio. Proposuit Theses i charta maiore cum Emblematis aeri incisis. Respondit vero illustris Pugil, ut ipsa verba referam, quibus ille actus in monimentis nostris notatus est: cum non minore suo, quan philos. Facultatis honore, ac merita laude doctrinae & diligentiae": Ioannes Nepomucenus Mederer, *Annales Ingolstadiensis Academicae*, vol. II (Ingolstadt, 1782), 332, 334.

[184] HStAM, Personenselekt Cart. 441. On the requirement of the *Proberelation*, see Heydenreuter, *Der Landesherrliche Hofrat*, 61–63.

[185] HStAM, Personenselekt Cart. 441: "Ir Churfrt. drt. anbei gehorsambst bittent, die geruehen mir hierauf mit gnaden Acta ad referendum auswolgen, die gebreichige probrelation hierbei vor dero hochlob. Hofrath abligen und nachdeme vermitls negst vorhabenter besuechend frembder Landten in exercitis und sprachen mich etwas mehrers qualificiert haben werde, mit Churfrt. diensten, damit

per standard procedure (*Kinder ausser Landes*), though the authorizing official was notably taken aback at the insinuation of any promise of office in
the future, which he laconically refused to acknowledge.

The *peregrinatio academica*, or grand tour, was a widely accepted rite
of passage among the European nobility in the early modern period.[186]
Viewed as a transition from the university to a life of politics, the *peregrinatio* tested the nobleman's emotional maturity and measured the weight of
his pocketbook. It also provided an opportunity to benefit first hand from
experiences at different universities and network at foreign courts, where
young traveling noblemen were received as honored guests. However, few
traveling scholars pursued serious courses of study at other European universities, remaining for a few days or weeks at each port-of-call on an established circuit.[187] Religious policies, while not officially prohibiting Bavarian
nobles from entering Protestant regions, did discourage travel to confessionally suspect areas, according to the stipulations of mandates regulating the
activities of territorial children abroad. The close proximity of Ingolstadt
to neighboring evangelical or bi-confessional cities meant that heterodox
ideas could not be shut out completely and a climate of controversy and
confrontation emerged at the university law faculty.[188] Italy remained by
far the most popular destination for a Bavarian *peregrinatio*.[189] With this
goal in mind, Leopold set off at age twenty-five, passing Benediktbeuern
to cross the Alps en route to the *Welschland* (Italy).

Eighteen months after the Aulic Council granted him his travel papers,
the *illustris Dominus* Francis Leopold Isidor arrived at Benediktbeuern on
April 15, 1662. He confessed to the custodian "fully and easily," recalling that, after completion of law studies, he had been sent to "far away
lands" to learn languages.[190] In 1661, he arrived in Siena, enrolling in
the Confraternity of the German Nation, one of many way-stations at
Italian universities for noblemen conducting their *peregrinatio*; his nominal one-scudo matriculation fee testifies to his presence in Tuscany.[191]
Shortly after leaving Siena, Taufkirchen was robbed of his senses. He

---

mein von Gott verliechnes weniges talentum zu Daselben und das Lieben Vatterlandts bevelch
schuldigistermassen applicirn möge . . ."
[186] Müller, *Universität*, 158.
[187] Fritz Weigle (ed.), *Die Matrikel der Deutschen Nation in Siena (1573–1738)*, vol. 1 (Tübingen,
1962), 1.
[188] Klaus Neumaier, *Ius Publicum. Studium zur barocken Rechtsgelerhsamkeit an der Universität Ingolstadt*
(Berlin, 1974).
[189] Ibid.; Müller, *Universität*, 77, 158.
[190] ". . . weit entlegne Lender geschickht worden, aldorten die sprachen zulehrnen, wie dann auch
geschehen . . .": AMB 620415.
[191] Weigle, *Die Matrikel*, 309.

fled to a wood, tore off his clothing and survived for three days without "human food," subsisting on a diet of oak leaves.[192] Two Spanish pilgrims found him in this state and, after persuading him to don a shirt, brought him to Livorno. From there, relatives had him transported by carriage to Benediktbeuern.

At the St. Anastasia shrine, Leopold Francis Isidor behaved violently and was repeatedly restrained in irons to prevent him from injuring curious onlookers. Exorcisms were conducted with the application of relics and twelve masses were read on his behalf. He remained at Benediktbeuern for eight days until regaining a calm and orderly disposition and attending auricular confession. Then he left with a page and several other servants, "with a good hope of his full recovery: may God grant him such."[193] Subsequent circumstances indicate he never fully recovered. According to an official genealogy, Leopold Francis Isidor never married, singular for male members of his lineage. His failure to find a suitable partner is attributable in part to ecclesiastical and legal prohibitions against marriage for those not of sound mind, rendering him unsuitable for the noble marriage market; in any case, his ultimate recovery remains in doubt.[194] His younger brother Johann Wolfgang inherited the family title and assumed the offices of Electoral Chamberlain and Aulic Councilor, despite a tradition of primogeniture. Again, there were legal prohibitions and social stigma attached to madness, so that Leopold Francis Isidor never gained a post in the territorial administration. Initial appearances indicate that, as the first son, he would have been set to inherit the title and advance into an administrative career. He completed legal studies at Ingolstadt with honors and traveled to Siena as part of a *peregrinatio*.[195] Whether Leopold Francis Isidor snapped under academic pressure, career difficulties or as a result of some mishap during his Italian journey is unknown.

The circumstances surrounding the affliction of Anna Maria Stremayer-Arnold from Mühlau near Innsbruck were similar to those of Leopold Francis Isidor, for both lost their reason in connection with a rite of passage, in her case courtship and marriage. Human sexual relationships were

---

[192] AMB 620415: ". . . so ist er ganz seines Sinnes beraubt worden, in einen Wald geflochen, sich selber seiner Khleider ganz entblest, 3 tag ohne menschliche speiss gelebt, als alleinig sich ergerzet mit den aichbletern . . ."

[193] Ibid.: "mit einen guetten Hoffnung seiner völligen gesundtheit: Gott wölle ihm solche mitthailen."

[194] Hübner, *Geneologische Tabellen*, vol. III, table 930. On marriage prohibitions, see Zedler, vol. XLIX, 2018–2020.

[195] His cousin, Wolfgang Joseph, also left a dissertation in HStAM, Personenselekt Cart. 441. On other members of the Taufkirchen clan who enrolled at Ingolstadt and in Siena during a *peregrinatio*: Müller, *Universität*, 178; Wiegle, *Die Matrikel*, 681.

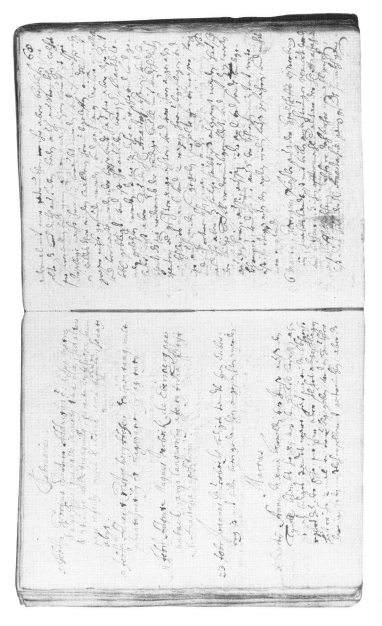

Plate 13. Anastasia miracle book: entry for the demoniac Anna Maria Arnold, March 3, 1662. (Permission of Central State Bavarian Archive, Munich.)

one of the leading causes of spiritual afflictions reported at the Anastasia shrine. Apart from complications in pregnancy and childbirth or marital difficulties, seventeen pilgrims mentioned courtship as the cause of their spiritual afflictions, while another ten claimed that they suffered as a direct result of wedding festivities. In yet another seventeen cases, persons concluded they had been driven to distraction by love magic. These cases contrasted sharply with that of Leopold Francis Isidor. Anna Maria herself did not descend from a venerable lineage, never attended a university, never wrote a thesis nor conducted a *peregrinatio*. Fortunately, the custodian at the Anastasia shrine meticulously recorded the details of her story and, in conjunction with good post-Tridentine parish registers, extraordinary court documentation and our present knowledge of early modern cultural practices, some of the custodian's more hermetic inferences from her plight become transparent.

Anna Maria, a demoniac, arrived at Benediktbeuern one month before Leopold Francis Isidor.[196] She explained that, while still single, a baker's apprentice proposed marriage to her, but she had refused.[197] Thereupon he twice gave her a "drink" laced with "a sugar," sharing the first round, but then ordering her to consume the second "to the last drop."[198] "After this drink, that same night, she was robbed of her senses."[199] For seven weeks thereafter, she wandered the forests "like a wild animal," was eventually found with great difficulty and was interned under guard.[200] Severely beset with demonic assaults, she was initially taken to a shrine at Mount St. Bartholomew for treatment.[201] For another three years thereafter, she experienced calm and peace. Subsequently, she then traveled to the Anastasia shrine complaining that the devil beset her once again with a variety of specters and visages. Small animals flew about before her eyes and she suffered suicidal temptations, as the devil tried to convince her that she could only be redeemed if she drowned herself.[202]

[196] AMB 620303.
[197] In the Anastasia miracle book, Mathias is referred to as a miller's apprentice (*Mälknecht*), which is restated in legal documentation (LaT Hofregistratur Protokolle Jahr 1661, vol. 1, 73r); see Schmeller, *Bayerisches Wörterbuch*, vol. 1, 1590.
[198] ". . . hat er ihr 2 mal ein trunckh gegeben, und ein Zuckher darein geschoben erstlich er selber mit getrunckhen, aber daß andermal nit mer getrünckhen, ihr aber befolchen, sie solte daß dickh auf den boden auch austrinckhen . . .": AMB 620303.
[199] ". . . nach disen Trunckh ist sie dieselbige nacht ihrer sin beraubt worden . . .": ibid.
[200] ". . .und 7 wochen als ein wildes Thier in den wäldern herumbgelaffen, endtlich mit grosser miehe gefunden worden, und noch lang dariber eingespert und verwarth worden . . .": ibid.
[201] Kramer, "Ein Mirakelbuch," 129, tentatively identifies the location of the St. Bartholomew shrine as Montafon.
[202] ". . . daß sie 3 Jahr ein ruche und frid gehabt, iezt aber du der Heiligen Anastasiae khomen, und bekhent, daß sie widerumb der laidige Teufl mit underschidlichen spectri oder gsichter angefochten,

Anna Maria's story illustrates the hazards inherent in a courtship ritual condemned by the post-Reformation authorities as clandestine marriage. She hailed from Imst, a Tyrolean market town in the Pitz valley
fifty kilometers west of Innsbruck. Domestic service, a common phase
in the life of young people, especially women, explains her residence in
Innsbruck.[203] The social status of her suitor, a baker's apprentice, Mathias
Arnold, reflected her own, since the social and economic implications
of courtship and marriage usually limited choice of prospective partners to one's peers.[204] In early modern Schwäbisch Hall, for example,
serving women charged with pre-marital sexual violations overwhelmingly chose their partners from among male servants, apprentices, masters
and their sons, or soldiers.[205] According to the ledger entry, the particular incident preceding her afflictions occurred three years prior to Anna
Maria's pilgrimage in 1662 and she was single at the time. Nocturnal trysts
between unmarried individuals were a common aspect of early modern
courtship, especially in Central and Northern Europe.[206] This custom,
known locally as "windowing" (*Fensterln*), recalls balcony scenes immortalized by Shakespeare in *Romeo and Juliet* and Rostand in *Cyrano de Bergerac*,
though a more accurate portrayal appears in Grimmelshausen's account of
the Thirty Years War, *Simplicissimus*.[207] In customarily comical form, the
scoundrel Simplicissimus describes his nocturnal visitation to a woman,
who allows him into her room, presses him for promises of marriage and

---

und vor ihren augen als ein khlaines maul und 2 rapen herumbgeflogen, und ihr auch in den Sin
gegeben, sie solte in wasser springen und sich ertrenkhen, wan sie anderst wolte seelig werden":
ibid.

[203] In some areas of early modern Bavaria, it has been estimated that servants made up more than
50 percent of the local population. Peasant servitude was an important phase of the life-cycle for
many; on this phenomenon, see Stefan Breit, "*Leichtfertigkeit*" *und ländliche Gesellschaft. Voreheliche
Sexualität in der frühen Neuzeit* (Munchen, 1991), 29–34; Michael Mitterauer, "Gesindedienst und
Jugendphase im europäischen Vergleich," *Geschichte und Gesellschaft* 11 (1985), 177–204. In rural
England, some 66 percent of women aged twenty to twenty-four were servants: Merry Wiesner,
Women and Gender in Early Modern Europe (Cambridge, 1993), 86–92.

[204] Richard van Dülmen, "Fest der Liebe: Heirat und Ehe in der frühen Neuzeit," in: van Dülmen,
Armut, Liebe und Ehre. Studien zur historischen Kulturforschung (Frankfurt am Main, 1988). On the
specific socio-economic aspects of courtship in early modern Central Europe, see Breit, "*Leichtfertigkeit*," 211–220; Rainer Beck, "Illegitimität und voreheliche Sexualität auf dem Land. Unterfinning,
1671–1770," in: Richard van Dülmen (ed.), *Kultur der einfachen Leute. Bayrisches Volksleben vom 16.
bis zum 19. Jahrhundert* (Munich, 1983), 112–150.

[205] Reante Dürr, *Mägde in der Stadt. Das Beispiel Schwäbisch Hall in der Frühen Neuzeit* (Frankfurt am
Main, 1995), 256.

[206] Michael Mitterauer, *Ledige Mutter. Zur Geschichte illegitimer Geburten in Europa* (Munich, 1983),
55–67, as well as Beck, "Illegitimität," and Breit, "*Leichtfertigkeit*."

[207] The balcony scenes of Shakespeare and Rostand are familiar enough. The comical account of
Simplicissimus' nocturnal tryst appears in chapter 21 of Hans Jacob Christoffe von Grimmelshausen,
Der abenteuerliche Simplicissimus (Stuttgart, 1970).

rewards him by allowing him to lie next to her in bed, where he falls asleep and is later surprised by the angry father. The overt features of this European cultural artifact are familiar enough; a young man secretly woos his beloved after dark, as she peers longingly from the windowsill of her parents' house.

Not infrequently, the man entered the woman's chamber, even her bed. In Swabia, David Sabean notes, once women reached marital age, they slept alone and were permitted to receive evening visitors with the tacit consent of the house-father, despite legal prohibitions. Sexual intercourse was not expected.[208] In 1585, the Frenchman Noël du Fail concurred: "In Germany, young men and women sleep together without this being considered shameful, and when their parents are asked about this familiarity, they answer 'caste dormiunt,' they sleep together chastely."[209] An anecdotal encounter between a Bavarian father confessor and a penitent implies the good-natured attitude toward "windowing" which prevailed as late as the eighteenth century: "'didn't you go windowing during Lent?', the father confessor asked the honest farm hand. 'Oh no, Father, that time is far too sacred; but, after Easter, if God wills, that can start again!'."[210]

An earthy, but innocent casualness toward courtship was not unusual in early modern Europe. What differentiated Mathias Arnold's visit to Anna Maria Stremayer from a casual nocturnal tryst was a marriage proposal. Like Grimmelshausen's *Courasche*, women generally avoided sexual intimacy before obtaining a firm matrimonial commitment, because the danger of conception threatened them with financial burden and the public shame of illegitimacy. Serving women found it particularly difficult to secure a marriage after pregnancy.[211] For that reason, women bringing paternity suits before Central European marriage courts nearly always asserted that they had slept with the alleged father only after a marriage proposal.[212] Theoretically, the verbal proposal of marriage served as

---

[208] Sabean, *Property*, 329–334. Note that the term "house-father" does not imply blood relation. Servants were also legally part of the household, and, in an attempt to fight clandestine marriages, Maximilian I of Bavaria issued a mandate (1635) ordering house-fathers to forbid "windowing" among their charges, but especially among servants (*Ehehalten*): HStAM GR F. 321 #7. On laws prohibiting fornication, see Breit, "*Leichtfertigkeit*," 78–83.

[209] Noël du Fail, *Contes et Discours d'Eutrapel* (ed. Jules Assézt) (1585), (Paris, 1874); cited from Beck, "Illegitimität," 143.

[210] "'Hast du die Fastenzeit durch nicht gefensterlet?' fragte ein Beichtvater einen ehrlichen Bauernknecht. 'Ach nein, Herr Pater, die Zeit ist gar zu heilig; aber nach Ostern, wills Gott, wirds wieder angehen!'": Schmeller, *Bayerisches Wörterbuch*, vol. I, 734.

[211] Dürr, *Mägde*, 252–258.

[212] Studies on this phenomenon are numerous: Beck, "Illegitimität," 132; Breit, "*Leichtfertigkeit*," 99–109; Sabean, *Property*, 331, 334; Max Safley, *Let No Man Put Asunder* (Kirkville, 1984), 15–17, 64–68.

a contractual offer with sexual intercourse representing acceptance. There-fore, Mathias Arnold's proposal contained an implicit sexual proposition. Ecclesiastical and secular authorities opposed such clandestine marriage contracts because they undermined parental authority. It was common for men to use the pretext of a marriage proposal to gain sexual favors with no real intention of fulfilling the promise. The proposal might be ver-bal or simply inferred through the presentation of a token, gift or shared drink of beer.[213] Marriage court records reveal just how difficult the sex-ual "signature" was to prove, but that proof was an essential component of a consummated (if clandestine) marriage agreement. Besides emotional uncertainties or potential insincerity on the part of her suitor, Mathias Arnold's proposal presented Anna Maria with yet another dilemma. In Bavaria, servants had been legally ineligible to marry since 1553.[214] The same was true of apprentices in the bakers' guild of Innsbruck, where Anna Maria's husband worked. A guild ordinance of 1590 not only required apprentices to attend auricular confession and communion according to the true Catholic religion, but also restricted them from marrying either outside the guild or before completing their apprenticeship, threatening breaches with forfeiture of credentials.[215]

Alone in a strange village, serving women were particularly vulnerable to exploitation, sexual and otherwise. Legislation threatened house-fathers for permitting male and female servants to share common sleeping quar-ters or participate in nocturnal visits, a state of affairs held responsible for widespread fornication and impregnation, especially among unmar-ried peasant servants and other vulgar individuals in the countryside.[216] Furthermore, the authorities added fornication to the litany of moral lax-ities responsible for internecine warfare and natural catastrophes.[217] How-ever, constant repetition suggests the failure of legal attempts to prohibit courtship and clandestine marriages according to a deeply ingrained pop-ular custom. One study of pre-marital sexual relations in early modern Bavaria has essentially stigmatized courtship between serving men and women in the countryside as rape-like.[218] Whether or not the applica-tion of modern values is appropriate here, serving women in early modern Europe certainly faced a catch-22 situation. Women entering paternity suits or accusing men of taking their honor were regularly fined for for-nication, even when the court awarded support in their favor or enforced

---

[213] On the shared drinking of beer, see Breit, "*Leichtfertigkeit*," 94–95.
[214] Ibid., 29; Strasser, *State of Virginity*, 27–56.   [215] Stadtarchiv Innsbruck, Cod. 53 #53.
[216] HStAM GR F. 321, #7.   [217] Breit, "*Leichtfertigkeit*," 5; Dürr, *Mägde*, 223.
[218] Breit, "*Leichtfertigkeit*," 217–218.

a marriage promise.[219] On the other hand, charges of rape were very serious. They jeopardized the stability of a village community by requiring the death penalty. Accusations of rape were also difficult to prove without witnesses or a full judicial confession. Already isolated by her status as an outsider in the community where she lived and worked, a serving woman often lacked the resources or access to social support mechanisms that would empower her to challenge a rapist in any other fashion than forcing him to marry, while leaving herself open to charges of fornication.

On June 16, 1657, four years and nine months before her pilgrimage, Anna Maria and Mathias had a baby girl legitimately baptized Anna at the parish church of Mühlau.[220] If the chronology of events described in the miracle book is accurate, the child was conceived on the night that Anna Maria went mad and became possessed. Apparently, the couple had their marriage recognized in the interim, otherwise the child would have been illegitimate. By succeeding in her wedlock to Mathias Arnold, Anna Maria was a rare exception. Indeed, Barbara Kammer, the honorable wife of a master baker of Innsbruck, served as the godmother, a fact not without significance. In 1658, a second child, Lucas, was baptized as a legitimate son of Mathias Arnold, honorable innkeeper (a reference to his father's profession), and Anna Maria Stremayer; this time, the godfather was Michael Kammer, the master baker himself.[221] The Arnold family appears to have been well situated socially, with powerful friends and economic security. They certainly needed them: while the local clergy accepted the marriage, the guild authorities did not. In March 1661, Mathias senior, the wealthy innkeeper in Mühlau, petitioned on behalf of his son to have him reinstated in the bakers' guild, after he was expelled for the crime of fathering an illegitimate child.[222] Inquiries by the archducal Aulic Council of the County of Tyrol with the City Council, the Mayor of Innsbruck, the district judge of Thaur, and his neighbors in Mühlau indicated that Mathias (who appeared in person before the Aulic Council) was a worldly and strong young lad, a capable baker's apprentice

---

[219] Ibid., 128–173.   [220] LaT, Pfarrregister, Film #631, 15.
[221] ". . . baptizani infante legitime natu coniungu honecti viri & hospitie in Millan Matheuß Arnold & matri Anna Maria Stremerin patrieo Michäel Cammer meister des Pekhenhandtwerchs zu Inssprugg": ibid., 19.
[222] LaT, Hofregistratur, Reihe F., F. 84, March 26, 1661. On Mathias senior's property holdings, see Eduard Widmoser, *Tirol A bis Z* (Innsbruck, 1970), 197–198, 397–398. According to LaT, Regierungskopialbuch 172, 185r–v, November 29, 1657: "Daß Christoph Miller in den Ime von Matheüß Arnoldt der 200 fl. Neüttlich verwendten Lehenbahren Zehenten auß dem gueth Kircher genant investiert werden solle."

with a good reputation.[223] On behalf of Archduke Ferdinand, an exception was granted by decree allowing Mathias to re-enter the trade, so long as he conducted himself honorably and continued to reside at his father's home.

Lest we presume all is well that ends well, we should recall that Anna Maria had initially turned down Mathias' proposal until he had given her a drink. The indication, initially at least, is that she objected to the marriage – at least this is how she described the circumstances years later at Benediktbeuern. Pressured by a well-positioned family to raise children in a precarious union to a man whose livelihood was threatened by a craft guild that questioned the legitimacy of their relationship drove Anna Maria to suicidal delusions, an affliction she attributed to a love potion. This leaves us to consider the phenomenology of exorcism in an attempt to understand the function of faith-healing in this case. At the Anastasia shrine, the devil announced his presence after the application of relics, screaming "out, out," and, before Anna Maria could set foot outside the chapel, he exited her body through her armpit and she was cured. What did Anna Maria Stremayer, the victim of an enchantment, gain from treatment at Benediktbeuern? Accusations against Mathias, a member of a locally respected family, would have been difficult to prove. They would certainly have harmed the Arnolds' reputation even more than charges of illegitimacy in an intimate community where "the psychological security of seventeenth-century villagers depended far more on maintaining good relations with one's neighbors than our peace of mind does."[224] At Benediktbeuern, far from Innsbruck, the accusation harmed no one and simultaneously unburdened Anna Maria from any feelings of guilt and nagging doubt. She could transfer guilt for the sexual indiscretion onto the love potion, while the devil eliminated the necessity for a public denunciation of her seducer – her husband and the father of her children – or an internalized denunciation of herself as a fornicator. The potion and the devil that entered her were the agents of possession, not the circumstances of that night, nor her rejection of the marriage proposal, her subsequent pregnancy and the tribulations of legal difficulties. In this case, charismatic faith-healing through exorcism represented a suspension of moral and legal imperatives against fornication, seduction and rape, offering salvation in the form of a culturally sanctioned ritual.[225]

---

[223] LaT, Hofregistratur, Reihe F., F. 85, May 11, 1661; LaT, Regierungskopialbuch, 175, 456r–v; 177, 413v–414r, 458v–459r; LaT Hofreistratur Protokolle Jahr 1661, vol. I, 25r, 73v; vol. II, 88v, 128v.

[224] MacDonald, *Mystical Bedlam*, 109–110.

[225] On the suspension of religious imperatives as part of the sacrament of auricular confession, see Drewerman, *Psychoanalyse*, 11.

CONCLUSIONS

The last two case histories reiterate the importance of examining nosology in a practical context. Furthermore, the phenomenology of spiritual physic revisits the questions of interpretation raised at the onset of this chapter. Spiritual physic incorporated treatments roughly equivalent to psychoanalytic explanations like suggestion, transferral, verbalization and removal to a neutral setting. It embraced medieval Christian traditions strengthened by the devotional renewal of the sixteenth century. Novelties associated with the post-Tridentine environment added to its stature – standardized training, institutional accreditation, formalized procedures and accountability. Popular beliefs and material contingencies motivated ordinary people to seek out spiritual physic. Readily available and not prohibitively costly, spiritual physic appealed to sufferers, kin and neighbors as an established form of treatment with a strong basis in their value system. Religious orthodoxy added to its reputation as it drew credibility and structure from the institutions of both church and, initially, the state. Despite elements of charismatic faith-healing, the power of Catholic spiritual physic ultimately rested in the institution. The priest healed through the sacrament of ordination and the power of the keys rather than any innate personal abilities or a state of grace, although the personality of the individual spiritual physician certainly played a role. In general, spiritual physic benefited from the spread of a standard vocabulary available to sufferers to structure their mental distresses. Healers at cult shrines also depended on the reputation of the specialist saint and their relics. At more traditional shrines like Pürten, wondrous relics acted as the sole basis of attraction. At the Anastasia shrine, on the other hand, the proactive involvement of the custodians insured Benediktbeuern a leading position in the mental health care sector.

Initially, sufferers accessed spiritual physic in the parish. We know very little about the process at this level, but Catholic priests relied heavily on shriving to identify symptoms and affect a simple cathartic cure through verbalization. Confession helped overcome anger, spitefulness and emotional discord. Should a confessor detect a serious affliction or one beyond his abilities, he might encourage sufferers to invoke a saint through a contractual vow. In more serious cases still, direct access to the saints and their relics proved necessary. Pilgrimage offered additional advantages, including disassociation from the context of the problem as a direct benefit of the journey. Like the triumphal stories of the journeys of the saints, a successful pilgrimage aimed to rebuild individual confidence. Sufferers also acquired social prestige at home through their contact with holy places and objects. They became a source of local pride and wonder, reifying a divine connection through their physical proximity to the relics of the special dead. In fact, as they neared Benediktbeuern, pilgrims attributed mood swings and symptoms directly to the proximity of St. Anastasia. At the shrine itself, her power focused on relics contained in the "head of Anastasia" (*Anastasia Kopf*; see Plate 14a), a reliquary bust of the saint containing her physical remains. At Pürten, all of the power of the Beata Alta focused on her evangelistary and not the place itself. Pilgrims borrowed the book, took it to an accommodation and slept on it as a pillow. Today, one can still see the sweat and oil from the heads of pilgrims on the cover pages of each gospel, upon which they slept (at least one pilgrim also entered an inscription to that effect in 1692), verifying its repeated use (see Plate 14b). Both relics suggest an association in the popular consciousness of spiritual afflictions with the head. In his *Bavarian Beacon*, Aemilian Biechler, a custodian and the first hagiographer of St. Anastasia, recommended the following prayer to pilgrims:

Greetings, oh comfort of all the helpless, oh remedy of all the sick. Look upon my misery, oh holy Anastasia. For my many sins cause me great tribulations . . . I fall to my knees in the deepest humility before God and you saints, here to renounce the evil enemy and all his temptations; to curse all sin and vice, I want to begin to love this very hour and no longer to offend. I am also consoled by the hope to receive forgiveness for all my sins . . . Take away everything from me that can hinder me from salvation and compensate with your good works that which is lacking from mine before God; so that I might achieve salvation of soul and body through your intercession. I will honor and love thee for all the days of my life, amen.[226]

Other common treatments included prayer, masses or the application of holy water. Auricular confession represented the most common treatment by far. The Anastasia ledger explicitly refers to auricular confession and communion as part of the healing process in some fifty cases. As chief spiritual physician at the shrine, the custodian heard the pilgrims' confessions

[226] "Seye gegrüsset O Trost aller hilfflosen/ O Artznei aller Krancken. Sihe an mein Elend O heilige Anastasia. Dann mich betrüben sehr meine grosse Sünd . . . also falle ich nider auff die Knye in tieffister demuth vor Gott und euch heyligen/ allda abzusagen dem bösen Feind/ und allen seinen eingebungen; zuverfluchen alle Sünd und Laster/ wil jetzt in dieser Stundt angangen zu lieben/ und nit mehr beleidigen. Bin auch einer getrösten hoffnung verzeihung aller meiner Sünden zuerlangen . . . Nimme hinweck alles von mir/ was mich an meinem hail verhindern kan/ und ersetze mit deinen Verdiensten/ was an den meinigen vor Gott abgehen wird; damit ich zugleich durch deine grosse Furbitt zu Seel und Leib das Heil erlangen kunden. Ich will dich ehren und lieben die zeit meines Lebens/ Amen": Biechler, *Bayerischer Pharos* (1663), 107–108.

Plate 14a. Reliquary bust of the St. Anastasia cult, *c.*1725. (Courtesy of the Salesians of Benediktbeuern; photograph by Photo Thoma, Benediktbeuern.) This ornate silver bust, which dates from the eighteenth century, bears witness to the success of the cult; in the seventeenth century, the relics were stored in a less valuable, wooden version.

Plate 14b. Evangelistary of the Beata Alta cult, *c.* tenth century. (Note the signs of wear from usage as a pillow. Permission of the Bavarian State Library, Munich.)

and administered communion.[227] Systematic recourse to auricular confession as spiritual physic reiterated the centrality of moral casuistry. This, in turn, amplified personal guilt in pathological perceptions of spiritual afflictions as the wages of sin, evil and moral turpitude. To offset feelings of shame, the anonymity of confession at shrines received a boost from the post-Tridentine move toward privatization. The confessional booth in Benediktbeuern mentioned in 1666 was either an original feature of the Anastasia chapel dedicated in 1606 or a later addition and it further enhanced the curative attributes of confession through the mystique of confidentiality.[228] For a variety of reasons, women exhibited moral afflictions to a larger extent than men, who predominated in legal and medical categories. Contemporaries often attributed a greater potential for immorality and sexual promiscuity to women. Women lacked analogous legal status in an increasingly patriarchal society. However, the proclivity to associate

[227] Hemmerle, *Die Benediktinerabtei*, 140–141, 251, 263.
[228] AMB 661006.

spiritual afflictions with a particular gender was never absolute; men suffered almost the entire range of spiritual afflictions, excluding those directly associated with childbirth.

Spiritual physicians tacked on ritual reintegration through consumption of the Eucharist after sacramental penance to symbolize closure. Vitus Heiss, "vexed by many insects," Georg Hauser, terrified at night in his bed, and Christoph Schmidt, a terrified old man: all had a mass read at Benediktbeuern, went to confession and took communion, "much relieved."[229] Maria Sper suffered tribulations as the result of a poor financial transaction, but slept well after confession and reception of the Eucharist.[230] Spiritual physicians treated persons suffering despair, the Hungarian fever, evil thoughts and raving madness with auricular confession followed up with communion.[231] Performance might bring only temporary relief. Contemporaries also interpreted the inability to perform an orderly confession or receive communion as a sign of mental disorder.[232] For example, when Catharina Megel, a melancholic, began to tremble after partaking of the Eucharist, the custodian interpreted this as a sign of demonic possession.[233] Mathias Ott refused to confess at his home in a state of despair, but finally did so at Benediktbeuern.[234]

Twenty-four-year-old Felicitas Jacob, forced by a fellow serving woman to drink what she euphemistically described as a "beer," became ill, could no longer perform her work and could not go to confession until her parents took her to the shrine.[235] Maria Leder was unable to confess for six months before her pilgrimage.[236] On her first day at the Anastasia shrine, Barbara Huber didn't want to confess, but recovered from her tribulations on the second day after shriving.[237] Maria Andre suffered tribulations arising from evil thoughts.[238] She desired neither to pray nor to confess, but left Benediktbeuern in peace after penance and communion. She verified her recovery eighteen years later in a communiqué. A perception of confession and communion as efficacious forms of spiritual physic was not limited to common persons. When Emperor Rudolf II and his son, Julius Caesar, had difficulties in confessing and taking communion, physicians and theologians interpreted these as sure signs of melancholy, enchantment and demonic possession.[239]

[229] ". . . mit vilen muken vexiert . . .": AMB 630114; 640329, 650110.   [230] AMB 660422.
[231] AMB 621109, 6303++ (no day), 660601, 660911, 670627, 680424.
[232] AMB 651121, 661110, 670307, 670627.   [233] AMB 660826.   [234] AMB 6303++ (no day).
[235] AMB 650331.   [236] AMB 650608.   [237] AMB 670228.   [238] AMB 680402.
[239] Midelfort, *Mad Princes*, 132–133, 142.

The autobiographic general confession provided an even more power-ful method of shriving. Catharina Hirsch (accompanied by her husband) thanked God for her recovery, but she still remained somewhat corrupt.[240] After the application of relics, she managed a complete general confession, communicated and experienced no further difficulties. The Tridentine requirement for a general confession following conversion from Prot-estantism also accompanied spiritual physic. Maria Pachleiter, an Eng-lishwoman "converted to the Christian faith" six months before her first pilgrimage to Benediktbeuern, returned two years later to perform a general confession.[241] Maria Elisabeth Siger, a former Zwinglian catechized by the Jesuits in nearby Landsberg, had already journeyed to several holy shrines before arriving at Benediktbeuern on May 19, 1662.[242] Not yet fully inte-grated into Catholic society, she still harbored grave reservations about her conversion. Siger arrived in the company of other pilgrims, requesting a general confession. The custodian administered the general confession in two stages. On the first day, the relics of St. Anastasia were laid upon her with no visible effect, but she confessed that since her youth she had never had peace of mind and suffered fainting spells. Then she suffered a fit in the presence of the custodian and consequently went completely out of her mind. Satan concealed his presence for four days, but during repeated applications of the relics on the fifth day, Maria Elisabeth began to tremble, rant and scream. Bound to a chair with metal cleats and restrained by several persons, she underwent the application of relics without ritual exorcisms until the evil spirit revealed itself in a torrent of laughter and mockery. Relics were applied again and again over the next four days to make the spirit do penance, forcing submission and liberating Maria Elisabeth from the need for restraint. On May 26, she confessed and the spirit exited her body in the form of a beetle. At first, the exorcist hesitated to believe that Satan had left her completely, so he continued to apply the relics for several days. As no further symptoms appeared, however, he became convinced of Elisabeth Maria's remarkable recovery, for which she thanked both God and St. Anastasia.

This leaves us to deal with the ultimate and perhaps most famous method of spiritual physic: exorcisms. Exorcisms represented an extraordinary heal-ing procedure, employed only after the exhaustion of all other conventional

[240] AMB 640120.
[241] ". . . zum Christlichen glauben bekhert worden vor 6 Monat . . .": AMB 660818, returned on 680924.
[242] AMB 620519.

sacraments and sacramental alternatives. Complaints of demonic possession rose toward the end of the sixteenth century and, not surprisingly,
exorcisms increased in frequency. Confronted by the devil on an unprecedented scale in the seventeenth century, distraught secular and ecclesiastical
officials reacted swiftly to regain control over madness, punishing what they
viewed as superstitious abuses and misappropriations by malingerers and
unauthorized healers. The changing history of demonic possessions and
exorcisms in early modern Bavaria evidences links between mental health
care, religion and contemporary politics more spectacularly than any other
form of spiritual physic. Historians of medicine, psychiatry and religion
are always quick to cite exorcism for a variety of reasons and, therefore, it
deserves special scrutiny.

CHAPTER 5

The decline of religious madness

Common sense is the best distributed commodity in the world, for
every man is convinced that he is well supplied with it.
René Descartes, *Discourse on Method*

. . . one always encounters monks more frequently than common sense.
Blaise Pascal, *Lettres Provinciales*

A DIABOLICAL CRISIS

We regularly associate the decline of religion and the rise of a secular society with enlightened philosophes. In mental health care, the pathological
insanity defense replaced religious explanations for madness. The history
of demonic possession and exorcisms provides perhaps the most dramatic
illustration of the transition to secular explanations for mental disorders in
the West. Histrionically charged, the highly visible ritual captured the contemporary imagination and possession still attracts the attention of modern
psychiatrists and historians for very good reasons. Cosmologically, the dramatic struggle between the demoniac and the exorcist literally embodied
the fight between good and evil, locating the celestial conflict of God and
Satan firmly in the *theatrum mundi*. The eschatological mood fixed on
possession and other forms of demonic activity during the general crisis.
Reports of possession surged suddenly at a time when witchcraft persecutions reached a terrible climax. Then, just as quickly, elite support for
exorcism and witch-hunting subsided, but largely for political rather than
medical, scientific or philosophical reasons. The profound shift in attitudes
about possession and exorcism at court reflected mounting political dis-
trust of metaphysical meddling in matters of state. Heated debate at court
over embarrassing public cases of demon possession in Bavaria coincided
with the end of the general crisis, contributing to the decline of religious
madness and the attendant rise of a secular insanity defense. As a radical
answer to blaring social incohesion, exorcism served its political purpose. It

197

achieved resounding popularity as spiritual physic as well. Then absolutist policies turned against exorcism, laying the groundwork for a psychological revolution.

Spiritual physic had always had both private and public moments. Since the introduction of the confessional, parishioners accessed auricular confession in an increasingly privatized form. The parish priest invited troubled members back into the community through public participation in the Eucharistic feast, marking recovery. The application of relics at cult shrines, while usually public, could also be private. While the bust of St. Anastasia was secured in a chapel, and application regularly occurred before large crowds (see Plate 9 above), sufferers removed the evangelistary from Pürten to sleep on. Exorcisms, too, could be public or private affairs. The Jesuits, consummate dramatists and demonologists who played on the internal sense of imagination, depicted exorcism as their most powerful weapon in the war on Satan. Their penchant for drama invited high-profile theatrics. Spectators witnessed the struggle between good and evil first-hand. Some participated and restrained demoniacs who raved with superhuman strength. Through intervention of the print media, local incidents emerged onto the regional or even the international stage, linking possession and exorcism to strategic policy decisions. At other times, access was restricted to committees of experts and officials. Sometimes, the relationship between demoniac and exorcist was strictly one on one.

Historians generally concur that the demand for exorcisms increased substantially from 1560 until the mid-seventeenth century. In 1975, the French historian and psychanalyst Michel de Certeau, SJ, intuitively estimated "thousands" of possessions in the seventeenth century.[1] One year later, William Monter dubbed the seventeenth century "the Golden Age of the demoniac."[2] H. C. Erik Midelfort's empirical analyses represent the first concerted efforts to quantify the extent of the phenomenon. His exhaustive analysis of pamphlets and broadsheets charts 121 locations in Germany witnessing demonic possessions between 1490 and 1650.[3] From 1490 to 1559, thirty-four different locations featured in famous media accounts of possession. After 1560, numbers increased dramatically. From 1560 to 1579,

---

[1] Michel de Certeau, *The Writing of History* (New York, 1988), 290; originally published as *L'écriture de l'histoire* (Paris, 1975).

[2] William Monter, *Witchcraft in France and Switzerland: The Borderlands during the Reformation* (London, 1976), 60.

[3] Originally published as "The Devil and the German People: Reflections on the Popularity of Demon Possession in Sixteenth Century Germany," in: Steven Ozment (ed.), *Religion and Culture in the Renaissance and Reformation* (Kirksville, 1989), 98–119, the results appear in slightly abridged form in Midelfort, *A History of Madness*, 55–67.

pamphlet literature cited twenty-five new locations, more than double the annual rate of the preceding seventy-year period. Reports climaxed in the twenty-year period between 1580 and 1599 (forty-seven, nearly doubling once again), declining thereafter to fifteen locations over the years 1600–1650, although this "decline" amounted to an annual rate still one and one-half times higher than the initial seventy years.[4]

Notably, data from manuscript miracle books contradict accounts of famous incidents, especially in chronological, gender and geographic terms. There were sixty-eight individual cases of demonic obsession and full-blown possession at Benediktbeuern from 1657 to 1668 alone. Therefore, although publicized accounts waned, a robust practice in exorcisms continued. Gender statistics gleaned from printed and manuscript sources diverge as well. The pamphlet and broadsheet literature indicates a ratio of less than two to three (59/38[5]), lower than Signori's ratio of two to one from published miracle books (30/14) and significantly lower than the ratio of nearly five to one from the unpublished miracle book of Benediktbeuern (48/10). The incidence of possessions among women mentioned in published miracle books is higher than in broadsheets and considerably higher in unpublished sources. The unpublished miracle books of Benediktbeuern and Pürten also confirm significant numbers of possessions and exorcisms in the Catholic southeast beyond the mid-seventeenth century.[6]

There are several possible explanations for the discrepancies between published and unpublished sources. In Bavaria, legal prohibitions against the comical devils' books (*Teufelsbücher*) limited reception.[7] Printed miracle books focused on Marian shrines, which attracted fewer demoniacs than did specialist shrines. Undoubtedly, as edited accounts, published pamphlets

---

[4] Midelfort, *A History of Madness*, 61.

[5] Sixteen other incidents involved unspecified mixed-gender demoniacs and another eight were unidentified.

[6] Complicating Midelfort's claim that, ". . . possession was not a dominant idiom of madness in the south. It may be surprising, but the evidence is clear that famous demonic possessions and controversial exorcisms were largely absent from southern Germany, and especially the Catholic southeast, during the sixteenth century": *A History of Madness*, 62.

[7] As in many things, the Jesuits were exceptional. The presses at Ingolstadt and Dillingen produced a fair amount of broadsheets depicting famous exorcisms in the late sixteenth century. Sebastien Khuller, *Kurtze unnd wahrhafftige Historia von einer Junckfrawen, wölche mit etlich unnd dreissig bösen Geistern Leibhafftig besessen . . .* (München, 1574); Sextus Agricola and Georg Witmer, *Erschröckliche gantz warhafftige Geschicht welche sich mit Apolonia, Hannsen Geisslbrachts Burgers zu Spalt Haussfrauen . . .* (Ingolstadt, 1584); Georg Scherer, SJ, *Christliche Erinnerung bey der Historien von jüngstbeschehner Erledigung einer Junckfrawen, die mit zwölfftausent sechs hunder zwey und fünfftzig Teufel besessen gewesen* (Ingolstadt, 1584); also M. Johann Schnabel (from Ingolstadt, but at the time, parish priest of Heidingsfeld), *Warhafftige und erschröckliche Geschichte, welch sich neulicher Zeit zugetragen hat, mit einem Jungen Handtwerks und Schmidsgesellen . . .* (Würzburg, 1584). Apart from the last, these

and miracle books also underreported possessions out of a sense of propor-tion. The former limited themselves to famous incidents with polemical value, while the latter presented a broad cross-section of complaints. For example, even the printed Anastasia hagiographies list only a fraction of cases from the manuscript miracle book and drastically skew the frequency of possessions as a percentage of the total case-load. The same is true for Tuntenhausen. The heavily edited 1646 compilation of miracles reordered them by type rather chronology (an unusual practice for a miracle book), summarizing all spiritual afflictions in a dedicated section limited to six pages.[8]

In short, while neither the manuscript nor the printed archival source is more reliable, their authors had different intentions. For example, in absolute terms, one could claim that possessions at Benediktbeuern from 1657 to 1668 equal a third of the cases charted by Midelfort for all of Central Europe over a period of 160 years. Arguably, based on statistics alone, Bavaria witnessed an outbreak of demonic possessions of nearly unprecedented proportions at that time. The truth, however, is far more mundane. Occasional cases of possession came to the media as occasions of scandal, but, in fact, ordinary people commonly availed of exorcism, which was related "less to the pathological than the normal."[9] Stuart Clark reminds us that "a considerable hinterland of possession behaviour lies lost to historical view in the lives of those who, all over Western Europe, resorted to local exorcists or to healers and magicians like Napier."[10] Therefore, rather than another example of a local mass *demonomania* on the level of Loudon, the Bavarian case histories witness the normalcy of exorcism as spiritual physic.

Custodians at neither Benediktbeuern nor Pürten struck a note of alarm at the trend, nor did they view it as peculiar. For them, and the sufferers as well, possession was hardly as unusual as the statistics might lead one to believe.[11] Commenting on highly publicized mass possessions in convents

---

do not include publications from Dillingen or other areas in present-day Bavaria. Many thanks to Ursula Krah for these references, treated in her forthcoming article, "'Vom boesen Feindt / dem Teuffel / eingenommen . . .': Das Motiv der Besessenheit in Flugschriften der Frühen Neuzeit," in: Hans de Waardt, Jürgen Michael Schmidt and Dieter R. Bauer (eds.), *Dämonische Besessenheit. Zur Interpretation eines kulturhistorischen Phänomens* (Bielefeld, forthcoming), 141–154.

[8] Hence the subtitle, *Denkwürdige Miracula*; see pp. 14–19 for spiritual afflictions.
[9] Ferber, *Demonic Possession*, 2, links this remark to exorcism. As she notes, the quote is originally from Natalie Zemon Davis, "The Rites of Violence," in: Zemon Davis, *Society and Culture in Early Modern Europe* (Stanford, 1965), 186.
[10] Clark, *Thinking with Demons*, 390.
[11] Ibid., 391: "Being possessed was undoubtedly an unpleasant and disturbing matter . . . But the very notion of demonic possession itself was not, so to speak, conceptually disturbing to many early

in early modern France, Moshe Sluhovsky asserts, ". . . it was these few, rather than the majority of cases, that proffered a dramatic narrative both to contemporaneous observers and recorders of these events and to historians, who mistook the voluminous documentation of these exceptional cases for a standard dynamic."[12] As a result, dramatic cases of possession are vastly overemphasized. Something at work at the grass-roots level is not reflected in the printed sources, highlighting the disjunctive nature of the discourse on possession. Mass possessions at Loudon (1634) and Salem (1692), spectacular though they were, represent a fraction of the larger context, and incidents of possession were neither isolated nor rare.[13] Sluhovsky proposes a chronological process of diffusion, popularity and demise in "their growing popularity in the sixteenth and seventeenth centuries, as well as their demise in the following [eighteenth] century."[14]

Demonic possessions, like legal witchcraft persecutions, declined in the eighteenth century, but unlike them, they never disappeared entirely. Both continued to the end of the *ancien régime* and, indeed, exorcisms continue throughout the world to the present day. The diachronic conjunctures of demonic possessions and witch-hunting in Bavaria are many, including the danger that complaints of possession might spill over into accusations of witchcraft.[15] Nevertheless, despite many parallels, the exact relationship between the two remains a significant historiographic problem. As de Certeau emphasizes, "Possession is not the same thing as sorcery. The two phenomena are distinct, and they alternate with one another, even though many early treatises associate the two, and even mix them up."[16] The "distinction became more and more blurred in cases of diabolic possession of individuals in the second half of the sixteenth century," when

---

modern minds. The condition was a regular feature of social life, as it was then perceived, and the concept seems to have fitted without offence into the patterns of thought of both ordinary people and the learned."

[12] Sluhovsky, "The Devil," 1380–1381.

[13] The story of Loudon is the subject of an Aldous Huxley novel, not to mention literary works by Alexandre Dumas and Jules Michelet, an opera by Penderecki and a movie by Ken Russell. The best critical account is Stephen Greenblatt's translation of Certeau, *The Possession*. De Certeau (2) refers to a "diabolical crisis." He suggests a paradigm shift as well: see page 202 and note 21. The historical literature on Salem is large, but three works bear particular mention: the gender analysis of Carol F. Karlsen, *The Devil in the Shape of a Woman: Witchcraft in Colonial New England* (New York, 1987); the valuable if problematic Marxist interpretation of Paul Boyer and Stephen Nissenbaum, *Salem Possessed: The Social Origins of Witchcraft* (Cambridge, Mass., 1974); and the controversial psychoanalytic study of John Putnam Demos, *Entertaining Satan: Witchcraft and the Culture of Early New England* (New York, 1982).

[14] Sluhovsky, "The Devil," 1381.

[15] "Demonic possession became common in Germany just as witchcraft was generally assuming the dimensions of an epidemic as well": Midelfort, *A History of Madness*, 67.

[16] De Certeau, *The Possession*, 3.

demonologists began attributing possession to witchcraft and the possessed subsequently accused witches and sorcerers as the agents of their affliction.[17] In Bavaria, talk of possessions and witchcraft provided proponents of reason of state with a convenient platform at court to dwell on the excesses of popular beliefs. Therefore, the two phenomena, possession and witchcraft, played a decisive role in the fight against popular culture.[18] In an article in the *Annales* attributed to Lucien Febvre, the specific decades of the Counter Reformation in France between 1590 and 1620 (and more generally the century from 1540 to 1640) are even portrayed as a "psychological revolution," part of the broader scientific revolution and thus no less significant than other critical revolutions in Western civilization.[19] The article has a spooky history all its own, but the notion of a psychological revolution has reverberated, at least in French historiography, ever since, most recently in Georges Minois' theory of a collective crisis of the Western conscience.[20] In reference to Loudun, de Certeau located the dynamic of the psychological revolution in a "diabolical crisis" of the early seventeenth century:

> But the great resurgences of sorceries and possessions, such as the one that invaded Europe at the end of the sixteenth and the beginning of the seventeenth century, mark serious fault lines within a religious civilization, perhaps the last that could be expressed by means of the religious apparatus – the last rifts before a new beginning . . . The possession of Loudun is situated almost at the end of a long epidemic, and during the very years (1632–1640) when reason took a brisk step forward with the publication of Descartes' *Discourse on Method* (1637).[21]

Traditional philosophers and intellectual historians will recognize Cartesian dualism as a decisive moment of rupture in the history of ideas, when

---

[17] Sluhovsky, "The Devil," 1386.   [18] Behringer, *Witchcraft Persecutions*, 321.
[19] The comparisons include the French Revolutions of 1789, 1830 and 1848 and the agricultural and industrial revolutions: Lucien Febvre, "Aspects méconnus d'un renouveau religieux en France entre 1590 et 1620," *Annales d'historie economique et sociale* 13 (1958), 639–650.
[20] Minois, *History of Suicide*, passim. The original article, attributed to Febvre, was actually from his lecture notes and published posthumously by Robert Mandrou, who received approbation from Fernand Braudel. Mandrou championed the history of mentalities and a psychological interpretation of early modern French history permeated his work. Febvre was a major force behind psychological interpretations of history, spelled out in his seminal 1942 essay on the question of disbelief (coining the phrase "une question mal posse") in the early modern period, translated as *The Problem of Unbelief in the Sixteenth Century: The Religion of Rabelais* (Cambridge, Mass., 1983). In the Annales "school," Mandrou fell heir to the field of collective mentalities; see Peter Burke, *The French Historical Revolution: The Annales School 1929–1989* (Stanford, 1990), esp. 43 on Mandrou's relationship to Braudel. Mandrou based his own *Introduction to Modern France 1500–1640: An Essay in Historical Psychology*, trans. R.E. Hallmark (London, 1975) on Febvre's notes. In his *Magistrats et sorciers en France au XVIIe siècle: une analyse de psychologie historique* (Paris, 1980), Mandrou investigated a similar shift in mood played out in tensions between the central state and local authorities over witch trials and possessions.
[21] De Certeau, *The Possession*, 2.

the separation of the metaphysical from the physical world baptized the scientific revolution. By 1649, Descartes addressed the dualism of the mind–body problem directly in his *Passions of the Soul*. In it, he postulated a "certain gland in the brain" as the nexus between sensory perception in the anatomical nervous system and human consciousness, challenging hylomorphic doctrine and faculty psychology.[22] He removed the passions from the physical body, but linked the two physically through the mythical pineal gland, rather than metaphysically through sympathy.[23] His pineal gland and planetary vortices (later replaced by Newton's gravitational laws) equally lacked any empirical basis, but Cartesian dualism marked a major philosophical departure from Aristotelianism. In a most relevant allegorical reference to the dualism of reason and light over unreason and darkness, Michel Foucault claims, "the Cartesian formula of doubt is certainly the great exorcism of madness," since it offered ideological support for physically segregating the mad from the sane.[24] Coincidentally, Descartes served as a lieutenant in the Bavarian forces during the Battle of the White Mountain in 1621. However, the psychological revolution in Bavaria played itself out in the bodies of demoniacs rather than in an unheated studio in Ulm.

All over Europe, the practical impetus behind the decline of religious madness and the subsequent rise of a secular insanity defense is found not in philosophy, nor on the battlefield, but in the pragmatic victory of reason of state policies over confessional strife. Conflicts with an ostensible religious basis, e.g. the Smalkaldic War in the Empire, the French Wars of Religion, the Dutch Revolts, the English Civil War and, most cataclysmic of all, the Thirty Years War engulfed Europe for a century. In France, Henry IV's conversion exemplified a policy of putting the welfare of the state

[22] Descartes, *Le passions de l'ame*, in *Oeuvres* ed. Charles Adam and Paul Tannery (Paris, 1909), vol. XI, 342, 351–352. In a stunning commentary on the implications of Descartes' theories within the context of contemporary debate, Stephen Gaukroger notes, "This opened the door to an abandonment of the Scholastic account in favour of Stoicism, notwithstanding well-known difficulties with the Stoic account; for, as Levi remarks, 'as in antiquity, the great asset of Stoic theory is that it restores unity to a fragmented soul'": *Descartes. An Intellectual Biography* (Oxford, 1995), 398. The reference is to Anthony Levi, SJ, *French Moralists. The Theory of the Passions 1585–1649* (Oxford, 1964). On this philosophical problem in Renaissance thought, see William Bouwsma, "The Two Faces of Humanism: Stoicism and Augustinianism in Renaissance Thought," in: Heiko Oberman and Thomas Brady (eds.), *Itinerarium Italicum* (Leiden, 1975), 3–60. On its moral implications, see Letizia Panizza, "Stoic Psychotherapy in the Middle Ages and Renaissance: Petrarch's *De remediis*," in: Margaret Osler (ed.), *Atoms, Pneuma, and Tranquility* (Cambridge, 1991), 39–66.
[23] Superbly detailed in Gaukroger, *Descartes*, 394–405. On the dualism inherent in Descartes' writing on the affects and passions, see Leibbrand and Wettley, *Des Wahnsinn*, 242–247.
[24] Foucault, *Madness*, 108–109; see 86 on Descartes and the passions. In the original *Histoire de la folie* (Paris, 1961), 56–59, Foucault discusses Descartes' significance in greater detail.

before religious considerations. In England, Hobbes advocated the absolute power of a state over atomized subjects whose liberties were secondary to the avoidance of a war of all against all. An essential precondition of the first international peace of modern times, the Treaty of Westphalia removed doctrinal issues from the bargaining table in favor of reason of state.

A comparison with changing notions of society illustrates the political nature of the psychological revolution. Crudely, we could compare the three faculties of Aristotelian faculty psychology with the idealized notion of three estates in the society of orders in the body politic. The first estate, the clergy, long represented the social equivalents of the highest faculty of the intellect, which humans shared with angels. The nobles of the second estate, like the animal properties of the second faculty, were held responsible for moving and shaking the body politic. Finally, like the vegetative faculty, the third estate performed basic metabolic functions in society. By the seventeenth century, a patriarchal order based on precipitous social hierarchy had, in practice, been superimposed over the estate structure. The new structure envisioned a society broken down into subjects and sovereign rulers. Like Justus Lipsius, Jean Bodin (one of the chief architects of divine right theory) had also witnessed the horrors of religious civil war and, in his *Daemonomania* (1586), he threw in his lot with the witch-hunters during the impending diabolical crisis. Gradually, as rulers consolidated their power, they rose out of the estates. In Bavaria, the concordat of 1583 secured the Wittelsbachs greater authority over the regional church. Jesuit father confessors slowly lost their influence over the prince. The aristocracy, too, suffered a decline in status. The Bavarian Fronde resulted in a domestication and confessionalization of the nobility. Proud aristocrats from venerable lineages, like Leopold Francis Isidor of Taufkirchen, found themselves relegated to the status of courtiers in the service nobility, forced to compete with bourgeois jurists on the learned bench of the Aulic Council and the nobility of the robe on their own. Serving women, like Anna Maria Streymayer-Arnold, faced the prospects of illegitimacy and shame because of the campaign to end clandestine marriage, establish stringent rules on virginity and restrict eligibility to wed based upon status. The inhabitants of Bavaria were subjugated through the social disciplining of a repressive penitential regime, which exacted a heavy psychological toll. Religious explanations for psychic suffering and spiritual physic fell under attack. Conceptually, the idealized society of orders gave way to the social reality of an amalgamation of a ruling elite set above a subject class. Even before the arrival of Descartes, psychology redefined society into a dualism of reason and unreason.

As Bavarian witch trials reached a brutal climax in the late 1620s, political and social frustration enhanced the platform of moderate opponents of the zealous religious phalanx at court. By 1650, the millenarian fears unleashed by the religious conflagrations and general crisis had proved unfounded. The world went on. Just as the ceiling frescoes of the human soul in the festive hall in Benediktbeuern celebrated a boom in the business of spiritual physic, metaphysical and theological interpretations of the mind–body relationship too had fallen out of favour at court.[25] Absolutism was hardly absolute,[26] but it was making deep inroads in Bavaria by 1650. Maximilian I, an admirer of Justus Lipsius, had already implemented neo-stoicist reforms based on reason of state.[27] The zealous supporters of spiritual physic and witchcraft persecutions invested great political capital in exorcism as the ultimate expression of their craft. In the end, however, with the accession of Ferdinand Maria and Henriette Adelaide, the Savoyard, the politics of a diabolical crisis ended in a psychological paradigm shift from religious madness and spiritual physic to a secular insanity defense.

Ironically, the primary impetus behind the shift to a secular insanity defense at the Bavarian court arose from among the ranks of the Jesuits. This aspect of spiritual physic concretely identifies an area of fruitful interplay between medicine and religion often passed over in psychology and psychiatry. The suggestion of an insanity defense against charges of witchcraft is usually attributed to Johann Weyer.[28] His influence on Bavarian witch trials is embodied in the Jesuit skeptic Adam Tanner, whose own work on the deluded condition of accused witches contributed to a climate of moderation. Later, Bernhard Frey, SJ, became the first official in Bavaria openly to use Tanner's arguments against demoniacs. Frey championed the cause of the secular insanity defense. More than anyone else, he was responsible for its practical implementation at court in the mid-seventeenth century. In their opposition to witch persecutions and exorcisms, neither Weyer, nor Tanner nor Frey advanced anything remotely similar to Cartesian dualism. Instead they employed traditional religious arguments and recommended moderation to avoid the persecution of innocents. The cautious application of strict procedural guidelines by institutions like the Spanish and Roman inquisitions had already prevented excesses, contributing to relatively low

---

[25] On parallel processes in England, see MacDonald, *Mystical Bedlam*, 11; MacDonald, "Religion, Social Change," 101–125.
[26] Generally, see Nicholas Henshall, *The Myth of Absolutism* (London, 1992). For a detailed socioeconomic critique of absolutism, see William Beik, *Absolutism in Seventeenth-Century France. State Power and Provincial Aristocracy in Languedoc* (Cambridge, 1985).
[27] Richard Tuck, *Philosophy and Government, 1572–1651* (Cambridge, 1993), 145.
[28] Midelfort, *A History of Madness*, 183–227.

rates of witch persecutions and skepticism toward exorcism in Spain, Italy and other parts of Germany.[29] Frey became a stickler for proper procedures, which he used along with other clergymen to debunk several cases of demonic possession. Ironically, therefore, in Bavaria, the moderate clergy contributed significantly to the decline of religious madness through orthodox methods of proofs. These neo-scholastic spiritual physicians played a critical role in the psychological revolution of the seventeenth century, a paradigm shift of truly Kuhn-esque proportions.[30] By supporting the shift with traditional arguments, they planted seeds of secular psychology and psychiatry, which germinated as hybrids, carrying traits of spiritual physic with them.

THE ROUTINIZATION OF EXORCISM

A number of practical guides already existed in the late sixteenth century to guide the aspiring exorcist.[31] Officially, the famous *Rituale Romanum* of 1614 supplanted them and systematized orthodox regulations for ritual exorcisms in the modern Catholic Church. Prior to that, however, several highly publicized exorcisms decisively molded the ritual into two distinct styles throughout Europe. Peter Canisius acted as the earliest prototype for the most lasting style of modern exorcism. We can refer to it loosely as the Jesuit style. Canisius had witnessed a mass possession at a convent in the Low Countries on his way to southeast Germany.[32] Upon his arrival in Augsburg in 1560, he endorsed ritual abjurations, supported Jesuit exorcisms and, eventually, performed a controversial exorcism at Altötting in 1570.[33]

In the history of exorcism, the 1566 Miracle of Laon overshadows Canisius' activities as a milestone in the history of exorcisms. Jean Boulaese first described the miraculous exorcism of the seventeen-year-old French demoniac Nicole Obry de Vervins in 1567, when he published a brief tract

---

[29] Indeed, the intervention of the Roman Inquisition led to the end of a series of related witch-hunts and exorcisms in the Empire; see Rainer Decker, "Die Haltung der römischen Inquisition gegenüber Hexenglauben und Exorzismus am Beispiel der Teufelsaustreibungen in Paderborn in 1657," in: Sönke Lorenz and Dieter Bauer (eds.), *Das Ende der Hexenverfolgung* (Stuttgart, 1995), 97–116.

[30] In the classic sense of Thomas S. Kuhn, *The Structure of Scientific Revolutions* (Chicago, 1962).

[31] Clark, *Thinking with Demons*, 414–416; these included the *Fuga satanae* (Como, 1597) of Pietro Stampa and Girolamo Menghi's immensely popular *Fustis daemonum* (Venice, 1583) and *Compendio dell'arte essorcistica* (Bologna, 1576).

[32] In 1563, Johann Weyer reported on several incidents, including the mass possession at the convent of St. Brigitte near Xanten: Johann Weyer, *De praestigiis daemonum* (Basle, 1563), 295–296, 417–418. Canisius, underway from Nijmegen, later commented on the same mass possession in 1566: *Beati Petri Canisii, Societatis Iesu, epistulae et acta*, ed. Otto Braunsberger, 6 vols. (Freiburg, 1896–1923), vol. v, 652–655; many thanks to Hans de Waardt for this reference.

[33] Reconsidered in Roper, *Oedipus*, 174–180.

and presented it to King Philip II of Spain. Boulaese personally witnessed a crowd of 150,000 onlookers, including King Charles IX and Queen Catherine de Medici, who attended the ceremony at the onset of the French Wars of Religion.[34] He intended to document the transubstantiated power of the Eucharist and thereby established a style of Eucharistic exorcisms, common in areas witnessing struggles between Catholics and Huguenots/Reformed Calvinists in France and the Low Countries, where it became a propaganda issue during the Dutch Revolt.[35] Boulaese published a more detailed and famous account, *Le Manuel de l'Admirable victoire du Corps de Dieu sur l'Esprit* (Paris, 1578), after traveling from Spain to Italy. There he received papal approbation for its publication and was exposed to stories about Canisius, which influenced the work, through his encounter with Jesuits in Rome, like his confidant, Guillaume Postel.[36] The Jesuit style, destined to outlive the French style, formed the basis for the *Rituale Romanum*. In the Jesuit style, the Eucharist played a subordinate role to relics, holy water and the intervention of the saints.[37] Eventually, the use of the Eucharist in exorcisms was forbidden because of the danger of profanation by the demoniac.[38]

The story of Canisius' activities in Augsburg and Altötting heavily influenced future cases of possession and exorcism in Bavaria. Nonetheless, it would be wrong directly to associate the genesis of modern exorcisms with the Society of Jesus as an institution per se. The order maintained an ambivalent attitude and frequently called on Canisius to moderate his stance. Nor can Canisius alone be held entirely responsible for the popularity of the ritual. Like Boulaese, he tapped into its latent potential to win converts in a climate of heightened religious sensibilities.[39] Canisius was a maverick; he acted primarily to secure the goodwill of the powerful Fugger family in the struggle to re-catholicize Augsburg.[40]

---

[34] Crouzet, "A Woman and the Devil." See also Walker, *Unclear Spirits*, esp. 20–22.
[35] The circumstances of internecine warfare also contributed to a greater proclivity for physical violence directed against the demoniac: Sarah Ferber, "Reformed or Recycled? Possession and Exorcism in the Sacramental Life of Early Modern France," in: Kathryn Edwards (ed.), *Witches, Werewolves and Wandering Spirits* (Kirksville, 2002), 58–59.
[36] Crouzet, "A Woman and the Devil," 191, 211–212, 215 (Appendix). Postel was a linguist, astronomer, Cabbalist, diplomat, professor, and religious universalist.
[37] Walker, *Unclear Spirits*, 19, 22–23.
[38] E.g. *Rituale Romanun Pauli V Pontificis Maximi* (Turonibus, 1926), Titulus XI, Caput I, 13 ("De Exorcizandis"), 389.
[39] Götz Freiherr von Pölnitz, "Petrus Canisius und das Bistum Augsburg," ZBLG 18 (1955), 352–394; Roper, *Oedipus*, 175; Duhr, *Geschichte der Jesuiten*, vol. I, 731–735, 740.
[40] Winfried Schulze, *Deutsche Geschichte im 16. Jahrhundert 1500–1618* (Frankfurt am Main, 1987), 254–255.

Canisius had a longstanding interest in exorcism and possession.[41] In response to his letter to Rome in 1545 describing an exorcism, Peter Faber, SJ, Loyola's lieutenant, warned him about the power of demonic illusions and deceptions.[42] In 1553, in a letter from Vienna to Martinus Gotfridus, SJ, Canisius discussed the links between sin, auricular confession, possession and mental health.[43] On arrival in Augsburg in 1560, he delivered a fiery anti-Lutheran polemic discussing demonic activity in the town and the saving power of exorcism; in 1562, he wrote to Rome about a demonically motivated suicide.[44] In a lengthy sermon on possession and witchcraft held in the cathedral of Augsburg on March 5, 1564, he laid out his theory about how Satan entered human bodies.[45] Canisius explained to the assembled throng how Satan tortured bodies psychically and physically, but only in a naturally explicable fashion and with the ultimate permission of God. He demonstrated that Solomon, Paul and the apostles ordained exorcism in biblical times. Finally, applying principles from Galenic humoral pathology and Aristotelian faculty psychology, he elaborated on the weakening effect of sin on the flesh, allowing Satan to enter and corrupt the body. This, in turn, affected the internal senses of imagination and fantasy, resulting in symptoms of blasphemy, sacrilegious outbursts and the loathing of sacred objects.[46] Furthermore, Canisius differentiated between obsession – when victims (like St. Anthony) saw and heard the devil, suffering from external assaults or temptations (*Anfechtungen*) – and full-blown possession – when victims lost complete control over their faculties and their body. In principle, obsession was an exogenous affliction, while possession was endogenous.[47]

The specifics of Canisius' activities in Augsburg and Altötting need not detain us here, since several notable accounts already exist. Lyndal Roper has referred to the years from 1560 to 1580 as "the years of the exorcism mania in the city"; Bernd Roeck identifes a "witch-psychosis," though it did not result

[41] Martha Schad, *Die Frauen des Hauses Fugger von der Lilie* (Tübingen, 1989).
[42] Canisius, *Beati Petri Canisi*, vol. I, 140–144.
[43] Ibid., 734, 724–726, and especially 743, recalling how auricular confession had brought women obsessed by the devil back to mental and physical health ("mulierem a daemone obsessam ad sanitatem mentis et corporis revocat").
[44] Duhr, *Geschichte der Jesuiten*, vol. I, 732. Canisius, *Beati Petri Canisi*, vol. I, 714f.
[45] Ibid., vol. IV, 868–885.
[46] His abilities as a physician of the soul were later detailed by Rader, *Bavaria Sancta*, vol. IV, 143–147. Further materials on his healing activities are found in manuscripts of the Jesuit order prepared in support of an application for Canisius' beatification: HStAM Munich Jesuiten 513 (*Vita, mores, litterae, miracula et beatifcatia Petri Canisii SJ 1553–1760*). Canisius was beatified in 1864 by Pope Pius IX and canonized in 1925 by Pope Pius XI.
[47] De Certeau, *The Possession*, 38.

in an actual persecution.[48] And Phil Soergel has also provided an excellent explication of the whimsical pamphlet war emerging from Martin Eisengrein's account of the exorcism in Altötting.[49] Perhaps it is worth recalling that, in 1567, Duke Albrecht V appointed Martin Eisengrein as superintendent of Altötting to rejuvenate veneration at the shrine. Like other shrines, Altötting suffered badly under the attacks of reformers. Eisengrein, raised as an Evangelical Protestant, studied in Tübingen and Ingolstadt in 1553. After his referral to the imperial court in Vienna, he converted to Catholicism in 1558/1559. Canisius, the Provincial of Upper Germany (including Vienna) and ex-Vice-Chancellor of the University of Ingolstadt, knew Eisengrein personally and probably orchestrated the conversion, a major coup for the Catholic cause in the Empire.[50] An influential figure at the Bavarian court, Canisius later secured Eisengrein posts at Ingolstadt and Altötting. The two remained life-long friends and corresponded frequently on matters of faith, politics and education. The potential for their collusion on the Altötting project can hardly be overstated. A number of themes recurring throughout that exorcism are also noteworthy. These included the virginity of the victim,[51] the devil gaining access to the victim's body after the utterance of a blasphemy, revelations of a false baptism or ill-intended marriage proposal, the interrogation of the devil by the exorcist, the physical battle over the victim's body waged between the devil and the saints, speaking in tongues, and the power of Catholic sacraments and sacramentals (i.e. the cult of the Virgin Mary and the saints, the application of relics, and auricular confession and communion).[52] These themes reappeared in later cases of demonic possession in Bavaria and throughout Europe.

The number of publications on famous exorcisms and possessions, such as Boulaese's 800-page account in 1578 of the Miracle at Laon, proliferated at an astounding rate thereafter. Some broadsheets were published in Munich and Ingolstadt, as well as nearby Dillingen and Augsburg. Outside Bavaria, systematic treatises on demonology began appearing with regularity. One particular author, Peter Thyraeus, SJ, deserves our special attention. Educated in Mainz and Trier before Bishop Julius Echter summoned him to

---

[48] Roper, *Oedipus*, 180; Roeck, *Eine Stadt*, vol. I, 112–116.
[49] Soergel, "Spiritual Medicine," *passim*.
[50] Luzian Pfleger, *Martin Eisengrein* (Freiburg, 1908), 4–12. Many thanks to Phil Soergel for this reference.
[51] An example of what Hsia, *Catholic Renewal*, 41, has termed "engendered sanctity." In Jesuit-style exorcisms, the relationship between demoniac and exorcist was essentially symbiotic. Whereas virginity was central to the empowerment of female demoniacs, healing power characterized the sanctity of the celibate male exorcist; ibid., 134–136. However, charges of "sexual perversities" in cases of possession might lead to accusations of witchcraft; ibid., 148–150.
[52] Roper, *Oedipus*, 174.

teach at the new university in Würzburg, Thyraeus produced a number of standard demonological works, including his *Daemoniaci* (Cologne, 1598), a handbook for exorcists. The story of Altötting figures prominently in his *Loca infesta* (Cologne, 1604). His brother, Hermann Thyraeus, SJ, taught theology from 1556 to 1560 at the University of Ingolstadt, where Canisius had just vacated his office at the university to assume the post of Provincial of Upper Germany. Contacts between members of the Jesuits order operating in a provincial community were virtually unavoidable, presenting us with a trail of information about the Altötting affair leading directly from Canisius through Hermann Thyraeus to his brother Peter. Canisius also influenced practicing physicians in the region. The Tyrolean medic Hippolyt Guarinonius employed artifacts associated with Canisius to treat plague victims, women suffering difficult pregnancies, as well as his own illnesses and infirmities. This type of good press insured the propagation of the legendary tale of Canisius and his style of exorcism.

By the mid-seventeenth century, there were many exorcists, including non-Jesuits, operating in Bavaria. One Benedictine monk, Aemilian Biechler, the author of *A Bavarian Beacon*, promoted exorcisms in Benediktbeuern. His career as a monastic exorcist was fairly typical. Aemilian (Eberhard) Biechler was born c.1614 in Sigmaringen, a Catholic enclave in the Duchy of Württemberg.[53] His parents, Agatha and Jacob Biechler (an official of the Hohenzollerns), were members of a prominent local family related through marriage to St. Fidelis.[54] That holy man provided Biechler with an early example of asceticism in an age when sainthood was a recognized career goal: Biechler's obituary describes a frivolous and tearful boyhood spent in the orchards, but through strict moral guidance and secret assistance from the saint, he matured into an upstanding young man, unaffected by the lascivious temptations of youth.[55] Through his familial connections, he became a choirboy in the Elector's chapel and entered the Jesuit college in Munich 1629, graduated two years later and transferred to the college in Ingolstadt.[56] In 1632, he professed vows at Benediktbeuern

---

[53] Hemmerle, *Die Benediktinerabtei*, 612.
[54] Ibid.; Alex Frick, *Häuserbuch von Sigmaringen* (Sigmaringen, 1971), no. 59, lists entries for Johann Bücheler, Untervogt, Johann Bücheler's widow, and Job Orth. On the influence of hagiographies on aspiring saints, see Gabor Klaniczay, "Legends as Life-Strategies for Aspirant Saints in the Later Middle Ages," in: Klaniczay, *The Uses of Supernatural Power: The Transformation of Popular Religion in Medieval and Early-Modern Europe* (Princeton, 1990), 95–111.
[55] "His namque vix superatio, mex/: doctus iam tunc à secretiore melioris Genij instinctu": HStAM KL BB 123.
[56] HStAM Jes. 2263, 349–350; Max Leitschuh (ed.), *Die Matrikeln der Oberklassen des Wilhelms Gymnasium in München*, vol. 1 (Munich, 1970), 60, 62.

and returned to Ingolstadt to study logic and casuistry in 1636.[57] At the university, Biechler fell in with conservatives and under the influence of a fellow Swabian and staunch Catholic convert, Prof. Christoph Besold.[58]

Biechler returned to Benediktbeuern with diploma in hand and his superiors immediately elevated him to the priesthood. In 1639, he took on additional duties as the custodian of the St. Anastasia shrine, the origin of his involvement with spiritual physic and exorcism.[59] Biechler, immensely popular in the parish, exhibited extraordinary skill as a diplomat and charismatic orator. Tasked with carrying tribute monies to the commander of the Swedish garrison in distant Landshut, Biechler hesitated when the imminent withdrawal of occupying forces endangered the delivery.[60] After the Swedish withdrawal, he returned to Benediktbeuern and personally redistributed the tribute among the abbey's peasants. In 1657, Biechler became parish priest of Benediktbeuern. "He was an excellent preacher, whose sermons distinguished themselves through successful disposition and great clarity."[61] Biechler's obituary praised his pastoral service administering the sacraments, catechizing the youth, tending to the sick and preaching.[62]

[57] HStAM KL BB 124, 386; Hemmerle, *Die Benediktinerabtei*, 612; Pirin Lindner, *5 Profeßbücher. 4: Benediktbeuern* (Munich, 1910), 39; Pölnitz, *Die Matrikel*, vol. II, 593–595.

[58] Like Eisengrein, Besold was another zealous convert to Catholicism from Württemberg recruited by the Wittelsbachs. A talented jurist, political theorist and mystic, he ceremoniously assumed a professorship in the legal faculty at Ingolstadt, a position he occupied until his death in 1638, coincidentally the year of Biechler's graduation; Mederer, *Annales*, vol. II, 277–279, 286–289. Whether or not the two native Swabians actually met during this time is uncertain, but with several hundred faculty and students, the university was a relatively small community. Besold's conversion from Lutheranism to Catholicism provoked a storm of controversy in the Empire at the height of the Thirty Years War. Formerly a professor at the Lutheran University of Tübingen, he converted "secretly" in 1630, only making his decision known after imperial Catholic forces occupied the Duchy of Württemberg following the Battle of Nördlingen in 1635; ADB, vol. II, 556–558. Immediately elevated to the status of councilor in the occupation government, Besold turned down appointments to the imperial court in Vienna and the University of Bologna to accept the chair offered by Maximilian I at Ingolstadt, because of his vehemence for Counter Reformation. There he published a number of anti-Protestant works, including a bitter critique of the unlawful dispossession of free imperial monasteries by Duke Ulrich the Mad of Württemberg, a legal case study based on archival research, later cited during the negotiations for the Peace of Westphalia in 1648: *Documenta rediviva monasteriorum preaecipuorum in Ducatu Wüstembergico sitorum* (Tübingen, 1636). Perhaps more relevant to the present consideration was his popular *Thesaurus Practicus* (Tübingen, 1624), a standard encyclopedia which ran into multiple editions. Besold's *Thesaurus* included numerous definitions of forms of spiritual physic and spiritual afflictions.

[59] Hemmerle, *Die Benediktinerabtei*, 565.

[60] Ibid., 612.

[61] Pfarrarchiv Benediktbeuern, Pfarregister, vol. II (1650–1710), "Pfarrvikaren zu Benediktbeuern"; HStAM KL BB 123; Hemmerle, *Die Benediktinerabtei*, 570; Lindner, *S Profeßbücher*, 39.

[62] "Ultimis, praecipire, undecim, paulo plus, annis, parochialis Ecclesiae intro Monasteium Curae suffectus, Monachum simul, et Parochum egit omnibus numeris absolutum: In administrandis Sacramentis, Catechizanda Juventute, visitandis aegrotis, instruendis ad patientiam, suaque praesentia allevandis, verè solectissimus Pastor": HStAM KL BB 123.

Biechler also compiled an ambitious manuscript entitled "Institutionis oratoris" in 1658, a work of classical rhetoric (see Plate 15).[63]

Biechler's tenure as parish priest coincided precisely with the entries in the Anastasia miracle book. Initiated in 1657, the last regular entry was made on June 11, 1668, less than a month before he died of illness and exhaustion, disregarding the advice of his physician to rest.[64] Biechler, the prime force behind the practice of spiritual physic described in the miracle book, also published in 1663 the first Anastasia hagiography, *A Bavarian Beacon*.[65] Coelestin Mosmiller, who occupied the office of custodian *c.* 1660, became active in the cult as well.[66] In his duties as exorcist, Biechler drew on the monastery's excellent library. It contained Besold's *Thesaurus*, Thyraeus' contemplations on nocturnal terrors, tracts on exorcism and demonology by Binsfield, Del Rio and Menghi (among others), along with a wide assortment of works on casuistry, the moral theology of sin, confessors' handbooks, and an arcane book of benedictions and exorcisms dating from the fifteenth century.[67]

Like Canisius, exorcism provided Biechler with a vehicle to realize his own career aspirations – beatification or even sainthood – as well as the political ambitions of his monastery and the Benedictine order. As the first author to promote the Anastasia cult in print, he stressed her virginity in a conscious allusion to the cult of the Virgin, extolling the sexual polemics of Counter Reformation Catholicism to enhance her prestige and, simultaneously, the purity of his order. For example, the hagiography recalled the possession of Anna Maria of Cannerhausen, a noblewoman from the Netherlands. When she refused to compromise her virginity in a marriage arranged by her parents, her suitor administered a satanic love potion with her mother's consent.[68] She immediately became possessed and wandered vainly for years in search of a cure. Finally, at Benediktbeuern, she was exorcised of the demon, as the virgin martyr Anastasia triumphed over Satan and his minions.

---

[63] BayStBi Clm 4731.
[64] Biechler continued working until two days before his death: HStAM KL BB 123.
[65] Biechler, *Bayerischer Pharos* (1663).   [66] Hemmerle, *Die Benediktinerabtei*, 565, 616.
[67] Some entries in the ledger, especially those pertaining to love magic, suggest derivation from Besold; see the *Thesaurus practicus* (Augusta Vindelicorum, 1641), 603. The library's catalogue, put together by Karl Meichelbeck during his tenure as cloister librarian from 1696, still exists: BayStBi Cgm C. 405, vol. I, 21r on Del Rio and Menghi (listed as "inter Prohibitos"), 32r on Thyraeus; vol. II, 6r on Binsfield. The book of exorcisms and benedictions is found in the Bavarian State Library: BayStBi Clm 4757.
[68] Biechler, *Bayerischer Pharos* (1663), 84–86.

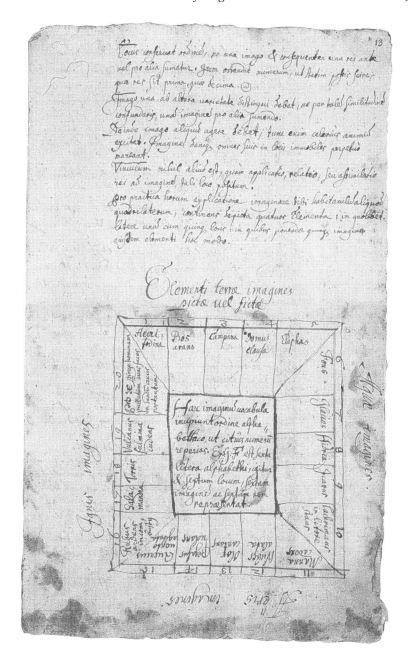

Plate 15. Rhetorical imagery of the four physical elements of classical physics from Biechler's "Institutionis oratoris." (Permission of the Bavarian State Library, Munich.)

With the figure of his ancestor St. Fidelius looming before him since childhood, Biechler aspired to sainthood as a valid career goal. By the seventeenth century, healer-saints figured as leading contestants for canonization. Like Canisius, Biechler sought to achieve this goal through charismatic leadership, rhetorical acumen and access to metaphysical power as a healer and exorcist.[69] Abbot Amand Thomamiller, who wrote his obituary, implied that Biechler deserved beatification at the very least.[70] Thomamiller, an outspoken advocate for the formation of a Bavarian Benedictine Congregation (formed in 1684), awarded the custodianship of the St. Anastasia shrine with unprecedented status as his right-hand official; the custodian alone possessed the keys to the sacristy and only surrendered them in case of illness and, then, only to the abbot directly.[71]

BOOTLEG EXORCISMS

Personally influenced by religious zealots at the University of Ingolstadt, Biechler's views were nonetheless out of step with the religious and political attitudes at court by the mid-seventeenth century. Things were different in the early seventeenth century, when exorcism – with or without ecclesiastical authorization – was a fairly common procedure in Bavaria. Shrines (e.g. Altötting, Benediktbeuern, Pürten or Tuntenhausen) claimed institutional support, especially at Benedictine abbeys (e.g. Andechs, St. Emmeram in Regensburg, Ettal, Ottobeuren or Wessobrunn). Indeed, the Benedictines gradually supplanted the Jesuits as the major practitioners of exorcism in the region. Certainly, St. Benedict enjoyed special status as the patron saint of exorcisms. In the eighteenth century, Pope Benedict XIV adopted his medal, sometimes called the "exorcism crucifix," for specific use in the ritual (Plate 17). If the Jesuit position remained ambiguous, while Benedictine exorcisms had the institutional backing of the order, unofficial healers entered the market as well, which was so thoroughly saturated by the early seventeenth century that one Bavarian monk converted to Calvinism and

---

[69] On career possibilities in sainthood, see Peter Burke, "How to be a Counter-Reformation Saint," in: Burke, *The Historical Anthropology of Early Modern Italy: Essays on Perception and Communication* (Cambridge, 1987), 48–62. On the characterization of a paradigm shift from the militant martyred saint to a model inspired by "simplicity, populism and healing," see Hsia, *Catholic Renewal*, 122–137.
[70] The obituary is entitled, "Vitae Bonae, Beatae Mortis}Echo{Beata Mors, Vita Beata": HStAM KL BB 123. On Thomamiller, see Hemmerle, *Die Benediktinerabtei*, 519–521.
[71] Ibid., 141. On Thomamiller's role in the formation of a Congregation, see ibid., 171–173. A second (and more famous) hagiographer of St. Anastasia, Karl Meichelbeck, also held this position, which was emblematic of career success: ibid., 629.

Plate 16. Copper etching from Biechler's *Bavarian Beacon* (fourth edition, 1690): "St. Anastasia, Patron of the Monastery of Benediktbeuern and Medicine for the Mad." (Permission of the Bavarian State Library, Munich.)

sought new clients in far-off Utrecht; Bavaria had become a net exporter of exorcists.[72]

The propagation of exorcisms in print after 1571 is a measure of both their popularity and their usefulness as political propoganda.[73] Their impact was twofold. On the one hand, they demarcated clear boundaries between orthodox practice and demonic superstition through the routinization of the ritual. On the other hand, they had the knock-on effect of spreading beliefs in demon possession and promoting the efficacy of exorcisms further still. The story of Pastor Johann Weiss of Martinsbuch exemplifies a paradoxical outcome, which juxtaposed popular or unauthorized spiritual physicians with the post-Tridentine campaign to suppress evil "*supersti-tiones.*" Weiss fell foul of both the ecclesiastical and secular authorities for his activities as an exorcist. In this sense, the church hierarchy viewed his superstitions as evil and effective. They represented satanic practice rather than unfounded prejudice, condemned supra-regionally by the papal bull *Coeli et terrae* in 1586 and the Bavarian Mandate against Witchcraft and Superstition of 1612, the most comprehensive secular legislation on the two subjects ever produced in Europe.[74] Weiss, born the son of a priest in Martinsbuch in 1517, inherited his father's parish.[75] During a visitation conducted by the Bishop of Regensburg in 1559, Weiss testified that he only preached authorized sermons (i.e. those of Johann Eck), recognized all sacraments as such, and spoke out for the veneration of saints and the practice of good works.[76] He admitted to frequenting taverns and, though he refrained from dance, he employed a female "cook," who attended weddings in his company, a euphemism for concubinage. In the course of the interview, some questions arose regarding his ignorance of the sacraments. For example, he granted absolution with the words, "God have mercy and

[72] On the career of Johannes Mauritius Bergerus, a former Franciscan monk from Ebersberg who later converted to Evangelical and then Reformed Protestantism before practicing exorcisms in Utrecht, see Benjamin Kaplan, "Possessed by the Devil? A Very Public Dispute in Utrecht," *Renaissance Quarterly* 49 (1996), 738–759; Kaplan, *Calvinists and Libertines. Confession and Community in Utrecht, 1578–1620* (Oxford, 1995), 210–219; Hans De Waardt, "Chasing Demons and Curing Mortals: The Medical Practice of Clerics in the Netherlands," in: Hilary Marland and Margaret Pelling (eds.), *The Task of Healing: Medicine, Religion and Gender in England and the Netherlands, 1450–1800* (Rotterdam, 1996), 173–302.
[73] For an overview, see Thorndike, *Experimental Magic*, 555–559.
[74] See also David Lederer, "Living with the Dead: Ghosts in Early Modern Bavaria," in: Kathryn Edwards (ed.), *Witches, Werewolves and Wandering Spirits* (Kirksville, 2002), 28–30.
[75] F. Markmiller, "Die Beschworungen des Martinsbucher Pfarrers Johann Weiss gegen ende des 16. Jahrhunderts," *Der Storchenturm* 9 (1970), 54–66. It is unclear whether Weiss was legally considered illegitimate. However, the fact that he inherited the parish implies at least tacit recognition of his lineage.
[76] Ibid., 57.

Plate 17. Reverse side of St. Benedict's cross (From author's collection)
The initials V R S N S M V – S M Q L I V B are an abbreviation for an exorcist's prayer:
Vade retro Satana! Nunquam suade mihi vana! Sunt mala quae libas. Ipse venena bibas! (Get
thee back, Satan! Do not suggest to me your vanities! Your offerings are evil. Drink your
own poison!). The letters inside the cross abbreviate a Latin rhyme: *Crux sacra sit mihi lux!*
Nunquam draco sit mihi dux! (The cross will be my light! Never will the dragon be my
leader!)

guide you to our Lord Jesus Christ free of sin and in hope of eternal life,"
instead of the more formal "ego te absolvo . . ."[77] Otherwise, although
he lived in open concubinage, the visitor reported that Weiss conducted
himself in a priestly fashion and provided well for his children.[78]

---

[77] Ibid., "Misereatur [et] ducat vos dominus noster Jesu Christus sine macula cum gaudio in vitam
aeternam."
[78] Ibid., 58.

Twenty years later, in 1579, the secular authorities invited Weiss to attend a hearing before the Duke in Landshut on the charge of practicing magic.[79] Weiss admitted to treating hundreds of persons, many robbed of their senses or possessed by the spirits of stillborn children from purgatory, reacting with dismay at their accusations.[80] In a state of fear, he skipped town the next day, defying an order to remain in Landshut. The Duke sent his chaplain to apprehend him. He found Weiss already back at the parish house and demanded the surrender of a suspicious book mentioned during the inter- rogation. The book, which ostensibly contained weather benedictions and exorcisms, could not be located despite a thorough search; Weiss claimed he had lost it. Weiss willingly returned with the chaplain to Landshut. There, Weiss confessed to none other than Peter Canisius, who had performed his own exorcism at Altötting nine years earlier. Canisius and the secular authorities questioned him extensively on his treatment of the mad, but released the simple old man after eliciting assurances he would never per- form another exorcism again. Later that year, Weiss was implicated in trying to cure a madman in Straubing, but he claimed the family begged him on numerous occasions and he was unable to refuse the money they forced upon him.[81] Until his death in 1594, no further complaints of unauthorized exorcisms were reported against him.

A similar case occurred in 1624, when the dean of Aufkirchen and the pastor of Fürstenfeldbruck denounced Wolfgang Faber, chaplain of Ober- alting, to the Ecclesiastical Council of Freising for practicing a variety of strange arts, healing the lame, the mad, demoniacs and other illnesses.[82] Faber responded to charges before the council, denying he ever exorcized the possessed, insisting instead he had sent them to Benediktbeuern. If he had healed one lame person, then it was only through the application of holy water and salt, standard sacramentals used in blessings. Occasion- ally, the abbots of Ettal and Benediktbeuern did send him possessed and deranged individuals for help, but he denied ever laying a hand on them. Instead, he sat them at a table and gave them the holy water and salt, after which they began to brawl and flail about senselessly. He admitted that some pilgrims, who found no solace at Benediktbeuern, were comforted in this fashion, but claimed his practices, which included a day of abstinence

---

[79] Ibid., 59–63; HStAM Staatsverwaltung F. 2792, f. 198r–v.
[80] On the contentious role of souls from purgatory as possessing spirits in popular culture and Catholic orthodoxy, see Lederer, "Living with the Dead," 31–35. Ferber, *Demonic Possession*, 64–74.
[81] Ibid., 63–66.
[82] "Ihme wie das Er mit allerlai seltzammen Khinsten umbgehe, also Khrimpe gerathmache mente captos, et diabolo obsessos restaurire, atque alios morbos incurabiles heile furgehalten et alia plura": AEM GR 61, 9–11. See also Leo Weber, *Veit Adam von Gepeckh* (Munich, 1972), 383.

in preparation for each healing, were prescribed in an exorcist's handbook, which he surrendered to the Ecclesiastical Council. Faber claimed that the formulas in the handbook, approved by the Pope himself, were drawn from old missals from the diocese of Brixen in Tyrol.

The court preacher of Freising and a learned theologian examined Faber independently, noting he actually knew very little of official procedures for the casting out of demons. Faber detailed his methods for them in six examples of cures he had worked. Specifically, he had healed a lame child, a wagon driver suffering from falling sickness, a deranged cooper, a girl from Ettal beset by two male spirits (one fiery and the other black), a dumb baker's apprentice from Munich (who paid for Faber's services), and Hans Biber of Fürstenfeldbruck, who was also lame. Furthermore, on St. Michael's Mass in 1623 (a terrible plague year), no fewer than six wagonloads of people suffering serious illnesses arrived at Oberalting seeking his help. Pater Faber insisted that he cured the poor for nothing, though he sometimes received food and drink as payment in kind or unsolicited largess from the wealthy. His use of holy water and salt was deemed in accordance with the *Rituale Romanum* without any hint of "necromancy."

The council subsequently referred Faber to the rector of the Jesuits in Munich for further questioning by qualified theologians and sent the handbook along for an assessment of its orthodoxy. The rector commented that Faber was an uneducated priest and although the handbook contained nothing erroneous or heretical, it was written "barbarically" (i.e. in the vernacular); the matter of approval by Sixtus IV was considered plausible. Since Faber led a decent and pious life, he was to be forgiven his naivety and ignorance. The Ecclesiastical Council forbade Faber to practice exorcisms in the future, the Jesuits confiscated the book and their rector recommended that inquiries be made with local officials and the Bishop of Augsburg, Faber's nominal ecclesiastical superior, to determine the extent of his activities. Investigated again in 1626 on suspicion of witchcraft and illegal blessings, Faber pleaded his innocence, stressing that no further cures had followed his last reprimand, because he sent all subsequent petitioners to Benediktbeuern.[83] Fortunately for Faber, another investigation in 1627 came up empty.[84] Otherwise, at the height of the witchcraft persecutions in southeast Germany, his life might easily have been forfeit. Certainly, the authorities took pains to investigate any possible connection between Faber's exorcisms, necromancy and witchcraft.

[83] AEM GR 62, 44; 63, 47, 50–51.   [84] AEM GR 64, 44.

Much as did Weiss, Chaplain Faber performed services as a spiritual physician to supplement a meager income from a parochial benefice. When they continued to perform healings after the authorities forbade them from doing so, both claimed at subsequent hearings that they had acted reluctantly and under pressure from desperate sufferers. Faber and Weiss were found negligent for conducting exorcisms without a license. In a move to control spiritual physic, the post-Tridentine church hierarchy sought to monopolize episcopal authority by censuring certain procedures without approbation, such as the absolution of heinous sins according to rules of reserved cases.[85] Unauthorized exorcisms performed by the uneducated lower clergy also cost official cults business, damaged the image of the ecclesiastical hierarchy and, after the Bavarian Mandate against Witchcraft and Superstition of 1612, they represented a very serious secular crime as well.[86] Several examples of applications for a license to exorcize serve to illustrate the difficulties encountered in the implementation of a policy of control, especially when it came to drawing a line between exorcism and sorcery, and between possession and witchcraft.

In the Bishopric of Augsburg, the Ecclesiastical Council took direct action to restrict licenses to exorcize on a number of occasions. In a lengthy hearing from August 1619 to April 1620, Chaplain Michael Spalt, another member of the lower clergy, was accused of conducting unlicensed exorcisms on Sabina N. in Lenzfried near Kempten.[87] On January 15, 1620, the Ecclesiastical Council publicly excommunicated Spalt, who insisted on defending his activities through scripture alone, thereby displaying evangelical tendencies. During the deliberations of March 14, the council charged the demoniac, Sabina N., with practicing witchcraft and ordered her examination by a Jesuit and a Franciscan at the University of Dillingen to establish whether or not she was actually possessed. The Dillingen theologians determined that her heretical tendencies justified a trial for witchcraft. The Ecclesiastical Council ordered the trial on April 9, 1620 and Chaplain Spalt was conducted to Rome for further examinations; the outcome of the case is not known. Clearly the authorities associated witchcraft, heresy and demonic possession in her case. It appears they harbored suspicions against the exorcist as well.

The exorcism of Walpurga Schmidt was forbidden after an examination in Dillingen failed to reveal signs of demonic possession.[88] As late as 1699, a certain Pater Marcus was refused a license to exorcize Anna Huber

---

[85] On the use of the reserved cases as a centralizing tendency, see Pallaver, *Das Ende*, 55–56.
[86] Behringer, *Mit dem Feuer*, 167–168; also 187–188, on sanctions against forbidden books (article 8).
[87] ABA GR 1618–1669, 25, 26, 34, 35.   [88] ABA GR 1690–1708, 120–121.

because of municipal laws against the rite within the city limits of Augsburg in effect since the time of Canisius.[89] In 1665, the Ecclesiastical Council flatly refused a woman from Füssen a license to exorcize on the grounds of her inexperience.[90] This reminds us that women were not specifically prohibited from conducting exorcisms. Indeed, midwives were authorized to practice a form of spiritual physic as part of the formula of emergency baptisms, driving out the devil from children they thought might die; in Protestant and especially Catholic areas of Europe, they were "responsible for the spiritual as well as the physical well-being of the children."[91]

From August 1657 to February 1660, an even lengthier dispute ensued over the activities of Pater Himbertus Vischer, a Benedictine monk from St. Afra and Ulrich in the city of Augsburg. He was suspected of conducting unauthorized exorcisms in nearby Liezheim, which the Ecclesiastical Council referred to as a scandal to the Catholic religion.[92] However, in this case, his order's strategic ambitions rather than supplemental sources of income for a lowly parish priest were at stake. The ban on public exorcisms in Augsburg since the days of Canisius forced Vischer's superiors to relocate his practice for the "treatment of souls" to the nearby abandoned monastery of St. Leonhard in Liezheim.[93] Vischer operated in strict accordance with the *Rituale Augustanum*, the locally authorized version of the *Rituale Romanum*, invoking SS. Ulrich and Afra in addition to St. Leonhard for his cures, and had already freed eight persons from the demon.[94] Pater Cellarium, also of SS. Ulrich and Afra, offered favorable testimony on Vischer's behalf, as did all the priests of the chapter house of Hochstätt. Under the protection of his monastic order, the only legal recourse for the council was to charge Vischer before his abbot.

After deliberations on October 25, 1657, the Ecclesiastical Council of Augsburg tried to persuade the abbot to prohibit Vischer from performing exorcisms because of his improper use of relics. The council argued that relics were intended for use against the devil, but no signs of actual possession had been determined, so Vischer employed them against witchcraft

---

[89] Ibid., 201.   [90] ABA GR 1618–1669, 169.

[91] Wiesner, *Women and Gender*, 69; Wiesner, "Women and the Reformation in Germany," in: Sherrin Marshall (ed.), *Women in Reformation and Counter-Reformation Europe* (Bloomington, 1989), 24. See also Karant-Nunn, *The Reformation of Ritual*, 63; Steven Ozment, *When Fathers Ruled: Family Life in Reformation Germany* (Cambridge, Mass., 1983), 108–112.

[92] ABA, 1618–1669, 87–89, 89–90, 107, 122, 123, 124.

[93] Ibid., 87–89: "missa esset a suo superiore, ad Monasterium extintum in Liezheim ut ibi propossitum ruralem ageret, et Curam animarum administaret, Et ibidem apud S. Leonardem multa miraculi fierent." On the prohibition against exorcism in Augsburg, see Roper, *Oedipus*, 174.

[94] ABA GR 1618–1669, 87–89: "et per preces et SS. Udalricum ibidem Sepulturarum, nec non S. Leonardi invocationem, octo personas a Daemone liberatas . . ."

instead.[95] Still, both the abbot and Vischer refused to give way. One year later, in September 1658, Vischer stated for the record that he had not actually exorcized, but merely applied relics to the suffering, a perfectly legitimate procedure; this forced the Ecclesiastical Council's hand.[96] In January 1660, the council had to acknowledge that Vischer's practices for the treatment of the bewitched still fell within the authority of reliquary cures and they dropped the case shortly thereafter.[97] Unlike members of the parish clergy, Vischer operated under the institutional protection of the Benedictines, thus serving as an instrument of his order's ambitions. However, in a savvy legal move to circumvent the monastical sanction, on November 3, 1662 – only shortly after Vischer had conducted another series of healings at the abandoned monastery in Liezheim – the Ecclesiastical Council of Augsburg officially restored custody of the property to the abbot of SS. Ulrich and Afra with the permission of the Duke of Pfalz-Neuburg and with papal approbation.[98] In a win–win situation, this placed the formerly masterless property under the same restrictions as the civic institution in Augsburg, while placating the abbot through the acquisition of a new property.

It was difficult for both secular and episcopal authorities to restrict exorcisms undertaken by the orders. In 1670, the Ordinary of Freising refused an application from a father confessor Gulius, a monk from the Salvator cloister in Altomünster, to exorcize the demoniac Ursula Wagner, commanding him instead to refer the possessed to Benediktbeuern for treatment.[99] Still, Pater Gulius persisted in his attempts to cure her with both spiritual and medical remedies, but met with unsatisfactory results. The Ordinary recommended medical treatment for melancholy from a corporal physician.[100] Nonetheless, Ursula's father, Georg Hafner, a smith and citizen of Altomünster, insisted on an exorcism. The Ordinary then inquired with the Abbot of Altomünster to verify that Gulius acted with his consent.[101] Gulius denied exceeding his authority and stated that the conventual, Pater Paul, acting on his behalf, had offered no spiritual phsyic or exorcism other than consolation in the confessional, though he believed that a public exorcism with relics might satisfy desperate demands voiced by the citizenry of the small town.[102] To quell public murmurings, the Ordinary authorized the application of the cranium of St. Altonus in private by the two padres. Pater Gulius admitted that the relics had no visible effect on the "imagined" devil and conceded it might be driven out more readily were Ursula remanded

---

[95] Ibid., 89–90.   [96] Ibid., 107.   [97] Ibid., 122, 123, 124.   [98] Ibid., 149.
[99] AEM GR 87, 211.   [100] Ibid., 266.   [101] Ibid., 273.   [102] Ibid., 282.

to honest work with a good beating; the Ordinary in Freising supported his verdict.[103] When Ursula's father again insisted on an exorcism in January 1671, he was rebuffed with an order from the Bavarian secular authorities to jail his daughter and remand her to work.[104] At that point, the ecclesiastical authorities intervened again. At the behest of Ursula's father, Pater Gulius approached the Ordinary again, who reordered the application of relics and a penitential cure for Ursula.[105] As long as certain orders, particularly the Benedictines, continued to condone exorcisms, their institutional position shielded them from both the ecclesiastical and secular authorities, whereas members of the lower clergy, like Johann Weiss, Wolfgang Faber and Michael Spalt, could offer little more than tacit resistance to bishops and the state.

Rosina Huber: ghost-buster extraordinaire

A concurrent increase in reported sightings of ghosts in the midst of the Thirty Years War is closely linked with perceptions of demonic possession and witchcraft. Ghosts were sighted in both urban and rural settings. At Augsburg in 1633, the watch at SS. Ulrich and Afra twice reported a ghost appearing at night in the form of a deer, but torchlight excursions led by the chaplain Hans Ferber on two occasions found nothing.[106] In 1640, the Ecclesiastical Council of Freising investigated reports of ghosts plaguing travelers in the Ebersberg Forest just east of Munich.[107] Some travelers met with deadly mishaps attributed to the supernatural and, for three consecutive nights, no one took to the roads for fear of ghosts. The Aulic Council in Munich registered similar sightings and requested reports from district judges and the *Rentmeister* in Landshut and in Straubing after ghosts were seen at night in the forests around Landshut.[108] After confirmation arrived from Straubing, the Aulic Council ordered patrols along the roads to insure the safety of travelers. When the former town clerk of Neustadt, Johann Fuhrmann, was found in a forest hung by a belt, the authorities feared the worst; a ghost must have been responsible.[109]

It was widely held that persons who died before performing a promised religious obligation were liable to haunt the living until the pledge had been fulfilled. However, the rise of ghost sightings in Bavaria at the height of the Thirty Years War paralleled growing ecclesiastical ambivalence toward

---

[103] Ibid., 311.   [104] AEM GR 88, 17.   [105] Ibid., 44.
[106] SStBA 2 Cod. S. 65, entry for November 6, 1633.
[107] AEM EG, communiqués to the Pastor of Kirchdorff and the Chaplain of Fraichoven.
[108] HStAM HR 267, 69r–v, 339v–340r, 493v.   [109] HStAM HR 268, 66v–67v.

reported apparitions. Though the church officially sanctioned the belief in spirits, its representatives proved more and more reluctant to recognize extraordinary spiritual attributes among unauthorized individuals outside the ecclesiastical hierarchy. This reluctance manifested itself in skepticism toward sightings of apparitions and demonic possessions in Bavaria. In 1643, a baker at Altomünster described to his father confessor the visit of a ghost from purgatory requesting the performance of an unfulfilled vow.[110] Only then could the spirit rest in peace. The monk repeated the baker's confession to the Ecclesiastical Council in Freising, which found itself in an awkward position: while they could not deny the possibility of an apparition outright, the council insisted that the story failed to meet certain critical criteria.[111] The council communicated ten discrepancies, among them the outward appearance of the ghost and the time of the apparition. The baker claimed that the spirit appeared brightly lit and joyous, in the day as well as at night. Ghosts from purgatory, the council reminded his confessor, were spirits of the dark, tending to sadness and usually showing themselves around midnight. The council recommended a re-examination of the baker to iron out inconsistencies in his story.

The extraordinary activities of Rosina Blökhl-Huber, the wife of a carpenter from Aresing in the district of Schrobenhausen, tell us a great deal about the blurred lines between popular and official culture in the back-and-forth campaign against superstitions.[112] Not an exorcist in the strictest sense, she exorcised ghosts from houses rather than demons from humans. Rosina Blökhl was arrested in 1641 for the illegal expulsion of ghosts (*Vertreibung der Geister*), summoned before the vicar of Augsburg and then taken to the territorial jail in Munich (the infamous *Falkenturm*). There, she underwent fifteen weeks of cruel interrogations conducted by monks under judicial torture.[113] After withstanding their examination, during which nothing suspicious was unearthed, she was released and informed personally by the court judge in Munich[114] that not only was she free to return home, but, as far as the Elector Maximilian I was concerned, she would not be prevented from redeeming lost souls in the future – so long as she consulted with her ecclesiastical superiors beforehand. In 1643, denunciations against Rosina

---

[110] AEM EG, report from the father confessor of Altomünster, September 4, 1643.
[111] Ibid., directive to the father confessor of Altomünster of October 1, 1643.
[112] Considered at length in Lederer, "Living with the Dead," 40–46.
[113] "In beisein allerlei geistlichen ordens Personen: wie nit weniger in alhiesigem Falckhenthurn 15 wochen lang außgestadtener gefenkhnus aufs schärpfste examiniert . . .": AEM EG, report of the Pastor of Our Lady in Munich, January 14, 1658. On her arrests in 1641 and 1643, see the Aulic Council protocols: HR 278, 373r–v.
[114] Rothaften, later *Rentmeister* of Straubing.

submitted to the Aulic Council by the district judges of Schrobenhausen and Friedberg were sharply rebuffed, and the council repeated the order to allow Rosina to practice without hindrance. Subsequently, she received a personal invitation from the Prince-Bishop of Freising[115] to drive the ghost of the apothecary's departed mother from his shop in the episcopal residence. After she succeeded, she became a celebrity throughout the region. Within a short period of time, the court chamberlain, Baron Haslang, Baron Hans Christoph of Preysing, Baron Johann Maximilian von Preysing, the court chamber president, Baron Johann Mändl von Deitenhoven, Mayor Ridler of Munich (the city's wealthiest patrician), and a member of the illustrious Welser banking family from Solln had all employed Rosina as a ghost-buster.

In the winter of 1657, Count Albrecht of Törring, the most propertied noble landholder in Bavaria, again requested Rosina's aid. For some time, a ghost had haunted his town house on the corner of Schwabinger and Cross lanes in Munich, terrorizing his housekeeper, who suffered horrible fits of falling sickness and became bedridden. The count approached the padres of the Society of Jesus to ban the ghost, but they categorically refused, attributing the difficulties to an evil spirit or witchcraft.[116] The count subsequently turned to the Capuchins and Carmelites for help and each order sent four monks to hold watch for two consecutive nights, blessing the house from top to bottom, hanging crucifixes above all the portals and spraying holy water about. When these methods failed, they decided that a spirit from purgatory was responsible rather than an evil one.

The reputation of the ghost in the count's home grew in town and members of high society urged him to seek Rosina's help. Count Albrecht wrote the district judge of Schrobenhausen, who relayed the message to Rosina at her private home and she agreed. The count also requested the permission of the pastor of Our Lady of Munich[117] to condone the ceremony in his parish, informing him that other ecclesiastics and the secular authorities already approved Rosina's services. Pastor Mändl sanctioned the "quasi-exorcism" (*sic*) as well, administering auricular confession and communion to Rosina on the night of December 22 in the presence of the count before

---

[115] Veit Adam of Gepeckh.
[116] "Also hat ermelter herr Graf zu entledigung des Geist anfenglich die hern Patres der Societet Jesu alhie angesprochen, welche es aber rotunde abschlagen, und solches nur für ein gespenst, oder hexerei gehalten": AEM EG, report of Johann Caspar Luzen, personal secretary to the Count of Törringen, January 10, 1658.
[117] Dr.Th. Anthony Mändl.

she went about her work. She took up watch along with several clergymen in that part of the house most frequented by the ghost. On Christmas Eve between eleven and midnight, the ghost arrived as an unseen woman, accompanied by the usual signs – a knocking at the doors and walls of the rooms. Without resorting to any suspicious means of communication or superstitious blessings, Rosina gently asked the ghost what it sought and how it could be helped.

With heavy sobs and sighs ("quite unlike the kind of noises emitted by the possessed"), the soul identified itself as a widow and former occupant of the house, who had died in the dark without the extreme unction and before fulfilling a promise to have six holy masses said, three each at Our Lady and at the Carmelite monastery of Munich. Rosina assured her that the masses would be said on her behalf and alms would be distributed among the poor. The promise of fulfilling the intended good works placated the ghost, and she departed with audible sighs of relief. The next day, the countess paid the Capuchins and Carmelites to hold the six masses and then distributed alms from her own hands. Three nights later, the ghost appeared again in the usual place, before a table on which a portrait of Our Lady of Altötting stood. In the presence of the countess and four men, Rosina asked whether the ghost was satisfied, to which it responded, yes, that was all and more than she desired.[118] The shadowy ghost disappeared with a sigh and was never seen in the house again. Both the count's private secretary and the Pastor Mändl praised Rosina in their personal correspondence as a pious, humble and simple woman, who had a good reputation for handling such cases with satisfactory results. The count and countess expressed their gratitude in coin. Rosina's authority to drive out ghosts, certified by a test of fire under torture, was further enhanced by the patronage of the court elite, elevating her above suspicion to celebrity status.

A POLITICAL MOOD SWING

Rosina Blökhl-Huber was an exceptional figure. Apart from the fact that she was a laywoman authorized to "exorcize" (albeit under male/ecclesiastical supervision) through blessings and sacramentals, she bucked a rising trend

---

[118] ". . . ist hernach ersagter Geist in der dritten nacht umb die ordinari stundt an das gewohnliche orth vor dem Tisch, auf denen unnser lieben frauwen biltnus von Altenötting gestandten, satsam hergekhommen, deme das weib in beisein der frau Gräfin und 4 benambsten Manspersohnen abermahlen gefragt, ob der Seelen an dem verrichten werkh ein bemögen geschehen sei, darauf die Seel geanntwortet, ia, es sei nun alles und mehr, als sie begert . . .": AEM EG, report of Johann Caspar Luzen.

of skepticism at court. Under Maximilian I, the central authorities had already begun to express cautious skepticism over mounting numbers of exorcisms and miraculous cures, sometimes referred to as "ecclesiastical abuses," in Bavaria from the early seventeenth century. In 1610, a noble-woman[119] wrote the Duke expressing concerns about cures at St. Peter's in the district of Riedenburg performed by a young virgin, Anna Nehmen, with the assistance of a "ghost or angel."[120] In a related case, the Privy Council initiated an investigation into possible witchcraft by a midwife, who used body parts from executed criminals (provided by the local executioner) to exorcize pregnant women.[121] In 1615, the Bavarian Ecclesiastical Council investigated reports of wonders performed on Bavarians at Mariazell in Austria, the shrine where Johann Christoph Haizmann later underwent his exorcisms.[122] A similar report was filed in 1652 regarding another Austrian pilgrimage shrine.[123]

A series of exorcisms during the reign of Ferdinand Maria attained such notoriety that they ushered in a pronounced mood of skepticism among the ruling elite in Bavaria, as well as in other areas of Germany.[124] The possession of Barbara Renner at Eichstätt and her fifteen-year treatment by the Jesuit exorcist Ulrich Speer initiated the spree in 1652.[125] Barbara was a Calvinist convert from the Upper Palatinate, annexed at the onset of the Thirty Years War by Maximilian, who initiated a re-Catholicization of the area after 1628.[126] This re-confessionalization coincided with the worst epidemic in Bavaria during the seventeenth century, as well as the high-point of witchcraft persecutions in Franconia between 1624 and 1630; a brutal hunt in the Prince-Bishopric of Eichstätt occurred in 1627 as well.[127] Pater Speer's activities as an exorcist met with sharp criticism from his superiors in

---

[119] Regina von Seyboldtsdorf.
[120] HStAM, GR. 1210/20 (*Die Aufhebung verschiedener Geistlichen Mißbräuche . . .*).
[121] Ibid. On the medical practice of executioners in Bavaria, including the use of dead body parts or "mummy," see Jutta Nowosadtko, *Scharfrichter und Abdecker. Der Alltag zweier "unehrlicher Berufe" in der Frühen Neuzeit* (Paderborn, 1994), 162–194. For Augsburg, see Kathy Stuart, "Des Scharfrichters heilende Hand – Medizin und Ehre in der Frühen Neuzeit," in Sybille Backmann, Hans-Jorg Künast, B. Ann Tlusty, and Sabine Ullmann (eds.), *Das Konzept der Ehre in der Frühen Neuzeit* (Augsburg, 1998), 316–348; Stuart, *Defiled Trades and Social Outcasts. Honor and Ritual Pollution in Early Modern Germany*, 153–163.
[122] HStAM, GR 1210/20.   [123] Ibid., miracles at the Holy Cross monastery.
[124] E.g. Paderborn: Decker, "Die Haltung," *passim*.
[125] Duhr, *Geschichte der Jesuiten*, vol. III, 753–755.
[126] Ziegler, "Die Rekatholisierung der Oberpfalz," 436–455.
[127] During the years 1627/1928, plague visited southeastern Germany so horribly that the Aulic Council in Munich set up a special commission to monitor the disaster. The effects of the plague were also disastrous in nearby Augsburg: Roeck, *Eine Stadt*, 630–654. On the witchcraft persecution in Franconia and Eichstätt during these years, see Behringer, *Witchcraft Persecutions*, 224–229.

the Society of Jesus,[128] who complained that he practiced unauthorized methods and placed too much faith in the utterings of the devil, whom Speer had naively forbidden to lie. Only the enthusiastic support of the Prince-Bishop of Eichstätt saved Speer from being sacked. The exorcisms finally ended when Barbara died unexpectedly in 1667. The society forbade Speer from publishing his accounts of the shameful spectacle.

In 1662, the Jesuit Pater Willibald Starckh, father confessor at the civic hospice in Straubing, reported the successful exorcism of a bewitched epileptic who had signed a pact with the devil, Elisabeth de la Haye, through the intercession of St. Francis Xavier. Starckh based his exorcisms on the accounts of a fellow Jesuit, Georg Stengel. A theologian at Ingolstadt and Dillingen and a zealous proponent of witch-hunting, Stengel devoted a whole chapter of his *De judiciis divines* (Ingolstadt, 1651) to Canisius' exorcism at Altötting and many elements of the Altötting affair reappeared in Starckh's own activities.[129] Starckh presented enough eyewitness accounts to persude his superiors to allow the publication of Elisabeth's exorcism in 1664. However, his superiors, highly disturbed by his activities quickly transferred him to Munich, where he could be monitored more closely. There, Starckh continued his former practice shortly after his arrival in the territorial capital.[130] Between 1667 and 1669, he promoted exorcisms on the demoniac Katharina Rieder in St. Joseph's Hospice and, not surprisingly, the intercession of St. Francis Xavier and the devil's pact comprised a central theme.[131] Katharina's possession is one of the rare instances for which we still enjoy her own autobiographic testimony in addition to the accounts of her exorcist and official correspondence.

Katharina's case illustrates the full extent of the penetration of the penitential regime into the popular psyche. She kept a running diary in the form of individual written confessions addressed to her assigned (and skeptical) Jesuit confessor, Pater Scharer, and a nun, Sister Johanna.[132] Rieder complained of tribulations, terrors, pusillanimity and despair. Although her visions of Francis Xavier indicate Starckh's powers of suggestion, her diary reads like a compendium of psychic pressures arising from a serious complex of Catholic guilt.[133] At the onset, Starckh convinced Katharina that auricular confession to anyone other than a Jesuit would be a heinous sin. However, she soon complained "confession helped no more" since "I

---

[128] General Nickel in Rome and Rector Mühlholzer in Munich.
[129] As White, *A History of the Warfare*, book II, 117, fn. 118, notes in his chapter "From 'Demonical Possession' to Insanity."
[130] Duhr, *Geschichte der Jesuiten*, vol. III, 756.   [131] HStAM Jes. 2428.
[132] HStAM Jes. 527.   [133] See chapter 2 above.

am no longer allowed to confess my matter to the Jesuits . . . during my accursed confession to Pater Scharer, my dear sister, I must have left the note in his confessional, ah, then the devil must have it, I know that he has it, but I may not say anything to the father confessor, I must keep silent . . ."[134] The note she referred to was a devil's pact. Pater Scharer expressly doubted its existence and wished to avoid implications of witchcraft that might potentially overshadow the eulogy of Francis Xavier. He even chastised Katharina, threatening that the Virgin Mary would find out if she had lied. His doubts about the pact drove Katharina to despair: "Pater Scharer is making everything so hard for me now, its no wonder that I am desperate at this moment, for now I should keep completely silent and say nothing about the matter . . . Oh God, how my error brought upon myself through this confession grieves me, and this confession grieves me from my heart . . ."[135] Two lightly penned slips of paper follow this entry in her file, stating, "Because of my false confession, I now surrender myself to the devil totally and completely with body and soul, with possessions and blood, irretrievably."[136] Suspecting she had been baptized incorrectly, Katharina Rieder contemplated asking her brother about the priest or midwife who conducted the ritual at her birth. She claimed the incorrect baptism allowed the devil access to her body and recalled how he entered her one night at age nine, when she awoke in the night screaming and saw a man in black standing by her bed.[137] Katharina now prayed to the Virgin, the blood of Christ and Francis Xavier for relief from an affliction that drove her to suicidal despair. In another confession to the nun assigned to her case, she revealed tribulations that drove her to seek relief in a pledged pilgrimage to Tuntenhausen, a vow she also contractualized in writing.[138]

---

[134] ". . . ich derf den Jesuidern mein sach nit mer beichtenn . . . mit meinem verfluchten beichten dem pater Scharer dan hab mein liebe schwester wo mueß der Zetel in seinen Beichtstuell gelegt ach es mueß der Teifel dan haben, ich weiß das er in gehabt hat, ich darf aber zu dem beichtvater nicht sagen, ich mueß schweigen . . .": HStAM Jes. 527. The diary, which exhibits a great deal of grammatical and syntactical confusion, is currently the subject of PhD dissertation research by Paul Clear.
[135] "Es macht mir iezt der pater Scharer alles so schwer, das kein wunder wer ich Deth den augenblik verzweiflen, iezt solt ich still schweigen und nichts von der sach sagen . . . Ach gott wie khimeret mich mein verschreiben, das ich mir mit diser beicht verursacht hab, und dise beicht khimbert mich auch von Herzen . . .": ibid.
[136] "Die teiffel ergib ich mich ganz und gar mit leib und seel mit gut und blut unwidter ruefflich" and "wegen der falschen beicht so ich gethon hab, iezt ergib ich mich dem teüffel ganz und gar mit leib und sell mit gut und blut unwider rueflich": ibid. The pacts are written so lightly that a quartz magnifying glass with ultraviolet light was needed to read them.
[137] HStAM Jes. 2428. [138] HStAM Jes. 527.

So great was the frustration at her inability to confess her tribulations and despair to Pater Scharer that she composed a seventeen-point written confession to him.[139] Starting at age ten, she doubted her faith and was sure she was damned, though knew not why. The elevation of the Eucharist in mass and sacred objects caused her nausea. Convinced that the Lutheran faith, not the Catholic, was correct, she mistrusted all the clergy, accusing them of rhetorical trickery. Tempted to kill herself in a variety of ways, Katharina doubted that anyone supported her in her struggle. She wished to accompany "the man [i.e. the devil]" to Augsburg. At age eleven, she drew a portrait of "the man," writing upon it in blood, but "confessed by her conscience" that, at the time, she was unaware who he was. With no hope in God, calling him a "Turk," she was tempted to go to live with pagans rather than stay among the Christians. She condemned prayer as useless, "just some poem, one simply writes them in books," and considered the beliefs of heathens "just a matter of the heart that I share with them." When she took communion, she wanted to spit out the host rather than allow it to enter her heart. As far as auricular confession was concerned, Katharina doubted whether God really forgave the sins confessed. She repeated the self-accusation of a false confession not in keeping with her catechisms and revealed the nagging desire to speak with her father confessor and "hit him in the face for it, but, for many reasons, I don't."

Humbly commending herself to her "spiritual Doctor," she accused herself of demonic whoring in an incident distinctly reminiscent of a witch's copulation with a paramour:

I also say to my father confessor, that this morning I found some money on my bed, which I know for certain is not mine, but am unsure from whence it comes. I ask your eminence – I am so pusillanimous today that I freely threw all the sacred objects in the stove and suffered the whole while from such despair that no one can help me anymore – whether the evil one also had his pleasure from the money, and it occurs to me, that if I knew the money was from him, then I would rather love him more, and surrender myself to him . . .[140]

On June 1, 1669, Katharina made good on her pledge to the Virgin and made a pilgrimage to Tuntenhausen, where she was miraculously relieved

---

[139] Ibid., a rare example of a confession recorded by a penitent.
[140] "Auch sag ich meinem beichtvatter das ich heuth morgen ein gelt auf dem beth gefunden hab, welches ich wol wais das dieses gelt nit von mir gewesen ist woher es aber ist wais ich auch nit. Frag Ehrwird ich bin so khleinmeitig hab heuth frue die geweichten sachen alle in ofen geworfen hab alleweil verzweifelt und es khan mir nement mer helfen obs der bes geist hab auch an dem gelt ein frid gehabt und mir gedenkch wan ich wiß das dises gelt von ihm wer so wolt ich ihn noch lieber haben, und mich ihm auf ein neues ergeben . . ": HStAM Jes. 527.

of her sufferings.[141] At a mass held back in Munich on August 26, Pater Scharer confirmed her recovery. Other representatives of the society condemned the procedure all the same. The Provincial in Munich[142] expressed complete disdain for the so-called "wonder of St. Francis Xavier," which seemed to him and others nothing more than a sequel to Pater Willibald Starckh's previous performance in Straubing. Pater Bernard Frey, SJ, professor of moral theology and later father confessor to Elector Ferdinand Maria, opposed the exorcism on the grounds that it opened the way for accusations of witchcraft.[143] Only fifteen years earlier, he recalled, a demoniac had been executed in nearby Augsburg for practicing witchcraft after she confessed to signing a devil's pact during an exorcism.[144] But for influential and pragmatic moderates like Frey, Katharina Rieder too might also have ended her days at the stake. He composed numerous legal briefs in cases of witchcraft and possession, damning the persecutions of women he considered deluded. That opinion decisively gained the upper hand in Bavaria after 1661, when Frey had the ear of the Elector in the confessional.

Paradoxically, the shift in mood is attributable to the same religious order whose members initiated the wave of exorcisms, produced systematic treatises on demonology and helped stoke the flames of legal witch-hunting. However, Bernhard Frey represented a new breed of Jesuit. He followed in the footsteps of the noted skeptic Adam Tanner, SJ. Tanner, the mouthpiece of an opposition group in Ingolstadt during the first quarter of the seventeenth century, who published a four-volume treatise on moral theology in 1626/1627. In the animus of moral casuistry as spiritual physic, Tanner argued diminished capacity as an insanity defense in cases of witchcraft. His ideas later influenced Friedrich Spee's more famous *Cautio criminalis.*[145] Frey too was a moral casuist and the first Bavarian official to openly cite Tanner's work.[146] Like Tanner (and unlike Aemilian Biechler, Canisius and Eisengrein), Frey had regional origins. He was born c.1609 in Oberstdorf, epicenter of a recent witch-hunt and peasants' revolt, events that moderated his outlook about the dangers of excess.[147] Frey studied in Ingolstadt during

[141] The official testimony from the shrine, signed and sealed on August 15, 1669, was placed at the end of the file: ibid.

[142] Jacob Rassler.   [143] Duhr, *Geschichte der Jesuiten*, vol. III, 756–757.

[144] On the devil's pact, exorcism, trial and execution of Maria Bihlerin in Augsburg, see Behringer, *Witchcraft Persecutions*, 329.

[145] Ibid., 245–246, 322–328, 354–357.

[146] Edited copies of attestations by Frey are found in a two-part article by Bernhard Duhr, SJ, "Zur Geschichte des Jesuitenordens. Aus Münchner Archiven und Bibliotheken," *Historisches Jahrbuch der Görresgesellschaft* 25 (1904), 126–167, and 28 (1907), 61–83.

[147] On Frey, see David Lederer, "Bernhard Frey," in: Richard Golden (ed.), *Encyclopedia of Witchcraft: The Western Tradition* (Santa Barbara, 2005).

Tanner's tenure and took orders in the Society in 1628, perhaps at the behest of Tanner himself. His experience of the moderates in Ingolstadt made a lasting impression. Frey went on to become the most outspoken proponent of the insanity defense in cases of witchcraft and exorcism at the Bavarian court.

Frey taught briefly in Freiburg before returning to Ingolstadt to complete studies in advanced theology and was ordained in 1637. Subsequently, he lectured in Augsburg, Ingolstadt, Innsbruck, Landshut, Munich and Lucerne, publishing on casuistry and moral theology, the soul/mind/body relationship, personal guilt and mental culpability. Spiritual physic represented his primary scholarly interest. In 1653, he was appointed to lead a mission to re-Catholicize the Pfalz-Neuburg. After 1654, he settled in Munich, leading the elite Marian congregation. From 1661 to 1679, Frey served as the last in an unbroken, century-long chain of Jesuit confessors to the Wittelsbach rulers.

Throughout his career, Frey argued for the moderate and compassionate treatment of mental disorders within the framework of neo-scholastic spiritual physic.[148] In 1670, he became the first Bavarian official publicly to refer to the arguments of Spee and Tanner on the excesses of torture and the dangers of chain reaction witch-hunting in an attempt to contain a series of accusations he duly condemned as "dangerous and dreadful trials against witches."[149] His stance on madness is clearly illustrated by his role in a serious incident. During a private meeting with the Bavarian Chancellor in 1679, his close personal friend Johann Rottgner stormed into the room, produced a pistol, shot and wounded Frey and then assaulted the Chancellor with a knife. Both escaped with their lives, but Rottgner was sentenced to the galleys. Through his influence as father confessor to Ferdinand Maria, Frey pleaded for leniency on his behalf with the Elector and succeeded in having the sentence mitigated on the basis of an insanity defense. Through his efforts in cases of madness, demonic possession and witchcraft, Frey became the primary architect for the practical implementation of an insanity defense in early modern Bavaria.

Of course, Frey's attitudes would have had little effect were it not for a growing climate of skepticism at court. In 1664, for example, a father requested poor relief to support his possessed daughter, but the Aulic Council categorically declined, ordering him to seek gainful employment

[148] Michael Schaich, "Frey, Bernhard," in: Laetitia Boehm, Winfried Müller, Wolfgang J. Smolka and Helmut Zedelmaier, *Biographisches Lexikon der Ludwig-Maximilians-Universität München* (Berlin, 1998), 130–132.
[149] Behringer, *Witchcraft Persecutions*, 323, 356.

to provide for his family properly. The council threatened any further laziness on his part with a stiff fine.[150] Simultaneously, two other exorcisms underway at the dynastic shrine in Altötting and in Munich met with colder responses from both ecclesiastical and secular authorities. The first incident, the case of Anna Mayer, has been treated by Duhr and need only be complemented here with additional material from the Anastasia miracle book.[151] Anna Mayer claimed to be possessed by the same seven demons driven out of Anna Bernhauser by Canisius in 1570. She also knew of the exorcisms of Pater Ulrich Speer from Eichstätt. From 1666, some 120 exorcisms performed on Anna at Altötting were recorded in hundreds of reports submitted to Elector Ferdinand Maria by their major advocate, the dean of Altötting, Gabriel Khupferle.[152] Khupferle had examined and validated Maximilian I's blood pact with the Virgin Mary in 1651. Obsessed with the reputation of Altötting, he also composed and published miracle books treating wonders at the shrine.[153] His handling of the possession of Anna Mayer damaged the reputation of the shrine, "not to mention the Catholic faith" and Bavaria by achieving unwanted notoriety throughout the Empire. It also aroused popular animosity against the Jesuits for their condemnation of the exorcisms. They were ended by the direct intervention of the Elector at the urgings of Bernhard Frey.

The local Jesuit rector at Altötting refused to cooperate with Khupferle from the start, engaging Frey to attend the procedure as an observer. Frey, convinced that evidence of demonic possession was lacking, recommended that the authorities turn Anna over to a respectable family for discipline, heavy work and fasting. His decision was based neither on disbelief in the possibility of supernatural agency nor in a dualistic world-view – to the contrary. Similar to the opponents of witchcraft persecutions, Tanner, Spee and Weyer, for example, Frey never disputed the possibility of demonic intervention in the affairs of humankind. Instead, he too engaged legalistic arguments from within the existing epistemological structure of learned beliefs to argue for other possibilities, particularly the possibility of insanity. Throughout his examination of the demoniac, Frey proved himself an adroit practitioner of spiritual physic, employing orthodox models from Aristotelian faculty psychology and Galenic humoral pathology to disprove

---

[150] HStAM HR 364, 423r.
[151] It has been cogently treated by Duhr, *Geschichte der Jesuiten*, vol. III, 757–766; Duhr, "Eine Teufelsaustreibung in Altötting," *Beiträge zur Geschichte der Renaissance und Reformation. Festschrift für Joseph Schlecht* (Munich, 1917), 63–76.
[152] HStAM KL AÖ 52.
[153] Gabriel Küpfferle, *Historii von der weitberühmten . . .* (Munich, 1661); Küpfferle, *Gnadenprozeß der Allerheiligsten Junckfrawen . . .* (Munich, 1664).

the possession. He conducted a systematic examination, scrutinizing the state of her intellect, will, imagination, memory, her speech patterns and the external senses of sight and sound for evidence of possession, obsession, or delusions of a mental, visual and aural nature, summarizing his findings in a lengthy brief.[154] After negotiations with the Archbishop in Salzburg and the Franciscan Provincial, Anna's father (a day laborer from the village of Zolling in the Bishopric of Freising) procured the services of Pater Lucas Glasberger as exorcist. Frey's opposition eventually led to the dismissal of Pater Lucas at the order of Ferdinand Maria, but not before the demoniac publicly denounced the Jesuits as "witchmasters" who wanted to turn the Chapel of Our Lady into a "dancehall." Anna physically assaulted the Jesuit rector at Altötting, jumping him from behind, scratching his face and trying to strangle him.[155] On March 29, 1668, by direct order of the Elector, Anna and her father, now indigent after selling all their worldly goods, were sent packing back to Zolling and refused permission to beg or receive alms. However, Jesuit opposition to this and other exorcisms further undercut the order's popularity. The Society had been the target of popular and ecclesiastical anger for its war on clerical concubinage in Bavaria.[156] The Jesuits had clearly been on the defensive after the arrival of the Theatines and they were detested by many other orders as well. Meanwhile, the Benedictines, who continued to meet a popular demand for spiritual healing at rural shrines like Benediktbeuern, stepped into the vacuum, thereby enhancing their reputation among the population at large.

Before appearing in Altötting, Anna Mayer had already made a pilgrimage to the Anastasia shrine on September 13, 1666, with little fuss over her possession.[157] Later, after the custodians at Altötting initially balked at an exorcism, she returned again to Benediktbeuern on October 6 and the Benedictines thoroughly exorcized her.[158] At the Anastasia chapel for a second time, Anna began to rave, revealing that a devil driven out of another person during her previous visit had transferred to her body because she had been improperly baptized. When the custodian inadvertently rubbed his nose on the sacred reliquary bust, she screamed at him, "See, it burns you, you've gotten a cold from our witch in the confessional, because you didn't kneel before hearing confession . . ."[159] Before Anna left on her fateful journey to Altötting, St. Anastasia forced Anna and her devil to provide

[154] HStAM KL AÖ 52.   [155] Ibid., f. 417, decree of Ferdinand Maria from November 8, 1667.
[156] At least according to Michel de Montaigne, *Journal du Voyage*, 109–111.   [157] AMB 660913.
[158] AMB 661006.
[159] "Gel es brant dich, hast mer ains bekhommen von unseren bäßl in dem beichtstuell, die weil du vor nit nider gekhniet vor dem beichthören . . .": ibid.

an herbal charm to serve as a cold remedy for the ailing custodian. This devil's recipe recommended pouring his excess phlegm into cut nettles, "because our bassl (that is the witch) has to roll around in them after she returns home from the dance and if that gets in her face then she will share in God again."[160] Her experience at Benediktbeuern left a lasting impression, evidenced by her repeated cries, "it burns, it burns" (a reference to the martyrdom of St. Anastasia) during subsequent treatment at Altötting.[161]

Another notorious exorcism held more severe consequences for the demoniac and reflects the growing intolerance of the ruling elite for spiritual afflictions that attracted the public eye. Anna Puchmayer became possessed after her husband died in 1657.[162] In 1666, Anna and Christina, her daughter, made a pilgrimage to St. Emmeram, a Benedictine monastery in Regensburg. The pair remained there for thirteen weeks while the monk Pater Aemilian performed exorcisms on Anna, during which "she became totally black and stuck out her tongue all long and black."[163] Once, at the instigation of the devil, she wandered into a nearby wood and prepared a noose to hang herself, but was saved in the nick of time by a passer-by. The exorcist drove out the "glutton devil" and the "quarrel devil," composing a written testimony for Anna to take with her "for official reasons" (*Amtswillen*). From Regensburg, the duo traveled on to Benediktbeuern (perhaps at the urgings of the Benedictines of St. Emmeram), where they arrived on August 25 and presented the official testimony to the custodian.[164] After vespers, Anna was led to the Anastasia chapel and immediately began to rage terribly until two men, sorely taxed, managed to restrain her in a chair. After a time, she calmed down. Upon their departure from Benediktbeuern, the couple journeyed on to the Benedictine monastery at Ettal, where the evil demon ranted considerably.[165] From there they went straight to Schlehdorf, staying for fourteen days. The abbot applied newly acquired relics causing the devil to rave frantically and he exorcized two devils, both of whom answered questions in German, having been forbidden to speak Latin. When they exited her body in the form of an insect (which only Anna saw), they left behind a bruise on her forehead and a

---

[160] "Noch mueß ich dir ains sagen, sprache er, daß wasser muest in die Prennössl giessen, Warumb frage ich? Rx: dan unser bäßl (daß ist die hex) wans von dem tanz haimb kumbt, mueß sie sich darein wölzen, und khombt ihr solches in daß gesicht, dan sie thail mer an Gott hat": ibid.

[161] See HStAM KL AÖ 52, ff. 2–5, Khupferle's report of the events of November 4, 1666.

[162] For a graphic reconstruction of her movements, see Map 2, above.

[163] AMB 661006: in her testimony, Anna Puchmayer may have confused the Regensburg monk with Pater Aemilian Biechler, the exorcist at Benediktbeuern.

[164] AMB 660825.   [165] BayStBi Cgm 2620, ff. 120–126.

drop of blood dripped from her hand. At each monastery, two or three men were always called upon to hold her down.

Wintering back in Munich, Anna Puchmayer traveled to Freising in the following year, where the Prince-Bishop[166] took a personal interest in her possession. This time, her companion was Stephan Hepperger, citizen and button-maker from Munich, who accompanied her "for the honor of God and Our compassionate Lady," as he later stated under oath.[167] In Freising, Anna revealed the source of her possession: as a child, a witch baptized her in the name of 100,000 devils. When relics were applied, she declared, "Pater Willibald [i.e. Starckh] in Munich will drive out the devil in the Holy Cross Chapel before Whitsuntide." How she knew of Starckh's exorcisms in Munich is unclear. Hepperger was completely convinced by everything he witnessed in Freising: Anna displayed knowledge of things hidden, had exposed his and other people's thoughts, and read the stars.[168]

The Prince-Bishop ordered an examination of witnesses and the demoniac in Munich by a committee of theologians. Headed by the Dean of St. Peter's,[169] it also included Bernhard Frey and the secretary of the Bavarian Electoral Ecclesiastical Council,[170] as well as nine others, mostly Capuchins, Carmelites and Augustinians.[171] The committee met on June 1 and questioned six witnesses before proceeding with the theological examination of the possessed at seven in the evening.[172]

The first witness, Scholastica Mayer, was single, forty years old and a lifelong resident of Munich now living on a benefice at the Holy Spirit hospice. Scholastica first met Anna in February 1667 and Anna frequented the hospice thereafter. From the first, Anna told Scholastica that demonic assaults and temptations had increased since her youth and the evil spirit "Blower" (*Blaserin*) possessed her. Anna suffered a fit in her presence, screaming "Phooey, phooey to the soldiers, we have to travel" and fell into exhaustion. Anna told her she had visited St. Michael's and stood at the grave of Jerimias Drexel – court preacher under Maximilian I and a notorious proponent of witch-hunting. She rambled about being baptized in the name of the devil, noting that the person responsible was already down in hell. Scholastica also knew the details of her pilgrimages to Benediktbeuern, Ettal, Schlehdorf and St. Emmeram.

---

[166] Duke Albrecht of Wittelsbach.   [167] BayStBi Cgm 2620 ff. 120–126.
[168] Ibid.: "Ihme aber und anderen habs die mainung wol gesagt und den Planeten gelesen."
[169] Dr. Johann Keller.   [170] Hans Georg Megehrl, Aulic Councilor.
[171] BayStBi Cgm 2620 f. 127; the episcopal order to conduct the examination is mentioned in a letter, ff. 132–135.
[172] Ibid., ff. 120–126, 128–130.

The second witness, Christina Puchmayer, provided detailed information about the pilgrimages undertaken with her mother. Since Anna visited Benediktbeuern, she had no peace. Anna told her that she was baptized in the name of a thousand devils and each night after midnight she ranted and screamed until exhausted; afterwards she couldn't remember a thing. Then Ursula Khuen, the hostel-keeper, reported on Anna's behavior as a lodger during the past three years. She too knew of the exorcisms at Benediktbeuern and Regensburg, but now the "windplay devil" was in Anna with five hundred companions. She had never seen one of Anna's fits, though her lodger once fell down the steps at the hostel. Anna suffered a fit in Freising and told Ursula about the creature who refused to come out until she was re-baptized. Then Pater Willibald would exorcize it in the Holy Cross church. Later, Anna hinted the "barefoots" (i.e. the Franciscans) might also be allowed to conduct the exorcism as well.

The fourth witness, Sebastian Heckh, was a priest at St. Anna's, where he once saw the demoniac kneel down before an iron grating and paw between the bars. After saying mass, he approached her, whereupon Anna yelled back at him, "she had never heard such a grave mass" and "Go away, you black devil, you're in cahoots with the Carmelites!" He offered her alms, which she accepted after an initial refusal. Anna's son Adam, a nineteen-year-old tailor from Landshut, was also summoned to testify. He recalled that as soon as she saw him, she flung herself at him calling him a whore-hunter (*Huern Jägerl*). She also told him that St. Anna's was an infernal house (*Brennhaus*), "Oh you burner, oh you burner, 500 were there in the old inferno," a reference to the martyrdom of St. Anastasia picked up during her visit to Benediktbeuern. The theologians of Munich concluded that none of the testimony gave any indication of possession, indicating that Anna either suffered from a melancholic mood disorder, or else her possession was outright fraud.

Later that evening, her children and the button-maker dragged Anna ranting and raving into St. Peter's for ritual examination. Ordered to stand still and answer the questions of the assembled theologians, she continued to flail about, spraying herself with holy water and then drinking it. Led by Frey, the skeptical ecclesiastics then applied an empty reliquary made of brass, while Anna screamed, "the pain, the pain" and blasphemously uttered the name "Jesus." Thereupon, concealed relics were secretly applied, but Anna made no response. As she was unable to understand commands in Latin, they silenced her in German and commanded her to pray. She peaceably repeated the *Our Father* and *Ave Maria*; her expression, her eyes and her forehead remained unchanged. On her way out of the church, she mistook one of her Minorite interrogators for Pater Lucas, the Franciscan exorcist at Altötting, calling him a "goose-neck" and condemning the Jesuits as "black devils." Then she left the church and the theologians convened for a verdict. Applying principles from Jesuit superiors issued during the exorcism of Barbara Renner in Eichstätt (*Judicium de Energumena Barbara*) and from the work of Peter Thyraeus, it was decided that Anna suffered from no unnatural or inhuman afflictions usually displayed by the possessed.[173] She was unable to identify things hidden, the relics had no effect and she could neither speak nor understand Latin. Her ranting was interpreted as purely natural and diagnosed as either melancholy or fraud, eliminating the need for further exorcisms or examinations. The Prince-Bishop of Freising agreed with the committee's recommendations and decreed on June 13 that Anna Puchmayer be remanded to the care of physicians for treatment with medicines. A suitable cleric was to hear her confession once every eight days, or more frequently if he saw fit, to encourage her to perform contrition often and to report back on any progress.[174] Formal inquiries were also lodged with the abbots of Benediktbeuern, Schlehdorf and St. Emmeram.

On June 23 and again on August 1, the stubborn Anna Puchmayer loosed a volley of petitions aimed at the Ecclesiastical Council in Freising, reporting worsening infestations by a devil, which now regularly spoke in Latin, Italian and Hebrew, and she reiterated that she had been baptized in his name.[175] After another supplication arrived on August 8, Prince-Bishop Albrecht ordered deliberations with one of her examiners as well as her father confessor at St. Peter's on the pros and cons of having Anna quietly re-baptized in the presence of two or three priests.[176] Ten days later, after conferring with Bernhard Frey, the Dean of St. Peter's in Munich hesitantly responded that inquiries with Anna's parish of birth were needed to confirm whether or not the original baptism had been defective in some way.[177] Frey continued to express doubts. On August 29, frustrated, the ecclesiastical authorities deferred the entire affair to the Aulic Council in Munich.[178]

On September 6, the Aulic Council responded negatively to the supplication from Freising for re-baptism. Instead, they warned the town council in Munich that Anna drew large crowds and ordered their dispersion by pressure and arrests if necessary to prevent unrest.[179] Anna continued to portray herself as possessed, causing disturbances in churches and the private homes of curious thrill-seekers. After several honorable and prominent persons accused her of damaging their good name and reputation, the Aulic

---

[173] Ibid., ff. 132–135, 142.   [174] Ibid., ff. 116–119; AEM GR 84, 218.   [175] Ibid., 236, 307.
[176] Ibid., 319–320.   [177] Ibid., 337.   [178] Ibid., 355.   [179] HStAM HR 375, 231v.

Council took quick action. Basing its decision on the findings from the theological committee and at the advice of Bernhard Frey, the Aulic Council declared that Anna suffered from fevers rather than possession and, on February 11, 1668, it ordered the town council to have her interned in a place "where such people belong."[180] On April 19, the council decreed further that Anna Puchmayer be permanently transferred from St. Joseph's Hospice to the quarters for the senseless at the Holy Spirit Hospice, and the exchequer was ordered to pay the annual 40 fl. in upkeep from the treasury.[181] At the request of the administrator of the Holy Spirit Hospice, she was permitted to attend mass at St. Peter's, albeit under proper supervision and so long as she caused no disturbances. Otherwise visits were limited to the church in the Holy Spirit Hospice. After mass, the administrator should return her directly to her cell to avoid any unpleasant incidents.[182] Later, in September, Pater Placidus, a Benedictine monk from the monastery at Weltenburg, requested permission from the Aulic Council to perform an exorcism on Anna in the Holy Spirit Hospice, but his request was flatly refused.[183] When the council received word that Pater Placidus had surreptitiously visited Anna at the hospice on several occasions to administer pastoral care, they revoked his visitation privileges in November.[184] Her fate in the Holy Spirit Hospice is unknown.

CONCLUSIONS

Like confession and pilgrimage, exorcism has a direct historical relevance for our discussion of spiritual physic. In some ways, the dramatic and unpredictable nature of demonic possession contributed more to both the rise and decline of religious interpretations of madness than any other form of affliction. Above all, the work of Canisius, the second apostle of the Germans, as a moral casuist and spiritual physician accounted for the widespread routinization of exorcisms and a corresponding growth in demand amongst a population catechized by him and Eisengrein on the dangers of demonic afflictions. They spawned a breed of imitators, both official and unofficial, like Aemilian Biechler, who pursued legitimate career aspirations in the burgeoning field of spiritual physic. Contingent upon social forces, the legitimacy of their activities often depended on institutional connections. Practitioners operating on the fringes fell under mounting pressure to conform to ecclesiastical and secular control. Ironically, they and their patients

---

[180] HStAM HR 377, 162r.   [181] HStAM HR 378, 76v.   [182] Ibid., 154v–155r.
[183] HStAM HR 379, 426r.   [184] HStAM HR 380, 236r.

often faced charges of practicing the very types of diabolism they sought to combat through their treatments.

By the mid-seventeenth century, moderate attitudes prevailed in the Society of Jesus and among representatives of the secular authorities. This is no doubt attributable to the continuing role of Jesuit father confessors at court, especially Bernhard Frey, a moderate acquainted with the dangers of religious zealotry from the witch-hunts of his birthplace. Coterminous with Biechler's custodianship of the Anastasia shrine at the rural abbey of Benediktbeuern, Frey spearheaded a psychological "revolution" with broad support at court. He argued fervently for incorporation of an insanity defense on traditional religious grounds and met with considerable success. The final outcome of Anna Puchmayer's case is indicative of the shift in mood, both at court and among the Jesuits. Through Frey's intercession, the authorities eventually remanded the demoniac to institutional custody. Two other cases of possession confirm the victory of the insanity defense at court. In 1667, the Privy Council ordered a raving demoniac removed from Altötting to another location for the duration of Ferdinand Maria's annual visit to the shrine, presumably at the instigation of the Elector.[185] Similarly, in 1669, the Privy Council ordered the Aulic Council to remand two demoniacs (one of whom was judged frenetic rather than possessed) to the custody of the Holy Spirit Hospice in Munich.[186]

The perils of religious zealotry experienced during the witch-hunts and the Thirty Years War, combined with the easing of the general crisis, promoted a shift in attitude toward moderate reason of state policies. Officials became less willing to countenance demonic possession and spiritual physic as forms of spirituality when they threatened state control over its subjects and public order, caused political embarrassments and damaged the reputation of the authorities both at home and abroad. Spiritual physic provided a useful tool to consolidate and mobilize Bavarians during the age of confessional strife under a Counter Reformation regime. In the end, however, it proved too unpredictable to meet the needs of the nascent absolutist state.

Nonetheless, in order to replace forms of spiritual physic they once supported, the authorities had to find viable alternatives. The Wittelsbachs and members of the Aulic Council in Munich toyed with strategies for dealing with the mad, searching for avenues to insure both the safety of society at large and the proper fulfillment of their increasingly paternal obligation to care for less fortunate subjects. In fact, a reliance on spiritual

---

[185] "Umb verfiegung , dass die alda vorhanden besesene Persohn in diesser Zeit, solang sich ihre chrflrt. Gn. Daselbts aufhalten, von danen an ein ander orthh gekhommen werden": HStAM, GR 1210/20.
[186] Ibid.

physic alone would never have been wholly adequate and other models were already available. These included a system of communal care based in the parishes and districts, as well as a jurisdictionally fragmented network of civic, dynastic and ecclesiastical hospices in limited use for confinement purposes. As the case of Anna Puchmayer indicates, the authorities came to favor the latter. These were the ideological and social preconditions for the growth of institutionalized care in Bavaria, though confinement came to dominate treatment only in the nineteenth century. In the early modern period, obstacles to confinement were great and, in many ways, insurmountable given the structural impediments of seventeenth-century society.

CHAPTER 6

Confinement and its vicissitudes

A date can serve as a landmark: 1656, the decree that founded, in Paris,
the Hôpital Général.

Michel Foucault, *Madness and Civilization*

Nowhere are absolutist designs in the care of the mad more in evidence than
in policies of spatial segregation, some negative, others positive. As early
expressions of the state's sovereignty over its subjects, the birth of prisons
and houses of correction like Amsterdam's *tuchthuis* in 1596 replaced a diversity of customs. Spatial segregation represented a long-term institutional
strategy described by Michel de Certeau as the victory of space over time.[1]
Segregation held important implications in the arena of mental health as
well and forms the basis for Foucault's thesis on the ideological origins of the
Great Confinement. The preferment of specific forms of segregation over
others also signifies the decline of religious and popular interpretations of
madness and the rising tide of a secular insanity defense. At court, policies
concerning two particular types of segregation – burial decisions in cases
of suicide and the confinement of the mad in the Holy Spirit Hospice in
Munich – exemplify elite skepticism. The historical segregation of the mad
illuminates the failures, successes and practical limitations on the power of
the early modern state to assert its sovereignty.

Popular attitudes toward suicide proved particularly stubborn. Popular
beliefs associated the devil with attacks on humans through evil thoughts
and despair as well as demonic obsession and possession. Mythically, witches
and self-murderers acted as agents of the devil, attacking agrarian fertility
and causing crop failures. Chronological patterns of suicide statistics for
Bavaria suggest striking parallels between all three diabolic phenomena,

[1] De Certeau, *The Practice*, xix.

which are difficult to dismiss as meaningless coincidences. For example, according to the records of the Bavarian Aulic Council, reports of self-killing peaked during the general crisis, just as witch-hunting and demonic possessions witnessed a surge. Between 1611 and 1670, the council deliberated more than three hundred cases of suicide. Of these, 89 percent (269 cases) occurred between 1611 and 1635, falling drastically over the subsequent thirty-five years thereafter.[2] Reported suicides clustered in individual crisis years, such as the crop failures of 1611/1612 (14 cases) and 1614/1615 (18), and the plagues of 1623 (19), 1627/1628 (32 – incidentally some of the worst years of witch persecutions in the region), and 1634 (14).

Faced with a spate of self-killing during the crisis, the Aulic Council proved ever more willing to employ the insanity defense in its deliberations over state of mind in burial decisions. Early modern Europeans usually attributed suicide to either of two motivations: a state of diminished capacity (*non compos mentis*) or intentional suicide (*felo de se*). The authorities attributed intentional suicide to demonic assaults or temptations, promoting symptoms of despair. Early modern despair implied a mental state resulting from diabolical temptations intended to raise doubts in sufferers over their salvation and to convince them to put an end to their lives. Desperate suicide damned one eternally and required an ignominious burial outside the communal cemetery. Demonic temptations (*Anfechtungen*), a condition prior to despair, resembled demonic obsession; an unidentified voice or the devil himself taunted the sufferer with the hopelessness of their situation.[3] Both Calvin and Luther described suicides possessed by the devil.[4] Similar attitudes held sway in Zwinglian Zurich and Elizabethan England.[5] Robert Burton noted that, "The principall agent and procurer of this mischief, is the Divell, those whom God forsakes, the Divell by his permission layes hold on."[6] In Bavaria, Aegidius Albertinus took a similar stance on demonic temptations and suicide.[7]

In Bavaria, increased recourse to the insanity defense for suicide resonated in similar attitudes toward witchcraft and demonic possession. Therefore, suicide provides another key register to measure the effects of the diabolical crisis, allowing for a methodological triangulation of the three

[2] Lederer, "Verzweiflung im Alten Reich," 259.   [3] Midelfort, *A History of Madness*, 309–312.

[4] Minois, *History of Suicide*, 72–74; Jeffrey R. Watt, *Choosing Death. Suicide and Calvinism in Early Modern Geneva* (Kirksville, 2001), 73–74.

[5] Michael MacDonald and Terence Murphy, *Sleepless Souls. Suicide in Early Modern England* (Oxford, 1994), 49–60; Markus Schär, *Seelennöte der Untertanen. Selbstmord, Melancholie und Religion im Alten Zürich, 1500–1800* (Zurich, 1985), 150–210.

[6] Robert Burton, *The Anatomy of Melancholy*, vol. III (Oxford, 1994), 411.

[7] Albertinus, *Lucifers Königreich* (1883), 348.

demon-related phenomena. An analogous shift at court in England cor-
roborates the shift from demonic guilt toward the insanity defense as part
of a broader trend among the European elite. In popular culture, however,
suicide not only constituted a heinous sin and a diabolical act, but also
provoked celestial displeasure. If improperly disposed of, the body of a suicide could cause physical dishonor to those handling it and the spirit could
reappear as a revenant to haunt the living. It was also widely feared that the
burial of a desperate suicide in hallowed ground caused inclement weather,
especially hail storms, resulting in crop devastation. The fear of the profanation of cemeteries as a cause of inclement weather is a well-documented
aspect of popular beliefs in both rural and urban areas throughout Europe.[8]
Recurrent plagues, crop failures and periods of high inflation during the era
of the general crisis validated those fears. The authorities in Bavaria began
diligent reporting of suicides for the first time. They recognized a connection between catastrophes and higher rates of reported suicides. They also
identified the storage of corpses during protracted suicide investigations as a
potentially dangerous source of infectious diseases, calling for rapid burials.
In the structure of popular beliefs, ordinary Bavarians too associated suicide with subsistence crises and disease, but inverted cause and effect. Many
held suicides responsible for the disasters, rather than noting the role of
disease as a cause of terminal suffering which resulted in suicide. Popular
beliefs followed a rudimentary logic: over the ages, people detected the conjuncture of suicides with poor harvests, disease and the death of livestock.
The nineteenth-century ethnographer Edward Tylor defined this mental
process as the "Association of Ideas."[9] Though his model is pejorative,[10] it
holds a certain merit for its explanatory value.

The burial of a suicide in hallowed ground represented a *causus belli* in the
popular mind. On at least nine separate occasions, Bavarian communities
rose up, taking arms in suicide revolts to prevent the profanation of a local
cemetery through the interment of suicides. On the other hand, some of

---

[8] See, for example, Hanns Bächtold-Stäubli (ed.), *Handwörterbuch des deutschen Aberglaubens*, vol. VII
    (Berlin, 1935/1936; reprint: Augsburg, 2005), 1628. See also Lederer, "Aufruhr"; Lederer, "Dishonor-
    able Dead"; and, most recently, Lederer, "Verzweiflung im Alten Reich."
[9] "The principal key to the understanding of the Occult Science is to consider it as based on the Asso-
    ciation of Ideas, a faculty which lies at the very foundation of human reason, but in no small degree
    of human unreason also": Edward Burnett Tylor, *Primitive Culture: Researches into the Development
    of Mythology, Philosophy, Religion, Language, Art, and Custom*, 2 vols. (London, 1873), vol. I, 115–117.
[10] Ibid.: "Man, as yet in a low intellectual condition, having come to associate in thought those things
    which he found by experience to be connected in fact, proceeded erroneously to invert this action, and
    to conclude that association in thought must involve similar connexion in reality." His suggestion
    that there are higher and lower intellectual states is a good example of nineteenth-century social
    Darwinism.

the same official opponents of witchcraft persecutions also recommended harsh measures to put down what they deemed unfounded superstitions that challenged the legitimate sovereignty of the state to dispose of the bodies of its subjects. And, like beliefs in magic and demon possession, popular prejudices against suicide continued in Bavaria well beyond the seventeenth century and evidenced the tenacity of popular culture.[11] Rather than a product of popular agitation, the insanity defense arose from an elite reaction to popular prejudices as a challenge to sovereign authority.[12]

One particular case history illustrates how the general crisis combined with popular fears to provoke public resistance, complicating the practical implementation of a secular insanity defense. A bad year in Bavaria, indeed in most of southeastern Germany, it was in 1612 that Maximilian I signed the Bavarian Mandate on Witchcraft and Superstition into law. Poor climatic conditions during the previous year caused a crop failure, an epidemic among humans and livestock, and in turn rapid grain price inflation.[13] Cyclic crises like this one were a common feature of the period. Reports of suicide in Bavaria shot up dramatically in 1612, a characteristic of subsistence crises throughout the period, when reported rates of suicide could achieve levels more than five times the annual norm.[14] The case of Anna Kirchberger, a Bavarian peasant, exemplifies that trend. On June 23, Anna, a mother and the wife of a one-half shareholder in the village of Feilnbach, brought a ladder into the house. She secured a noose to it and hanged herself.[15] One of the dishonorable people charged with handling the dead (probably a knacker) cut the corpse down and packed it in a barrel for storage until an investigation into the circumstances of death

---

[11] For example, see Georg Karl Mayr (ed.), *Sammlung der Churpfalz-Baierischen allgemeinen und besonderen Landes-Verordnungen*, vol. IV (Munich, 1788), 823.

[12] One recent study has claimed that the movement for the decriminalization of suicides received a strong impetus from below in eighteenth-century Schleswig-Holstein. However, even in this case, the push came from intermediary and local representatives of the state after 1740 rather than the general populace: Vera Lind, *Selbstmord in der Frühen Neuzeit: Diskurs, Lebenswelt und kultureller Wandel am Beispiel der Herzogtümer Schleswig und Holstein* (Göttingen, 1999), e.g. 465. Changing bureaucratic attitudes at this time are indicative of changes in imperial legislation, for example the *Reichsabschluss* of 1731 regarding the prejudices of the common people against those who handled the corpses of self-killers.

[13] The plague, inflation, harvest failures and livestock diseases during the agrarian crisis of 1611/1612 are characterized in Behringer, *Witchcraft Persecutions*, 95, 291–292.

[14] Lederer, "Aufruhr." In 1613, for example, a broadsheet appeared in Alsace, depicting a father who hanged his three children and then himself to escape starvation after his brother refused them assistance. His wife stabbed herself thereafter: Karin Schmidt-Kohberg, ". . . und hat 'sich selbsten . . . an ein Strickhalfter hingehenckt . . .' Selbstmord im Herzogtum Württemberg im 17. und 18. Jahrhundert," in: Johannes Dillinger (ed.), *Zauberer – Selbstmörder – Schatzsucher. Magische Kultur und behördliche Kontrolle im frühneuzeitlichen Württemberg* (Trier, 2003), 132.

[15] StAM, Pfleggericht Aibling B41, 190v; AEM GR 34, 67v.

determined its final resting place. Only the central authorities could reach
the burial decision in cases of self-murder, dictating that local judges report
the findings of their investigation directly to the Aulic Council. However,
confident in his assessment, the district judge[16] dispatched his report to
the council without formal inquiry. He identified chronic illness as the
motivation. Given the circumstances, he judged the deceased *non compos
mentis* and recommended interment in consecrated ground.

The Aulic Council replied via courier on June 27.[17] They reminded the
judge of proper procedure and to conduct a complete inquiry by gath-
ering sworn testimony from neighbors and relatives. However, since his
assessment appeared correct, the council ordered him to confer with the
local clergy concerning burial in consecrated ground. If the parish priest
agreed, then Anna could be buried in the parish cemetery. Otherwise, they
authorized him to dispose of her body at minimum cost to the chancellery.

Days later, the district judge summarily served Adam Pruggmayer, the
parish priest of Au (and acting priest of the filial church of Feilnbach),
with the writ from Munich. According to the writ, Anna had killed herself
while suffering from plague and, unless the priest harbored any serious
reservations, circumstances dictated her interment in consecrated ground
as soon as possible. For the moment, her corpse stayed put in the barrel
pending the parish priest's evaluation. However, the priest sought advice
from the local dean, who admonished Pruggmayer not to allow a burial
in the parish cemetery. Although the parish priest agreed in principle with
his advice, he expressed concern over the writ from the Aulic Council in
Munich. The dean urged him to travel to Freising and obtain counsel
directly from the bishop.

Pruggmayer returned to his parish and prepared for the ninety kilometer
journey to Freising, several days on foot. Meanwhile, the elders of Feilnbach
held a village counsel and called up the local militia under their captain.
Four ringleaders advocated marching on the cemetery to deter the burial. A
band armed with pole-arms and farm implements arrived at the cemetery,
setting up watch day and night, awaiting instructions from the bishop.

Several days later, Pruggmayer arrived in Freising accompanied by two
communal representatives. Before the bishop's Ecclesiastical Council, he
suddenly revealed an inconsistency in the district judge's account of the
suicide. He claimed that everyone in the neighborhood, including Anna's
own relatives, knew that she committed the despicable act not to escape

---

[16] Andre Rieder; see Georg Ferchl, *Bayerische Behörden und Beamte 1550–1804* (Munich, 1908), 18.
[17] HStAM HR 104, 293v.

the sufferings of illness, but out of demonic despair. In that case, having lost hope of resurrection and eternal life, canon law forbade her burial in consecrated ground. On those grounds, acting on the priest's testimony and a supportive letter from his local superior, the Ecclesiastical Council pronounced Anna unworthy of a Christian burial. The council denied burial in the cemetery, but in view of the district judge's insistence and the writ of the Aulic Council from Munich, it left the choice of another location to the secular authorities – naturally at their expense. Upon his return, Pruggmayer communicated the decree to his local secular and ecclesiastical superiors. Incensed by Pruggmayer's blatant contradiction of his own report, the district judge in turn proclaimed the episcopal decree "a blank scrap of paper."[18] He called on the skinner to remove Anna Kirchberger's body from the barrel (where it had been interred in the summer heat for over two weeks) and to take it to the cemetery without further hesitation. There, the judge confronted the village militia. After dispersing the crowd under threat of force and fines, he had the body interred in the consecrated ground of the communal cemetery adjacent to the church of Feilnbach.[19]

The community and their parish priest expressed outrage and indignation. Pruggmayer threatened to suspend all religious services at the church next to the cemetery. He sent a full report of the incident to the Ecclesiastical Council in Freising. The council deemed the matter serious enough to inform the provost of the cathedral chapter, the bishop's direct subordinate. On behalf of Pruggmayer and the parish assembly, the council requested that the bishop intervene personally with Duke Maximilian in Munich. In his report, the parish priest also queried whether or not he should withhold services in the church, now deemed profaned by the burial. With the acknowldgment of the provost, the Ecclesiastical Council forwarded the complaint to the bishop personally, calling for the exhumation of Anna Kirchberger's body and its immediate removal to a "proper" place, with assurances that such a shameful intrusion on the autonomy of a free parish never occur again.

Simultaneously, the Aulic Council in Munich ordered the district judge to conduct a complete inquiry into the uprising, with particular attention to the ringleaders and the activities of the parish priest. Pruggmayer's threat to suspend church services made them especially wary; the Aulic Council instructed the district judge to prevent this from happening under any circumstances. They also issued a communiqué to the bishop, initiating direct negotiations between Munich and Freising.

---

[18] AEM GR 34, 73r–74v.   [19] HStAM HR 105, 41v.

It soon became evident to the ecclesiastical authorities that the priest's claims regarding the circumstances of the suicide were inaccurate. Sworn testimony gathered by the judge from members of the community corroborated the original claim that Anna suffered from a serious and longstanding illness prior to the suicide, affecting her sanity. The parish priest received an official reprimand from Freising for instigating the incident, warning him to follow the dictates of the secular authorities in this matter obediently and without delay. For the sake of her honest survivors, who suffered public degradation and disadvantage, the Ecclesiastical Council had Anna's corpse commended to consecrated ground. They also admonished Pruggmayer to refrain from popular "superstitions," particularly the notion that hail and disaster are occasioned by the interment of a suicide in hallowed ground, ordering him to sermonize against the belief from the pulpit.

Three months later, *Rentmeister* Bernhard Barth conducted a public trial in the matter of Anna Kirchberger's suicide during his annual rounds through the districts.[20] Barth, renowned as a bitter opponent of witchcraft persecutions in Bavaria, summoned the ringleaders before the assembled community, charged them with rebellion, and fined them eight pounds each, a harsh, but hardly draconian sentence.[21] Afterwards, he publicly chastized the entire parish, threatening fines and exile for participation in future acts of disobedience and unrest.

The case of Anna Kirchberger is exemplary and hardly singular. Between 1619 and 1630, the Aulic Council reported four other incidents of communal resistance to the choice of burial site in cases of suicide. They investigated another four reports between 1631 and 1670. In eight cases, women had committed suicide, in the ninth a village priest. In the latter case, rather than objecting to burial in consecrated ground, the community swarmed the priest's house in a *ravage*, the ritual plundering of the goods of a suicide.[22] The parish community was the source of all nine protests. In 1619 and 1621, for example, the Aulic Council in Munich again ordered severe penalties for the ringleaders of two separate suicide uprisings near Dachau. In 1630, the community of Landsberg actually succeeded in forcing the authorities to bury Magdalena Knoller in a desolate place, instead of in the cemetery for unbaptized children, as originally intended. In Markt Schwaben, the parish priest and his local superior both intervened, unsuccessfully, on behalf of the parish in 1647 to have Elisabeth Pichlmayer buried

---

[20] StAM RL 112, 622v–624v.
[21] Ferchl, *Bayerische Behörden*, 671; Behringer, *Witchcraft Persecutions*, 272–280.
[22] Vandekerckhove, *On Punishment*, 119–120.

in a desolate place, threatening communal resistance with force and judicial action once again. Twenty years later, representatives of a parish near Markt Schwaben protested personally before the Aulic Council, procuring a dishonorable interment for another suicide, even though considerable evidence indicated that the old widow suffered from faintheartedness and had an otherwise upstanding reputation for her piety. In effect, suicide revolts challenged the authority of the state both judicially and in terms of its sovereign monopoly of violence. And, not unusually, the challenge succeeded.

Legally enshrined in the sixteenth century, the authority of the state over suicide had a long history. The first imperial legal code, the *Carolina*, outlined legal procedure for the Holy Roman Empire in 1532. It categorized self-killing (Article 135: *Straff eygener tödung*) as a felony alongside manslaughter, murder, infanticide and poisoning.[23] However, it limited the only penalty, forfeiture, to those who took their own life to avoid criminal prosecution. In that case, the suicide forfeited heritable properties to the authorities. Apart from that, article 135 did not affect the eligibility of heirs to inherit, whether or not the court judged the suicide *non compos mentis* (specifically melancholy brought on by illness, infirmity of mind or similar forms of imbecility). The *Carolina* theoretically superseded customary practices. Never uniformly implemented throughout the Empire, the provisions of the *Carolina* manifested the centralizing tendencies of resurgent Roman law; in fact, the conditional forfeiture precisely replicated penalties for suicide in classical Rome.[24]

In 1616, Maximilian I reformed territorial law and published a new, comprehensive criminal code.[25] In actual practice, the *Carolina*'s provisions against self-killing applied in Bavaria for some time. Unlike the *Carolina*, however, Bavarian judicial sources universally refer to self-killing either by the means employed (self-hanged, self-drowned, self-shot, etc.) or simply as self-executed (*selbst hingerichtet*). Self-execution implied the usurpation of the sovereign power of the authorities over life and death.[26] The Aulic

---

[23] Gustav Radbruch (ed.), *Die Peinliche Gerichtsordnung Kaiser Karls V. von 1532 (Carolina)* (6th edn, Stuttgart, 1991), 87–102.
[24] The similarities are outlined in Zedler, vol. xxxvi, 1603. On the development of practice from Roman law, see Alexander Murray, *Suicide in the Middle Ages, vol. II: The Curse on Self-Murder* (Oxford, 2000), 154–181.
[25] Though it contained no specific reference to suicide, the code contained a catchall article assuming penalties from the *Carolina* for crimes it otherwise omitted; *Landts und Policey Ordnung der Fürstenthumben Obern und Nidern Bayern . . .* (Munich, 1616), 827: *Malefizprozeßordnungen Tit. 8, Art. 10.*
[26] In accordance with Roman law, Zedler, vol. xxxvi, 1598, considered suicide to escape penalties an insult against the legitimate authorities.

Council treated self-execution as a very serious offense and, like madness, identified it as an affair of princely concern (*in causae domini*, or *landesherrliche Interessensachen*). Procedure required local judges to report suicide directly to the Aulic Council. As the intermediate superior of local judges, the *Rentmeister* seldom became involved.[27] At the local level, district judges and parish priests took the most active role in suicide investigations. The primary purpose, to determine cause of death, required a ruling of death by misadventure, foul play or suicide.[28] In the latter case, the Aulic Council's decision on motive determined place of burial.

The protocols of the Aulic Council and the district courts allow for a reconstruction of the specific procedural guidelines of the investigations. Upon discovering the deed, local officials obtained the corpse's ritual removal from the locus of death, by either the executioner or the skinner, to temporary storage, often in a barrel, until the investigation could be completed.[29] A local inquiry ensued with sworn testimony gathered from neighbors and family to establish the circumstances of death and, in the case of suicide, the person's state of mind.[30] The central authorities lodged a legion of complaints against local officials arising from negligent handling of investigations: district judges questioned witnesses unofficially or without prepared interrogatories; testimony went unrecorded; burials occurred before the Aulic Council reached a decision on cause of death.[31] Frequently, they leveled reprimands and fines against district judges for non-compliance. The Council ordered local officials to view the body personally and provide a detailed report.[32] Occasionally, they requested expert medical testimony by a physician or a barber-surgeon.[33] The Council authorized the collection of testimony under duress, if the suicide seemed in any way

---

[27] The Aulic Council requested that the *Rentmeister* provide information to determine whether or not a local official who attempted suicide had done so to escape punishment for some indiscretion: HStAM HR 261, 109v–110v. The council ordered the *Rentmeister* to punish the leaders of a peasant revolt brought about by its insistence that a suicide be buried in the cemetery: HStAM HR 106, 47v. The *Rentmeister* was Bernhard Barth, a bitter opponent of witchcraft persecutions: Behringer, *Witchcraft Persecutions*, 253. When witchcraft was suspected in a suicide, the council ordered the *Rentmeister* to apprehend and punish the offender: HStAM HR 117, 198r–199r.

[28] The procedure followed in seventeenth-century Bavaria was common throughout the Empire; see Zedler, vol. xxxvi, 1604–1605.

[29] The use of the barrel as a temporary sepulcher was tied to the method of water disposal: AEM GR 34, 73r–74v. On the role of the executioner in handling suicides in Bavaria, see Nowosadtko, *Scharfrichter und Abdecker*, 69–85.

[30] StAM Pfleggericht Tölz, Gerichtsrechnungen #39 (1641), 50v–51r; HStAM GR 139, 110.

[31] Some examples: HStAM HR 157, 58v; HR 175, 251r–v; HR 104, 293v; HR 166, 76v; HR 155, 289r; HR 252, 103v; HR 297, 205v; HR 330, 14v–15r; HR 316, 458r–v.

[32] HStAM HR 118, 186; HR 225, 313v–314r; HR 235, 13v.

[33] HStAM HR 133, 189v; HR 172, 137v (danger of plague); HR 200, 395r–v (attempted suicide).

suspicious, recommending the judicial torture of spouses, lovers or accused witches.[34]

In Bavaria, where forfeiture penalties depended solely on the criminal status of the self-killer, the fisc seldom confiscated. After a lengthy legal dispute in 1609, even fewer confiscations occurred; in one case, the exchequer explicitly spared the dowry of a self-executioner's wife as independent property after he killed himself to avoid punishment.[35] Out of 300 cases of reported suicide between 1611 and 1670, the Aulic Council requested inventories of property in only twenty-five suicides, fewer than 10 percent of all cases. The results of nine are indeterminate, while the other sixteen ended in a clear decision that favored heirs, though the costs of burial were usually deducted from the estate. In one case, the authorities even remitted a self-executioner's debts rather than passing them on to his widow and young children.[36] One poor woman with seven children inherited the paltry estate of their father under questionable circumstances.[37] As a rare occurrence, therefore, confiscation played a relatively minor role as a motivating factor in the decisions of the Aulic Council and offered little enrichment for officials or coroners. Evidence from the *Rentamt* of Landshut confirms few actual confiscations (*confiscierlicher delicti*) in Lower Bavaria as well.[38]

Given the lack of a broad legal basis for penalization through forfeiture, the conditions of burial occupied the concerns of the central authorities. In Bavaria, the most shameful forms of burials included cremation, disposal in a river, interment under the scaffold, and interment "at a secluded place where neither man nor beast treads," the most common of all.[39] In cases of unintentional suicide or diminished capacity, which dictated leniency, the body of a self-executioner could be interred either in the cemetery at night without the pealing of bells, along the outside wall of the cemetery, or in the place of burial reserved for unbaptized children. Physical proximity to the cemetery approximated the degree of dishonor associated with each particular suicide.

Before, during and after the Thirty Years War, decisions of the Aulic Council on the state of mind in cases of suicide reflect a trend toward rationalized procedures and leniency in meting out honorific sanctions. One of the oldest penalties, disposal of the body in water, declined rapidly in popularity at the beginning of the seventeenth century. Between 1611 and 1615, the Aulic Council recommended disposal in water for 25 percent of all

---

[34] HStAM HR 117, 198v–199r, 228v–229r; HR 175, 251r–v; 210, 171v; 272, 227r.
[35] HStAM HK 190, 190r.   [36] HStAM HR 95, 72r–v.   [37] HStAM HK 227, 159v.
[38] Lederer, "' . . . welches die Oberkeit," 177–178.
[39] "Am Ort und Ende wo weder Mensch noch Vieh hinkommt."

suicides. After placing the corpse in a barrel, the authorities had it thrown into a nearby river. Known as "running" (*rinnen*), the custom appeared in the Middle Ages, but fell out of favor by the seventeenth century.[40] Some historians link its original intent to a belief in the cleansing power of water to wash away danger (*weggeschwemt*), while Alexander Murray promotes a view of the suicide's corpse as simple waste for efficient disposal.[41] The authorities employed this method on two final occasions in 1620 and 1623.[42] Analogously, sinking the corpse in a wild swamp also went out of vogue after 1615, at the time plague became endemic for a period of two decades. Briefly, in 1628, the Aulic Council dabbled with burial under the scaffold. Usually reserved for criminals convicted of very serious crimes, such as infanticide, it was extremely dishonorable.[43] Although the authorities used the method throughout the seventeenth century, they only did so on an occasional and sporadic basis.

Banal as customs for the spatial segregation of corpses seem, they illustrate the trend toward procedural rationalization and centralization in two ways. First, practical limitations associated with water or swamp interments precluded universal implementation, since one could only conduct such rituals in the immediate vicinity of swamps or rivers, thereby reinforcing local differentiations. By insisting on uniform procedures for all burials, the authorities enhanced their legal sovereignty. Second, the abrupt change in method coincided with severe outbreaks of plague. After 1615, water and swamp burials quickly declined in popularity. The last employment of the water method during a horrific plague in 1623 marked a clear procedural break with the past. In that year, the Aulic Council recorded more self-executions than in any before: nineteen, almost four times the yearly average from 1611 to 1670. High rates of suicide coupled with the factor of contagion led the Aulic Council to increase its recommendations for speedy cremation.

Cremation, sporadic before 1615, began to be employed more regularly. By 1623, the Aulic Council ordered cremation in one-third of all cases. The authorities cremated regularly from that point onward and it ranked second

---

[40] Bächtold-Stäubli, *Handwörterbuch*, vol. VII, 1630, suggests that water-disposal of the corpse was already out of practice by the sixteenth century, but it was regularly employed in neighboring Augsburg well into the seventeenth century.

[41] Murray, *Suicide*, 37–41.   [42] HStAM HR 157, 68r, 185r; HR 182, 227v.

[43] Burial of suicides under the scaffold was practiced throughout the Empire: Zedler, vol. XXXVI, 1605. The prosecution of infanticide witnessed an increase as well during this time. On the exemplary and deterrent function of punishment in early modern Germany, see Richard van Dülmen, *Theater of Horror. Crime and Punishment in Early Modern Germany* (Cambridge, 1991), 43, for an example of burial rites.

only to burial in remote sites as the most favored method for disposing of self-executioners. The Aulic Council intentionally employed cremation and burial in remote sites to prevent the spread of contagion. Investigations of self-executions could drag on for weeks, as decomposition of the body set in. For example, a habeas corpus dispute over jurisdiction between the Bishop of Freising and Bavaria in 1628 postponed the burial of a woman for so long that the corpse began to "smell horribly."[44] The Aulic Council urged local officials to persuade the bishop that fear of contagion motivated them to press for immediate burial in a remote location, rather than any desire to infringe upon Freising's sovereign authority over the bodies of its subjects. In other cases, the Aulic Council specifically commanded local officials to cremate "without delay" during the warm summer months in order to prevent decomposition and the threat of contagion.[45] Cremation gained a certain preferment, rising gradually to 31 percent for the years 1661–1670.

Naturally, the status of the self-murderer represented an important variable in burial decisions; according to Georges Minois, *the* most important factor.[46] Suicide patterns among members of the first and second estates, especially the nobility, are difficult to establish since they were usually exempted from normal channels of prosecution and were in a better position to withhold or distort information concerning their immediate circle. The reported suicide of a monk from the monastery of Bernried who hanged himself with his cincture was exceptional, having occurred in a public inn.[47] Startled by the news, both the secular and ecclesiastical authorities agreed, in light of the summer heat, to bury the body at an isolated site. Members of the lower clergy received little preferential treatment when it came to self-execution; both a pastor and a sexton were buried at remote sites.[48] For the rest of the population, nominal occupational status exercised little influence on the choice of burial procedure. Mayors and public officials fared no better than servants or carters when it came to dishonorable burials. Penalties for individuals on the margins of the community were harsher, particularly for soldiers, beggars and the unidentified; the Aulic Council was keen to find symbols of Catholic orthodoxy in the possession

---

[44] HStAM HR 219, 328r–v.   [45] HStAM HR 229, 234v; HR 235, 335v.

[46] According to Minois, *History of Suicide*, 16–18, 248–301, the social class of the self-killer played a central role in perceptions of suicides from the Middle Ages throughout the *ancien régime*; see also Jean-Claude Schmitt, "Le suicide au Moyen Age," *Annales ESC* 31 (1976), 7, on the methodological difficulties in identifying suicides among the social elite.

[47] HStAM HR 366, 213v–215r, 337r; HR 367, 73r, 105r; AEM GR 82, 286v–287r.

[48] HStAM HR 161, 46v, 50r, 61r, 120r–v, 206v; HR 112, 90r.

of vagrants, such as medallions or books, before reaching a decision on burials.[49]

However, an increased willingness of the Aulic Council to recommend lenient interment for self-executioners is perhaps the most significant change in the pattern of burial rituals. While the actual numbers of recommendations for honorable or semi-honorable burial either in the cemetery, along the cemetery wall, or in the burial grounds for unbaptized children fluctuated in relation to suicide rates, these requests increased steadily as a percentage of the whole. Orders for lenient burials fell slightly from 16 percent between 1611 and 1620 to 15 percent during the catastrophic decade of the twenties. State of mind of the self-murderer influenced the official choice of burial site more than any other factor. The council strongly recommended burial in the cemetery for individuals considered of good reputation, dutiful in prayer, neighborly, pious or god-fearing.[50] Interment in either the cemetery or the burial grounds for unbaptized children was suggested for a woman who displayed "strong signs of regret" just prior to taking her life.[51] Another man had recently converted to Catholicism, winning him similar privileges.[52] The reputation of living relatives received consideration in the choice of burial rite as well. The Ecclesiastical Council of the Bishop of Freising noted that burial in unconsecrated soil worked to the ultimate derision and disadvantage of even honorable relations.[53] When circumstances unavoidably dictated a disgraceful burial outside the cemetery, shame to the survivors could be ameliorated by a discreet or "quiet" interment.[54]

Individual state of mind at the time of suicide attained central importance in the seventeenth century as a mitigating factor in the determination of burial method (see Table 6.1). State of mind played a decisive role in 15 percent of all cases during the first half of the period considered (1611–1640), but then jumped to 25 percent in the later half (1641–1670). The council recognized two mental conditions affecting choice of burial location: religious despair (*desperation, Verzweiflung*), a serious form of apostasy, and

---

[49] There are no details at all on twenty-three of the suicides. The occupations of some 102 could be ascertained. Servants were most numerous (16), followed by day laborers (9) and carters (8), all professions of low status.

[50] For example: HStAM HR 330, 115r–v; HR373, 69r–v, 306r–v; HR 379, 342r, 313r–v.

[51] HStAM HR 239, 109v: "starke Zeichen der Reue von sich gegeben."

[52] HStAM HR 128, 267v: "zuvor der Catholischen Religion zugethon."

[53] AEM GR 34, 73v–74v: "auch derselben negst ehrlichen befreundten höchstem Spott und Nachteil geraichen thue."

[54] Occurring "in der Stille": HStAM HR 139, 158v; HR 330, 115r–v.

Table 6.1 *The rise of the insanity defense: state of mind as a factor in burial decisions*

Year	Reported suicides	Despair		Non compos mentis		Physical infirmity	
		No.	%	No.	%	No.	%
1611–1619	57	4	7	4	7	1	2
1620–1629	96	4	4	5	5	2	2
1630–1639	47	2	4	5	11	1	2
1640–1649	30	0		6	20	1	3
1650–1659	29	0		9	31	0	
1660–1670	37	0		8	22	0	

Source: HStAM HR 1611–1670.

mental and/or physical infirmity.[55] A declaration of desperation implied that the self-murderer had acted freely (*compos mentis*) and probably at the instigation of the devil in an attempt to kill the soul. A verdict of despair invariably resulted in dishonorable burial.[56] Infirmity or madness, on the other hand, mitigated individual culpability and justified leniency. The most common varieties of mental infirmities mentioned in the records were melancholy, senility and pusillanimity, all of which indicated diminished capacity. Physical illness as a source of mental anguish also justified an insanity defense. Physical infirmities included bodily weakness, headaches, Hungarian fever and plague. In cases specifically addressing state of mind at the time of death, determinations of madness and infirmity steadily overshadowed diabolic despair; after 1640, religious despair disappeared as a category of suicide from the protocols of the Aulic Council, replaced by madness.

Slight though this evidence might seem, its trajectory is significantly unidirectional and it validates independent qualitative proofs in the areas of opposition to witchcraft persecutions, skepticism toward demonic possession, support for a secular insanity defense, and the rationalization of burial practices in cases of suicide. As a cumulative pool, all areas indicate a decreased concern with diabolical agency at court. Additionally, in European comparison, MacDonald's figures for England display a striking similarity. Specifically, although the absolute number of *felo de se* verdicts

---

[55] On despair as a religious category, see Lederer, "Dishonorable Dead," 349–365; Murray, *Suicide*, 369–395.
[56] Besold, *Thesaurus*, "Begräbniß der Todten," 22; Zedler, vol. xxxvi, 1605.

dominated throughout the early modern period, rising from 90 percent in
1530 (just prior to the Act of Supremacy) to 99 percent by 1610 (in the midst
of the general crisis), they declined gradually in the 1620s and 1630s. After
1660, verdicts of *non compos mentis* returned to King's Bench progressed
throughout the rest of the seventeenth century, from 7 percent in 1660–
1664 to 41 percent by 1700–1704.[57] After 1660, both at King's Bench in
England and the Aulic Council in Bavaria, the insanity defense in suicide
verdicts advanced, though the policy of confiscation retarded the decline of
felo de se verdicts in England, since (unlike Bavaria and the Empire, where
Roman law prevailed) confiscation offered coroners and judges there a
potential source of enrichment. Nonetheless, patterns of suicide verdicts
are indicative of a diabolic crisis and a psychological revolution, coinciding
with the forward march of the insanity defense throughout Europe in the
later seventeenth century.

    For example, in a decisive resolution of September 18, 1668 ("Super
Questione Sepultura aliunium vel ex Melancholia vel Desperation sus-
pecti"), Elector Ferdinand Maria reached a substantive agreement with
ecclesiastical authorities over the necessity to complete a full investigation
into a self-killer's state of mind before a parish priests could either grant or
reject the right to a Christian burial.[58] In its decisions on such an essential
matter of the soul, the Aulic Council consistently deferred to the expert
opinion of parish priests as recognized spiritual physicians for a psychological profile of the individual. The parish priest played a crucial role in the
tragedy of suicide. His opinion influenced the decision on the final resting-
place, because cemeteries fell under his nominal jurisdiction. The priest,
as the local representative of his ordinary, retained authority over burial
rites in Bavaria until the end of the *ancien régime*, another limitation on
state sovereignty over the bodies of its subjects. The protocols of the Aulic
Council in Munich explicitly ordered district judges to consult with the
local priest about burial procedures for suicides on more than fifty separate
occasions between 1610 and 1670.[59] Although verdicts of suicide by despair
nearly disappeared from the Aulic Council protocols, communities and the
ecclesiastical authorities continued to challenge insanity verdicts. The state
could threaten their subjects and dissenting parish priests with pressure,
fines and threats of force, but attempts to rule by executive fiat also met
with reversals. In fact, electoral mandates reconfirmed pastoral prerogative
late into the eighteenth century until the authors of the Bavarian secularization finally revoked ecclesiastic jurisdiction over cemeteries in 1809,

---

[57] MacDonald and Murphy, *Sleepless Souls*, 15–16, 29, 81, 122.   [58] HStAM GR 1191.
[59] The wording of these orders constituted a strong reminder to district judges to observe an established
    policy.

both for hygienic reasons and because of an (ostensibly) enlightened public attitude toward suicide.[60]

As a local spiritual physician, the parish priest possessed an intimate knowledge of his parishioners and their mental health. To obtain said knowledge, a post-Tridentine parish priest had a number of devices at his disposal. Ritually linked to all rites of passage in the lives of his parishioners (birth/baptism, marriage, death), he spiritually guided and consoled them from earliest childhood through unsettling and dangerous phases that often played a role in suicidal behavior. In Bavaria since the beginning of the seventeenth century, the parish priest compiled extensive parish registers, enabling him to reconstitute personal biographies from the records of his predecessors and keep track of compliance with the sacraments. One sacrament in particular, auricular confession, offered parish priests an unusually penetrating view into the private lives of their parishioners. Ecclesiastical sanctions rendered parishioners ineligible for burial in consecrated ground if they died without attending yearly confession, a further incentive to participate in the sacrament.[61] Confidentiality notwithstanding, the secular authorities regularly questioned the parish priest regarding a penitent's state of mind as revealed during auricular confession just prior to suicide. In one case, a priest cradled the bleeding head of suicidal woodsman in his lap for nearly five hours, encouraging him to a sign of contrition so that he might perform final absolution: "Jacob, do you know who you are? Give me just one sign, that you are sorry . . . that you have harmed yourself and thereby have insulted God; if you regret it, raise your head."[62] When the woodsman, who had shot himself, mumbled "AHHH" (*sic*), the priest absolved him and consoled him, wiping the blood from his head until he died. The priest then recorded the entire confession, including references to other privy conversations in the confessional. Of course, the secular authorities' primary interests in confessions included heretical tendencies, deviant behavior, illness and an evaluation of sanity that might influence their burial decisions.[63] Input on burial decisions rested on the recognition of the parish priest's psychological acumen and this is one area where the spiritual physician continued to play an active role. However,

---

[60] Mayr, *Sammlung der Churpfalz-Baierischen allgemeinen*, 125; Georg Karl Mayer (*sic*) (ed.), *General-Index über alle Landes-Verordnungen* (Munich, 1809), 630.

[61] A decree to that effect was published in 1603 in nearby Catholic Tyrol: Pallaver, *Das Ende*, 58. Carl Borromeo, the Archbishop of Milan, ordered physicians to break off treatment of the sick after four days if they refused confession. In 1566, Pope Pius V required physicians to swear an oath to that extent; see Prosperi, "Beichtväter," 129.

[62] AEM GR 87, ff. 102r–105v; considered in detail in Lederer, "Dishonorable Dead."

[63] For example, HStAM HR 221, 251; HR 261, 109v–110v; HR 339, 137v; HR 346, 351v–352r; HR 373, 69r.

declining verdicts of suicidal despair and fewer orders for dishonorable burials suggest that the insanity defense made headway among the parish clergy as well. Perhaps they too had changed their attitudes, although, as in the case of the parish priest Pruggmayer in 1612, it seems more likely that they caved in under pressure from the ordinary and, after the resolution of 1668, the secular authorities. In either case, they read the writing on the wall and recognized the need to move away from diabolical explanations for suicide in order to retain any legitimate authority over such matters.

CHAINS BIND BOTH WAYS

Officially, the protocols of the Ducal/Electoral Aulic Council in Munich usually identified persons with severe spiritual afflictions as mad or, literally, senseless or sufferers of unreason (*sinnlos, Unsinnig*). Unofficial descriptions, like miracle books, depicted persons who had "slipped from reason" (*vom ihrem Verstand verrückt*), "lost their senses" (*ihr Sinn verloren*), or had been "robbed" of reason (*ihres Verstandts beraubt*). Reason and sense represented social capital which the mad lacked, had lost or had had stolen. Official nosology implied a lack of the accoutrements of legal majority, while unofficial nosology suggested an accident, an inadvertent displacement or a forceful estrangement. In either case, few additional mechanisms existed for removing the dangerously insane from communities threatened by raving persons or burdened by the rules of Christian charity. Often, restraint offered the only option available to families and communities to control unruly members.

Initially, sufferers might be bound to their beds, but a chronic condition forced the costly step to contract with the local smith for the casting of chains, the classic devotional symbol of madness (Plate 18). The late medieval miracle books of Altötting record early examples. In 1497, Conrad Hauser lost control of his spirit and reason and had to be tied to his bed.[64] Votive paintings of Margret Eyseleis (1520), Conrad Scheuirlen's son (1523) and Jörg Lästrider's wife depicted their restraint with chains and still adorn the chapel at Altötting today. Sufferers arrived at Pürten in chains as well.[65] In remembrance of his affliction, Wolfgang Reid paid homage to

---

[64] Reported later in the *Oetinga eruderate 1623* and edited in Bauer, "P. Johannes Saller," 67–68, 91–92. Saller cited a number of early miracles to substantiate the power of spiritual physic over the remedies of physicians.

[65] For example: PMB 630831, 650728, 800130.

Plate 18. *The Veneration of St. Anastasia*: implored by devoted sufferers, including a madman who casts off his chains and a reclining demoniac; to the left, a devil exits his mouth in a puff of black smoke (Meichelbeck, *Leben/Leyden/Todt/Ehreburg . . .*, 1710) (Permission of the Bavarian State Library, Munich.)

St. Anastasia at Benediktbeuern with a wax chain.[66] Maria Kronbacher lay in chains for some time before their removal at the Anastasia shrine.[67] A certain barber-surgeon became confused and "had to be chained."[68] Melchior Vendt lay in chains nearly a whole year before relatives transported him to Benediktbeuern.[69] Maria Bernhard visited gypsies to have her fortune told, but they enchanted her instead and she had to be bound by two chains.[70] Dangerous persons were usually restrained in chains only when necessary, since restraint kept them from work and involved considerable capital expenditure. Vitus Linhart erred from his senses for a whole year, had to be put in chains, but periodically came to his senses long enough to work for three or four weeks at a time, only to be chained again.[71] Other pilgrims were chained simply to facilitate the journey to a shrine.[72] Simon Hueber was restrained with three chains and led to Benediktbeuern.[73] In the warm months, sufferers were chained to a wagon for transport.[74] Bartel Ruger, robbed of his reason fourteen days prior, was chained to a sled and transported to the Anastasia shrine in the winter.[75] Melchior Vendt, a wealthy brewer's servant deranged as a result of an inheritance conflict, was transported from Swabia on a wagon with chains on his feet, but even as he neared Benediktbeuern, he cast off his chains and rode on to the shrine in full possession of his faculties.[76]

The confinement of sufferers burdened communities. Their continued presence in the locale disrupted communal and familiar relations in a civil and reproductive sense. Confinement of the mad at home, in the community or in an institution posed additional financial burdens for families and the parish. Margaretha Haderin, initially confined in chains at her brother-in-law's house, supported herself by alms until her health improved somewhat and she recovered her senses.[77] The authorities ordered Ulrich Gail confined either in the hospital of Aichach or elsewhere in his village until he got better.[78] Rudimentary care at the local level often gave rise to cruelties and neglect, offering little hope for a recovery. Under the circumstances, families and communities predictably sought alternatives to public begging, costly restraint by chains or long-term confinement in homes, hospices or houses of incarceration.

During the seventeenth century, Bavarian families comprised the first echelon of care and finance, followed by parishes. The heavy burden often

[66] AMB 630514.   [67] AMB 651121.
[68] ". . . in ein solche verwirung gerathen das er hat miessen an kheten geschlagen werden . . .": AMB 600725.
[69] AMB 650414.   [70] AMB 670707.   [71] AMB 600415.   [72] AMB 610923, 641117.
[73] AMB 600424.   [74] AMB 650530, 650601.   [75] AMB 630129.   [76] AMB 650530.
[77] HStAM HR 207, 154v.   [78] HStAM HR 254, 194v–195r.

led to maltreatment. The Aulic Council in Munich regularly intervened on paternalist grounds to insure families and communities fulfilled their obligations toward afflicted members. In 1611, the Aulic Council ordered the district judge of Traunstein to seek financial assistance from the family of a senseless man.[79] At Wolfratshausen in 1612, they ordered care for Wolfgang Häfel's senseless wife at his expense. If he was unable to pay, she should apply for alms from the parish community. The Aulic Council remanded widow Haderin to chains at her brother-in-law's home with alms collected for her support until such time as she regained her reason and health.[80] The need for the central authorities to intervene and the reluctance on the part of families, communities and individuals to bear the burden of costs alone underscores the potential for neglect before regular state intervention began in the seventeenth century.

The authorities harbored three primary concerns: shelter, sustenance and the safety of the community at large. The case of Margaretha Pichler, temporarily restrained in the local jail in 1616, demonstrates the rudimentary nature of official expectations for care. The district judge of Dachau required her relatives to contribute money to construct a cell (*Khötterl*) for her temporary confinement in a comfortable place away from the jail. He authorized the construction of a pauper's hut (*almuesen Haus*) built with voluntary contributions of wood from the local community and had her chained therein and supported through the collection of alms in the community.[81] Similarly, Anna Bärtler's father built a crate of wood, had her chained there and supported her by the collection of alms in the parish, adding a small oven to protect her against the winter cold – a common feature of local care.[82] The Aulic Council reminded district judges to avoid any threat of danger or damage to the community, but also intervened to insure the safety of the sufferers if threatened.[83] In 1640, workers set out to construct a pauper's hut near a mill to lodge the senseless Sebald Reitter, but the miller came in the night and angrily demolished the entire structure along with its oven. Arrested, the miller spent four days in jail on bread and water and had to pay for the hut's reconstruction. Ironically, the Aulic Council later judged the miller mad as well, resulting in investigations into his home of origin.[84]

Until the mid-seventeenth century, communal subventions for the raving regularly originated from voluntary alms collected for the afflicted in

---

[79] HStAM HR 93, 228r.   [80] HStAM HR 207, 154v.
[81] HStAM HR 130, 5r; HR 130, 136v–137r; HR 131, 125v, 188v.   [82] HStAM HR 227, 70v.
[83] HStAM HR 111, 54r; HR 305, 453v–454r; HR 313, 126v–127r; HR 320, 111r–v; HR 333, 374r–v.
[84] HStAM HR 269, 140v–141r, 290v.

her or his respective parish. The new territorial criminal code of 1616 recognized the need to collect alms at the parish level. It envisioned voluntary
contributions by parish communities in response to entreaties from the
pulpit ordered by the state, which expressly associated folly (*Narrheit*) with
poverty and begging.[85] Procedurally, Maximilian's *Ordinance . . . for the
Support of the Domestic, Needy, Local Poor* (*Hausarmen*) of 1627 laid out specific guidelines for this traditional method of parish relief.[86] The *Ordinance*
assigned responsibility for the maintenance of "all poor needy persons who,
because of age, illness and other infirmities, are unable to support themselves without alms" to the parish community of birth or longstanding residence and distinguished them from the undeserving poor.[87] Ultimately, the
authorities lumped the legally senseless together under the category of
the deserving poor since at least 1611, ordering district judges to authorize
the collection of alms for their support.[88]

The classic portrait of uncontrolled begging in Catholic territories juxtaposed with an orderly welfare system among Protestants is somewhat
misleading. Whereas Ursula Mittenzwain, citizen of Freising married to a
member of the tin-workers guild, could beg the two pounds of wax for
a votive offering in her community in 1620, the *Ordinance* of 1627 forbade all public and house-to-house begging in Bavaria, at least in theory.[89]
Outdoor poor relief may have been collected and distributed in a decentralized fashion at the parish level, but district judges administered relief.[90]
Well-established procedures for a communal system of voluntary donations
and the local distribution of alms operated according to provisions three
through seven and eleven of the *Ordinance*. Village leaders (*Dorfhauptleute*)
or a beggars' judge (*Bettelvogt*) identified the needy, or they came forward

[85] *Landts und Policey Ordnung*, 686–687: "Damit auch die arme dürfftigen desto stattlicher mögen
unterhalten werden/ so sol denselben in Stätten/ Märckten/ und auffm Landt/ bey den Kirchmenigen
das Allmuesen gesammlet; auch das Volck durch die Prediger auff den Cantzeln/ mit fleiß ermahnht
werden/ daß sich ein jeder in solchen loblichen Werck der Barmherzigkeit mitleydig und willig
erzaig und halt." Examples of baroque sermons treating beggars and fools in the same context are
found in Moser–Rath, *Dem Kirchenvolk*, 95–98.

[86] *Landgebot/ Gesaz/ und Ordnung/ wie es im ChurFürstenthumb Bayrn/ so wol mit Unterhaltung der
Inlendischen dürfftigen Haußarmen Leuten/ als mit vertreibung und außreitung aller fremder starcker
Bettler . . . gehalten werden soll* (Munich, 1627). Edited in Ziegler, *Dokumente*, 994–999. Maximilian's
first mandate on poor relief appeared in 1599 and the Ordinance of 1627 was reprinted in 1630:
HStAM, *Kurbayern Mandatensammlung* 1599 IX 26, 1627 XI 19, 1630 II 6.

[87] Ziegler, *Dokumente*, 994–995. In Europe the distinction between shame-faced and undeserving poor
was universal: Jütte, *Poverty*, 8–14.

[88] HStAM HR 93, 228r; HR 105, 252v–253r. Again, a general feature of European poor relief: Jütte,
Poverty, 17, 24–25.

[89] Bauer, "P. Johannes Saller," 63, 86.

[90] On centralized and decentralized systems of poor relief in early modern Europe, see Jütte, *Poverty*,
100–139.

directly with a supplication. District judges chose parish leaders and tasked them with the orderly collection of alms on a weekly basis; should communities display undue "coldness" toward the needy, then district judges stepped in and collected alms under the supervision of the parish clergy, who stood by adjuring their flocks. Collection in church on Sundays and holy days was the preferred method; fair distribution among the needy followed.

In official practice, the authorities awarded entitlement to alms by written patent and issued a beggar's license (*Bettelbrief*) in response to a formal petition to the *Rentmeister*.[91] The procedure subsumed even the mendicant orders; in the second quarter of June 1644, for example, they received over twenty petitions for support from soldier's wives, Franciscans and others in the *Rentamt* of Munich.[92] Besides the local poor, the *Ordinance* of 1627 made provisions for authorized foreigners, lepers and pilgrims in possession of a valid beggar's license.[93] Parish members who owned their own homes, real estate, prebends, stipends or livestock, those deemed physically able to conduct a trade, as well as carousers observed frequenting in taverns, were ineligible for communal support.[94] The *Ordinance* threatened vagabonds, demobilized soldiers and other wandering idlers (*Müssigänger*) with arrest, forced labor and banishment.[95]

Like other disciplinary measures, prohibitions on begging proved difficult to implement in actual practice and met with public opposition. Pastor Hans Nenner, operator of a wine tavern (*Weinschenke*) in the district of Vohburg, was denounced to the Aulic Council in Munich in 1628, when he spoke out in a sermon against the new poor laws. He could "give no other or better counsel to poor Germans, than that they should take a noose and hang themselves."[96] In 1629, the Aulic Council explicitly referred to Anna Weber, the senseless daughter of Bärtl Weber, as one of many local poor and an eligible recipient of alms collected on her behalf from the community according to the provisions of the beggars' *Ordinance* (*Bettlmandat*).[97] Other senseless individuals obtained special authorization from the Aulic Council, which modified restrictions on their behalf, both before

[91] The beggars' license was another common feature of early modern poor relief, as in England; they were sometimes counterfeited to circumvent the application procedure: ibid., 122, 190.
[92] HStAM HR 283, 3r, 5r, 16r, 19r, 26v, 28r, 29v, 43v, 48r, 81v, 88v, 118r, 154r, 159r, 167v, 168v, 226r, 261v, 324v, 334r, 341r, 355r, 355v, 403r, 421v.
[93] Ziegler, *Dokumente*, 996. [94] Ibid., 995. [95] Ibid., 998.
[96] ". . . den armen Teutschen keinen anderen und bessern rath Zugeben, als das sie ainen Strickh nemmen, und sich selber erhenken solle . . .": HStAM HR 325v–326r. On the failure of Maximilian's disciplining strategy in the area of poor relief, see Elisabeth Schepers, *Als der Bettel in Bayern abgeschafft werden sollte. Staatliche Armenfürsorge in Bayern im 16. und 17. Jahrhundert* (Regensburg, 2000).
[97] HStAM HR 227, 70v.

and after 1627. In 1613, an order conditionally permitted Margaretha Wagner to collect alms in front of her parish church on Sundays and holy days.[98] In 1630, the Aulic Council authorized the district judge of Schwaben to build a lunatic's cell (*Kötterl*) for a senseless farmhand in a comfortable place. They made provisions for a special collection from passing travelers should the regular collection prove insufficient for his upkeep, but otherwise ordered the farmhand supported like the other local poor.[99] Presumably, such mad persons became the subjects of public display for local onlookers and passers-by.

The law did not require parishes to accept responsibility for support if the afflicted individual in question originated from outside the local community. Not surprisingly, communities callously tried to shift responsibility onto a sufferer's birthplace whenever possible. In such cases, the Aulic Council in Munich investigated to fix accountability. In the case of the aforementioned farmhand, the community sought internment in the central hospice of the Holy Spirit in Munich, since he was a "stranger and foreigner," despite the fact that work away from home was a regular condition among the large serving class in Bavaria.[100] Again, in his case, the Aulic Council ordered additional collections from "strangers passing through," a concession attributable to his non-local status.[101] When the district judge of Aichach balked at providing support for Barbara Rast, the Aulic Council ordered an investigation to determine her place of birth.[102] After it became apparent that she was not from Bavaria, they provided her with warm winter clothing and transported her to the border, "so that she might seek her nourishment and support elsewhere."[103]

Complex negotiations between representatives of the central authorities and communities resulted when a person's familial status, and therefore eligibility for local alms, was disputed. Georg Kolb, a resident of the district of Wolfratshausen, married a resident of the Hofmark of Reichertsbeuren and moved into her household.[104] Shortly thereafter, in 1611, he fathered a son, Wolf. At the age of ten, Wolf left his impoverished parents' household in search of work, moving back to relatives in Deining, a village on the estate of

---

[98] HStAM HR III, 54v.   [99] HStAM HR 232, 440v.
[100] "daß hierin vermelte absünige Persohn als ein frembdling, unnd außlender, zu anndern absünigen persohnen alhie eingenommen unnd unnderhalten wurdte . . .": HStAM HR 232, 440r.
[101] ". . . frembden durchraisenden personen . . .": ibid.
[102] HStAM HR 124, 14v.
[103] "Dem Pfleger zue Aichach hinwider zuschreiben, weil die hierinn benambste weibspersohn zue den iezt bevorstehenden wintterrlichen Zeitten, so übel mit claidungen versehen, als soll er sie von gesambeltenn gelt nach notturfft khlaiden, und als dann auf die Gränz fhüeren lassen, damit sie anderwerths Ihr narung suechen und sich erhalten möge": ibid., 62v.
[104] HStAM HR 312, 370v–371r; HR 313, 126v–127r.

the abbey of Schäftlarn in the district of Wolfratshausen. There he worked for thirty years as a common herder of livestock and a day laborer, later marrying. However, when he lost his reason in 1651, the family and the village community refused support. After weeks of negotiations, the Aulic Council finally ordered the residents of the district of Wolfratshausen to establish a fund for his care. Simultaneously, they ordered the Abbot of Schäftlarn and Sir Christoph of Preysing (lord of the Hofmark of Reichertsbeuren, Wolf's district of birth) to gather alms from their subjects and contribute as well. By the mid-seventeenth century, as this case illustrates, Bavaria was moving towards a more centralized system of outdoor poor relief based on judicial districts rather then parishes, as the authorities proved less willing to rely on communal charity and good will.

THE "DUNGEON" OF THE HOLY SPIRIT HOSPICE

Alternatives to spiritual physic and local care for the insane existed since the late Middle Ages. Direct access to university-trained physicians was limited.[105] Under Maximilian, the Bavarian health care system witnessed a fundamental restructuring.[106] Together with the Privy Council, the Duke/Elector represented the highest instance in medical policy decisions. Maximilian released a barrage of mandates, decrees and instructions for health care procedures, such as the plague decrees of 1599, 1606, 1613, 1625, 1634 and 1649, all following shortly after severe pandemics in Bavaria.[107]

Organizationally, the Aulic Council supervised and implemented control of territorial health policies, followed by the *Rentmeister*, the district judges and civic councils (see Figure 6.1). The authorities subjected towns, villages and individuals to quarantines. The council forbade imports of tainted meats or linens from infected areas and prosecuted quacks, unauthorized medical practices and cures violating the 1612 mandate against superstitious practices and witchcraft.[108] During the particularly catastrophic plague years 1627/1628, Maximilian set up the first special commission, the Deputation on Infection (*Infektionsdeputation*), to monitor the pandemic, a

---

[105] For a study on a *Narrenarzt* (mad doctor), see George Windholz, "The Case of the Renaissance Psychiatrist Peter Meir," *Sixteenth Century Journal* 22 (1990), 163–172. Midelfort examines changes in professional and academic psychiatric care during the sixteenth century, both at court (*Mad Princes*, 47–70) and in the academy (*A History of Madness*, 140–181).

[106] Some of these structural innovations are outlined in: Heydenreuter, *Der Landesherrliche Hofrat*, 256–257; Alexander Hofmeister, *Das Medizinalwesen im Kurfürstentum Bayern* (Munich, 1975).

[107] HStAM *Mandatensammlung* 1599 X 4, 1606 IX 9, 1613 IX 5, 1613 IX 24, 1634 VIII 19, 1649 XI 1. The decree of 1634 is reprinted in Ziegler, *Dokumente*, 1073.

[108] An edition of the mandate appears in Behringer, *Mit dem Feuer*, 165–191.

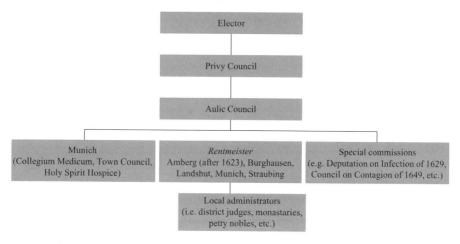

Figure 6.1. Administration of public health under Maximilian I (by author)

step taken again with the organization of a standing Council on Contagion (*Kontagionsrat*) during the plague of 1649.[109] In the residential capital, three administrative bodies simultaneously monitored health care: the Aulic Council, the Collegium Medicum and the Munich town council. Maximilian founded the Collegium Medicum, a council of his personal court physicians, at the end of the sixteenth century.[110] They interviewed newly arrived physicians to establish their qualifications and analyzed medications brought into the city.[111] The Collegium also regularly inspected the city's apothecaries.[112] In special cases, they provided professional testimony as well, stepping in to investigate the case of the hermaphrodite Barbara Khrabler, for example.[113] Naturally, the Collegium counted attendance to the personal health of the prince as its primary duty. The Munich Civic Council, with its venerable privileges and exemptions, became directly responsible for implementing territorial medical policies and quarantines in the residential city. It also held medieval privileges over admissions to the Holy Spirit Hospice, a thirteenth-century

---

[109] The voluminous protocols of the *Infektionsdeputation* are found in three volumes of the Aulic Council protocols, HStAM HR 215–217.
[110] The Collegium is described in the *Landts- und Policey Ordnung.*
[111] HStAM HR 212, 152v–153v; HR 266, 76r–v.   [112] HStAM HR 139, 28v, 118r; HR 197, 235v.
[113] "Caa. Dni. an das Collegium Medicorum in München umb bericht wegen der Barbara Khrablerin heimblich im leib habenden Mannβglidts": HStAM HR 199, Index "M," April.

institution re-established as an independent parish under civic control after a fire in 1333.[114]

The Bavarian health care system witnessed a substantial institutional boost during the reign of Maximilian I. He founded a ducal hospice (*Herzogspital*, 1601), the St. Rochus Hospice for chronically ill plague victims (1607), the St. Nicholas Hospice (1617) and the St. Joseph Hospice (1626), all in Munich, as well as numerous plague houses (*Siechenhäuser*) throughout the Duchy. At times, St. Joseph's and St. Elisabeth's hospices in Munich sheltered the mad, but only on a temporary basis. The Holy Spirit Hospice in Munich, a medieval civic institution, remained the central repository for the incurably insane in Bavaria until the end of the *ancien régime*.

The first mention of violent inmates at the Holy Spirit appears in two fifteenth-century testaments of philanthropic donations of 10d. each for the "fools there in the plague room."[115] From the early sixteenth century, two specific petitions for the admission of violent persons to the Holy Spirit survive. One came from Christoph of Haslang, district judge of Pfaffenhofen in 1523, who petitioned the administrator of the hospice, an old friend, to admit a senseless woman from his jail and assume 20kr. in indemnities from a smith, presumably for chains; both requests bore the approval of the prince.[116] The other petition, addressed to Maximilian in 1599, came from Wolf Schmidt to have two of his seven children committed.[117] They had lain in chains robbed of their senses for over three years, could not eat human food and represented a fire hazard to the neighborhood, which no longer tolerated them. The Munich town council had already turned down a previous supplication and Wolf humbly begged the prince to intercede directly on his behalf and that of his raving sons. By the early seventeenth century, a separate repository for the mad in the Holy Spirit Hospice had been established. Known locally as the *Keichenhaus* (literally a jail or dungeon) and officially as the chamber of the mad (*Stube der Sinnlosen*), it should not be confused with public cages for drunkards (*Narrenhäuser*), a regular feature of late medieval German towns.[118] This wing for the mad at

[114] On the history of the Holy Spirit Hospice, see Adalbert Huhn, *Geschichte des Spitales, der Kirche und der Pfarrei zum Heiligen Geist in München* (Munich, 1893).

[115] Hubert Vogel, *Die Urkunder des Heiliggeistspitals 1250–1500* (Munich, 1960), 469, 341–342. ". . . den ellenden kindlein und den narren daselbs in der siechstuben jeweils 10 Münchner Pfennig umb semel zu ainer pesserung irer pfrunde geben sollen."

[116] StdAM Heiliggeistspital 281.   [117] HStAM GR 1190.

[118] Huhn, *Geschichte des Spitales*, 84, 92. Schmeller, *Bayerisches Wörterbuch*, vol. 1.2, 1219, defines the *Keichen* (high German = *Kerker*) as "a cell, a bad, dark chamber." Although Schmeller mentions the incarceration of drunks in *Keichen* generally, the *Keichenhaus* was a specific term in Munich for

the hospice already contained individual cells for the insane rather than one large chamber. It resembled other medieval asylums, both large and small, throughout Germany, such as the "Revilien" of early modern Cologne; behind each heavily bolted numbered door, a cell equipped with a latrine of sorts confined a sufferer, fed by slipping food under the door; four times a year, cell and inmate were cleaned.[119] Care for the residents in the *Keichenhaus* in Munich was, at best, rudimentary. A hospice ordinance of 1485 ordered careful segregation of the mad from other inmates – the poor, the elderly and especially the children residing in the hospice (Figure 6.2).[120]

Besides simple incarceration, pastoral care and spiritual physic was administered by the father confessor of the Holy Spirit parish church. Especially in cases of demonic possession, the state placed strict limitations on spiritual physic to avoid scandal and public disorder. In the aforementioned case of Anna Puchmayer, the Aulic Council restricted access to a potential exorcist, Pater Placidus. Spiritual care of the mad, to include confession and attendance at mass, were at a minimum. Hardly innovative, care at the Holy Spirit revolved around incarceration, rather than treatment. The dungeon for the mad in the Holy Spirit represented the end of the line in early modern mental health care.

Bavarian hospices never witnessed the innovative reforms of specialized institutions on the style of the Counter Reformation Echter Hospice of Würzburg or the Protestant hospice at Haina. The state relied heavily on the civic institution to hold the most troublesome cases and never developed its own system of dedicated hospitals during the early modern period.

the madhouse and did not refer to a local cage on a public square for shaming drunkards and other unruly persons. Urban drunkenness was compared with foolishness (*Narrheit*) and prosecuted by overnight lock-up in the *Narrenhaus* since the late Middle Ages in places like Augsburg: Tlusty, *Bacchus*, 85. During a vintagers' strike in Kitzingen two years before the outbreak of the Peasants' War, the participants, who passed the morning drinking in a tavern instead of reporting to work as migrant grape-pickers, were incarcerated on bread and water and a public decree threatened them with the *Narrenhaus*: MSUSpC MS 1256, BayStBi Cgm 5037. In 1625, a Bavarian priest was illegally locked in a *Narrenhaus*, presumably for drunkenness, by a district judge, but the judge subsequently received an official reprimand for exceeding his authority over ecclesiastical privilege: HStAM Geist. Rat 40, f. 101r.

[119] On Cologne, see Robert Jütte, *Ärzte und Patienten in der frühen Neuzeit* (Munich, 1991), 183. The most detailed analysis of hospice care for the mad is found in Midelfort, *A History of Madness*, 322–384. As he notes, the Juliusspital in Würzburg was extremely progressive for its day. By comparison, conditions in Munich were very poor.

[120] "Item sy soll auch zuuoran in der kindstuben sein und daselbs auch aufsehen und ob den kinden sein, das der durch di diern ordennlich gewartet werde, das auch di narren und die das vallennd haben nicht unter den kinden, sonndern in der rauch oder grossern stuben sein und pleiben sullen": Vogel, *Die Urkunden des Heiliggeistspitals*, 541, Hospice Ordinance of 1485; "Besonders wird auch darauf aufgesehen, daß in der Kinderstube keine Narren und keine solchen Leute kommen, welche die fallende Sucht haben, denn diese gehören in die Keiche oder in die Rauchstube": Huhn, *Geschichte des Spitales*, 84.

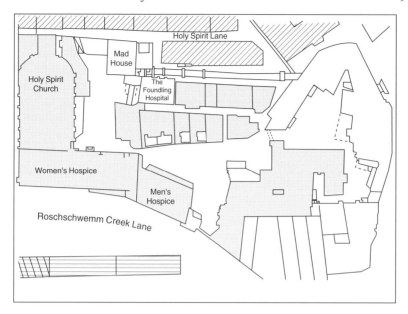

Figure 6.2. Plan of the Holy Spirit Hospice in Munich. (Source: Huhn, *Geschichte Des Spitales*, Appendix: Situationsplan)

At best, patients could avail of the smoke-room (*Rauchstube*), a common medicinal practice of fumigating madness with burnt herbal preparations.[121] Inmates received regular rations of food and yeast beer; the Aulic Council expressed outrage after discovering that construction workers consumed the beer intended for inmates.[122] In 1657, the administrator of the Holy Spirit[123] ordered renovations, including a cast-iron oven installed in the *Keichenhaus* to provide warmth for the inmates.[124] As with care for the raving in the countryside, the authorities concerned themselves primarily with the rudimentary provision of sustenance, shelter, warmth and restraint. In the final analysis, the absolutist state remained beholden to a corporate institution.

The central authorities could avail of other options. Regionally, jails served as transitory holding centers until a hut or cell could be erected locally or space became available at the Holy Spirit. Margaretha Pichler had to be interned in the jail in Dachau until her relatives could be tracked down.[125]

---

[121] Smoke was also used to treat Landgrave Wilhelm II of Hesse in 1508 and Duke Philip of Mecklenburg in 1538: Midelfort, *Mad Princes*, 44, 50.
[122] HStAM HR 289, 135v–136r, 205v–206r.   [123] Ferdinand Hörl of Wettersdorf.
[124] StdAM, HGS Rechnungsbücher 1657, 91.   [125] HStAM HR 129, 92r–v.

After Matheus Diechtel beat an elderly man to death, he was consigned
to the district jail in Pfaffenhofen, but later released after provisions were
made for local restraint and alms.[126] Senseless persons confined in jails
on a transient basis received special treatment. In 1620, the couple Georg
and Susanna Stelzhaimber were held in temporary custody at the jail in
Dachau, "though without bonds and not as criminals," until the origin of
their melancholy could be determined.[127] Georg Morreitter, who suffered
amnesia, was taken into custody after acting senselessly in the village of
Grossberghofen. The Aulic Council ordered that he be confined at the
jail in Dachau for eight days and nights for constant observation, during
which time they interrogated him about his identity and place of origin.[128]
Shortly thereafter, he regained his memory and, after only six days, the Aulic
Council authorized his release, exempting him from payment for his upkeep
(*Atzung*) during his stay, as was usual in criminal cases.[129] The Falkenturm
(Munich's infamous central jail) also served as a temporary repository for the
senseless until the Aulic Council reached a decision on their disposition.[130]
Apart from paternalistic concerns for proper care, raving individuals had
to be kept out of jails because they were unpredictable. For example, after
another prisoner turned up dead in his jail cell, the Aulic Council transferred
Hans Jobst Khueffer with all haste from the Falkenturm to the Holy Spirit
"in view of his madness."[131]

Monasteries interned their own, but cloister records reveal very little
about this practice.[132] On one occasion, in 1612, a monastery (*Bruederhaus*)
in Burghausen maintained an unidentified senseless man, presumably a
monk, on alms.[133] The cloister at Neustift interned another monk on an
endowment as late as 1688.[134] Otherwise, options were limited. During
the first half of the seventeenth century, only the hospice in Reichenhall, a wealthy center of salt mining, contained limited facilities to house
lunatics.[135] In 1612, the Aulic Council ordered the district judge of Erding
to construct a cell at the local hospice to restrain Egidius Pürg.[136] Forty
years later, the administration of the re-Catholicized Upper Palatinate in

[126] HStAM HR 159, 197r–v.   [127] HStAM HR 161, 191v–192r
[128] HStAM HR 321, 526v.   [129] HStAM HR 322, 393r.
[130] HStAM HR 197, 256v–257r; HR 304, 82v.
[131] ". . . demnach wür den begangner entleibung halber hiehero in unser Fronfest des falckhenthurms
herbrachten und darinen biß dato enthaltenen Hannsen Jobst Khueffern von Otterzhoven, unsers
dir gnedigst anverthrauten Pfleg Gerichts, in verbleibung seiner wohnsinnigkeit in daß heil. Geisst
Spital alhie gegen raichanged 40fl. Jehrlich Cosstgelts transferiern lassen . . .": HStAM HR 331,
136v–137r.
[132] For the case of a crazed Jesuit murderer in Cologne, see Jütte, *Ärzte und Patienten*, 185–187.
[133] HStAM HR 105, 137v.   [134] HStAM HR 456, 201r–v.   [135] HStAM HR 305, 453v–454r.
[136] HStAM HR 105, 133r.

Amberg constructed two cells to house two, poor, senseless individuals.[137] The Aulic Council decreed in 1636, 1648 and 1658 that lunatics in Aichach, Landsberg and Weilheim either should be admitted to the local hospice or, if that proved unmanageable, should be maintained by contributions and held directly in their villages until such time as they recovered.[138]

The state never considered confinement terminal and, as in cases of community care, all parties concerned hoped for a speedy recovery to end the burden of charity on society at large as well as individual suffering. Just as a lengthy court battle over apportioning the costs of his care at the hospice in Reichenhall reached its climax, senseless Oswald Casstenstainer began to show signs of recovery and was released to resume his trade as dyer.[139] However, the simple hope of improvement did not automatically ensure an individual's social rehabilitation as a productive member of society. When Caspar Meillinger, a butcher from the Au near Munich, began to show signs of improvement in 1655, the Aulic Council sent physicians from the Collegium Medicum to his cell in the Holy Spirit to investigate the matter and determine what his condition was and whether he could be released without danger.[140] If the *medici* held the opinion that he posed no threat to the community, then representatives of the town council of Munich should interrogate him further to ascertain whether or not he might voluntarily leave Bavaria and take up a new residence elsewhere. Unfortunately, midway through the medical portion of his examination, Meillinger began to rave uncontrollably, forcing the authorities to abandon their attempt to exile him.[141] The magistrates of Cologne employed a similar policy of banishment in their treatment of the insane.[142] In this respect, the politics of the body differed precious little when applied to the body politic. The widespread employment of banishment, a standard legal method of ridding a territory of deviates, ultimately represented a policy of capitulation.[143]

THE STRUCTURAL LIMITS OF ABSOLUTISM

Absolutism was never absolute, as the gap between the ideological origins and practical failure of the seventeenth-century policy of confinement demonstrates.[144] One cannot overemphasize that confinement in the

---

[137] HStAM HR 315, 486v–487v.   [138] HStAM HR 254, 194v–195r; HR 302, 55r–v; HR 341, 182v.
[139] HStAM HR 308, 325v–326r.   [140] HStAM HR 330, 21v–22r.
[141] HStAM HR 331, 136v–137r, 244v–245r, 498r.   [142] Jütte, *Ärzte und Patienten*, 183.
[143] The intricacies of expulsion as a form of punishment are discussed in Scribner, "The Mordbrenner."
[144] The structural and fiscal inadequacies of the absolutist state are highlighted in Anderson, *Lineages*; again, see also Henshall, *The Myth* and Beik, *Absolutism*.

Keichenhaus of the Holy Spirit Hospice represented a desperate last resort in the limited absolutist system of mental health care management. Families and parishes provided long-term support for the vast majority of the insane until the end of the *ancien régime*. The state intervened when the primary concerns of public order, safety and minimal care could not be met by these means. Initially, district judges reminded communities and families of their Christian responsibility to care for their own unfortunates before proceeding to apportion the burden of care at the district level.

From the mid-seventeenth century, the central authorities also supported and encouraged institutionalization as a desirable alternative to spiritual physic and parish charity. The popularity of that policy is reflected in a gradual increase in petitions to the Aulic Council to commit persons to the Holy Spirit Hospice from outlying localities, pronounced after the Thirty Years War. Between 1610 and 1639, communities petitioned the Aulic Council for admission to the Holy Spirit on only three occasions, once per decade. Then, from 1640 to 1647, seven requests came to the attention of the council, roughly one per year. At the conclusion of the war, no fewer than eighteen admissions were sought. Although numbers fluctuated thereafter, they never again fell to pre-war levels.[145] Although the general population stubbornly clung to beliefs in the moral casuistry of mental disorders and the role of the devil, they appeared more than willing to avail of the regime's institutional strategy of confinement and embraced the insanity defense, when it involved an avoidance of the social and economic burdens associated with local care. The social desire to institutionalize the insane became an irreversible trend.

However, an imbalance of resources and desires subsequently saved many from the *Keichenhaus*. Bed-space was at a premium in most early modern hospices, and the Holy Spirit in Munich was no exception.[146] As early as 1551, Albrecht V promised every mad Bavarian a place in the Holy Spirit if proper local care from families and communities was unavailable. It is impossible to ascertain whether that promise was tenable (and that is doubtful) *before* Maximilian I officially elevated the care of insanity to a matter of princely concern (*Causae domini*),[147] but by 1640 the spatial limits of institutionalized segregation were splitting at the seams. Time and again, the Aulic Council apologized for the necessity to restrain the mad

---

[145] During the 1660s, another seven petitions appeared before the council; an additional five petitions were lodged in the two-year period of 1687 to 1688.

[146] Jütte, *Poverty*, 63–65.

[147] On this legally distinct category applied to criminal and administrative matters of particular importance appearing before the Aulic Council, see Heydenreuter, *Der Landesherrliche Hofrat*, 158–167.

at home, in the parish, district or *Rentamt* because "presently, no empty space is available here [at the Holy Spirit] among the mad so that support might be provided."[148] During the 1640s, four requests were turned down outright, two were tabled and only one person was admitted. A run of petitions from the 1650s met with similar apologetic denials. In 1653, the baker Georg Lehner attained the dubious honor of provisional admittance "should a cell become empty here at the Hospice of the Holy Spirit before long."[149] In 1655, Caspar Hufschmidt's wife was refused because, "presently, as we will verily report, the hospice is as of late packed with mad people to such a great extent, that the supplicant's wife cannot be admitted at this time." Caspar's stubborn insistence eventually gained her provisional entry "as soon as a cell becomes available," presumably upon release or death of one of the inmates.[150] By 1659, the day laborer Balthasar Müller literally had to wait for a young female inmate to die before he could have his wife committed.[151] As late as 1700, only thirty-one persons from the entire region inhabited the confines of the *Keichenhaus*.[152] The state policy of centralized institutionalization and the enthusiastic response embodied in rising numbers of petitions shows that subjects were perfectly willing to "share in the fruits of their own domination"[153] to a calculating degree, but the facilities to implement the policy simply did not exist.

Medieval procedures governing admission to the Holy Spirit acted as a further obstacle to the smooth implementation of a centralized policy of institutionalization. The Holy Spirit was a venerable civic institution and, as such, access to its facilities fell under the jurisdiction of the Munich town council. Each attempt by the Aulic Council to commit a mad person from outside the city to the hospice met with opposition from the town council, just as did Prince-Bishop Julius Echter in Wurzburg, whose social

[148] For example: "dermahlen alhie khein Ledigst orth, darinen der Sünlosen Persohnen Ir underkhommen verschafft werden möchte, vorhanden . . .": HStAM HR 271, 365r; "dieweilen aber gestaltsame gelegenheit für den Sünlosen Camerer alhiesiger orthen nicht vorhanden . . .": ibid., 421r; "Dem Landrichter zu Fridtberg wider zuschreiben, weilen der Zeit für dise Persohn, bei denen von München alhie khein gelegenheit verhanden . . .": HStAM HR 273, 2r.
[149] "Solte aber dem negsten alhie beim Spital zum Heil. Geist ein khötterl lehr werden, sovil selbige verwalter erbietig Ihne Pekhen einzunemmen . . .": HStAM HR 322, 393r.
[150] ". . . dieweils wür dann glaublich bericht werden, daß aniezo der Spital dermassen mit Sinlosen Leüth bestekht, daß des Suppl. weib dermahlen nit eingenommen werden khan . . .": HStAM HR 329, 405r; "die von München erkhlärth, besagtes weib, wann ein köttel ledig werde, einzunemen . . .": ibid., 519r–v;
[151] ". . . daß durch absterben eines Mädleins ein stell bei einem khetterl erledigt worden . . .": HStAM HR 343, 238v–239r.
[152] Huhn, *Geschichte des Spitales*, 92.
[153] Thomas Robisheaux, *Rural Society and the Search for Order in Early Modern Germany* (Cambridge, 1989), 4.

welfare policies were hampered by the question of civic control in the 1580s until he established a purpose-built structure.[154] In 1617, the Aulic Council politely and deferentially requested the cooperation of the town council to accept the senseless Gilg N. from suburban Haidhausen into the "mad house" (*Unsinigen Haus*) at the hospice.[155] At Duke Maximilian's personal behest, Balthasar Dischinger could be committed in 1620.[156] Then, in the 1630s, Maximilian began gnawing generally at all civic privileges, a tactic symbolically manifest in Hans Krumper's Marian column erected illegally in the town square. In his first direct confrontation with the town council on the matter of admissions to the Holy Spirit, the councilors rebuffed his request to have Ulrich Gail admitted in 1636, citing civic privilege. On legal grounds, they argued that "their hospice was endowed and built for their citizens afflicted with madness and not for outsiders," an argument they persisted in until the end of the *ancien régime*.[157] A tactic employed often in the past, it left the Aulic Council with no other alternative than to have Gail interned locally. In 1644, the Aulic Council referred a petitioner directly to the town council, although the civic fathers had fled temporarily before a Swedish incursion; the request was later denied.[158] At the end of the war, the electoral administration flexed its muscles, commanding the town council to have Elisabeth Steinberger transferred from the *Falkenturm* to the Holy Spirit, because incarceration in the jail violated paternalistic directives for care of insanity.[159] However, when the town council expressed reservations over her citizenship, the Aulic Council conceded once again, apathetically instructing the civic fathers to conduct their own investigation and apprise them of their deliberations.[160]

At the end of his reign, Maximilian and his councilors deferred less graciously to civic councils in other Bavarian metropoles. One of the last petitions for commitment during his reign arrived in September 1649 from Reichenhall – the aforementioned case of the dyer Oswald Casstenstainer. The district judge wished to have Oswald committed to the civic hospice in Reichenhall, to prevent "all kinds of mishaps and danger."[161] The Aulic

---

[154] Hans-Christoph Rublack, *Gescheiterte Reformation. Frühreformatorische und protestantische Bewegungen in süd- und westdeutschen geistlichen Residenzen* (Stuttgart, 1978), 134–137. The internment of the mad at the Juliusspital, however, appears to have been a major success story, far ahead of its time; Midelfort, *A History of Madness*, 372.

[155] HStAM HR 133, 213v.   [156] HStAM HR 155, 185r.

[157] ". . . das sie allerhandt entschuldigungen sonderlichen aber wie hievor schon öffters beschehen, diß vorwerden wurden, das gedachte Ihr Hospice nicht für frembde sonder Ihr verburgerte und mit der absinnigkheit behaffte Leüt gestifft und erbaut worden sei . . .": HStAM HR 254, 194v–195r.

[158] HStAM HR 283, 107v, 279v–280r.   [159] HStAM HR 304, 84r.   [160] Ibid., 82v.

[161] HStAM HR 305, 453v–454r.

Council apportioned payments for internment onto the entire communities through the collection of alms. However, the mayor and town council opposed his admission to the civic institution on the grounds that Reichenhall was not his place of birth. Finally, the Aulic Council in Munich went over the head of the district judge and intervened directly, ordering the town council to accept Oswald either at the hospice or at some other fitting venue and support him with the contributions.[162] Within weeks, the district judge and the town council engaged in another legalistic war of words and the Aulic Council became adamant. It ordered both parties to desist from quarreling, and reprimanded the town council for the "wicked passions" expressed in their correspondence – to no effect.[163] Numerous briefs in the same impassioned tone changed hands over the next seven months until Oswald was finally accepted in the hospice in May, with the city reneging on most of its own obligations of financial support.[164] Ironically, one month later, Oswald recovered fully and was released from the civic hospice.[165]

This case was indicative of a new policy, in terms of both central intervention in civic affairs and the organization of relief for the mad. While Maximilian paid lip-service to longstanding civic prerogatives, his successor, Ferdinand Maria, attempted to trample on traditional privilege by executive fiat. Through legal precedents set in 1651 and 1652, Ferdinand Maria established contractual obligations with the Munich town council ostensibly granting the electoral administration permission to remand any person deemed mad to the *Keichenhaus*, provided room was available and the annual costs of 40fl. were paid by the central authorities. Ferdinand Maria also restructured and formalized the system of contributions for support and care of the insane by families, communities and whole districts.[166] The resolution of 1652 was invoked again in 1654.[167] However, spatial constraints forced Ferdinand Maria to establish a contingency policy, offering cells in the *Keichenhaus* provisionally on a waiting list. The Elector's assault on civic privilege had already begun before his *de facto* majority, since his mother, Maria Anna, held the reins of power at the time. However, his was more than an attempt to flex political muscle on an issue of tangential importance. He acted in a fashion perfectly consistent with his later policies toward exorcisms and the insanity defense during the 1660s. Together with formalized reliance on district-level contributions, it should have represented a strong move toward centralized management of mental health

---

[162] Ibid., 85v.   [163] HStAM HR 306, 107v–108v.
[164] HStAM HR 307, 257r–259r, 267r; HR 308, 214r.   [165] Ibid., 325v–326r.
[166] HStAM HR 317, 295v–296r; HR 334, 372r–373r.   [167] HStAM HR 323, 346v.

care and provided a viable alternative to spiritual physic, especially through ritual exorcisms.

Nevertheless, although civic privilege diminished by the end of the seventeenth century, it embodied a legal thorn in the side of the regime. In 1657, the Aulic Council consigned Johann Baptist Aicher[168] to the Holy Spirit after he became humorally "corrupted"(*corrumpiert*). The council saw no reason why the subjects of the district of Dachau should bear any burden of care, since he had surely been there at the time, but had neither lived nor owned property there.[169] Predictably, the Munich town council felt no obligation to admit him to the *Keichenhaus*, but Ferdinand Maria intervened personally, demanding a cell for Aicher among the mad funded by his brother.[170] A special commission set up to deliberate on the contentious matter confronted the town council, which wasted no time in reminding the authorities that, according to their "famous privileges," the Holy Spirit Hospice fell under their civic, not dynastic jurisdiction.[171] When the commission cautiously apprised Ferdinand Maria of the situation, he became so frustrated that he laconically left it to the town council to decide "on some place or another" where Aicher might be restrained and cared for.

The town council's resistance to the policy of centralized institutionalization at the Holy Spirit Hospice represented a response to wounded civic privilege, but it had economic dimensions as well: someone had to pay for long-term care. Their medieval system of local care was based upon alms, endowments and pious bequests intended specifically for members of the community.[172] The economic system of voluntary charitable contributions for care proved a major stumbling block to centralization. Indeed, at the strategic level, the entire Bavarian state budget depended upon a medieval system of contributions from the estates (the *Landtag*, composed of the prelates, nobility and wealthy burgers) until the end of the *ancien régime*. Maximilian flirted with direct taxes in 1612 and Ferdinand Maria levied a bureaucratically unprecedented territorial audit in 1672, but neither provided the basis for a lasting system of direct taxation.[173] Structurally, the prince either had to elicit charity to support lunatics or had to pay out of his own pocket.

---

[168] Brother of Johann Hartmut Aicher, an electoral official in Friedberg.
[169] HStAM HR 334, 263v–264r.   [170] Ibid., 372r–373r.   [171] Ibid., 493r.
[172] The benefices, investments, interest payments and other income of the Holy Spirit Hospice were listed annually in StdAM HGS, *Rechnungsbücher* under "Einnahmen."
[173] The latter audit produced massive records revealing socioeconomic conditions in Bavaria in the aftermath of the Thirty Years War, records which have yielded several important studies including Schlögl, *Bauern, Krieg und Staat*; Schepers, *Als der Bettel*.

At first, Maximilian worked within the local system of contributions, applying disciplinary pressures on families and communities to force them to assume their responsibilities for rudimentary care and the protection of communities. During the first three decades of the seventeenth century, twenty disputes over custody of the mad included only three petitions for admission to the Holy Spirit. In the other cases, the central authorities had to intervene locally when families and communities shirked their responsibilities. The case of Margaretha Pichler from the district of Dachau illustrates some of the difficulties encountered in adjudicating responsibility. In 1616, Duke Maximilian personally ordered inquiries with her closest relative to determine whether he was willing to take custody of Margaretha after her release from the district jail.[174] The district judge tried to coax him to provide her with support and protect the community from danger out of sympathy and common propriety. Instead, her relatives offered a lump sum for the construction of a cell to contain her, with the surplus added to a collection of alms to meet her general upkeep.[175] A suggestion from the district judge to save money by retaining her in the jail was rebuffed as illegal and an extra collection had to be taken up to provide wood for a shelter; legally, the authorities could not force the community to do so, since all contributions were voluntary.[176] After five months, proper measures had not been taken, so a cell for Margaretha had to be added on to the local poor house. By then, the district judge had already spent 40fl. of official funds on the matter; he was encouraged to take up negotiations with the family again and make up any discrepancy from fines he imposed on local adulterers.[177] After the district judge tried to avoid this disposition as well, the Aulic Council in Munich insisted at last that Margaretha be admitted to the poor house, but yielded to the economic dilemma, notifying the exchequer in Munich to assist in the situation.[178]

Another financial innovation promoted after 1640 to provide for supporting the senseless was to liquidate their assets. The assets were then turned over to an agent, usually a close relative, identified as the legal custodian. The Aulic Council ordered Georg Lehner to take custody of his insane brother and provide for him from his estate.[179] Georg Attermoser's fortune from his bakery provided enough for his family to care for

---

[174] HStAM HR 129, 92r–v.   [175] HStAM HR 130, 5r.
[176] ". . . doch nit in der fronvesst, sonder in ainem anndern füeg- und bequemblichen orth abweegs von der Gemainden holtz und Ihrer etlichen befreündten geuttwillig anerbottenen gelt (weil mahn die übrige von rechts wegen nit darzue nöthen khan) erpauen . . .": Ibid., 136v–137r.
[177] "Die 40fl. alberait aufgeloffenen uncossten belangendt, so zuee abstattung desselben ins khunfftig ein Ehebruch straff deputiert werden.": HStAM HR 131, 125.
[178] Ibid., 188v.   [179] HStAM HR 283, 279v–280r.

him until his death.[180] By selling the possessions of Maria Mägelein and another unnamed "soldier's girl," the district judge of Rain raised 102fl. and, through careful management, he established a fund for their immediate needs.[181] The butcher's shop of Hans Meillinger was auctioned off to provide his brother with the money required for the madman's safe custody.[182]

A more positive move toward centralized funding of support involved setting up a fund at the district level through a generally enforced collection (*gemeine/proportionierte Anlag*). The first recorded collection of this type was set up for Balthasar Zimmerman in 1620.[183] Noting that Martin Strobl lacked any substantial assets, the district judge of Rosenheim collected local alms and then instituted a general collection at the district level in 1646.[184] Reliance on this procedure increased as time went on and difficulties in raising requisite funds from families and communities led the authorities to apportion the burden at the district level. This solution was certainly amenable to families and parishes, but met with resistance from neighboring communities as well as the district judges, who resented the additional bureaucratic responsibilities of enforcement and collection. Parish priests also needed to be persuaded to exhort their charges to contribute during special masses for the afflicted individuals, since such contributions diminished their already tenuous ability to collect their own wages.[185]

Ferdinand Maria exerted heavier pressure on communities and local officials to provide for the upkeep of the mad. The resolutions established by legal precedent at the onset of his reign formed a conscious policy toward the centralized management of insanity. He eventually raised the enforced collection to a standard feature of support, established the yearly fee for incarceration in a cell at 40fl., and fixed the dates for quarterly contributions to the exchequer, from whence they were transferred to the Court Office of Expenditures (*Hofzahlamt*) and paid directly to the administrator of the Holy Spirit. In the model precedent of September 3, 1652, Ulrich Weissen applied to the Aulic Council to have his "corrupted" brother Stephan committed to the Holy Spirit Hospice.[186] However, the report of the district judge of Starnberg indicated that Ulrich, a day laborer, lacked sufficient assets to cover the 40fl. in yearly costs. Ferdinand Maria resolved the situation, decreeing a quarterly collection at the district level by the district judge of Tölz to be submitted to the Court Office of Expenditures for as long as Stephan resided in the hospice. However, the order had to be

[180] HStAM HR 292, 325v.　　[181] HStAM HR 298, 7v.　　[182] HStAM HR 304, 473v.
[183] HStAM HR 182, 54r.　　[184] HStAM HR 292, 79r.　　[185] Beck, "Der Pfarrer," *passim*.
[186] HStAM HR 317, 295v–296r.

repeated two years later, indicating that it met with resistance.[187] In 1656, quarterly confinement costs of the raving murderer Hans Jobst Khueffer were assumed by the state.[188] Ferdinand Maria finally decreed substantial legislation apportioning the costs of care in 1668, the same year he cut a deal with the regional bishops on burial decisions in cases of suicide.[189] Decisions on the spatial segregation of the insane had, by that time, come full circle. The decree officially recognized the collection of support at the district level and represented a legal turning point in funding care for the mad in Bavaria.

In practice, however, these procedural innovations became bogged down in legal battles. The wife and father-in-law of Wolf Steger, a council of nine representing the market town of Aibling and the district judge of Aibling all faced off over this complex of issues in 1653. Although Wolf's estate included quantities of horses, cattle, pigs, sheep and other livestock, fields and pastures, movable goods and liquid assets, his father-in-law claimed that the entire property, to include livestock, was deeply indebted, a claim for which documentation was requested.[190] This left the judge in the precarious position of persuading the nine-member council of Aibling to come up with the funds to support Wolf or otherwise raising it from an enforced collection taken at the district level.

Twenty-five years later, Elector Maximilian Emanuel, the bellicose "blue king," had yet to find a solution for the material problems of central-ized institutionalization. In 1690, Andreas Rumpfinger's wife had to be turned away from the Holy Spirit Hospice for lack of space.[191] By then, the legal reallocation of costs from the community to the district level had been forced through, but this only relocated the problem of negotiating with parishes onto the backs of district judges; communities resented the burdensome collection of contributions, especially for mad persons from neighboring towns and villages. Habeas corpus presented a tactical method to haggle over costs. Or, once a lunatic entered the Holy Spirit Hospice, the local authorities might simply "forget" their obligation to provide quarterly support. When Hans Jacob Langgasner died in the cells of the Holy Spirit Hospice, several communities in his district refused to meet demands for a proportion of the back support payments in excess of 220fl.[192]

Sometimes communities insinuated that they had borne the burden of support long enough by refusing continued payments. In 1687, a legal

[187] HStAM HR 323, 346v.   [188] HStAM HR 331, 136v–137r.
[189] Mayr, *Sammlung der Churpfalz-Baierischen*, 127.
[190] HStAM HR 319, 302v–303v; HR 320, 110v.
[191] HStAM HR 464, 207r.   [192] HStAM HR 455, 138v; HR 456, 201r–v.

battle broke out over contributions to the endowment to support Melchior Krundtner in the Holy Spirit, resulting from a renewed decree on the payment of support at the district level, which sought to strengthen the policy of centralized institutionalization.[193] On October 6, Maximilian Emanuel issued a warning to the noble landlord of the Hofmark Leibersdorf after he received word from the hospice administrator that payments for one of his subjects were in arrears.[194] He was fined 12Rt. and ordered to make up the difference within fourteen days or face further penalties. In this instance, dealings with a nominally autonomous noble jurisdiction further complicated the problem of enforced contributions. Sir Johann Sigmundt Zeller of Leibersdorf, a minor free-imperial knight, claimed an enclave subordinate to the Prince-Bishopric of Freising. The Aulic Council subsequently reminded the district judge of nearby Kranzberg that subjects of the Hofmark held a liability to pay their proportion of the collection just as other subjects in the district. However, he should see to it that the district also contributed accordingly, since the burden on the smaller Hofmark was too great to be borne alone. The judge then submitted 560fl. in payments, calming the council in Munich.

Sir Johann Sigmundt Zeller of Leibersdorf wrote to the Prince-Bishop of Freising, Duke Joseph Clement of Wittelsbach, questioning the legality of another quarterly payment, "because with these already heavy fiscal burdens in the territory, such a renewal has never occurred before."[195] He complained further that the burden of care "to this date *in naturo*" for Georg Khopp of Niederhummel and Philip Gilgenover of Marzling (two other alms recipients in his jurisdiction) relieved his subjects from any requirement to "pay double" for Melchior Krundtner's incarceration in the Holy Spirit. The Aulic Council simultaneously received a report from the district judge of Kranzberg announcing that Leibersdorf was again in arrears and disputed his responsibilities. On March 9 of the following year, the judge of Kranzberg wrote Leibersdorf, insisting that his subjects "contribute, namely from each full share holder 18kr. according to the proportion of goods for the year 1687, and turn this sum in for a receipt at the court," so that the matter would not give rise to any disturbances.[196] Another complaint to the Prince-Bishop from Leibersdorf followed on March 17. The case set an important precedent. The system of collecting alms at the

[193] Mayr, *Sammlung der Churpfalz-Baierischen*, 651.   [194] HStAM HR 455, 64v–65r.
[195] ". . . weiln dises bei ohnedeme schweren Landthpurdten ain solche neuerung, die vormahl nie gewesst . . .": HStAM GRF. 1190.
[196] ". . . nemblich von iedem hof 18 xer unnd also nach Proportion der Güetter für an. 1687 heisens einraichen, und gegen Schein beigericht erlegen . . .": ibid.

district level, enshrined in law, was extended to include semi-autonomous noble jurisdictions. In order to prevent the smaller noble territories being overcome by a "miserable condition," the central authorities ordered district judges and nobles to work together to share the burden of support. The practice based on this precedent continued until the late eighteenth century, when it was reconfirmed in territorial legislation.[197]

CONCLUSIONS

The ideology of spatial segregation, whether in criminal or lunacy reform, eluded the early modern absolutist state in practice. The absolutist state lacked the fundamental structures of a modern one, economically, institutionally and socially, to implement its policy goals of centralization and sovereignty over the bodies of its subjects. In the realm of suicide reform, it attempted to relegate self-murderers to hallowed ground under the auspices of the insanity defense, but met with serious resistance from communities, still deeply imbued with popular conceptions about the role of Satan in the physical realm. In this regard, the state bore substantial guilt for its earlier reliance on metaphysical explanations for catastrophes during the general crisis. It succeeded far too well in its catechistic and propagandistic campaigns and subsequently suffered attendant difficulties in challenges to previously acceptable normative explanations of suffering in society at large. The populace took the message to heart and, even when the crisis passed, they still found metaphysical explanations superior to physical ones in their own experience of day-to-day tribulations, including the perennial problem of mad persons, who deviated from social expectations. The state had done its job only too well and the ruling elite themselves still had to accept responsibility for the confessional paradigm. Pathological explanations for madness were reserved for coming generations.

Always a tentative matter, the spatial segregation of the mad in Bavaria revolved around negotiations with communities, the church and town councils. With each looking out for a justification that fit its own advantage, conflicts were bound to arise. Earlier pressure on communities voluntarily to provide care for the mad at the parish level according to the provisions of beggars' mandates failed for two reasons: they were counterproductive to the goals of political centralization and they proved impractical or were easily circumvented. Redistribution of costs at the district level gave the authorities greater flexibility, but in the end, made the central authorities

---

[197] Mayr, *Sammlung der Churpfalz-Baierischern*, 127, 651 #116.

dependent upon the largess both of the localities and of religious institutions. In the struggle for authority before, during and after the general
crisis, each social stratum played upon previous models to enhance their
relative political stance, laying the grounds for continued conflict. In the
battle of space over time, the immediate dependence of the state upon
limited resources placed it squarely back at the bargaining table in nearly
each and every instance. There was never a settlement, simply an enduring
political struggle. Even in the residential capital, Munich, the town council
took every begrudging step possible to remind the Wittelsbachs of their
place in the society of orders by referring to ancient traditions and customs.
And the church maintained a right to hegemonic control over cemeteries.
True centralization in the area of mental health care eluded the Electors
who, despite their international reputation, still needed to count on the
fiscal and institutional contributions of their subjects in a political body of
estates.

The ideological shift to a policy of institutionalization foundered in the
structural atavisms of the feudal fiscal system of contributions. Unfortunately, although the populace clung to metaphysical explanations for mental
disorders, families and communities proved perfectly willing to defer the
mad to the central authorities for institutionalization and relief from the
burdens of care. In that regard, they truly profited from the fruits of their
own domination. This was a burden that the absolutist state, however willing, could ill afford. The resultant confusion in the area of mental health
care management meant that the state turned away from spiritual physic
without offering a viable alternative, a situation further exacerbated by the
collapse of the Bavarian state after the War of the Spanish Succession and
the Habsburg occupation in the early eighteenth century. The structural
problems in the realm of mental health care could only be solved through
the implementation of sweeping constitutional reforms. Make no mistake
about it: the ideal and the intentions were there. The will to sovereignty
over the bodies of subjects lay at the heart of political culture at court in
the seventeenth century. However, the structures necessary to implement
state-sponsored lunacy reform and police the secularization of suicide only
became available after the implementation of a Josephine-style secularization in 1803 and the Napoleonic reorganization of Bavaria as a kingdom
in the Confederation of the Rhine. Until that time, the ideological origins
of the Great Confinement remained purely ideological, a promise that the
absolutist state proved woefully incapable to deliver.

CHAPTER 7

The legacy of spiritual physic

The refusal of modern "enlightenment" to treat "possession" as a hypothesis to be spoken of as even possible, in spite of the massive human tradition based on concrete experience in its favor, has always seemed to me a curious example of the power of fashion in things scientific. That the demon theory will have its innings again is to my mind absolutely certain. One has to be "scientific" indeed, to be blind and ignorant enough to suspect no such possibility.

William James, *Report on Mrs. Piper's Hodgson-Control*

The history of madness in early modern Bavaria is a prime example of the political and social forces at work in mental health care. As doctors of the human soul, spiritual physicians combined a legalistic interpretation of sin with the contemporary rhetoric of immorality as the prevailing causes of spiritual afflictions. Christian values, Galenic humoral pathology and Aristotelian faculty psychology informed their moral etiology. For example, in Bavaria, spiritual physicians intended auricular confession as consolation, a humoral purgative to expunge guilt. However, the constant bombardment of moral preaching by zealots like Eisengrein and Albertinus, coupled with the unrelenting scheme of catechism and coercion from childhood, afforded at least some people little in the way of consolation. The case history of the demoniac Katharina Rieder painfully illustrates a downward spiral from the pressures of religious guilt and the penitential regime.

For the secular authorities, enforced compliance with the yearly requirement aimed first and foremost at the religious homogenization of the subject population. Through a system of surveillance, they achieved eminent successes in rooting out heresy by catechizing the populace on the mannerisms of outward compliance. Enforced penance was an important tool in the formal confessionalization of Bavaria. Whether or not it achieved inner compliance of conscience is another matter entirely. During the reign of Maximilian I, when the system of surveillance expanded to its fullest dimensions, the enforcement of the yearly requirement sorely tested the limits of

the well-ordered police state. The authorities also had difficulties ideologically linking their subjects' inner pangs of guilt to natural catastrophes and
wars. Subjects fixed on problems of a personal nature and, as the general
crisis subsided, so too did the complex of religious controls.

On the face of it, one might then interpret the penitential regime as a
failure. The undiminished popularity of auricular confession in the eighteenth century suggests otherwise. For example, although the new chapel
constructed in Andechs contained no fewer than thirteen confessionals
along its internal circumference (practically one every fifteen feet), it could
not satisfy the desire of devotees to confess. For nine days during the dedication jubilee in 1755, thirty-three padres heard confessions daily from three
in the morning until nine at night; penitents overflowed the building into
the transept of the adjacent cloister.[1] Thirty thousand pilgrims received
the Eucharist after confession during the jubilee. In an anecdote, a local
chronicler depicted a visiting Franciscan confessor who, perplexed by the
onslaught of penitents, made this request of a woman in the confessional:

My dear! You certainly don't deserve a heavy penance, but I have an urgent request
for you. As I've already heard confessions for five or six days without a pause and
find no time for sleep, I am presently overcome by exhaustion. Please be so kind as
to pray a rosary here in the confessional, so that I might give myself over to sleep
for a few minutes. When you've finished, then wake me. I would heartily thank
you for this.[2]

Such outpourings of popular devotion sorely taxed the early modern system of surveillance, but under the circumstances the enthusiastic response
rendered controls redundant. Whether external compliance justifies declaring the penitential regime a success or failure of social disciplining is difficult
to say, but high attendance indicates the popularity of spiritual physic as
psychic consolation. People attended auricular confession frequently, in
large numbers and of their own volition. Either the internal disciplinary
message of guilt drove them to do so or auricular confession offered a
welcome opportunity to voice personal insecurities and seek advice and
consolation in an otherwise rigid moral climate. In either case, enforced
confession became unnecessary. To that extent, auricular confession as spiritual physic and social discipline appears to have been a resounding success
for both subjects and the authorities.

Patterns of popular devotion to the cult of the dead are also indicative
of the give-and-take between rulers and subjects. The Reformation badly

---

[1] Willibald Mathäser, OSB, *Andechser Chronik* (Munich, 1979), 114–115.   [2] Ibid., 115.

damaged the reputation of the cult of the saints, but the Wittelsbachs contributed heavily to its reinvigoration during the sixteenth century. Maximilian I orchestrated his histrionic Marian dynastic program particularly well, mobilizing the saints in a hierarchical and militant structure through theatrics, art and literature. In history and sacred geography, Maximilian I patronized a specific version of Marian devotion conducive to political centralization and the ideological unity of space. Artistic and literary images of the *Patrona Bavariae* and the *Bavaria Sancta* welded a baroque network of holy places and macabre relics into a mythic cliché. Today, they are enduring symbols of regional self-identification. There can be little doubt of either their success or popularity. Another Marian monument in the main square of Munich that carries her name has become a major tourist attraction and an internationally recognized landmark of the city.

However, and despite the best intentions of the authorities, pilgrimage was a poor method of inculcating discipline. Ironically, freeing subjects from everyday social controls legitimized extraordinary behavior through direct access to sacred power. Public processions and annual mass pilgrimages took on carnivalesque features of anti-Lenten proportions. They facilitated unruly, disorderly and potentially criminal behavior under the guise of piety. Annually, the authorities fought a running battle against "riff-raff," the hawkers, fornicators, drunkards, thieves and other stock characters at huge devotional gatherings. As a consequence, the absolutist state never mastered the social disruption inherent in its own peregrinational summons to the people. The authorities gradually disassociated themselves from massive devotional events. By the late-eighteenth century Enlightenment, the state legislated against processions, passion plays and uncontrolled popular devotion.

The consumption of the official literary and artistic promotion of the Marian program also had an unexpected knock-on effect for other cults. In competition, the monastic orders successfully adapted, employing the same images to enhance the prestige of their local shrines. Even if the Wittelsbachs regretted the competition, it would have been manifestly cynical to approve of some saints and disapprove of others. The Wittelsbach-sponsored reinvigoration of pilgrimage not only provided the orders with an effective public relations model, but also encouraged spontaneous popular devotion of the type noted by Marc Forster in southwest Germany almost a hundred years later.[3] Pürten benefited from its location along the main pilgrimage route to Altötting. The Anastasia shrine received spontaneous

---

[3] Forster, *Catholic Revival*, especially 84–88.

and supra-regional attention through purely oral transmission, until the custodian Aemilian Biechler initiated a hagiographic tradition with his *Bavarian Beacon* in 1663. The hagiography went into four editions and both cults flowered into the late seventeenth century, a testimonial to the continued demand for spiritual physic after the general crisis. The complaints of pilgrims and seasonal patterns of pilgrimage demonstrate the predominance of personal and material concerns associated with mental disorders. When ordinary Bavarians undertook pilgrimages, their driving motivation remained local, not directly related to the state or society at large.

Personal concerns of individual sufferers come to the fore in their own characterizations of spiritual afflictions. Relatively minor spiritual afflictions, above all common tribulations, predominated. We should avoid trivializing their complaints, because the motivation to conduct a pilgrimage justified the arduous journey. Therefore, when tempted to translate spiritual afflictions into modern terms, extreme caution is advised. This is not to say that the language of spiritual afflictions is so foreign that it defies translation, but the idiomatic expression of mental anguish demands careful reconstruction within a specific historical context. More often than not, cultural and social relationships attached meanings to spiritual afflictions, especially during liminal stages in a person's life-cycle. Additionally, unexpected misfortunes, unfulfilled expectations, personal frustrations, and failures all gave use to mental anguish.

From the perspective of gender, the authorities evinced patently bureaucratic concerns in their blanket generalizations of spiritual afflictions as madness, a psychologically imprecise, collective legal term. Madness implied a violent threat to society, but the Aulic Council applied the category indiscriminately to some who were dangerous and others who were obviously harmless. A state of diminished capacity, madness resolved questions of legal culpability and legitimized legal intervention. In keeping with the patriarchal ideal of the early modern state, the Aulic Council described men as "mad" far more often than women, by a ratio of more than two to one, because of their legal advantage over women. For example, mental disorders among men commanded the attention of the authorities because they might require jurisprudence to establish an executor of the estate, whereas a husband could more easily perform that function for his wife than vice versa.

Therefore, the overwhelming predominance of women in cases of spiritual afflictions and religious madness is not perplexing. Sheilagh Ogilvie characterizes the systematic legal discrimination regularly practiced against women in early modern Germany as "gender tutelage."[4] Mental disorders among women had fewer legal implications, since immediate responsibility for a woman fell to familial and communal patriarchs. One could also argue the predominance of women as sufferers of spiritual afflictions on the basis of physiological explanations, without necessarily invoking the presumption that women are more universally prone to psychic disorder.[5] In the Bavarian sources, for example, physiology played a demonstrable role in specifically female mental disorders resulting from complications during pregnancy and childbirth, including miscarriage, postpartum depression, stillbirth and infant mortality. Obviously, men did not face a comparable dilemma. Otherwise, more women than men sought devotional treatments in every category of spiritual affliction *except* somatic disorders. Contemporaries tended to explain female afflictions spiritually.

In an age obsessively focused on sin, contemporaries viewed the female body as more permeable by moral corruption than the male.[6] The spiritualized image of the virgin saint or beata (whether the Virgin Mary, the virgin Beata Alta or the virgin St. Anastasia) also influenced the depiction of female mental disorders as spiritual. It was no coincidence that Del Rio discussed "psychiatry" and the healing of souls in a Marian tract.[7] The mother of God, forgiving and accessible to the laity, represented the purity of virginity, a palpable material condition infused with deep spiritual and moral meaning in early modern Catholicism. The reaffirmation of sacerdotal celibacy by the Council of Trent confirmed the preferred status of sexual abstinence as an attainable goal, reinforcing the prestige of chastity.[8] In a world experienced alternately as chaotic and repressive, virginity, celibacy and chastity seemed to offer at least one area over which the individual could exercise a modicum of self-control. However, courtship in early modern Europe was a contact sport: people were regularly injured, both physically and mentally. Several women considered in this study went mad after refusing an unwanted marriage proposal, a circumstance they shared with St. Anastasia herself.

If some women suffered frustration in their efforts to gain empowerment through sexual continence, others empowered themselves through their suffering, expressing afflictions as demoniacs. Bernhard Frey suspected as

---

[4] Sheilagh Ogilvie, "How Does Social Capital Affect Women? Guilds and Communities in Early Modern Germany," *American Historical Review* 109 (2004), 325–359.
[5] MacDonald, *Mystical Bedlam*, 35–40, esp. 38.   [6] Roper, *Oedipus, passim*.   [7] Del Rio, *Florida*.
[8] Discussed in regard to female virginity in Strasser, *State of Virginity*, and to clerical celibacy in Marc R. Forster, *The Counter Reformation in the Villages: Religion and Reform in the Bishopric of Speyer, 1560–1720* (Ithaca, 1992); Forster, *Catholic Revival*.

much and while he never contested their sincerity, he tested demoniacs thoroughly and insisted on remanding most to industry instead of to the care of exorcists. In the end, no one reason can adequately explain the motivations of women to avail of spiritual physic, but one thing is clear. Whatever their reasons, the overwhelming predominance of women as sufferers of spiritual afflictions in early modern Europe is empirically irrefutable.

In the final analysis, men too made up a significant, though lower proportion of sufferers. To paraphrase a scholar of the witch-hunt, mental disorders in early modern Europe were sex related, but not sex specific.[9] As the explication of two case histories – a nobleman and a common serving woman – demonstrates, neither gender nor social status contributed uniformly to mental disorders. Despite the successful completion of his university career, Leopold von Taufkirchen went mad during his grand tour under the pressures of his passage to majority and the world of the patriarchal elite. Anna Maria Arnold lost her senses during another contemporary rite of passage, courtship. Marriage pressures contributed to a demonic possession, despite the prospect of social advancement from service into the world of the guild professions. Therefore, gender roles and social status alone do not explain spiritual afflictions. In both cases, mental disorder was also contingent upon personal expectations, wants and desires. In neither case did gender, social status nor access to personal gain guarantee mental balance. Given these complexities, the present study confirms that the effort to analyze individual case histories sheds new light on social expectations and helps us to recover history's lost people from obscurity and to locate them in a comprehensible and meaningful framework.

The story of exorcism in Bavaria from Canisius to Biechler parallels the rise and fall of spiritual physic as a story of belief, authority and skepticism. Like many moralists active in Bavaria at the time, both Canisius and Biechler came from outside the region. Both fought to revitalize exorcism, a practice with roots in late antiquity. Jesuit intellectuals systematized practices during the Confessional Age. Then, the general crisis of the seventeenth century ushered in a diabolic crisis, ending in what Lucien Febrve once championed as a psychological revolution in France during the Counter Reformation. In Bavaria too, when the possessed personifications of the Eschaton and their exorcists failed to resolve the general crisis, skepticism took hold among the ruling elite. Upon closer examination, the authorities in both France and Bavaria began to suspect that religious

---

[9] Christina Larner, *Enemies of God: The Witch-Hunt in Scotland* (Baltimore, 1981); see also Brian P. Levack, *The Witch-Hunt in Early Modern Europe* (London, 1987), 124.

zealotry actually contributed to social disorder. Subsequently, they lost faith in the power of the devil to act in the material world.

By the mid-seventeenth century, official support for exorcisms waned. Even a Jesuit, casuist and nominal spiritual physician like Bernhard Frey expressed growing skepticism about demonic possession, advising caution about the dangers of witch-hunts. Like Weyer, Tanner and other opponents of persecution before him, he did not refute the possibility of demonic agency, but simply pointed out other possibilities, including natural explanations, within the existing ideological paradigm. We might consider the rise of skepticism and the move to an insanity defense as aspects of the diabolical crisis and a psychological revolution, or, if one prefers, we could also place events within the context of a broader paradigm shift. In a comment on the scientific revolution of the seventeenth century, Thomas Kuhn described attempts at the resolution of systemic crises from within a paradigm as precondition for the emergence of novel theories:

Part of the answer, as obvious as it is important, can be discovered by noting first what scientists never do when confronted by even severe and prolonged anomalies. Though they may begin to lose faith and then to consider alternatives, they do not renounce the paradigm that has led them into crisis . . . once it has achieved the status of a paradigm, a scientific theory is declared invalid only if an alternate candidate is available to take its place.[10]

Steeped in Christian morality, Galenic humoral pathology and Aristotelian faculty psychology, spiritual physic held explanatory power logically consistent with contemporary cosmology. For casuists, faculty psychology linked individual morality with the social causes of catastrophic events in accordance with Aristotelian physics. Initially, as events portended the general crisis, promoters of spiritual physic like Canisius spotlighted possession as immanent proof of rising demonic activity in a binary eschatology, the penultimate struggle between good and evil.

It took almost a century before the Wittelsbachs and their Jesuit father confessors agreed that exorcisms only exacerbated social disorder. This was the first major fissure in the systematic reliance on spiritual physic. Bernhard Frey from Oberstdorf was no radical. He urged restraint and applied orthodox principles to discourage exorcisms. He expressed concerns that cases of demonic possession might end in witch trials, like those Canisius had earlier agitated for when Conrad Stoeckhlin was burned at the stake in Oberstdorf just before Frey's birth. Perhaps the skepticism of the new generation of spiritual physicians he represented lies in their homespun roots.

[10] Kuhn, *Scientific Revolutions*, 77.

They had no need to prove their loyalty. As a generation, they had also experienced the worst of the witch trials and the cataclysm of war first hand. When they argued for restraint, however, they still did so within the existing cosmological paradigm, rather than turning to Cartesian dualism. The insanity defense had always been available, and a tainted acquaintance with calamities, religious bigotry and social disruption now favored it. Exorcists like Aemilian Biechler continued to practice in Bavaria for some time, at least in the countryside. They were popular, because ordinary Bavarians had been taught to invoke demonic explanations to justify personal travails. Only tangentially concerned with learned eschatology, they applied popular practices concerned with individuals. However, as a career goal, the era of achieving sainthood through exorcism had passed. For representatives of the state, possession and exorcism proved difficult to control, too unpredictable to channel. They discouraged public exorcisms in favor of judicious admonitions to industry, quiet individual pilgrimages to official Wittelsbach shrines, religious reprogramming through a dependable father confessor and, finally, a theoretical preferment of confinement.

Nevertheless, imposing the insanity defense and confinement posed numerous challenges, including the potential for further social and ideological disintegration. The absolutist state confronted corporate privilege and the threat of popular unrest. The treatment of suicide was another prominent mental health issue associated with demonic agency. Baroque necrolatry placed a special premium on final resting places. Decisions regarding the honorable interment of suicides still depended upon their state of mind and the input of the church authorities. Until the parish clergy could be won over to an attitude of restraint, they represented another disruptive social force. Popular prejudices, at times encouraged by the parish clergy, prevailed among large segments of the population. When the central authorities disagreed with communities over the role of the devil in suicides, only threats of fines and violence succeeded in overcoming deep-seated resistance to the burials of suicides in hallowed ground. Imperial decrees of the eighteenth century still had to confront these prejudices, so engrained had the fear of the demonic become in the popular consciousness. Nevertheless, as in England after 1660, the *non compos mentis* defense had gained the upper hand among the ruling elite, gradually forcing its way down the bureaucratic ladder. Official skepticism about demonic causation, the essence of the diabolical crisis, touched Europe from Bavaria in the southeast to England in the northwest.

This makes the enthusiastic popular support for a policy of confinement seem almost paradoxical, unless one views it in terms of material conditions.

Families and communities willingly allowed the state to relieve them of the burden of mad persons, simultaneously demonstrating a marked reluctance to pay for relief, motivated by tactical opportunism. One might rationalize about contrite ideological change, but, like the popularity of auricular confession and pilgrimage, evidence of strategic concern on the part of ordinary individuals and communities is lacking. Despite paternalistic intentions to care for the mad properly, the old regime struggled to rise to the challenge and largely failed; the Wittelsbachs could ill afford to pay for centralized institutionalization out of their own dynastic funds and their subjects stubbornly refused to cooperate. A novel policy of confinement required a steady budget for current expenditures. Initially, the authorities relied on the existing parish-based system of contributory poor relief. When that failed, relief was reapportioned at the district level, an almost equally unsatisfactory fiscal solution.

The authorities also lacked adequate institutional space to house and care for the mad. They recognized that it was unethical and probably illegal to lodge the mad in jails and could not prevail in the struggle for jurisdictional authority over civic hospices. Prominently, the absolutist state did not even have the authority to impose its will by executive fiat upon the town council of Munich, the electoral residence. In order to avail of the facilities in the Holy Spirit Hospice, privileged by Emperor Louis the Bavarian since the Middle Ages, the Electors had to negotiate with the city fathers on a tenuous case-by-case basis. As a result, tensions mounted when the state withdrew support for exorcisms without either buying wholesale into a novel cosmology or providing a viable method of alternative care.

The history of clinical psychiatry in Bavaria did not progress linearly. It followed a serpentine path from spiritual physic toward psychological medicine with several sudden switchbacks. This forces us to rethink MacDonald's pessimistic conclusion on developments in eighteenth-century England, where private asylums and the lunacy trade took up the slack in state-sponsored mental health care.[11] MacDonald suggested that the disappearance of ambulatory treatment for the insane in the eighteenth century was a "disaster" and that "Many of the successful practices employed by Napier and his contemporaries were discarded because they were associated with religious radicalism and popular superstition."[12]

---

[11] On the lunacy trade and the eighteenth-century history of British asylums, see Scull, *Most Solitary of Afflictions*; Roy Porter, *Mind-Forg'd Manacles: A History of Madness in England from the Resotration to the Regency* (London, 1987).
[12] MacDonald, *Mystical Bedlam*, 230–231.

Did the decline of spiritual physic have disastrous consequences for sufferers in Bavaria? What of the leniency shown toward self-killers and their
survivors? The simple answer is, society could not have one without the
other. The gradual banning of Satan from state affairs and the rise of the
insanity defense also had a deterrent effect on witch persecutions, a development we ought to greet with applause. Some things were lost, others gained.
But, on the whole, the eighteenth century found issues of mental health
care in Bavaria largely unresolved. No comprehensive system of madhouses
emerged until the mid-nineteenth century. Spiritual physicians continued
to practice, if less vocally, while the state preferred the insanity defense
and institutionalization in serious cases, but lacked the material resources
for their complete implementation. Rudolf Schlögl has suggested that the
Bavarian state also had no compelling impetus for economic reform after
the Thirty Years War, since recovery followed without grave difficulties.[13]
Financial stimulus after 1640 coincided with ideological changes toward
madness policies and positive change did occur; the state moved away from
the characterization of suicides, mad persons and witches as demonic cases.
Nevertheless, without a definitive resolution, which could only be achieved
by fundamental structural reforms, the problems would simply not disappear. They stewed at the popular level and finally resurfaced at the very
end of the *ancien régime*, like ghosts haunting the Enlightenment. By that
stage, however, official sanction had long passed squarely onto the shoulders
of bourgeois luminaries and medical experts, who replaced pious peasant
women like Rosina Huber as the new secular exorcists of spirits, demoniacs
and witches.

RÉSUMÉ: MADNESS, RELIGION AND THE STATE IN
EIGHTEENTH-CENTURY BAVARIA

A tentative foray into the continued difficulties surrounding the issue of
mental health care in the eighteenth century is far too tempting to pass up.
If the eighteenth century was a disaster, then it was one not only for the
mad, but also for Bavarians in general. The Wittelsbach dynasty focused its
attention abroad and Elector Maximilian Emanuel's unfortunate alliance
with France during the War of the Spanish Succession ended in nearly fifty
years of foreign occupation. Maximilian Emanuel briefly reconquered Tyrol
after centuries of Habsburg domination, but the gain proved ephemeral.
By 1704, his army routed, the Blue King fled for Brussels, seriously entertaining the idea of a territorial exchange for Flanders or Sicily. However, he

---

[13] Schlögl, *Bauern, Krieg und Staat*, 360–367; synopsized in Asch, *The Thirty Years War*, 187–189.

found no takers and, in his absence, the Habsburgs invaded and occupied Bavaria. His son, Karl Albrecht, inherited the Electorate with 25,000,000fl. in debts. When Karl Albrecht won the imperial election in 1742, he fulfilled a centuries-old dynastic aspiration. The resultant struggle with Maria Theresa drained the state coffers still further, with the deficit reaching a staggering 32,000,000fl. Karl Albrecht narrowly averted bankruptcy through French contributions and papal approval for the first tithe on regional monasteries. However, the tithe concession enabled the powerful monasteries adroitly to block state-sponsored plans for direct taxation until 1768.[14] As Emperor Charles VII, Karl Albrecht acted as little more than a figurehead in an anti-Austrian coalition backed by Frederick II of Prussia and Louis XV of France. When he died in 1745, the Habsburgs forced his heir, Maximilian III Joseph, to renounce dynastic claims to the imperial title before agreeing to withdraw their forces from Bavaria. Finally, after 1745, Maximilian III Joseph reasserted the dynasty's ancestral hold over Bavaria.

In the interim, political uncertainty decayed the efficient bureaucratic infrastructure carefully crafted since the reigns of Albrecht V and Maximilian I. This is reflected in the sources: the Aulic Council protocols are far less systematic and comprehensive after 1705. As a consequence, the history of madness is more difficult to trace in official records during the first half of the eighteenth century. There is also a corresponding deficit of miracle books, which declined in popularity. The international spread of scientific naturalism altered patterns of devotion, moral casuistry, spiritual physic and religious madness among the social elite. Bourgeois sentimentality and moral pathology began to replace sin and humoral pathology, preparing the ground for alienist psychiatry.[15]

In his study of self-reflections on suicide during the Enlightenment, Andreas Bähr identifies a transitional period, when religious morality and bourgeois sentimentality overlapped in the mid-eighteenth century.[16] One hagiographic example illustrates a similar transitional stage in the history of Bavarian devotional piety and spiritual physic. In 1710, the historian Karl Meichelbeck of Benediktbeuern published the final Anastasia hagiography, *The Life, Suffering, Death and Elevation of the Great Holy Martyr Anastasia.*[17] Meichelbeck, an adherent of the enlightened Maurinist historical school,

---

[14] Behringer, *Witchcraft Persecutions*, 378–379
[15] On the "invention" of bourgeois psychiatry in the eighteenth century, see Doris Kaufmann, *Aufklärung, bürgerliche Selbsterfahrung und die "Erfindung" der Psychiatrie in Deutschland, 1770–1850* (Göttingen, 1995).
[16] For an excellent account of the enlightened semantics of suicide, see Andreas Bähr, *Der Richter im Ich. Die Semantik der Selbsttöttung in der Aufklärung* (Göttingen, 2002), 44–91.
[17] Meichelbeck, *Leben/ Leyden/ Todt*.

Plate 19. *The Wonder of Kochel Lake*, copper etching, *c.*1728. On the bottom right, destruction threatens Benediktbeuern; on the left, the invaders are driven off by inclement weather; in the middle, demons fly out of the possessed. (Courtesy of Archiepiscopal Archive, Munich; photograph by Foto Thoma, Benediktbeuern.)

studied arts at the Benedictine University of Salzburg.[18] After 1696, he assumed the posts of cloister librarian, archivist and custodian at the St. Anastasia shrine. His other publications included an excellent diocesan history of Freising and monastic histories of Andechs and Benediktbeuern. He also rationalized and catalogued the abbey's rich archival and library holdings.

Although Meichelbeck opened his Anastasia miracle book with the biography of the saint, largely recapitulating Biechler's earlier narrative from the *Bavarian Beacon*, his enlightened training resulted in several novelties. For example, demonic possession makes its appearance on the cover page, but spiritual afflictions only figured in one-third of the miracles described throughout the text. Meichelbeck certainly had not forgotten the propagandistic value of the miracle book. His most innovative chapter proclaimed a recent miracle, the Wonder of Kochel Lake. He described the Wonder against the backdrop of the collapse of the Bavarian state under Maximilian Emmanuel. Meichelbeck recalled how, in 1704, the abbey and nearby villages were abandoned by electoral troops, but saved from certain destruction on the eve of the feast of St. Anastasia.[19] When Habsburg levies (the feared Croats and Pandurs, popular bogey-men in parental reprimands as late as the twentieth century[20]) attempted to cross the frozen Kochel Lake directly south of the abbey, an unseasonably warm wind (*Föhn*[21]) melted the ice and prevented the enemy's advance (see Plate 19). Meichelbeck's enlightened interpretation of St. Anastasia's intervention introduced a novel effect. In the absence of protection by their secular ruler, the saint had interceded through a naturally occurring weather-related miracle. By the eighteenth century, Benedictine literary and theatrical productions often served as propaganda weapons against competing religious orders or secular hegemony rather than against Protestants.[22] For example, Meichelbeck's Wonder of Kochel Lake supported a jurisdictional claim over disputed lands and fishing rights.

[18] The leader of the Maurists, the luminary Jean Mabillon, had already visited Benediktbeuern in 1683 to study at its renowned library. He arrived during the translation festival of St. Anastasia, when the volume of pilgrims forced the French dignitary to seek lodgings at a distant inn, a haphazard reception blamed for his unflattering portrayal of the cloister: Hemmerle, *Die Benediktinerabtei*, 70.

[19] Meichelbeck, *Leben/ Leyden/ Todt*, 196–281.

[20] Cultural remnants of the deprivations suffered under Habsburg occupation by Hungarian and Croat troops were reflected in the habit, widespread until the early twentieth century, of threatening misbehaved children with the *Panduren* and the *Krawaten*: Bosl, *Bayerische Geschichte*, 134.

[21] A common occurrence in the foothills of the Bavarian Alps, *Föhn* is a familiar phenomenon in the region. Caused by a sudden high-pressure front of warm winds from the African continent, locals often complain of headaches and use the *Föhn* to excuse excessive behavior.

[22] Hermann Hörger, "Geistliche Grundherrschaft und nachtridentinisches Frömmigkeitsbedürfnis. Die Abtei Benediktbeuern im Kampf gegen das Eremitorium Walchensee (1687–1725)," ZBLG 47 (1978), 83. On the propagandistic use of high baroque theater by the Bavarian Benedictine

The Wonder occurred after Maximilian Emanuel's defeat and its retelling served as a rhetorical device to create a political vacuum.[23] According to the legend, the Bavarian army abandoned the southern counties, leaving the Habsburg mercenaries to ravage the pious inhabitants. Thereupon, the monks of Benediktbeuern vowed to build St. Anastasia a new chapel and she delivered the abbey and local peasants from the encroaching hordes. A Bavarian state commission coincidentally witnessed the Wonder of Kochel Lake. The commission was engaged in the arbitration of a border dispute between Benediktbeuern and Schlehdorf, a neighboring monastery on Kochel Lake. According to Meichelbeck:

> It just so happened at that time that the cloister Benediktbeuern was involved in a jurisdictional conflict with the neighboring cloister Schlehdorf over a certain part of Kochel Lake, previously transferred to it in return for recognition of our jurisdiction over the neighboring moraines . . . by the Elector's Court Chamber representative. And on the aforementioned 28th day of January, the parties agreed that they should set the new district boundary markers in Kochel Lake, which was frozen hard as stone (and would have been impossible in summer), and in the moraines . . .[24]

A perennial component of their neighborly relationship, border conflicts between Benediktbeuern and Schlehdorf accompanied a running dispute with the Electors over Benediktbeuern's judicial competence in capital crimes;[25] this particular dispute flared up in 1702.[26] In his capacity as local archivist, Meichelbeck was perfectly cognizant of the abbey's dispute with Schlehdorf over fishing rights and a nearby brewery.[27] The Wittelsbachs had taken the side of Schlehdorf since 1687. In 1710, when Meichelbeck published his Anastasia hagiography, the Abbot of Benediktbeuern had the Augustinian brewery shut down. He refused to allow the miller (who was a subject of Benediktbeuern) to go to work. The Wonder of Kochel Lake concretely proved the power of St. Anastasia to the electoral officials – not in the realm of spiritual physic, but in international warfare. Meichelbeck subsequently led a delegation to Rome to secure restrictions on Schlehdorf

---

Congregation, see Klaus Zelewitz, "Propaganda Fides Benedictina. Salzburger Ordenstheater im Hochbarock," in: Jean-Marie Valentin (ed.), *Gegenreformation und Literatur. Beiträge zur interdiszi-plinären Erforschung der katholischen Reformbewegung* (Amsterdam, 1979), 201–215.

[23] Columbus has been accused of employing a similar literary strategy against Native Americans: Greenblatt, *Marvelous Possessions.*

[24] Meichelbeck, *Leben/ Leyden/ Tödt*, 203–204.

[25] Which the abbey claimed according to a document signed by Louis the Bavarian, presumably a forgery.

[26] Hildebrand Troll, *Kirche in Bayern. Verhältnis zu Herrschaft und Staat im Wandel der Jahrhunderten* (Munich, 1984), 139.

[27] Hemmerle, *Die Benediktinerabtei*, 237; Hörger, "Geistliche Grundherrschaft."

from the Curia in 1712.[28] In 1715, a play enacted by children to entertain the Bishop of Freising while on a visit to Benediktbeuern referred to the dispute.[29]

As the one and only success over the invading Habsburg army, the Wonder of Kochel Lake provided a rallying cry for popular resistance in Bavaria. The succession of financial and military disasters under Maximilian Emanuel meant untold hardships for the inhabitants of Bavaria, especially during the enforced quartering of Habsburg troops. Bavarians sorely needed a hero. On Christmas Day, 1705, an uprising broke out in Sendling at the gates of Munich, instigated by a group of bourgeois administrators.[30] Legend has it that the leader of the uprising was Balthasar, the smith of Kochel. According to the legend, the smith fell that Christmas day in the massacre of Bavarians by the Austrian occupiers at Sendling. Oddly, however, the smith seems actually to have died of natural causes in 1720 and he was buried in the cemetery in Kochel.[31] As a symbol of resistance, the mythical smith of Kochel outlasted the Wonder of Kochel Lake, being immortalized in bronze both in the town square of Kochel and in Sendling to celebrate the bicentennial of the battle during an era of rabid nationalism.[32] The smith (sculpted as a virile figure with a spiked club) embodied a male vision of heroism, both patriotic and martial, that had eclipsed the healer-saint of the Counter Reformation.

By the eighteenth century, the ruling elite no longer associated St. Anastasia with spiritual physic, madness and the fight against Satan. In a travel diary kept during a journey to Italy by Elector (later Emperor) Karl Albrecht in 1737, an entry records a brief visit to Benediktbeuern before crossing the Alps. The party arrived at the monastery, dined with the abbot in the festival hall and attended mass in the Anastasia chapel. The abbot blessed each member of the party with the relics of S. Anastasia, inspiring the Elector's lack-luster comment, "she is a great patron of afflictions of the head."[33] When Maximilian III Joseph stopped at Benediktbeuern during a hunting trip in 1749, the relics were applied to him and the other cavaliers as well,

---

[28] Hemmerle, *Die Benediktinerabtei*, 237–238, 630.
[29] Ibid., 281. The play was written and directed by Pater Marus Sartori of Benediktbeuern; a fellow Benedictine from Andechs composed the musical score.
[30] The so-called *Sendlinger Mordweihnacht*.
[31] Patriotically remembered in Christian Probst, *Lieber Bayerisch Sterben. Der bayerische Volksaufstand der Jahren 1705 und 1706* (Munich, 1978), 348–349.
[32] The speeches from the event and a romanticized biography were published as J. N. Sepp, *Festschrift zur zweiten Jahrhundertwende der Schlacht von Sendling* (Munich, 1905).
[33] "Nach der Tafel wobey wir köstlichen Wein vom Prälaten getrunken, giengen wir in die Kirche, der Segen zu empfangen, und uns das Haupt der Heil. Anastasia aufsetzen zu lassen, welche eine große Patronin in Kranckheiten des Hauptes ist": HStAM KL BB 137.

but as a simple blessing without reference to any curative powers.[34] Eventually, the Wittelsbachs clamped down on popular devotion, prohibiting a number of passion plays, holy days and processions to pilgrimage shrines. An edict of 1770 forbade the performance of all passion plays in Bavaria on the official grounds that "the great mysteries of our Religion do not belong on stage"; the edict threatened some 160 local productions.[35] In its attack on popular devotion, the state displayed little concern for the financial ramifications for local communities.[36]

The Wittelsbachs also declared war on the tradition of "blue Monday" and the all-too-numerous local saints' days. Previously tolerated, they were literally wiped from the calendar. However, censors complained that smugglers operated a thriving trade in calendars from the neighboring Bishopric of Salzburg, which enjoyed great popularity, because they marked the prohibited feast days. An eighteenth-century apogee of ritual pilgrimages and processions is directly attributable to the communal effort to resist the anti-devotional policies of the enlightened absolutist state.[37] In 1770, for example, locals flaunted an official ban on a procession to Hohenpeissenberg, flocking in the thousands to the pilgrimage shrine in protest.[38] The Ecclesiastical Council in Munich and the town council in nearby Weilheim cited the standard catalogue of immoral behavior (excessive drinking, disorderliness and fornication) in their justification of the ban.

The struggle between the state and popular devotees came to a head in the Bavarian War on Witchcraft from 1766 to 1770. Witch-hunting continued to have statutory force, renewed as late as 1751. The last legal persecutions for witchcraft took place in Landshut, when a fourteen-year-old girl was executed in 1756.[39] In that particular case, the victim suffered the torments, demonic assaults and suicidal tendencies indicative of demoniacs and diagnosed as madness or fraud in the mid-seventeenth century by Frey. However, the Bavarian government grew intent to introduce reforms modeled on those of Joseph II in Austria. In 1766, a Theatine historian, Don Ferdinand Sterzinger, initiated an ideological battle against common superstitions in a speech held before the Elector in the recently instituted Bavarian Academy

[34] ". . . den Segen vor und nach mit dem H. Haubt S. Anastasia gegeben und solches beeden durchl. Und and. Cavallier aufgesezt nach welchen man sich augenblicklich auf die große Jagd am Hirsch . . .": ibid.

[35] Georg Brenninger, "Passionsspiele in Altbayern," in: Michael Henker, Ebeshard Dünninger and Evamaria Brockhoff (eds.), *Hört, sehet, weint und liebt. Passion spiele in alperlärdischen Raum* (Munich, 1990), 61–65.

[36] Hörger, *Kirche*, 106.

[37] See Rebekka Habermas, *Wallfahrt und Aufruhr. Zur Geschichte des Wunderglaubens in der frühen Neuzeit* (Frankfurt am Main, 1991).

[38] Ibid., 131–150.   [39] Behringer, *Witchcraft Persecutions*, 350–351.

of Sciences. A tragic-comical war of words ensued, pursued in public sermons and pamphlets by eponymous authors with apocryphal pseudonyms or humorous epigrams: 'the lover of truth', 'the lover of decent freedom', 'a healthy sane mind from this side of the Danube', a 'Godly scholar', a certain 'F. N. Blocksberger', 'J.F.Z.', 'F.L.' or 'A.E.I.O.U.'[40] On the one side, the proponents of witch-hunting (including the Jesuits of Altötting, who took pains to record actual tests of Satan's power) attacked the dangerous free-thinkers, 'witch-stormer' Sterzinger and his supporters in the Academy.[41] In 1767, the luminary Peter von Osterwald delivered a decisive blow in another speech before the Academy. This led to the adoption of sweeping legal reforms, eliminating the ecclesiastical censorship board, restructuring the Ecclesiastical Council and successfully encroaching upon the privileges of the monasteries in a Mandate on Cloisters (*Klostermandat*) of 1768, to allow for taxation.[42]

Almost immediately, the luminaries of the Academy found themselves up against a renewed challenge in the form of an anti-secularizing reaction from the general populace. The suppression of the Society of Jesus by papal decree in 1773 only exacerbated the situation.[43] Large numbers of ex-Jesuits, cut loose from institutional control, became troublesome vendors of magical folk beliefs to whip up popular support against their enlightened detractors. This time, spiritual physic and exorcism provided the stuff of the conflict. In 1774, Johann Joseph Gassner achieved prominence throughout southern Germany as a wonder healer. Gassner condoned exorcisms to cure all types of illness.[44] He claimed that demons and witches were the primary causes of ill health in the present godless world. Although he failed to cure the daughter of Prince-Bishop Ignaz Anton Fugger of her blindness, more than twenty thousand admirers (both Catholic and Protestant) flocked to Ellwangen seeking his help. They celebrated him "as the Apostle sent to oppose free thinkers."[45] From July 10 to August 10, Gassner performed exorcisms on more than thirteen hundred persons.[46] Although the Prince-Bishop of Constance disapproved of these "treadmill exorcisms," Gassner's cures were verified by physicians and churchmen in

---

[40] Ibid., 363.   [41] Ibid., 361–381.

[42] "Apparently, these far-ranging plans were intended to erode the position of the surrounding episcopates, in addition to mediating the power of the territorial monasteries": ibid., 378–379.

[43] HStAM Kurbayern Mandatensammlung 1773 XI 2.

[44] On Gassner, see H. C. Erik Midelfort, *Exorcism and Enlightenment: Johann Joseph Gassner and the Demons of Eighteenth-Century Germany* (New Haven, 2005).

[45] Behringer, *Witchcraft Persecutions*, 381–387.

[46] Ernst Florey, *Ars magnetica. Franz Anton Mesmer 1734–1815, Magier vom Bodensee* (Constance, 1995), 85–86.

the ecclesiastical principalities of Eichstätt, Freising and Regensburg, where an episcopal commission confirmed a further 375 *bona fide* cures. Not surprisingly, the ex-Jesuits of Augsburg, Dillingen, Ingolstadt, Landsberg and Munich vocally supported Gassner. A subsequent pamphlet battle raged from 1774 to 1777 and took on many aspects of the previous Bavarian War on Witchcraft, including a derisive tract against Gassner's exorcisms, which, it complained, promoted the metaphysical principle of sympathy as a wonder cure.[47]

Sterzinger penned a condemnation of Gassner's work in a review published by the Academy of Sciences. He warned that Gassner threatened the entire medical establishment and closed with the polemic, "Good night, my lord physicians, if from now on cures can only be had through exorcisms."[48] The Academy moved swiftly to contain the situation, dispatching its own commission to Ellwangen, headed by Sterzinger and a prominent physician, Dr. Wolter. Wolter fell under Gassner's influence after the exorcist practiced successfully on his daughter, but Sterzinger remained adamant.[49] With Osterwald's help, he procured the consent of the new secular college of censors to ban Gassner's publications in Bavaria. Their efforts to keep Gassner out of Munich met with success; he never personally conducted an exorcism in Bavaria. However, Gassner found imitators among the ex-Jesuits, who made use of what little social capital was left to them. By 1776, two exorcists were already active in Munich, a priest named Riedmayer and the ex-Jesuit Gogler. In a panicked letter to Elector Maximilian III Joseph, the civic pastor Joseph Felix Effner described a virtual outbreak of demonic possessions in Munich:

The extraordinarily enthusiastic preacher in the Holy Spirit Hospital, the ex-Jesuit Priest Gogler, has very vehemently sermonized, among other related sorts of exaggerated matters, against the free thinkers and their evil books. His listeners – mostly inmates of the hospital and other common people among whom there is most certainly no danger of either free thinking or book reading – have been rendered pusillanimous in the sure belief that, above all, the authorities and nearly every person of high estate are infected by such Godless persons. In doing so, the preacher creates the immediate impression that he is more concerned to convince his listeners to hate persons of high estate and the authorities, rather than to see to the betterment of their morals . . . Oh most gracious Lord Elector! I leave it to more learned men to decipher what evil against the true Christian Catholic

[47] Anonymous, *Die Sympathie, ein Universalmittel wider alle Teufeleyen* (Sterzingen im Tyrol, 1775).
[48] Florey, *Ars magnetica*, 86.
[49] Andreas Kraus, *Die naturwissenschaftliche Forschung an der Bayerischen Akademie der Wissenschaften im Zeitalter der Aufklärung* (Munich, 1978), 144. Many thanks to Erik Midelfort, who is currently investigating the Gassner phenomenon.

religion may spring from such steps, but must dutifully remind you only that if these exorcisms are allowed to continue, indeed if these things are supported publicly from the pulpit, then at least two-thirds of the populace in the city of Munich will be transformed in the perception, most damaging to both soul and body, that they are possessed.[50]

These developments alarmed Sterzinger. Like most contemporaries, he was willing to accept that Gassner could heal, but concluded in frustration that, "God does not do it, the devil cannot, therefore it must be nature . . . either a magnetic, or electrical or sympathetic force."[51] In order to establish the natural forces at work, Sterzinger persuaded Maximilian III Joseph to invite an expert to Munich to judge the case. Simultaneously, an anonymous pamphlet appeared in 1775: It recommended that an invitation be extended to the Viennese wonder healer, Franz Anton Mesmer. Mesmer, it claimed, could be counted on for an impartial judgment, because his "wonderful and magnetic operations are most analogous to those of Mr. Gassner."[52] The Prince-Bishop of Rodt, who previously hosted Mesmer and was convinced of the scientific nature of his theories on animal magnetism, recommended him personally to the Elector.

Mesmer arrived in Munich in 1775. He convinced the Academy of the efficacy of Gassner's cures, but reassured them that they were in fact scientifically explicable. He agreed with Sterzinger that Gassner was sincere and possessed of a special talent – to heal through animal magnetism. Mesmer's demonstrations met with approval from the Academy, so much so that they elected him to their membership at the instigation of Osterwald (who hoped to recover from his own ill health through Mesmer's methods). On the basis of Mesmer's scientific experiments, Gassner was prohibited from entering Bavaria; Emperor Joseph II subsequently decreed a prohibition on exorcisms throughout the Empire.[53] Mesmer succeeded in turning the Academy into a platform to sell his own theories on animal magnetism. The enthusiastic members conducted a public competition in 1776 on the question, "Whether there is a true analogy between electrical and magnetic forces? And, if demonstrable: one must ask, whether and how these forces affect the animate body? To this end, these questions must be explained through actual experiments."[54] Mesmer won first prize; Mesmer seemed *scientific*. What impressed the luminaries at the Academy most was his reliance on purely natural explanations, even if many of his ideas on natural physics

[50] HStAM GR 1210/20. [51] Kraus, *Die naturwissenschaftliche Forschung*, 144–145.
[52] Florey, *Ars magnetica*, 89–90. [53] Ibid., 91.
[54] Kraus, *Die naturwissenschaftliche Forschung*, 227.

were fundamentally Aristotelian in character.[55] However, what was most important was his expressed disavowal of metaphysical explanations for the sufferings of Gassner's patients.

Amidst the Academy's deliberations over the causes and cures of illnesses, Maximilian III Joseph died of smallpox in 1777. Heirless, the elder line of the Wittelsbach dynasty died with him. When Karl Theodor, a successor chosen from the younger Zweibrücken line, refused to relocate to Munich, another vacuum of authority offered popular religiosity a temporary reprieve and Oberammergau procured a special permit to perform its famous passion play after a lengthy legal battle.[56] The relentless efforts of Karl Theodor's successor, Maximilian IV Joseph, and his enlightened ministers Montgelas[57] and the American Benjamin Thomas (alias the Count of Rumford) culminated in the legal secularization of Bavaria from 1803 to 1806. Montgelas, connected to the Masonic *Illuminati*, represented the reform party in the Academy of Sciences.[58] Two brief French occupations of Bavaria in 1796 and from 1799 to 1801 offered him "a laboratory opportunity to enact the perfect late-Enlightened absolutist reforms."[59] The Josephine secularization of more than eight hundred Austrian monasteries between 1780 and 1790 provided Montgelas with a structural precedent. The secularization represented nothing less than a sweeping constitutional reform of the Bavarian state.

[55] The literature on Mesmer is voluminous. Briefly, however, the natural basis of Mesmer's claims, established in his 1766 *Dissertatio physico-medica de Planetarum influxu*, was structurally analogous to Gassner's metaphysical premises of hylomorphic sympathy. The fundamental difference between the two was Mesmer's insistence on natural as opposed to metaphysical causes, enhancing his reputation with luminaries like Osterwald. Nonetheless, Mesmer's theory of animal magnetism was laced with occult references to sympathies between macrocosm and microcosm, between general gravitation and animal attraction: Kraus, *Die naturwissenschaftliche Forschung*, 145–146. This is hardly surprising, when one considers that Mesmer, born in Meersburg, had studied at the Jesuit universities of Dillingen and Ingolstadt, where an Aristotelian curriculum was still taught in the early eighteenth century. Initially, Mesmer's belief in the omnipresence of invisible fluids influenced by magnets was inspired by the experiments of the Viennese Jesuit and charismatic healer Maximilian Hell. By the time he appeared before the Bavarian Academy of Sciences, he had replaced the magnets entirely with the force of his own body as the cosmic vessel of magnetic power. The rest of Mesmer's meteoric rise and fall is well known. After offending Vienna's most prominent physicians, he traveled to France in 1778 and became a popular pre-revolutionary figure in the salons of Paris. Finally, he received a stiff rebuke from the Royal Society at the hands of Antoine-Laurent Lavoisier and Benjamin Franklin, who denied the existence of his invisible fluids; see Robert Darnton, *Mesmerism and the End of the Enlightenment in France* (Cambridge, Mass., 1968). Eventually, one of his methods – initially known as mesmerism and later as hypnotism – greatly influenced later treatments by Pinel, Charcot and, subsequently, Freud, who carried it back to Vienna from Paris.
[56] Brenninger, "Passionsspiele," 63.
[57] See Eberhard Weis, *Montgelas 1759–1799. Zwischen Revolution und Reform* (Munich, 1971).
[58] Ibid.; Richard van Dülmen, *Der Geheimbund der Illuminaten. Darstellung, Analyse, Dokumentation* (Stuttgart, 1975).
[59] Isabel Hull, *Sexuality, State, and Civil Society in Germany, 1700–1815* (Cornell, 1996), 337–342.

With the elevation of Bavaria to a kingdom in the Confederation of the Rhine under Napoleon, Maximilian IV Joseph ruled as king over a powerfully centralized and modern state with the authority to expropriate the holdings of most monasteries in the region.[60] The central state pushed through ideological reforms favored by luminaries since the mid-eighteenth century.[61] The state benefited primarily from a reorganized economic structure and a system of direct taxation. The loss of the Bavarian monasteries, highly efficient managers of agriculture, schools and other public works, would have been an insufferable blow had it gone uncompensated. Secularization was a costly affair, and backers had to be found to prop up the administration during the transition with loans of 7,500,000fl. However, strategic efforts to dismantle popular piety still met with resistance. In 1803, for instance, when charged with the enforced secularization of monastic property in Benediktbeuern, a commissioner[62] received special permission to leave the ornate St. Anastasia bust in the parish, "because the people in this area look upon this Anastasia bust with unbelievable trust and I fear unpleasant unrest, if one was to take it from them so suddenly."[63]

In the final quarter of the eighteenth century, enlightened bureaucrats also addressed the issue of lunacy reform. Apart from the return of demonic possessions to the Holy Spirit Hospice, several specific and troubling incidents in Straubing came to the attention of the authorities in Munich. In 1782, and again in 1788, the *Rentmeister* of Straubing[64] wrote Munich about the brutal murder of a young girl committed by a local smith "in a most wretched manner."[65] No local facility was available to hold the maniac, and he was "left to rot in the local jail, to the shame of mankind."[66] Another lengthy report written in 1795 by his successor[67] stressed the threat to public safety arising from the lack of a proper system of madhouses (*Tollhäuser*), forcing the administration to allow identifiably dangerous persons to wander about freely.[68] As a consequence, another child had been murdered and such persons represented an immanent fire hazard: in nearby Regensburg, a madman recently burned the Chapel of the Holy Blood (built to commemorate the execution of Jews charged with host-desecration in the sixteenth

---

[60] Manfred Treml, "Die Säkularisation und ihre Folgen," in: Josef Kirmeier and Manfred Treml (eds.), *Glanz und Ende der Alter Klöster. Säkularisation im Bayerischen Oberland 1803* (Munich, 1991), 122–131.
[61] Behringer, *Witchcraft Persecutions*, 387.   [62] Maximilian von Ockel.
[63] Wolfgang Jahn, "Die Aufhebung des Klosters Benediktbeuern," in: Kirmeier and Treml, *Glanz und Ende*, 74, 144. The Anastasia bust is still carried in local processions and it remains in her chapel to this day.
[64] Johann Maria Freiherr von Weichs.   [65] He had decapitated her.
[66] HStAM GR 1190 #63 (*Obere Landesregierung*) and #62 (*General Acta Die Errichtung einiger Tollhäuserin Baiern betr. 1788–1870*).
[67] Johann Nepomuk Anton Felix, Count Zech von Lobming.   [68] HStAM GR 1190 #62.

century) to cinder and ashes. The *Rentmeister* claimed that another man, accused of poor household management, languished in prison for six years, when in fact he belonged in a hospital. This type of imprisonment, he noted, violated the laws and exposed him to common criminals and bad air, worsening his already pitiable condition.

In 1792 and 1793, the exchequer collated a group of supplications for admittance to the Holy Spirit Hospice from areas outside Munich as evidence of the pressing need for a state asylum.[69] In 1794, the Privy Council concurred that five mad persons (none from Munich) were currently held in the *Falkenturm* jail and the new house of correction.[70] The council offered a four-point argument, deploring the situation. The persons in question, they noted, already suffered the loss of their reason and should, under no circumstances, suffer additionally at the hands of a godless immoral horde of thieves, robbers and murderers. A cure was impossible under the circumstances. Furthermore, the mad disrupted the work regimen at the house of correction and endangered weak and ill prisoners. Finally, the house of correction was filled to overflowing and the warden had enough on his hands to prevent breakouts, maltreatment or murder among the inmates, not to mention suicides. The remarks of the Privy Councilors underscore the belief that madness represented a pathological and curable condition. They envisioned an institution to cure the insane, expressing concern for their safety and the safety of others.

In 1794, a government commission investigated the viability of a public asylum in Bavaria. The government followed the lead of other territories, where a rapid succession of madhouses had been founded since the beginning of the eighteenth century.[71] The commission encouraged district judges to lodge petitions for central relief from the costs of care for dangerous individuals associated with the policy of enforced contributions at the district level in effect since the seventeenth century. The intermediary officials (i.e. the *Rentmeisters* of Landshut, Straubing and Burghausen)

---

[69] Ibid.

[70] These included Joseph Oelinger from Reichenberg in the province of Landshut; the son of Michael Holzmiller, an acolyte from Achering in the district of Kranzberg; Katharina Kornbrust, who had killed a child in the private jurisdiction of the nobles of Weissensteig; Mathias Schlauderer of Gräfelfing; and Georg Heinrizi, who had burned down his father's farm in Wolfratshausen.

[71] E.g. Celle (1710), Waldheim (1716), Mannheim (1749), Ludwigburg (1749), Schwabach (1780), Bayreuth (1788) and, most recently, the infamous *Narrenturm* in Vienna (1789): Dieter Jetter, *Grundzüge der Geschichte des Irrenhauses* (Darmstadt, 1981), 21–33. On the history of the creation of the Viennese institution under Joseph II, the Foucauldian thesis of Jasmine Köhle's analytical study, *Der Narrenturm in Wien oder das Paradigma des Wahnsinns* (Vienna, 1991) is quite useful; see also the more recent work of Alfred Stohl, *Der Narrenturm oder die dunkle Seite der Wissenschaft* (Vienna, 2000).

highly recommended the creation of a central repository for the mad. It goes without saying that centralized care offered obvious fiscal advantages to both the local and intermediary bureaucracies. Between 1794 and 1798, the commission investigated a number of potential sites for an asylum, including abandoned castles and underused hospices.[72]

Gradually, discussion shifted to a plague and fever hospital of the electoral household in Giesing, a transfluvial suburb of Munich. Prominent burgers had already suggested Giesing as a possible location for an asylum during the reign of Karl Theodor and the commission's substantive findings evidenced its superior qualities. Nearly empty since the last major epidemic of 1773, it already had an annual endowment of 3,000fl. from the electoral household and provisions for an existing staff of one physician, a barber-surgeon, an administrator, four orderlies and two cooks.[73] By terminating a commission for the Pauline monks to hold daily masses, the asylum saved an additional 373fl. In the interests of the *securitas publica*, Giesing was safely located across the Isar on the outskirts of town. Yet it was still close enough to the physicians and hospitals of Munich in case of emergencies. It already contained fifteen cells and could easily house up to thirty inmates. The existing walled garden "is especially suitable for the amusement of mad persons, with whom no danger is associated." One consultant physician[74] voiced disapproval and submitted a proposal for a purpose-built structure modeled after an asylum he had seen in England. The commission responded negatively to his proposal, since "here, the person would be handled far too much like an animal," deciding instead for an asylum styled after Ludwigshafen and the Juliusspital in Würzburg.[75] Under the direction of the electoral protomedicus,[76] the commission finalized the

---

[72] HStAM GR 1190 #62. The commission immediately dismissed the dilapidated castle in Burghausen as a possible site. The exchequer did not favor the Ducal Hospital in Munich. No adequate lands were available to compensate the owner of the castle at Berg am Laim. A donor proposed his castle at Leuting in return for minor relief, but the commission failed properly to investigate the property. In Landshut, an abandoned plantation was deemed structurally unsound, while the civic hospice could only convert three cells at a cost of 468fl. The costs of converting ten cells in the leprosium in Straubing were estimated at over 2,300fl. In a predictable argument, representatives of the Holy Spirit Hospice in Munich vehemently protested "that the few cells here, which are already occupied, are not even sufficient to care for the fools in this city."

[73] Ibid.   [74] Dr. Georg Öggl.

[75] On the institutional history of asylums in south Germany, see Alexandra Chmielowski, "Reformprojekt ohne Zukunft: Die Heilanstalt und psychiatrische Klinik in Heidelberg (1826–1835)," in: Erik J. Engstrom and Volkes Roelcke (eds.), *Psychiatrie in 19. Jahrhundert. Forschunger zur Geschichte van psychiatrischen Institutionen, Debatten und Praktiken in deutschen Sprachraun* (Basle, 2003), 49–66; Ann Goldberg, *Sex, Religion, and the Making of Modern Madness: The Eberbach Asylum and German Society 1815–1849* (Oxford, 1999). The Juliusspital is considered in Midelfort, *A History of Madness*, 365–384, stressing the relative progressiveness of this early modern Catholic hospital.

[76] Dr. Franz Joseph Besnard.

Giesing proposal and ordered the Secret Finance Department to draw up three alternative blueprints for alterations to the existing structure in conjunction with consultant physicians. On November 5, 1798, the so-called Schneidheim plan was submitted. Ratified by special order of the Elector in 1800, the renovations commenced on July 17, 1801, when the former hospice was officially dissolved.[77] Two years later, on July 1, 1803 (and just as the secularization of the Bavarian monasteries began), the Electoral Bavarian Insane Asylum opened its doors in Giesing to patients for the first time. The secularization provided substantial capital for running expenses. In 1806, Elector Maximilian IV Joseph became King Maximilian I Joseph and the asylum was elevated to royal status. To many, it seemed that the riddle of mental health care had been solved. Nonetheless, as the early history of the institution demonstrates, the asylum was woefully inadequate in terms of space and funding.[78] It hardly represented the successful culmination of a Great Confinement. By the mid-nineteenth century, confinement had assumed massive proportions, but had still proved unable to solve the problem of mental disorders in Bavaria. For every new asylum that opened its doors, it seemed that more than enough patients could be found to fill it.

THE LEGACY OF SPIRITUAL PHYSIC:
A PSYCHOANALYTIC EXCURSUS

One can surely give oneself over to a train of thought and follow it as far as it leads purely out of scientific curiosity or, if one will, as a devil's advocate, who nevertheless has not signed a pact with the Devil.[79]
(Sigmund Freud, *Beyond the Pleasure Principle*)

I do not think our successes can compete with those of Lourdes. There are so many more people who believe in the miracles of the Blessed Virgin than in the existence of the unconscious.
(Sigmund Freud, *New Introductory Lectures*)

To avoid any confusion, it needs to be stated clearly that the end of the *ancien régime* and the foundation of a Bavarian insane asylum did not spell the end of spiritual physic. As aspects of pastoral care in Catholicism, pilgrimages are still conducted, confessions are still heard and exorcisms continue to be

---

[77] StAM RA (Regierung von Oberbayern) Fasz. 278, No. 4396, September 6, 1822: "Nach einen Antrage der ehemaligen churfurt. General Landes Direktion vom Jahren 1800 wurde dieses Gebäude durch allerhochstens Reskript vom 17. Juli 1801 zur Lokalität für eine neu zu errichtende Irrenheilungsanstalt Anstalt überlassen, für diesen Zweck in der folgenden zwei Jahren ausgebaut, und errichtet, so dass die ersten Aufnahmen im Jahre 1803 statt finden konnten."

[78] On the early history of the asylum after 1803, see David Lederer, "Die Geburt eines Irrenhauses: Die königlich-bayerische Irrenanstalt zu Giesing/München," in: Engstrom and Roelcke, *Psychiatrie in 19. Jahrhundert*, 67–94.

[79] Author's translation.

practiced, though in a manner more analogous to the cautious outlook of Bernhard Frey than Peter Canisius. Alienists rooted some of their premises in spiritual physic as well. Spiritual physic was particularly influential in the psychic interpretation of mental health, the counterpart to somatic psychiatry. One of the pioneers of psychic psychiatry in Germany was Karl Philipp Moritz, who dedicated a psychiatric journal to the art of curing souls (*Seelenheilkunde*).[80] His case histories portrayed the social causes of insanity in a fashion sympathetic to bourgeois philanthropy. Moritz sought the causes of insanity in wayward life-styles, poverty and bad upbringing, freely mixing pathological and moral categories of analysis. The psychic school had powerful representatives in the early alienist movement: both Johann Christian Heinroth (the first chair of psychiatry in Germany at Leipzig from 1811) and Jean-Etienne-Dominique Esquirol, Pinel's most famous student, subscribed to a view of mental illness influenced by a metaphysical and moralizing understanding of the human soul.[81] By the late nineteenth and early twentieth century, many leading psychologists, psychiatrists and psychoanalysts expressed a direct interest in the cures of the early modern period, especially demonology. William James, the first American professor to lecture in psychology at Harvard (significantly, he lectured in the philosophy department; psychology was still considered a branch of philosophy in America at that time), was a noted spiritualist, requesting that a medium be hired to contact him after his death. C. G. Jung was fascinated by the psychological implications of early Christian theology from Tertullian to Luther.[82] He neither disputed their premises, nor did he claim them as his own. However, he doubted that ancient intuitive practices, such as humoral pathology or astrology, were suitable criteria for modern psychological typologies.[83] Of all the secular practitioners of psychiatry and psychoanlaysis, however, Sigmund Freud deserves special attention here for his analysis of the case history of another seventeenth-century Bavarian demoniac, Johann Christoph Haizmann. Freud applied retrospective medicine to Haizmann's case history in order to prove the universal applicability of his own psychoanalytic principles.

[80] Karl Philipp Moritz published *Anton Reiser. Ein psychologischer Roman* between 1785 and 1790 in his own journal, *Gnothi sautón oder Magazin zur Erfahrungsseelenkunde als ein Lesebuch für Gelehrte und Ungelehrte, 1783 – 1793* (Berlin, 1793–1793; reprint: Nördlingen, 1986).
[81] Michael Kutzer is convinced that the debate between the psychic and somatic schools of the early nineteenth century was a red herring; for details of Heinroth's role, see his "'Psychiker' als 'Somatiker' – 'Somatiker' als 'Psychiker': Zur Frage der Gültigkeit psychiatriehistorischer Kategorien," in: Engstrom and Roelcke, *Psychiatrie in 19. Jahrhundert*, 27–48.
[82] Carl G. Jung, *Psychologische Typen* (Zurich, 1921; Rsmt: Düsseldorf, 1995), 7–67; many thanks to Sonu Shamdasani for this reference.
[83] Ibid., 566–567.

In 1920, Dr. Rudolf Payer-Thurn introduced Sigmund Freud to the case history of a Bavarian painter and demoniac, Johann Christoph Haizmann. In his capacity as archival director of the *Fideikomiss* library, Payer-Thurn requested an expert medical opinion from his distinguished Viennese colleague and sent him the transcription of a curious historical document – the "diary" of that possessed artist.[84] Haizmann's case instantly captured the pioneering psychoanalyst's imagination. The transcription recounted his initial seizures and the horrified reaction of the Sunday congregation gathered in the church of Pottenbrunn, Austria on August 29, 1677. Haizmann's unnatural convulsions subsided temporarily after he made a confession, received absolution and communion, only to flare again, persisting into the following day. The local prefect came to examine him, but questions alluding to forbidden arts (the Austrian authorities suspected him of witchcraft) prompted Haizmann to beg another private audience with the parish priest. He now confessed an extraordinary tale of a pact with Satan signed nine years before.

Startled, the anxious curé remanded Haizmann to the custody of Benedictine monks at the nearby shrine of the Holy Virgin of Mariazell, where he suffered through three anguished nights of exorcisms. On the feast of the birth of the Virgin (September 8) around 11:30 p.m.,[85] Satan returned a blood-signed pact and was driven from his body in the guise of a dragon. However, this recovery was short-lived. That winter, while visiting his sister in Vienna, Haizmann complained of fantastic visions and renewed demonic molestation. Soon thereafter, he returned to Mariazell for protracted exorcisms, but not until May could he retrieve a second pact from the devil. Out of gratitude, Haizmann entered the Hospitaller order, dying "piously" at Neustatt on the Mettau in 1700. Although sometimes tempted by the devil "when he had drunk a little too much wine,"[86] Haizmann nonetheless resisted Satan's subsequent efforts to coax him into another diabolical contract.

---

[84] The manuscript, entitled *The Trophy of Mariazell*, is in fact an eighteenth-century copy of the original, with an attestation to that effect from Abbot Kilian of St. Lambert. An English translation appears in Hunter and MacAlpine, *Schizophrenia 1677*, 57–86. Payer-Thurn published his own interpretation of the case with the title, "Faust in Maria-Zell," *Chronik Wiener Goethe-Vereins* (1924), 1–18. Haizmann was born in 1651 in Traunstein in the Electorate of Bavaria: Gaston Vandendriessche, "Johann Christoph Haizmann (1651–1700). Barocke Teufelsaustreibung in Mariazell," in: Rupert Feuchtmüller and Elisabeth Kovács, *Welt des Barock* (Vienna, 1986), 141–145.

[85] Hunter and Macalpine, *Schizophrenia 1677*, 63, incorrectly translate *circa horam mediam duodecimam noctis* as midnight; a correction is offered by H. C. Erik Midelfort, "Catholic and Lutheran Reactions to Demon Possession in the Late Seventeenth Century: Two Case Histories," *Daphnis* 15 (1986), 623–648.

[86] Hunter and Macalpine, *Schizophrenia 1677*, 84.

In 1923, Freud published his analysis of the case, *A Seventeenth-Century Demonological Neurosis*,[87] in which he explored its amenability to his own psychoanalytic theories. He regarded Haizmann's possession experience as a manifestation of grief over the loss of his father. The devil symbolized the "primal Father" (*Urvater*[88]), providing Haizmann with a father-substitute (*Vaterersatz*).[89] The demonic pacts never existed, but represented a "neurotic fantasy," a parapraxis, quite literally a Freudian slip. From them Freud inferred that Haizmann harbored feelings of ambivalent hatred toward the deceased, provoked by his father's tacit disapproval of his career choice as an artist.[90] Consumed by contradictory emotions of love and hate, Haizmann suffered simultaneously from two contradictory neuroses. On the one hand, he displayed an uncontrollable urge for self-punishment, a castration complex reflected in a fantasized pregnancy (Freud's interpretation of the number nine as a recurrent motif). On the other hand, he yearned to castrate his father, hence the artist's androgynous caricatures of the devil/father-figure with fully developed mammae. Freud's final diagnosis of the case alluded to his previous analysis of the Saxon judge Daniel Paul Schreber.[91] Haizmann suffered from obsessional neuroses caused by an irreconcilable personality conflict between his female and male inclinations (fear of castration/desire to castrate), complicated by masochistic fantasies of hellish torture and ultimately arising from the repression/denial of an early infantile love-fixation for the father.[92]

Freud was not a professionally trained historian and has been accused of committing several misdemeanors in his zeal to analyze the Haizmann case

---

[87] The original, "Eine Teufelsneurose im Siebzehnten Jahrhundert," appears in the *Gesammelte Werke* (hereafter cited as GW), vol. XIII (1949), 315–353. This English translation is found in *The Standard Edition of the Complete Psychological Works of Sigmund Freud*, ed. James Strachey (hereafter cited as SE), vol. XIX (1961), 67–105.

[88] A concept elaborated two years earlier in "Group Psychology and the Analysis of the Ego," SE vol. VIII, 67–143, especially 122–124.

[89] Freud, "Demonological Neurosis," 83–92.

[90] Ibid., 88. There are obvious parallels here to the famous psychohistoric analysis of Martin Luther's rebellion against his father and his later rebellion against the Pope; see Erikson, *Young Man Luther*. However, although the manuscript states that Haizmann "began to despair of his art and the possibility of earning a living by it" (Hunter and Macalpine, *Schizophrenia 1677*, 59), the original document never actually indicates that his father forbade him to pursue a career in art.

[91] His 1911 piece on Schreber appears as "Psychoanalytic Notes on an Autobiographical Account of a Case of Paranoia (*Dementia Paranoides*)," in SE, vol. XII, 3–82.

[92] Freud, "Demonlogical Neurosis," 92. Schreber, whose father was renowned as the inventor of the *Schrebergarten* (many thanks to Zvi Lothane for this information), presided over a panel of judges, but suffered a crushing defeat as the national liberal candidate of Chemnitz in the 1884 *Reichstag* elections and, subsequently, a severe breakdown. For a critical analysis of his case, see Lothane, *In Defense of Schreber*; for his edited autobiography, see Hunter and MacAlpine, *Memoirs of my Nervous Illness*, with a fine introduction by Samuel Weber.

history.[93] For example, he relegated the events in question to those "dark times" of the "Middle Ages."[94] In doing so, however, he merely adopted the conventional enmity toward things smacking of traditional religion from the prominent historical wisdom of his day. In fact, the Haizmann case post-dated Descartes and was situated foursquare in the Age of Reason. Therefore, Freud's assumption reveals more about misconceptions of "modernity" and problems of historical periodization than about exorcism, witchcraft persecutions or the use of judicial torture, all of which persisted well into the eighteenth century and beyond.[95] A certain philological problem lies in his translation of the phrase "ex morte parentis" ("because of the death of a parent," i.e. gender non-specific), taken as a specific reference to Haizmann's father. Although Freud's translation has been vigorously disputed as offering only a slight foundation for a theory of ambivalent filial devotion, the original phrase is surely ambiguous in the context of the original source.[96] Indeed, given a lack of evidence about Haizmann's mother, Freud may be justified in his rendering. His dismissal of devil's pacts as "pure fantasy" is questionable in light of existing pacts, such as Katharina Rieder's, though again, this is not Freud's fault alone. We can no longer simply interpret the pacts away as the warped intellectual products of fanatical theologians, as the scholarly consensus on the "cumulative concept of witchcraft" sometimes does.[97] Existing pacts are rare, because contemporary practice required their destruction by burning as blasphemies.[98] Nevertheless, early modern Europeans undoubtedly contracted devil's pacts, albeit unilaterally. While only a handful survive

[93] Gaston Vandendriessche offers a most scathing critique in his *The Parapraxis in the Haizmann Case of Sigmund Freud* (Louvain, 1965).
[94] Freud, "Demonological Neurosis," 72.
[95] See the compelling synthesis of institutionalized forms of torture from antiquity to the present by Edward Peters, *Torture* (Philadelphia, 1996). The last legal burning of a witch was held at Glarus, Switzerland, in 1793. Obviously, exorcisms are still conducted to this day.
[96] Midelfort, "Catholic and Lutheran Reactions," 628.
[97] On the cumulative concept and the pact, see Levack, *The Witch-Hunt*, 27–45, esp. 32–35. Richard van Dülmen suggests that these beliefs were alien to popular culture, "Imaginationen des Teuflischen. Nächtliche Zusammenkünfte, Hexentänze, Teufelssabbate," in: van Dülmen (ed.), *Hexenwelten. Magie und Imagination* (Frankfurt am Main, 1987), 94–130.
[98] Regarding the Haizmann issue, archivists have clearly sided with Payer-Thurn, viewing the devil's pacts as a manifestation of the Faust phenomenon: Günther Mahal, "Fünf Faust-Splitter aus drei Jahrhunderten," *Bausteine zur Tübinger Universitätsgeschichte* 1 (1981), 98–121; Volker Schäfer, "Tübinger Teufelspakte," in: Uwe Jens Wandel (ed.), *". . . helfen zu graben den Brunnen des Lebens." Historische Jubiläumsausstellung des Universitätsarchivs Tübingen* (Tübingen, 1977), 72–77. Many thanks to Dr. Schäfer, director of the University Archive at Tübingen, for fueling my curiosity about such matters. The demonologist and lawyer Martin Del Rio described another demoniac who signed two pacts with the devil, subsequently burned by the Bishop of Graz in 1600. See Del Rio, *Disquisitiones* (1608), 513–516, Bk. 6, ch. 2, sec. 3, ques. 3.

in the archives today, second-hand references to their existence are more common than one might expect.[99] Again, if the cultural context of their production seems peculiar to us, we have already learned something about our own preconceived notions of modernity through our perception of their "otherness."

For, despite these trivialities, Freud's most persuasive assertion remains his claim for the universal and metahistorical validity of his psychoanalytic method, still highly influential among later generations of historians. In the *Demonological Neurosis*, he asserts ironically, almost jokingly:

> I will instead say quite simply that I know very well that no reader who does not already believe in the justifiability of the psychoanalytic mode of thought will acquire that belief from the case of the seventeenth-century painter, Christoph Haizmann. Nor is it my intention to make use of this case as evidence of the validity of psychoanalysis. On the contrary, I presuppose its validity and am employing it to throw light on the painter's demonological illness.[100]

Of course, statements like these might leave one with the impression of an intellectual imperialist boldly sailing off to colonize the seventeenth-century mind of Haizmann, regally patronized as "our painter." This, at least, is the interpretation that moved the historian and psychoanalyst Michel de Certeau to wave the red flag of anachronism:

> First of all Freud shows a very typical attitude toward the Mariazell manuscript. For if he uses his tools on these still-fallow lands that have yet to be "cultivated" in psychoanalytic terms – that is, on these writings originating in the seventeenth century – it is not because the terrain is foreign, supposedly different, and set apart as times past. To the contrary, it is because the times are his own. The documents that he reads are part of his own context. They belong to his present time, but that time has not been analyzed – a revealing sign.[101]

References to Freud's other psychoanalytic case studies reinforce the suspicion that Freud's interests were cynically centered on the broader implications of his psychoanalytic agenda. At least, this is what his detractors, the "Freud bashers" of the 1980s and 1990s, would have us believe.[102] In addition to mentioning the Schreber case, a *parapraxis* and the *Urvater/Ersatzvater*, he wistfully commences the *Demonological Neurosis* with a rhetorical comparison of historical and depth analyses of case histories. Freud stated that

---

[99] Despite Midelfort's (1986) initial skepticism, documented evidence of pacts is mounting. See Heiss, "Konfessionelle Propaganda," and David Lederer, "Pact with the Devil," in: Richard Golden, *Encyclopedia of Witchcraft: The Western Tradition* (Santa Barbara, 2005).

[100] Freud, "Demonological Neurosis," 84.   [101] Certeau, *The Writing*, 291.

[102] This is the central message of Webster, *Why Freud was Wrong*; see the critical review by Peter Swales, "Once a Cigar, Always a Cigar," *Nature* 378 (November 1995), 107–108.

the facts of the Haizmann case spoke for themselves, since their meaning could "be brought to light without much interpretation – much as a vein of pure metal may sometimes be struck which must elsewhere be laboriously smelted from the ore."[103] In other words, Freud thought the case was a psychoanalytical gold mine.

Educated in the classics, Freud demonstrated some understanding of the hermeneutic difficulties associated with the analysis of a case history based solely on documentary evidence. For example, he recognized that the Haizmann text actually consisted of two documents: the Latin report of a monastic scribe and the "patient diary" in German. Hence, he was conscious of the critical problem of translating and interpreting sources according to the circumstances of their production and the status of the author. Freud's attitude toward religion (he viewed it as a self-indulgent form of human consolation) fluctuated between appreciation and skepticism. Although he expressed grave concerns about accepting the products of "monastic super-stition" at face value, he pointed out how the initial rhetoric of failure actually damaged the shrine's reputation. Consequently, he observed how self-deprecating admissions rhetorically reinforced the story's credibility, an indication of a critical eye.[104] Freud had other experiences of working with historical material. A cursory perusal of the bibliography at the end of *On Dreams* substantiates at least a rudimentary acquaintance with historical literature relevant to psychoanalysis. Apart from the classical interpreta-tions by Aristotle and Artemidoros, the sixteenth-century *Little Book of Dreams* by the pseudo-physicus Walther Ryff of Strasbourg also figures in the extensive reading list of pre-nineteenth-century works at the end of the book, although he only considered them *en passant* in the introductory comments.[105]

To his credit, Freud respected the beliefs of past cultures, acknowledging that they too possessed distinctive psychiatric categories, if only we were prepared to recognize them as such.[106] In the *Demonological Neurosis*, he interspersed original categories with his own without differentiation, expla-nation or critical interpretation. For example, he noted that the Bavarian painter suffered from pusillanimity and melancholy,[107] but categorized then them as "depressions," a term alien to seventeenth-century nosology. More

[103] Freud, "Demonological Neurosis," 73.   [104] Ibid., 74–77.
[105] See "On Dreams," SE, vol. v, 687–713. More commonly known as *The Interpretation of Dreams*, the work was first published in 1900.
[106] Freud, "Demonological Neurosis," 72.
[107] The latter is still widely regarded as a psychiatric condition, e.g. Michael Schmidt-Degenhard, "Versteinertes Dasein – zur Problemgeschichte und Psychopathologie der Melancholie," *Forschung und Medizin*, 45–56.

precisely, he classified them as emotional depressions,[108] like Haizmann's contemporaries, who similarly identified them as affective afflictions.[109] Previously, in *Beyond the Pleasure Principle*, Freud had also insisted that three affective disorders discovered among veterans of the First World War (angst, fear and shock), though related, were actually separate psychiatric maladies – coincidentally, a belief common in Haizmann's day.[110] In his own words, whereas "the neuroses of our unpsychological modern days take on a hypochondriacal aspect and appear disguised as organic diseases, the neuroses of earlier times emerge in demonological trappings."[111] This was not merely a statement of antiquarian interest on his part, but instead reflects the historical relevance of demonic possession for his own agenda.

Freud's interest in demonology transcended terminological sympathy to embrace theory as well. "The demonological theory of those dark times has won in the end against all the somatic views of the period of 'exact' medicine."[112] This indictment of somatic psychiatry represents a subliminal critique of positivism with a hauntingly postmodern ring to it. More surprisingly, Freud's expressed affinity for early modern theories on exorcism and demonology translated into actual psychotherapeutic practice. Earlier, in his *Studies on Hysteria* (1893–1895), Freud described a therapy of suggestion involving the laying on of hands, a procedure he "borrowed" from Bernheim to overcome the resistance of patients who could not be hypnotized. He described the procedure as follows:

"I placed my hand on the patient's forehead or took her head between my hands and said: 'You will think of it under the pressure of my hand. At the moment at which I relax my pressure you will see something in front of you or something will come into your head. Catch hold of it. It will be what we are looking for . . .'"[113]

---

[108] In the Strachey version, this term is translated somewhat inaccurately as "a state of depression": Freud, "Demonological Neurosis," 79–81. See the original terms, GW, vol. XIII, 325–326. For a synopsis of his ideas on affective disorders, see Arnold H. Modell, "Affects: Freud's Theory," in: Benjamin B. Wolman (ed.), *International Encyclopedia of Psychiatry, Psychoanalysis and Neurology* (New York, 1977), vol. I, 299–303.

[109] See Zedler, vol. X, 829–830: *Gemüths = Kranckheiten werden diejenigen genennet, welche von Gemüths = Bewegungen und Unruhe der Seelen entstehen.*

[110] GW, vol. XIII, 10.   [111] Freud, "Demonological Neurosis," 72–73.

[112] Ibid. Despite his vehement critique of purely somatic and organic interpretations of psychiatric illness, Freud began his career as a neurologist, was heavily influenced by the work of William Wundt and, as Frank J. Sulloway demonstrates in his controversial book, *Freud, Biologist of the Mind* (New York, 1979), he remained convinced that the anatomical nervous system was ultimately responsible for neuroses. In that sense, Freud essentially continued in a psychological tradition from Aristotle to Pavlov which attempted to locate the nodal point (e.g. Decartes' pineal gland) where sensory impulses affecting the anatomical nervous system are translated into conscious perceptions.

[113] SE, vol. II, "Studies on Hysteria (1893–95)," 110.

This therapy was successfully employed on the analysand Miss Lucy R., again on Fräulein Elisabeth von R. and subsequently on many others, leading Freud to exclaim, "I can no longer do without it"; it eventually replaced his use of hypnosis altogether.[114] He characterized the psychoanalyst "as a father confessor, who gives absolution, as it were, by a continuance of his sympathy and respect after the confession has been made."[115] Freud's candid allusions to Catholic ritual hardly resulted from chance. Another therapeutic method employed on Elisabeth von R. (curiously reminiscent of early modern witch-hunters) tested the insensitivity of certain body parts by pricking them with a needle.[116] Such methods attest to a concrete ideological interlocutor between Freud and his monastic precursors at Mariazell. What could possibly explain the nature of that interlocution?

Freud's encounter with Catholicism in the *fin de siècle* Austro-Hungarian Empire began in childhood.[117] We know that he remained in the care of a devout Catholic nanny until her dismissal for theft when the boy was two and a half. She used to tell him pious stories about the saints, instructed him in the concepts of Heaven and Hell, and took him to hear mass at St. Mary's, the local church in predominantly Catholic Freiburg, Moravia, where the family lived until shortly after his third birthday, in 1859, when they moved to Vienna.[118] His mother once commented, "when you got home, you would preach and tell us what God Almighty does."[119] In his own *Autobiographical Study*, Freud recalled a youthful engrossment with his own copy of the Philippson Bible that began almost as soon as he had learned to read.[120] However, despite any latent residues from an early childhood encounter with Christianity, and indeed despite his own

---

[114] Ibid., 106–11, 145, 270–272. It should be noted that the introduction of hypnotism as a method of psychiatric treatment coincided with the Josephine secularization of the late eighteenth century, which put an end to official support for exorcisms and witch-hunting.

[115] Ibid., 282.

[116] Ibid., 135–136. Freud was also perfectly aware that "inquisitors prick with needles to discover the devil's stigmata": *The Complete Letters of Sigmund Freud to William Fliess (1887–1904)*, ed. Jeffrey Moussaieff Masson (Cambridge, Mass., 1985), 225, letter of January 17, 1897; see also the German text in Sigmund Freud, *Briefe an Wilhelm Fliess*, ed. Michael Schröter (Frankfurt am Main, 1986), 238.

[117] Much has been made of this encounter by Peter J. Swales; see his "Freud, Minna Bernays, and the Conquest of Rome: New Light on the Origins of Psychoanalysis," *The New American Review* (Spring/Summer 1982), 1–23. Swales has gone so far as to claim that Freud's seduction of Minna Bernays manifested his childhood desire to seduce the Virgin Mary, represented by his Catholic nanny, and thereby conquer Christianity's "lie of the salvation of mankind" through a secular salvation.

[118] Ernest Jones, *The Life and Work of Sigmund Freud* (New York, 1953), vol. 1, 6–12.

[119] Peter Gay, *Freud. A Life for our Times* (London, 1988), 7.

[120] "An Autobiographical Study," SE, vol. xx, 8; Jones, *The Life*, 19.

adamantly declared secular life-style, Freud maintained, "My parents were Jewish and I have remained a Jew myself."[121]

In fact, Freud unambiguously revealed that his scientific debt to early modern Christian demonologists and exorcists did not arise from a casual encounter with Catholic culture, but instead was the conscious product of his own medical studies and research. Throughout his works, he consistently employs the term "soul" or "psyche" (*Seele*) when discussing the human mind and mental processes.[122] In a telling letter penned to William Fliess on January 17, 1897, he compared his own theories of psychiatric etiology with those of "medieval" theologians:

What would you say, by the way, if I told you that all of my brand-new prehistory of hysteria is already known and was published a hundred times over, though several centuries ago? Do you remember that I always said that the medieval theory of possession held by the ecclesiastical courts was identical with our theory of a foreign body and the splitting of consciousness? But why did the devil who took possession of the poor things invariably abuse them sexually and in a loathsome manner? Why are their confessions under torture so like the communications made by my patients in psychic treatment? Sometime soon I must delve into the literature on this subject . . .[123]

One week later, Freud wrote to Fliess to confirm that he had indeed ordered a book on the subject and intended to "study it diligently."[124] That book was none other than the now infamous *Malleus maleficarum*, once considered a collaborative effort of the Dominican inquisitors Heinrich Kramer (alias Institoris) and Jacob Sprenger, first published in 1486.[125] Nonetheless, it would be incorrect to presume that an intellectual genealogy from early modern demonology to Freud's ideas originated from a chance perusal of the *Malleus*, for three very specific reasons. First, this reference postdates the aforementioned methods outlined in the *Studies on Hysteria* by at least two years. Second, as the above letter of January 17 clearly demonstrates, his interest in the *Malleus* was to corroborate suspicions he already held. Finally and most conclusively, there is evidence indicating that Freud's introduction

---

[121] "An Autobiographical Study," SE, vol. xx, 7.
[122] And, in this sense, the Strachey *Standard Edition* of the complete works, which translates *Seele* as "mind" or "mental," gives the erroneous impression of a more secularized version of Freud's concepts. Many thanks to Lyndal Roper for bringing this significant detail to my attention.
[123] *Complete Letters*, ed. Moussaieff Masson, 224, letter of January 17, 1897; *Briefe*, ed. Schröter, 237.
[124] *Complete Letters*, ed. Moussaieff Masson, 227, letter of January 24, 1897; *Briefe*, ed. Schröter, 239–241.
[125] The most recent edition demonstrates that the *Malleus* was almost certainly the singular effort of Heinrich Kramer and may even have been published without the approval of Sprenger: Günther Jerouschek and Wolfgang Behringer (eds.), *Der Hexenhammer. Malleus maleficarum* (Munich, 2000).

to demonological theory occurred in an institutional setting as part of his formal medical training. He offers us a valuable clue in the *Demonological Neurosis*, where he notes decisively that "Several authors, foremost among them Charcot, have, as we know, identified the manifestations of hysteria in the portrayals of possession and ecstasy that have been preserved for us in the productions of art."[126] This is a direct reference to *Demoniacs in Art*,[127] a volume containing artistic representations of the possessed from the fifth to the eighteenth century, edited by Freud's revered mentor, the founder of modern French psychiatry and originator of retrospective medicine, Jean-Martin Charcot.[128]

James Strachey's editorial note to the *Demonological Neurosis* in the *Standard Edition* of the complete works also traces the genealogy of Freud's long-standing interest in demonology and spiritual possession back to his studies with Charcot at the Salpêtrière Hospital in Paris in 1885/1886.[129] In his *Report on my Studies in Paris and Berlin* (1886), Freud stated his unqualified admiration for "the Professor," whose astute comparisons between modern hysteria and the "medieval" phenomena of possession, witchcraft and devil beliefs greatly impressed his young Viennese protégé.[130] The subject of demonology achieved prominence in France long before Freud's arrival. The Russian-born, French-educated doctor Alexander Axenfeld began an influential public lecture series on the history of medicine for physicians at the Paris faculty of medicine in 1865.[131] His most controversial lectures focused on the life and legacy of a sixteenth-century scholar, Johann Weyer. Weyer has often been attributed with metamorphosing the modern insanity defense when, in 1563, he published the *De praestigiis daemonum*, which claimed that women accused of witchcraft probably suffered from hallucinations, fantasies or terrible dreams.[132] Philippe Pinel, famed

---

[126] Freud, "Demonological Neurosis," 27.

[127] Jean-Martin Charcot and Paul Richer, *Démoniaques dans l'art* (Paris, 1887).

[128] On Charcot and the use of images of demonic possession in retrospective medicine, see H. C. Erik Midelfort, "Charcot, Freud and the Demons," in: Kathryn Edwards (ed.), *Witches, Werewolves and Wandering Spirits* (Kirksville, 2002), 199–215; also Ruth Harris' introduction to her translation of Jean-Martin Charcot, *Clinical Lectures on Diseases of the Nervous System* (London, 1991).

[129] SE, vol. xiix, 69–70.

[130] Ibid., vol. I, 3–15, esp. 10–11; these remarks, as well as his respect for Charcot, are echoed in Freud's translation of the lectures on hysteria: SE, vol. I, 39–59, esp. 41–45.

[131] Jan Goldstein, *Console and Classify. The French Psychiatric Profession in the Nineteenth Century* (Cambridge, 1987), 355. The accusation of partisanship had already been raised, albeit in less systematic form, in Patrick Vandermeersch, *Psychiatrie, godsdienst en gezag. Psychiatry, religion and authority* (Löwen, 1984), esp. 306–311.

[132] Most convincingly, H. C. Erik Midelfort, "Johann Weyer and the Transformation of the Insanity Defense," in: Ronnie Po-Chia Hsia, *The German People and the Reformation* (Ithaca, 1988), 234–262.

for freeing the mad from their chains, had already mentioned Weyer in his *Traité médico-philosophique sur l'alienation mentale ou la manie* (Paris, 1801). Pinel's own method of moral treatment evidenced earlier forms of religious treatments.[133] He offered a subtle, if skeptical lesson to contemporaries on the therapeutic value of exorcism as an emotional shock treatment for those suffering severe delusions of possession:

The enlightened physician knows how he has to understand this religious cere-mony, but he has to credit it to the dexterity of the priests of all times and all places, that they knew the art of dominating people and of gaining their respect by means of spectacular ceremonies tackling the sense for the marvelous and by means of strong and lasting emotions.[134]

Sixty-four years later, Axenfeld reintroduced Weyer as a forerunner of enlightened science, the champion of humanitarian medicine fighting against the brutal fanaticism of religion.[135] In doing so, Axenfeld employed Weyer vicariously to challenge theories of criminal culpability and capi-tal punishment in nineteenth-century France based upon free will: "We continue to kill, with perfect tranquillity, criminals who are not insane because, apart from insanity, moral liberty seems indisputable . . . The will is free, that is the dogma."[136] Ulteriorly, Axenfeld's critique targeted the recent alliance of the Second Empire with the Catholic Church – the champion of social theories on the free will against the behavior-ist philosophy of Comtian positivism. His lectures drew record crowds, but were quickly suppressed; one of Axenfeld's most promising students also had his career destroyed. However, his ideas reverberated among col-leagues. Bourneville, a neurologist at the Salpêtrière, subsequently founded

---

Whether or not the attribution of the modern insanity defense to Weyer is a myth has yet to be definitively proved, but an otherwise useful overview of the textbook arguments fails convincingly to challenge the theory of continuity: Patrick Vandermeersch, "The Victory of Psychiatry over Demonology: The Origin of the Nineteenth-Century Myth," *History of Psychiatry* 2 (1991), 351–363. On the other hand, an extensive history of the insanity defense offers weak argumentation to suggest a continuity lying even further back than the sixteenth century: Daniel N. Robinson, *Wild Beasts and Idle Humours: The Insanity Defense from Antiquity to the Present* (Cambridge, Mass., 1996). The modern legal insanity defense remains a modern phenomenon.

[133] Goldstein, *Console*, 72–80. She refers to these methods as charlatanism, noting Pinel's use of purga-tives, bleeding and hellebore for mania: "With Pinel, recognition of the efficacy of charlatanistic treatments of insanity not only continued but was taken further: Selected aspects from charlatanism were to be deliberately appropriated by official medicine and transformed by it – transformed rather more in status than in content" (72). Further she suggests that moral treatment derived from the methods of Francis Willis, John Haslam and others, posing the rhetorical question, "Why should learned medicine look for guidance to such a motley crew?" Their methods were popularism "Scientized" (73).

[134] Vandermeersch, "The Victory," 357.   [135] Goldstein, *Console*, 356.   [136] Ibid.

the *Bibliothèque diabolique*, a series reprinting accounts of possession and witchcraft. In the introduction to the first French translation of the *De praestigiis daemonum* appearing as volume three of the series in 1885 (fatefully, just prior to Freud's arrival in Paris), Bourneville canonized Weyer as the father of modern psychiatry and an unbeliever ("un impie").[137] Historians of medicine have since debunked the myth of Weyer, recognizing that he too believed in the works of Satan, the existence of witchcraft and the possibility of demonic possession.[138] However, the eulogy of Weyer by the budding French psychiatric profession needs to be considered against the backdrop of tense church–state relations in late nineteenth-century Europe. An ultramontane policy against secularism, Gallicanism and conciliarism had triumphed at the Vatican Council with a declaration on papal infallibility (*Pastor aeternus*, 1870) and mounting anti-modernist suspicions. Simultaneously, forceful eruptions of popular piety accompanied an era of agricultural dearth and economic crisis, taking the shape of Marian apparitions at Knock, Lourdes and Marpingen.[139] In turn, national governments reacted by seeking either to channel the forces of official and popular religion into political support or to repress them outright. The French psychiatric profession found itself caught up in a doctrinal debate between liberal and clerical factions that outlived the Second Empire. The wary authorities of the Third Republic continued to spy on Charcot, whose anti-clerical sentiments were no secret at the medical faculty in Paris.[140] The conflict climaxed in a victory for the liberals and an endowed chair for Charcot dedicated to the study of nervous disorders – an unconditional official affirmation of his universal laws on hysterical seizure. Dubbed "retrospective medicine," Charcot politicized the hysteria diagnosis in the anti-clerical campaign by equating hysteria with demonic possession and condemning the inhumane treatment of demoniacs at the hands of the Catholic Church. Naturally, the crusading figure of Johann Weyer figured prominently in this equation.[141]

The influence of Charcot's retrospective approach to psychiatry, his comparative analyses of hysteria and demon possession, and the stature of Johann Weyer at the Salpêtrière can hardly be overstated in the genesis of Freud's ideas, even in his own personal estimation. In 1906, for example,

[137] Vandermeersch, "The Victory," 361.
[138] The twentieth-century continuation of the myth of Weyer as a champion of secular organic medicine is outlined in Kutzer, *Anatomie*, 13–18.
[139] For a very successful account of nineteenth-century Marian devotion, see David Blackbourn's *The Marpingen Visions: Rationalism, Religion and the Rise of Modern Germany* (Oxford, 1993).
[140] Goldstein, *Console*, 359–369.   [141] Ibid., 359–373.

Freud answered a questionnaire distributed to members of the intelligentsia by a Viennese newspaper. In response to a request for a list of ten good books, Freud noted circumspectly that a list of the most important books of all time would have to include the great achievements in natural science by Copernicus, Charles Darwin and the physician Johann Weyer.[142] That Freud associated himself most closely with Weyer is demonstrated by another list he composed ten years later for the journal *Imago*. In the updated version of irreparable blows to the narcissism of humankind brought about through scientific progress, Freud cited Copernicus for removing the earth (and hence humanity) from the center of the universe, Darwin for revealing that humans shared an affinity with other animals, and finally himself for demonstrating that the ego was not "master in its own house"[143] – effectively usurping Weyer's position in his previous list.

Freud was not only professionally, but personally interested in demonology. The devil is mentioned 121 times in the complete works, overwhelmingly in the *Demonological Neurosis*.[144] Freud displayed a marked penchant for diabolical literature in later life. His favorite books included Flaubert's *Temptation of St. Anthony*, Milton's *Paradise Lost*, Hugo's *Notre Dame of Paris* and Dante's *Inferno*; there is no evidence that he ever read the more famous *Madame Bovary*, or *Paradise Regained*, the *Purgatorio* or the *Paradiso*; his favorite opera was *Don Giovanni*.[145] It is also well known that Freud (not to mention many nineteenth-century celebrities, possibly even a pope) was an avid cocaine user from 1884 to at least 1895.[146] However, Swales' discovery that Freud's first cocaine encounter on the night of April 30, 1884 coincided with *Walpurgisnacht* is striking.[147] Add to this Freud's fastidiousness in choosing to purchase the cocaine from the chemist

---

[142] Peter J. Swales, "Freud, Johann Weier, and the Status of Seduction: The Role of the Witch in the Conception of Fantasy" (printed privately by the author, 1982); see also Swales, "Freud, Krafft-Ebbing, and the Witches: The Role of Krafft-Ebbing in Freud's Flight into Fantasy" (printed privately by the author, 1983). Swales notes that the information dates from 1906 and not 1907, as is usually believed. My thanks to Paul Vitz for obtaining a copy of these and other works by Swales. Swales can still be contacted at 285 Mott St., New York, NY 10012.

[143] Jones, *The Life*, vol. II, 225–226; SE, vol. XVI, 284–285; Ernst Gellner, *The Psychoanalytic Movement or the Cunning of Unreason* (London, 1985), 216–218.

[144] According to Samuel Guttman, Randall Jones and Stephen Parrish, *The Concordance to the Standard Edition of the Complete Psychological Works of Sigmund Freud* (Boston, 1980), vol. II, 129 (*Devil, Devil's, Devils*).

[145] A superb argument for Christian influences on Freud through demonic *belles lettres* is provided by Paul C. Vitz, *Sigmund Freud's Christian Unconscious* (New York, 1988), 100–128.

[146] Sigmund Freud, *Cocaine Papers* edited with an introduction by Robert Byck, notes by Anna Freud (New York, 1974).

[147] Peter J. Swales, "Freud, Cocaine and Sexual Chemistry: The Role of Cocaine in Freud's Conception of the Libido" (privately printed by the author, 1983).

Emanuel Merck. As Freud knew, Merck was the head of the German drug
company founded by Johann Heinrich Merck. The elder Merck, a close
friend of Goethe, consciously served the romantic author as a tragic model
for the mad poetic genius Torquato Tasso, as well as Mephistopheles in
Faust.[148] Faust, the figure in Goethe's most famous drama, signs a pact with
the devil. The Faust legend had medieval origins, but the first printed text
appeared in German in 1587.[149] In most early modern versions, Faust sells
his soul in pursuit of knowledge and power. The original 1587 collection of
Faust stories went into multiple editions and spawned countless imitators,
including novels, plays and operas by Marlowe, Lessing, Berlioz, Heine,
Mann, to name just a few, making it one of the most popular motifs in
modern literature. Freud's own fascination with the legend has led one
author to hypothesize that Freud actually empathized with the Antichrist
himself and that "an important part of him was involved in a neurotic
fantasy pact with the Devil" – a state he blames on Freud's sensitivity,
traumatic experiences, cocaine use and reading contemporary works by
Nietzsche.[150]

However, if Weyer and Goethe represented (for Freud at least) a critical
link between modern psychoanalysis and early modern demonology, this
study suggests a more orthodox historical evolution from early modern
spiritual physic to eighteenth-century psychiatry. Retrospective medicine
implied the universality of nineteenth-century psychiatric principles, but
its theories and methods borrowed from early modern spiritual physic to
provide a secularized form of pastoral medicine. Sarah Ferber has even
suggested that psychiatrists' "use of early modern texts might be seen in
part as a means not only of establishing a distance between themselves and
the clergy, but also a way of establishing a kind of heredity and lineage."[151]
This does not challenge psychoanalysis simply because it is based, at least
in part, on religion.[152] Instead, in keeping with William James as well as
current psychiatric text books, we recognize that experiences like demonic

---

[148] Hermann Bräuning-Oktavio, "Der Einfluss von Johann Heinrich Mercks Schicksal auf Goethes
'Faust' (1774) und 'Tasso' (1780/88)," *Jahrbuch des Freien Deutschen Hochstifts* (1962), 9–57.

[149] A critical overview of the early editions is available in Cornel Anton Zwierlein, *Das semantische
Potential des Fauststoffes um die Wende vom 16. zum 17. Jahrhundert* (unpublished MA thesis, Munich,
1999).

[150] Vitz, *Freud's Christian Unconscious*, 170–171. Vitz (149–157) also speculates that Freud may have in
fact contracted two actual devil's pacts himself on the evening of his first experiment with cocaine,
years before he even became aware of Haizmann, which would help to explain his fascination with
the case.

[151] Ferber, "Charcot's Demons," 134.

[152] Recently, revisionist evidence for a neurological basis to Freud's claims has been reasserted; see Mark
Solms, "Freud Returns," *Scientific American* 290 (2004), 82–89.

possession are certainly possible under peculiar cultural circumstances. And psychoanalysis is possible because of the cultural tradition out of which it grew. The true historical legacy of spiritual physic, then, lies not in its defeat in "warfare" at the hands of enlightened science, but in its contribution to a revolution in psychology, its relationship to changing political and social structures, and its secularized influence on modern psychiatric care. Europe's inner demons are still with us; we seem unable to do without them entirely.

Bibliography

ARCHIVAL SOURCES

AUGSBURG

Archiv des Bistums Augsburg (ABA)

Geistlicher Rat (GR) 1618–1669, 1690–1708

Staat- und Stadtsbibliothek Augsburg (SStBA)
2 Cod. S. 65

Stadtsarchiv Augsburg (StAA)
Reichschronik (RC) 20

BENEDIKTBEUERN

Pfarrarchiv Benediktbeuern
Pfarrmatrikel

INNSBRUCK

Landesarchiv Tirol (LaT)
Hofregistratur Protokolle Jahr 1661, vol. I, vol. II
Hofregistratur, Reihe F., Fasz. 84, 85
Pfarrregister, Film #631.
Regierungskopialbuch 172, 175, 177

MUNICH

Archiv des Erzbistums München (AEM)
Erscheinungen von Geistern (EG)
Geistlicher Rat (GR) 31, 34, 61, 62, 63, 64, 82, 84, 87, 88

Bayerisches Hauptstaatsarchiv (HStAM)

Blechkasten (BlK) 34, 35
Geistlicher Rat 40
General Register (GR) 139, 321, 1190, 1191, 1210/20
Hofkammer (HK) 190, 227
Jesuitica (Jes.) 513/III, 527, 2263, 2428
Kloster Urkunde (KU) *Benediktbeuern* (BB) 1272, 1275, 1286, 1317
Klosterliteralien (KL) Altötting (AÖ) 52
Klosterliteralien (KL) Andechs 40, 41
Klosterliteralien (KL) *Benediktbeuern* (BB) 121 ⅟₂ (AMB = Anastasia Miracle Book),
    123, 124, 137
Kurbayern Hofrat (HR) 93, 95, 103–106, 110–112, 117, 118, 121, 122–124, 128–131, 133,
    135–137, 139, 141, 143, 146, 148, 150, 152, 155, 157, 159, 161, 164, 166, 168, 170,
    172, 174, 175, 177, 180, 182, 184, 186, 189, 191, 193, 195, 197, 199, 200, 202, 203,
    205, 207, 209, 210, 212, 214, 215–217, 218, 219, 221, 223, 225, 227, 229–233, 235,
    238–241, 243–246, 248, 250–265, 266, 267–269, 271–276, 278–281, 283, 288–
    290, 292, 293, 295–299, 302–324, 326, 328–337, 339–344, 346–349, 351–369,
    371–373, 375–380, 454–457, 464, 467, 468, 484, 486.
Kurbayern Mandatensammlung 1599 X 4, 1599 IX 26, 1606 IX 9, 1613 IX 5, 1613 IX 24,
    1627 XI 19, 1630 II 6, 1634 VIII, 1649 XI 1, 1773 XI 2
Personenselekt Cart. 441
Rentmeister Literalien (RL) 26, 40, 80
Staatsverwaltung f. 2792

Bayerische Staatsbibliothek (BayStaBi)

Codex germanicus monacensis (Cgm) C. 207–245, 405, 1309, 2620, 5037
Codex latinus monacensis (Clm) 4731, 4757, 5250

Staatsarchiv München (StAM)

Briefprotokolle, Gericht Tölz, Hofmark Benediktbeuern
Pfleggericht Aibling B41
Pfleggericht Tölz, Gerichtsrechnung #39
Regierung van Oberbayen, (RA) Fasz. 278
Rentamt München (RM) Fasz. 278
Rentmeister Literalien (RL) 112

Stadtarchiv München (StdAM)

Heiliggeistspital (HGS) 281.
Heiliggeistspital (HGS) Rechnungsbücher 1657
Universitätsarchiv München (UAM)
LI 8, October 23, 1654.

324 *Bibliography*

PÜRTEN

Pfarrarchiv Pürten

Pürtner Mirakelbuch (PMB)

PUBLISHED PRIMARY SOURCES

Agricola, Sextus, and Georg Witmer, *Erschröckliche gantz warhafftige Geschicht welche sich mit Apolonia, Hannsen Geisslbrachts Burgers zu Spalt Haussfrauen . . .* (Ingolstadt, 1584).

Albertinus, Aegidius, *Christi Königreich und Seelengejaidt* (Munich, 1618).

Erschröckliche doch warhaffte Geschichte/ Die sich in der Spanischen Statt/ Madrileschos genannt/ mit einer verheuraten Weibsperson zugetragen/ welche von einer gantzen Legion Teuffel siben Jar lang besessen gewest (Munich, 1608).

Flagellum Diaboli, oder des Teufels Gaissl (Munich, 1602).

Der Fürsten und Potentaten Sterbekunst (Munich, 1599).

Gusman de Alfaryr (Munich, 1615).

Der Hirnschleifer (Munich, 1618).

Historia vom Ursprung/ auff abnemmen der Ketzereyen/ und was sie seyter Anno 1500 schief aller orten in der Welt . . . für wunderbarliche veränderungen/ weitläuffigkeiten/ jammer/ noth und höchste gefarlichekeiten verursacht (Munich, 1614).

Der Seelen-Compaß. Das ist: von den Vier letsten dingen deß Menschen: Vom Todt/ Jüngsten Gericht/ der Höllen und Ewigen Leben (Munich, 1617).

Von den Sonderbaren Geheimnusse deß Anti Christi (Munich, 1604).

Anonymous, *Denkwürdige Miracula . . . unser Lieben Frawen Gottshauß und Pfarrkirchen zu Tunderhausen* (Munich, 1646).

Anonymous, *Geistliche Artzney in Zeit der Pest, ansteckenden Kranckheiten, und betrübten Zeiten* (n.l., n.d.).

Anonymous, SJ, *Geistliches Trost-Büchlein/ . . . doch wegen unterschidlicher Zufäll und Scruplen geängstigte Seel trösten und auffmuntereren soll/ zu sonderbarem Trost und Hülff viler betrübten Gemüther* (Munich, 1699).

Anonymous, *Looke about you: The Plot of Contzen, the Moguntine Jesuite, to cheate a Church of the Religion Established therin and to serve in Popery by Art, without noise or tumult; As it is by him drawne out in his 18. and 19. Chapters of his second Booke of Politickes, Translated by a Catholicke Spy* (London, 1641).

Anonymous, *Newer Beichtform* (Munich, 1635).

Anonymous, *The political question, whether a wise ruling territorial prince can be indifferent about Gassner's cures without disadvantage to his subjects* (Munich, 1775).

Anonymous, *Die Sympathie, ein Universalmittel wider alle Teufeleyen* (Sterzingen im Tyrol, 1775).

Aristotle, *De anima* (New York, 1986).

Ay, Karl-Ludwig (ed.), *Dokumente zur Geschichte von Staat und Gesellschaft in Bayern. Abteilung I: Altbayern vom Frühmittelalter bis 1800*, 2 vols. (Munich, 1977), vol. II, *Altbayern von 1180–1550*.

Bacon, Francis, *The Advancement of Learning* (London, 1605).

Baradinus, Daniel, *Geistliche Artznei für Ketzergifft* (Munich, 1600).

Bauer, Robert (ed.), "Das älteste gedruckte Mirakelbüchlein von Altötting," *Ostbairische Grenzmarken. Passauer Jahrbuch für Geschichte, Kunst und Volkskunde* 5 (1961), 144–151.

(ed.), "Die Altöttinger Votivtafel," *Ostbairische Grenzmarken. Passauer Jahrbuch für Geschichte, Kunst und Volkskunde* 13 (1971), 176–183.

(ed.), "Das Büchlein der Zuflucht zu Maria. Altöttinger Mirakelberichte von Jacobus Issickemer," *Ostbairische Grenzmarken. Passauer Jahrbuch für Geschichte, Kunst und Volkskunde* 7 (1964/1965), 206–236.

(ed.), "P. Johannes Saller SJ – Das ausgegraben Oeting. Die Mirakelberichte 1623," *Ostbairische Grenzmarken. Passauer Jahrbuch für Geschichte, Kunst und Volkskunde* 35 (1993), 54–108.

Besold, Christoph, *Thesaurus Practicus* (Tübingen, 1624; Augusta Vindelicarum, 1641).

Biechler, Aemilian, *Bayerischer Pharos S. Anastasia von Gott in Obern-Bayern vor 600 Jahren in dem Closter Benedictbaiern angezündet . . .* (Augsburg, 1663; Munich, 1668; Munich, 1681; Munich, 1690).

Blumhardt, Johann Christoph, *Die Krankheitsgeschichte der Gottliebin Dittus*, ed. Gerhard Schäfer (Göttingen, 1978).

Boulaese, Jean, *Le Manuel de l'Admirable victoire du Corps de Dieu sur l'Esprit* (Paris, 1578).

Bucelin, Gabriel, *Germaniae Topo-Chrono-Stemmatographicae Sacrae et Profanae*, 4 vols. (Ulm, 1699).

Burton, Robert, *The Anatomy of Melancholy* (Oxford, 1621).

The Anatomy of Melancholy, 6 vols. (Oxford, 1989–2000).

Canisius, Peter, *Beati Petri Canisii, Societatis Iesu, epistulae et acta*, ed. Otto Braunsberger, 8 vols. (Freiburg, 1896–1923).

Beicht und Communion Büchlein (Dillingen, 1579).

Der kleine Catechismus (Ingolstadt, 1584).

Charcot, Jean-Martin, *Clinical Lectures on Diseases of the Nervous System*, ed. and trans. Ruth Harris (London, 1991).

Charcot, Jean-Martin and Richer, Paul, *Démoniaques dans l'art* (Paris, 1887).

Contzen, Adam, *Politicorum libri decem* (Mainz, 1620).

Corbeius, Theodorus, *Pathologia* (Noribergum, 1647).

Croll, Oswald, *Tractat von den innerlichen Signaturen oder Zeichen aller Dinge* (Frankfurt, 1623).

Del Rio, Martin, *Disquisitiones magicarum Libri Sex* (Antwerp, 1599–1600; Antwerp 1608; Mainz 1617).

Florida mariana (Antwerp, 1598).

Investigations into Magic, ed. and trans. P. G. Maxwell-Stuart (Manchester, 2000).

Denkwürdige Miracula und Wunderzaichen in Zwölff underschidliche Ordnungen außgethailt . . . zu Tundenhausen (Munich, 1646).

Descartes, René, *Oeuvres*, vol. XI, ed. Charles Adam and Paul Tannery (Paris, 1909).

    Les Passions de L'âme (Amsterdam, 1649).

Documentra rediviva monasteriorum Preacipuorum in Ducatu Würtenbergico sitorum (Tübingen, 1636).

Du Flail, Noël, *Contes et Discours d'Eutrapel* (1585) ed. Jules Assézt (Paris, 1874).

Eck, Johann, *Enchiridion* (Ingolstadt, 1529).

    De poenitentia et confessione secreta semper in Ecclesia Dei observata, contra Lutherum (Ingolstadt, 1533).

    Der viert tail Christlicher Predigen von den siben H. Sacramenten nach auß wesung Christlicher Kirchen und grund Byblischer gschrifft/ den alten frummen Christen zu gut (Ingolstadt, 1534).

Eisengrein, Martin, *Beichtbuch* (Ingolstadt, 1579).

    Trewherzige Vermanung an alle Catholische Christen/ das sie sich/ durch den Teuffel und seine Diener/ von der Beicht nit lassen abwendig machen (Ingolstadt, 1566).

    Unser Lieben Fraw zu Alten oetting (Ingolstadt, 1571).

Erasmus, Desiderius, *Praise of Folly*, trans. Betty Radice (London, 1993).

Feucht, Jacob, *Fünff kurtze Predige/ zur Zeit der grossen Theurung/ Hungersnot/ und Ungewitter . . .* (Cologne, 1573).

Freud, Sigmund, *Briefe an Wilhelm Fliess*, ed. Michael Schroter (Frankfurt am Main, 1986).

    Cocaine Papers, ed. Robert Byck (New York, 1974).

    The Complete Letters of Sigmund Freud to William Fliess (1887–1904), ed. Jeffrey Moussaieff-Masson (Cambridge, Mass., 1985).

    Gesammelte Werke, ed. Anna Freud, 19 vols. (London, 1952–1987).

    The Standard Edition of the Complete Psychological Works of Sigmund Freud, ed. James Strachey, 24 vols. (London, 1953–1974).

Freytag, Joannes, *Kurzer Bericht von der Melancholia Hypochondriaca* (Frankfurt am Main, 1643).

Geiler von Kaysersberg, Johann, *Das irrig Schaf. Sagt von kleinmütikeit und verzweiflung* (n.l., [Strasburg] *c.*1510).

Giustoboni, P. A., *Il medico spirituale al punto, aggiuntovi in questa impressione dallo stesso autore l'esorcista istrutto* (Milan, 1694).

Goclenius, Rudolf, ΨΥΧΟΛΟΓΙΑ: *hoc est de hominis perfectione, animo, ortu huius* (Marburg, 1594).

Gretser, Jacob, *De sacromento poenitentiae* (Ingolstadt, 1591).

Guarinonius, Hippolyt, *Die Grewel der Verwüstung Menschlichen Geschlechts . . .* (Ingolstadt, 1610).

Guerry, Phillip, SJ, *Philosophia universi* (Antwerp, 1738).

Hazlitt, William (ed. and trans.), *The Table Talks of Martin Luther* (London, 1895).

Hübner, Johann, *Geneologische Tabellen*, 4 vols. (Leipzig, 1728).

Ignatius of Loyola, *The Spiritual Exorcises of Ignatius Loyola*, ed. and trans. George E. Ganss, SJ (St. Louis, 1992).

On Witchcraft: An Abridged Translation of Johann Weyer's De Praestigiis Dae-monum, eds. and trans. Benjamin G. Kohl, H. C. Erik Midelfort and John Shea (Asheville, 1998).

Zedler, Johann Heinrich, *Grosses vollständiges Universal-Lexikon*, 68 vols. (Halle and Leipzig, 1732–1754; reprint: Graz, 1964).

Ziegler, Walter (ed.), *Dokumente zur Geschichte von Staat und Gesellschaft in Bayern. Abteilung I: Altbayern vom Frühmittelalter bis 1800*, vol. II: *Altbayern von 1550–1651* (Munich, 1992).

SECONDARY SOURCES

Albrecht, Dieter, *Maximilian I von Bayern 1573–1651* (Munich, 1998).

Anderson, Perry, *Lineages of the Absolutist State* (London, 1974).

Andree-Eysn, Marie, *Volkskundliches aus dem bayerisch-österreichischen Alpengebiet* (Braunschweig, 1910).

Ariew, Roger, "Descartes and Scholasticism: The Intellectual Background to Descartes' Thought," in: Cottingham, John (ed.), *The Cambridge Companion to Descartes* (Cambridge, 1992), 58–90.

Asch, Ronald G., *The Thirty Years War. The Holy Roman Empire and Europe, 1618–1648* (London, 1997).

Babb, Lawrence, *The English Malady. A Study of Melancholia in English Literature from 1580 to 1642* (East Lansing, 1951).

Bach, Hermann, "Mirakelbücher bayerischer Wallfahrtsorte (Untersuchung ihrer literarischen Form und ihrer Stellung innerhalb der Literatur der Zeit)" (unpublished Ph.D. dissertation, Munich, 1963).

Bächtold-Stäubli, Hanns (ed.), *Handwörterbuch des deutschen Aberglaubens*, 10 vols. (Berlin, 1935/1936; reprint: Augsburg, 2005).

Bähr, Andreas, *Der Richter im Ich. Die Semantik der Selbsttötung in der Aufklärung* (Göttingen, 2002).

Baker, Herschel, *The Image of Man: A Study of the Idea of Human Dignity in Classical Antiquity, the Middle Ages, and the Renaissance* (New York, 1961).

Baron, Hans, *In Search of Florentine Civic Humanism. Essays on the Transition from Medieval to Modern Thought* (Princeton, 1988).

Bary, Roswitha von, *Henriette Adelaide von Savoyen. Kurfürsten von Bayern* (Munich, 1980).

Bauerreiss, Romuald, OSB, *Kirchengeschichte Bayerns*, vol. VII (St. Ottilien, 1977).

Beck, Rainer, "Illegitimität und voreheliche Sexualität auf dem Land. Unterfinning, 1671–1770," in: Dülmen, Richard van (ed.), *Kultur der einfachen Leute. Bayrisches Volksleben vom 16. bis zum 19. Jahrhundert* (Munich, 1983), 112–150.

"Der Pfarrer und das Dorf. Konformismus und Eigensinn im katholischen Bayern des 17./18. Jahrhunderts," in: Dülmen, Richard van (ed.), *Armut, Liebe, Ehre. Studien zur historischen Kulturforschung* (Frankfurt am Main, 1988), 107–143.

Unterfinning. Ländliche Gesellschaft vor Anbruch der Moderne (Munich, 1993).

Becker, Constantin, "Thyraeus," in: *Dictionnaire de Spiritualité*, vol. xv (Paris, 1991), 913–916.

Beek, Henri Hubert, *De Geestesgestoorde in de Middeleeuwen. Beeld en Bemoeienis* (Haarlem, 1969), 184–186.

Behringer, Wolfgang, *Chonrad Stoecklin und die Nachtschar* (Munich, 1994).

    Mit dem Feuer vom Leben zum Tod. Hexengesetzgebung in Bayern (Munich, 1988).

    "Mörder, Diebe, Ehebrecher. Verbrechen und Strafen in Kurbayern vom 16. bis 18. Jahrhundert", in: Dülmen, Richard van (ed.), *Verbrechen, Strafen und soziale Kontrolle. Studien zur historischen Kulturforschung III* (Frankfurt am Main, 1990), 85–132, 287–293.

    Shaman of Oberstdorf: Chonrad Stoeckhlin and the Phantoms of the Night, trans. H. C. Erik Midelfort (Charlottesville, 1998).

    "Weather, Hunger and Fear: Origins of the European Witchhunts in Climate, Society and Mentality," *German History* 13 (1995), 1–27.

    Witchcraft Persecutions in Bavaria: Popular Magic, Religious Zealotry, and Reason of State in Early Modern Europe, trans. J. C. Grayson and David Lederer (Cambridge, 1997).

    "Witchcraft Studies in Austria, Germany and Switzerland," in: Barry, Jonathan, Hester, Marianne and Roberts, Gareth, *Witchcraft in Early Modern Europe: Studies in Culture and Belief* (Cambridge, 1996), 64–95.

Behringer, Wolfgang, Lehman, Hartmut and Pfister, Christian, *Kulturelle Konsequenzen der "Kleinen Eiszeit"* (Gottingen, 2005).

Beik, William, *Absolutism in Seventeenth-Century France. State Power and Provincial Aristocracy in Languedoc* (Cambridge, 1985).

Ben-Chorin, Schalom, "Die Polster, das Schwarzbrot und der Antisemitismus. Randbemerkungen zum Oberammergauer Passionsspiel," in: Henker, Michael, Dünninger, Eberhard and Brockhoff, Evamaria (eds.), *Hört, sehet, weint und liebt. Passionsspiele im alpenländischen Raum* (Munich, 1990), 215–220.

Berg, Karin, "Der ehemalige 'Bennobogen' der Münchner Frauenkirche," in: Glaser, Hubert (ed.), *Wittelsbach und Bayern II/1: Um Glauben und Reich. Kurfürst Maximilian I. Beiträge zur bayerischen Geschichte und Kunst 1573–1657* (Munich, 1980), 312–317.

Berggren, Erik, *The Psychology of Confession* (Leiden, 1975).

Berman, David, "Simon Browne: The Soul-Murdered Theologian," *History of Psychiatry* 7 (1996), 257–263.

Bierbrauer, Katharina, *Die vorkarolingischen und karolingischen Handschriften der bayerischen Staatsbibliothek* (Wiesbaden, 1990).

Bilinkoff, Jodi, "Confessors, Penitents, and the Construction of Identities in Early Modern Avila," in: Diefendorf, Barbara and Hesse, Carla, *Culture and Identity in Early Modern Europe (1500–1800). Essays in Honor of Natalie Zemon Davis* (Ann Arbor, 1993), 83–100.

Bireley, Robert, *The Counter-Reformation Prince. Anti-Machiavellism or Catholic Statecraft in Early Modern Europe* (Chapel Hill, 1990).

"Hofbeichtväter und Politik im 17. Jahrhundert," in: Sievernich, M. and Switek, G., *Ignatianisch. Eigenart und Methode der Gesellschaft Jesu* (Freiburg, 1990), 386–403.

Maximilian von Bayern, Adam Contzen, SJ und die Gegenreformation in Deutschland 1624–1635 (Göttingen, 1975).

Blackbourn, David, *The Marpingen Visions: Rationalism, Religion and the Rise of Modern Germany* (Oxford, 1993).

Blasius, Dirk, *"Einfache Seelenstörung". Geschichte der deutschen Psychiatrie 1800–1845* (Frankfurt am Main, 1994).

Blickle, Peter, *Deutsche Untertanen. Ein Widerspruch?* (Munich, 1981).

Obedient Germans? – A Rebuttal: New View of German History, trans. Thomas A. Brady (Charlottesville, 1998).

Böck, Robert, *Volksfrömmigkeit und Brauch. Studien zum Volksleben in Altbayern* (Munich, 1990), 19–59.

Boer, Wietse de, *The Conquest of the Soul. Confession, Discipline, and Public Order in Counter-Reformation Milan* (Leiden, 2001).

"The Politics of the Soul: Confession in Counter-Reformation Milan," in: Lualdi, Katherine Jackson and Thayer, Anne T. (eds.), *Penitence in the Age of Reformations* (Aldershot, 2000), 116–133.

Bosl, Karl (ed.), *Andechs: der heilige Berg; von der Frühzeit bis zum Gegenwart* (Munich, 1993).

Bayerische Geschichte (Munich, 1976).

Bossy, John, "The Social History of Confession in the Age of the Reformation," *Transactions of the Royal Historical Society* 25 (1975), 21–38.

Bouwsma, William, "The Two Faces of Humanism: Stoicism and Augustinianism in Renaissance Thought," in: Oberman, Heiko and Brady, Thomas (eds.), *Itinerarium Italicum* (Leiden, 1975), 3–60.

Boyer, Paul and Nissenbaum, Stephen, *Salem Possessed: The Social Origins of Witchcraft* (Cambridge, Mass., 1974).

Brandmüller, Walter (ed.), *Handbuch der bayerischen Kirchengeschichte*, 3 vols. (St. Ottilien, 1993).

Bräuning-Oktavio, Hermann, "Der Einfluss von Johann Heinrich Mercks Schicksal auf Goethes 'Faust' (1774) und 'Tasso' (1780/88)," *Jahrbuch des Freien Deutschen Hochstifts* (1962), 9–57.

Breit, Stefan, *"Leichtfertigkeit" und ländliche Gesellschaft. Voreheliche Sexualität in der frühen Neuzeit* (Munich, 1991).

Brenninger, Georg, "Passionsspiele in Altbayern," in: Henker, Michael, Dünninger, Eberhard and Brockhoff, Evamaria (eds.), *Hört, sehet, weint und liebt. Passionspiele im alpenländischen Raum* (Munich, 1990), 61–65.

Breuer, Dieter, "Hippolytus Guarinonius als Erzähler," in: Zeman, Herbert (ed.), *Die österreichische Literatur. Eine Dokumentation ihrer Literarhistorischen Entwicklung* (Graz, 1986), 1117–1133.

Broderick, James, SJ, *Petrus Canisius, 1521–1597* (Vienna, 1950).

Brosnahan, Timothy, "Casuistry," in: New Advent Encyclopedia online [http://www.newadvent.org/cathen/03415d.htm (accessed 10 December 2004)].

Brown, Peter, *The Cult of the Saints. Its Rise and Function in Latin Christianity* (Chicago, 1981).

Brückner, Wolfgang, "Beichte," in: *Lexikon für Theologie und Kirche*, vol. II (Freiburg, 1994), 157–159.

Brunner, Herbert, Hojer, Gerhard and Seelig, Lorenz, *Nympherburg: Residenz München* (Munchweiles, 1986).

Bücking, Jürgen, "Hippolytus Guarinonius (1571–1654), Pfalzgraf zu Hoffberg und Volderthurn," *Österreich in Geschichte und Literatur* 12 (1968), 65–80.

Kultur und Gesellschaft in Tirol um 1600. Des Hippolytus Guarinonius' "Grewel der Verwüstung Menschlichen Geschlechts" (1610) als kulturgeschichtliche Quelle des frühen 17. Jahrhunderts (Lübeck, 1968).

Burke, Peter, *The French Historical Revolution: The Annales School 1929–1989* (Stanford, 1990).

"How to be a Counter-Reformation Saint," in: Burke, *The Historical Anthropology of Early Modern Italy: Essays on Perception and Communication* (Cambridge, 1987), 48–62.

The Italian Renaissance: Culture and society in Italy (Oxford, 1986).

Burkardt, Albrecht, *Les clients de saints: maladie et quête du miracle à travers les procès de canonisation de la première moitié du XVIIe siècle en France* (Rome, 2004).

Buxbaum, Engelbert Maximilian, *Petrus Canisius und die kirchliche Erneuerung des Herzogtums Bayern, 1549–1556* (Rome, 1973).

Cameron, Euan, *The European Reformation* (Oxford, 1991).

Certeau, Michel de, *Heterologies. Discourse on the Other* (Minneapolis, 1986).

The Possession at Loudun, trans. Stephen Greenblatt (Chicago, 1996).

The Practice of Everyday Life (Berkeley, 1984).

The Writing of History (New York, 1988); originally published as *L'écriture de l'histoire* (Paris, 1975)

Chambers, Liam, "Defying Descartes: Michael Moore (1639–1726) and Aristotelian Philosophy in France and Ireland," in: Harrison, Stephen (ed.), *The Medieval World and the Modern Mind* (Dublin, 2001), 11–26.

Chartier, Roger, *Cultural History: Between Practices and Representations*, trans. Lydia G. Cochrane (Ithaca, 1988).

Chatellier, Louis, *The Europe of the Devout* (Cambridge, 1989).

Chmielowski, Alexandra, "Reformprojekt ohne Zukunft: Die Heilanstalt und psychiatrische Klinik in Heidelberg (1826–1835)," in: Engstrom, Eric J. and Roelcke, Volker (eds.), *Psychiatrie im 19. Jahrhundert. Forschungen zur Geschichte von psychiatrischen Institutionen, Debatten und Praktiken im deutschen Sprachraum* (Basle, 2003), 49–66.

Christian, William, *Local Religion in Sixteenth-Century Spain* (Princeton, 1981).

Clark, Stuart, *Thinking with Demons: The Idea of Witchcraft in Early Modern Europe* (Oxford, 1997).

Clasen, Claus-Peter, "The Anabaptists in Bavaria," *Mennonite Quarterly Review* 39 (1965), 243–261.

Cohen, Esther, "The Animated Pain of the Body," *American Historical Review* 105 (2000), 41–47.

Collins, James B., *The State in Early Modern France* (Cambridge, 1995).

Crouzet, Denis, "A Woman and the Devil: Possession and Exorcism in Sixteenth-Century France," in: Wolfe, Michael (ed.), *Changing Identities in Early Modern France* (Durham, N.C., 1997), 191–215.

Darnton, Robert, *Mesmerism and the End of the Enlightenment in France* (Cambridge, Mass., 1968).

Decker, Rainer, "Die Haltung der römischen Inquisition gegenüber Hexenglauben und Exorzismus am Beispiel der Teufelsaustreibungen in Paderborn in 1657," in: Lorenz, Sönke and Bauer, Dieter (eds.), *Das Ende der Hexenverfolgung* (Stuttgart, 1995), 97–116.

Delumeau, Jean, *Le catholicisme entre Luther et Voltaire* (Paris, 1970).
Fear in the West (New York, 1989).
Sin and Fear: The Emergence of a Western Guilt Culture 13th–18th Centuries (New York, 1990).

Demos, John Putnam, *Entertaining Satan: Witchcraft and the Culture of Early New England* (New York, 1982).

Deutscher, Thomas, "The Role of the Episcopal Tribunal of Novara in the Suppression of Heresy and Witchcraft, 1563–1615," *The Catholic Historical Review* 77 (1991), 403–421.

Diemer, Dorothea, "Hans Krumper," in: Glaser, Hubert (ed.), *Wittelsbach und Bayern II/1: Um Glauben und Reich. Kurfürst Maximilian I. Beiträge zur bayerischen Geschichte und Kunst 1573–1657* (Munich, 1980), 279–311.

Dotterweich, Heinz, *Der Junge Maximilian. Jugend und Erziehung des bayerischen Herzogs und späteren Kurfürsten Maximillian I. von 1573 bis 1593* (Munich, 1962; reprint: Munich, 1980).

Drewermann, Eugen, *Psychoanalyse und Moral Theologie 1: Angst und Schuld* (Mainz, 1982).

Duggan, Lawrence G., "Fear and Confession on the Eve of the Reformation," *Archive for Reformation History* 75 (1984), 153–175.

Duhr, Bernhard, SJ, "Zur Geschichte des Jesuitenordens. Aus Münchner Archiven und Bibliotheken," *Historisches Jahrbuch der Görresgesellschaft* 25 (1904), 126–67, and 28 (1907), 61–83.

Duhr, Bernhard, SJ, *Geschichte der Jesuiten in den Ländern deutscher Zunge*, 4 vols. (Freiburg, 1907–1913)
"Eine Teufelsaustreibung in Altötting," *Beiträge zur Geschichte der Renaissance und Reformation. Festschrift für Joseph Schlecht* (Munich, 1917), 63–76.

Dülmen, Richard van, "Fest der Liebe: Heirat und Ehe in der frühen Neuzeit," in: van Dülmen, *Armut, Liebe und Ehre. Studien zur historischen Kulturforschanged* (Frankfurt am Main, 1988).
Der Geheimbund der Illuminaten. Darstellung, Analyse, Dokumentation (Stuttgart, 1975).
"Die Gesellschaft Jesu und der bayerische Späthumanismus," *ZBLG* 37 (1974), 358–415.

"Imaginationen des Teuflischen. Nächtliche Zusammenkünfte, Hexentänze, Teufelssabbate," in: van Dülmen (ed.), *Hexenwelten. Magie und Imagination* (Frankfurt am Main, 1987), 94–130.

Theater of Horror. Crime and Punishment in Early Modern Germany (Cambridge, 1991).

Dürr, Renate, *Mägde in der Stadt. Das Beispiel Schwäbisch Hall in der Frühen Neuzeit* (Frankfurt am Main, 1995).

Eco, Umberto, *The Island of the Day Before* (New York, 1995).

Eichhorn, Gertraud K., *Beichtzettel und Bürgerrecht in Passau 1570–1630. Die administrativen Praktiken der Passauer Gegenreformation und den Fürstbischöfen Urban von Trenbach und Leopold I., Erzherzog von Österreich* (Passau, 1997).

Elias, Norbert, *Court society* (New York, 1983).

Ellenberger, Henri F., *The Discovery of the Unconscious. The History and Evolution of Dynamic Psychiatry* (New York, 1970).

Ellington, Donna Spivey, *From Sacred Body to Angelic Soul: Understanding Mary in Late Medieval and Early Modern Europe* (Washington, DC, 2002).

Elton, Geoffrey R., "Crime and the Historian," in: Cockburn, J. S. (ed.), *Crime in England, 1550–1800* (Princeton, 1977), 1–14.

Engstrom, Eric J. and Roelcke, Volker (eds.), *Psychiatrie im 19. Jahrhundert. Forschungen zur Geschichte von psychiatrischen Institutionen, Debatten und Praktiken im deutschen Sprachraum* (Basle, 2003).

Erikson, Erik, *Young Man Luther* (New York, 1958).

Ernst, Cecile, *Teufelsaustreibungen. Die Praxis der katholischen Kirche im 16. und 17. Jahrhundert* (Berne, 1972).

Esguerra, Jorge Cañizares, "New World, New Stars: Patriotic Astrology and the Invention of Indian and Creole Bodies in Colonial Spanish America, 1600–1650," *American Historical Review* 104 (1999), 33–68.

Evans, Robert John Weston, *Rudolf II and his World. A Study in Intellectual History, 1576–1612* (Oxford, 1973).

Febvre, Lucien, "Aspects méconnus d'un renouveau religieux en France entre 1590 et 1620," *Annales d'histoire économique et sociale* 13 (1958), 639–650.

The Problem of Unbelief in the Sixteenth Century: The Religion of Rabelais (Cambridge, Mass., 1983).

Ferber, Sarah "Charcot's Demons. Retrospecive Medicine and Historical Diagnosis in the Writings of the Salpêtrière School," in: Gijswifjt-Hofstra, Marijke, Marland, Hilary and de Waardt, Hans, *Illness and Healing Alternatives in Western Europe* (London, 1997), 120–141

Demonic Possession and Exorcism in Early Modern France (London, 2004).

"Reformed or Recycled? Possession and Exorcism in the Sacramental Life of Early Modern France," in: Edwards, Kathryn (ed.), *Witches, Werewolves and Wandering Spirits* (Kirksville, 2002), 58–59.

Ferchl, Georg, *Bayerische Behörden und Beamte 1550–1804* (Munich, 1908–1910).

Fleischer, Manfred P., "'Are Women Human?' – The Debate of 1595 between Valens Acidalius and Simon Gediccus," in: *The Sixteenth Century Journal* 12 (1981), 107–120.

Florey, Ernst, *Ars magnetica. Franz Anton Mesmer 1734–1815, Magier vom Bodensee* (Constance, 1995).

Forster, Marc R., *Catholic Revival in the Age of the Baroque: Religious Identity in Southwest Germany, 1550–1750* (Cambridge, 2001).

The Counter Reformation in the Villages: Religion and Reform in the Bishopric of Speyer, 1560–1720 (Ithaca, 1992).

Foucault, Michel, *Histoire de la Folie* (Paris, 1961).

The History of Sexuality, vol. I: An Introduction (New York, 1980).

Madness and Civilization. A History of Insanity in the Age of Reason (New York, 1965).

"The Politics of Health in the Eighteenth Century," in: Foucault, *Power/Knowledge: Selected Interviews and Other Writings, 1972–1977* (New York, 1980), 166–182.

Freitag, Werner, *Volks- und Elitenfrömmigkeit in der Frühen Neuzeit. Marienwallfahrten im Fürstbistum Münster* (Paderborn, 1991).

Frick, Alex, *Häuserbuch von Sigmaringen* (Sigmaringen, 1971).

Friedman, Saul S., *The Oberammergau Passion Play: A Lance against Civilization* (Carbondale, 1984).

Gareis, Balthasar, *Psychotherapie und Beichte* (St. Ottilien, 1988).

Gaukroger, Stephen, *Descartes. An Intellectual Biography* (Oxford, 1995).

Gay, Peter, *Freud. A Life for our Times* (London, 1988).

Geary, Patrick, *Furta Sacra. Thefts of Relics in the Central Middle Ages* (Princeton, 1990).

Gelder, Michael, Gath, Dennis and Mayou, Richard, *Concise Oxford Textbook of Psychiatry* (Oxford, 1994).

Gellner, Ernst, *The Psychoanalytic Movement or the Cunning of Unreason* (London, 1985).

Gemert, Guillaume van, "Tridentinische Geistigkeit und Moraldidaxis in Guarinonius' 'Grewel'. Der Artzt als geistlicher Autor," in: Locher, Elmar (ed.), *Hippolytus Guarinonius im interkulturellen Kontext seiner Zeit* (Bozen, 1995), 45–64.

Die Werke des Aegidius Albertinus (1560–1620). Ein Beitrag zur Erforschung des deutschsprachigen Schrifttums der katholischen Reformbewegung in Bayern um 1600 und seiner Quellen (Amsterdam, 1979).

Gentilcore, David, *From Bishop to Witch: The System of the Sacred in Early Modern Terra d'Otranto* (Manchester, 1992).

"Contesting Illness in Early Modern Naples: Miracolati and the Congregation of Rites," *Past and Present* 148 (1994), 117–148.

"The Fear of Disease and the Disease of Fear," in: Naphy, William and Roberts, Penny (eds.), *Fear in Early Modern Society* (Manchester, 1997), 184–208.

Healers and Healing in Early Modern Italy (Manchester, 1998).

Bibliography

Gierl, Irmgard, *Bauernleben und Bauernwallfahrt in Altbayern. Eine kulturkundliche Studie auf Grund der Tuntenhausen Mirakel-Bücher* (Munich, 1960).

Gijswijt-Hofstra, Marijke, Marland, Hilary and Waardt, Hans de, *Illness and Healing Alternatives in Western Europe* (London, 1997).

Ginzburg, Carlo, *The Cheese and the Worms: The Cosmos of a Sixteenth-Century Miller* (New York, 1980).

   Night Battles (Baltimore, 1983).

Glaser, Hubert (ed.), *Wittelsbach und Bayern II/1: Um Glauben und Reich. Kurfürst Maximilian I. Beiträge zur bayerischen Geschichte und Kunst 1573–1657* (Munich, 1980).

Goldberg, Ann, *Sex, Religion, and the Making of Modern Madness: The Eberbach Asylum and German society 1815–1849* (Oxford, 1999).

Goldstein, Jan, *Console and Classify. The French Psychiatric Profession in the Nineteenth Century* (Cambridge, 1987).

Goleman, Daniel, *Destructive Emotions: How Can We Overcome Them?: A Scientific Dialogue with the Dalai Lama* (New York, 2003). .

Greenaway, Peter, *The Baby of Macon* (Darwin, 1993).

Greenblatt, Stephen, *Marvelous Possessions: The Wonder of the New World* (Chicago, 1991).

Grell, Ole Peter and Cunningham, Andrew, "Medicine and Religion in Seventeenth-Century England," in Grell and Cunningham, *Religio Medici: Medicine and Religion in Seventeenth Century England* (Aldershot, 1996).

   (eds.), *Religio Medici: Medicine and Religion in Seventeenth Century England* (Aldershot, 1996).

Grimmelshausen, Hans Jacob Christoffe von, *Der abenteuerliche Simplicissimus* (Stuttgart, 1970).

Gutting, Gary, "Foucault and the History of Madness," in: Gutting, *The Cambridge Companion to Foucault* (Cambridge, 1994), 47–70.

Guttman, Samuel, Jones, Randall and Parrish, Stephen, *The Concordance to the Standard Edition of the Complete Psychological Works of Sigmund Freud,* 6 vols. (Boston, 1980).

Habermas, Rebekka, *Wallfahrt und Aufruhr. Zur Geschichte des Wunderglaubens in der frühen Neuzeit* (Frankfurt am Main, 1991).

   "Wunder, Wunderliches, Wunderbares: Zur Profanisierung eines Deutungsmusters in der frühen Neuzeit," in: Dülmen, Richard van (ed.), *Armut, Liebe und Ehre: Studien zur historischen Kulturgeschichte* (Frankfurt am Main, 1988), 38–66.

Haemig, Mary Jane, "Communication, Consolation and Discipline: Two Early Lutheran Preachers on Confession," in: Lualdi, Katherine Jackson and Thayer, Anne T. (eds.), *Penitence in the Age of Reformations* (Aldershot, 2000), 30–48.

Hahn, Alois, "Zur Soziologie der Beichte und anderer Formen institionalisierter Bekenntnisse: Selbstthematisierung und Zivilizationsprozess," *Kölner Zeitschrift für Soziologie und Sozialpsychologie* 34 (1982), 407–434.

Haliczer, Stephen, *Sexuality in the Confessional. A Sacrament Profaned* (Oxford, 1996).

Halm, Philipp, "Die Mirakelbilder zu Altöting," *Bayerischer Heimatschutz* (1925), 1–27.

Harley, David, "Spiritual Physic, Providence and English Medicine, 1560–1640," in: Grell, Ole Peter and Cunningham, Andrew (eds.), *Medicine and the Reformation* (London, 1993), 101–117.

Harvolk, Edgar, *Votivtafeln* (Munich, 1979).

Hatfield, Gary, "Descartes' Physiology and its Relation to his Psychology," in: Cottingham, John (ed.), *The Cambridge Companion to Descartes* (Cambridge, 1992), 334–370.

Heil, Dietmar, *Die Reichspolitik Bayerns unter der Regierung Herzog Albrechts V. (1550–1579)* (Munich, 1999).

Heiss, Gernot, "Konfessionelle Propaganda und kirchliche Magie. Berichte der Jesuiten über den Teufel aus der Zeit der Gegenreformation in den mitteleuropäischen Länder der Habsburger," *Römische Historische Mitteilungen* 32 and 33 (1990/1991), 122–125.

Helm, Jürgen, "Die Galenrezeption in Philipp Melanchthons De anima (1540/1552)," *Medizinhistorisches Journal* 31 (1996), 891–902.

Hemmerle, Josef, *Die Benediktinerabtei Benediktbeuern* (Berlin, 1991).

Henker, Michael, Dünninger, Eberhard and Brockhoff, Evamaria (eds.), *Hört, sehet, weint und liebt. Passionspiele im alpenländischen Raum* (Munich, 1990).

Henshall, Nicholas, *The Myth of Absolutism* (London, 1992).

Heydenreuter, Richard, *Der Landesherrliche Hofrat unter Herzog und Kurfürst Maximilian I. von Bayern (1598–1651)* (Munich, 1981).

Hofman, Philip, *Church and Community in the Diocese of Lyon 1500–1789* (New Haven, 1984).

Hofmeister, Alexander, *Das Medizinalwesen im Kurfürstentum Bayern* (Munich, 1975).

Hojer, Gerhard and Schmid, Elmar, *Nymphenburg* (Munich, 1991).

Hörger, Hermann, "Geistliche Grundherrschaft und nachtridentinisches Frömmigkeitsbedürfnis. Die Abtei Benediktbeuern im Kampf gegen das Eremitorium Walchensee (1687–1725)," *ZBLG* 47 (1978), 69–84.
Kirche, Dorfreligion und bäuerliche Gesellschaft: Struktur-analysen zur gesellschaftsgebundenen Religiosität ländlicher Unterschichten des 17. bis 19. Jahrhunderts, aufgezeigt an bayerischen Beispielen, 2 vols. (Munich, 1978/1983).

Houston, R. A., *Madness and society in Eighteenth-Century Scotland* (Oxford, 2000).

Hsia, Ronnie Po-Chia, *The Myth of Ritual Murder: Jews and Magic in Reformation Germany* (1988).
Society and Religion in Münster 1535–1618 (New Haven, 1982).
Trent 1475: Stories of a Ritual Murder Trial (New Haven, 1992).
The World of the Catholic Renewal 1540–1770 (Cambridge, 1998).

Hubensteiner, Benno, "Maximilian I" in: Glaser, Hubert (ed.), *Wittelsbach und Bayern II/1: Um Glauben und Reich. Kurfürst Maximilian I. Beiträge zur bayerischen Geschichte und Kunst 1573–1657* (Munich, 1980), 185–195.

Huber, Otto, Klinner, Helmut and Lang, Dorothea, "Die Passionsaufführungen in Oberammergau in 101 Anmerkungen," in: Henker, Michael, Dünninger, Eberhard and Brockhoff, Evamaria (eds.), *Hört, sehet, weint und liebt. Passionspiele im alpenländischen Raum* (Munich, 1990), 163–180.

Hubula, Erich, "Vom europäischen Rang der Münchner Architektur um 1600," in: Glaser, Hubert (ed.), *Wittelsbach und Bayern II/1: Um Glauben und Reich. Kurfürst Maximilian I. Beiträge zur bayerischen Geschichte und Kunst 1573–1657* (Munich, 1980), 141–151.

Huhn, Adalbert, *Geschichte des Spitales, der Kirche und der Pfarrei zum Heiligen Geist in München* (Munich, 1893).

Hull, Isabel, *Sexuality, State, and Civil Society in Germany, 1700–1815* (Cornell, 1996).

Hunt, Morton, *The Story of Psychology* (New York, 1994).

Hunter, Richard and MacAlpine, Ida (eds.), *Memoirs of my Nervous Illness* (Cambridge, Mass., 1988).

(eds.), *Schizophrenia 1677. A Psychiatric Study of an Illustrated Autobiographical Record of Demoniacal Possession* (London, 1956).

(eds.), *Three Hundred Years of Psychiatry 1535–1860* (London, 1963).

Hüttl, Ludwig, *Max Emanuel. Der Blaue Kurfürst 1679–1726* (Munich, 1976).

Imhof, Arthur (ed.), *Historische Demographie als Sozialgeschichte: Giessen und Umgebung vom 17. Zum 19. Jahrhundert* (Darmstadt, 1975).

The International Classification of Diseases and the Diagnostic and Statistical Manual of Mental Disorders (DSM IV) (Washington, 1994).

Jedin, Hubert, *Geschichte des Konzils von Trient*, vol. III (Freiburg, 1970).

Jetter, Dieter, *Grundzüge der Geschichte des Irrenhauses* (Darmstadt, 1981).

Jöcher, Christian Gottlieb, *Allgemeines Gelehrten-Lexicon*, 4 vols. (Leipzig, 1750/1751).

Jones, Ernest, *The Life and Work of Sigmund Freud*, 2 vols. (New York, 1953).

Jung, Carl G., *Psychologische Typen* (Zurich, 1921; reprint: Düsseldorf, 1995).

Jungmann, Josef Andreas, SJ, *Die lateinischen Bußriten in ihrer geschichtlichen Entwicklung* (Innsbruck, 1932).

Jütte, Robert, *Ärzte und Patienten in der frühen Neuzeit* (Munich, 1991).

Poverty and Deviance in Early Modern Europe (Cambridge, 1994).

Kamen, Henry, *European society 1500–1700* (London, 1992).

The Iron Century (London, 1971)

Kapferer, Bruce, *A Celebration of Demons: Exorcism and the Aesthetics of Healing in Sri Lanka* (Bloomington, 1983).

Kaplan, Benjamin, *Calvinists and Libertines. Confession and Community in Utrecht, 1578–1620* (Oxford, 1995).

"Possessed by the Devil? A Very Public Dispute in Utrecht," *Renaissance Quarterly* 49 (1996), 738–759.

Karant-Nunn, Susan, *The Reformation of Ritual: An Interpretation of Early Modern Germany* (London, 1997).

Karlsen, Carol F., *The Devil in the Shape of a Woman: Witchcraft in Colonial New England* (New York, 1987).

Kaufmann, Doris, *Aufklärung, bürgerliche Selbsterfahrung und die "Erfindung" der Psychiatrie in Deutschland, 1770–1850* (Göttingen, 1995).

Kirmeier, Josef and Treml, Manfred (eds.), *Glanz und Ende der Alten Klöster. Säkularisation im bayerischen Oberland 1803* (Munich, 1991).

Klaniczay, Gabor, "Legends as Life-Strategies for Aspirant Saints in the Later Middle Ages," in: Klaniczay, *The Uses of Supernatural Power: The Transformation of Popular Religion in Medieval and Early-Modern Europe* (Princeton, 1990), 95–111.

Klibansky, Raymond, Panofsky, Erwin and Saxl, Fritz, *Saturn and Melancholy: Studies in the History of Natural Philosophy, Religion and Art* (New York, 1964).

Kneschke, Enrst Heinrich, *Neues allgemeines deutsches Adels-Lexicon*, 9 vols. (Leipzig, 1870; reprint: Neustadt an der Aische, 1995–1996).

Knöpfler, Alois, *Die Kelchbewegung in Bayern unter Herzog Albrecht V* (Munich, 1891).

Köhle, Jasmine, *Der Narrenturm in Wien oder das Pardigma des Wahnsinns* (Vienna, 1991).

König, Maria Angela, *Weihegaben an U. L. Frau von Altötting vom Beginn der Wallfahrt bis zum Abschluss der Säkularisation* (Munich, 1939).

Koslofsky, Craig, *The Reformation of the Dead. Death and Ritual in Early Modern Europe, 1450–1700* (London, 2000).

Krah, Ursula, "'Vom boesen Feindt / dem Teuffel / eingenommen . . .': Das Motiv der Besessenheit in Flugschriften der Frühen Neuzeit," in: Waardt, Hans de, Schmidt, Jürgen Michael and Bauer, Dieter (eds.), *Dämonische Besessenheit. Zur Interpretation eines kulturhistorischen Phänomens* (Bielefeld, 2005), 141–154.

Kramer, K. S., "Die Mirakelbücher der Wallfahrt Grafath," *Bayerisches Jahrbuch für Volkskunde* (1951), 80–102.

"Ein Mirakelbuch der heiligen Anastasia in Benediktbeuern," *Bayerisches Jahrbuch für Volkskunde* (1991), 111–136.

Kraus, Andreas, *Maximilian I. Bayerns Großer Kurfürst* (Regensburg, 1990).

Die naturwissenschaftliche Forschung an der Bayerischen Akademie der Wissenschaften im Zeitalter der Aufklärung (Munich, 1978).

Kriedte, Peter, *Peasants, Landlords, and Merchant Capitalists: Europe and the World Economy, 1500–1800* (Cambridge, 1983).

Kriss-Rettenbeck, Lenz, *Bilder und Zeichen Religiösen Volksglauben* (Munich, 1971).

Ex Voto. Zeichen, Bild, und Abbild im christlichen Votivbrauchtum (Munich, 1972).

Das Votivbild (Munich, 1958).

Kuhn, Thomas S., *The Structure of Scientific Revolutions* (Chicago, 1962).

Kutzer, Michael, *Anatomie des Wahnsinns. Geisteskrankheit im medizinischen Denken der frühen Neuzeit und die Anfänge der pathologischen Anatomie* (Hürtgenwald, 1998).

"'Psychiker' als 'Somatiker' – 'Somatiker' als 'Psychiker': Zur Frage der Gültigkeit psychiatriehistorischer Kategorien," in: Engstrom, Eric J. and Roelcke, Volker (eds.), *Psychiatrie im 19. Jahrhundert. Forschungen zur Geschichte von psychiatrischen Institutionen, Debatten und Praktiken im deutschen Sprachraum* (Basle, 2003), 27–48.

Labouvie, Eva, *Andere Umstände. Eine Kulturgeschichte der Geburt* (Vienna, 1998).

Landersdorfer, Anton, *Das Bistum Freising in der bayerischen Landesvisitation des Jahres 1560* (St. Ottilien, 1986).

Lang, Gottfried O., *"Die Wechselwirkung wirtschaftlicher und nicht wirtschaftlicher Faktoren im Fortbestand der Oberammergauer Passionsspiele,"* in: Henker, Michael, Dünninger, Eberhard and Brockhoff, Evamaria (eds.), *Hört, sehet, weint und liebt. Passionsspiele im alpenländischen Raum* (Munich, 1990), 203–210.

Larner, Christina, *Enemies of God: The Witch-Hunt in Scotland* (Baltimore, 1981).

Le Goff, Jacques, *The Birth of Purgatory* (Aldershot, 1984).

Lea, Henry Charles, *History of Auricular Confession and Indulgences in the Latin Church*, 3 vols. (Philadelphia, 1896).

Lederer, David, "Aufruhr auf dem Friedhof. Pfarrer, Gemeinde und Selbstmord im frühneuzeitlichen Bayern," in: Signori, Gabriela (ed.), *Trauer, Verzweiflung und Anfechtung. Selbstmord und Selbstmordversuche in mittelalterlichen und frühneuzeitlichen Gesellschaften* (Tübingen, 1994), 189–209.

"Bernhard Frey," in: Golden, Richard (ed.), *Encyclopedia of Witchcraft: The Western Tradition* (Santa Barbara, 2005).

"De cultuurgeschiedenis van de zelfdoding in Vlaanderen: een uitdaging," *Archiefink* 2 (2002), 4–5.

"The Dishonorable Dead: Elite and Popular Perceptions of Suicide in Early Modern Germany," in: Backmann, Sibylle, Künast, Hans-Jörg, Tlusty, B. Ann and Ullmann, Sabine (eds.), *Das Konzept der Ehre in der Frühen Neuzeit* (Augsburg, 1998), 347–363.

"Die Geburt eines Irrenhauses: Die königlich-bayerische Irrenanstalt zu Giesing/München," in: Engstrom, Eric J. and Roelcke, Volker (eds.), *Psychiatrie im 19. Jahrhundert. Forschungen zur Geschichte von psychiatrischen Institutionen, Debatten und Praktiken im deutschen Sprachraum* (Basle, 2003), 67–94.

"Living with the Dead: Ghosts in Early Modern Bavaria," in: Edwards, Kathryn (ed.), *Witches, Werewolves and Wandering Spirits* (Kirksville, 2002), 25–53.

"Pact with the Devil," in: Golden, Richard (ed.), *Encyclopedia of Witchcraft: The Western Tradition* (Santa Barbara, 2005).

"Popular Culture," in: Jonathan Dewald (ed.), *Europe 1450–1789: Encyclopedia of the Early Modern World* (New York, 2004), 1–9.

"Selbstmord im frühneuzeitlichen Deutschland: Klischee und Geschichte," *Psychotherapie* 4 (1999), 196–202.

"Verzweiflung im Alten Reich. Selbstmord während der kleinen Eiszeit," in: Behringer, Wolfgang, Lehman, Hartmut and Pfister, Christian, *Kulturelle Konsequenzen der kleinen Eiszeit* (Göttingen, 2005), 255–280.

"'. . . welches die Oberkeit bey Gott zuverantworten hat.' Selbstmord im Kerker während der frühen Neuzeit," *Comparativ* 5/6 (2003), 177–188.

Lehmann, Hartmut, "Frömmigkeitsgeschichtliche Auswirkungen der Kleinen Eiszeit," in: Schieder, Wolfgang (ed.), *Volksreligiosität in der modernen Sozialgeschichte* (Göttingen, 1986), 31–50.

Leibbrand, Werner and Wettley, Annemarie, *Der Wahnsinnn. Geschichte der abendländischen Psychopathologie* (Freiburg, 1961).

Levack, Brian P., *The Witch-Hunt in Early Modern Europe* (London, 1987).

Levi, Anthony, SJ, *French Moralists. The Theory of the Passions 1585–1649* (Oxford, 1964).

Levi, Giovanni, *Inheriting Power: The Story of an Exorcist*, trans. Lydia G. Cochrane (Chicago, 1988).

Lewis, C. S., *The Discarded Image* (Cambridge, 1964).

Lewis, I. M., *Ecstatic Religion: An Anthropological Study of Spirit Possession and Shamanism* (Harmondsworth, 1971).

Liliencron, Rochus Freiherr von, "Albertinus, Aegidius", ADB vol. I (Leipzig, 1875), 217–219.

Lind, Vera, *Selbstmord in der Frühen Neuzeit: Diskurs, Lebenswelt und kultureller Wandel am Beispiel der Herzogtümer Schleswig und Holstein* (Göttingen, 1999).

Lindemann, Mary, *Medicine and society in Early Modern Europe* (Cambridge, 1999).

Lischka, Marion, "Der Mensch zwischen Humanismus und Reformation. Die Anthropologie Philipp Melanchthons und ihre Bedeutung im Zeitalter der Konfessionalisierung" (MA thesis, Bochum University, 1993).

Lothane, Zvi, *In Defense of Schreber: Soul Murder and Psychiatry* (Hillsdale, 1992).

Low, David B., "Religious Affects in Spinoza: A Topology of Emotions Understood as a System of Spirituality" (Ph.D. dissertation, Temple University, 1998).

MacDonald, Michael, *Mystical Bedlam: Madness, Anxiety, and Healing in Seventeenth-Century England* (Cambridge, 1981).

"Religion, Social Change, and Psychological Healing in England, 1600–1800," in: Sheils, W. J. (ed.), *The Church and Healing* (Oxford, 1982), 101–126.

MacDonald, Michael and Murphy, Terence, *Sleepless Souls. Suicide in Early Modern England* (Oxford, 1994).

Macfarlane, Alan, *Witchcraft in Tudor and Stuart England* (London, 1970).

Mahal, Günther, "Fünf Faust-Splitter aus drei Jahrhunderten," *Bausteine zur Tübinger Universitätsgeschichte* 1 (1981), 98–121.

Maher, Winifred Barbara and Maher, Brendan, "The Ship of Fools: *Stultifera Navis* or *Ignis Fatuus?*," *American Psychologist* 37 (July 1982), 756–761.

Malone, Dumas (ed.), *Dictionary of American Biography* (New York, 1933).

Mandrou, Robert, *Introduction to Modern France 1500–1640: An Essay in Historical Psychology*, trans. R. E. Hallmark (London, 1975).

Magistrats et sorciers en France au XVIIe siècle: une analyse de psychologie historique (Paris, 1980).

Matejovski, Dirk, *Das Motiv des Wahnsinns in der mittelalterlichen Dichtung* (Frankfurt an Main, 1996).

Mathäser, Willibald, O S B., *Andechser Chronik* (Munich, 1979).

Mauer, Benedikt, *"Gemain Geschrey" und "teglich Reden". Georg Koelderer – ein Augsburger Chronist des konfessionellen Zeitalters* (Augsburg, 2001).

Mayer, Anton and Westermayer, Georg, *Statistische Beschreibung des Erzbisthums München-Freising*, vol. II (Regensburg, 1880), 161–167.

Meinecke, Friedrick, *Die Idee der Staatsräson in der neueren Geschichte* (Munich, 1976).

Midelfort, H. C. Erik, "Catholic and Lutheran Reactions to Demon Possession in the Late Seventeenth Century: Two Case Histories," *Daphnis* 15 (1986), 623–648.

"Charcot, Freud and the Demons," in: Edwards, Kathryn (ed.), *Witches, Werewolves and Wandering Spirits* (Kirksville, 2002), 199–215.

"The Devil and the German People: Reflections on the Popularity of Demon Possession in Sixteenth Century Germany," in: Ozment, Steven, *Religion and Culture in the Renaissance and Reformation* (Kirksville, 1989), 98–119.

Exorcism and Enlightenment: Johann Joseph Gassner and the Demons of Eighteenth-Century Germany (New Haven, 2005).

A History of Madness in Sixteenth-Century Germany (Stanford, 1999).

"Johann Weyer and the Transformation of the Insanity Defense," in: Hsia, Ronnie Po-Chia, *The German People and the Reformation* (Ithaca, 1988), 234–262.

The Mad Princes of Renaissance Germany (Charlottesville, 1994).

"Madness and the Problems of Psychological History in the Sixteenth Century," *Sixteenth Century Journal* 12 (1981), 5–12.

"Sin, Melancholy, Obsession: Insanity and Culture in 16th Century Germany," in: Kaplan, Steven L. (ed.), *Understanding Popular Culture* (New York, 1984), 113–145.

Witch-Hunting in Southwest Germany, 1562–1684: The Social and Intellectual Foundations (Stanford, 1972).

Miller, Uwe, "Der Versuch Herzog William V. von Bayern, das Reichsheiltum in seine Besitz zu bringen," *Mitteilungen des Vereins für Geschichte der Stadt Nürnberg* 72 (1985), 117–135.

Minois, Georges, *History of Suicide: Voluntary Death in Western Culture* (Baltimore, 1999).

Mitterauer, Michael, "Gesindedienst und Jugendphase im europäischen Vergleich," *Geschichte und Gesellschaft* 11 (1985), 177–204.

Ledige Mutter. Zur Geschichte illegitimer Geburten in Europa (Munich, 1983).

Modell, Arnold H., "Affects: Freud's Theory," in: Wolman, Benjamin B. (ed.), *International Encyclopedia of Psychiatry, Psychoanalysis and Neurology* (New York, 1977), 299–303.

Monter, William, "The Historiography of European Witchcraft: Progress and Prospects," *Journal of Interdisciplinary History* 2 (1971/1972), 435–453.

Witchcraft in France and Switzerland: The Borderlands during the Reformation (London, 1976).

Morford, Mark, *Stoics and Neostoics. Rubens and the Circle of Lipsius* (Princeton, 1991).

Moser-Rath, Elfriede, *Dem Kirchenvolk die Leviten Gelesen. Alltag im Spiegel süddeutscher Barockpredigten* (Stuttgart, 1991).

Müller, Rainer A., *Universität und Adel. Eine soziostrukturelle Studie zur Geschichte der bayerischen Landesuniversität Ingolstadt 1472–1648* (Berlin, 1974).

Müller, Winfried, "*Hofbeichtväter und geistliche Ratgeber zur Zeit der Gegenreformation,*" in: Müller (ed.), *Universität und Bildung* (Munich, 1991), 141–155.

Murray, Alexander, "Confession as a Historical Source in the Thirteenth Century," in: Davis, R. H. C. and Wallace-Hadrill, J. M. (eds.), *The Writing of History in the Middle Ages. Essays Presented to Richard William Southern* (Oxford, 1981), 275–322.

Suicide in the Middle Ages, vol. I: The Curse on Self-Murder (Oxford, 2000).

Murray, David J., *A History of Western Psychology* (Englewood Cliffs, 1988).

Myers, W. David, "*Poor Sinning Folk*": *Confession and Conscience in Counter-Reformation Germany* (Ithaca, 1996).

Neumaier, Klaus, *Ius Publicum. Studium zur barocken Rechtsgelerhsamkeit an der Universität Ingolstadt* (Berlin, 1974).

Nowosadtko, Jutta, *Scharfrichter und Abdecker. Der Alltag zweier "unehrlicher Berufe" in der Frühen Neuzeit* (Paderborn, 1994).

O'Neil, Mary R., "Sacerdote ovvero strione: Ecclesiastical and Superstitious Remedies in 16th Century Italy," in: Kaplan, Steven L. (ed.), *Understanding Popular Culture* (New York, 1984), 53–84.

Oestreich, Gerhard, *Neostoicism and the Early Modern State*, ed. Brigitta Oestreich and Helmut Georg Koenigsberger, trans. David McLintock (Cambridge, 1982).

Ogilvie, Sheilagh, "How Does Social Capital Affect Women? Guilds and Communities in Early Modern Germany," *American Historical Review* 109 (2004), 325–359.

Oswald, Julius, SJ and Rummel, Peter (eds.), *Petrus Canisius – Reformer der Kirche. Festschrift zum 400. Todestag des zweiten Apostels Deutschlands* (Augsburg, 1996).

Ott, Martin, *Die Entdeckung des Altertums. Der Umgang mit der römischen Vergangenheit Süddeutschlands im 16. Jahrhundert* (Kallmünz, 2002).

Ozment, Steven, *The Age of the Reformation, 1250–1550* (New Haven, 1980).

The Reformation in the Cities (New Haven, 1975).

When Fathers Ruled: Family Life in Reformation Germany (Cambridge, Mass., 1983).

Pallaver, Günther, *Das Ende der Schamlosen Zeit. Die Verdrängung der Sexualität in der frühen Neuzeit am Beispiel Tirols* (Vienna, 1987).

Panizza, Letizia, "Stoic Psychotherapy in the Middle Ages and Renaissance: Petrarch's *De remediis*," in: Osler, Margaret (ed.), *Atoms, Pneuma, and Tranquility* (Cambridge, 1991), 39–66.

Parker, Geoffrey and Smith, Lesley M. (eds.), *The General Crisis of the Seventeenth Century* (London, 1978).

Parker, Kenneth, "Richard Greenham's 'Spiritual Physicke': The Comfort of Afflicted Consciences in Elizabethan Pastoral Care," in: Lualdi, Katherine Jackson and Thayer, Anne T. (eds.), *Penitence in the Age of Reformations* (Aldershot, 2000), 71–83.

Paula, Georg and Wegener-Hüssen, Angelika (eds.), *Denkmäler in Bayern, Band I.5: Landkreis Bad-Tölz-Wolfratshausen* (Munich, 1994).

Payer-Thurn, Rudolf, "Faust in Maria-Zell," *Chronik Wiener Goethe-Vereins* (1924), 1–18.

Peters, Edward, *Torture* (Philadelphia, 1996).

Pfeiffer, Samuel, "Demonic Attributions in Nondelusional Disorders," *Psychopathology* 32 (1999), 252–259.

Pfister, Christian, *Raum-zeitliche Rekonstruktion von Witterungsanomalien und Naturkatastrophen, 1496–1995* (Zurich 1998).

Pfleger, Luzian, *Martin Eisengrein* (Freiburg, 1908).

Pölnitz, Götz Freiherr von, *Die Matrikel der Ludwig-Maximilians Universität Ingolstadt-Landshut-München* (Munich, 1939).

"Petrus Canisius und das Bistum Augsburg," *Zeitschrift für bayerische Landesgeschichte* 18 (1955), 352–394.

Porter, Roy, *Mind-Forg'd Manacles: A History of Madness in England from the Restoration to the Regency* (London, 1987).

"The Patient in England, *c.*1660–*c.*1800," in: Wear, Andrew (ed.), *Medicine in society: Historical Essays* (Cambridge, 1992), 91–118.

Prantl, Carl, *Geschichte der Ludwig-Maximilians Universität in Ingolstadt-Landshut, München*, 2 vols. (Munich, 1872).

Prinz, Friedrich, *Frühes Mönchtum im Frankenreich. Kultur und Gesellschaft in Gallien, den Rheinland und Bayern am Beispiel der monastischen Entwicklung (4. bis 8. Jahrhundert)* (Munich, 1988).

Probst, Christian, *Lieber Bayerisch Sterben. Der bayerische Volksaufstand der Jahren 1705 und 1706* (Munich, 1978).

Prosperi, Andriano, "Beichtväter und Inquisition im 16. Jahrhundert," in: Reinhard, Wolfgang and Schilling, Heinz, *Die katholische Konfessionalisierung* (Güterslohe, 1995).

Rabb, Theodore K., *The Struggle for Stability in Early Modern Europe* (Oxford, 1975).

Rayez, André, "Del Rio," in: *Dictionnaire de spiritualité ascétique et mystique*, vol. III (Paris, 1957), 131–132.

Riezler, Sigmund, *Geschichte Bayerns, 1597–1651*, vol. V (Gotha, 1903).

Rittgers, Ronald K., "Private Confession and Religious Authority in Reformation Nürnberg," in: Lualdi, Katherine Jackson and Thayer, Anne T. (eds.), *Penitence in the Age of Reformations* (Aldershot, 2000), 49–70.

Robinson, Daniel N., *Wild Beasts and Idle Humours: The Insanity Defense from Antiquity to the Present* (Cambridge, Mass., 1996).

Robisheaux, Thomas, *Rural society and the Search for Order in Early Modern Germany* (Cambridge, 1989).

Roeck, Bernd, *Eine Stadt in Krieg und Frieden. Studien zur Geschichte der Reichsstadt Augsburg zwischen Kalenderstreit und Parität*, 2 vols. (Göttingen, 1989).

Roepke, Claus-Jürgen, "Die evangelische Bewegung in Bayern im 16. Jahrhundert," in: Glaser, Hubert (ed.), *Wittelsbach und Bayern II/1: Um Glauben und Reich. Kurfürst Maximilian I. Beiträge zur bayerischen Geschichte und Kunst 1573–1657* (Munich, 1980), 101–114.

Romeo, Giovanni, *Inquisitori, esorcisti e streghe nell'Italia della Controriforma* (Florence, 1990).

Roper, Lyndal, *Oedipus and the Devil. Witchcraft, Sexuality and Religion in Early Modern Europe* (London, 1994).

Rößler, Hans, *Geschichte und Strukturen der evangelischen Bewegung im Bistum Freising 1520–1571* (Nuremberg, 1966).

"Kontakte und Strukturen als Voraussetzung für die evangelische Bewegung des 16. Jahrhunderts im Herzogtum Bayern," ZBLG 32 (1969), 355–366.

"Wiedertäufer in und aus München 1527–28," *Oberbayerisches Archiv* 85 (1962), 42–53.

Rothkrug, Lionel, "Holy Shrines, Religious Dissonance and Satan in the Origins of the German Reformation," *Historical Reflections* 14 (1987), 143–286.

"Religious Practices and Collective Perceptions: Hidden Homologies in the Renaissance and Reformation," *Historical Reflections* 7 (1980), 206–213.

Rublack, Hans-Christoph, *Gescheiterte Reformation. Frühreformatorische und protestantische Bewegungen in süd- und westdeutschen geistlichen Residenzen* (Stuttgart, 1978).

"Lutherische Beichte und Sozialdisziplinierung," *Archive for Reformation History* 84 (1993), 127–155.

"Political and Social Norms in Urban Communities in the Holy Roman Empire," in: Greyerz, Kaspar von (ed.), *Religion, Politics and Social Protest: Three Studies on Early Modern Germany* (London, 1984), 24–60.

Rublack, Ulinka, "Fluxes: The Early Modern Body and the Emotions," *History Workshop Journal* 53 (2002), 1–16.

Sabean, David Warren, *Power in the Blood: Popular Culture and Village Discourse in Early Modern Germany* (Cambridge, 1984).

Property, Production, and Family in Neckarhausen, 1700–1870 (Cambridge, 1990).

Safley, Max, *Let No Man Put Asunder* (Kirkville, 1984).

Sargent, Steven, "A Critique of Lionel Rothkrug's List of Bavarian Pilgrimage Shrines," *Archive for Reformation History* 80 (1989), 351–358.

"Religion and society in Late Medieval Bavaria: The Cult of St. Leonard" (unpublished Ph.D. dissertation, University of Michigan, 1988).

Sauermost, Heinz Jürgen, "Zur Rolle St. Michaels im Rahmen der Wilhelmisch-maximilianischen Kunst," in: Glaser, Hubert (ed.), *Wittelsbach und Bayern II/1: Um Glauben und Reich. Kurfürst Maximilian I. Beiträge zur bayerischen Geschichte und Kunst 1573–1657* (Munich, 1980), 167–174.

Schaching, Otto von, *Maximilian I, der Große, Kurfürst von Bayern* (Freiburg, 1876).

Schad, Martha, *Die Frauen des Hauses Fugger von der Lilie* (Tübingen, 1989).

Schäfer, Volker, "Tübinger Teufelspakte," in: Wandel, Uwe Jens (ed.), *". . . helfen zu graben den Brunnen des Lebens," Historische Jubiläumsausstellung des Universitätsarchivs Tübingen* (Tübingen, 1977), 72–77.

Schaich, Michael, "Frey, Bernhard," in: Boehm, Laetitia, Müller, Winfried, Smolka, Wolfgang J. and Zedelmaier, Helmut, *Biographisches Lexikon der Ludwig-Maximilians-Universität München* (Berlin, 1998), 130–132.

Schär, Markus, *Seelennöte der Untertanen. Selbstmord, Melancholie und Religion im Alten Zürich, 1500–1800* (Zurich, 1985).

Scheer, Monique, "From Majesty to Mystery: Change in the Meanings of Black Madonnas from the Sixteenth to Nineteenth Centuries," *American Historical Review* 107 (2002), 1412–1440.

Schepers, Elisabeth, *Als der Bettel in Bayern abgeschafft werden sollte. Staatliche Armenfürsorge in Bayern im 16. und 17. Jahrhundert* (Regensburg, 2000).

Schilling, Heinz, "'History of Crime' or 'History of Sin'? – Some Reflections on the Social History of Early Modern Church Discipline," in: Kouri, E. J. and Scott, Tom (eds.), *Politics and society in Reformation Europe. Essays for Sir Geoffrey Elton on his 65th Birthday* (London 1987), 289–310.

Schlögl, Rudolf, *Bauern, Krieg und Staat. Oberbayerische Bauernwirtschaft und frühmoderner Staat im 17. Jahrhundert* (Göttingen, 1988).

"Zwischen Krieg und Krise," *Zeitschrift für Agrargeschichte und Agrarsoziologie* 40 (1992), 133–167.

Schlombs, Wilhelm, *Die Entwicklung des Beichtstuhls in der katholischen Kirche: Grundlagen und Besonderheiten im alten Bistum Köln* (Düsseldorf, 1965).

Schmeller, Johann Andreas, *Bayerisches Wörterbuch*, 2 vols. (Munich, 1872–1877; facsimile reprint: Munich, 1985).

Schmid, Alois, "Geschichtsschreibung am Hofe Kürfurst Maximilians I. von Bayern," in: Glaser, Hubert (ed.), *Wittelsbach und Bayern II/1: Um Glauben und Reich. Kurfürst Maximilian I. Beiträge zur bayerischen Geschichte und Kunst 1573–1657* (Munich, 1980), 330–340.

Schmidt, Hans, "Pfalz-Neuburgs Sprung zum Niederrhein. Wolfgang Wilhelm von Pfalz Neuburg und der Jülich-Klevische Erbfolgestreit," in: Glaser, Hubert (ed)., *Wittelsbach und Bayern II/I: Um Glauben und Reich. Kurfürst Maximilian I. Beiträge zur bayerischen Geschichte und Kunst 1573–1657* (Munich, 1980), 77–89.

Schmidt-Degenhard, Michael, "Versteinertes Dasein – zur Problemgeschichte und Psychopathologie der Melancholie," *Forschung und Medizin*, 45–56.

Schmidt-Kohberg, Karin, ". . . und hat 'sich selbsten . . . an ein Strickhalfter hinge-henckt . . .' Selbstmord im Herzogtum Württemberg im 17. und 18. Jahrhundert," in: Dillinger, Johannes (ed.), *Zauberer – Selbstmörder – Schatzsucher. Magische Kultur und behördliche Kontrolle im frühneuzeitlichen Württemberg* (Trier, 2003), 113–220.

Schmitt, Jean-Claude, *The Holy Greyhound: Guinefort, Healer of Children since the Thirteenth Century* (Cambridge, 1983).

"Le suicide au Moyen Age," *Annales ESC* 31 (1976), 3–28.

Schnauerte, Heinrich, *Die Bußlehre des Johannes Eck* (Münster, 1919).

Schnell, Hugo, *Der baierische Barock. Die volklichen, die geschichtlichen und die religiösen Grundlagen sein Siegeszug durch das Reich* (Munich, 1936).

Schreiber, Anton Wilhelm, *Maximilian I. der Katholische, Kurfürst von Bayern und der dreißigjährige Krieg* (Munich, 1868).

Schreiner, Julia, *Jenseits vom Glück. Suizid, Melancholie und Hypochondrie in deutschsprachigen Texten des späten 18. Jahrhunderts* (Munich, 2003).

Schüling, Hermann, *Bibliographisches Handbuch zur Geschichte der Psychologie des 16. Jahrhunderts* (Hildesheim, 1967).

Schulze, Winfried, *Deutsche Geschichte im 16. Jahrhundert 1500–1618* (Frankfurt am Main, 1987).

Vom Gemeinnutz zum Eigennutz: über den Normenwandel in der ständischen Gesellschaft der frühen Neuzeit (Munich, 1987).

"Untertanenrevolten, Hexenverfolgung und 'kleine Eiszeit': Eine Krisenzeit um 1600," in: Roeck, Bernd, Bergdolt, Klaus and Martin, Andrew John (eds.), *Venedig und Oberdeutschland in der Renaissance. Beziehungen zwischen Kunst und Wirtschaft* (Sigmaringen, 1993), 289–309.

Schwaiger, Georg (ed.), *Bavaria Sancta. Zeugen des christlichen Glaubens in Bayern*, 3 vols. (Regensburg, 1970–1973).

Screech, M. A., *Montaigne and Melancholy: The Wisdom of the Essays* (Selinsgrove, 1983).

Scribner, Robert, "Cosmic Order and Daily Life: Sacred and Secular in Pre-Industrial German society," in: Greyerz, Kaspar von (ed.), *Religion and society in Early Modern Europe 1500–1800* (London, 1984), 17–32.

Scribner, Robert, "The Impact of the Reformation on Daily Life," in: Scribner, *Popular Culture and Popular Movements in Reformation Germany* (London, 1987). Reprinted in Scribner, Robert and Roper, Lyndal (eds.), *Religion and Culture in Germany, 1400–1800* (Leiden, 2004), 275–301.

"Mobility: Voluntary or Enforced? Vagrants in Württemberg in the Sixteenth Century," in: Jaritz, Gerhard and Müller, Albert (eds.), *Migration in der Feudalgesellschaft* (Frankfurt am Main, 1988), 64–88.

"The Mordbrenner Fear in Sixteenth-Century Germany: Political Paranoia or the Revenge of the Outcast?" in: Richard, J. (eds.), *The German Underworld: Essays in the Social History of Crime in German from the Sixteenth Century to the Present* (London, 1988), 29–56.

Scull, Andrew, *The Most Solitary of Afflictions: Madness and society in Britain 1700–1900* (New Haven, 1993).

Seidl, Siegfried, "Der volkstümliche Maler Johann Bapt. Reisbacher sen. in Kollnburg bei Viechtach (Bayer. Wald)," *Bayerisches Jahrbuch für Volkskunde* (1980-1981), 29–30.

Seifert Arno, "Die 'Seminarpolitik' der bayerischen Herzöge im 16. Jahrhundert und die Begründung des jesuitischen Schulwesens," in: Glaser, Hubert (ed.),

Wittelsbach und Bayern II/1: Um Glauben und Reich. Kurfürst Maximilian I. Beiträge zur bayerischen Geschichte und Kunst 1573–1657 (Munich, 1980), 125–132.

Seils, Ernst Albrecht, *Die Staatslehre des Jesuiten Adam Contzen, Beichvater Kurfürst Maximilian I. von Bayern* (Lübeck, 1968).

Sepp, J. N., *Festschrift zur zweiten Jahrhundertwende der Schlacht von Sendling* (Munich, 1905).

Shamdasani, Sonu, *Jung and the Making of Modern Psychology: The Dream of a Science* (Cambridge, 2003).

Shapiro, James, *The Troubling Story of the World's Most Famous Passion Play* (New York, 2000).

Shorter, Edward, *A History of Psychiatry. From the Era of the Asylum to the Age of Prozac* (New York, 1997).

Signori, Gabriela, "Aggression und Selbstzerstörung. 'Geistesstörungen' und Selbstmordversuche im Spannungsfeld spätmittelalterlicher Geschlechterstereotypen (15. Und beginnendes 16. Jahrhundert)," in: Signori, Gabriela (ed.), *Trauer, Verzweiflung und Anfechtung. Selbstmord und Selbstmordversuche in mittelalterlichen und frühneuzeitlichen Gesellschaften* (Tübingen, 1994), 113–148.

(ed.), *Trauer, Verzweiflung und Anfechtung. Selbstmord und Selbstmordversuche in mittelalterlichen und frühneuzeitlichen Gesellschaften* (Tübingen, 1994).

Simplicio, Oscar di, "Confessionalizzazione e identità collettiva – Il caso italiano: Siena 1575–1800," *Archive for Reformation History* 88 (1997), 380–411.

Peccato, Penitenza, Perdono: Siena 1575–1800. La formazione della coscienza nell'Italia moderna (Milan, 1994).

Skultans, Vieda, "Affliction: An Overview," in: Eliade, Mircea (ed.), *The Encyclopedia of Religion*, vol. 1 (New York, 1987), 51–55.

Sluhovsky, Moshe, "The Devil in the Convent," *American Historical Review* 107 (2002), 1379–1411.

Smith, Jeffrey Chipps, *Sensuous Worship: Jesuits and the Art of the Early Catholic Reformation in Germany* (Princeton, 2002).

Snoeck, Andreas, *Beichte und Psychoanalyse* (Munich, 1960).

Soergel, Philip, "Spiritual Medicine for Heretical Poison: The Propagandistic Uses of Legends in Counter-Reformation Bavaria," *Historical Reflections* 17 (1991), 125–149.

Wondrous in his Saints. Counter-Reformation Propaganda in Bavaria (Berkeley, 1993).

Solms, Mark, "Freud Returns," *Scientific American* 290 (2004), 82–89.

Spindler, Max (ed.), *Handbuch der bayerischen Geschichte*, vol. II (Munich, 1988).

Sprandel, Rolf, "Die Seele der Analphabeten im Mittelalter," in Jütteman, Gerd, Michael, Sonntag and Wulf, Christoph (eds.), *Die Seele. Ihre Geschichte im Abendland* (Weinheim, 1991), 97–103.

Sreenivasan, Govind P., *The Peasants of Ottobeuren, 1487–1726: A Rural Society in Early Modern Europe* (Cambridge, 2004).

Steiner, Peter Bernhard, "Der gottselige Fürst und die Konfessionalisierung Altbayerns," in: Glaser, Hubert (ed.), *Wittelsbach und Bayern II/1: Um Glauben und Reich. Kurfürst Maximilian I. Beiträge zur bayerischen Geschichte und Kunst 1573–1657* (Munich, 1980), 252–263.

Stieve, Felix, *Die kirchliche Polizeiregiment in Baiern unter Maximilian I. 1595–1651* (Munich, 1876).

Stohl, Alfred, *Der Narrenturm oder die dunkle Seite der Wissenschaft* (Vienna, 2000).

Strasser, Ulrike, *State of Virginity. Gender, Religion and Politics in an Early Modern Catholic State* (Ann Arbor, 2004).

Stuart, Kathy, *Defiled Trades and Social Outcasts. Honor and Ritual Pollution in Early Modern Germany* (Cambridge, 1999).

Stuart, Kathy, "Des Scharfrichters heilende Hand – Medizin und Ehre in der Frühen Neuzeit," in Backmann, Sibylle, Künast, Hans-Jörg, Tlusty, B. Ann and Ullmann, Sabine (eds.), *Das Konzept der Ehre in der Frühen Neuzeit* (Augsburg, 1998), 316–348.

Sulloway, Frank J., *Freud, Biologist of the Mind* (New York, 1979).

Swales, Peter, "Freud, Cocaine and Sexual Chemistry: The Role of Cocaine in Freud's Conception of the Libido" (privately printed by the author, 1983).

"Freud, Johann Weier, and the Status of Seduction: The Role of the Witch in the Conception of Fantasy" (printed privately by the author, 1982).

"Freud, Krafft-Ebbing, and the Witches: The Role of Krafft-Ebbing in Freud's Flight into Fantasy" (printed privately by the author, 1983).

"Freud, Minna Bernays, and the Conquest of Rome: New Light on the Origins of Psychoanalysis," *The New American Review* (Spring/Summer 1982), 1–23.

"Once a Cigar, Always a Cigar," *Nature* 378 (November 1995), 107–108.

Tentler, Thomas N., *Sin and Confession on the Eve of the Reformation* (Princeton, 1977).

"Sacramental Privacy: The Myth, Law and History of the Seal of Confession, 1215–1965," unpublished paper.

Thayer, Anne T., "Judge and Doctor: Images of the Confessor in Printed Model Sermon Collections, 1450–1520," in: Lualdi, Katharine Jackson and Thayer, Anne T. (eds.), *Penitence in the Age of Reformations* (Aldershot, 2000), 10–29.

Theopold, William, *Mirakel. Heilung zwischen Wissenschaft und Glauben* (Munich, 1983).

Votivmalerei und Medizin (Munich, 1981).

Thomas, Keith, *Religion and the Decline of Magic* (London, 1970).

Thorndike, Lynn, *A History of Experimental Magic and Science, vol. VI: The Sixteenth Century* (New York, 1941).

Tlusty, Ann, *Bacchus and Civil Order. The Culture of Drink in Early Modern Germany* (Charlottesville, 2001).

Tönnies, Ferdinand, *Gemeinschaft und Gesellschaft. Abhandlung des Communismus und des Sozialismus als empirischer Kulturformen* (Leipzig, 1887); translated as *Community and Civil Society*, ed. Jose Harris, trans. Margaret Hollis (Cambridge, 2001).

Treml, Manfred, "Die Säkularisation und ihre Folgen," in: Kirmeier, Josef and Treml, Manfred (eds.), *Glanz und Ende der Alten Klöster. Säkularisation im bayerischen Oberland 1803* (Munich, 1991), 122–131.

Trevor-Roper, Hugh, *Religion, the Reformation and Social Change* (London, 1967).

Trexler, Richard, *Public Life in Renaissance Florence* (New York, 1980).

Troll, Hildebrand, *Kirche in Bayern. Verhältnis zu Herrschaft und Staat im Wandel der Jahrhunderten* (Munich, 1984).

Tuck, Richard, *Philosophy and Government, 1572–1651* (Cambridge, 1993).

Tylor, Edward Burnett, *Primitive Culture: Researches into the Development of Mythology, Philosophy, Religion, Language, Art, and Custom* (London, 1873).

Vandekerckhove, Lieven, *On Punishment. The Confrontation of Suicide in Old Europe* (Leuven, 2000).

Vandendriessche, Gaston, "Johann Christoph Haizmann (1651–1700). Barocke Teufelsaustreibung in Mariazell," in: Feuchtmüller, Rupert and Kovács, Elisabeth, *Welt des Barock* (Vienna, 1986), 141–145.

The Parapraxis in the Haizmann Case of Sigmund Freud (Louvain, 1965).

Vandermeersch, Patrick, *Psychiatrie, godsdienst en gezag. Psychiatry, religion and authority* (Löwen, 1984).

"The Victory of Psychiatry over Demonology: The Origin of the Nineteenth-Century Myth," *History of Psychiatry* 2 (1991), 351–363.

Vitz, Paul C., *Sigmund Freud's Christian Unconscious* (New York, 1988).

Vogel, Hubert, *Die Urkunden des Heiliggeistspitals 1250–1500* (Munich, 1960).

Waardt, Hans De, "Chasing Demons and Curing Mortals: The Medical Practice of Clerics in the Netherlands," in: Marland, Hilary and Pelling, Margaret (eds.), *The Task of Healing: Medicine, Religion and Gender in England and the Netherlands, 1450–1800* (Rotterdam, 1996), 173–302.

Wagenhals, Margaret Hamilton, "Report on Saint Thomas Aquinas' Concept of the Emotions as Contained in the Summa Theologica, I–II, Quaestiones XXII–XLVIII" (unpublished MA thesis, Smith College, 1907).

Waldkraiburger Nachrichten, 3.III.1993, 24.

Walker, D. P., *Unclean Spirits. Possession and Exorcism in France and England in the Late Sixteenth and Early Seventeenth Centuries* (Philadelphia, 1981).

Waterworth, J. (ed.), *The Council of Trent: Canons and Decrees* (Chicago, 1848).

Watkins, Oscar D., *A History of Penance*, vol. II (London, 1920).

Watt, Jeffrey R., *Choosing Death. Suicide and Calvinism in Early Modern Geneva* (Kirksville, 2001).

Weber, Leo, *Der frühbarocke Festsaal und seine Deckenbilder im Kloster Benediktbeuern* (Munich, 1996).

St. Benedikt zu Benediktbeuern als Wallfahrtsort (Benediktbeuern, 1981).

Veit Adam von Gepeckh (Munich, 1972).

Weber, Mathias M., *Ernst Rüdin. Eine kritische Biographie* (Berlin, 1993).

Weber, Wolfgang, "Im Kampf mit Saturn. Zur Bedeutung der Melancholie im anthropologischen Modernisierungsprozeß des 16. und 17. Jahrhunderts," *Zeitschrift für Historische Forschungen* 19 (1992), 154–192.

Webster, Richard, *Why Freud was Wrong: Sin, Science and Psychoanalysis* (New York, 1995).

Wedgewood, C. V., *The Thirty Years War* (London, 1938).

Weigle, Fritz (ed.), *Die Matrikel der Deutschen Nation in Siena (1573–1738)*, 2 vols. (Tübingen, 1962).

Weis, Eberhard, *Montgelas 1759–1799. Zwischen Revolution und Reform* (Munich, 1971).

White, Andrew D., *A History of the Warfare of Science with Theology in Christendom* (New York, 1896; reprint: Buffalo, 1993).

Widmoser, Eduard, *Tirol A bis Z* (Innsbruck, 1970).

Wiesner, Merry, *Women and Gender in Early Modern Europe* (Cambridge, 1993).

"Women and the Reformation in Germany," in: Marshall, Sherrin (ed.), *Women in Reformation and Counter-Reformation Europe* (Bloomington, 1989), 8–29.

Working Women in Renaissance Germany (New Brunswick, 1986).

Windholz, George, "The Case of the Renaissance Psychiatrist Peter Meir," *Sixteenth Century Journal* 22 (1990), 163–172.

Wolfart, Johannes C., *Religion, Government and Political Culture in Early Modern Germany: Lindau, 1520–1628* (London, 2001).

"Why was Private Confession so Contentious in Early Seventeenth-Century Lindau?" in: Scribner, Robert and Johnson, Trevor (eds.), *Popular Religion in Germany and Central Europe, 1400–1800* (London, 1996), 140–165.

Wunder, Heidi, *He is the Sun, She is the Moon: Women in Early Modern Germany* (Cambridge, Mass., 1998).

Wüst, Wolfgang, "Kurbayern und seine westlichen Nachbarn. Reichsstadt und Hochstift Augsburg im Spiegel der diplomatischen Korrespondenz", ZBLG 55 (1992), 255–278.

Zelewitz, Klaus, "Propaganda Fides Benedictina. Salzburger Ordenstheater im Hochbarock," in: Valentin, Jean-Marie (ed.), *Gegenreformation und Literatur. Beiträge zur interdisziplinären Erforschung der katholischen Reformbewegung* (Amsterdam, 1979), 201–215.

Zemon-Davis, Natalie, "The Reasons of Misrule," in: Zemon-Davis, *Society and Culture in Early Modern France* (Stanford, 1965), 97–123.

"The Rites of Violence," in: Zemon-Davis, Natalie, *Society and Culture in Early Modern Europe* (Stanford, 1965), 152–188.

Ziegler, Walter, "Die Rekatholisierung der Oberpfalz," in: Glaser, Hubert (ed.), *Wittelsbach und Bayern II/1: Um Glauben und Reich. Kurfürst Maximilian I. Beiträge zur bayerischen Geschichte und Kunst 1573–1657* (Munich, 1980), 436–455.

Zinsser, Hans, *Rats, Lice and History. A Study in Biography* (New York, 1934).

Zwierlein, Cornel Anton, *Das semantische Potential des Fauststoffes um die Wende vom 16. zum 17. Jahrhundert* (unpublished MA thesis, Munich, 1999).

Index

Provincial Power and Absolute Monarchy
The Estates General of Burgundy, 1661–1790
JULIAN SWANN

People and Politics in France, 1848–1870
ROGER PRICE

Nobles and Nation in Central Europe
Free Imperial Knights in the Age of Revolution, 1750–1850
WILLIAM D. GODSEY, JR

Technology and the Culture of Modernity in Britain and Germany, 1890–1945
BERNHARD RIEGER

The Russian Roots of Nazism
White Émigrés and the Making of National Socialism, 1917–1945
MICHAEL KELLOGG

The World Hitler Never Made
Alternate History and the Memory of Nazism
GAVRIEL D. ROSENFELD

Madness, Religion and the State in Early Modern Europe
A Bavarian Beacon
DAVID LEDERER

also available in paperback